COUNTRIES AT
THE CROSSROADS

COUNTRIES AT THE CROSSROADS

A Survey of
Democratic Governance

Sanja Tatic
Christopher Walker
EDITORS

FREEDOM HOUSE
NEW YORK • WASHINGTON, D.C.

ROWMAN & LITTLEFIELD PUBLISHERS, INC.
LANHAM • BOULDER • NEW YORK • TORONTO • OXFORD

ROWMAN & LITTLEFIELD PUBLISHERS, INC.

Published in the United States of America
by Rowman & Littlefield Publishers, Inc.
A wholly owned subsidary of The Rowman & Littlefield Publishing Group, Inc.
4501 Forbes Boulevard, Suite 200, Lanham, Maryland 20706
www.rowmanlittlefield.com

Estover Road
Plymouth PL6 7PY
United Kingdom

British Library Cataloguing in Publication Information Available

Library of Congress Cataloging-in-Publication Data

Countries at the crossroads : a survey of democratic governance / Sanja Tatic,
Christopher Walker, editors.
    p. cm.
  Includes bibliographical references and index.
  ISBN-13: 978-0-7425-5800-7 (cloth : alk. paper)
  ISBN-13: 978-0-7425-5801-4 (pbk. : alk. paper)
  ISBN-10: 0-7425-5800-2 (cloth : alk. paper)
  ISBN-10: 0-7425-5801-0 (pbk. : alk. paper)
  1. Democracy—Case studies. 2. Representative government and
representation—Case studies. I. Tatic, Sanja. II. Walker, Christopher.
JC423.C7196 2006
321.803—dc22   2006027743

Printed in the United States of America

⊖™ The paper used in this publication meets the minimum requirements of American
National Standard for Information Sciences—Permanence of Paper for Printed Library
Materials, ANSI/NISO Z39.48-1992.

CONTENTS

COUNTRIES AT THE CROSSROADS
2005–2006

2005 COUNTRIES	2006 COUNTRIES
Algeria	Armenia
Angola	Azerbaijan
Bangladesh	Bahrain
Bhutan	Cambodia
Bolivia	East Timor
Burkina Faso	Georgia
China	Guatemala
Colombia	Guyana
Ecuador	Indonesia
Egypt	Jordan
Eritrea	Kazakhstan
Ethiopia	Kenya
Honduras	Kyrgyzstan
Iran	Malawi
Laos	Malaysia
Libya	Morocco
Mauritania	Nepal
Mozambique	Nicaragua
Paraguay	Nigeria
Peru	Pakistan
Philippines	Sierra Leone
Russia	South Africa
Rwanda	Sri Lanka
Swaziland	Tanzania
Syria	Uganda
Tajikistan	Ukraine
Thailand	Venezuela
Tunisia	Vietnam
Turkey	Yemen
Zambia	Zimbabwe

ACKNOWLEDGMENTS

Countries at the Crossroads is the product of the collective contributions of numerous Freedom House staff members and consultants. This study was also made possible by the generous support of the Bureau of Democracy, Human Rights, and Labor at the U.S. Department of State.

Country report authors made an outstanding contribution to this effort, working to produce 30 clear, informed analyses of a highly diverse group of countries. The report authors are: Zachary Abuza, Adam Albion, Mick Andersen, Dominique Arel, Edward Aspinall, Peter Bartu, Ravi Bhatia, Carolyn Bull, William Case, John Damis, Emil Danielyan, David Dye, Ivelaw Griffith, Hussein Haqqani, Anita Isaacs, Paul Kaiser, Nelson Kasfir, Brian Katulis, Darren Kew, Stanley Khaila, Tom Lansner, Fred Lawson, Robert Lloyd, Ned McMahon, Robert Oberst, Martha Brill Olcott, Karen Polglaze, William Reno, Mark Rosenberg, Sanja Tatic, and Christopher Walker.

A group of distinguished regional experts served on the advisory committee, providing valuable input on the narratives and scores. They are: Joel Barkan, Linda Beck, John Carey, Elizabeth Carlson (Fuller), Catharin Dalpino, John Entelis, Gregory Gause, Jeffrey Herbst, Tom Lansner, Amit Pandya, Robert Rotberg, Jillian Schwedler, Michael Shifter, Peter Sinnott, Timothy Snyder, Bridget Welsh, and Coletta Youngers.

The *Countries at the Crossroads* methodology was originally developed with the expert contribution of a group of senior advisers, including Larry Diamond, Hoover Institution; Paul Martin, Columbia University; Rick Messick, World Bank; Ted Piccone, Open Society Institute; Louise Shelley, American University; and Ruth Wedgwood, Johns Hopkins University. Jay Verkuilen of the University of Illinois, Urbana-Champaign, provided invaluable guidance, in addition to his participation in the methodology committee.

Freedom House staff devoted extensive time and energy to develop this project. Sanja Tatic was the managing editor of the study. Christopher Walker, directory of studies; Arch Puddington, director of research;

and Jennifer Windsor, executive director of Freedom House provided overall guidance and support for the project, in addition to serving on the survey's internal review committee. Research assistant Camille Eiss supplied important research, editorial and administrative support, as did staff members Thomas Webb and Astrid Larson, and interns David Emery and Kathryn Hannah. Nancy van Itallie copyedited the volume. Ida Walker was the proofreader, and Beverly Butterfield designed and typeset the volume.

EXPERT ADVISORY COMMITTEE

JOEL BARKAN
Professor of Political Science,
University of Iowa

LINDA BECK
Assistant Professor of Political Science,
University of Maine-Farmington

JOHN CAREY
Associate Professor, Government
Department, Dartmouth College

CATHARIN DALPINO
Adjunct Professor of Southeast Asian
Studies, Edmund A. Walsh School of
Foreign Service, Georgetown University

JOHN ENTELIS
Professor of Political Science and
Director, Middle East Studies Program,
Fordham University

ELIZABETH FULLER
Caucasus Analyst, Radio Free Europe/
Radio Liberty

GREGORY GAUSE
Associate Professor of Political Science,
University of Vermont

JEFFREY HERBST
Provost and Executive Vice President
for Academic Affairs, Miami University

THOMAS LANSNER
Adjunct Associate Professor, Columbia
University School of International and
Public Affairs

AMIT PANDYA
Attorney at Law and Consultant
Washington, D.C.

ROBERT ROTBERG
Director, Program on Intrastate
Conflict and Conflict Resolution,
Belfer Center, Harvard University

MICHAEL SHIFTER
Vice President for Policy,
Inter-American Dialogue

PETER SINNOTT
Lecturer, Columbia University School
of International and Public Affairs

JILLIAN SCHWEDLER
Assistant Professor of Government
and Politics, University of Maryland

TIMOTHY SNYDER
Professor, Department of History,
Yale University

BRIDGET WELSH
Assistant Professor of Southeast Asia
Studies, Johns Hopkins University,
School of Advanced International Studies

COLETTA YOUNGERS
Independent Consultant and Senior
Fellow, Washington Office on Latin
America

ENTRENCHED CORRUPTION AND THE CHALLENGE TO DEMOCRATIC ACCOUNTABILITY

Sanja Tatic and Christopher Walker

The increase in the number of electoral democracies, the spread of democratic ideals, and the proliferation of human rights values over the last three decades have generated domestic and international pressure for reform on autocratic states, one-party dictatorships, and monarchies. Emerging democracies are similarly scrutinized as to whether their newly formed democratic institutions are sustainable. While a wide range of states now face growing pressure to make crucial choices about liberalization and reform, world leaders, foreign assistance providers, and the international business community are eager to have at their disposal effective tools for monitoring and measuring political development among countries standing at the crossroads of democratic governance.

Countries at the Crossroads provides detailed written analysis and comparative statistics on two sets of 30 states at this very juncture—typically middle-performing countries that qualify neither as failed states nor as clear beacons of democracy. The countries evaluated represent a range of governments: traditional or constitutional monarchies, one-party states or outright dictatorships, states where reforms have stalled or lagged behind, and states that suffer from insurgencies. Every other year each edition evaluates 30 countries; over a two-year time period a report is issued on each of the 60 countries identified for analysis.

In this way, *Crossroads* covers an extensive set of countries while offering readers useful time series data as well as comprehensive narrative evaluation of the progress and backsliding under way in the countries covered. The survey examines four main aspects of governance: public voice and accountability, civil rights, the rule of law, and anticorruption and transparency. The 2006 edition marks the third year of the survey and thus allows for drawing clear conclusions regarding some of the evaluated countries' progress toward democratic norms and others' growing authoritarian tendencies since 2004.

1

As illustrated in so many of the narratives in this edition, entrenched corruption stands out as a major obstacle to reform in transitional countries. In 2006, as was the case in 2004, Anticorruption and Transparency saw the weakest performance of the four main areas evaluated, averaging a score of 2.71 (on a scale of 0–7, with 7 being strongest), more than a full point lower than the strongest overall category, Civil Liberties. Across country types and geographical regions, none of the 30 evaluated countries has ever scored above a 4.0 on the anticorruption measure.

The crumbling of authoritarian regimes in the midst of popular protests in Georgia, Kyrgyzstan, and Ukraine was in no small part spurred by public frustration with corrupt governance. Although these countries still confront profound challenges, particularly in the spheres of anticorruption reform and the rule of law—common to many post-transition countries—the political changes represent a significant development in the two-year period since this set of countries was last examined.

Not all countries covered in the survey have demonstrated an improvement. Most countries have maintained the status quo, while others, such as Zimbabwe, Nepal, and Nigeria, showed a decline as a result of the growing authoritarian tendencies of their leaders. Arguably, the case of Nepal has been the most extreme: "King Gyanendra has suspended Nepal's entire democracy, dismissed parliament, and appointed a hand-picked prime minister and cabinet. The rule of law has been subverted through the creation of a number of extrajudicial bodies, and human rights have been profoundly compromised."

The survey presented a number of other significant findings:

- Respect for the rule of law has dramatically declined across the survey since 2004, with decreased scores in nearly half of the countries examined.
- Torture in police custody remains the most pressing human rights problem in more than half of the countries examined.
- Countries that have achieved particular improvement in the past two years include Kyrgyzstan, Georgia, Morocco and Ukraine. Those that have declined the most are Nepal, Zimbabwe and Nigeria.
- In nearly two-thirds of the reports, experts' recommendations emphasize a need to balance the political playing field, especially

in the context of election campaigns, where incumbents often dominate and prevent the press from providing useful information to the public.

Entrenched Corruption Poses Enormous Challenge to Reform

Crossroads' Anticorruption and Transparency section analyzes a government's performance in fighting corruption by evaluating the existence of laws and standards to prevent and combat corrupt practices, the enforcement of such measures, and overall governmental transparency. Scores in this category are remarkably low across regions and country typologies. Even in those countries with relatively sound performance in accountability and public voice, such as South Africa and Kenya, the scores for corruption remain low.

Crossroads analysts and regional specialists found Zimbabwe, Azerbaijan, Yemen, Kazakhstan, and Bahrain to be the five weakest performers in this category among the 30 countries evaluated in this year's edition. In these countries, powerholders effectively maintain an institutional chokehold on the state, maximizing private benefits while assigning a secondary role to the public interest. Zimbabwe was the worst performer in this category. The report observes that "the primary interest of the Mugabe government is to retain power through a system of patronage that includes access to both state and private assets. The ruling ZANU–PF party owns a wide range of businesses, allowing party elites to profit personally."

In another example, in Kazakhstan, where President Nursultan Nazarbayev has ruled for a decade and a half, the report finds that "the government of Kazakhstan is unlikely to take decisive steps to eliminate corruption as long as Nursultan Nazarbayev remains president of the country. . . . It is hard to imagine that he will support a complete overhaul of the existing system, which has brought significant wealth to his family."

Even in the states that have recently experienced transition, where a new generation of leaders took power amid tremendous public enthusiasm, with strong mandates to stamp out corruption, meaningful anticorruption reform remains elusive. The Ukraine report, for example, finds that the breakthrough in the exposure of corruption on a grand scale following the Orange Revolution "was not accompanied by a change in the structural incentives for politicians and civil servants to blur the line between private and public interests."

The issue of corruption is particularly pernicious in countries where citizens are dependent on the government for their most fundamental needs. In such settings, entrenched corrupt networks feed on weak and insular state institutions that were designed to deliver political goods to the public. Absent sufficiently strong countervailing institutions, even new governments principally dedicated to reform are often unable to unshackle themselves from the narrow, private interests that subsume the public interest. In Yemen, for example, "a culture of bribery permeates the state apparatus including hospitals, schools, and universities." Bribes are necessary for such basic activities as obtaining hospital treatment, and those who raise objections publicly often face criticism or even worse.

In any democracy, the news media is a vital institution with the responsibility to report on government activities, increase transparency, help ensure government integrity, and serve the public interest. However, *Crossroads'* Accountability and Public Voice measures suggest that media itself is often subject to influence by powerful political and economic interests that leads to self-censorship and a muzzling of the sort of reporting that would ameliorate corrupt practices.

Journalists and editors are frequently co-opted by officials and business interests. Moreover, reporters who expose government corruption or are particularly critical of regime practices are often subject to arbitrary arrest or threats or acts of violence. In Armenia, for example, at least four journalists were severely beaten by special police while covering the brutal break up of an antigovernment demonstration in Yerevan in 2004. The fear of such retribution leads to poor government transparency, allows corruption to remain ingrained, and serves to prevent any meaningful discussion of issues that could lead to policy reform.

The governments, for their part—whether long-standing procedural democracies, countries newly in transition, or autocratic states—often list rooting out corruption as their top priority. Many have waged aggressive anticorruption campaigns throughout the two years under study, including passing important anticorruption legislation and some high-profile arrests, often cited as evidence of their progress. Yet none of the 30 countries have reduced corruption to levels where it no longer presents a serious obstacle to sustained economic growth and further political development. In fact, between 2004 and 2006, anticorruption and transparency scores have declined in nearly one-third of all countries surveyed.

Latin America

Regionally, Latin America is the highest-performing region in this edition. Of particular note is the strength of civil society, which contributes to the Latin American countries' relatively strong performance in the sphere of Accountability and Public Voice. Nevertheless, the region confronts a major political battle today between liberal democrats of the left and right and authoritarian populists. Venezuela, the worst performer of the Latin American countries reviewed this year, which also underwent the most significant drop among the countries of the region since the last review (in the spheres of Accountability and Public Voice and Anticorruption and Transparency), exemplifies the populist-authoritarian model.

Sub-Saharan Africa

The countries of sub-Saharan Africa were the second-best performing regional group. South Africa was the strongest overall within this region. As a region, Africa underwent the greatest decline on issues under the indicator measuring "Protection Against State Terror, Imprisonment, and Torture." Zimbabwe, the worst-performing country in the region, has suffered a considerable decline in performance since the last review, dropping nearly four full points in the aggregate. President Robert Mugabe has dragged Zimbabwe into a political, social, and economic morass. ZANU-PF economic policies have transformed one of Africa's most diversified economic sectors into a pre-industrial, peasant-based economy. Mugabe's manipulation of food shortages has generated untold misery in his country. Some 75 percent of Zimbabweans now live in poverty; the country is facing a crisis of major proportions, one created by Zimbabwe's leadership. Violence and intimidation have been used to control what remains of a free press and to convert the country's once highly respected and independent judiciary into a reliable instrument for implementation of the president's policies. As a result of its increasingly brutal and antidemocratic rule, Robert Mugabe's regime's precipitous descent into the ranks of the world's most repressive systems was reflected in the survey findings: Of all 30 countries examined, Zimbabwe received the poorest scores in three of the four main categories.

Asia-Pacific

In Asia, Nepal, which faced one of the most important political crises in its history, underwent the most precipitous decline, with significant backsliding in the areas of Accountability and Public Voice, Civil Liberties, and Anticorruption and Transparency. The Nepal report notes that during the coverage period, "the rule of law has been subverted through the creation of a number of extrajudicial bodies, and human rights have been profoundly compromised." A 15-point code of conduct issued by the government to regulate nongovernmental organizations (NGOs) was among the factors that contributed to the decline in Nepal's scores. East Timor also suffered a decline due to the effects of the withdrawal of the United Nations administration from the country. The unresolved political cleavage between East Timor and Indonesia, one for which an effective strategy is still required, threatens to undo the progress that was achieved after hostilities were brought to an end in October 1999. As the East Timor report notes, "the most pressing concerns include achieving justice for the atrocities and human rights violations from 1974 to 1999 in a way that is broadly accepted, dealing with the wide range of issues related to veterans of the resistance, and implementing an effective land and property title regime and a means for resolving disputes."

Middle East and North Africa

The countries of the Middle East and North Africa received the lowest scores in this survey. Yemen saw a significant drop, owing chiefly to severe restrictions on press freedom. During the two years covered in the survey, Yemeni journalists faced numerous incidents, including "violence, death threats, arbitrary arrests, and convictions under weak laws governing the freedom of the press." In Jordan, freedom of association and assembly became even more restricted after Interior Minister Samir Habashneh demanded that professional associations completely halt all activities deemed political, and after the governor of Amman announced that "any kind of event, gathering or meeting, save for weddings, should obtain prior approval."

However, there were some signs of modest progress in the MENA region. Morocco has enjoyed gains since the last review, principally in the spheres of Accountability and Public Voice and Civil Liberties. In a significant development, the country's interior commission in the Chamber of Deputies approved new legislation to reform the process involved in the formation of political parties and the campaign finance law, including providing parties with an annual subsidy.

Eurasia

The three countries of the Caucasus, Kazakhstan, Kyrgyzstan, and Ukraine, comprise the Eurasia region; among the countries visible crosscurrents were at work. Improvements in Georgia, Kyrgyzstan, and Ukraine were among the most significant of all countries in the survey, first and foremost in the sphere of Accountability and Public Voice, a rubric that includes such areas as elections, civil society, and media (a more detailed review of the "color revolution" countries is below). Azerbaijan, on the heels of severely flawed parliamentary elections in 2005, was the poorest performing country in this regional grouping.

Georgia, Ukraine, and Kyrgyzstan

The events of the last two years in Georgia, Ukraine, and Kyrgyzstan involved at least to a degree examples of systems in which incumbent leadership was unable to bring sufficient reform to bear in order to meet the expectations of their citizens. On the strength of popular pushback against unresponsive and corrupt political leadership, the "revolutions"— the "Rose" variety in Georgia, "Orange" in Ukraine, and "Tulip" in Kyrgyzstan—enabled a rotation of power, and with it an opportunity to set in motion a degree of democratic reform not before experienced in the post-Soviet era.

In the non-Baltic former Soviet Union such a rotation of power has been a rare achievement. Since the implosion of the USSR, hopes for institutionalization of free and fair elections and functioning succession mechanisms largely slipped from reach. Instead, with the consolidation of authoritarian or semi-authoritarian regimes, lopsided political campaigns, sham elections, and extended presidential terms in office have become the norm. Genuine expressions of public will have more often than not taken a back seat to interests of the relative few in the ruling elite who have assigned to themselves public policy decision-making prerogatives.

While the three color revolution countries registered some of the strongest improvements in this survey, the challenges confronting these states are both enormous and emblematic of the deeper reform challenges that confront such transitional countries. The exuberance of these people-power movements against corrupt, autocratic governance has given way to recognition that consolidating democratic reform will be an exceedingly difficult and long-term effort.

One aspect of the color revolution phenomenon that has received insufficient attention to date from policy makers and the scholarly community is the critical difference between two forms of mobilization. In the first instance, there is mobilizing to open political space and to induce a rotation of power. The second dimension, mobilization to bring about meaningful institutional reform, is an effort that requires far more time to achieve. For this reason, it is not surprising that Georgia, Ukraine, and Kyrgyzstan have managed considerable improvement in their Accountability and Public Voice scores from 2004 to 2006, while seeing far less movement or improvement in the areas of Rule of Law and Anticorruption and Transparency. This suggests that these countries are coming up against institutional friction many years in the making. It also suggests that policy makers and assistance organizations must recalibrate their expectations about the pace of reform in transitional countries confronting such serious institutional challenges.

The interpretation of these events and the lessons to be drawn from them are the subject of intense debate. One thing is clear, however. The election process served as a catalyst that enabled what is so uncommon in the FSU: a rotation of power among different political forces or factions. In these cases it was not the elections per se that determined the rotation of political power, but the public's reaction to a defective election process that ultimately led to the removal from power of seemingly entrenched leadership.

Expert Recommendations

Countries at the Crossroads includes recommendations that highlight priorities for government action in the four thematic categories in each country. Analysts are encouraged to focus on issues that need to be addressed most urgently in devising their recommendations. Therefore, variation from one set of recommendations to the next is considerable. However, several recommendations stand out. In nearly two-thirds of the reports, experts emphasize the need for balancing the media playing field, especially in the context of election campaigns, when incumbents often dominate and prevent the press from playing a meaningful role in providing information to the public. Moreover, the authors of these reports recommend that media freedom should be increased, whether through less restrictive laws or practices, less government interference, or better protections for journalists who cover controversial issues.

The second most frequently recurring recommendation is for efforts to combat torture. In particular, experts cited the need for improving police training and professionalism. Of the 30 reports, 13 call for measures to improve police reform and encourage better training. The countries for which this recommendation was highlighted were Kazakhstan, Kyrgyzstan, Armenia, Azerbaijan, Georgia, Morocco, Bahrain, Jordan, Uganda, Venezuela, Guatemala, Cambodia, and Indonesia.

Moreover, along with the most recurrent recommendations are also calls for more effective enforcement of financial disclosure laws that prevent conflicts of interest among public officials. Most countries have these laws on the books; however, in many cases the agencies in charge of enforcing the regulations are either too weak or lack independence to prosecute individuals who breach them.

The 2006 edition of *Countries at the Crossroads* also revisits the recommendations first made in 2004 for these countries (these recommendations and their updates can be found in the appendix). In far too many cases, little or no action has been taken on these critical reform priorities, suggesting that governments have not devoted sufficient attention and political will to these issues.

Conclusion: Democracy's Fragility and Resilience

The global trends toward democratization paint a promising picture of the world. However, sound institutions and democratic governance do not develop overnight. With good governance increasingly being acknowledged as one of the key factors in encouraging growth, a reality that has been recognized by the Millennium Challenge Account among others, it is important that policy makers remain focused on the basic elements that constitute accountable and responsive governance. The evaluation of the states examined in *Countries at the Crossroads* is designed to enhance understanding of the progress that states should make if they are to achieve transparent and accountable governance. By focusing on state performance, *Crossroads* puts primary responsibility for the protection of basic rights and good governance on governments.

These countries at the crossroads are by definition neither optimal nor irredeemably poor performers. They are countries whose leadership can make policy choices to ensure basic human rights and to enable these states to join the community of stable, free, and democratic nations. And they should be encouraged to do so.

Sanja Tatic and **Christopher Walker** are co-editors of *Countries at the Crossroads.*

COUNTRY SCORES

	Accountability and Public Voice	Civil Liberties	Rule of Law	Anticorruption and Transparency
Armenia	3.51	3.81	2.69	2.62
Azerbaijan	2.43	3.21	2.29	1.27
Bahrain	2.52	3.73	3.67	2.07
Cambodia	3.28	3.33	2.22	2.46
East Timor	3.83	4.64	3.81	2.62
Georgia	4.78	4.27	3.96	3.87
Guatemala	4.35	3.42	3.16	3.10
Guyana	4.53	4.76	4.79	3.99
Indonesia	4.70	3.70	2.97	2.45
Jordan	2.83	3.12	3.12	2.28
Kazakhstan	2.51	4.01	2.62	2.04
Kenya	5.16	4.58	3.90	3.24
Kyrgyzstan	4.17	4.17	3.38	2.54
Malawi	4.75	4.58	4.37	3.50
Malaysia	3.04	2.97	4.01	2.87
Morocco	3.30	3.67	3.04	2.14
Nepal	2.23	2.80	2.73	2.30
Nicaragua	4.49	4.20	3.61	3.40
Nigeria	3.51	3.34	2.90	2.51
Pakistan	2.15	1.76	1.83	2.14
Sierra Leone	4.65	4.15	3.78	3.17
South Africa	5.06	4.98	4.44	3.91
Sri Lanka	4.27	4.45	4.15	3.71
Tanzania	3.82	3.82	3.37	2.82
Uganda	3.99	3.81	3.66	3.74
Ukraine	4.85	4.34	3.65	3.01
Venezuela	3.00	4.07	2.98	2.13
Vietnam	1.63	3.00	2.75	2.61
Yemen	2.64	3.35	2.88	1.93
Zimbabwe	1.07	2.45	1.26	0.88

ACCOUNTABILITY AND PUBLIC VOICE

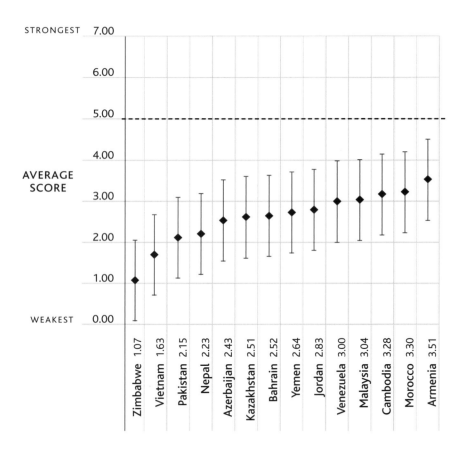

Note: Horizontal bars represent margin of error. Margin of error = 0.69, which is derived from an approximate 95 percent confidence interval based on using ±2* (standard error of measurement).

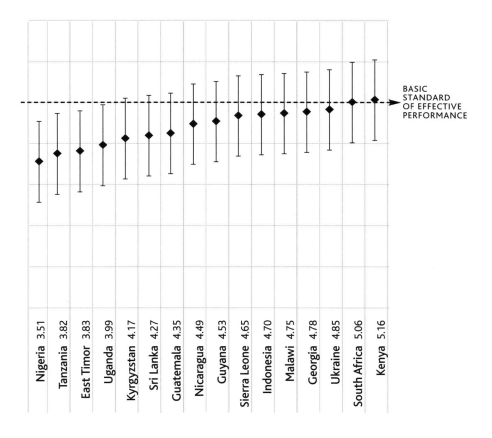

BASIC
STANDARD
OF EFFECTIVE
PERFORMANCE

Nigeria	3.51
Tanzania	3.82
East Timor	3.83
Uganda	3.99
Kyrgyzstan	4.17
Sri Lanka	4.27
Guatemala	4.35
Nicaragua	4.49
Guyana	4.53
Sierra Leone	4.65
Indonesia	4.70
Malawi	4.75
Georgia	4.78
Ukraine	4.85
South Africa	5.06
Kenya	5.16

CIVIL LIBERTIES

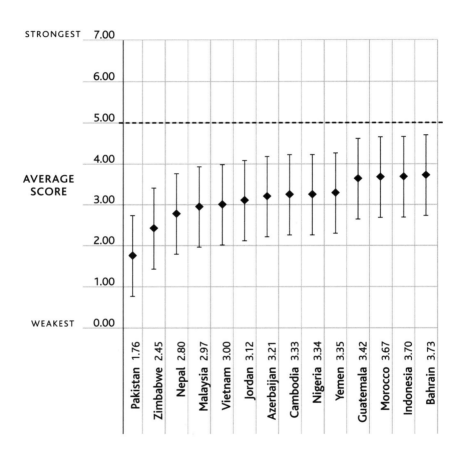

STRONGEST 7.00

AVERAGE SCORE

WEAKEST 0.00

Pakistan 1.76
Zimbabwe 2.45
Nepal 2.80
Malaysia 2.97
Vietnam 3.00
Jordan 3.12
Azerbaijan 3.21
Cambodia 3.33
Nigeria 3.34
Yemen 3.35
Guatemala 3.42
Morocco 3.67
Indonesia 3.70
Bahrain 3.73

Note: Horizontal bars represent margin of error. Margin of error = 0.82, which is derived from an approximate 95 percent confidence interval based on using ±2* (standard error of measurement).

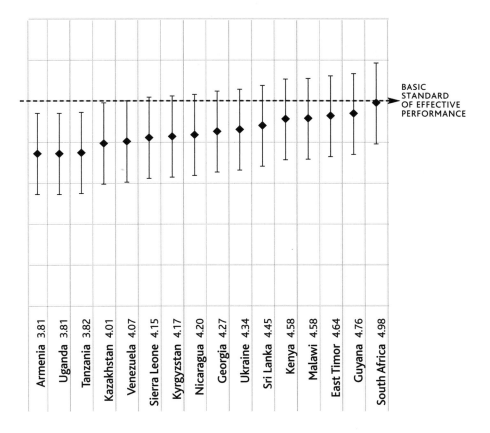

BASIC
STANDARD
OF EFFECTIVE
PERFORMANCE

Armenia 3.81

Uganda 3.81

Tanzania 3.82

Kazakhstan 4.01

Venezuela 4.07

Sierra Leone 4.15

Kyrgyzstan 4.17

Nicaragua 4.20

Georgia 4.27

Ukraine 4.34

Sri Lanka 4.45

Kenya 4.58

Malawi 4.58

East Timor 4.64

Guyana 4.76

South Africa 4.98

RULE OF LAW

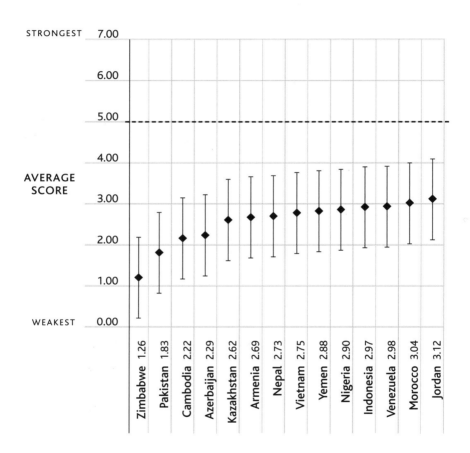

STRONGEST

AVERAGE
SCORE

WEAKEST

7.00
6.00
5.00
4.00
3.00
2.00
1.00
0.00

Zimbabwe 1.26
Pakistan 1.83
Cambodia 2.22
Azerbaijan 2.29
Kazakhstan 2.62
Armenia 2.69
Nepal 2.73
Vietnam 2.75
Yemen 2.88
Nigeria 2.90
Indonesia 2.97
Venezuela 2.98
Morocco 3.04
Jordan 3.12

Note: Horizontal bars represent margin of error. Margin of error = 0.69, which is derived from an approximate 95 percent confidence interval based on using ±2* (standard error of measurement).

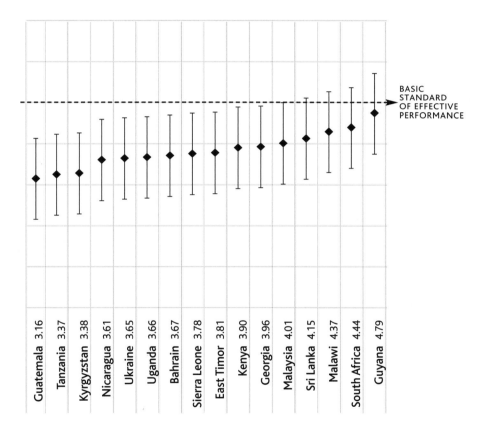

BASIC
STANDARD
OF EFFECTIVE
PERFORMANCE

Guatemala 3.16
Tanzania 3.37
Kyrgyzstan 3.38
Nicaragua 3.61
Ukraine 3.65
Uganda 3.66
Bahrain 3.67
Sierra Leone 3.78
East Timor 3.81
Kenya 3.90
Georgia 3.96
Malaysia 4.01
Sri Lanka 4.15
Malawi 4.37
South Africa 4.44
Guyana 4.79

ANTICORRUPTION AND TRANSPARENCY

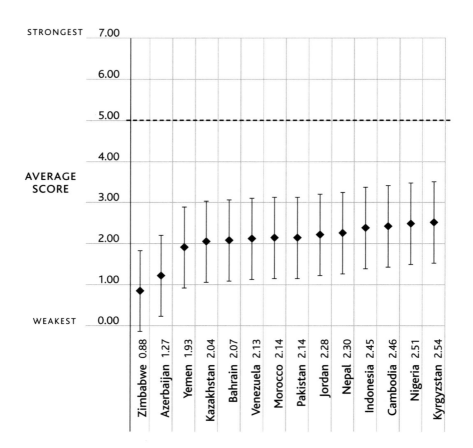

Note: Horizontal bars represent margin of error. Margin of error = 0.54, which is derived from an approximate 95 percent confidence interval based on using ±2* (standard error of measurement).

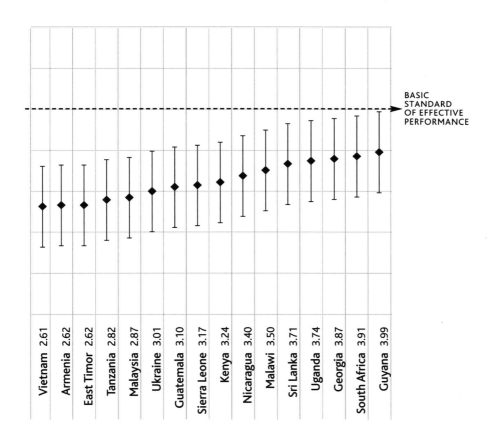

BASIC
STANDARD
OF EFFECTIVE
PERFORMANCE

Vietnam 2.61
Armenia 2.62
East Timor 2.62
Tanzania 2.82
Malaysia 2.87
Ukraine 3.01
Guatemala 3.10
Sierra Leone 3.17
Kenya 3.24
Nicaragua 3.40
Malawi 3.50
Sri Lanka 3.71
Uganda 3.74
Georgia 3.87
South Africa 3.91
Guyana 3.99

INTRODUCTION TO COUNTRY REPORTS

The *Countries at the Crossroads 2006* survey contains reports on 30 countries. Each report begins with a section containing basic political and economic data arranged in the following categories: **capital, population,** and **gross national income** (GNI) **per capita.** In addition, numerical ratings are provided for **Accountability and Public Voice, Civil Liberties, Rule of Law,** and **Anticorruption and Transparency.**

The **capital** was obtained from the CIA *World Factbook 2005.* **Population** data were obtained from the Population Reference Bureau's *2006 World Population Data Sheet.* Data on **GNI per capita** were obtained from the World Bank World Development Indicators database (www.worldbank.org) and from Internet World Stats (www.internetworldstats.com).

The **Accountability and Public Voice, Civil Liberties, Rule of Law,** and **Anticorruption and Transparency** categories contain numerical ratings between 0 and 7 for each country, with 0 representing the weakest performance and 7 representing the strongest performance. For a full description of the methods used to determine the survey's ratings, please see the chapter on Survey Methodology.

Following the political and economic data, each country report is divided into five parts: an introduction, and analyses of **Accountability and Public Voice, Civil Liberties, Rule of Law,** and **Anticorruption and Transparency.** The introduction provides a brief historical background and a description of major events. The **Accountability and Public Voice, Civil Liberties, Rule of Law,** and **Anticorruption and Transparency** sections summarize each government's degree of respect for the rights and liberties covered in the *Countries at the Crossroads* survey. Each section contains a set of recommendations highlighting the specific areas of most immediate concern for the government to address.

ARMENIA

CAPITAL: Yerevan

POPULATION: 3 million

GNI PER CAPITA: $950

SCORES	2004	2006
ACCOUNTABILITY AND PUBLIC VOICE:	2.98	3.51
CIVIL LIBERTIES:	3.96	3.81
RULE OF LAW:	3.26	2.69
ANTICORRUPTION AND TRANSPARENCY:	2.75	2.62

(scores are based on a scale of 0 to 7, with 0 representing weakest and 7 representing strongest performance)

Emil Danielyan

INTRODUCTION

Armenia was one of the first Soviet republics to rid itself of Communist rule after a democratic election in 1990. The small South Caucasus state's transition to democracy and a market economy had a very promising start as its new, young leaders embarked on sweeping political and economic reforms that earned them acclaim in the West. However, the process slowed considerably with the outbreak of a war with neighboring Azerbaijan over the disputed Nagorno-Karabakh region following the collapse of the Soviet Union. The fighting in Karabakh, coupled with armed conflicts elsewhere in the region, cut off Armenia's key routes of communication with the outside world. The country's gross domestic product (GDP) shrank by more than half from 1992 through 1993. The new regime, meanwhile, developed authoritarian tendencies that increased following a May 1994 ceasefire agreement with Azerbaijan that sealed Armenian victory in the bitter war.

The democratic regression manifested itself in a December 1994 government ban on a major opposition party and the closure of the newspapers it controlled. It culminated in the disputed parliamentary election of July 1995, which marked the beginning of Armenia's post-Soviet history of electoral fraud. Armenia's first president, Levon Ter-Petrosian, secured reelection in a reputedly rigged presidential ballot in September

Emil Danielyan is a Yerevan-based journalist and political analyst.

1996 that provoked serious unrest in Yerevan. Ter-Petrosian's lack of legitimacy enabled his government rivals to force him to resign 16 months later. His successor and the current president, Robert Kocharian, cannot boast a democratic track record either. Kocharian was twice (in 1998 and 2003) declared the winner of presidential elections marred by serious fraud. His political opponents likewise refuse to recognize his legitimacy.

The Armenian authorities' systematic failure to hold free and fair elections was highlighted by a November 2005 referendum on a package of constitutional amendments put forward by Kocharian and his governing coalition. Official results, which showed a crushing "yes" vote, sharply contrasted with largely empty polling stations and reports of massive vote rigging.

The Kocharian administration's human rights record has repeatedly been described as poor by the international community. It hit a new low in 2004 with an unprecedented government crackdown on the Armenian opposition that involved mass arrests and even violence. The ruling regime tightened its grip on electronic media in 2002 by closing the country's sole television station critical of Kocharian.

The past two years have also seen an erosion of the civil liberties enjoyed by Armenians since the collapse of Communism. The Armenian law enforcement bodies have effectively been given the new roles of political policing and keeping track of and bullying opposition activists, especially in the regions outside the capital.

ACCOUNTABILITY AND PUBLIC VOICE – 3.51

"Power in the Republic of Armenia belongs to the people," reads Article 2 of the nation's post-Soviet constitution, adopted in 1995. It provides for free and fair elections at all levels. However, all national elections held in Armenia since independence have been marred by some degree of ballot stuffing, vote rigging, and similar irregularities. Observers from the Organization for Security and Cooperation in Europe as well as the Council of Europe reported serious fraud during the most recent Armenian presidential and parliamentary elections, held in 2003. They concluded that the elections fell short of Western standards, giving weight to opposition claims that they were blatantly rigged.

The disputed constitutional referendum held on November 27, 2005, underscored the country's culture of electoral fraud. A monitoring team from the Council of Europe cast serious doubt on the credibility of the official results, according to which nearly two-thirds of Armenia's 2.3 million eligible voters took part in the referendum, and over 93 percent of them backed President Kocharian's constitutional changes. "The extremely low voting activity did not correspond to the high figures provided by the electoral commissions," the observers said in a statement.[1] The Armenian opposition, which boycotted the vote, put the turnout at about 16 percent.

The disputed referendum reinforced the widely held belief that Armenians cannot change their leadership through elections. The nation's sole post-Soviet regime change, in February 1998, was the result of government infighting rather than the expression of popular will. Free and fair elections have proved elusive despite frequent changes to electoral legislation that are supposed to inhibit chronic vote rigging. But the legal amendments have been rendered meaningless by the Armenian leaders' evident reluctance to let the public decide whether or not they should remain in power. Furthermore, the amendments have not weakened the regime's tight grip on the election commissions. The legally guaranteed equal campaigning opportunities exist only on paper, with state television and the private networks controlled by Kocharian routinely providing extremely biased coverage of opposition activities. Campaigning for the referendum was no exception.

The ruling regime has also relied heavily on its status and extensive financial resources, which are often used to buy votes, a phenomenon that again came to light during nationwide local elections held over the course of 2005. The local polls, boycotted by the opposition, were won mostly by wealthy candidates representing various business clans and even quasi-criminal elements loyal to the regime. The latter increasingly relies on government-connected oligarchs.

The authorities' poor human rights record deteriorated further in the spring of 2004, when the Armenian opposition launched a campaign of antigovernment protests in a bid to replicate the November 2003 Rose Revolution in neighboring Georgia. Kocharian's regime responded with an unprecedented crackdown on opposition supporters across the country. Hundreds were arrested and sentenced to up to 15 days in prison on trumped-up petty charges under the Soviet-era code of administrative offenses. Very few of them had access to lawyers or a public trial.

Police also arrested several opposition leaders in April 2004 and charged them with calling for a "violent overthrow of the government." The authorities released the leaders three months later under pressure from the Council of Europe. Around that time, two other prominent opposition figures and a human rights activist were assaulted in Yerevan. The assailants were never brought to justice. The victims described them as burly men with very short haircuts, resembling in their appearance bodyguards for government-connected oligarchs. Two dozen such men attempted to disrupt an opposition rally in Yerevan on April 5, 2004. Scores of police stood by and looked on as they smashed the cameras of photojournalists who were filming their actions. Only two of the thugs were subsequently prosecuted and given symbolic fines.

Tension came to a head on the night of April 12–13, 2004, when security forces dispersed an opposition demonstration outside Kocharian's residence, using water cannons, stun grenades, and even electric-shock equipment. They went on to ransack the Yerevan offices of the main opposition parties. Facing criticism by various domestic and international organizations, the authorities argued that heavy-handed tactics were justified because they staved off a coup d'etat.[2]

Armenia's democratization has also been hampered by an extremely lopsided system of governance that gives sweeping powers to the president of the republic. The constitutional amendments, approved in the referendum and adopted, gave some of those powers to the cabinet of ministers and parliament. The president, for example, will no longer be able to sack the prime minister and dissolve the National Assembly at will. His authority to appoint and dismiss virtually all judges will also be somewhat restricted. The United States, the European Union, and the Council of Europe endorsed those amendments. But the Armenian opposition dismissed them as insignificant and said the authorities should respect the existing laws in the first place.

Despite the constitutional reform, the Armenian president will remain by far the most powerful state official. In particular, he will continue to form single-handedly the State Civil Service Council that oversees the government bureaucracy. This council was set up in 2002 in accordance with a new law intended to protect civil servants against arbitrary dismissal, cleanse government agencies of incompetent officials, and create a merit-based system. The council, according to its chairman, Manvel Badalian, fired about 350 civil servants and hired more than 1,350 others on a competitive basis by November 2004.[3] But critics say that the selection process, which includes an oral interview, is discretionary and open to abuse.

Armenia boasts more than 3,000 nongovernmental organizations (NGOs) registered with the Ministry of Justice. Although most of them hardly operate in practice, the figure suggests that the registration process is rather simple. The NGOs engage in a wide range of activities, including benevolence, human rights protection, women's and minority affairs, and consumer rights. The most successful usually have external sources of funding. The government rarely interferes with their activities, but the impact of NGOs on government policies and decisions has been minimal.

Local civic groups rarely dealt with political affairs until the 2004 government crackdown on the opposition, which was trying to unseat Kocharian. From April through June 2004, some groups held rallies and picketed the prosecutor general's office in Yerevan in protest of mass arrests of opposition activists and Armenia's perceived transformation into a police state.[4] Following the campaign, some three dozen NGOs created a coalition advocating political reform. The coalition, called Partnership for Open Society, unsuccessfully lobbied for more serious changes in the Armenian constitution and electoral code throughout 2005. The government did, however, give in to pressure from local environmental protection groups in June 2005, when it decided to reroute a planned new highway that would have passed through one of Armenia's last remaining virgin forests.

The Armenian media operate in a more hostile environment than the NGOs, with the authorities continuing to maintain tight control over the state-owned Armenian Public Television and virtually all private channels, which are owned by businesspeople loyal to Kocharian and rarely air reports critical of his administration. Their reporters are believed to operate under editorial censorship. The only TV station critical of the authorities, A1+, was controversially pulled off the air in 2002. Its repeated attempts to resume broadcasting have been thwarted by the Kocharian-controlled National Commission on Television and Radio.

The regulatory body likewise rejected an A1+ bid to obtain an FM radio frequency in February 2005. The Armenian newspapers (virtually all of them privately owned) are far more diverse and free, but their low circulation seriously limits their ability to inform the public.

From 2003 to 2005, virtually no libel suits were filed against the media. Nor did the authorities use a controversial clause in the Armenian criminal code that allows them to prosecute journalists for defamation of character. Still, the year 2004 saw the worst-ever government-sanctioned violence against journalists. At least four were severely beaten by special police while covering the brutal break up of an antigovernment demonstration in Yerevan. The beatings were never investigated by law enforcement authorities. "The impunity surrounding these attacks made journalists more vulnerable," the New York–based Committee to Protect Journalists said in a subsequent report.[5] In a separate incident, a photojournalist was assaulted by several men after photographing luxury villas belonging to senior government and law enforcement officials. Although one person was sentenced to six months imprisonment for the attack in October 2004, the bodyguard of a senior police officer, who reportedly provoked the assault, was not prosecuted.

Internet users as well as writers, musicians, and other artists are not known to have faced any government restrictions. Economic problems and poor enforcement of copyright laws are far more serious obstacles to free cultural expression.

Recommendations
- The Armenian authorities should make firm and resolute efforts to curtail election fraud.
- The authorities should at last start enforcing legal provisions that make vote buying a serious crime.
- President Kocharian must end the de facto impunity enjoyed by increasingly feared oligarchs.
- Armenia needs a deeper, consensus-based reform of its flawed constitution.
- The ruling regime should lift restrictions on the electronic media, permit A1+ to resume broadcasting, investigate instances of unwarranted violence against journalists, and bring those responsible to trial.

CIVIL LIBERTIES – 3.81

The constitution makes it clear that "no one may be subjected to torture and to treatment and punishment that are cruel or degrading to the individual's dignity." However, ill-treatment of detainees, the most common form of human rights violation in Armenia according to domestic and international watchdogs, remains widespread, with law enforcement officers routinely beating criminal suspects to extract confessions. The situation does not seem to have improved since the Armenian parliament's ratification in 2002 of the European Convention for the Prevention of Torture and the European Convention on Human Rights. The move led to the first-ever inspection of Armenia's prisons and detention sites by the European Committee for the Prevention of Torture (CPT). In a report made public in July 2004, the Council of Europe concluded that individuals arrested or interrogated by Armenian law enforcement bodies run a "significant risk" of torture, humiliation, and psychological pressure.[6] The report said members of a CPT delegation who met with Armenian detainees heard "numerous and consistent allegations of physical ill-treatment. . . . The ill-treatment alleged consisted essentially of punches and kicks, and of striking the persons concerned with truncheons and/or other hard objects, such as chair legs, thick metal cables or gun butts."

Human Rights Watch likewise noted in its 2005 *World Report* that "Torture and ill-treatment in police custody remain widespread in Armenia."[7] The illegal practice has continued unabated due to the atmosphere of impunity in which the Armenian police and other security agencies operate. No officer is known to have been prosecuted for such abuses in 2003–04. Furthermore, the Armenian government challenged the CPT's conclusion, saying that "the facts indicated in the report were not concrete."[8]

In April 2004, an opposition activist in the southern town of Artashat, Grisha Virabian, had to undergo urgent surgery after enduring a reportedly brutal interrogation at a local police station. The authorities refused to investigate his harrowing account of torture. Furthermore, Virabian himself was nearly prosecuted for resisting one of his police interrogators.

The country's human rights ombudsperson, Larisa Alaverdian, said in July 2005 that a large proportion of the citizen complaints filed with her office concern violations of due process of law. She said many Armenians believe that court rulings against them and their relatives are based on testimony extracted under duress. An annual report by the ombudsperson's office said that the local courts' bias in favor of state prosecutors is "constantly evident" and that the law enforcement agencies rarely investigate torture allegations.[9] Law enforcement agencies are often eager to keep criminal suspects in pretrial detention, making it easier for them to extract "confessions."

The maximum legal period of pretrial detention in Armenia is one year. Detainees are less likely to be mistreated by law enforcement officials after being convicted and sentenced. Conditions in local Soviet-era prisons have reportedly improved since 2002, when Armenia's penitentiary system was transferred from police to Justice Ministry jurisdiction. But they were deemed unsatisfactory by a monitoring group comprising representatives of a dozen NGOs that conducted a yearlong inspection of prisons across the country. Their report, released in June 2005, said most Armenian prisons remain overcrowded and unsanitary and are in urgent need of repairs.[10] Justice Ministry officials accepted the criticism but blamed the problem on a lack of funds.[11] The Council of Europe has repeatedly demanded the abolition of the code of administrative offenses, under which hundreds of opposition activists were arrested in 2004. However, Kocharian's regime continues to use the code on a vast scale whenever the opposition threatens its grip on power.

Aside from the 2004 opposition crackdown, the Armenian opposition has been generally free to hold rallies, although virtually none of its 2004 protests in Yerevan was formally permitted by the authorities. In May 2004, at the height of the opposition campaign, the Kocharian-controlled parliament passed a new law on rallies that many saw as an infringement of citizens' constitutionally guaranteed freedom of assembly. The law was amended a year later in line with recommendations of experts from the Council of Europe. In particular, a provision was scrapped that allowed police to disperse a street gathering if it posed a threat to public and state security. But another controversial clause that bans demonstrations outside the presidential palace in Yerevan was kept in force.

The state largely respects citizens' constitutional right to freedom of association, as evidenced by the existence of over 60 political parties and thousands of NGOs. Citizens are not forced to belong to any organization. Still, many civil servants and other public sector employees have been compelled to campaign for incumbent presidents and ruling parties during elections. They were similarly instructed to campaign for the passage of Kocharian's constitutional amendments in November 2005. Several trade unions unite mainly public sector workers. The bulk of the private sector workforce is not unionized due to high unemployment and weak government protection of workers' rights.

The creation in 2003 of Armenia's Office of the Human Rights Defender gave citizens an important new avenue for seeking justice. Despite having been appointed by the president, Ombudsperson Alaverdian has proven quite vocal in condemning and tackling abuses committed by various government bodies. Her relations with the government markedly deteriorated over the course of 2005. Alaverdian complained in July 2005 about a lack of legal powers, saying that her office is able to look into only a fraction of citizen petitions against courts and law enforcement bodies.

The Armenian constitution guarantees gender equality, and there are no laws discriminating against women. Nevertheless, Armenia is a conservative, male-dominated society in which few women hold senior government posts. Local women's organizations say domestic violence is not uncommon, but they have yet to determine the precise scale of the problem. Trafficking of Armenian women abroad is seen as a more serious problem. In 2003, the U.S. State Department upgraded Armenia from its so-called Tier 3 group to its Tier 2 group of states, which the United States believes are making "significant efforts" to tackle illegal cross-border transport of human beings. However, the department's latest annual report on the issue, released in June 2005, put Armenia on a Tier 2 watch list because of its "failure to show evidence of increasing efforts to combat trafficking over the past year." [12] Washington's warning to Yerevan followed an independent journalistic investigation that implicated senior Armenian law enforcement officials in prostitution rings operating in the United Arab Emirates. [13]

The constitution gives equal rights and protection to ethnic minorities (mostly Yezidi Kurds, Russians, and Assyrians), which make up less than 3 percent of the country's population. Even though the minorities rarely report instances of overt discrimination, they often complain about difficulties with receiving education in their native languages, partially due to financial constraints, including the lack of textbooks and resources for teacher training.

Armenia also has constitutional guarantees for freedom of conscience, with about 50 religious organizations reportedly operating in the country. Their members have been generally free to practice their religious beliefs. The Armenian Apostolic Church, to which over 90 percent of the population belongs, enjoys a quasi-official privileged status. One of the constitutional amendments put to referendum in November 2005 upholds that status by recognizing the ancient church's "exceptional mission" in the spiritual and cultural life of the Armenian people.

The church advocates restrictions on activities of nontraditional religious groups, notably Jehovah's Witnesses. The U.S.-based group was for years denied official registration primarily due to its strong opposition to military service, which is compulsory in Armenia. Dozens of its young male members have been imprisoned for refusing the two-year duty. Jehovah's Witnesses was finally legalized in October 2004, shortly after the entry into force of a new law on alternative civilian service. At least two dozen Jehovah's Witnesses enlisted for the new service, mostly as hospital attendants. However, most of them had deserted their civilian places of service by May 2005 on the grounds that they were overseen by military officials. Seven of them were sentenced to between two and three years in prison in October 2005 on desertion charges.[14]

Recommendations

- The Armenian authorities should stop tolerating ill-treatment of detainees and should investigate persistent torture reports. Law enforcement officials should be ordered explicitly to discontinue the practice.
- Persons taken to police stations for questioning should be given access to lawyers from the very moment of detention, rather than after being formally declared criminal suspects.
- The Armenian authorities should finally abolish the Soviet-era administrative code in line with Council of Europe recommendations.
- The Armenian ombudsperson should be given greater authority to investigate human rights abuses.
- Authorities should clamp down in earnest on human trafficking.

RULE OF LAW – 2.69

Armenia's judicial system remains under strong government influence, despite having undergone substantial structural changes since the Soviet collapse. It is mistrusted by the population, which perceives it as riddled with corruption. The current Armenian constitution introduced a three-tier structure of courts of general jurisdiction topped by the Court of Appeals. It also created a separate nine-member Constitutional Court empowered to overturn government decisions, impeach the president, and invalidate elections. On paper, these judicial bodies are protected against state interference. But they have been highly subservient in practice, rarely ruling against the government and prosecutors. This is not least because of the fact that all Armenian judges, except five members of the Constitutional Court, are appointed by the president of the republic without parliamentary confirmation.

In a study conducted in 2004, the American Bar Association's Central and East European Law Initiative (ABA/CEELI) found no fundamental progress in judicial independence and corruption in recent years. It rated Armenia negatively on 13 out of the 30 indicators making up its judicial reform index, used to assess the rule of law in emerging democracies.[15] Among the factors negatively rated were the selection and appointment of judges and the courts' susceptibility to improper influence. The ABA/CEELI study, based on interviews with Armenian judicial officials and legal experts, concluded that "legal culture in Armenia, mainly in the criminal law field, is still dominated by Soviet-era thinking that puts the procuracy at the top of the legal system, followed by judges and lastly defense advocates."[16]

The mass imprisonment of opposition activists in 2004, when Armenian judges rubber-stamped police fabrications, was a vivid manifestation of this reality. Another indication of their subordination to the executive is the fact that the local courts sanction pretrial detentions of criminal suspects in the vast majority of cases. According to official statistics unveiled by a senior judge at the Armenian Court of Appeals, Mher Khachatrian, more than 96 percent of 5,116 arrest petitions filed by prosecutors in 2003 were approved by judges at various levels.[17] Less than half of those remanded were convicted and sentenced to prison terms in subsequent trials. Khachatrian admitted that many judges "seem to be scared" of rebuffing prosecutors, who are usually guided by the Soviet-style presumption of guilt.

Some of the key constitutional amendments enacted by the Armenian authorities in 2005 are meant to strengthen the judiciary by making Armenia's Council of Justice, a body that has the exclusive authority to recommend to the president the appointment and removal of judges, more independent. Until now all the council's members were named and dismissed exclusively by the head of state. The constitutional reform empowered Armenian judges to elect nine council members by secret ballot. The president and the parliament each appoint two of the remaining four members of the body. It will take years before the practical impact of this change emerges.

It also remains to be seen whether the authorities will make any changes in the procedure for the selection of judicial candidates. The process involves oral interviews with the justice minister. The ABA/CEELI study noted a "widespread public perception that this process is guided by bribery, nepotism, and partisanship." In addition, Armenian law does not require prospective judges to have practiced before a tribunal or to undergo relevant training before taking the bench. This might explain why many judges are perceived to be incompetent.

"All persons are equal before the law," proclaims one of the constitutional amendments pushed through in the disputed referendum. It is hard to imagine this provision being enforced under Armenia's existing law enforcement and judicial systems. Armenian law may prohibit any discrimination based on a person's gender or ethnic origin, but the reality has been very different. Innocent citizens lacking money and government connections are practically unprotected against mistreatment in custody, while criminals may have cases against them dropped in exchange for a bribe.

Trials in Armenia are usually open to the media and the public in general. Criminal suspects have a legal right to hire defense attorneys. If they cannot afford to do so, the state is required to provide them with a lawyer free of charge. However, government-appointed counsels are notorious for secretly collaborating with prosecutors. The Office of the Prosecutor General is tightly controlled by the president, which is why politically motivated trials are not uncommon in Armenia. The procuracy, the police, the National Security Service (the former KGB), and the military are directly subordinate to Kocharian. Parliament and even the Cabinet of Ministers have little control over their activities.

Ruling regimes in Armenia have always used the security apparatus for carrying out and covering up vote falsifications. Law enforcement bodies have also become powerful tools of political repression in recent years, with police departments across the country detaining opposition activists whenever Kocharian's hold on power is challenged by his foes. This was evident in the run-up to and in the wake of the November 2005 referendum. Local human rights groups saw more and more elements of a police state in Armenia during 2003–05.

It is little wonder that there were virtually no reported instances of senior law enforcement officials prosecuted for abuse of power. Most of these officials, wealthy individuals with extensive business interests, operate in utter disregard for human rights. Prosecutor General Aghvan Hovsepian, for example, is believed to control a dairy firm, a TV channel, and other businesses. Another powerful official, Deputy Police Chief Hovannes Varian, was described by a newspaper as Armenia's richest policeman, who has made a "very serious fortune" fed by at least a dozen businesses.[18] Not incidentally, Varian has been present at just about every major opposition rally in Yerevan and personally led the brutal break up of the April 2004 protest outside Kocharian's palace.

The constitution gives everyone the right to own private property, which the state can take away only in exceptional cases and with commensurate compensation defined by law. This provision appears to have been generally respected until the start of a massive government-sanctioned redevelopment project in central Yerevan in 2004. Hundreds of old houses were torn down to give way to expensive residential and office buildings constructed by private investors. Many of the house owners protested against the amount of financial compensation offered by the municipal authorities, saying it was well below the market value of their property. Some even sued the government, accusing officials overseeing the scheme of corruption. However, Yerevan courts sided with the government in virtually all cases, and a human rights lawyer who represented the last resisting house owners was arrested by former members of the KGB on dubious fraud charges in October 2005. Most of those low-income residents were forcibly evicted from their homes by the end of 2005.

In a special report issued in September 2005, Ombudsperson Alaverdian condemned the entire process as unfair and even illegal. She argued in particular that the properties were alienated in accordance with government directives rather than under a special law, as is required by the constitution.[19] The government ignored the report.

Recommendations

• The Armenian authorities should enact additional safeguards for judicial independence, such as a parliamentary endorsement of all judicial candidates, and put an end to the justice minister's involvement in their selection.
• The government and law enforcement agencies should stop pressuring courts into handing down verdicts favorable to their interests.
• State prosecutors should scale down recourse to pretrial detentions.
• The ruling regime must stop using the police and the former KGB operatives to deal with political opponents.

ANTICORRUPTION AND TRANSPARENCY – 2.62

Armenia's business environment has long been regarded by Western lending institutions as one of the most liberal in the former Soviet Union. The government appears to have liberalized it further in recent years under pressure from the International Monetary Fund (IMF) and the World Bank. In an extensive study on the Armenian economy, a group of IMF economists pointed to a simplification of licensing procedures, a higher "quality of [government] regulations," and their increased accessibility to the local business community. "These changes led to an improvement in the business environment and put Armenia ahead of most CIS countries in a variety of governance indicators," they wrote.[20] The World Bank arrived at a similar conclusion in a September 2005 survey that assessed "the ease of doing business" in 155 countries on the basis of ten factors such as taxation, business registration, and labor legislation. Armenia was 46th in the rankings, ahead of all other CIS countries.[21]

Still, government connections remain essential for doing business in Armenia. Some forms of large-scale economic activity, such as importation of fuel, wheat, and other basic commodities, have effectively been monopolized by oligarchs. Another form of excessive state involvement in the economy is a notoriously corrupt and arbitrary tax and customs administration. The IMF and the World Bank have been pressing the authorities to tackle the problem, but harassment from tax authorities remains the number one subject of complaints by Armenian business-people. They usually avoid publicly challenging the government for fear of retribution.

In a very rare exception to this rule, the coffee importing company Royal Armenia publicly accused the leadership of the Armenian customs authority throughout 2004 and 2005 of illegally penalizing it for its refusal to engage in a scam that would have enriched senior customs officials. The extraordinary allegations, denied by the Armenian customs authority, were widely covered by the Armenian press. But the embattled company faced serious consequences as a result, when it was all but driven out of the coffee business and its two top executives were arrested on dubious fraud charges in October 2005. Their example will hardly encourage whistle blowing by other entrepreneurs.

Many ministers and other senior government officials are themselves involved in business, directly or indirectly owning companies. Armenian newspapers regularly carry reports about their and their relatives' extravagant lifestyles. Their questionable self-enrichment is clearly facilitated by the absence of any laws on conflicts of interest. Armenia did enact a law in 2002 that obligated senior public officials to declare their assets. However, the law has proven ineffectual, with many officials routinely underreporting their conspicuous wealth.

This reality is a reflection of the widespread corruption that has engulfed all areas of life in Armenia, including the education sector. Bribery remains a serious problem in the selection of students for the prestigious programs of state-run universities. In November 2003, the government unveiled a long-awaited plan of mainly legislative actions aimed at fighting corruption. Throughout 2005, the government claimed to be successfully implementing the program endorsed by the World Bank, but indications that it has actually reduced the scale of graft were absent. For example, Armenia scored 2.9 out of 10 on Transparency International's 2005 Corruption Perceptions Index (CPI)—down from 3.1 in the 2004 global survey conducted by the Berlin-based watchdog.[22]

There is a widely held belief, shared by Transparency International representatives in Yerevan, that the Armenian authorities lack the will to combat corruption in earnest. During 2003–05, no senior officials are known to have been prosecuted for bribery and other corrupt practices. Law enforcement authorities claimed to have solved 227 corruption-related crimes in the first half of 2005 but refused to identify any of the individuals who allegedly committed those crimes.[23]

Although Armenian laws and regulations are published on time and are even accessible on the Internet, government transparency has generally been lacking. In September 2003, the Armenian parliament passed a potentially significant law that gives citizens the right to obtain important information from both public and private legal entities. Under that law, government agencies cannot turn down citizen inquiries that deal with "cases of emergency threatening citizens' health and security," the economic situation in the country, education, health care, and environmental protection. Such information must be provided, normally free of charge and in writing, within 30 days of the receipt of an application. Public awareness of these important provisions has so far been weak, and it is therefore premature to gauge their overall impact on government transparency.

At least one government structure, the Yerevan municipality, has clearly failed to comply with the law by refusing to release copies of all of its decisions regarding lucrative land allocations in the Armenian capital in recent years. The information was requested by Hetq.am, an online investigative publication that extensively covered the process, which was tainted with reports of high-level corruption and nepotism. The copies had still not been provided by the municipality as of November 2005, despite successful legal action taken by Hetq.

The government's budget-making process has been reasonably transparent, with the National Assembly publicly debating and even altering spending bills submitted by the executive. The government also reports to parliament and must secure its approval for the execution of the national budget. The government's detailed execution reports must be considered by lawmakers after being examined by parliament's Audit Chamber. However, although the oversight body, the most important in Armenia, has repeatedly criticized the government's use of public finances and external loans, it lacks the legal and administrative muscle to affect government policies.

The authorities also claim to have cracked down on corrupt practices in the awarding of government contracts with a 2000 law that mandates competitive bidding for every single government purchase of goods and services worth more than $500. But the head of a government agency handling state procurements, Gagik Khachatrian, admitted in February 2005 that many potential suppliers avoid taking part in such tenders, presumably because of lack of faith in their integrity.[24] Much of the foreign assistance in Armenia comes from the United States and Europe, who administer its distribution themselves.

Recommendations

- The Armenian authorities should stop tolerating endemic corruption in their ranks and should enforce relevant laws by prosecuting corrupt high-level officials.
- The authorities should enact a stringent law on conflicts of interest and amend the existing law on financial disclosure to allow for the verification of declared assets.
- Tax and customs officials must be explicitly banned from collecting state revenues in an arbitrary and discretionary manner.
- The freedom of information law should be amended to specify sanctions against government agencies illegally refusing to provide data requested by citizens.

NOTES

[1] "Statement by the Council of Europe Observer Mission for the referendum on constitutional amendments in Armenia" (Strasbourg: Council of Europe [COE], 28 November 2005).

[2] *Cycle of Repression: Human Rights Violations in Armenia* (New York: Human Rights Watch [HRW], Briefing Paper, 4 May 2005), http://hrw.org/backgrounder/eca/armenia/0504/.

[3] Hrach Melkumian, "Armenian Civil Service Watchdog Sums Up Two-Year Work," in *RFE/RL Armenia Report* (Prague and Washington, D.C.: Radio Free Europe/Radio Liberty [RFE/RL]), 4 November 2004, http://www.armenialiberty.org.

[4] Hrach Melkumian, "Civic Groups Protest Against 'Police State,'" *RFE/RL Armenia Report,* 15 April 2004.

[5] "Armenia," in Attacks on the Press 2004 (New York: Committee to Protect Journalists [CPJ]), http://www.cpj.org/attacks04/europe04/armenia.html.

[6] *Report to the Armenian Government* (Strasbourg: COE, European Committee for the Prevention of Torture and Inhuman or Degrading Treatment or Punishment, 28 July 2004), http://www.cpt.coe.int/documents/arm/2004-25-inf-eng.htm.

[7] *World Report 2005* (HRW), http://hrw.org/wr2k5/.

8 *Final Response of the Armenian Government to the Report of the European Committee for the Prevention of Torture and Inhuman or Degrading Treatment or Punishment* (Strasbourg: COE, European Committee for the Prevention of Torture and Inhuman or Degrading Treatment or Punishment, 28 July 2004), http://www.cpt.coe.int/documents/arm/2004-27-inf-eng.htm

9 Anna Saghabalian, "Ombudsman Criticizes 2004 Crackdown on Opposition," *RFE/RL Armenia Report,* 26 April 2005.

10 Karine Kalantarian, "Civic Groups Want Better Prison Conditions in Armenia," *RFE/RL Armenia Report,* 30 June 2005.

11 Ibid.

12 *Trafficking in Persons Report 2005* (Washington, D.C.: U.S. Department of State, Office to Monitor and Combat Trafficking in Persons, 3 June 2005), http://www.state.gov/g/tip/rls/tiprpt/2005/.

13 Edik Baghdasarian, "Prosecutors are Hard at Work, But Human Trafficking is Booming," *Hetq-Online* (Investigative Journalists of Armenia), 30 March 2005, http://www.hetq.am/eng/society/0503-dub-9.html.

14 Vahan Ishkhanian, "Convictions for Conviction: Alternative service recruits sentenced on AWOL charges," *Armenia Now,* 11 November 2005, http://www.armenianow.com/?action=viewArticle&CID=1378&IID=1055&AID=1202.

15 "Armenia," in *Judicial Reform Index* (Chicago and Washington D.C.: American Bar Association, Central and East European Law Initiative [ABA/CEELI], December 2004), http://www.abanet.org/ceeli/publications/jri/home.html.

16 Ibid, 2.

17 Karine Kalantarian, "Arrest Data Highlight Court Weakness In Armenia," *RFE/RL Armenia Report,* 27 April 2004.

18 Karen Mikaelian, "Adherents of the Criminal Underworld," *Chorrord Ishkhanutyun,* 6 December 2005.

19 Vahan Ishkhanian, "Is Anybody Listening?" *Armenia Now,* 25 September 2005.

20 E. Gelbard, J. McHugh, C. Beddies, and L. Redifer, "Growth and Poverty Reduction in Armenia: Achievements and Challenges" (Washington, D.C.: International Monetary Fund [IMF], December 2005), 10.

21 Atom Markarian, "Armenia's Business Environment 'Best In CIS,'" *RFE/RL Armenia Report,* 21 September 2005.

22 *2005 Corruption Perceptions Index* (Berlin: Transparency International, 18 October 2005), http://www.transparency.org/policy_and_research/surveys_indices/cpi/2005.

23 Ruzanna Stepanian, "Government Reports Rise In 'Corruption Crimes,'" *RFE/RL Armenia Report,* 2 November 2005.

24 Nane Atshemian, "Official Admits Business Distrust Of State Procurements," *RFE/RL Armenia Report,* 16 February 2005.

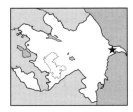

AZERBAIJAN

CAPITAL: Baku
POPULATION: 8.4 million
GNI PER CAPITA: $820

SCORES	2004	2006
ACCOUNTABILITY AND PUBLIC VOICE:	2.63	2.43
CIVIL LIBERTIES:	3.78	3.21
RULE OF LAW:	2.92	2.29
ANTICORRUPTION AND TRANSPARENCY:	1.57	1.27

(scores are based on a scale of 0 to 7, with 0 representing weakest
and 7 representing strongest performance)

Christopher Walker

INTRODUCTION

Azerbaijan is an energy-rich state of eight million inhabitants located in
the politically fragile south Caucasus region. Energy resources and strategic location render the country of serious interest to its immediate neighbors and global powers alike.

Azerbaijan's principal challenge in the near term is to identify a course
to enable genuine political reform and to open the country's now tightly
controlled institutions to more democratic participation. In this regard
the November 2005 parliamentary elections and the presidential elections in October 2003 are emblematic of the profound institutional
challenges that confront the country. These two flawed elections also
represent the political bookends of the Ilham Aliyev era to date.

International observers and reformers in Azerbaijan looked to the
parliamentary elections of 2005 as a potential turning point in Azeri
politics. However, these elections, like the presidential ballot of November 2003, were beset by irregularities and failed to meet international
standards. The authorities took some modest, positive steps during the
2005 election cycle, including lifting a ban on election monitoring by
local nongovernmental organizations (NGOs) that receive more than
30 percent of their funding from outside sources and creating a public
television station. These measures were, however, offset by extensive

Christopher Walker is Director of Studies at Freedom House.

flaws in the vote tabulation process and intimidation of opposition candidates. The authorities' controlling approach to this election ensured that the opposition would not achieve a competitive threshold.

The poor conduct of the election process is in essence a symptom of far deeper and fundamental challenges confronting the country. The source of the problem rests in an entrenched political culture that retains Soviet-era governance features, among them flawed institutions incapable of achieving sufficient levels of accountability.

The slow progress on implementing democratic reforms has not gone unnoticed by key Western institutions and monitoring organizations. While Azeri government officials cite gradual improvements in the country's governance, domestic critics and outside organizations assert that little meaningful reform has been implemented under Ilham Aliyev's leadership. The Organization for Security and Cooperation in Europe (OSCE) and the Council of Europe (COE), for instance, have repeatedly chided the authorities for the sluggish pace of reform.

The June 2005 final resolution of the Parliamentary Assembly of the Council of Europe (PACE) on "Functioning of Democratic Institutions in Azerbaijan" was particularly scathing in its critique of the country's lack of progress. The report cited an extensive list of deficiencies in what are the building blocks of a democratic system, including open and fair elections, freedom of assembly, and independence of the news media and of the judicial and legislative branches of government.[1] The nongovernmental sector likewise finds itself under great pressure and pushed to the fringes of Azeri society. The marginalization of organizations and forces not aligned with the regime presents a dilemma that confronts many other unreformed post-Soviet regimes: namely, how to include alternative voices in the political process and move away from zero-sum politics.

In the short to mid term, oil revenues and energy-sector driven economic growth should provide a social cushion. The year 2005 saw the official inauguration of the Baku-Tbilisi-Ceyhan pipeline, which has the potential to help bring about a previously unknown degree of prosperity for the citizens of Azerbaijan. Oil is slated to flow through the 1,100 mile-long pipeline in earnest later in 2006. Nevertheless, weak rule of law and the absence of independent institutions capable of holding powerful actors accountable suggest that the system may fall prey to the resource curse, a phenomenon that afflicts many states with substantial natural energy wealth and substandard institutions.

The "frozen" conflict of Nagorno-Karabakh, which created some 800,000 internally displaced persons (IDPs) in Azerbaijan, is another issue that looms large on the Azeri political scene. These IDPs include a generation of children who have been born and are growing up in appalling conditions, and may well be ripe for recruitment into radical Islamic groups in the not-too-distant future. So long as this conflict remains frozen, it will also act as an obstacle to regional cooperation and maintain a dangerous degree of mutual enmity between Armenians and Azerbaijanis.

While the November 2005 elections revealed that the ruling powers remain determined to prevent political opposition from reaching a competitive threshold, the ballot also offered evidence to suggest that the opposition is ill equipped to mount a serious challenge. The suffocating grip on Azerbaijan's politics by the ruling Yeni Azerbaijan Party (YAP) presents a singular challenge for the country's political development. At the same time, a poorly organized opposition has not distinguished itself, leaving an enormous reform vacuum in the country's political life.[2] Weak political competition and the absence of meaningful checks and balances feed into a system in which the ruling elite can and does operate with impunity.

ACCOUNTABILITY AND PUBLIC VOICE – 2.43

Azerbaijan's constitution assures its citizens the right to change their government peacefully. However, in practice this right is effectively denied. Indeed, all of the elections conducted under the stewardship of former President Heidar Aliyev and more recently under his son, Ilham Aliyev, have fallen short of international standards for democratic elections. The parliamentary elections held in November 2005 were no exception.

The obstacles to free and fair elections are manifold. Opposition parties are at a severe disadvantage in terms of resources. The authorities use the full complement of state administrative resources to advance the interests of the ruling YAP, systematically denying the opportunity for political opposition to reach a competitive threshold. The November parliamentary vote represents a case in point.

In the November 2005 elections, the YAP captured 58 seats in the 125-member parliament, while opposition parties won 13, of which the Azadliq (Freedom) bloc won eight. The majority of the 42 independents with no party affiliation are believed to be beholden to the government.[3] The Constitutional Court annulled the results in 10 districts, whose races were to be rerun on May 13, 2006. Apart from technical and administrative obstacles in the election process, the authorities also employ more brutal tactics in managing political competition. In the weeks leading up to the election, the main opposition bloc (Azadliq) faced a state media smear campaign, as well as arrests, beatings, and intimidation by the authorities.[4] International observers criticized the vote, but given the control of content on the airwaves and the authorities' downplaying of the Western monitors' findings, it was unclear in the immediate aftermath of the election whether the Azeri public was aware of the independent observers' critical assessment.[5]

As has been the case in other recent election periods, the most recent election cycle was characterized by highly polemical political rhetoric. The government and principal opposition parties in Azerbaijan tend to speak at or past each other. As a result, little in the way of meaningful policy debate on the major public issues confronting the country takes place. The absence of a serious policy dialogue on Azerbaijan's ballooning oil wealth is of particular concern. Moreover, in the wake of the popular democracy movements in Georgia, Ukraine, and Kyrgyzstan, political discourse in Azerbaijan has in many ways become a zero-sum affair, whereby incumbents assert that political opposition seeks only to upend the existing order. Meanwhile, the regime's invoking of a potential revolution scenario provides a rationale for taking even more restrictive action against the opposition.

Among the most damaging by-products of this distorted political dynamic is that incumbents systematically deny a meaningful level of opposition participation in the policy-making and political process. This denial of even a modicum of political space inflames resentment and frustration within the opposition, all of which perpetuates an environment of recrimination and suspicion.

Given the authorities' track record in previous elections, a host of international monitoring bodies was particularly attuned to the conduct of the 2005 elections. For example, the OSCE's Office for Democratic Institutions and Human Rights conducted a comprehensive needs assessment (NAM) in 2004, which spelled out the areas in which the Azeri authorities should improve electoral practice. The OSCE issued a report five months in advance of the November 2005 election that enumerated key areas requiring reform.

Among the reforms the NAM cited were: the composition of election commissions at all levels should be reconfigured in a manner that ensures they enjoy public confidence, and in particular the confidence of those running for office; election officials who committed fraudulent actions leading to invalidation of results in 694 polling stations in the 2003 presidential elections—as well as persons in charge of Constituency Election Commissions where serious violations occurred—should be prosecuted and should not be involved in administering the November 2005 parliamentary elections; the powers given to the local authorities to restrict political gatherings should be curtailed, and freedom of assembly should be respected during the election period; the authorities should implement previous recommendations to use inking of voters' fingers as a public confidence and transparency measure; and the reconsideration of provisions in the law that prohibit NGOs that receive more than 30 percent of their funding from foreign sources from monitoring elections.[6]

The OSCE NAM report represents a broad critique of the Azeri electoral infrastructure and process. However, Azeri authorities took a distinctly minimalist approach to the OSCE critique, implementing only a handful of measures too late in the election process to make a serious positive impact.

For example, on October 28—only a week before election day—the authorities lifted the ban on NGOs receiving 30 percent of their funding from foreign sources to send election observers. This modification of the Law on Public Unions and Foundations was encouraged by the Council of Europe and the OSCE/ODIHR, but due to the extremely short interval between its adoption and election day, it had little practical effect on the November 6 election.[7]

During the weeks leading up to the November election there was no shortage of political intrigue. What the regime characterized as a planned coup resulted in the arrest of a number of former cabinet ministers and business leaders. They included minister of economic development Farhad Aliyev, former finance minister Fikrat Yusifov; Fikrat Sadyqov, the former head of Azerbaijan's state-controlled Azerkimya petrochemical company; former health minister Ali Insanov; and former presidential administration official Akif Muradverdiyev. Yusifov was arrested on October 16, shortly in advance of the expected return to Azerbaijan of exiled opposition leader Rasul Quliyev. Azerbaijan's law-enforcement agencies say Yusifov's initial confessions made possible all subsequent arrests. Authorities claimed that some 13 former cabinet ministers, government officials, business executives, and police officers were detained on charges that include preparation of a coup, illegal possession of weapons, embezzlement, and corruption.[8]

The net result of the existing political structure is that no credible opportunity arises for the effective rotation of power among a range of different political parties representing competing interests and policy options.

Given the heavy hand of the state in so much of Azeri life, one of the spheres that could help in the larger democratic reform effort is civil society. Here, too, however, the authorities have taken an adversarial posture. Azerbaijani law prohibits nongovernmental groups from taking part in political activity, and, more generally, the civic sector is not able to influence public affairs or policy choices in a significant and consistent manner.

NGOs continue to face serious problems in registering with the Ministry of Justice. A joint assessment report prepared by the International Monetary Fund and the International Development Association, however, recognized progress in the consultative process among a number of communities in discussing poverty reduction. At the same time, the assessment report stressed the need to institutionalize this behavior and to make it a regular and integral part of policy formulation in the country.[9]

A more comprehensive report issued in 2005 by the OSCE was highly critical of the obstacles NGOs confront in the registration process. The OSCE monitors concluded that no serious improvements had been made in the registration process for NGOs since the adoption of the new Law on State Registration and State Register of Legal Entities in late 2003.[10] Moreover, NGOs in Azerbaijan are sustained principally through international donors; a reduction in international support would have a debilitating effect on the already precarious position of indigenous NGOs.

Azerbaijan's media sector also confronts major obstacles. Authorities use a variety of tools to manipulate and intimidate the press. State businesses in Azerbaijan, for example, do not advertise in opposition newspapers. A private business with interests in state contracts in an economy still dominated by the state will usually decide that caution is wiser than advertising in such publications. Publications not aligned with the authorities must obey the rules of state-owned printing facilities. Distribution of opposition publications outside the capital city of Baku is often obstructed. The court system is subordinated to the executive, and therefore journalists, editors, and publishers do not have consequential legal recourse.

Journalists are also subject to physical abuse, risking death. In March 2005, Elmar Huseinov, editor at the opposition magazine *Monitor,* was gunned down in the stairwell of his apartment building in Baku. Why he was killed and by whom is unclear. The whole story behind the murder of this opposition journalist may never be known, but the case, with its opaque investigation and doubts about the vigor with which it is being pursued, is emblematic of the difficult environment for the press in Azerbaijan.

The scope of the authorities' intimidation and restrictions are laid out in detail in a report issued in July 2005 by the OSCE's rapporteur on freedom of the press, Miklos Haraszti, who paints a troubling picture.[11] While there is still some degree of pluralism in Azerbaijan's print media, in television there is virtually none. Azerbaijan has 16 television channels, six of which broadcast to a national audience (AzTV1, ANS, Lider, Space, ATV, Public TV). A number of the channels with national reach have clear or believed links to the regime. For example, Lider TV is run by President Aliyev's cousin, Adalat Aliyev. Space TV is owned by the president's sister. ATV is widely believed to be controlled by the president's powerful chief of staff, Ramiz Mehtiev.

During the 2005 election campaign, in its prime time news and current affairs programs, ATV demonstrated a clear bias. Media monitoring of election campaign content revealed that in the two months leading up to election day ATV devoted 97 percent of its political and election prime time coverage to the activities of President Aliyev, the presidential administration, the government, and the YAP.[12] Private stations Lider, Space, and ATV reflected a pattern of political favoritism similar to that of state-funded broadcasters during the 2005 campaign.[13] All of this occurred despite President Aliyev's decree in May 2005 that mandated complete media access for all parties, freedom of assembly during the election campaign, and the ability of independent organizations to conduct exit polls without interference.

One noteworthy development on the Azeri media scene was the unveiling of the country's first public-service broadcasting channel, which hit the airwaves in August 2005. Following the flawed 2003 presidential election, the Council of Europe adopted a resolution demanding that the government of Azerbaijan immediately implement a series of steps that included the creation of public-service television to allow all political parties to communicate better with the country's citizens.[14] While the Council of Europe for months exhorted the authorities in Baku to establish a genuinely independent and professional public broadcasting channel, the regime dragged its feet. Nevertheless, candidates did have more free airtime than in past election cycles, a welcome step that should be institutionalized going forward.[15] Whether the authorities will ease control of the new public broadcasting channel to permit discussion of serious social and political issues is an open question. Given the relatively limited resources available to public broadcasting and the lopsided composition of the nine-member public broadcasting steering committee that oversees programming content and strategy, the prospects for a truly independent station are rather doubtful.

Recommendations
- The last-minute action to enable NGOs receiving 30 percent or more of their funding from foreign sources to send election observers was too late to have a meaningful impact on the November 2005 parliamentary elections. For future elections, the authorities should enable the NGO community to play a significant watchdog role in the election process.
- The capacity and independence of the new public broadcasting station should be ensured by the authorities. Toward this end, the composition of the public broadcasting steering committee should be balanced with members possessing a range of political affiliations and reflecting a diversity of views. In addition, the fledgling station should receive sufficient resources to fulfill its promise as a genuine, independent information source for Azerbaijan's citizens.
- The authorities should make an affirmative effort to enable the activities of independent NGOs and civic groups.

• Television and radio licensing procedures need to be reformed to make them more transparent and fair.

CIVIL LIBERTIES – 3.21

Azerbaijani law prohibits torture or other cruel or degrading treatment or punishment. However, in practice the government is believed to commit numerous human rights abuses.

Four deaths occurred in custody over the course of 2004, allegedly due to beatings. Police tortured and beat persons in custody and used excessive force to extract confessions. In most cases, the government took no action to punish abusers. Prison conditions remained harsh, and some prisoners died as a result of these conditions; however, the government did permit independent monitoring of prison conditions by local and international humanitarian groups. Arbitrary arrest and detention and lengthy pretrial detention continued to be problems.[16]

Authorities often arbitrarily arrested and detained persons without legal warrants. The law allows police to detain and question individuals for three hours without a warrant. The constitution also states that individuals who are detained, arrested, or accused of a crime should be advised immediately of their rights and the reason for arrest and should be accorded due process of law. The authorities did not respect these provisions in practice, however.[17] In March 2004, President Aliyev pardoned more than 100 persons, whom the Council of Europe had designated as political prisoners.[18]

In the months leading up to the November elections, the authorities in a number of instances resorted to the use of force in suppressing public protests. On May 21, 2005, riot police armed with shields and batons intervened to prevent scores of would-be participants from reaching the venue for a planned opposition rally in Baku. Officials rejected the organizers' request for permission to hold the rally, arguing that it was inappropriate to hold such a mass action in advance of the arrival in Baku of foreign heads of state scheduled to attend the official inauguration on May 25 of the Baku-Tbilisi-Ceyhan export pipeline.[19] The Azerbaijani authorities have had a poor record on freedom of association and assembly, sometimes resorting to force to disperse opposition rallies not sanctioned by the authorities. In September, police in Baku violently dispersed a small gathering of demonstrators who had gathered to protest the detention of a member of the youth group Yeni Fikir (New Thinking).[20]

A month earlier, in August, Ruslan Bashirli, the head of Yeni Fikir, which is the youth wing affiliated with the Azerbaijan Popular Front Party (AHCP), was arrested on charges of receiving funds from the Armenian secret services as part of a coup attempt. According to the Azerbaijani Prosecutor-General's Office, Bashirli traveled in July 2005 to Tbilisi at the behest of his mentor, AHCP chairman Ali Kerimli. While in Tbilisi, Bashirli allegedly met with three men, an ethnic Georgian and two Armenians, all of them Armenian intelligence agents, and told them he was working on instructions from a U.S.-based assistance organization to prepare for a revolution in Azerbaijan.[21]

In the aftermath of this affair, questions persisted about the facts behind the events. Whether the Azeri authorities used the episode in Tbilisi to discredit the AHCP and its leader Ali Kerimli in a fashion similar to the arrests of cabinet and other senior officials in Baku three weeks before the election is a question that may never be fully answered.

Azerbaijan's constitution provides for equality between men and women. Nonetheless, Azerbaijan is a traditional, male-dominated society, where women hold few formal high positions of power. While there is some NGO activity to promote the rights of the disabled, the authorities have not made meaningful efforts to advance such rights.

Azerbaijan is classified as a "Tier 2 – Watchlist" country by the U.S. State Department's Office to Monitor and Combat Trafficking in Persons. This indicates that the government of Azerbaijan does not fully comply with the minimum standards for the elimination of trafficking; however, it is making significant efforts to do so. In June 2005, the parliament (Milli Majlis) passed a Law on Fighting Human Trafficking. Azerbaijan is primarily a country of origin and transit for women and children trafficked for the purpose of sexual exploitation. Azerbaijani, Russian, Ukrainian, and Central Asian women and girls were trafficked from or through the country to the United Arab Emirates (U.A.E.), Turkey, Pakistan, and India. Internal trafficking of women and girls appeared to be an increasing problem.[22]

On April 2, 2004, a three-judge panel convicted Ilgar Ibrahimoglu, the imam of the independent Juma mosque, of inciting and committing violence in connection with a postelection demonstration in October 2003 that turned violent. He was given a five-year suspended sentence and released immediately, having served four months in pretrial detention. On July 30, 2004, authorities detained the imam again, together with 25 members of the Juma mosque, in connection with activities of the mosque but released him the same day.[23]

While independent unions tend to be weak and generally are kept in check by the government, workers at the McDermott oil services company, a U.S. concern, were the exception to the rule. On November 22, 2005, some 1,500 workers at the company's construction yards walked off the job in what was the first mass strike action since Azerbaijan achieved independence in 1991. The strike lasted only one day, but workers signaled their intention to halt work again if their demands were not met. McDermott officials, together with representatives from the Azerbaijani state oil company SOCAR, made an offer, which the strikers rejected. On November 28, workers halted their activity. On November 29, McDermott officials agreed to give their Azerbaijani workers a 20 percent pay increase, effective December 1, and then a further 12 percent raise January 1, 2006.[24]

Recommendations

- The Azerbaijani authorities must take most aggressive steps to ensure that torture is no longer a feature in the criminal system.
- The Azerbaijani authorities must respect freedom of assembly and ensure that peaceful public protest is permitted.
- The government of Azerbaijan should implement a victim referral and protection system, provide adequate anti-trafficking training for police, and properly vet officers on the anti-trafficking unit.
- The authorities should release all remaining persons designated as political prisoners by the Council of Europe.
- The Azerbaijani government should be encouraged to work in tandem with the independent trade union representing oil-sector workers to minimize discrimination by foreign companies against Azerbaijani employees.

RULE OF LAW – 2.29

Azerbaijan's judiciary is corrupt, inefficient, and politicized. It suffers from a number of critical deficiencies, including heavy influence on its work from the executive branch. These realities have the practical effect of denying average citizens access to justice. Due to the pivotal role of the judiciary in ensuring that the rule of law prevails in day-to-day life, its weakness and lack of independence also has a spillover impact on other key sectors of Azeri society. Judicial corruption and poor administration, for example, have aroused the concern of Azerbaijan's business community, which increasingly see these deficiencies as serious impediments to business development.[25]

Criminal matters remain under the influence of Soviet-era practice whereby investigations are conducted as much to obtain confessions as to gather and analyze evidence. Recognizing the weaknesses of the country's legal profession, several international organizations have sought to work with the authorities to advance legal reform. In an assessment of the legal profession in Azerbaijan issued in March 2005, the OSCE and ABA/CEELI deemed the situation for lawyers in Azerbaijan to be "critical."[26]

Azerbaijan's Law About Advocates and Advocates' Activities, which mandated the creation of a new bar association, was adopted in 1999. No new members were admitted to the Collegium of Advocates, an association of attorneys over which the authorities have maintained de facto control, between 1999 and 2004.[27] In August 2004, President Aliyev signed amendments to this law, which came into effect in 2005. The spirit and intent of the law is to expand the number of advocates available to defend individuals in criminal matters. Indeed, one of the principal limitations on the right to choose legal representation freely in criminal cases has been the small number of lawyers entitled to represent clients in Azerbaijan. With one lawyer for every 22,887 people, the ratio of lawyer to citizen is among the lowest in the Newly Independent States.[28]

The new law was to have opened up the initial membership of the new Collegium to more than 200 licensed lawyers. This would almost double the number of advocates in the country. However, the Ministry of Justice and the Organizational Committee for the new Collegium of Advocates interpreted the law's provision on licensed lawyers in a very narrow and restrictive manner, effectively limiting to 36 the number of qualified lawyers.[29]

Generally speaking, lawyers' work is not highly valued, and typical fees are egregiously low. For example, by one estimate an hour of a state barrister's time is valued at 2,250 manats (approximately US46¢). The average fee of a barrister per case is 300,000 to 600,000 manats (US$61–122).[30]

Amendments to the law governing the selection of judges, which included a more rigorous exam procedure, came into effect in 2005. International observers have assessed the new selection process to be an improvement, demonstrating greater transparency and fairness.

Defendants' access to legal counsel is uneven, and there have been cases in which detained individuals were not allowed to communicate with an attorney or were held in detention longer than permitted by law. This was a particular issue in the case of the arrests in connection with the alleged coup attempt that the authorities claimed was orchestrated by Rasul Guliyev and a number of prominent government ministers and officials, including economic development minister Farhad Aliyev, his brother and Azpetrol chairman Rafig Aliyev, and health minister Ali Insanov.

Given the overall capriciousness of the Azerbaijani legal system, it is not entirely surprising that the system does not afford consistent protection of property rights. In lucrative strategic sectors, individuals closely aligned with the regime have significant advantages in acquiring control of assets.[31]

Civil control of police, security services, and the military is recognized in legislation and in the constitution. However, given the concentration of power in the executive and limited checks on it, as a practical matter security forces and the military are considered to be under civilian control to the extent they obey the president. The only potential check on the president in this context is the Constitutional Court, which, at least in theory, can challenge the president. However, presidential appointment of the Constitutional Court's judges limits such accountability in practice.

In a story that captured national headlines in March 2005, officials from the Ministry of the Interior were found to be involved in a kidnapping ring. As part of this drama, the Ministry of National Security launched an operation on March 10 that secured the release of Zamira Hajieva, wife of the president of the International Bank of Azerbaijan, who had been abducted a month earlier by a group that demanded several million dollars in return for her safe release. Hajieva was found in a concrete bunker belonging to a senior police official who was apprehended together with some 20 other people, seven of them interior ministry officials. On March 23, Minister Usubov dismissed his first deputy, Zakhid Dunyamaliyev, Criminal Investigations Department head Zakir Nasirov, and two of Nasirov's deputies. The National Security Ministry and the Prosecutor-General's Office released a joint statement the same day on additional crimes allegedly committed in recent years by a criminal gang headed by former interior ministry official Haji Mamedov.[32]

Article 25 of the constitution asserts the principle of equality of all persons before the law and courts. However, in practice those with close ties to the regime and ruling party have significant advantages. Moreover, the regulatory and administrative capriciousness that is a day-to-day reality vitiates the right to property enshrined in the constitution. Protections are frequently not upheld within the legal system.

Recommendations

- The authorities should redouble efforts and make judicial reform a first-order priority. Building on the positive steps achieved in the judicial examination process should be a part of this effort.
- Within the context of the larger legal reform effort, the Azerbaijani authorities should take priority action to ensure private property rights are ensured.
- The authorities must make more effective efforts to ensure that the new Collegium of Advocates has a sufficient quantity and quality of lawyers to meet society's needs. To this end, the Ministry of Justice and the organizational committee for the new Collegium should interpret the new law's provision on licensed lawyers in an expansive manner to promote a significant increase in the number of qualified lawyers.
- Azerbaijan's leadership must take steps to ensure that power institutions, such as the interior ministry, are subject to greater accountability and transparency.

ANTICORRUPTION AND TRANSPARENCY – 1.27

High levels of corruption plague all sectors of the Azeri system. Corruption therefore represents one of the country's biggest obstacles to political, economic, and social development. The absence of political competition is a fundamental contributing factor to the persistently corrupt environment. Azerbaijan ranks 101 out of 177 in the United Nations Human Development Index, below its resource-poor neighbors in Georgia and Armenia. The country was ranked 137 out of 159 countries surveyed in the 2005 Transparency International Corruption Perceptions Index.

Like those of many of its post-Soviet neighbors, the bureaucracy in Azerbaijan has a life of its own, creating an environment in which average citizens are at the mercy of unaccountable and often capricious bureaucratic behavior. The ruling YAP tends to integrate the personal interests of officials with the public offices they hold. In Azerbaijan, corrupt clans treat large state corporations as private fiefdoms and maintain monopolies in consumer goods, trade, and other non-oil sectors, strangling the creation of other businesses. Although Azerbaijan has enjoyed solid economic growth in the last two years, much of the country suffers from poverty, especially in rural areas.[33]

A web of regulations and bureaucratic requirements provides fertile terrain for corruption, on both petty and grand scales. Of course, this reality is reinforced by the weakness of critical institutions, such as the judiciary and news media, which could exert a positive impact against the pervasive corruption that afflicts Azeri society.

Grand corruption manifests itself in a number of ways, including excessive state involvement in the economy, with many officials believed to be enjoying significant stakes in strategic industries. While there is a critical absence of meaningful political competition among a range of different political parties representing varying interests and policy options, intraparty competition within the YAP can be fierce, especially when it comes to controlling interests in strategic industries.

Opaque, oligarchic competition plays out in a number of ways. For example, as part of a preelection action undertaken by President Aliyev in October 2005, Economic Development Minister Farhad Aliyev was fired from his post. Law enforcement agency sources suggested that both Farhad Aliyev and his brother, Rafik, president of the Azpetrol oil company, were arrested on suspicion of preparing a coup against the government. Farhad Aliyev reportedly came into conflict with senior officials, including Kamaladdin Heydarov, head of the State Customs Committee. In late 2004, Farhad Aliyev had launched an anti-monopoly campaign, naming customs impediments for imports as a main tool relied on by monopolies to preserve their business domains. The campaign appeared to divide members of parliament from the ruling YAP into two camps. Rafik Aliyev, Farhad Aliyev's brother, as president of Azpetrol Oil Company, controlled 90 percent of Azerbaijan's gas stations. Farhad Aliyev is believed to control companies dealing with cement and aluminum production, electricity distribution, and telecommunications. Meanwhile, as part of this intra-elite competition, Heydarov is alleged to control banks, part of the construction sector, fisheries, and part of the mobile communications market.[34]

The authorities created a number of anticorruption bodies in 2004 and 2005. President Aliyev issued decrees in March and September 2004 endorsing, respectively, a law on combating corruption and Azerbaijan's State Program on Fighting Corruption. In August 2005 President Aliyev issued a decree on financial disclosure by public officials. Under the decree, the president, the speaker of the parliament, the head of the presidential executive staff, the prime minister, deputy ministers, Supreme Court judges, and ambassadors abroad must submit information on their incomes to an anticorruption commission, which was formed under the State Service Management Council. The powerful chief of the presidential administration, Ramiz Mehtiyev, supervises both the anticorruption commission and the State Service Management Council.

Formal anticorruption structures have therefore been put in place. However, given the organization of the political system and these anticorruption bodies' lack of independence in their current form, it is more likely in practice that these entities will follow a pattern of being used for factional score-settling than for fair and systematic addressing of the country's pervasive corruption.[35]

The education sector also falls prey to corruption. Bribes are commonplace for admission to university, receiving good grades, and graduation. In June 2005, a protest against corruption in the education system was organized by a group calling itself "No to corruption in the education system" and the electoral bloc Yeni Adlar (New Names) but was dispersed immediately by the police.[36]

In September 2005, the government instituted a significant pay raise for traffic police, who in Azerbaijan and much of the former Soviet world have an almost legendary capacity for fleecing average citizens. Under the new salary structure, some 1,400 traffic policemen earn

US$350 per month. Officers earn between US$500 and US$700, as much as seven times more than their previous salaries. Whether this measure makes an enduring impact may depend on the extent to which it can affect the larger pyramid system of bribery in which payoffs are demanded by superiors throughout the chain of command.[37]

While the opposition media write on allegations of corruption within the government, the accusatory and often inflammatory tone of this reporting renders it ineffectual. Moreover, the profound weakness of independent media makes reporting on corruption issues more difficult. This is especially true of national broadcast media, from which most average citizens obtain their news, and which is largely controlled by the ruling elite and therefore rarely offers fair or vigorous scrutiny of official corruption.

With more than $2 billion in infrastructure projects expected largely to be financed through oil revenues in 2006,[38] safeguards on public spending will become even more important. Bureaucratic regulations and a general lack of transparency contribute to an environment where corruption can flourish on the awarding of public contracts.

Sufficient public access to official information is a serious problem, contributing to a legal and regulatory environment that is nontransparent. As part of the country's larger challenge of improving transparency, information on governmental budget making is not accessible to the general public, nor is the extent of the legislative branch's access to and scrutiny of executive branch budget matters known. A comprehensive access to information law was adopted and is to come into effect in December 2005. The authorities have one year to implement the provisions of the new law, which would among other things require public access to legislation and laws, and post key information to the World Wide Web.

Recommendations
- The authorities must establish an anticorruption body that is genuinely independent and capable of exercising influence on and making a dent in the country's considerable corruption problem.
- A vigorous public discussion of Azerbaijan's corruption is essential. Toward this end, the authorities must do more to enable national broadcast media to report on allegations of official corruption.

- The authorities should take a cooperative posture toward civil society organizations and leverage the nongovernment sector's capacity and expertise in the effort to solve Azerbaijan's massive corruption problem.
- The authorities should fully implement the important law on access to information, which would enable sorely needed transparency across the official bureaucracy.

NOTES

[1] Andreas Gross and Andrea Herkel, "Functioning of Democratic Institutions in Azerbaijan (Doc. 10569, Report of the Committee on the Honoring of Obligations and Commitments by Member States of the Council of Europe [Monitoring Committee])" (Strasbourg: Parliamentary Assembly of the Council of Europe, Resolution 1456, 22 June 2005).

[2] Guy Chazan, "Protest Over Azerbaijan Elections Fails to Draw Huge Crowds – Azerbaijan's Unpopular Revolt, Opposition Fails to Muster Support Seen in Other Democracy Drives," *Wall Street Journal,* 10 November 2005, A15.

[3] Margarita Akhvlediani and Shahin Rzayev, "Azerbaijan: A Question of Change" (London: Institute for War and Peace Reporting [IWPR], Caucasus Reporting Service, No. 315, 23 November 2005).

[4] "A Rocky Past and Hazy Future for Azerbaijan's Opposition," Agence France-Presse (AFP), 30 October 2005.

[5] C. J. Chivers, "Observers Criticize Azeri Vote: Findings Lend Support to Fraud Accusations," *New York Times,* 8 November 2005, 3.

[6] "Needs Assessment Report Ahead of Parliamentary Elections in Azerbaijan, November 2005" (Warsaw: Organization for Security and Co-operation in Europe [OSCE]/Office for Democratic Institutions and Human Rights [ODIHR], 17 June 2005).

[7] "Statement of Preliminary Findings and Conclusions, International Election Observation Mission, Parliamentary Election, Republic of Azerbaijan, 6 November 2005" (OSCE/ODIHR), 11.

[8] Jean-Christophe Peuch, "Alleged Plotters Confess on State Television" (Prague and Washington, D.C.: Radio Free Europe/Radio Liberty [RFE/RL], 30 November 2005). See also Rovshan Ismayilov, "Arrests of Entrepreneurs in Azerbaijan Likely Linked to Political Re-shuffle," EurasiaNet.org, 19 December 2005.

[9] "Poverty Reduction Strategy Paper Progress Report: Joint Staff Assessment, Azerbaijan Republic" (Washington, D.C.: International Monetary Fund [IMF] and International Development Association [IDA], 12 August 2004), 3.

[10] Anar Kazimov and Hafiz Hasanov, "Report on the Registration Procedure of Non-Governmental Organizations" (Baku: OSCE, 6 May 2005).

[11] Miklós Haraszti, "Assessment Visit to Azerbaijan, Observations and Recommendations" (OSCE, The Representative on Freedom of the Media, 14 July 2005).

12 "Statement of Preliminary Findings and Conclusions" (OSCE/ODIHR), 8.

13 Ibid., 9.

14 Council of Europe Resolution 1358 (2004).

15 Elizabeth Fuller, "Candidates Benefit from More Media Access," RFE/RL, 30 November 2005.

16 Country Report (U.S. Department of State, 2005).

17 Ibid.

18 "Azerbaijani President Pardons Rebel Ex-Colonel, Other Political Prisoners," Newsline, Volume 8, Number 52, RFE/RL, 18 March 2004.

19 Fuller, "Azerbaijani Police Quash Rally in Capital," RFE/RL, 22 May 2005.

20 "Azerbaijan Police Crack Down on Protest over Activist," AFP, 23 September 2005.

21 Fuller, "Spy Scandal Continues to Raise More Questions than Answers," RFE/RL, 10 August 2005.

22 "Trafficking in Persons Report" (Washington, D.C.: U.S. Department of State, Office to Monitor and Combat Trafficking in Persons, 3 June 2005).

23 Country Report (U.S. Department of State, 2005).

24 Rufat Abbasov, "Azerbaijan:Famous Victory for Striking Oil Workers" (IWPR, Caucasus Reporting Service, No. 317, 6 December 2005).

25 "Entrepreneurs Confederation Chair Welcomes Judiciary Reforms," *Financial Times* Information, Asia Africa Intelligence Wire, BBC Monitoring, 5 July 2005; "Azeri Businessmen Welcome Dismissal of Top Judges," *Financial Times* Information, Asia Africa Intelligence Wire, BBC Monitoring, 21 April 2005.

26 "Report on the Situation of Lawyers in Azerbaijan" (Baku: OSCE and American Bar Association Central European and Eurasian Law Initiative [ABA/CEELI], March 2005), 1.

27 "Report from the Trial Monitoring Project in Azerbaijan 2003–2004" (Baku: OSCE/ODIHR), 14.

28 "Report on the Situation of Lawyers in Azerbaijan" (Baku: OSCE and ABA/CEELI, March 2005), 2.

29 Ibid.

30 Samira Ahmedbeyly, "Azerbaijan Lawyers Up in Arms" (IWPR, Caucasus Reporting Service, No. 264, 1 December 2004).

31 2006 Index of Economic Freedom, Azerbaijan report, Heritage Foundation, 2006.

32 "Large Scandal due to Participation of High-Ranking Officials of the Ministry of Interior in Kidnapping has Started in Azerbaijan," *Turan* Information Agency (Baku), 10 March 2005.

33 Henry Meyer, "Azerbaijan Revels in Oil Boom but Graft Keeps Much of the Country Poor," Associated Press, 31 October 2005.

34 Rovshan Ismayilov, "Azerbaijani Minister Fired, Allegedly Arrested for Coup Attempt," EurasiaNet.org, 19 November 2005, http://www.eurasianet.org/departments/insight/articles/eav101905a.shtml.

35 "TV Doubts Azeri Anti-Corruption Body to be Effective," ANS TV (Baku), BBC Monitoring, 25 April 2005.

36 "Azeri Police Foil Protest Against Corruption in the Education System," ANS TV, BBC Monitoring, 28 June 2005.

37 Rufat Abbasov and Gulnaz Gulieva, "Azerbaijan: Traffic Cops' Pay Raise Unlikely to Curb Graft" (IWPR, Caucasus Reporting Service, No. 306, 30 September 2005).

38 "Public Finance: Transparency and Efficiency,"No. 6, p. 36. Public Finance Monitoring Center, Local Government and Public Service Reform Initiative, Baku, 2005.

BAHRAIN

CAPITAL: Manama

POPULATION: 0.7 million

GNI PER CAPITA: $12,410

SCORES	2004	2006
ACCOUNTABILITY AND PUBLIC VOICE:	3.32	2.52
CIVIL LIBERTIES:	3.59	3.73
RULE OF LAW:	3.33	3.67
ANTICORRUPTION AND TRANSPARENCY:	2.83	2.07

(scores are based on a scale of 0 to 7, with 0 representing weakest and 7 representing strongest performance)

Fred H. Lawson

INTRODUCTION

Bahrain is the least wealthy of the oil-producing Arab Gulf states, and boasts an exceptionally well-educated and politically sophisticated citizenry. A brief period of constitutional and parliamentary government was brought to an abrupt end by order of the ruler (amir) in August 1975. Persistent popular agitation to reinstate the electoral order exploded into widespread violence from 1994 to 1999. During the course of the uprising, tensions heightened between the dominant Sunni population and the subordinate Shia. Long-standing agreement among liberal reformers in the two communities began to erode, opening the door to more radical movements in both camps.

After proclaiming Bahrain a monarchy in February 2002, Sheikh Hamad bin 'Isa Al Khalifah has presided over a steady contraction of the package of political reforms that was introduced during 2000–01. Liberal and radical activists who applauded the restoration of the National Assembly (al-Majlis al-Watani) were greatly disappointed by the regime's decision to accord the appointed upper house, the Consultative Council (Majlis al-Shura), the same legislative powers as the popularly elected

Fred H. Lawson is professor of Government at Mills College. He is author of *Bahrain: The Modernization of Autocracy* (Boulder, CO: Westview Press, 1989) and "Repertoires of Contention in Contemporary Bahrain," in Quintan Wiktorowicz, ed., *Islamic Activism* (Bloomington: Indiana University Press, 2003).

lower house, the Chamber of Representatives (Majlis al-Nuwwab). Furthermore, the Amended Constitution of 2002 takes away the right of elected representatives to introduce bills for parliamentary debate and instead requires that all draft laws be referred to committee and introduced to the assembly by the Council of Ministers. In October 2002, King Hamad promulgated a revised Press and Publications Law, which imposes severe penalties for publishing any report that criticizes the monarchy, jeopardizes national unity, advocates changes to the country's political system, or denigrates Islam. That same month, the monarch issued Decree Number 56, which grants blanket immunity from criminal and civil prosecution to any official suspected of inflicting torture or otherwise violating human rights in the past.

ACCOUNTABILITY AND PUBLIC VOICE – 2.52

According to the amended constitution, the 40 members of the Chamber of Representatives are to be selected by popular vote every four years. The first parliamentary election under the terms of the revised constitution took place in October 2002, in an atmosphere that proved to be largely free of outright fraud and intimidation. Nevertheless, the Council of Ministers enacted a new citizenship law three months before the balloting that permitted citizens of the other five member-states of the Gulf Co-operation Council (Saudi Arabia, Kuwait, Qatar, the United Arab Emirates and Oman) to obtain concurrent Bahraini nationality, with full voting rights, thereby diluting the influence of natural-born citizens. The cabinet also issued a political rights statute that blocked popular societies and civic organizations from "participating in any electoral campaign on behalf of any candidates" and prohibited "campaigning in religious places, universities and schools, public squares, roads and government buildings."[1] After critics of the regime won a majority of the seats contested in municipal council elections in May 2002, electoral districts were reconfigured to improve the chances of pro-regime candidates and give greater weight to the country's Sunni population. More important, thousands of Syrians, Yemenis, and Baluchis who held positions in the armed forces, police, and intelligence services were granted the right to vote. Reformers immediately condemned this administrative move, which they labeled "political naturalization," that is, citizenship conferred for largely illegitimate "political" motives.

In response to such machinations, and to protest the general terms of the amended constitution, four major popular societies boycotted the parliamentary election. These were the Islamic National Accord Society (al-Wifaq), the National Democratic Action Society (al-Amal al-Watani al-Dimuqrati or al-Wa'ad), the National Bloc (al-Tajammu' al-Qawmi), and the Islamic Action Society (al-Amal al-Islami). Just over 53 percent of eligible voters participated in the first round of balloting for the Chamber of Representatives, while no more than 45 percent turned out for the second round. Twenty-eight Sunnis and 12 Shias ended up being elected to the Chamber of Representatives. A majority of the Sunni members belonged to the local branch of the Muslim Brotherhood (Ikhwan al-Muslimin), most of whom hailed from the association's more moderate mainstream, while a small number came from the more radical (or salafi) wing.

Political parties are prohibited by law, although the Chamber of Representatives periodically raises the question of whether formal parties should be permitted to emerge. The king is on record as saying that the establishment of organized political parties is an issue for the legislature to decide. A proposal to allow the formation of political parties was rejected by the parliamentary legislative and legal affairs committee in May 2004.[2] Two months later, the Bahrain Chamber of Commerce and Industry took an important step toward breaking the impasse by setting up a political action committee to lobby the National Assembly on matters of concern to local businesspeople.[3]

Nothing of consequence was discussed in the National Assembly during the first year after the elections. But as 2003 came to a close, it became apparent that the country's two primary social welfare and retirement agencies were rapidly approaching insolvency. A special commission selected from the Chamber of Representatives by the chamber's speaker drew up a report charging three cabinet ministers with "mismanaging the funds" held by these agencies and engaging in "a number of failed investments" that had drained their coffers.[4] When the government showed little interest in the report, five members of the commission called for a public "parliamentary interrogation" of the three ministers. This step was strongly resisted by the Speaker, on the grounds that too much parliamentary activism might prompt the king to suspend the National Assembly, as his father had done 30 years earlier. Although two of the ministers eventually submitted to questioning by the commission, both retained their posts as a result of various legal technicalities.[5]

In the wake of this episode, reformist members of parliament have become increasingly outspoken in voicing demands for change. Representatives in August 2004 called for the resignation of the minister of electricity following a power failure that plunged the country into a 12-hour blackout.[6] Seven months later, the Chamber of Representatives amended its rules to permit any future questioning of cabinet ministers to take place in full session rather than in closed committee. A group of 15 influential representatives, including the first deputy speaker, introduced a sweeping proposal in June 2005 to increase the size of the elected lower house from 40 to 45 members, to give the Chamber of Representatives the authority to question the prime minister, and to require that cabinet ministers receive parliamentary approval before taking office.[7] These initiatives had not been overturned by the Council of Ministers by the end of the year.

Beyond the confines of the National Assembly, the range of public debate remains tightly constrained. In February 2004, the four organizations that had boycotted the 2002 parliamentary elections announced plans to hold a two-day conference to discuss what they called the constitutional crisis confronting the country. Government officials riposted that no such crisis existed and that the activities of the four associations demonstrated the overall health of Bahrain's political system. As the conference opened, one senior official remarked that the gathering was "illegal because the organizers failed to get the required license from the Ministry of Labor and Social affairs."[8] Foreign participants were stopped at the airport and prevented from entering the country. The minister of the royal court, Sheikh Khalid bin Ahmad Al Khalifah, remarked that "it is necessary that all public discussions on domestic matters stipulated by the constitution be confined to Bahrainis, and no one else should be involved."

In September 2004, the prestigious 'Urubah Club hosted a public forum on the problem of persistent poverty in Bahrain. During the course of the program, one of the featured speakers, the vice president of the

Bahrain Center for Human Rights (BCHR), insisted that the government should be held accountable for its failure to alleviate poverty and unemployment and that the cabinet should accept its collective responsibility by resigning. These remarks sparked a firestorm of condemnation. The speaker, 'Abd al-Hadi al-Khawajah, was arrested on charges of insulting high-ranking officials and "inciting hatred of the regime, spreading rumors that may disturb the public stability and harming the public interest"; the 'Urubah Club was closed down for 45 days; and the king, after taking the unusual step of personally chairing a meeting of the Council of Ministers, issued a proclamation denouncing those who "incite sedition and create divisions in the community, especially in the political forums that abuse the political openness and freedom of expression."[9] Shortly thereafter, the BCHR was shut down by the Ministry of Labor and Social Affairs on the grounds that its actions had contravened the provisions of the 1989 Associations Law that prohibited civic associations from engaging in political affairs. Al-Khawajah was sentenced to one year in prison, but in late November 2004 the king granted him clemency.

In October 2004, the Ministry of Labor and Social Affairs sent notices to 80 civic associations and nongovernmental organizations warning them to set up permanent headquarters and abide by the terms of the 1989 Associations Law or else face immediate closure.[10] A month later, the cabinet introduced a draft law requiring any public meeting or popular demonstration to obtain prior approval from the provincial governor. It also prohibits motor vehicles from being used in rallies, unless permission is granted in advance by the minister of the interior.[11] The Ministry of Labor and Social Affairs shut down the opposition Islamic Action Society for 45 days in July 2005 after speakers at an event it had sponsored at the Bahrain Society of Engineers made remarks that were openly critical of the government and the ruling family. An even more stringent set of regulations governing the activities of licensed political societies was adopted in the wake of this event.

Nevertheless, popular societies and civic organizations continue to proliferate. By the spring of 2005, the number of officially recognized associations was approaching 400. Of these, 24 have been licensed as political societies and are thereby allowed to sponsor public workshops, conferences, and debates on policy-related issues with the permission of the Ministry of Labor and Social Affairs.

A revised Associations Law was adopted in July 2005. It imposes tighter restrictions on the internal procedures and fund-raising operations of political societies and makes it illegal for such organizations to be based on class, profession, geographical domain, or confessional character.[12] Penalties for violating the statute include lengthy jail sentences, even life imprisonment.[13] Existing political societies were required to apply to the Ministry of Justice and Islamic Affairs for re-licensing by early October. Some societies, particularly ones based in such predominantly Sunni districts as al-Muharraq but also the major Shia organization al-Wifaq, complied with the new requirement, while a number of others, including the prominent liberal association The Forum (al-Muntada), opted not to do so and reverted to being purely social and civic organizations.

Petitioning the authorities directly continues to be an important means by which Bahraini citizens express demands for change. In July 2003, al-Wifaq presented a petition to the royal court (*diwan*) signed by 33,000 individuals that called for the immediate repeal of Decree Number 56; the petition went unanswered. The society then shifted its efforts to obtaining as many signatures as possible on a petition that demanded basic revisions in the amended constitution. In response, the minister of the royal court issued a statement that called the petition campaign illegal, as "no other party [except the king and cabinet] has the right to call for changes in the constitution."[14] In May 2004, police raided four signature-collection stations across the country and arrested 19 activists. When the authorities agreed not to prosecute the detainees, al-Wifaq temporarily suspended the petition drive.

A group of women organized as the Women's Petition Committee presented the diwan with a petition in December 2004 urging the adoption of a unified personal status code in place of the existing system of religion-based family laws.[15] Two months later, after 75,000 citizens had attached their signatures to it, the petition for constitutional revision was presented to the diwan. It was once again refused, this time on the grounds that all political demands should be handed over to the National Assembly.

Restrictions mandated by the 2002 Press and Publications Law impose severe limitations on local journalists including severe penalties for publishing any report that criticizes the monarchy, jeopardizes national unity, advocates changes to the country's political system, or denigrates Islam. In August 2003, the Ministry of Information circulated a memorandum among foreign news agencies that instructed them not to dispatch reports regarding the government's policy of political naturalization. However, the editors of Bahrain's major newspapers have been granted weekly meetings with the heads of various government departments. The journalists take advantage of these sessions to ask tough, unscripted questions. If the audience is small enough, state officials are reported to offer surprisingly frank and direct answers. Ministers have even taken steps on occasion to change policy or revise official procedures in response to the questions and comments raised in these forums. On the whole, major newspapers enjoy a degree of latitude and freedom from official harassment that is not accorded to smaller publications. Local television and radio stations, by contrast, remain government owned and only broadcast reports that praise or congratulate the regime for its activities.

State agencies have routinely blocked local access to a variety of internet sites with the assistance of the country's primary service provider, the Bahrain Telephone Company (Batelco). The justification for doing so has usually been either that the proscribed sites incite sectarianism or that they impugn the good name of the nation. State officials routinely monitor postings and weblogs on sites run by local activists, including such community forums as Diraz.net and al-Muntadayyat. In February 2005, police went a step further and arrested the moderator of the Arabic-language web forum www.bahrainonline.org, 'Ali 'Abd al-Imam. The moderator and two of his technical assistants were charged with "defamation of the king, inciting hatred against the regime and spreading rumors and lies that could cause disorder."[16] The three were released after a series of well-organized popular protests.

Recommendations
- The king should announce a firm date by which members of the Consultative Council (Majlis al-Shura) will be chosen by popular election rather than by royal appointment.
- The regulation that requires any group that wishes to organize a public debate or workshop to obtain a license from the authorities (whether from the Ministry of Labor and Social Affairs, the Ministry of Justice and Islamic Affairs, or the provincial governor) should be abolished.

- The palace should agree to accept formal petitions from societies and associations rather than only from individuals.
- The 2002 Press and Publications Law should be rescinded or drastically revised to permit greater freedom of speech.

CIVIL LIBERTIES – 3.73

In early 2003, the government-sponsored BHRS released a report stating that all political prisoners had been released and that those individuals who had been dismissed from employment in state agencies (including the University of Bahrain) for their political activities during the 1990s had been reinstated.[17] In addition, the report noted that the law that prohibited societies and organizations from campaigning on behalf of candidates for the National Assembly had been amended to permit such activity in the future.[18] It pointed out as well that peaceful demonstrations and public gatherings no longer elicit brutal and indiscriminate responses from the police, as they had done as recently as the spring of 2002.

Representatives of popular societies and civic organizations confirm the main points of the BHRS's 2003 report. Leading figures of al-Wifaq concur that there is at present no institutionalized or systematic torture or imprisonment of political activists but only isolated incidents of mistreatment and harassment. The killing of protesters has always been a rare occurrence in Bahrain, even at the height of the popular uprising of 1994–99. The three dozen persons who died as a result of actions by the police during the course of the uprising are still honored openly as martyrs by their home communities, giving the authorities an added incentive to behave with restraint.

Long-term detention without trial is prohibited by the amended constitution and has been abandoned in practice in recent years. Following the repeal of the draconian State Security Law in 2001, anyone who is suspected of committing a crime is routinely charged or released within 48 hours of arrest. The courts are reported to have rejected occasional requests from the police to hold suspects for longer periods of time.[19] The constitution also protects the country's citizens from all forms of mental and physical torture and prohibits information gathered by means of torture from being used in judicial proceedings. Oddly enough, the amended constitution fails to guarantee explicitly that Bahraini citizens will not be forced into exile, a measure that was an important instrument of government policy toward political dissidents in the 1990s. It does, however, protect citizens from any imposed limitations on their freedom of movement, which may imply a constitutional guarantee against forced exile. Exile is not being used as a punishment at the present time.

The situation confronting Bahraini women remains fundamentally ambiguous. On the one hand, Article 5 of the amended constitution guarantees full equality between men and women. In addition, Article 18 states that "people are equal in human dignity, and citizens are equal before the law in public rights and duties. There shall be no discrimination among them on the basis of sex, origin, language, religion or creed." The government is a signatory to the United Nations Convention on the Elimination of All Forms of Discrimination against Women (CEDAW). In 2003, the authorities embarked on a highly publicized campaign to end all trafficking in women and children in the country and created a special task force to deal with the problems faced by the large number of vulnerable female domestic servants.[20] Major societies and civic organizations, including such overtly Islamist associations as al-Wifaq, openly advocate greater educational and career opportunities for women and actively recruit female members. A small number of outstanding women have risen to top positions in local business, including enterprises closely linked to the state.

On the other hand, Article 5 of the revised constitution also notes that the guarantee of equality between men and women is bounded by "the provisions of Islamic canon law (Shari'ah)." Similarly, Bahrain's adherence to the CEDAW is predicated on the stipulation that the convention's implementation must conform to the tenets of Islamic law and that traditional restrictions on the movements of female family members must be recognized.[21] Women are routinely treated differently from men in the proceedings of both the civil and religious courts. By early 2004, a law had been enacted that prohibited all female students from entering or leaving the campus of the University of Bahrain with any man who was not her father, brother, or husband.[22] Furthermore, women occupy significantly fewer senior posts in private and public companies and government agencies than might be expected given the fact that females currently account for almost one-quarter of the total labor force. Discrimination against women takes a variety of forms, from a passive adherence to long-standing misogynistic practices and attitudes to an outright refusal to hire and promote females to positions of real responsibility. Most galling to many is the continued importation of non-Bahraini expatriates to work as teachers, health-care professionals, and clerical staff at a time when Bahraini women who have been trained for these same occupations remain unemployed.

Eight women stood as candidates for the lower house of parliament, distributing themselves among the various electoral districts so as not to compete directly with one another. None of them won a seat, despite strong hints from the government that women should be represented in the National Assembly. Some female candidates complained afterward that they had been blocked from speaking and distributing flyers in public places. Others attributed their lack of success to widespread social and cultural biases against women.

After months of campaigning by the government-sponsored Higher Council for Women, the Chamber of Representatives in October 2005 started to debate a draft personal status law that would supersede the existing corpus of customary Islamic law (Sharia) that deals with such matters as divorce, alimony, child support, and inheritance. Several influential Shia scholars quickly condemned the statute, and one recommended that it be submitted to Grand Ayatollah 'Ali al-Sistani in Najaf for advice. Local Shia notables orchestrated a series of popular demonstrations against the draft law, many of which drew large numbers of women. The head of the Council of Shia Scholars ('Ulama) charged that the bill was intended "to please the United States" and predicted that violence might break out if it were adopted.[23] The controversy left the otherwise proreform organization al-Wifaq in a quandary; educated younger women make up a large proportion of the society's active membership, yet the leadership hesitated to take a position that might split the Shia into opposing factions. The head of al-Wifaq took the guarded position that the government has no right to draft legislation that deals with religious matters and that the amended constitution should be revised to ensure that such issues are left in the hands of individuals well versed in Islamic doctrine.[24] Still, female members of al-Wifaq played a key role in organizing demonstrations against the draft personal status law, and by November senior figures in the society had begun to follow their lead.

Members of the country's most important political minority—Arabic speakers who follow the Shia branch of the Islamic faith, who make up between one-half and two-thirds of the native-born population—maintain that active and sustained discrimination by Sunnis in general and the ruling family in particular explains their generally disadvantaged position in local society. The poorest neighborhoods of Manama and the most dilapidated villages in the surrounding countryside are invariably inhabited by Shias. Districts populated by Sunnis contain attractive houses, paved streets, and well-maintained public buildings, whereas many Shia areas contain older, run-down dwellings, lack paved roads, and have no public offices. Shia neighborhoods also tend to be overcrowded, often with clusters of school-age children playing or loafing in the streets.

On the other hand, Article 17 of the amended constitution stipulates that citizens are protected against discrimination on the basis of religion. More specifically, Article 22 guarantees "the inviolability of worship, and the freedom to perform religious rites and hold religious parades and meetings in accordance with the customs observed in the country." These provisions are aimed directly at the local Shia community, whose periodic celebrations include a wide range of public demonstrations of collective and personal piety. The neighborhood institutions in which many of these festivities are organized and planned, the mourning houses dedicated to the memory of al-Imam Husain, remain largely outside the purview of state agencies. Government officials also tend to keep their distance from Shia mosques, and tolerate a good deal of freedom of expression on the part of preachers who enjoy popular respect. Sunni mosques, by contrast, are more closely regulated by the central administration.

Other national and cultural minorities fare rather well in economic terms, although few of the thousands of Indians, Pakistanis, Bangladeshis, Filipinos, and Palestinians who reside in the country have been granted Bahraini citizenship. Those expatriates who do become citizens possess it only in the third class. This means that they cannot vote in municipal and parliamentary elections or run for elective office, although they do enjoy the right to bring cases before the criminal and civil courts. Unlike their counterparts in neighboring Arab Gulf states, naturalized and resident expatriates are usually permitted to bring their immediate families with them to Bahrain. Nevertheless, in March 2005, the United Nations Committee on the Elimination of Racial Discrimination formally requested that the government of Bahrain prepare a detailed report on the measures it was undertaking to end discrimination against both the indigenous Shia and other minority communities.[25]

The council of ministers refused on four different occasions to rescind an official ban on labor unions imposed in 1977. When it became evident that the cabinet was going to refuse for the fifth time, King Hamad promulgated a decree in September 2002 authorizing workers and salaried employees to form organizations to promote their economic interests. The decree grants workers the right to strike, so long as three-quarters of the members of the affected union vote to do so by secret ballot and the company involved is given at least two weeks' warning. A General Federation of Workers' Unions (GFWU) was formed in January 2004 by the country's 40 legally sanctioned trade unions.[26] On May 1 of that year, hundreds of workers took part in a spontaneous demonstration to demand pay increases, better working conditions, and greater efforts to combat unemployment. The federation in March 2005 took the Civil Service Bureau to court to force it to allow government workers to set up unions. Several hundred GFWU members marched on May Day 2005 to demand fair representation on the boards of the public and private sector social security agencies.[27]

Sporadic popular protests are met with a variety of countermeasures. In May 2004, a march in central Manama by more than a thousand Shi'is demanding the immediate withdrawal of U.S. troops from the Iraqi cities of Najaf and Karbala was broken up by police, who lobbed tear gas canisters and shot rubber bullets into the crowd. The king immediately fired the long-standing minister of the interior and replaced him with the chief of staff of the Bahrain Defense Force, General Rashid bin 'Abdullah bin Ahmad Al Khalifah.[28] Clashes between protesters and police erupted once again in late October 2004 following the arrest of the human rights campaigner 'Abd al-Hadi al-Khawajah. Participants in a sit-in at the offices of the royal court to show solidarity with unemployed workers in June 2005 were roughed up by the police and placed under arrest.[29] A young woman active in the campaign to reduce unemployment was reported to have been sexually assaulted by police in late November.[30] The incident sparked an outburst of violent demonstrations across the country. By contrast, successive protests in favor of constitutional change throughout the spring and summer elicited less violent re-actions from police and security personnel.

Overtly religious demonstrations encounter greater restraint. When marchers commemorating the death of al-Imam Husain on the occa-sion of 'Ashurah in February 2005 displayed banners bearing the pic-ture of Iran's spiritual leader, Ali Khamenei, and symbols of Lebanon's Party of God (Hizbullah), the minister of Islamic affairs summoned prominent Shia scholars to his office to "express the government's dis-may over such unpatriotic actions."[31] No arrests were made, and a min-istry spokesperson remarked that the government was "keen to solve the issue through dialogue."

Recommendations
- The government should expand both educational and employment opportunities and social services for the most disadvantaged groups in Bahraini society.
- State officials should permit public employees to form trade unions to promote their economic interests.
- Police and security officers who develop and implement ways to respond to nonviolent public demonstrations without the use of excessive force should be rewarded.
- The government must rescind Decree Number 56 and thoroughly investigate and punish perpetrators of torture against political activists.
- The authorities should work with local civic and religious associa-tions to formulate a mutually acceptable personal status law that guarantees the legal rights of women.

RULE OF LAW – 3.67

It is difficult to assess comprehensively the degree to which Bahrain operates according to the rule of law. A large majority of the country's citizens hoped, and perhaps even expected, that an updated version of the 1973 constitution would be instated as the permanent basis of Bahrain's political system. There is now almost no possibility that this will happen, and the amended constitution of 2002 has supplanted the earlier document as the foundation of political and economic life. Crit-ics of the amended constitution have largely resigned themselves to this state of affairs, and have begun to demand not that the new constitution be replaced by the previous one but instead that it be revised so as to include some of the more liberal provisions of the National Action Charter, which won overwhelming approval from voters in a February 2001 plebiscite.

Extensive political, juridical, and economic prerogatives remain firmly in the hands of senior members of the ruling family, the Al Khalifah. Members of the Al Khalifah are virtually exempt from civil and criminal law, although they do answer to a family council headed by senior sheikhs. Since independence in 1971, the justice minister has been a prominent Al Khalifah sheikh. Moreover, the king himself, in his capacity as the country's highest judicial authority, decides especially sensitive matters, including ones that involve members of the ruling family, according to his own judgment.

Various groups in Bahrain agree that the situation confronting anyone accused of a political crime is much more satisfactory now than it has been in the recent past. The amended constitution states that those who are charged with a crime are considered innocent until proven guilty. Any defendant who cannot afford legal counsel may request that a lawyer be appointed by the Ministry of Justice and Islamic Affairs. Most individuals who find themselves charged with breaking the law, even the comparatively strict Press and Publications Law, appear in open court and are permitted to present evidence and arguments in their own defense. Defendants are usually released with only minor penalties, and charges are often dismissed even before guilt or innocence has been formally determined. In fact, it is the very uncertainty that pervades the operation and deliberations of the judicial system that causes the most anxiety for defendants and the greatest concern among those who champion further reforms. There is no question that the judiciary currently exercises considerable leniency in dealing with political cases, but it is impossible to ascertain how long this extraordinary degree of tolerance may last or where its precise boundaries may turn out to lie.

Bahrain's regular armed forces are entirely subject to civilian control. In the first place, the highest ranks of the officers' corps are dominated by members of the ruling family. In addition, mid-level and junior posts tend to be occupied by a wide range of expatriates, who remain in the country at the sole discretion of the regime. Furthermore, the regular army plays almost no role in domestic affairs. Conventional police units are complemented by an extensive internal security apparatus. These formations have exercised greater restraint in dealing with protesters in the wake of the 1994–99 uprising, although allegations that police employ excessive force to subdue demonstrators continue to crop up on a regular basis.

Private property rights appear to be particularly susceptible to contravention by the Al Khalifah. Influential members of the ruling family continue systematically to requisition extensive tracts of productive agricultural land. These lands are quickly cleared of trees, denuded of topsoil, and then sold or leased to developers at a considerable profit. Such activity is particularly widespread along the northern coast, where confiscated properties are attached to land that has been newly reclaimed from the sea at public expense to yield valuable parcels of commercial real estate.

Recommendations
- King Hamad should begin to relinquish the absolute authority that he exercises with regard to judicial affairs.
- Current judicial practices that protect the rights of defendants should be codified in an explicit form.
- All encroachments on private property should be adequately compensated.

ANTICORRUPTION AND TRANSPARENCY – 2.07

The National Action Charter of 2001 clearly states that "public funds are sacred, and every citizen has a duty to protect them. Public authorities have to take all measures to safeguard them."[32] The document goes on to assert that "economic openness must be accompanied by a change in the general management towards easing procedures, transparency, the elimination of overlapping responsibilities, the improvement of services, and the modernization of economic legislation, all of which must be governed by the principles of honesty and the equality of opportunities." To this end, the charter envisaged the establishment of "an office for financial control and an office for administrative control," to be responsible for supervising "the increase of work transparency in all state institutions." These two agencies have yet to be created, and all mention of them was omitted from the amended constitution.

The long-time prime minister, Shaikh Khalifah bin Salman Al Khalifah, plays a key role in economic affairs. He is reputed to be involved in virtually every major business deal in the country, amassing great wealth as a result. Other members of the ruling family also receive handsome side payments from business transacted on the islands, either in the form of large commissions that are required or expected as part of all contracts and investments involving foreign companies, or by being appointed to lucrative positions on the boards of directors of local subsidiaries of transnational corporations.

It is generally hard to distinguish between the perquisites of office and corrupt administrative practices in Bahrain. High-ranking officials enjoy magnificent houses, large staffs of personal servants, and expensive automobiles. State-funded construction projects tend to benefit individuals and families with close ties to the Al Khalifah. Oil revenues flow directly into the central treasury, obviating the need for taxes and fees to fund the operation of government agencies. As a result, licenses and contracts represent political arrangements rather than economic ones and are subject to a wide degree of latitude depending on the actors involved. The process by which government contracts are awarded is kept hidden from public view. Considerable speculation about the illicit activities of the rich and powerful circulates in the form of rumor and innuendo, but no mechanisms currently exist to obtain reliable information about the finances of state agencies and public sector enterprises. At present, Bahrain ranks 36th (out of 158) on a scale of perceived corruption published by Transparency International. This puts the kingdom below Oman, the United Arab Emirates, and Qatar, but above Kuwait, Saudi Arabia, and the remaining Arab countries.[33]

Allegations of large-scale or sustained corruption on the part of government officials, particularly if they might implicate members of the ruling family, can be reported in the local press only in the most oblique fashion. By the same token, the head of the Women's Petition Committee was put on trial for asserting publicly that the presiding judges in the country's network of family courts were for the most part "corrupt, biased and unqualified."[34] In November 2005, the first deputy speaker of the National Assembly announced that he intended to push for the establishment of a transparency commission that would investigate charges of corruption and propose new ways to clean up corrupt administrative practices. Immediately after this announcement, the prime minister told reporters that greater attention should be paid to economic growth and less energy devoted to political controversies. The president of the pro-regime al-Mithaq society elaborated: "It is great to have a parliament and to expand freedom of expression, but what Bahrain really needs is politicians who think of the country's national interests and look for ways to consolidate its modern trends in an increasingly globalised world."[35]

Recommendations

- The government should encourage the National Assembly to adopt and implement measures that heighten the transparency of contracts and agreements drawn up by state agencies and public-sector enterprises.
- The offices of financial and administrative control should be established and allowed to function as envisaged in the National Action Charter.
- State officials should work with the ruling family council and transnational corporations to stop all demands for or expectations of illicit commissions as a precondition for economic projects and investments.
- State agencies and public sector companies should begin to draw up and publish detailed accounts of their annual income and expenditures.

NOTES

1. Nadeya Sayed Ali Mohammed, "Political Reform in Bahrain: The Price of Stability," *Middle East Intelligence Bulletin* 4 (September 2002).
2. Mohammed Almezel, "Plan to Legalise Bahrain Political Parties Shot Down," *Gulf News,* 18 May 2004.
3. Tariq Khonji, "Businessmen Push for Political Role," *Gulf Daily News,* 5 July 2004.
4. Almezel, "Bahrain MPs to Quiz Ministers Despite Speaker's Warning," *Gulf News,* 21 January 2004.
5. Abdulhadi Khalaf, "Bahrain's Parliament: The Quest for a Role," *Arab Reform Bulletin* 2 (May 2004).
6. Almezel, "MPs Demand Resignation of Bahraini Minister," *Gulf News,*25 August 2004.
7. Almezel, "Call to Change Constitution Gathers Steam in Bahrain," *Gulf News,* 20 June 2005.
8. Almezel, "Bahrain Allows Opposition Forum," *Gulf News,*15 February 2004.
9. "King Denounces Bid to Divide Bahrainis," BBC, 27 September 2004.

10 Almezel, "Dozens of NGOs and Societies Face Closure," *Gulf News*, 20 October 2004.

11 Almezel, "Battle Looms Over Proposed Law to Regulate Rallies," *Gulf News*, 7 November 2004.

12 Habib Toumi, "Political Societies Divided over New Regulation," *Gulf News*, 10 August 2005.

13 Mazen Mahdi, "Move to Regulate Groups Draws Flak," *Gulf News*, 28 September 2004.

14 Almezel, "Bahrain Warns Opposition Groups," *Gulf News*, 28 April 2004.

15 "Activists Call for Judicial Reforms," *Gulf News*, 14 December 2004.

16 "Bahrain Detains Moderator of Online Forum for 'Defaming King,'" Agence France Presse (AFP), 1 March 2005.

17 *Annual Report 2001–2002* (Manama: Bahrain Human Rights Society [BHRS], 2003), 4.

18 Ibid., 13.

19 "Bahrain," in *Country Reports on Human Rights Practices 2002* (Washington, D.C.: U.S. Department of State, 31 March 2003).

20 "Kingdom Lauded for Protection of Expats' Rights," *Bahrain Tribune*, 19 June 2003.

21 Sabika al-Najjar, "Bahrain," in *Women's Rights in the Middle East and North Africa: Citizenship and Justice* (New York: Freedom House, 2005) 54.

22 Gerald Butt, "Undercurrents of Change in Bahrain?" *Middle East Economic Survey*, 16 February 2004.

23 "Bahraini Shiite Cleric Warns against Family Law," AFP, 4 November 2005.

24 Toumi, "Al Sistani's Opinion Urged on Bahrain's Draft Family Law," *Gulf News*, 29 October 2005.

25 "Bahrain Human Rights Record Gets a Boost from Sottas" Deutsche Presse-Agentur, 28 September 2005.

26 Almezel, "Bahrain's First Federation of Labour Unions Formed," *Gulf News*, 13 January 2004.

27 "Federation to Rally for Unions," Gulf News, 1 May 2005.

28 Mahdi, "King Hamad Orders Probe into Clashes in Manama," *Gulf News*, 23 May 2004.

29 Nora Bustany, "In Bahrain, Doubts About Reform," *Washington Post*, 24 June 2005.

30 "Bahrain on Verge of Turmoil after Rape of Activist" (Washington, D.C.: Institute for Gulf Affairs, 29 November 2005), www.gulfinstitute.org/artman/publish/article_33.shtml.

31 Almezel, "'Unpatriotic Displays' during Ashura Processions Anger Government," *Gulf News*, 8 March 2005.

32 "Draft National Charter," *Bahrain Tribune*, 24 December 2000.

33 *Corruption Perceptions Index 2005* (Berlin: Transparency International, 2005).

34 "Bahraini Activist Tried Over Insulting Judiciary," ArabicNews.com, 6 June 2005.

35 Toumi, "Focus More on Economy than Politics: Khalifa," *Gulf News*, 16 November 2005.

CAMBODIA

CAPITAL: Phnom Penh
POPULATION: 13.3 million
GNI PER CAPITA: $300

SCORES	2004	2006
ACCOUNTABILITY AND PUBLIC VOICE:	3.04	3.28
CIVIL LIBERTIES:	3.05	3.33
RULE OF LAW:	2.04	2.22
ANTICORRUPTION AND TRANSPARENCY:	2.11	2.46

(scores are based on a scale of 0 to 7, with 0 representing weakest and 7 representing strongest performance)

Carolyn Bull

INTRODUCTION

After decades of civil conflict, Cambodia has made significant progress in restoring peace and political stability, reducing social tensions, and building the institutions of democratic governance. Major obstacles remain, however, to the establishment of a pluralist democratic society in which those goals may be realized fully. The UN intervention of 1992–93 and more than a decade of international development assistance have brought Cambodia the institutional rudiments of a democracy built on respect for human rights and the rule of law, but the state appears both unwilling and unable to guarantee either. Very few elements of a modern chain of public accountability are in place, resulting in poor governance and extensive corruption. Governmental dysfunction has obstructed the development process, with the greatest cost borne by the poor and vulnerable. Despite large injections of foreign aid, basic social indicators have seen scant improvement over the last decade. Ranked 130th of 177 countries in the UN's human development index,[1] Cambodia trails its neighbors in literacy, life expectancy, and infant mortality rates.

Cambodia thus sits at a fragile juncture in its transition from a hierarchical political system that prioritizes stability and control to a more liberal democratic society. Some 80 percent of the population are

---

Carolyn Bull is a PhD candidate in Politics at the University of New South Wales.

engaged in the subsistence rural economy, and to a large extent Cambodian social and political structures remain driven by traditional hierarchical patron-client relationships. Such ties rely on inequalities of wealth, status, and power and personalized interactions between the powerful and weak, in contrast to the impersonal guarantees of physical and economic security, such as the rule of law, that underpin liberal democracies. This lends itself to authoritarian forms of power politics antithetical to the principles of deliberative democratic interaction.

Against the legacy of the Khmer Rouge period, this poses a difficult reform environment even for the most committed government. Developing a decentralized, open democracy based on formal rules of law and a diversified market economy would alter the rule-and-incentive system under which the entire country operates. Powerful vested interests threatened by this objective have inevitably sought to obstruct reformists.

The 11-month political deadlock that followed the July 27, 2003, National Assembly elections highlighted the fundamental lack of legitimacy of the democratic process in Cambodian realpolitik. The prime minister, Hun Sen, consolidated his political and economic patronage system in response to an ambitious reform program proposed by the Alliance of Democrats (a coalition of FUNCINPEC and Sam Rainsy Party [SRP] opponents backed by former king Norodom Sihanouk, elements of the Cambodian People's Party [CPP], and prodemocracy urban civil society groups), which aimed to moderate Hun Sen's grip on power and level the political playing field.[2] Whether Hun Sen will take advantage of this consolidated power base to stall reform remains an open question.

ACCOUNTABILITY AND PUBLIC VOICE – 3.28

Cambodia's constitutional monarchy is headed by the king, Norodom Sihamoni. Executive authority is vested in the Royal Government of Cambodia, led by the prime minister. The bicameral parliament comprises a 123-seat National Assembly and a 61-seat Senate. The king appoints the prime minister and council of ministers from among the elected National Assembly representatives. Since 1993, National Assembly elections have been held regularly every five years. Cambodia's Election Law is fair; suffrage is universal and equal for Khmer citizens over 18 years, and voting is conducted by secret ballot.

National Assembly elections are open to multiple parties, although political pluralism is not well established. Since Cambodia's first democratic elections, in 1993, the CPP has used its dominance of the state apparatus to restrict opportunities for the effective rotation of power, including through the use of violence. Following the 1993 elections, in which FUNCINPEC won a greater share of the votes than the CPP, the latter forced the formation of a coalition that did not reflect the election outcome and enabled it to dominate its FUNCINPEC counterparts, gaining progressively greater control over Cambodia's administrative and security apparatuses. An ongoing power struggle between the CPP and FUNCINPEC co–prime ministers erupted in a coup of July 5–6, 1997, in which Cambodian elites demonstrated their continued unwillingness to resolve their differences through peaceful democratic means. Although FUNCINPEC remained part of the government, Hun Sen further consolidated political control and weakened FUNCINPEC's role in day-to-day governance.

The CPP increased its share of the vote in the most recent election, on July 27, 2003, winning 73 of 123 seats, but fell short of the two-thirds majority needed to form a government unilaterally. A protracted deadlock in negotiating a coalition under the leadership of the prime minister, Hun Sen, destabilized the political climate and further stalled reform efforts. The CPP finally reached a power-sharing agreement with the National United Front for an Independent, Neutral, Peaceful and Cooperative Cambodia (FUNCINPEC) on June 30, 2004, although the legality of this arrangement has been questioned. On July 15, the National Assembly approved the new coalition government by means of an Additional Constitutional Act, without meeting the stipulations of Article 119 of the constitution requiring formal appointment by the king. Questioning the legality of this act, all 24 opposition SRP National Assembly members boycotted the session.

The Senate, established in March 1999, resulted from a power sharing compromise between the CPP and FUNCINPEC following the 1998 National Assembly elections. The first Senate's 63 members comprise three CPP/FUNCINPEC nominees, two senators nominated by the king, and a further 56 senators nominated by political parties in proportion with their standing in the National Assembly. Constitutional amendments in 1999 allowed for the indirect election of all but three senators beginning in 2004. In the event, this election was delayed, reflecting the endemically slow nature of political change in Cambodia and exacerbating concerns over Hun Sen's commitment to the political reform process. Following the eventual passage of the Senate Election Law in May 2005, a senate election is now scheduled for January 22, 2006. An electoral college of 11,384 commune council and National Assembly members will elect 57 senators by secret ballot for a six-year term, under a proportional representation system that, given that electors are expected to vote along party lines, is unlikely to affect the political balance of power. A further two senators will be appointed by the king, with the remaining two elected by a majority vote of the National Assembly.

At the provincial level, governors are appointed by the prime minister and are currently distributed between the CPP and FUNCINPEC. At the local level, commune councils were elected for the first time in 2002, as part of the government's policy to devolve public administration and decision making to the commune level. The Law on Commune Administration provides for commune councils to select the commune chiefs; in practice the CPP generally appoints them at the national level. The CPP's dominance over commune authorities in rural areas, where 80 percent of the population resides, has limited public participation in democratic debate. Opposition parties have found it difficult to establish themselves and oppositional social movements are rare. Local politics replicates traditional authoritarian structures, whereby commune chiefs make most decisions with little participation by villagers. Democratic participation in Cambodia thus remains an elite, urban affair, and there tends to be little popular awareness of politics as a multiparty sphere of debate.[3]

State-sanctioned political violence continues, generally with impunity. Although the 2003 National Assembly election was less violent than those of 1998 and 2002, at least 14 killings were recorded during the election process, including those of a FUNCINPEC politician and a senior judge.[4] Killings continued during the postelection deadlock, including the assassination in October 2003 of a FUNCINPEC radio station editor and the shooting of a pop star linked to FUNCINPEC.

State-sponsored intimidation of the SRP, Cambodia's only significant opposition party, casts doubt on the government's commitment to genuine pluralist politics. Of particular concern was the revocation by the National Assembly in February 2005 of the parliamentary immunity of Sam Rainsy and fellow SRP legislators Chea Poch and Cheam Channy. In August 2005, the latter was sentenced by a military court to seven years' imprisonment for allegedly trying to recruit an armed group, despite the court's lack of civilian jurisdiction or any evidence to prove the case. [*Editor's note:* On December 22, 2005, Sam Rainsy was convicted in absentia of defaming Prime Minister Hum Sen and Prince Norodom Ranariddh. He was sentenced to 18 months in prison and remains in self-imposed exile.]

Despite some irregularities, election conduct has been creditable in terms of registration, polling, and vote counting, with little evidence of police or military interference. Elections have nonetheless been marred by uneven campaign opportunities, fraud, political violence, and intimidation. The majority of election-related instances of corruption occur in rural areas, where party leaders are embedded in traditional patron-client social networks. Although all parties campaigned freely in 2003, the CPP used its control of the primary mechanisms by which Cambodians receive information—the broadcast media and the commune chiefs—to malign its political opponents. It also used state resources, including transportation, personnel, and office space, to further its campaign. All the major parties engaged in vote buying, and the campaign environment was further sullied by government restrictions on and arrests of political opponents.

Election administration is politically biased. The National Election Commission (NEC) is controlled by the CPP, and provincial commune election committees are almost exclusively affiliated with the CPP or FUNCINPEC. The NEC's administrative capacity is weak, and it has proven ineffective in investigating and penalizing electoral offenses and in operating an effective complaints system. Campaign finance regulations are inadequate. The 2006 Senate election, the first to be conducted wholly by the NEC without international assistance, will provide an acid test of the NEC's capacity to oversee a free and fair election.

Although the principle of separation of powers is enshrined in the constitution, the CPP's dominance over state institutions blurs the distinction between the ruling party and the state, particularly at the commune level. The National Assembly does not provide a significant check on the executive due to its inexperience in drafting legislation and inadequate resources for its secretariat, as well as the CPP's dominance, although it is gradually becoming a more significant forum for debate. There is no active policy requiring the government to discuss its programs with the National Assembly.[5] The Senate's role is largely perfunctory.

Appointment, promotion, and dismissal of civil servants are not merit based or transparent. A large proportion of civil servants were appointed because of their support for either the CPP or FUNCINPEC.

Cambodia's independent civic sector has expanded rapidly since the first nongovernmental organization (NGO) was registered in 1991. Citizens are not compelled by the state to belong to associations, and with the exception of armed groups, which are banned, the state seldom inhibits membership in associations. Civic, business, and cultural organizations operate with relative freedom and comment publicly on government policy. However, state-sponsored intimidation and attacks still occur, particularly on civil society organizations active in the political sphere. There are few established channels for government-civic dialogue, although pressure from international donors, which have strongly backed the development of civil society, has sometimes been effective in securing such dialogue.

The constitution protects freedom of expression, press, and publication, as long as these do not adversely affect "public order," "national security," and "political stability." The 1995 Press Law prohibits prepublication censorship and imprisonment for expression of opinion. However, a national security caveat empowers the government to fine, suspend, and confiscate newspapers.

The print media are relatively free and accessible to all major parties. Newspapers have contributed to both government accountability and freedom of expression, although they reach less than 10 percent of the population. The two largest newspapers are considered pro-CPP, but many of the dozen or so Khmer- and English-language newspapers that publish regularly carry a wide range of items critical of the government, the prime minister, and the CPP. At least two dailies are controlled by the SRP.

By contrast, the CPP exerts tight control over the broadcast media. Cambodia's 20 radio stations and seven TV channels reach more than half the population and are the main sources of information in many rural areas. CPP coverage overwhelmingly dominates that of its opponents, and licensing of television and radio frequencies is politically biased. The SRP has continued to be denied a radio license.[6] The internet is unrestricted but has limited reach.

Media self-censorship is common. In addition, state censorship has included prohibiting rebroadcasts of Voice of America and Radio Free Asia reports, censoring live telecasts of National Assembly sessions, and banning the sale of publications. The government has also controlled media content through defamation provisions in the penal code and Press Law and threatened, detained, and suspended journalists. This included detaining Radio Free Asia and *Cambodia Daily* journalists in July 2004 and the arrest in October 2005 of the head of the independent radio station Beehive.

Recommendations

- The government should reform the NEC and its provincial counterparts, including by amending the Election Law, to establish clear recruitment and selection procedures that will ensure electoral officials are not politically affiliated.
- The government should take full responsibility for developing legislation on Senate elections and for the timely organization of this election.
- The government should take measures to improve state accountability and transparency, including establishing regular channels for government dialogue with civil society on policy making, merit-based civil service appointments, and strengthening the monitoring role of the National Assembly.
- The government must desist from interfering with and intimidating the media and ensure that media licensing procedures are not subject to bias.
- The government must end its intimidation of Sam Rainsy Party members and restore parliamentary immunity in accordance with the constitution.

CIVIL LIBERTIES – 3.33

Article 38 of the constitution prohibits coercion and physical ill-treatment of detainees and prisoners, as well as arbitrary arrest and detention.

Torture, arbitrary arrest, and detention provisions exist in Cambodia's principal criminal legislation, the 1992 Provisions Relating to the Judiciary and Criminal Law and Procedure Applicable in Cambodia during the Transitional Period (hereafter the penal code) and the 1993 Law on Criminal Procedure. However, these provisions do not fully meet Cambodia's international obligations as a signatory to the Convention Against Torture.

In practice, numerous instances have been documented of physical and psychological torture of prisoners in police and prison custody, the vast majority of which occur immediately after arrest. There are few practical safeguards to protect against this.

The constitution and the Law on Criminal Procedure permit victims of state breaches of the law to file claims, but judicial corruption, reluctance to institute investigations, and bias in favor of state actors undermine the effectiveness of these provisions.[7] State perpetrators of torture generally operate with complete impunity and, indeed, endorsement by high-level state actors. State actors routinely protect security forces and officials from prosecution or disciplinary action and consistently fail to investigate allegations of torture in detention, particularly of political opponents. In the minority of cases in which investigations are conducted, evidence is seldom uncovered, investigations are often deficient, and court delays are lengthy.[8]

Arbitrary arrest is common, and pretrial detention, often without access to lawyers or family members, routinely exceeds the legal limit of six months. A bail system has been introduced, but many prisoners do not have the resources to utilize it. Prison conditions are poor. Although banned in 1993, shackling remains widespread. Access by prisoners to food and medical care is restricted, particularly for those without family support, and prison overcrowding is a problem.[9] Money and personal connections are the only effective guarantees of legal representation and release.

Citizens have few protections from abuse by nonstate actors, although the government's success in eliminating the Khmer Rouge and restoring stability since the 1997 coup has significantly improved the security environment for most Cambodians.

Cambodia has made significant progress in institutionalizing the rights of women. Gender equality is constitutionally guaranteed. The Labor Law prohibits gender-based employment discrimination, including sexual harassment, and laws also guarantee relatively equal voting and property rights. The Marriage and Family Law establishes gender equality in the family; the enactment of a Law on Domestic Violence in September 2005 was a major step toward improving the legal environment.

Cambodian women are nonetheless significantly underrepresented in government and the state, comprising only 9 percent of civil servants, 7 percent of judges, 8.5 percent of commune council members, and 12 percent of National Assembly members.[10] In the paid labor market, female employment is largely restricted to the garment sector, which faces an uncertain future following Cambodia's WTO accession in September 2004. Women struggle to gain management positions, and average wages are 33 percent lower than those of men.[11] Maternity leave, while legally guaranteed, is offered only in the state sector and a minority of private businesses. In the rural subsistence economy, which occupies 75 percent of the workforce, the ability of women to protect land rights or to gain access to credit or other agricultural services is limited.

The gender gap in paid employment is influenced by educational disparities. In upper secondary and tertiary institutions, fewer than 50 girls are enrolled for every 100 boys. Some 45 percent of female adults are completely illiterate, compared to 24.7 percent of men.[12]

The state is partially engaged in addressing these issues, particularly through the ministry of women's affairs, although it devotes few resources in this area. Efforts to combat gender discrimination are hindered by poor enforcement of institutional protections, resource shortfalls, and sociocultural discrimination.

The constitution prohibits commerce in humans, and trafficking is proscribed in the 1996 Law on Suppression of Kidnapping, Trafficking and Exploitation of Humans. The government has signed on to the relevant international protocols and participates in regional anti-trafficking initiatives, importantly with Vietnam. Despite this, state efforts to combat trafficking are generally ineffective, hindered by the involvement of the military, officials, and police, a weak judicial system, a lack of resources, and low technical capacity. Since the first child-trafficking conviction in 2002, the government has tended to prosecute only high-profile cases, remaining reluctant to press charges in the majority of instances, especially if the cases involve the police or military.[13]

The rights of non-Khmer ethnic minorities, who constitute 10 percent of the population, are inadequately protected. Discriminatory practices relate to citizenship and legal residence; electoral, natural resource, and cultural rights; and access to education and health care. Ethnic Chinese, Muslim Cham, and indigenous tribes are generally not discriminated against, but Khmers from southern Vietnam and ethnic Vietnamese are subjected to widespread animosity and racist propaganda. The state's treatment of indigenous minority asylum seekers from the central highlands of Vietnam remains problematic, and freedom of movement for Phnong indigenous people in Mondulkiri Province has also emerged as an issue.[14] The legal rights of non-Khmer citizens are ambiguous. The constitution guarantees equality before the law only for Khmer citizens, and eligibility requirements for Khmer nationality under the 1996 Law on Nationality make it difficult for persons belonging to minority groups to establish their citizenship. This allows legal discrimination, particularly with respect to voting and land ownership, to which only citizens of Khmer nationality enjoy constitutional rights.

The rights of Cambodian children are routinely violated, despite legal protections. Child abuse, commercial sexual exploitation and other child labor, and sale for adoption are common. People with disabilities—who constitute up to 20 percent of the population, a legacy of protracted war and mine injuries in particular—are discriminated against at all levels of society. Disabled women and children are especially vulnerable to exploitation and discrimination in education and employment.

Buddhism is the state religion, but minority religions—Islam, Christianity, Baha'i and Cao Dai—are well integrated and experience little social or official discrimination. The constitution guarantees freedom of religious belief and worship, subject to a public order and security caveat. The state generally respects these rights, although it has occasionally banned Christian proselytizing and in September 2004, deported 12 Vietnamese Cao Dai followers. The state refrains from appointing religious leaders, and there are no significant restrictions on religious ceremony or education.

With unionization at less than 1 percent of the workforce, the union movement is small but growing. The 1997 Labor Law accords workers the right to form and join labor unions of their own choosing, to bargain collectively, and to strike. However, there is little political will to enforce this. Employers engage freely and regularly in antiunion activity and discriminate against trade union members, and the state has arrested union leaders for allegedly inciting violence. The assassination in 2004 of Chea Vichea, a trade union leader with SRP connections, and of garment factory union leader Ros Sovannareth, highlighted the continued impunity for politically motivated crimes.[15] Although in August 2005 two persons were sentenced to 20 years' imprisonment for Chea Vichea's murder, fundamental principles of a fair trial were contravened.[16]

State intervention in demonstrations has for the most part been restrained, although demonstrations in 1998 and December 2002 were violently suppressed. The constitution guarantees the right to nonviolent demonstration, but under the 1991 Law on Demonstrations the state may ban gatherings deemed "detrimental to public tranquillity, order or security." The government has frequently refused to authorize demonstrations since the violent anti-Thai riots of January 2003, banning or otherwise intervening in at least 16 demonstrations in Phnom Penh in 2004, sometimes with excessive police or military force.[17]

Recommendations

- The government should fully and promptly investigate allegations of state torture and ensure appropriate prosecution and punishment of perpetrators. Practical safeguards in police stations and prisons should include regular independent inspections; guaranteed access for NGOs, doctors, and lawyers; administrative and criminal sanctions for police misconduct; recording of injuries sustained in detention; and procedures to ensure that evidence obtained through torture is inadmissible in court.
- The government should review its tightening of restrictions on demonstrations since January 2003.
- The government must prioritize strategies to promote gender equality, and in particular to upgrade the literacy and vocational skills of girls and women. This should include programs to improve access to services for women in rural areas.
- The government must step up efforts to combat human trafficking and the sexual and commercial exploitation of women and children, including prompt prosecution of trafficking cases involving state actors.

RULE OF LAW – 2.22

The justice system remains one of the weakest elements of the Cambodian state. The government has consistently failed to meet judicial reform benchmarks, including those agreed upon with donors at the

2002 and 2004 Consultative Group meetings (the key forum for bilateral and multilateral donors to discuss and coordinate international assistance for Cambodia's development process).

The constitution guarantees judicial independence, but separation of powers is not upheld in practice. Executive interference in the conduct of judges and prosecutors, all of whom are CPP appointees, is rife. This has included instructions for charges to be dropped, the dismissal of judges, the re-arrest of suspects released by the courts, and open intimidation of judges by members of the armed forces.[18] Politically related crimes are seldom prosecuted; the politically powerful and their families enjoy impunity for even the most serious crimes.[19] Judicial independence has been further undermined by the government's recent iron-fist policy to combat judicial corruption, which it has used to impose sanctions against court officials without following proper disciplinary procedures.[20]

Court budgets are not separate from the Ministry of Justice, and there is no declaration of assets requirement for judicial officials. The Supreme Council of Magistracy (SCM), which appoints, oversees, and disciplines judges and prosecutors, lacks independence, is unable to fulfill its disciplinary function, and has made questionable judicial appointments.[21] The Cambodian Bar Association has become increasingly politicized, both through the admission of several senior CPP members in 2004, despite their lack of legal qualifications, and as a result of a continuing dispute over the election of its president.[22]

Cambodia's legal framework relies on an incomplete set of laws drafted hastily by the United Nations Transitional Authority in Cambodia, which implemented the Cambodian peace settlement from 1992 to 1993 and oversaw Cambodia's first democratic elections in May 1993. Drafts of a new penal code, a code on criminal procedure, a civil code, and a code on civil procedure have been prepared with international assistance, but there appears to be little political will to enact them.

The court system lacks both resources and an adequate institutional framework, resulting in lengthy delays and chronic maladministration. Corruption is endemic, due in part to extremely low salaries. There is an acute shortage of educated judges and lawyers; only one in six judges has a law degree, and only one of the nine Supreme Court judges does.[23] Specialist legal education is now offered, including at the Royal School of Judges and Prosecutors established in November 2003, but it will be some years before this has a positive impact. Ultimately, better education and remuneration are unlikely to improve judicial conduct until political interference ceases.

Civil and criminal disputes are frequently resolved extrajudicially. The use of summary and mob justice is widespread, particularly in rural areas, and police are often complicit or reluctant to intervene. Citizens tend to ignore the law in favor of less transparent patronage systems, especially the intervention of senior officials. Court officials and the police often pressure victims to settle disputes extrajudicially. Both state and nonstate actors enjoy impunity across all areas of law. Public officials, as well as ruling party actors and members of their families, are seldom brought before the courts.

Legally, trials are public and defendants have the right to be present, to consult with a lawyer, to question witnesses, and to bring witnesses and evidence before the courts. Cambodians are also constitutionally entitled to the presumption of innocence and the right of appeal. In practice, however, investigative and trial procedures are generally well below international standards. Shaped by its Vietnamese/Soviet predecessor, the trial system is characterized by a high conviction rate and forced confessions. Defendants are often detained without warrants and denied prompt trial. Investigative procedures tend to be deeply flawed, and trials usually lack adequate evidence or cross-examination. The right of presumption of innocence is routinely violated; judges often predetermine trial outcomes after consultation with the Ministry of Justice or provincial authorities, the capacity of a defendant to bribe judges being a key determinant of the verdict. There is no effort to ensure that evidence obtained through torture is inadmissible, and defendants are often tried in absentia.[24]

Police and prison officials frequently deny defendants access to legal representation. As there is no state legal aid program and the majority of citizens cannot afford legal representation, citizens routinely appear in court without counsel.[25] Illiterate defendants are often not informed of the content of the written confessions they have signed. NGO-funded legal aid has helped improve access to legal counsel and acquittal rates for the poor.

The National Assembly ratified the Khmer Rouge Tribunal Law in October 2004, establishing a special mixed tribunal comprising a majority of Cambodian and a minority of international judges. Funding remains an issue, as does the question of whether the tribunal will deliver just outcomes and adequately protect victims and witnesses.

Although the national police and armed forces fall nominally under civilian control, the state lacks the institutional capacity or political will to exercise that control. The armed forces exert excessive influence over politics, the economy, and state policy and are the most powerful authority in many rural areas.[26] Creditable progress has been made toward demobilization, but trust-building and employment creation remain key issues.

Military and police personnel enjoy widespread impunity, although there have been some convictions for political killings in recent years. In cases involving military personnel heard within the civilian court system, military officers have pressured judges to release defendants without trial. The military court system is partisan and poorly resourced. There is no independent authority to investigate complaints against the police.

Insecurity of land tenure has been a major source of conflict since forced collectivization under the Khmer Rouge. Around 75 percent of Cambodia's land area is technically managed by the state, including most natural resources and large agricultural properties.[27] Much of this is outsourced through concessions to private companies. This, combined with land grabbing by powerful military and local officials, has displaced the poor and exacerbated conflict between villagers and state actors in rural areas.

Recognizing the scale of the problem, the government has made progress in developing a sound resource management policy, including the passage of a Land Law in 2001 and the suspension of some concessions pending a more effective concessions policy. As ever, substantive progress depends on strengthening responsible institutions. Key subsidiary regulations to implement the Land Law have not yet been adopted, including any on collective land titling and indigenous status. Illegal logging and the misuse of state resources have continued. The courts remain largely unable to enforce land rights, with disputes subject to political interventions, particularly when military or police are involved. In August 2005, for example, the courts dismissed charges against some 120 police and military officers implicated in the deaths of five villagers in Bantay Meanchey Province during a forced land eviction.

The establishment in 2002 of cadastral commissions to conciliate land disputes at local, provincial, and national levels was an important step toward reconciling conflicts outside the courts. With donor technical assistance, the commissions are just beginning to function, but concerns remain about their interpretation of jurisdiction and about the ability of poor families without documentation to prevail over powerful opponents.

Recommendations

- The executive must commit to ending interference in judicial affairs. Strong leadership is required at the highest levels, including the Ministry of Justice, the Supreme Council of Magistracy, and the Supreme Court.
- The government should upgrade the legal framework by enacting the draft penal code, code on criminal procedure, civil code, and code on civil procedure, as well as subsidiary regulations.
- The government should reform the SCM to ensure its independence. In particular, it should ensure that the Ministry of Justice does not participate in decisions relating to the dismissal or reassignment of judges and that council members are not affiliated to political parties. The SCM should be funded adequately.
- Judicial corruption must be addressed, including through the establishment of an independent anticorruption commission; support for independent monitoring of the judiciary; improved transparency of criminal processes including the mandated presence of lawyers for the accused and the prohibition of trial judges' reviewing evidence prior to trials; and improved personal security and adequate remuneration for judges and prosecutors.
- Access to justice should be improved through the establishment of a state-funded legal aid program.

ANTICORRUPTION AND TRANSPARENCY – 2.46

Corruption drains off an estimated 10 percent of Cambodia's gross domestic product.[28] It is a way of life in business and for state agents, notably the judiciary, customs and business licensing officials, the police, and the tax authority.[29] The ruling party appropriates resources on a massive scale to maintain its dominance over the security forces and state infrastructure.[30]

Opportunities for state corruption are extensive. The bureaucracy is cumbersome, politicized, and unregulated, while the broader regulatory environment is nontransparent. Cash-based payments systems (as opposed to bank-transfer payments systems, which are easier to track) and the weakness of internal and external accountability mechanisms make the risk of engaging in corruption very low. Civil service salaries are typically less than 20 percent of the living wage, making corruption essential for survival.[31]

The government has repeatedly committed itself to fighting corruption but has not matched rhetoric with action. The state does not adequately protect against conflicts of interest in public office or the private sector. The constitution prohibits government members from professional involvement in trade or industry and from holding positions in the civil service, and the Common Statute of Civil Servants forbids civil servants to use their positions for personal profit or to manage private enterprises. These prohibitions are not upheld in practice, and provisions for internal sanctions are seldom, if ever, activated. The legislature and executive are not expressly forbidden from using state assets for business or political ventures.

Although the state itself refrains from excessive involvement in the economy, with relatively few government-owned companies or assets, no accountability mechanism exists to check the business interests of members of the government or National Assembly. Officials flagrantly abuse position for commercial privilege. The business interests of the CPP's top clique, for example, are estimated at US$400 million annually.[32]

Cambodia is not a signatory to the UN Convention Against Corruption. Although the government has been working toward national anticorruption legislation since 1995, a draft anticorruption law is yet to be passed and no anticorruption authority exists. As it currently stands, the draft anticorruption law falls short of international standards. Problems include a weaker definition of corruption, vague requirements for assets declaration, and a failure to prohibit laundering.[33] Although at present it is possible to prosecute for corruption under the penal code, the political environment is not supportive of this. Government officials continue to enjoy almost complete impunity for corruption. Some arrests of state officials relating to trafficking have reportedly been made, but the government is not known to have prosecuted any cases of official corruption despite committing itself at the 2002 and 2004 donors' meetings to do so with immediate effect.

Financial disclosure procedures are similarly inadequate. No legislation covers the declaration of assets and liabilities of state officials, nor are there processes for public scrutiny or verification of financial assets. The enactment in 2000 of an Audit Law for external and internal audit arrangements was a key step toward adequate financial management, but scant progress has been made in implementing an effective audit regime, through either external or internal systems. Cambodia's first external audit body, the National Audit Authority (NAA), was created in January 2002. It has its own budget and reports directly to the National Assembly. However, lack of legal infrastructure, experience, and resources have impeded its effectiveness. Senior NAA positions are politicized. The establishment of an ombudsman's office was mooted in the government's 2002 National Poverty Reduction Strategy, but little progress has been observed.

Higher education suffers from pervasive corruption. Schemes to obtain illegal payments for manipulating the deployment and promotion of teachers are common, as are unofficial payments to teachers (who do not receive a living wage), charges for additional lessons that students are pressured to attend, and payments to secure university admission and passing grades on exams. This adversely affects access to education for the poor.[34]

The judicial system, itself arguably the country's most corrupt institution, offers little recourse for corruption victims to pursue their rights. Although allegations of government corruption—including at the highest levels—receive widespread coverage in the media, there are few avenues by which corruption can be monitored and the government pressured to improve accountability. Anticorruption activists risk persecution, while the National Assembly and Senate are ineffective checks on government performance.

Although gradually improving, public access to government information and public participation in government decision-making processes are poor, and citizens lack effective means to express their preferences to policy makers. Lawmaking and enforcement are generally not transparent. Televised legislative debates have increased the transparency of the legislative process somewhat, but there is no notice and comment period prior to the approval of laws or regulations. Public input is limited to irregular consultations between the government and civil society groups. National Assembly and Senate members seldom receive copies of laws, regulations, or government decisions, further weakening their role in the accountability process. The government has begun periodically publishing and distributing an official gazette of new Cambodian laws and subsidiary regulations, but this has only partly addressed the need for a comprehensive archive of laws.

Cambodia's weak and nontransparent budget process hinders policy implementation and provides extensive opportunities for corruption. Legal and technical deficiencies in the public accounting system make it easy to divert funds illegally. Agencies generally fail to comply with budget law requirements, and funds are seldom disbursed or utilized in accordance with budget plans.[35] The National Assembly's Finance and Banking Committee scrutinizes the budget, but it lacks the technical capacity to do a meaningful job and is not public. It is as yet unclear how effective the NAA will be in performing its role. The recent establishment of a public financial management reform committee within the Ministry of Economics and Finance was a positive step but will need to be matched by serious political commitment and practical assistance.

The government has made little progress in implementing and enforcing 1995 legislation on public procurement. Procurement processes are notoriously corrupt, nontransparent, and lacking in effective control procedures. No specific legal penalties exist for procurement-related corruption. The official introduction in 2003 of a requirement for competition in procurement has not yet translated into effective competition or transparency.

Cambodia has no freedom of information law and few established procedures for gaining access to information. Information disclosure is patchy and generally at the discretion of the government. Budget, national account, and other economic and social indicators are available to the public on a regular and timely basis but with variable accuracy.[36] Defense and other sensitive information is kept secret and business and corporate information guarded closely.[37] Negotiations on key policy decisions are secretive as well.

The 1995 Press Law grants journalists the right to publish accurate official information and right of access to government-held records, albeit subject to national security and other caveats. It does not, however, cover the general public or sanction officials who deny access to information. Ordinary citizens must generally present written requests in person and in many cases experience lengthy or indefinite delays, while journalists rely on personal connections rather than established procedures. Deterred by excessive bureaucracy, the requirement for bribery, illiteracy, and perceptions that the state is impenetrable, citizens rarely attempt to obtain information.

The government enables the legal administration and distribution of foreign assistance, although the distribution of such assistance is susceptible to procurement-related corruption. Aid comprises some 60 percent of the national budget, and the government is therefore heavily dependent on it. This dependence has had a profound effect on Cambodia's political development. Although instrumental in creating an electoral democracy, political institutions, and a civil society, the superficiality of many aspects of the Cambodia political process demonstrate the equally profound limitations of this "donor democracy." Donors have struggled to build real commitment to democratic reform on the part of the Cambodian elite and have in some senses distorted the democratization process. The development of civil society, which in Cambodia owes its very existence to foreign donors, is one such example. Many civil society organizations are not robustly grounded in existing social structures and have experienced both credibility problems due to their close association with the international donor community and dislocation as a result of changing donor agendas. This has affected their already limited ability to channel community concerns and to provide a counterweight to the authority of the state.

Recommendations
- The government should impose stiff anticorruption measures, such as enacting laws on anticorruption, assets declaration, and conflict of interest; establishing an independent anticorruption commission; ensuring the independence of the NAA and strengthening its technical capacity; and establishing an ombudsman's office.
- The civil service needs reform, including increased salaries and extensive education to change entrenched behavior. This could be funded by streamlining the civil service.
- The government should improve parliamentary oversight processes, especially with respect to the capacity of the finance and banking

committee to monitor government performance in budget formulation and expenditure.

- Public finance reform must continue, particularly public procurement and budget disbursement and reconciliation procedures. Reform should include a shift from a cash-based to a bank-transfer payments system.
- Access to information needs to be improved, including through enacting freedom of information legislation and strengthening the information infrastructure.

NOTES

[1] "Cambodia" in *Human Development Report 2005* (New York: United Nations Development Program [UNDP], 2005), http://hdr.undp.org/statistics/data/countries.cfm?c=KHM.

[2] Steve Heder, "Hun Sen's Consolidation: Death or Beginning of Reform?" *Southeast Asian Affairs 2005* (Singapore: Institute of Southeast Asian Affairs, 2005), 114.

[3] Caroline Hughes, "Candidate Debates and Equity News: International Support for Democratic Deliberation in Cambodia," *Pacific Affairs* 78 (Spring 2005): 79.

[4] Kingdom of Cambodia: The Killing of Trade Unionist Chea Vichea (London: Amnesty International [AI], AI Index: ASA 23/008/2004, 3 December 2004), http://web.amnesty.org/library/Index/ENGACT230082004?open&of=ENG-KHM.

[5] *Cambodia at the Crossroads: Strengthening Accountability to Reduce Poverty* (Washington, D.C.: World Bank, 2004), 5, http://siteresources.worldbank.org/INTCAMBODIA/Resources/Cover-TOC.pdf.

[6] *Human Rights Overview: Cambodia. Country Summary January 2005* (New York: Human Rights Watch [HRW], 2005), 3, http://hrw.org/wr2k5/pdf/cambod.pdf accessed 25 July 2005.

[7] In June 2004, the deputy director of the National Police, General San Phan, said that torture during interrogation was sometimes necessary. He reportedly retracted the statement after a complaint from the UN Special Representative of the Secretary General. See *Kingdom of Cambodia: The killing of trade unionist Chea Vichea* (AI).

[8] *2004 UN Commission on Human Rights: Mission: To Promote and Protect Human Rights* (AI, AI Index: IOR 41/001/2004, 1 January 2004), http://web.amnesty.org/library/Index/ENGACT400082003?open&of=ENG-KHM.

[9] *Situation of human rights in Cambodia: Report of the Special Representative of the Secretary-General for Human Rights in Cambodia, Peter Leuprecht* (Geneva: UN Commission on Human Rights Economic and Social Committee, E/CN.4/2004/105, 19 December 2003), 3.

[10] *A Fair Share for Women: Cambodia Gender Assessment.* April 2004 (Phnom Penh: UNIFEM, World Bank, ADB, UNDP, DFID/UK and Ministry of Women's and Veteran's Affairs, 2004), 11, http://siteresources.worldbank.org/INTCAMBODIA/Resources/ExecutiveSummar.pdf.

11 Ibid, 6.

12 Ibid, 8.

13 Abigail Schwartz, "Sex trafficking in Cambodia," *Columbia Journal of Asian Law* 17 (Spring 2004), 410.

14 *Quarterly Report, Third Quarter of 2005* (Phnom Penh: UN Office of the High Commissioner for Human Rights Field Office Cambodia, 2005), 7.

15 *Cambodia: Trade Unionist's Murder Shows Up Judicial Flaw* (AI, AI Index: ASA 23/009/ 2004, 3 December 2004), http://web.amnesty.org/library/Index/ENGACT230092004 ?open&of=ENG-KHM.

16 *The Special Representative Calls for Continued Investigation into the Murder of Trade Union Leader Chea Vichea and for the Immediate Release of Cheam Channy* (Phnom Penh: UN Special Representative of the Secretary-General for Human Rights in Cambodia, 16 August 2005), http://www.ohchr.org/english/press/docs/Leuprecht16august.pdf. See also *Quarterly Report, Third Quarter of 2005* (UN Office of the High Commissioner for Human Rights Field Office Cambodia, 2005), 1.

17 *Human Rights Overview* (HRW, 2005), 3.

18 *Kingdom of Cambodia: Urgent Need for Judicial Reform* (AI, AI Index: ASA23/004/2002, 19 June 2002).

19 *Cambodia: Getting Away with Murder* (AI, AI Index ASA 23/010/2004, 22 December 2004), http://web.amnesty.org/library/Index/ENGACT230102004?open&of=ENG-KHM.

20 *The Special Representative Calls for Continued Investigation* (UN Special Representative of the Secretary-General, 16 August 2005).

21 *Kingdom of Cambodia: The Killing of Trade Unionist Chea Vichea* (AI, 3 December 2004).

22 *Human Rights Overview* (HRW, 2005), 2.

23 *Cambodia at the Crossroads* (World Bank, 2004), 5.

24 *Cambodia: Governance Reform Progressing, But Key Efforts are Lagging* (Washington, D.C.: U.S. General Accounting Office [GAO], GAO-02-569, June 2002), 8.

25 *Situation of Human Rights in Cambodia* (UN Commission on Human Rights Economic and Social Committee, 19 December 2003), 10.

26 Sorpong Peou, *Intervention and Change in Cambodia: Towards Democracy?* (Chiang Mai: Silkworm Books, 2000), 366.

27 *Cambodia at the Crossroads* (World Bank, 2004), 19.

28 *Cambodia: Governance Reform* (U.S. GAO, June 2002), 9–10.

29 *Cambodia Governance and Corruption Diagnostic: Evidence from Citizen, Enterprise and Public Officials Survey* (World Bank, 2000), 5. See also *Cambodia at the Crossroads* (World Bank, 2004), 4.

30 *The Run-Up to Cambodia's 2003 National Assembly Election: Political Expression and Freedom of Assembly Under Assault* (HRW, June 2003), 2.

31 *Cambodia: Governance Reform* (U.S. GAO, June 2002), 10–11.

32 Christopher Gunness, "Cambodia's 'Missing' PM," BBC News/Asia Pacific, 25 July 2003, http://news.bbc.co.uk/1/low/world/asia-pacific/3097393.stm.

33 Christine Nissen, "Cambodia," in *Global Corruption Report* (Berlin: Transparency International, 2005), 121, http://www.globalcorruptionreport.org/download/english/ country_reports_a_j.pdf.

[34] "Education" in *NGO Statement to the 2004 Consultative Group meeting on Cambodia* (Phnom Penh: NGO Forum on Cambodia, 6–7 December 2004), http://www.ngo forum.org.kh/Development/Docs/CG%202004/Education.htm.

[35] Clay G. Westcott, ed., *Key Governance Issues in Cambodia, Lao PDR, Thailand and Vietnam* (Manila: Asian Development Bank, 2001), 9, http://www.adb.org/Documents/Books/Key_Governance_Issues/Chapter_2.pdf.

[36] *Cambodia Development Review* 7 (Phnom Penh: Cambodia Development Resource Institute, April–June 2003), http://www.cdri.org.kh.

[37] Peter Eng, "Cambodia: Restricted Information in a Semi-democracy," in Sheila Coronel, ed., *The Right to Know: Access to Information in Southeast Asia* (Manila: Philippine Center for Investigative Journalism, 2001), 43–63.

EAST TIMOR

CAPITAL: Dili
POPULATION: 0.9 million
GNI PER CAPITA: $550

SCORES	2004	2006
ACCOUNTABILITY AND PUBLIC VOICE:	4.77	3.83
CIVIL LIBERTIES:	4.62	4.64
RULE OF LAW:	4.76	3.81
ANTICORRUPTION AND TRANSPARENCY:	2.42	2.62

(scores are based on a scale of 0 to 7, with 0 representing weakest and 7 representing strongest performance)

Karen Polglaze

INTRODUCTION

East Timor became fully independent in 2002 after more than 400 years of Portuguese colonial rule and 24 years of Indonesian occupation. Portuguese control was largely characterized by neglect, and when a new government came to power in Lisbon in 1974, it began decolonization.[1] The rapid development of indigenous political parties, as well as cross-border interference by Indonesia, interrupted this process. A brief conflict between the main political groups ended when the Revolutionary Front for an Independent East Timor (FRETILIN) declared independence on November 28, 1975. Independence was short-lived: on the morning of December 7, 1975, Indonesian troops landed in Dili and began an occupation that would cost up to 183,000 Timorese lives.[2]

Regime change in Indonesia in 1998 created the opportunity for a new policy allowing the East Timorese to hold a referendum on whether to become an independent state or an autonomous region within Indonesia. Months of violence and intimidation marred the August 1999

Karen Polglaze first traveled to East Timor in 1998 as a correspondent for Australian Associated Press. She reported on the conflict in 1999 and returned to East Timor in 2001–2002 as an adviser for the Timor Lorosa'e Journalists Association. From 2003 to 2005, she managed the National Democratic Institute for International Affairs Security Sector Reform Program in East Timor, working with parliament, the government, and civil society.

101

UN–administered ballot, in which 78 percent of the population voted for independence.[3] Anti-independence militias, supported by the Indonesian military, swiftly retaliated, unleashing a wave of violence that left more than 1,400 dead and half the population displaced.[4] More than 70 percent of the country's buildings were completely or partly destroyed, and essential infrastructure was dismantled.[5] A UN-mandated international military force arrived to restore order, and in October 1999, a UN administration was established to facilitate the transition to independence.

Today, East Timor has made significant progress toward democracy despite being Asia's poorest country.[6] It has had to create the institutions of modern democracy from scratch with few indigenous resources and little experience. That it has come this far with little internal conflict or threat of disintegration is an almost unparalleled achievement. But much more time and support are needed to entrench the institutions of democracy, and there is a significant power imbalance in which the executive dominates. Understanding and implementation of the rule of law is poor, and the government is inadequately separated from the police.[7] On paper, East Timor has many of the attributes of a modern democracy, such as constitutional protection of a wide range of rights. However, this is not reflected in daily life; the administration's lack of experience and understanding of how such rights are translated into practice tends to render meaningless those protections. The impact of this lack of capacity has become increasingly apparent as East Timorese institutions have assumed full responsibility for running the country.

Poverty also threatens the fragile gains. Transport and communications are difficult, infant and maternal mortality are high, and access to health care can be problematic. Many have no access to clean water, and few outside the two largest cities have regular electricity.

While the legacy of external control continues to shape politics and society, outstanding issues from the past will threaten the country's fragile stability unless resolved. The most pressing concerns include achieving justice for the atrocities and human rights violations from 1974 to 1999 in a way that is broadly accepted,[8] dealing with the wide range of issues related to veterans of the resistance, and implementing an effective land and property title regime and a means for resolving disputes. Also crucial is the development of an effective strategy that enables East Timor and Indonesia to resolve problems without threatening their bilateral relations. Above all, efforts to ensure meaningful citizen involvement in the decision-making processes of government must be strengthened so the people can at last feel truly represented.

ACCOUNTABILITY AND PUBLIC VOICE – 3.83

In August 2001, the United Nations sponsored a nationwide election for the Constituent Assembly, a transitional body charged with drafting the new constitution. The vote was contested by 16 parties; the majority party, FRETILIN, won 55 of 88 seats. In March 2002, the Assembly approved the constitution, which designated the president as head of state and a prime minister as head of government. The electoral law, through transitional arrangements in the constitution, provided the possibility for the Constituent Assembly to transform itself into the first parliament without another election. The members so voted, and on May 20, 2002, they became East Timor's first national parliament. New electoral laws are in the process of being drafted for the 2007 parliamentary and separate presidential elections.

Village (*suco*) and sub-village (*aldeia*) elections held on a rolling basis between December 2004 and September 2005 provided an insight into how the next national elections might unfold. They were run by the new State Technical Administration for Elections (STAE), which is part of the Ministry of State Administration. The National Electoral Commission, a body of prominent citizens appointed to these honorary positions, supervised the conduct of the polls. It is expected that both bodies will preside over the 2007 elections.

In general, the elections were rated free and fair, although independent observation was limited. Alleged irregularities were referred to the Court of Appeal, and repeat elections for certain village councils were held. The most significant problem arose when the electoral authority enrolled voters according to the new delineations of *sucos* and *aldeias,* which resulted in some voters' enrollment in villages and sub-villages other than those in which they believed they lived. This problem was later resolved by ensuring that polling places in each village had copies of nearby village rolls as well as their own.[9] Consequently, fewer problems were reported in later rounds.

A major concern for political parties was the government's late presentation to parliament of the electoral law for the local elections and the lack of consultation and involvement of the other political parties and the public in its development. Although the law was promulgated more than six months before the first rounds, its full implications were not recognized. This resulted in some parties being unprepared for its requirements, especially the one calling for political parties to be registered in order to endorse candidates.

As the elections unfolded, the nongovernment parties began to allege abuses—including the failure to allow the nomination of several non-FRETILIN candidates, the late nomination of FRETILIN candidates, and the hiring of FRETILIN party members as casual electoral officers. The parties also alleged that government officials used government vehicles to campaign and that voters were warned that voting for a nongovernment party might mean that local development projects would not go ahead.

Some anxiety has emerged over the timing of the next parliamentary elections, reflecting uncertainty over orderly succession and transitional arrangements. Sections 75 and 93 of the constitution make it clear that parliamentary and presidential terms last up to five years; those of the current members of parliament (MPs) and the president began on May 20, 2002. The next elections must therefore be resolved in time to allow the new parliament and president to be sworn in by May 20, 2007. This anxiety has also been fueled by repeated statements from leading FRETILIN figures that theirs is the only party able to govern and that FRETILIN will be in power for the next 50 years. These statements and the conduct of some FRETILIN officials during the local elections, combined with the lack of public trust in the nation's new institutions, have helped create doubts about the fair conduct of elections.

East Timor has not experienced an election with a government in place. It has not yet established rules and procedures to regulate government behavior during electoral periods. For example, there is nothing to prohibit the incumbent government from entering into contracts during the election that bind subsequent governments. Clearly, this could produce results that run counter to the will of the people expressed during the poll.

Laws establishing the military and police prohibit partisan activities by members of the armed forces. Other groups that might exert undue influence in voter choice, such as economic groups, are small, unorganized, or so far seem uninterested in doing so.

Most opposition political parties were formed in 2001 and have created their internal structures, policies, and processes since then. They have few resources—financial or human—and are still struggling to establish themselves in the districts. The state of all opposition parties militates against any one of them, or even an alliance, having a real chance of winning control of the government. Political party development assistance has been relatively meager. The reduction in size of the next parliament, in accordance with section 93 of the constitution, could weaken or destroy some opposition parties.

Development assistance has helped to strengthen the capacity of the government and the civil service. The same level of assistance has not been available to either the parliament or the judiciary, and this has contributed to an imbalance of power already inherent in the East Timor constitution and exacerbated by the weakness of the recently formed opposition parties. The government and donors have recognized this and are seeking increased assistance for the parliament and the judiciary. The constitution provides for a semipresidential system with little real power in the hands of the president. The majority parliamentary party or alliance chooses the prime minister, who determines the membership, size, and structure of the government. The concept of the parliament as a check on government power is not fully understood here, and many members do not yet see such monitoring as being among their responsibilities. The FRETILIN members sometimes struggle with conflicting loyalties between the party, as represented by its most senior members in the government, and the parliament as the lawmaking authority. Recent amendments to legislation regulating protests and demonstrations that reduced the required minimum distance from public buildings for protesters and the acceptance of court-advised changes to make other aspects of the same law constitutional are encouraging signs that the parliament is beginning to understand its separate role.

Despite impediments to its development, the parliament has reached many milestones in its three years of existence. MPs across party lines are beginning to understand the elements of representative democracy and are growing louder in their demands for the resources to enable them to carry out their tasks. However, parliament lacks human and financial resources, making it difficult for members to develop and institute democratic processes. Parliamentary committees are still coming to grips with their roles and functions. Legislative scrutiny is rudimentary, and the lack of legislative drafting capacity means that amendments are rare. Legislation is prepared only in Portuguese, and not all MPs have parliamentary staff and/or the level of fluency required for proper scrutiny. Research staff are nonexistent, and library facilities are extremely limited. Records of committees' public proceedings and reports are not properly archived or publicly available. Vehicles to enable MPs to consult their far-flung constituents became available only in 2005 and are inadequate in number and quality. The immense barriers parliamentarians face in trying to perform the simplest of tasks discourage even the most dedicated from undertaking basic duties such as communicating with constituents.

Civil servants are recruited, promoted, and trained through a process that lacks transparency. Disciplinary procedures are opaque, particularly in the armed forces, and prompt much complaint and debate. Capacity and a professional service ethos will take time to build. Effective administration is further hampered by excessive bureaucracy, arbitrary and unclear rules, and a failure to delegate responsibility effectively. All of these issues are recognized and being addressed by the government in cooperation with the United Nations and donors.

Nongovernmental organizations (NGOs) have a self-administered registration system. Laws regulating NGOs have been in development for several years, and responsibility for them has been shifted among several ministries. Donors and funders of civic organizations are largely free of government pressure, although occasional government comments about the roles and functions of NGOs have caused concern and prompted speculation that future regulations may restrict their activities. The government develops policy and legislation largely in secret, providing little opportunity for civic groups to influence it. Further, the state does not have any institutionalized mechanism for hearing the views of NGOs, and there is little evidence that such a mechanism will be developed in the near future.

The NGO sector in East Timor lacks experience; NGO criticisms of the government have often been ill informed or much too personal. This is often due to the difficulty in obtaining even basic public information from state bodies. Draft laws and policies are not routinely circulated. Parliamentary committees examine all legislation within their areas of responsibility, but most committees do not seek public input. Public comment is usually sought on draft legislation only when there is significant donor support for its development.

The media has operated freely since late 1999; the constitution contains significant support for freedom of expression (sections 40 and 41). However, the new penal code, which has been developed through a closed process, criminalizes defamation. The new code, scheduled to enter into force in early 2006, is likely to reduce legitimate reporting and comment due to journalists' fear of imprisonment or financial penalties. Public figures have proven sensitive to criticism, threatening journalists and outlets. Civil servants and police officers acting without legal authority have even confiscated cameras from reporters.

Prime Minister Alkatiri claimed that criminalizing defamation was necessary because the Timorese media are immature. Lack of experience and economic capacity mean that research and fact-checking are less than optimal and that reporters can misconstrue stories. However, the media have a legitimate information-supplying and watchdog role in a modern democracy, and a tolerant approach to error should prevail until the media sector becomes more developed.

Still, the media face significant capacity and economic barriers that make their existence precarious and predispose them to errors. Three daily newspapers and a weekly are based in Dili, while community radio stations regularly operate in most districts. Low literacy levels and publication language have an impact on readership, and maintaining circulation is difficult. Widespread poverty means that buying a paper is an unaffordable luxury for most. There are no laws regulating the Internet, although limited and expensive telephone coverage and poor electricity supply affect access.

A partly government-funded public broadcaster provides nationwide radio coverage, but its television broadcasts are limited to Dili and Baucau. The public broadcaster has largely operated on a combination of a national budget allocation and donor funding, although it has earned some income through sponsored programs. The government has not used its budget allocation to influence program content.

The public broadcaster is obligated to reflect cultural traditions and expressions in its programming and has made some effort to do this within a very small budget. There are no legal impediments to freedom of cultural expression, and music, poetry performance, storytelling, photographic and other visual art exhibitions are thriving. Economic constraints are the main barrier to publication of written works. Laws regulating other broadcasters are being developed, and no licensing regulations apply to the print media.

Recommendations

- The government should release a draft electoral law for wide public comment well before the 2007 elections. The parliament should seek donor funding for expert analysis and commentary on the draft.
- The electoral law should provide clear guidelines for dealing with the use of government resources, including salaries and transport, as well as an accessible mechanism for complaints.
- The government needs to seek more input from various non-governmental groups in the development of policy and legislation.
- Increased development support should be allocated to the national parliament, possibly to coincide with the preparation of the next parliament following the 2007 elections.
- The government should decriminalize defamation. Any new legal protection of personal reputation should be developed in consultation with the media, should take into account the media's real financial capacity, and should emphasize corrections and apologies rather than penalties.

CIVIL LIBERTIES – 4.64

East Timor has ratified all major international human rights treaties, including the treaty on torture, and has incorporated into its constitution the obligation to assess rights judicially in line with those treaties.[10]

A 2005 research study that analyzed documents dealing with war crimes committed between 1974 and 1999 found that the transitional justice system instituted to deal with serious crimes had failed to fully investigate and prosecute allegations of torture within its mandate.[11] It also noted that the judicial and prosecutorial approach to torture was out of line with standards in treaties East Timor has joined. Reports of serious beatings and other maltreatment of prisoners and police suspects increased during 2004 and 2005.[12]

Prison conditions are comparable with the very basic living standards generally prevailing in East Timor. The ratio of prison officers to inmates is reasonable by regional standards, and there are few reports of violence inside prisons, although a complaints mechanism is lacking. Prison officers are receiving training across a range of issues. Access to prisons is allowed to independent observers but is discretionary. Some concerns have been raised over the housing of juveniles with adults and the internment of minor offenders with serious habitual violent criminals.[13]

In districts without detention facilities, detainees may be locked in offices or other unsuitable locations while in police custody, and no budget is provided for food or transport for these detainees.[14] This has sometimes resulted in a reluctance to detain people or privation for detainees. Improvements in devolution of responsibility and budgets are being implemented.[15] Problems in the judicial system have contributed to excessive time in pretrial detention for many alleged offenders. A system for reducing excessive pretrial detention was introduced in late 2005.

Several members of dissenting political groups have been arrested on dubious legal grounds, although few successful prosecutions have been reported.[16] Public figures have done little to address this problem. Arrests on spurious grounds may be due to a lack of police knowledge, but they point to the potential for the abuse of the power of arrest.

Laws protecting people from abuse by private and nonstate actors are in place, but the civil court is barely functioning due to a paucity of human and financial resources. Complaints procedures for people who feel their rights have been violated by the state are beginning to be put in place. The police have developed such a procedure, although the process is still unclear. An ombudsman's office has been established that will begin receiving complaints in 2006. Some abuses of government processes can be reported to the Office of the Inspector General.

Gender equity is enshrined in the constitution, but some traditional practices will take time to change. The Office for the Promotion of Equality actively raises relevant issues, and political and civic leaders make positive statements about equality, although these have yet to be translated into widespread concrete action. While the civil service has no barriers to women's entry, few women hold senior positions. Women are less likely to receive job offers than men, as they are generally less well educated and are pressed into domestic and family support roles, but there is little public discussion about this lag.

Political parties included many women on their party lists for the 2001 elections, with the result that they hold 26 percent of parliamentary seats. However, no women preside over committees or fill other senior parliamentary positions. There is some discussion inside political parties about how to ensure that women are represented at senior levels. This will be especially important when the parliament is reduced after the 2007 elections.

The incidence of domestic violence is very high. The problem is well recognized, with public education campaigns backed by strong statements of support from political and other leaders. Surveys show that the police view domestic violence as a serious crime, although they tend to prefer using customary law to resolve it. Familial relationships and local power plays can influence decision making in customary law, which is usually arbitrated by local male leaders, further disadvantaging women and doing little to change the behavior of perpetrators. The number of successful prosecutions in the formal system therefore remains low, with little impact on public awareness and deterrence. The inconsistencies in imposed sentences also point to a range of different perceptions about the severity of domestic violence as an offense.[17]

Prostitution is illegal but thriving. A report from the Alola Foundation showed that trafficking in women and children into East Timor does occur, mainly from Indonesia, Thailand, China, and the Philippines.[18] The National Parliamentary Committee on Foreign Affairs, Defence and National Security investigated information received about trafficked women and children working as prostitutes in Dili. Their inquiries revealed that police are aware of the problem and that some women have been detained, although it is not clear whether they were prosecuted, convicted, or legally deported. No legal action has been reported against traffickers or brothel owners.

The constitution guarantees basic human rights in line with the major international human rights treaties; however, most are not yet reinforced by subsidiary legislation. Language remains a great source of discontent among the general population. None of the indigenous languages are taught in the education system, and few are transmitted in a written form. Early primary education is delivered in Portuguese, which is understood by fewer than 20 percent of people in the country; later education is delivered in Bahasa Indonesian, which older students still find most comfortable for reading and writing. Furthermore, much government information is produced in Portuguese, prompting negative responses from many East Timorese who consider it a foreign language. Tetum, the most widely understood language, is still developing a standardized written form, largely because the country's colonial rulers ignored it.

Although there are at least 13 different indigenous languages, the East Timorese generally consider themselves fairly homogeneous. There is a small ethnic Chinese minority, and a difference between people from the east of the country and those from the west is traditionally recognized. However, issues of ethnicity are rarely raised.

Conditions for people with disabilities are very difficult. In some cases, especially those involving chronic mental health conditions, communities do not understand the needs of disabled individuals. Poverty and a dearth of facilities for care compound these problems.

While the overwhelming majority of East Timorese identify as Catholic, there are also groups of Protestants and Muslims, and all can freely practice their beliefs. Although some reports of tensions resulting from proselytizing and conversions by Protestant preachers have surfaced, particularly in the Liquiça district, no serious incidents have occurred.[19]

The state refrains from involvement in the internal affairs of religious organizations and places no restrictions on observance or ceremonies. Large public demonstrations occurred in Dili in April and May 2005, when the Catholic Church objected to government plans to make religious education optional in state schools. After 20 days of peaceful demonstrations, which involved thousands of people, the government and the church negotiated an agreement whereby schools would offer religious education and parents could decide whether to send their children to those classes.

Freedom of association and assembly is guaranteed by the constitution (sections 42 and 43) and regulated by subsidiary law. Trade unions are legally protected, and citizens are not compelled to belong to any associations directly or indirectly. Laws regulating NGOs and other associations are yet to be developed, although provisions in the immigration and asylum law restrict some activities of noncitizens, and the formation and organization of political parties is regulated. Business and professional associations are unregulated. A draft law on a bar association has been criticized as fundamentally flawed because it gives the government too much say over private lawyers and because interested parties have not been involved in its development.[20]

Demonstrations and public protests are regulated by law and must be authorized in advance.[21] Two days of rioting in December 2002 prompted the government to be wary of future protests, while a forceful clampdown on a peaceful protest by veterans in mid-2004 provoked much public discussion and condemnation of police violence. The April 2005 Catholic Church demonstration stoked fears of a repeat performance, but the government and police remained calm, allowing the demonstrators to protest in a peaceful and orderly manner.

Recommendations
- Further training of police is required to reduce the number of people arrested and detained on spurious grounds.
- Continuing programs are needed to monitor and reduce pretrial detention periods.
- The government should make a greater effort to publish all public information in the most widely understood language in East Timor, Tetum.
- Efforts to combat trafficking of women and children should be increased and should focus on prosecuting those who profit from it.

RULE OF LAW – 3.81

At independence, East Timor inherited existing Indonesian law and received a new constitution, as well as a series of regulations and directives issued under the UN administration. Most laws introduced since independence are based on models from Portuguese-speaking countries and are published in Portuguese only.[22]

Timorese people had never held senior civil service positions under Indonesian rule, so none had experience as judges. As of the end of 2005, all indigenous judges were in full-time training initiated after they had failed a standardized qualification examination for the bench in late 2004. The district courts are now presided over by five international justices from Portuguese-speaking countries, none of whom speak Indonesian.[23] Two Timorese judges sit on the Court of Appeal, as it is illegal for this court to convene without an indigenous judge. However, their qualifications are questionable as they also failed the examination.[24]

Infrastructure damage and the lack of organizational and administrative capacity inhibit the functioning of the district courts outside Dili. In 2004 and 2005, these courts began to operate, noticeably improving the speed of justice, although a backlog of about 3,000 cases remains.

Unlike during the occupation, a judgment cannot easily be bought in East Timor, but some allegations of corruption have been made against certain court actors, mainly prosecutors.[25] The main factors affecting the independence of the judiciary include the single, government-provided training option; the concentration of administrative power in the position of chief justice of the Court of Appeal;[26] the lack of sufficient resources for the courts; and the low level of capacity among many of the court actors, including judges, prosecutors, public defenders, and clerks.[27] There are no reports of direct interference with judicial decision making by the executive or legislative branches, nor by other influential sectors of society.

Judicial decisions have little impact on the way civil servants carry out their daily tasks. Few cases have occurred in which a judicial decision was contrary to government policy, but in the most significant case, when the Court of Appeal decided that Portuguese law was applicable, the government and parliament both responded by writing a new law to make it clear that Indonesian law was applicable.

The judicial appointment, promotion, and dismissal system remains untested, and the adequacy of the training system cannot yet be judged as no one has thus far qualified based on it. The hybrid legal system and the history of judicial appointment have made consistent knowledge and application of the laws difficult.

The presumption of innocence is guaranteed by the constitution (section 34) and reinforced in the new penal code. However, timely court appearances, especially bail hearings, have been difficult to attain. This problem has been recognized, and many improvements have been made, although delays can still occur. The lack of judges has had a negative impact on the speed of trials, especially in the outer districts. District courts have also suffered from problems associated with poor electricity supply, a lack of administrative capacity, and difficult transport and communications, which may mean, for example, that accused people and witnesses are not notified of court dates.[28] Proceedings are generally held in public unless there are good legal reasons not to, and public defenders are part of the legal system.[29] While these defenders are undertaking compulsory training their role has been filled by private lawyers; there is some concern that a new law regulating the bar association could affect their ability to act as public defenders.

In general, prosecutors act independently of government control. However, the government's unwillingness to prosecute senior Indonesian figures over their alleged roles in the violence of 1999 has led the prosecutor general to abstain from issuing arrest warrants. As well, criminal accusations against some government figures have not been transparently investigated. The Office of the Inspector General has carried out many inquiries into allegations involving public officials, and 11 cases have been referred to the prosecutor, but no further progress has been reported.[30]

The requirement that the security sector to be accountable to civilian authorities is entrenched across the senior command of both branches of the armed forces and by their civilian leaders in government and parliament. Decrees establishing both armed forces branches reinforce civilian primacy; citizens understand that members of the armed forces are not above the law. The negative experience during the occupation has resulted in an active understanding that the armed forces should not be partisan, and this is reinforced by the constitution and subsidiary law. Generally, the police and military refrain from interference in politics; however, exceptions do occur.

Virtually all levels of the police lack a consciousness that officers who act criminally should be liable to court as well as disciplinary proceedings. Police disciplinary procedures are unaccountable, opaque, and secret. The rights of nonpolice complainants have not been properly addressed, and complaints procedures are unclear and unpublicized.

Public complaints about the behavior of military officers are rare except for the continuing cases of violence between members of the two armed forces branches. An independent inquiry into the military (FALINTIL-FDTL) following one of the most severe of these incidents of violence between the two armed forces, on January 25, 2004, resulted in a series of recommendations, many of which could be implemented within current resources, including the development of manuals, the production of material in Tetum, and the overhaul of the promotions system.[31]

Land and property ownership is a major challenge for lawmakers and affects both internal stability and future economic growth. During the Portuguese period, Portuguese land law existed alongside customary law. When Indonesia invaded, its legal regime applied to land; however, customary and traditional law continued to apply in some places. Many people were displaced during the occupation. Some property previously owned by the Portuguese government or by Timorese people who had fled the Indonesian invasion was taken over by the Indonesian administration or by Indonesian or other Timorese individuals. Property might have been divided, modified, improved, and sold during that time. In the violence that followed the ballot in 1999, most buildings and records were destroyed. After the restoration of order, most people returned, including those who had been in exile for more than 20 years. Many properties are now subject to competition for ownership by claimants asserting title obtained through different means conferred in different eras.[32]

The constitution (section 54) entrenches the rights of East Timorese nationals to own property and to transfer it during life or at death and to receive fair compensation for compulsory acquisition of private property. Communal land use exists in many areas, with exploitation of resources and stewardship responsibilities locally recognized as vested in certain communities.[33] Subsidiary legislation covering land ownership, leasing between private individuals, and administration and leasing of state-owned property has come into effect. Laws to complete the process of land regulation—on land dispute mediation and on property transfer, registration of preexisting rights, and title restitution—are under government consideration.[34]

Disputed claims to land have been registered, and several cases are before the courts, although criminal cases are prioritized. One case of disputed ownership received a great deal of publicity because one claimant is a prominent opposition party leader and the other is the government. The government forcibly removed the opposition leader, who had lived in the house since Indonesian times. Political motives were debated, but the case is progressing slowly through the courts like other civil cases. Mindful of the instability it could engender, the government is generally reclaiming property over which it asserts ownership in an orderly and gradual manner. Due to the general lack of progress in civil matters, no trends in land claim decisions are discernible.

The constitution guarantees equality before the law for all citizens and prohibits discrimination on the grounds of color, race, marital status, gender, ethnic origin, language, social or economic status, political or ideological convictions, religion, education, and physical or mental condition (Section 16). In practice, exercising these rights is more difficult for those with low literacy and education levels or who do not speak Portuguese, Tetum, or Bahasa Indonesian. Subsidiary laws on discrimination have not yet been drafted. The human rights ombudsman will report to the parliament.

Recommendations
- Findings of all investigations by the Office of the Inspector General should be made public unless it would prejudice a fair trial, in which case publication should be delayed rather than abandoned.
- Police disciplinary procedures need to be opened up; those suspected of committing crimes should be investigated and prosecuted.
- A police complaints system open to the public and responsive to complainants should be established and publicized.
- The laws to complete regulation of land and property should be implemented as a priority and the operation and administration of the land law system publicized.

ANTICORRUPTION AND TRANSPARENCY – 2.62

Business and other transactions with the government are frequently complicated by opaque requirements, heavy bureaucracy, and arbitrary rules not based in legislation. For example, as part of the complicated transitional approvals process for work permits for in-country foreign nationals, the police required a color passport-style photograph of the applicant wearing a bowtie and jacket. The government aims to develop a one-stop shop for customs clearance, which would remove the need to obtain separate approvals by a range of ministries, each of which can have different and/or overlapping requirements. This is an example that could be usefully repeated in many other areas.

The government has created a free-market economic system and has proven very resistant to frequent demands by interest groups seeking government intervention in the economy through measures such as food subsidies.

Measures to deal with conflict of public and private interests remain to be developed for both public and private sectors. People generally believe that government members and senior civil servants profit from their offices, although this is unproven, as no cases have been prosecuted through the courts. The Office of the Inspector General has referred at least 11 cases to the prosecutor general, but at the time of writing no further movement had been reported on those cases. The general suspicion of the population has been reinforced by a number of incidents, such as the prime minister's brother winning a monopoly contract to import various arms and other materiel including tanks and helicopters for the military, which highlight the need for transparency. Financial disclosure procedures for government members, members of parliament, and other holders of public office have been discussed but not developed.

The parliament has passed legislation creating the civil service, introducing disciplinary procedures, and establishing a code of ethics. Allegations of corruption may be reported to and are investigated by the Office of the Inspector General.

Citizens are highly aware of the illegality of bribery, which was a particularly detested feature of the Indonesian regime. Solicitations are generally refused and exposed; they have not been publicly reported in the higher education system.

The constitution provides for a High Administrative Tax and Audit Court to monitor public spending and audit state accounts (Section 129), but as it is not yet established, the Ministry of Planning and Finance currently performs the audit function. This court will also have responsibility for appeals against judgments made in relation to decisions by civil servants and organs of the state.

Legislative and administrative processes to prevent and punish corruption are still being developed. Public officials have yet to develop a high level of corruption awareness and procedures to combat it. The main corruption watchdog, the Office of the Inspector General, has made efforts to become more open over the course of 2005. This office is very active; it can now refer cases directly to the prosecutor general, strengthening its independence. As it reports to the prime minister, it is unclear whether the office is subject to political pressure or whether allegations are investigated without prejudice. Whistle-blower protection legislation has not been developed.

Allegations of corruption are often aired in the media, but follow-up to these allegations is rarely publicized. This has a negative impact on those implicated and reduces public confidence in the system.

Public access to government information is severely limited; gaining access to specific documentation that should be publicly available is very difficult. The resources and capacity to provide information are lacking. Moreover, most officials tend not to perceive the benefits of providing information to the public. Freedom of access to personal stored information is guaranteed by the constitution (Section 38), but subsidiary enabling legislation remains undeveloped. Most civil servants refuse to release information unless their superiors formally instruct them. No special arrangements are made to ease access to information for people with disabilities.

The national budget is drawn up through a comprehensive, closed internal process that has not been publicly explained. Parliament is routinely given only two to three weeks to scrutinize budget documents, a situation which always provokes complaint. Ministers were previously called in by parliamentary committees to explain the details of the budget, but in 2004 the government halted these appearances. For the past two budgets, the prime minister and the finance minister have answered questions before the parliament as a whole, a forum that is not conducive to the detailed questioning of line items that is required. Parliamentary committees have yet to seek alternative sources of information, such as from civil servants or interest groups. Interest groups have difficulty obtaining an advance copy of the budget, so trying to influence the debate would be virtually impossible. In any case, the capacity of most groups to undertake this work is limited.

The published financial information in the national budget lacks the detail necessary for appropriate scrutiny. The information is provided through the publication of the legislation and through the World Bank, which has been assisting the government in this area.[35]

The government contracting and tender procedure is not open. Tenderers likely to win government contracts often have family or other ties to leading government or other public figures, increasing public distrust of the system.

Foreign assistance has directly funded the national budget and contributed to reconstruction, with information on gross amounts publicly available. Non-governmental and other organizations have access to development assistance from a range of overseas donors and agencies without government intervention or legal impediment, except for restrictions on some funding of political parties.

Recommendations

- Financial disclosure procedures need to be developed so that the financial interests of senior officeholders and members of government and parliament are made public.
- Conflict-of-interest provisions for the public and private sectors must be formulated and routinely implemented.
- The parliament should implement a better budget scrutiny process, which would include input from civil servants and interest groups.
- Clear and transparent procedures must be developed for government tendering and contracting; information about successful tenders, as well as an explanation of why the bids were accepted, should be made public.

NOTES

[1] For East Timor's history, see J. Dunn, *Timor: A People Betrayed* (Brisbane, Australia: Jacaranda Press, 1983), or J. G. Taylor, *Indonesia's Forgotten War: The Hidden History of East Timor* (Sydney, Australia: Pluto Press, 1991).

[2] P. Walsh, "Media Misrepresentations of the CAVR Report," e-mail circulated by the East Timor Action Network, 4 January 2006. The report of the Commission for Reception, Truth and Reconciliation (CRTR), which has the most accurate estimates of the number of conflict-related deaths from 1974 to 1999, was not available at the time of writing, although some information has been made public.

[3] *Summary of the Report to the Secretary General of the Commission of Experts to Review the Prosecution of Serious Violations of Human Rights in Timor-Leste (then East Timor) in 1999* (New York: UN Security Council, 26 May 2005), 9.

[4] Ibid.

[5] "At a Glance: Timor-Leste," in *State of the World's Children 2006* (New York: UNICEF), http://www.unicef.org/infobycountry/Timorleste.html; *Strategy for Timor-Leste FY 06–08* (World Bank), 1.

[6] *World Bank Country Assistance Strategy for Timor-Leste FY 06–08* (Washington, D.C.: World Bank, Report No. 32700-TP, 18 August 2005), 15.

[7] *Report of the United Nations High Commissioner for Human Rights on Technical Cooperation in the Field of Human Rights in Timor-Leste* (New York: United Nations Economic and Social Council [UNECOSOC], Commission on Human Rights, 22 March 2005), 6.

[8] Much has been published about efforts to deal with the violent crimes of 1974 to 1999 in East Timor. The report of the Commission of Experts, cited above, provides a wealth

of information. East Timor truly stands at the crossroads over the soon-to-be published report of the CRTR. The president and the government are urging East Timorese people to look toward the future and not to seek retribution for the violent crimes Indonesia and some East Timorese committed in the past. This is because they believe that a peaceful future depends on harmonious relations with Indonesia, which has refused so far to cooperate with any serious effort to bring the perpetrators of these crimes to justice. It is doubtful whether most ordinary East Timorese people agree with this position; events since October 1999 have reinforced their expectations that the perpetrators would be punished. This is a very difficult issue for all in East Timor. The international community also has a stake in bringing human rights violators and war criminals to justice. Efforts to find a way forward should include significant public education and involvement in decision making so that the threat of disintegration is minimized. The international community must support these efforts.

9   K. Annan, *End of Mandate Report of the Secretary-General on the United Nations Mission of Support in East Timor* (New York: UN, S/2005/310, 12 May 2005), 1.

10 Treaties ratified by East Timor can be traced through the official government gazette, *Jornal da Republica,* http://www.mj.gov.tl/jornal/.

11 *Torture and Transitional Justice on Timor Leste* (Dili, Timor Leste: Judicial System Monitoring Program [JSMP], April 2005), 13–25, http://www.jsmp.minihub.org.

12 "Progress Report of the Secretary-General on the United Nations Office in Timor Leste (for the period 13 May to 15 August 2005)" (UN, 18 August 2005); *Report 2005: Timor Leste,* "Covering events January –December 2004" (London: Amnesty International [AI]), http://web.amnesty.org/report2005/tmp-summary-eng; "East Timor," in *World Report 2005* (New York: Human Rights Watch [HRW], 13 January 2005), http://hrw.org/english/docs/2005/01/13/eastti9825.htm.

13 *Technical Cooperation in the Field of Human Rights in Timor-Leste* (UNECOSOC), 5. Additional information supplied to the author by expert visitors to the prisons.

14 Information provided to public hearings held by the National Parliamentary Committee on Foreign Affairs, Defence and Security; World Report 2005 (HRW).

15 *Strategy for Timor-Leste FY 06–08* (World Bank), 9.

16 *Technical Cooperation in the Field of Human Rights in Timor-Leste* (UNECOSOC), 7.

17 *Police Treatment of Women in Timor Leste* (JSMP, January, 2005); *Women in the Formal Justice Sector: Report on the Dili District Court* (JSMP, 7 April 2004); *Statistics on Cases of Violence Against Women in Timor Leste* (JSMP, February 2005).

18 *Trafficking in Timor-Leste: A Look into the Newest Nation's Sex Industry* (Dili and Melbourne: Alola Foundation, October 2004), http://www.alolafoundation.org/HT%20report.php.

19 This information was reported by community leaders at a public hearing with the National Parliamentary Committee on Foreign Affairs, Defence and National Security in Liquiça in 2004.

20 "The Government Seeks to Regulate Private Lawyers" (JSMP, press release, 27 May 2005).

21 For an analysis of this law see the *Report on Draft Law 29/I/3A: Freedom of Assembly and Demonstration* (JSMP, October 2004).

[22] "Recent Developments in the Courts," *Justice Update* (JSMP) 22/2005 (October/ November 2005). Language difficulties beset all aspects of life in East Timor, but this is especially apparent in the judicial system. Most of the law that applies in East Timor is still Indonesian law, and none of the international judges speaks Indonesian; however, English copies of the laws are reportedly available. Timorese judges, public defenders, and prosecutors were largely educated in the Indonesian system but were given some short, but intensive, Portuguese training before they sat for the qualifying examinations in 2004 (which all judges failed). The training is being delivered in Portuguese. JSMP has noted that court actors who have been working alongside international staff do not appear to be significantly influenced by the training, probably because their Portuguese is not yet adequate. It is unlikely that many of the defendants speak Portuguese, and while interpreters are provided, many accused would not speak Tetum or Indonesian either. Legislation is published in Portuguese, which means that ordinary people are unlikely to understand it, in the improbable event that they are able to get a copy and, importantly, neither are police officers, who are also not likely to see copies of legislation, as the only method of circulation appears to be the *Jornal da Republica* (government gazette), which is not widely available. The electronic version is often out of date and not accessible to most people, who have no electricity or telephones. See also *The Impact of the Language Directive on the Courts in East Timor* (JSMP, Report, August 2004).

[23] "Recent Developments in the Courts," *Justice Update 22/2005* (October/November 2005).

[24] "Continued Trial of Serious Crimes Suspects," *Justice Update* 16/2005 (August 2005): 3–4.

[25] *Strategy for Timor-Leste FY 06–08* (World Bank), 5.

[26] *Overview of the Justice Sector: March 2005* (JSMP, March 2005), 25.

[27] See, in general, *Justice Updates* (JSMP).

[28] "Recent Developments in the Courts," *Justice Update* 22/2005 (October/November 2005).

[29] "Closure of Detention Review Hearings," *Justice Update* 15/2005 (15–25 July 2005).

[30] *Background Paper for the Timor-Leste and Development Partners Meeting* (World Bank, 25–26 April 2005), 8.

[31] X. Gusmao, "On the Findings of the Independent Inquiry Commission (IIC) for the FALINTIL-FDTL" (Washington, D.C.: East Timor and Indonesia Action Network, press release, 24 August 2004), http://www.etan.org/et2004/august/22/24onthe.htm.

[32] *Land Law Report* (JSMP, 27 September 2005).

[33] C. D'Andrea, *The Customary Use and Management of Natural Resources in Timor-Leste* (Fitzroy, Victoria, Australia: Oxfam, November 2003), http://www.oxfam.org.au/ world/asia/east_timor/reports.html.

[34] *Land Law Report,* (JSMP, 27 September 2005).

[35] An example of the Timor Leste national budget can be downloaded at http://extsearch .worldbank.org/servlet/SiteSearchServlet?q=Timor%20Leste%20budget.

GEORGIA

CAPITAL: Tbilisi

POPULATION: 4.5 million

GNI PER CAPITA: $770

SCORES	2004	2006
ACCOUNTABILITY AND PUBLIC VOICE:	3.68	4.78
CIVIL LIBERTIES:	3.92	4.27
RULE OF LAW:	3.89	3.96
ANTICORRUPTION AND TRANSPARENCY:	2.30	3.87

(scores are based on a scale of 0 to 7, with 0 representing weakest and 7 representing strongest performance)

Sanja Tatic

INTRODUCTION

Since gaining independence from the Soviet Union in 1991, Georgia has made mixed progress in promoting democracy and strengthening the rule of law. The country's first democratically elected president, Zviad Gamsakhurdia, was overthrown in a military coup after only a year-and-a-half-long rule. His downfall, largely provoked by his decision to abolish the post of commander of the Georgian National Guard and subordinate several senior officials to the Georgian Ministry of Internal Affairs, came amid accusations by the opposition that his presidency had become overly authoritarian. Gamsakhurdia's successor, Eduard Shevardnadze, was invited by a military council to lead the country as the acting chairman of the state governing council and was elected president in a 1995 vote.

Although Georgia succeeded in holding successful elections in the early and mid-1990s, Georgia's government did not rest on a strong set of democratic institutions; it mainly relied on Shevardnadze's paternalistic relationship with different sectors of society.[1] As a result, the administration became increasingly authoritarian after the growing opposition

Sanja Tatic is Managing Editor of *Countries at the Crossroads,* a survey of government accountability, civil liberties, corruption, and the rule of law in 60 countries. She is also a Southeast Europe and Caucasus analyst for Freedom House's annual *Freedom in the World* and *Press Freedom* surveys.

challenged its rule in the late 1990s and early 2000s. Shevardnadze won the 2000 presidential election by approximately 80 percent of the vote, but the poll was marred by myriad incidents of serious electoral fraud, including group voting, ballot-box stuffing, police presence in polling stations, and a lack of transparency in vote-counting and tabulation. These events, coupled with discontent over ailing economic reforms and a dwindling standard of living, contributed to a significant drop in support for the regime. During that time, the country's civil society became better organized, more active, and increasingly critical of the government's policies.

Hence, it was not a surprise that civil society played an essential role in the events of November 2003—better known as the Rose Revolution—in which the masses flooded the streets to protest the parliamentary elections deemed fraudulent by international and domestic observers. The events prompted Shevardnadze's resignation and brought to power a group of reformers, led by Mikhail Saakashvili and the coalition of the National Movement and the United Democrats. The new leaders consolidated their power after overwhelming electoral victories in January and March 2004, amid tremendous public enthusiasm and high expectations for the future of the country.

After his inauguration, Saakashvili found himself immersed in problems inherited from the old regime. The judicial system was plagued by incompetence, limited impartiality, and a lack of independence. Corruption was omnipresent in every segment of the society including government, the judiciary, law enforcement, utility companies, the educational system, and health institutions. Organized crime influence on politics and the economy was paramount and growing. In addition, Georgia's human rights record was mixed at best, with reports of torture and police brutality in prisons and pre-trial centers.

Amid the challenges, the government did make significant gains in several areas. New anticorruption measures successfully reduced corruption by instituting important laws on conflicts of interest, increasing salaries for judges and police, and prosecuting corrupt officials at all levels of government. A crackdown on graft in tax-auditing bodies considerably improved tax collection. Independent units were created to oversee and punish police officers who practiced brutality and torture. These undertakings, however, were offset by some questionable developments, evoking doubts about the administration's commitment to democratic values. For example, changes to the constitution skewed the balance of power in favor of the presidency and weakened the parliament. Moreover, journalists seem to have become less willing to criticize the government in the face of pressures, and the judiciary became increasingly subject to executive interference.

Georgia's political developments unfolded against a backdrop of wars for independence in South Ossetia and Abkhazia. Following Georgia's secession from the Soviet Union, the newly elected Georgian authorities, who were facing increasing levels of nationalism from Georgians wishing to establish an ethnic identity for their new state, stripped Abkhazian and South Ossetian minorities of their autonomy. Furthermore, Georgia's institutions at the time were not sufficiently developed to engage the minorities in the process of democratic compromise.[2] As a result, a civil war erupted, and both territories declared de facto independence from Georgia. Since the revolution, Saakashvili has attempted to reintegrate South Ossetia with the rest of the country; however, this effort has been largely unsuccessful and seems to have worsened the situation.

ACCOUNTABILITY AND PUBLIC VOICE – 4.78

The Georgian constitution provides for universal, equal, and direct suffrage through secret ballot. However, in the period preceding the Rose Revolution, electoral standards were low, and various irregularities were commonplace. Elections were meaningful in that a multiparty system existed and the franchise was inclusive, but there was little competition among the candidates, and the process was heavily skewed in favor of the incumbents. Massive fraud surrounding the November 2003 parliamentary elections prompted a peaceful popular uprising, eventually forcing Shevardnadze to resign.

The snap presidential and parliamentary elections of January and March 2004 were hailed as an improvement over the November 2003 vote, despite concerns about the continued lack of a clear separation between state administration and political party structures. The Organization for Security and Cooperation in Europe (OSCE) noted many positive aspects, including progress in the administration of the election process, greater secrecy of the ballot, and efforts to increase the participation of national minorities. Conversely, they also recorded officials' interference in the functioning of local election commissions and reduced scrutiny by the domestic monitoring organizations. The elections clearly evidenced improvements in the freedom of expression through the wide range of media campaign coverage; however, the pro-Saakashvili parties had a distinct advantage on state television through extensive and overwhelmingly positive coverage and paid advertisements. By contrast, opposition parties took a more passive campaigning approach, making only a few low-key appearances, mainly due to lack of funds.[3]

A total of 16 political parties and electoral blocs participated in the elections, none of which succeeded in challenging Saakashvili's National Movement–United Democrats (NMD). After a sweeping victory, the NMD gained 135 out of 150 unfilled seats in the parliament. Such one-party dominance remains a concern, as it hinders the opportunity for an effective rotation of power among a range of competing interests and policy options. Parties that did not participate in the revolution lost a great number of supporters, while the former ruling party, the Citizens Union of Georgia, disappeared completely from the political scene. The Conservatives and the Republicans, which broke away from the National Movement, as well as the New Rights Party and the Industry will Save Georgia now contest the ruling party's policies in parliament, although with a little success due to their limited representation. In the by-elections, held in October 2005, the National Movement won all five contested seats despite the opposition's decision to present a unified candidate in four of the races.

The election administration in Georgia is comprised of the Central Elections Commission (CEC), 75 District Election Commissions, and 2,860 Precinct Electoral Commissions, which contain both the ruling and the opposition parties. Saakashvili's appointment of several persons close to his administration to the CEC in 2004 provoked criticism among the opposition parties and some analysts. Political party financing is determined by the Law on Political Association; parties that crossed the required threshold in the preceding elections qualify for public funding. The CEC is tasked with monitoring the funds received by political parties.

The Georgian constitution calls for the separation of powers among the executive, legislative, and judiciary branches of government, although state power increasingly rests in the hands of the executive. In February 2004, the parliament passed constitutional amendments that created the post of prime minister, introduced the principle of governmental accountability to the parliament, and allowed the president to dismiss the parliament and call for new elections if the state budget is not passed in three attempts.[4] Many Georgians argue that the creation of a stronger executive office was necessary to overcome the crisis created by the revolution, but others point out that such a concentration of power undermines the system of checks and balances. Yet, there is some evidence that the legislative branch is slowly gaining more influence and independence. For example, in March 2005 the parliament passed the resolution against the Russian military bases in Georgia despite pressure from the executive to modify its language. In October 2005, Prime Minister Zurab Noghaideli dismissed Foreign Minister Salome Zourabichvili after members of parliament questioned her professionalism and asked for her discharge. The constitution grants the Constitutional Court the power to adjudicate on the constitutionality of laws and normative acts of the president and the government.

As in many other post-Communist countries, entry into and promotion within Georgia's civil service remains plagued by nepotism and cronyism. Efforts to combat this trend have been systematized through legislation on public service, which posits that employees must be recruited through an interview process. However, in reality, these procedures are often ignored in favor of preferential treatment for relatives and friends of high-ranking officials.[5]

Georgia's vibrant civil society does not face any major legal or registration impediments. Considering the weakness of opposition parties, the civic sector has taken the role of opposing governmental actions perceived as less democratic. Georgian non-governmental organizations (NGOs) have the ability to influence legislation and the political process. Parliamentary regulations provide for public hearings by committees on bills, and input from the civic sector is frequently sought. Furthermore, civic organizations are often included in various government commissions; Saakashvili has met with NGO representatives a number of times. Civil society's main critique of the current administration is that it sometimes does not provide enough time for public discussion when important decisions are made. For example, the motion to amend the constitution in February 2004 was initiated without much deliberation and consultation with the public.

Donors and funders of civic organizations are free from state pressures; however, most NGO financing still comes from abroad. The tax code, which was passed in December 2004, allows businesses to spend up to 8 percent of their earnings on such donations without paying taxes on that amount. A culture of charitable business activities is still underdeveloped, and only a small number of companies participate.

Freedom of speech and the press is enshrined in the Georgian constitution. However, media continue to be influenced by political interests. Further, journalists are still subjected to extralegal intimidation and physical violence; it remains unclear who is behind such attacks. For example, the editor of the weekly *Imedi* in the eastern city Gurjaani, Gela Mtiulishvili, was brutally beaten while returning home in June 2005; in a separate incident in November, a hand grenade was thrown at his home. In September 2005, five assailants attacked Saba Tsitsikashvili, an investigative journalist for the local daily *Saxalxo Gazeti,* in the northern city of Gori. Police later arrested Mr. Tsitsikashvili's assailant, who turned out to be a relative of one of the mayor's bodyguards. The state does not restrict access to the internet, and it protects freedom of cultural expression.

In June 2004, the parliament passed the Law on Freedom of Speech and Expression. The new act, widely praised as one of the most progressive laws in the region, formalized the right to free political speech and debate, editorial independence, and freedom to expose official wrongdoing; it also provided a set of new rules on defamation cases, ensured the right of journalists to protect the confidentiality of their sources, and relaxed provisions on disclosing state secrets. Moreover, defamation was officially decriminalized on the same day the Law on Freedom of Speech and Expression was introduced.

Despite these positive developments, the government continues to exercise indirect control over broadcast and print outlets. Journalists routinely receive informal directions from members of the government and media owners. Media owners frequently perceive that "doing favors" for high-ranking government officials and fostering a good relationship with the government is good for their business; they then exhort pressure on journalists working at their media houses.[6] Moreover, due to the poor economic conditions in the country, the media suffer from a lack of advertising revenue and frequently struggle to remain commercially viable. As a consequence, many are forced to depend on local officials and businesspeople for financial support, becoming subject to their editorial influence.

Recommendations

- The administration needs to ensure that all political parties receive equal campaigning opportunities in state-owned media by enforcing penalties against the stations that do not respect this rule.
- The government needs to implement stricter measures to prevent undue interference in elections by local officials and ensure due legal measures against individuals who do interfere.
- The administration needs to do better at enforcing the system of hiring and promotion based on civil service exams. Stricter laws on nepotism and patronage should be imposed; a special commission should be created to oversee implementation of the civil service laws.
- The administration needs to make certain that the membership of the Central Election Commission is more equitably divided among various parties.
- The government needs to ensure the safety of journalists by investigating attacks against the media more rigorously.

CIVIL LIBERTIES – 4.27

Torture of prisoners and pretrial detainees has been documented in Georgia for a number of years, representing the country's most pressing human rights problem. Georgia's prisons lack basic humanitarian necessities; prisoners have been subjected to overcrowding and a shortage of basic hygiene and nutrition.[7] However, of even greater concern are tactics used in pretrial detention centers that often include various forms of torture. In the past, the Shevardnadze regime tried to institute reforms that would reduce the occurrence of such abuses, but many of the anti-torture proposals and prison reforms were never fully developed or implemented.

In the months following the revolution, these problems were exacerbated as the new administration reportedly used torture to extract confessions from those they believed had escaped justice under Shevardnadze, especially if they were involved in corruption. In this context, the government did not shy away from unlawful practices such as arbitrary arrests or planting evidence in order to detain individuals, frequently without ever making a record of the arrest. The law in Georgia stipulates that citizens can be held in pretrial detention for a maximum of four months. In practice, suspects tend to be held for much longer due to a lack of judicial independence and the prosecutors' ability to order judges to keep the suspect detained as long as the prosecution desires.

In recent months, the government has demonstrated some willingness to tackle the issue of torture. At the end of 2004, the national ombudsman and several NGOs published a report documenting over 1,100 cases of torture and ill-treatment in Tbilisi alone since the revolution, forcing the authorities to take notice. Since then, several legal amendments have been introduced to the criminal and criminal procedure codes that in some way address the issue. For example, a measure was passed stipulating that testimonies obtained in pretrial detention could be used as evidence only if the defendant confirms their truthfulness in the court. In addition, witness testimonies obtained outside the courtroom can now be read during a trial only if the witness agrees to it while in court. Reform was also initiated from within the institutions: the offices of human rights and monitoring within the General Prosecutor's Office and the Ministry of Internal Affairs have been largely staffed with former representatives of the NGO community, recordkeeping in detention facilities has improved, and the police academy has been working to develop a new curriculum emphasizing human rights issues. In January 2005, a new department within the Ministry of Internal Affairs was set up to investigate cases of prisoners brought to detention centers with signs of abuse or torture, but due to the lack of resources, its work so far is limited to Tbilisi.[8]

Despite the progress, officers responsible for the ill-treatment of pretrial detainees still often go unpunished. In 2004, there were over 1,000 reported cases of torture by law enforcement, yet investigations were initiated in only 192 cases, resulting in the sentencing of 27 officers.[9] In 2005, of 154 investigations into torture by law enforcement, only 23 officers were officially charged, of which 21 were found guilty.[10] The sole channel through which defendants can petition for redress of their rights is the prosecutor-general's office; however, these complaints often do not receive appropriate attention due to the prosecutor's close relationship with the police.

The Georgian constitution guarantees equality between men and women; however, this is not always respected in practice. Although the status of women has improved somewhat in recent years, Georgian women are paid less than men with the same professional credentials and hold lower skilled positions. Furthermore, representation of women in politics is limited: only 4 out of 20 members of the Cabinet of Ministers are women. Domestic violence in Georgia is not criminalized, and the police rarely respond to reports from the victims of such violence. Moreover, reports of rape and sexual assault often go uninvestigated.

The trafficking of women remains a problem, and Georgia is a source and transit point for individuals forced into international sex labor. The criminal code stipulates a sentence of 5 to 20 years for this offense, depending on whether an organized group was involved or the trafficking resulted in the death of a victim. The government has made significant progress in its attempts to comply fully with the international standards against trafficking, yet its efforts still fall short of fulfilling all its promises. In January 2005, Saakashvili approved the latest anti-trafficking action plan and has established a special commission under the National Security Council responsible for developing a dialog with civil society organizations and creating proposals on how to strengthen the current anti-trafficking legislation.[11] Under the same action plan, the authorities created a new anti-trafficking unit, which thus far has functioned effectively, with more than 30 arrests reported in 2005 alone.

Approximately 16 percent of Georgia's population is composed of ethnic minorities, whose rights are constitutionally guaranteed and generally respected in the territories under the government's control. Yet, less than 3 percent of the candidates in the March 2004 elections belonged to a national minority group. Furthermore, no relevant political party represents national minorities, although some parties include minority candidates on their lists. Minorities frequently find it difficult to participate in the political process due to insufficient knowledge of the state language. Even though the government organizes free language courses, many members of minority groups do not speak Georgian, which in turn creates employment difficulties, particularly for persons wishing to work for the state. Some experts argue that the lack of language skills could be partially attributed to the physical isolation of many groups. For example, roads connecting some of these regions with the rest of Georgia are in very poor condition, often worse than the roads connecting the same regions to Armenia; this contributes to the export of more agricultural products from these areas to that country than to the rest of Georgia. In order to alleviate the problem, the state allocated a special budget in 2005 for the rebuilding of several roads. The government also created a number of initiatives aimed at reintegrating minorities into mainstream Georgian culture. For instance, the administration has provided for rebroadcasts of Georgian television news programs in translation and free legal consultations for ethnic Armenian and Azeri populations in certain regions. Furthermore, in order to quell persisting societal prejudices, Saakashvili has urged media not to report the ethnic origins of criminal suspects. Ethnic groups in Georgia, including Armenians, Abkhaz, Ossetians, Russians, and Greeks, are permitted to learn at schools in their respective native languages.

Despite improvements, religious minorities continue to report acts of intimidation and discrimination by local authorities. After the Rose Revolution, the new government permitted Jehovah's Witnesses to register the Watchtower Society, their staple organization. Yet several other minority churches, including the Armenian Apostolic Church and the Catholic Church, reported intimidation and difficulties in building new places of worship. According to a report by Amnesty International, the number of instances in which religious minorities were attacked decreased in 2004, but they still happened.[12] The government has successfully prosecuted and convicted some of the perpetrators, including a defrocked Orthodox priest who admitted to mobilizing members of his church to vandalize the premises of Jehovah's Witnesses and burn Bibles of the Baptist Evangelical Church.

The state refrains from involvement in the appointment of religious leaders and from placing restrictions on religious ceremonies, although the Georgian Orthodox Church has been awarded a special role in the constitution for its position in the country's history. Under a special agreement between the two entities, the government has a right to use the church's official symbols and also produce and distribute religious articles. In addition, the Orthodox Church is the only religious entity in Georgia that enjoys tax-exempt status.

Discrimination against people with disabilities, particularly in domains such as employment and education, remains a problem. While the law mandates that the government should ensure appropriate conditions for disabled people and should provide special preferences and policies for these groups, due to the lack of funds and a certain social stigma, persons with disabilities do not have access to much assistance and are frequently subject to discrimination and bias.

The state recognizes every person's right to freedom of association and has generally respected this right in practice. There are no barriers to the formation of political parties, NGOs, or trade unions, and citizens are not pressured to belong to any particular association. Moreover, employers who discriminate against union members may be prosecuted and forced to reinstate employees and pay their lost wages. However, as only a small percentage of workers are unionized, this law is not frequently tested. The government officially permits public demonstrations; however, on several occasions the police used excessive force to break up peaceful protests. In one example, law enforcement used batons to beat participants in a protest in Terjola on January 11, 2004, against imprisonment of a local man charged with firearms possession. Saakashvili later defended this violent response. On January 28, 2004, police violently dispersed the protests of street traders who were objecting to a recent decision to prohibit street trading in Tbilisi.[13]

Recommendations
- Police officers accused of torturing pretrial detainees or prisoners need to be adequately investigated and prosecuted.
- The activities of the special bureau in the Ministry of Internal Affairs charged with investigating torture should be expanded beyond Tbilisi.
- Basic conditions in Georgia's prisons need to improve; officials must ensure that prisoners are not malnourished and that they receive medical treatment when required.
- Domestic violence in Georgia should be criminalized, and law enforcement personnel should receive better training on how to protect the rights of women.
- The state should institute more thorough legal protections for people with disabilities and ensure that all public buildings are wheelchair accessible.
- The government needs to ensure that citizens are guaranteed their right of assembly and should institute measures of punishment for any police officer who uses force to break up peaceful protests.

RULE OF LAW – 3.96

Georgia implemented several successful reforms to its legal system in the wake of the Soviet Union's collapse. Additional measures to reduce corruption within the judiciary have been ushered in by Mikhail Saakashvili since his January 2004 inauguration. Despite this progress, Georgia's legal system continues to be mired in incompetence, corruption, and limited impartiality.

The Georgian constitution provides for an independent judiciary, protected by law from the influence of actors within the legislative or executive branch; it also gives judges personal immunity from prosecution without the consent of the head of the Supreme Court. However, the reforms pushed through parliament in February 2004 gave the president sole authority to appoint and dismiss common court judges. According to a Human Rights Watch briefing paper, this amendment has substantially reduced judicial independence by stoking fears among judges that decisions that displease the government may lead to their dismissal.[14] As an example, analysts point to the August 2004 presidential decree that called for a reduction in the number of judges without specifying the criteria to be used in deciding who would be dismissed.[15] The vagueness of the decree is likely to have caused many jurists to weigh the preferences of the government before handing down court decisions.

Furthermore, judicial authorities report that prosecutors and officials in the executive branch do not hesitate to use more direct methods of pressuring judges into making decisions or delivering convictions sought by the government. For example, in cases deemed sensitive, judges often receive intimidating phone calls, and many are threatened with physical violence.[16] In November 2005, the Speaker of the parliament, Nino Burjanadze, requested an investigation following allegations by a judge that authorities were attempting to influence his decisions. The same day, three Supreme Court justices accused Kote Kublashvili, the chairman of the Supreme Court, and Valery Tsertsvadze, the chairman of the Justice Council, of pressuring court judges at various levels.[17]

The Supreme Council of Justice, whose members are selected by all three branches of government, develops proposals for judicial reforms, initiates disciplinary proceedings, and organizes qualification exams for legal professionals wishing to become judges. In order to qualify to take the judgeship exam, candidates must have adequate legal education and at least five years of experience in practicing law. Despite the requirements, many judges in Georgia are poorly educated, lack professional pride, and are prone to graft. In an effort to curb these problems, the Georgian government has increased pay to jurists and has recently begun cracking down on judges suspected of taking bribes. In 2002, the average monthly salary for a judge on the Supreme Court was $280, whereas in 2005 most judges were earning between $1,000 and $2,000. With the increase in judicial salaries, bribery has decreased but was not completely eradicated. In October 2004, Alexandre Taliashvili, a Batumi judge, was arrested while taking a $500 bribe;[18] only ten days later, police arrested a judge in the town of Rustavi for illegally obtaining $10,000.[19]

In efforts to improve judicial training, the Supreme Court has outlined plans to create the Advanced School of Justice, which will encompass 14-month training for all newly appointed judges starting in 2007. The school will be supervised by an independent board whose members will be appointed by the Supreme Court, High Council of Justice, and the Office of the Prosecutor General.[20]

The law in Georgia stipulates that everyone accused of a criminal offense is presumed innocent and has a right to public trial. However, the conviction rates are extremely high: only 1.1 percent of all verdicts by first instance courts in 2005 were "not guilty," presenting a very slight improvement over the 0.5 percent figure in 2004.[21] According to the criminal code, the accused are guaranteed legal counsel before interrogation, and an attorney is provided to detainees who cannot afford adequate representation. However, the rights of the accused are not always observed in practice. Throughout 2004, authorities frequently limited attorneys' access to detainees, and the prosecutor's office exercised substantial control over court-appointed lawyers.[22] In July 2005, the prosecutor's office started drafting a new criminal code that would introduce jury trails for certain severe crimes. The new criminal code is scheduled to become effective in 2007.

The military in Georgia is managed by the Ministry of Defense, which in recent years has increasingly employed civilians in some of its top posts. The Georgian president acts as commander in chief of the armed forces and appoints the defense minister. The law proscribes military officers from involvement in politics, although the army and paramilitary organizations were a visible political force in the early 1990s.

In contrast to his predecessor, who largely stayed away from military affairs, Saakashvili has made army reforms a high priority, hoping to bring military standards closer to those of NATO. Yet many modifications still need to be implemented, as the Georgian Defense Ministry lacks transparency as well as critical legislative and judicial oversight. Military spending is subject to parliamentary approval; however, the parliament does not have much access to the details of how the money is being spent. Most problematic is the secrecy surrounding the Army Development Fund, which is financed by private individuals—frequently "patriots living abroad"—and used for activities that are not reported to the public.[24] Many NGOs are concerned that the Ministry of Defense has become a closed institution and that it has been extremely difficult to monitor the levels of corruption and abuse within the military ranks. In one instance, the defense minister publicly lambasted prosecutors for attempting to investigate allegations of abuse against an army officer.[25] In a different case, the minister refused to launch an investigation following a public demonstration of approximately 60 troops who were protesting their inadequate living conditions, which prompted the military ombudsman to resign.[26]

The right to own land and inherit property is enshrined in the constitution; expropriation of personal property is allowed only under limited circumstances and with the requirement that full compensation be made. However, in recent years several NGOs have published reports about irregularities in the process of land acquisition connected to the construction of the Baku-Tbilisi-Ceyhan (BTC) oil pipeline, including illegal leasing of individuals' land by local government officials. In 2005, as the new offenses were being brought to light, the administration made very little effort to resolve these disputes. For example, neither have private properties damaged during construction been repaired nor have their owners received appropriate compensation. Moreover, the affected villagers have faced intimidation and threats of physical violence from BTC employees after expressing their intent to organize public demonstrations.[27]

Recommendations

- The administration needs to work toward establishing a truly independent judiciary by encouraging legislation to restore the parliament's role in approving nominated judges and to eliminate the executive's ability to fire judges.

- Saakashvili needs to take more seriously allegations of judges' being pressured by prosecutors and other government officials by enforcing the current law and introducing stricter penalties.
- The administration needs to ensure that those accused of crimes have access to their attorneys at all times. Those not able to afford a private attorney need to be able to access a qualified public defender.
- The military should allow for more transparency and be required to submit to the parliament detailed reports on its expenditures.

ANTICORRUPTION AND TRANSPARENCY – 3.87

Corruption in Georgia, as in most post-Soviet states, is widely perceived as a major impediment to the country's economic development. The previous government was frequently criticized for not punishing corrupt civil servants and failing to enforce existing anticorruption laws. After coming to power, Saakashvili pledged to make the fight against corruption a centerpiece of his administration. While it is too early to assess the long-term effects of his policies, citizens of Georgia exude optimism: According to a survey measuring public attitudes within the country, three-fifths of Georgians predict that corruption will decrease a little or a lot in the next three years.[28] The progress was also recorded in Transparency International's 2005 Corruption Perceptions Index, in which Georgia scored 2.3 out of 10 points, a 0.3 point upgrade from the previous year.

Within the last two years, the government has undertaken a substantial number of anticorruption measures. It has created specialized anticorruption bodies and passed legislation in line with international standards. A new department was established within the National Security Council to take charge of anticorruption policy. In February 2004, the parliament passed a law for the creation of financial police, designated to fight economic crime; this agency is also in charge of uncovering corruption and has the full authority to carry out audits. In addition, the government established a specialized auditing body responsible for overseeing the use of public funds and started a hotline through which citizens can report wrongdoings in various agencies. In October 2005, legislation calling for the creation of a new special anticorruption division within the prosecutor-general's office and for bolstering the independence and power of this body was introduced in the parliament.

In a far-reaching attempt to institute systematic changes, the Ministry of Internal Affairs completely dismantled the old police force, notorious for its extortion practices, and created a new, much smaller, Western-style force in June 2004. In the process, about 16,000 police officers lost their jobs; the majority of these remain unemployed. Such a large number of dismissed police officers alarmed analysts concerned that, without a solid social security net, these former policemen could turn to organized crime. Yet, the police restructuring remains one of the most successful reforms undertaken by the new government. The new force is well trained and has received substantial pay raises, making it less disposed to corruption.

As a result of the ongoing anticorruption efforts, a number of high-ranking officials who served in the current and previous administrations, among them former ministers and deputies, department heads, and even Shevardnadze's son-in-law, were arrested on charges of corruption and embezzlement. These investigations and arrests have received significant attention from the media, although some experts charge that journalists have become less investigative and analytic in their reporting since the revolution.

One of the most controversial anticorruption reforms is the system of so-called plea-bargaining introduced in February 2004, which gives suspects the option of being released without trial if they agree to repay the state a predetermined amount of money, presumably equal to the amount they obtained through illegal deeds. While this practice is aimed at increasing budget revenues and bolstering the effectiveness of anticorruption reforms, it also creates doubts about a process that allows for criminal charges to be dropped if a suspect pays a specified amount in cash. Moreover, Transparency International maintains that while a portion of this money is destined to the state budget and the remaining funds are returned to law-enforcement agencies, the degree of tracking of this money is highly unsatisfactory.[29]

Georgia has a relatively well-developed framework of laws aimed at preventing conflicts of interest among public officials; however, the main challenge so far has been the implementation of those regulations. The

Law on Conflict of Interest and Corruption in Public Service requires financial disclosures for all public servants and their families; the law also prohibits public servants from engaging in economic activities while in office. Starting in February 2004, all public officials have been obligated to submit proof of legality for their property purchases. However, the special bureau that is in charge of monitoring compliance with this and other similar laws does not have the capacity to verify these statements. Georgia has instituted basic protections for whistle-blowers through the 2004 Law on Freedom of Speech and Expression, which stipulates that no person is legally liable "for the disclosure of a secret if that disclosure aimed to protect a lawful societal interest and the public interest in disclosure outweighs the damage done by the disclosure."[30]

As a legacy of the old system, the state remains considerably involved in the economy; however, the government has made substantial efforts to speed up privatization of state-owned enterprises. The perception of pervasive corruption and the lack of law enforcement had kept many Western entrepreneurs from investing in Georgia. In July 2004, the Ministry of Economy published a list of 300 state-owned enterprises, including the State Telecommunications, Tbilisi International Airport, and Vartsikse hydropower plant, all of which were put up for sale. In order to make the climate in Georgia more business-friendly, the administration eased many regulations and registration requirements. For instance, a June 2005 law reduced the number of businesses requiring a special license from 900 to 159.[31] At the same time, a new system was introduced under which individuals wishing to set up a business can obtain all information, forms, and licenses from a single state body.

The tax collection system in Georgia has suffered through the years due to corruption in tax-auditing bodies. In one of the largest scandals of 2005, the police arrested several senior tax officials on suspicion of soliciting an $80,000 bribe from a foreign businessman to write off $3 million in taxes he owed to the state. Despite the problems, tax revenue collection has improved due to the new tax code introduced in January 2005 and a timely payment of public sector wages, which resulted in an increase in consumer demand.[32]

The Law on Public Procurement requires all government agencies to publish and conduct government contracts according to internationally accepted standards. However, enforcement of this regulation has been weak due to poor training among public officials, as well as the lack of awareness of the law.[33] Noncompliance with this law is evidenced by a report on spending in the Defense Ministry that uncovered numerous cases in which large quantities of military supplies were purchased through direct contracts rather than competitive bidding. [*Editor's note:* In efforts to make the procurement system more transparent, the Ministry of Defense now posts all open tenders on their website].

The executive budget-making process in Georgia is fairly transparent and subject to legislative review; however, the parliament has no amendment powers and holds no public hearings. The budget and expenditures are published online and include mid-year and year-end reports, although the description of policy goals is often limited, making it unclear how some budget allocations connect to specific policy outcomes.[34] Moreover, the president's reserve fund, the annual budget designated for funding "special circumstances of state importance, such as natural and other types of calamities and unforeseen state obligations," often contains ambiguous charges such as business travels abroad for parliamentarians and one-time payments to various public persons and law enforcement agencies, without specifying the purpose.[35] In July 2005, the Georgian Association of Young Lawyers alleged misuse of presidential funds after it was uncovered that 33,000 laris (US$16,500) were used to cover the costs of a Georgian delegation's recent trip to Italy, while only 4,000 laris (US$2,250) were used as emergency aid to citizens of Dushenti, whose homes were destroyed in a flood. Nonetheless, budgetary performance in Georgia has improved in 2005 due to increased tax collection.

The right to obtain information about government operations was institutionalized in Chapter 3 of the general administrative code of Georgia. This law gives citizens the right to petition government agencies for most types of public information. Yet, the Law on State Secrets requires that information that might impact the country's sovereignty and political and economic interests be classified for up to 20 years. Several reports state that public offices often delay or ignore citizen requests, although they are required under law to provide information within 10 days.[36]

Corruption in higher education is widespread; it is common for students to pay significant amounts of money to gain admission to top schools or to get good grades. In efforts to ameliorate the situation, Saakashvili fired rectors of all state universities and arrested directors of several other schools on charges of bribery. The government recently introduced standardized university entrance exams, which are evaluated by independent agencies instead of universities as was previously the case. This measure provoked protests and hunger strikes at Tbilisi State University. Students protested mainly because in the past they were automatically granted an option to enroll at Tbilisi State Medical University after three years of college courses. However, some administrators protested because such a standardized system reduced their opportunities for extralegal income, as many students were bribing university admission officials with amounts up to $10,000.[37]

Following the Rose Revolution, Georgia has had an influx of foreign aid estimated at approximately $1 billion.[38] Most recently, the United States signed a package giving Georgia $295 million through the Millennium Challenge Account. Some NGOs claim that these funds are not scrutinized closely enough, as the supervisory board in charge of the money is made up almost exclusively of officials from the ruling party.[39] While no reports have surfaced of gross misappropriation of foreign aid in the new administration, some irregularities do exist at the lower levels of government. In one instance, Saakashvili warned local governors about misdeeds in the distribution of humanitarian diesel fuel: The lists of eligible farmers have been inflated over the past year and it seems likely that local officials pocketed what was left over.

Recommendations

- The administration should ensure a more effective enforcement of the Law on Conflict of Interest by giving more power to the special bureau in charge of the law's implementation.
- The government needs to increase the knowledge of public officials on the procurement laws and their successful implementation.
- Additional safeguards are necessary to prevent misappropriation of foreign aid, especially at the local levels of government.

NOTES

[1] Jack Snyder, *From Voting to Violence: Democratization and Nationalist Conflict* (New York: Norton, 2000).

[2] Ibid.

[3] "Repeat Parliamentary Election: Georgia" (Vienna: Organization for Security and Cooperation in Europe [OSCE], 28 March 2004).

[4] Zaal Anjaparidze "Opposition Doubts Fairness of Georgia's New Electoral Comission" in *Eurasia Daily Monitor* (Jamestown Foundation: 14 June, 2005) http://jamestown.org/edm/article.php?volume_id=407&issue_id=3365&article_id=2369878.

[5] David Losaberidze et al., "Local Government in Georgia," in *Local Governments in Eastern Europe, Caucasus, and Central Asia* (Open Society Institute, 2002), http://lgi.osi.hu/publications/2001/84/Ch5-Georgia.pdf.

[6] Freedom House interview (Tbilisi: 15 March, 2006)

[7] "Agenda for Reform: Human Rights Priorities after the Georgian Revolution" (New York: Human Rights Watch [HRW], 24 February 2004).

[8] "Europe and Central Asia: Summary of Amnesty International's Concerns in the Region: January–June 2005" (London: Amnesty International [AI], AI Index: EUR 01/012/2005).

[9] Statistics on the number of investigations and sentenced individuals are from the General Prosecutor's Human Rights Department provided to Freedom House through e-mail correspondence with Ako Minashvili, Executive Director, Liberty Institute, received on June 19, 2006.

[10] Statistics from the General Prosecutor's Human Rights Department provided to Freedom House through e-mail correspondence with Ako Minashvili, Executive Director, Liberty Institute, received on June 19, 2006.

[11] Otar Kakhidze, "Overview of Georgia's Efforts to Prosecute Perpetrators of Trafficking in Persons" (Tbilisi: Georgian Young Lawyers' Association, July 2005).

[12] "Europe and Central Asia: Summary" (AI, AI Index: EUR 01/012/2005), 5.

[13] Sidiki Kaba and Ucha Nanuashvili, "Open letter to Javier Solana, Secretary-General of the Council of the EU and High Representative for the Common Foreign and Security Policy," (Paris: Human Rights in Georgia, 9 July 2004) http://www.humanrights.ge/eng/stat24.shtml.

[14] "Georgia and the European Neighborhood Policy" (HRW, 2005).

[15] Ibid.

[16] "Georgia: Torture and Ill-treatment Still a Concern after the "Rose Revolution" (AI, November 2005).

[17] "Judges Say they are Under Pressure," *Civil Georgia,* 23 November 2005, http://www.civil.ge/eng/article.php?id=11201, accessed 27 November 2005.

[18] "Judge Arrested for Suspected Bribe-Taking," *Civil Georgia,* 11 October 2004, http://www.civil.ge/eng/article.php?id=8038, accessed 27 November 2005.

[19] "Judge Arrested for Alleged Bribe-Taking," *Civil Georgia,* 21 October 2004, http://www.civil.ge/eng/article.php?id=8135, accessed 27 November 2005.

[20] "Main Directions of the Court Reform" (Tbilisi: Supreme Court of Georgia) http://www.supremecourt.ge/georgian/strategia_eng.htm. Accessed on July 1, 2006.

[21] Statistics from the Supreme Court of Georgia provided to Freedom House through e-mail correspondence with Ako Minashvili, Executive Director, Liberty Institute, received on June 22, 2006.

22 "Georgia," in *Country Reports on Human Rights Practices 2004* (Washington, D.C.: U.S. Department of State, 2005).

23 "CEELI in Georgia" (Washington D.C.: Central European and Eurasian Law Initiative, July 2006) http://www.abanet.org/ceeli/countries/georgia/program.html.

24 Jean-Christophe Peuch, "Georgia: Civic Groups Criticize Defense Secretiveness, Militarization" (Prague and Washington, D.C.: Radio Free Europe/Radio Liberty [RFE/RL], 12 April 2005).

25 John Mackedon, "Georgian Government's Image Takes Hit Over Rights Abuse Incidents," *Eurasianet* Online Magazine, 26 April 2005, http://www.eurasianet.org/departments/civilsociety/articles/eav042605a.shtml.

26 Jean-Christophe Peuch, "Georgia: Civic Groups Criticize Defense Secretiveness, Militarization" (Prague and Washington, D.C.: Radio Free Europe/Radio Liberty [RFE/RL], 12 April 2005).

27 "Baku-Tbilisi-Ceyhan Oil Pipeline: Human Rights, Social and Environmental Impacts" (Oxford: Baku-Ceyhan Campaign, September 2005), http://www.bakuceyhan.org.uk/publications/FFM_sep_05.pdf.

28 *Global Corruption Barometer* (Berlin: Transparency International [TI], 2004), http://www.transparency.org/surveys/index.html#barometer.

29 "The Results of Background Research Within the Framework of State Expenditure Monitoring Program" (Tbilisi: TI Georgia, September 2005).

30 "Guide to the Law of Georgia on Freedom of Speech and Expression" (London: Article 19, April 2005).

31 "Georgia: Country Report" (London: Economist Intelligence Unit, August 2005).

32 Ibid.

33 "Georgia: Report on the Observance of Standards and Codes—Fiscal Transparency Module" (Washington, D.C.: International Monetary Fund [IMF], Country Report No. 03/333, October 2003), http://www.imf.org/external/pubs/ft/scr/2003/cr03333.pdf.

34 Pamela Gomez, "Opening Budgets to Public Understanding and Debate"(Washington, D.C.: Center on Budget and Policy Priorities, International Budget Project, 2004), http://www.internationalbudget.org/openbudgets/Summary.pdf.

35 ". . . State Expenditure Monitoring Program" (TI Georgia, September 2005).

36 David Banisar, "The Freedominfo.org Global Survey: Freedom of Information and Access to Government Record Laws Around the World" (Washington, D.C.: freedom info.org, May 2004), http://www.freedominfo.org/survey/global_survey2004.pdf.

37 Natia Janashia, "Fighting Corruption in Georgian Universities," *Academe,* September/October 2004, http://www.findarticles.com/p/articles/mi_qa3860/is_200409/ai_n9440963.

38 "EU Extends Cooperation with Georgia, but Expresses Caution on Accession Issue," *EurasiaNet,* 17 June 2004.

39 Tamar Khorbaladze and Manana Khidasheli, "Georgia: Foreign Aid Challenge" (London: Institute for War and Peace Reporting, 20 October 2005), http://www.reliefweb.int/rw/RWB.NSF/db900SID/RMOI-6HD4XX?OpenDocument.

GUATEMALA

CAPITAL: Guatemala City
POPULATION: 12.7 million
GNI PER CAPITA: $1,910

SCORES	2004	2006
ACCOUNTABILITY AND PUBLIC VOICE:	3.84	4.35
CIVIL LIBERTIES:	3.54	3.42
RULE OF LAW:	2.66	3.16
ANTICORRUPTION AND TRANSPARENCY:	2.47	3.10

(scores are based on a scale of 0 to 7, with 0 representing weakest
and 7 representing strongest performance)

Anita Isaacs

INTRODUCTION

Nine years after the signing of accords officially ending a brutal 36-year armed internal conflict that claimed some 200,000 mostly indigenous Mayan lives, the fragility of Guatemala's peace has been revealed once again. Two events shook the country during the summer and fall of 2005. In July, firefighters, summoned to investigate a possible gas leak in a munitions plant, found a vast police archive instead. The plant's vermin-infested rooms contained piles of documents lying in bundles, tossed in plastic bags, and meticulously filed in cabinets, their drawers labeled with their content—"assassinations," "disappearances." The firefighters had stumbled upon an official history of Guatemala's 36-year counterinsurgency (1960–1996), data that security forces had consistently denied existed.

One month later, massive mudslides coming on the heels of Hurricane Stan buried indigenous communities in the western highlands. Stan destroyed the lives and livelihoods of those who had already lost everything once, or in some cases twice, before—during the civil war and earlier, during a powerful earthquake that shook parts of those same highlands in 1976. It was in the rubble of the earthquake that the

---

Anita Isaacs is an associate professor of Political Science and the Benjamin Collins Professor of Social Sciences at Haverford College. She is completing a book on the challenges of truth and justice in postwar Guatemala.

145

military lost its struggle for the hearts and minds of Guatemala's indigenous poor, leaving room for a guerrilla movement to capitalize on the state's total disregard for their suffering.

Because the fault lines of peace and democracy remain so close to the surface in Guatemala, the outcome of these events in large part hinges on how the state responds. Government resolve to catalogue and to disseminate archive contents, currently under the control of the human rights ombudsman's office, and to use emerging evidence to provide justice and reform the country's security forces would offer the ruling Berger administration an unprecedented opportunity to deepen Guatemalan democracy. Similarly, by coming to the assistance of survivors of Stan in ways that affirm their human dignity, the government can turn another historic page, fostering a new relationship between state and society that is based on an elite commitment to respect, tolerance, and equality for the country's majorities that is more than rhetorical.

ACCOUNTABILITY AND PUBLIC VOICE – 4.35

November 9, 2003, closed an electoral campaign marred by intimidation, violence, and fraud. Legal battles and street clashes pitted supporters of the governing Guatemalan Republican Front (FRG) against those who sought unsuccessfully to block a constitutional reform permitting the presidential candidacy of the former dictator, General Rios Montt. The contest was further tainted by widespread allegations of misuse of state funds by the FRG, murky campaign financing, and vote buying.

These concerns notwithstanding, the elections themselves were regarded as mostly free and fair by a contingent of international intergovernmental and nongovernmental organization (NGO) observers, joined for the first time by a local observer team composed of civil society organizations. They commended the country's Supreme Electoral Tribunal for its professional oversight job. Turnout was higher than expected, with roughly 57 percent of registered male and 43 percent of registered female voters waiting in long lines to cast their ballots. Voters chose among 11 presidential candidates, representatives from 21 different political parties and coalitions competing for congressional seats, and a plethora of civic committees, locally based organizations contesting mayoralties. Choices encompassed a variety of ideological perspectives, ranging from the conservative Grand National Alliance (GANA) coalition, the National Advancement Party (PAN) and National Unity for Hope (UNE) parties, to the populist FRG and the political left, represented by the Guatemalan National Revolutionary Unity (URNG), the former guerrilla organization turned political party, and the newly formed Alliance for a New Nation (ANN), which competed only for congressional seats.[1]

The electoral outcome was cause for renewed optimism about the prospects for democracy in Guatemala. Rios Montt's third-place finish excluded him from a runoff round in which GANA candidate and former Guatemala City mayor Oscar Berger beat his rival by an eight-point margin. Not only was the former mayor regarded as an honest political figure—a welcome contrast to outgoing president Alfonso Portillo—but GANA's election signaled the triumph of yet another new political force, the third to govern the country since the signing of peace accords in December 1996.

Nevertheless, these elections highlighted persistent challenges to deepening democracy in Guatemala. Elections again took place without the political party and electoral reforms stipulated in the 1996 peace accords. Potentially significant numbers of eligible poor and indigenous voters were denied the ballot, unable to afford travel to distant polling centers, deterred by a cumbersome voter registration process, or turned away at polling booths because they lacked the requisite documents. In addition, in the absence of legislation regulating campaign finance and access to a media heavily controlled by a handful of elite interests, the political playing field remains highly uneven. The array of ideologically diverse parties masks circumstances in which incumbents have unregulated access to state resources; conservative forces, most notably the incumbent GANA, count on extensive and favorable media coverage as well as generous campaign donations.[2]

While the independence of Guatemala's branches of government is constitutionally guaranteed, the ruling party's legislative majorities during both the PAN (1996–2000) and FRG administrations (2000–2004) afforded the executive so much autonomy that the legislature became a virtual rubber stamp. GANA's razor-thin margin of victory—49 seats to the 42 secured by the FRG—should have enabled Congress to exercise its full range of deliberative, legislative, and oversight powers. Yet it has not lived up to its promise. Internal party divisions (within 18 months, 36 deputies resigned from the party on whose slate they had been elected) limit the opposition's capacity to provide effective oversight and initiative, fostering policy logjams.[3] Not surprisingly, two-thirds of Guatemalans surveyed in October 2005 believed the Berger government has done nothing to resolve their problems.[4]

In mid-2004, the government approved an initial electoral reform mandating a combined identity and voter registration card and the establishment of voting centers outside the major towns. Under pressure from civil society organizations, Congress agreed to introduce a second generation of laws, likely to encounter greater resistance, focusing on tightening campaign finance and political party structures.[5]

During the first year of the Berger administration, the clandestine groups that permeated official structures during the FRG government seemed to have retreated. They have reemerged more recently however, and political leaders have continued to receive threats.[6] The creation of a proposed UN Commission to Investigate Illegal Armed Groups and Clandestine Security Apparatus (CICIACS), which would have demonstrated the much-needed political resolve to combat entrenched impunity, remains bogged down in political and judicial wrangling.[7] Meanwhile, the Berger administration is criticized as overly captive to business interests. Individuals with close links to industry and the agricultural export sector head 23 of the 35 ministries, secretariats, and presidential commissions. The civil service has also come under scrutiny for its cronyism. Vice President Eduardo Stein has personally urged the introduction of merit criteria, to reverse a trend in which 18 percent of all civil servants are currently political appointees, by far the highest proportion in Latin America.[8]

The peace negotiations and resulting accords generated unprecedented opportunities for ongoing international and civic engagement in the implementation process. The international donor community operates without restrictions, its support designed to deepen democracy in such crucial areas as the administration of justice.[9] Civic groups, which do not face especially onerous registration requirements, have participated alongside government officials in commissions established to consider public sector reform, tackle pressing policy issues, and formulate legislation. Nevertheless, increasingly disillusioned by the slow pace of reform, those engaged in the discussion of socioeconomic and indigenous rights issues claim their recommendations are ignored and denounce what they consider a ploy by the government to substitute dialogue for action.[10]

The state protects freedom of cultural expression and seeks neither to control media content nor to limit access by government critics. In June 2005, the courts took an initial step to ban libel laws, ruling that provisions permitting the jailing of journalists for the slander of government officials were unconstitutional.[11] In contrast with the confrontational relationship that prevailed during the FRG administration, the Berger government enjoys almost too close a relationship with a print media now criticized for failing to feature critical views articulated by civil society. Additionally, the state has done little to protect journalists. During the first six months of 2005 alone, some 31 reporters suffered threats and violence while covering public protests or investigating the activities of those involved in the counterinsurgency of the 1980s and in organized crime today. Only one individual has been tried and convicted for acts of violence against journalists.

Recommendations
- Urgent steps must be taken to establish the CICIACS.
- Dialogue with civic actors must not be an end in itself; the resulting policy proposals should be formalized and incorporated in legislation.
- The Supreme Electoral Tribunal must receive the funding needed to enable the implementation of enacted electoral reforms.
- Initial electoral reforms must be complemented by second-generation political party and finance reform, which are as crucial to the consolidation of democracy as the initial set of reforms.
- To truly guarantee freedom of the press, those who threaten and harass journalists must be prosecuted to the full letter of the law, with consideration given to increasing penalties as further deterrence.

CIVIL LIBERTIES – 3.42

Although the Guatemalan constitution forbids the practice of torture, the National Civilian Police Force (PNC) is reported to use it systematically in securing confessions during interrogation of alleged criminals and in the treatment of inmates.[12] The police are also suspected of sexual abuse. Some 25 women registered formal complaints during the first 10 months of 2005, while an internationally funded study by the Comparative Institute of Penal Studies found that 99 percent of all women detained by the PNC have been victims of harassment, torture, or rape.[13] Few such cases are investigated, and while probes into police mistreatment of detainees have resulted in the dismissal of more than 500 officers over the past year, they have rarely led to the punishment of offenders; some 640 new cases now require investigation.[14]

Desperately overcrowded and underfunded prisons have been the scene of a recent rash of riots and daring escapes. The quality of food and medical care is abysmal, most guards are poorly trained and paid, pretrial detainees are often held together with convicts, and female prisoners are sometimes kept with male inmates. Making matters worse, prisons have become a bastion for gangs in recent years, with rival gangs often held in the same facility, contributing to an alarming increase in prison violence.

The constitution prohibits arbitrary arrest and detention, guarantees habeas corpus, limits pretrial detention to three months, and allows every citizen the ability to defend his rights by appealing for constitutional shelter. In practice, however, many of these rights are routinely violated without prospect of redress, notably in the case of minors, suspected gang members, and those too poor to post bail, who subsequently languish in overcrowded detention facilities. The Public Defenders Institute estimates that as many as 65 percent of all inmates have yet to be convicted of a crime.[15]

Clandestine groups and members of organized crime, holdovers from the FRG era, continue to intimidate opposition leaders and social activists. Peasant activists have received anonymous threats, while squatters have been violently evicted and even killed by security forces or landowners. Representatives of popular sector organizations protesting Guatemala's ratification of the Central American Free Trade Agreement (CAFTA) in March 2005 were brutally repressed, with one member killed. During 2005, 214 human rights workers were threatened and two were assassinated.[16] Although not directly implicated, the Berger administration has failed to provide adequate security, investigate the crimes, or confront the illegal groups and clandestine security apparatus it publicly blames for grave abuses against the human rights community.[17]

Initially, the GANA fared better in confronting crimes of the past, and seemed more willing than its predecessors to acknowledge state responsibility for massacres committed during the armed conflict. Forensic anthropologists even worked unimpeded, and for the first time ever, a senior official, Vice President Stein, visited the site of an exhumation. It was also on the Berger administration's watch that the police files were discovered and turned over for safekeeping to the human rights ombudsman. In early 2006, however, violations again increased and the director of the forensic anthropology foundation, Fredy Peccerelli, received renewed death threats that have yet to be satisfactorily investigated.

Men and women enjoy equal civil and political rights, Guatemala has ratified all international conventions protecting women's rights, and an active women's movement has fostered gender equality through legal reform. Structural obstacles, however, continue to militate against gender equality. Between 1999 and April 2005, 1,877 mostly young, urban women have been raped, tortured, and killed. Little effort has been made either to prevent or to solve these crimes. Only one of a paltry 151 cases investigated has resulted in a conviction. At fault are poor police training, inadequate resources, and ingrained societal attitudes, which tend to dismiss the crimes as "passionate problems" or the victims as prostitutes.[18]

Party structures discriminate against women, placing them so low on party lists that their electoral prospects are seriously diminished. The proportion of female deputies dropped from 13.8 percent to 8.9 percent between 1995 and 2003. Although their numbers doubled during the same period, only eight women are mayors today.[19] Other appointive offices display the results of similar gender bias, with the welcome exception of the Supreme Court, to which Congress elected a female president in October 2005. Female voter registration increased between 1999 and 2003, although this remains an uphill battle given higher rates of female illiteracy and the fact that women are more likely than men to lack the requisite birth certificates and identity cards. The government has passed reforms calling for attention to the education of girls and orphaned children.

Guatemalan women face discrimination in other spheres of life as well. Women's annual income is one-third that of men—despite the disproportionately high numbers of women employed in industry and services.[20] Women's groups also blame *machista* attitudes for the laxness with which the penal code continues to treat sexual offenders.

Guatemala is a country of origin, transit, and destination in the trafficking of women and children for the purposes of sexual exploitation and illegal adoption.[21] As many as 2,000 young girls may be working as prostitutes in Guatemala, and some 1,500 children are illegally adopted from Guatemala each year.[22] Evidence suggests that security forces, immigration officials, and elements of organized crime are complicit. The government has pledged to become more aggressive in breaking up trafficking rings and to pass legislation, still under discussion in Congress, that increases trafficking penalties and formally regulates the adoption process.

The constitution pledges respect for the customs, traditions, and social organization of Guatemala's indigenous people, who make up 45 percent of the population. This is echoed in a 1996 peace accord on the Identity and Rights of Indigenous Peoples, which urges the construction of a pluricultural, pluriethnic, and plurilingual state. The Berger government moved forward to establish a National Reparations Commission (CNR), which had been announced by the outgoing FRG administration, to compensate the mostly indigenous victims of the 36-year armed internal conflict, and recently announced the creation of a commission to investigate the fate of the disappeared. The country's most prominent female indigenous leaders have been appointed to official positions: Nobel Peace Prize winner Rigoberta Menchu as goodwill ambassador for the peace accords, and Rosalina Tuyuc, director of the Widows Association (CONAVIGUA) as president of the CNR.

Some legal and institutional progress has been registered. The passage of a decentralization law guarantees indigenous representation on local development councils, and new legislation requires state services to be provided in Mayan languages. The criminalization of racial discrimination paved the way for the April 2005 conviction of five Guatemalan politicians for hurling racist epithets at Rigoberta Menchu and for other rulings upholding the right to wear indigenous dress and practice Mayan spirituality.[23] School curriculums are to be revised to include a pluricultural focus; the numbers of bilingual teachers, judges, and court interpreters are gradually increasing; and state institutions have been established to protect indigenous rights.[24]

Despite these advances, embedded structures of inequality and discrimination have yet to be dismantled. Discriminatory practices continue in a culture that concedes its own intolerance. Three-quarters of the indigenous population are poor and one quarter extremely poor, a stark contrast with a ladino population in which 38 percent live in poverty and 6.5 percent in extreme poverty. Indigenous Guatemalans have on average completed 3.5 years of schooling, in contrast to 6.3 years for the ladino population. And indigenous women are paid roughly 80 percent less than their ladino counterparts, indigenous men 64 percent less than theirs.[25]

Guatemala is a signatory to conventions guaranteeing the rights of people with disabilities, has its own laws mandating equal access and opportunity in all spheres of life, and has committed itself to a peace accord that addresses the needs of those disabled by the armed conflict. Yet little effort has been made to enforce the provisions outlined in any of these, or even to identify the disabled population. It is only in recent years that the human rights community has begun to include a focus on people with disabilities.[26]

The free practice of religion is constitutionally enshrined; the state does not seek to regulate either faith-based organizations or religious instruction in schools. Obstacles to the practice of Mayan spirituality do arise, however, at times leading to violent clashes. Landowners forbid access to sacred sites located on their holdings, while Catholic and Protestant leaders sometimes prevent the use of ceremonial places situated near their churches.[27]

The right to freedom of association is recognized, but membership is not compelled. In the case of unions, however, that freedom is observed primarily in the breach. Despite common violations of international labor standards, including landowners' failure to pay minimum wage and *maquila* owners' dismissal of pregnant workers, less than 3 percent of the labor force is unionized. Only three legally recognized unions exist in the *maquila* sector, where 40 percent of the economically active population works. Fear of reprisal and lack of recourse militate against unionization. Labor organizers reported 45 death threats in 2004 alone. Decisions to unionize often result in the dismissal of employees, and although labor courts may uphold workers' rights, employers routinely circumvent their decisions without fear of sanction.

Procedural hurdles also make it difficult to stage strikes. In determining the legality of a strike, labor courts assess whether workers are conducting themselves peacefully and whether other forms of mediation have been exhausted. "Illegally" striking workers can be fired, and the government reserves the right to suspend any strike deemed prejudicial to essential activities and services.

The year 2005 was marked by a series of marches and demonstrations as popular sector, Mayan, and women's organizations protested discrimination, femicide, working conditions, the granting of foreign mining contracts, and the signing of CAFTA. Workers precluded from striking by existing labor legislation increasingly resort to illegal work stoppages. Several protests have engendered a violent official response, culminating in the injury and death of demonstrators.[28] Alarmed by the scale of protests, Congress introduced legislation to permit the prosecution of illegal strike participants and organizers.[29]

Recommendations

- The government must take decisive measures to ensure greater respect for political and civil liberties. Initial steps should involve concerted efforts to dismantle clandestine groups and to prosecute their members, as well as to reform the police to end the prevalence of torture.
- The government must also devote greater resources to the investigation and prosecution of femicide. In an effort to deter and solve these crimes it should hire female investigators and police officers, while also working to change deeply ingrained *machista* attitudes through education.
- Wholesale reform of the penitentiary system is urgently needed to address the pressing problems of arbitrary and extended pretrial detention. The reform should include a census of the inmate population, accompanied by measures to upgrade facilities, improve treatment of detainees, weed out guards with ties to organized crime and gangs, and augment the pay and training of new hires.
- The elimination of ethnic and gender discrimination requires addressing its embedded structural causes: poverty, inequality, and the continued political exclusion of women and indigenous people.
- The government must review labor legislation to ensure that it meets international standards, including the rights to form unions, engage in collective bargaining, and stage strikes.

RULE OF LAW – 3.16

Guatemala's laws affirm the independence of the judiciary, the presumption of innocence of those charged with criminal offenses, and the right to fair, public, and timely hearings with access to independent counsel. In practice, however, the country's judicial system falls short on all counts—so short, in fact, that the current vice president recently declared the rule of law in Guatemala to be "an international embarrassment."[30]

The Peace Agreement on Strengthening Civil Society and the Role of the Army calls for judicial modernization and reform to counteract the corruption that constrains judicial independence. In response, the 1999 passage of a judicial career law and code of ethics provided for the adoption of standardized, transparent practices in the recruitment, selection, training, and evaluation of judges, the establishment of a disciplinary board mandated to investigate and sanction ethical breaches, and standardized training programs targeting both entry-level and sitting magistrates.

The enactment of several of these measures has modernized the judiciary, notably in terms of selection, training, and oversight of judicial personnel. Other efforts have been offset by financial constraints, judicial impunity, and the politicization of the judicial process. The judiciary has consistently been denied the resources it requires to function effectively. Its proposed budget for 2006 is 637 million quetzals, approximately $850,000, which is roughly half the requested amount. As a result, reform is stymied. Guatemala lacks courtrooms and qualified personnel (judges, prosecutors, and investigators) to process the enormous backlog of cases that the overburdened justice system faces as it confronts the dual challenges of a decade-long transition to peace and the rule of law and the conversion from a Spanish inquisitorial model to the standard European model, which is evidence based and prosecutorial.[31] As a result, it frequently takes more than a year from the time an accused criminal is apprehended for a trial date to be set—indigent defendants, in particular, often languish in prison—and suits tend to drag on, sometimes for years thereafter. Not surprisingly, citizens tend to take justice into their own hands, as expressed in the alarming rise of vigilantism.

Judges and prosecutors who investigate and try individuals with ties to drug trafficking and organized crime are also susceptible to bribes and vulnerable to intimidation. During the first five months of 2005, 38 judges, magistrates and prosecution lawyers were threatened and two judges and three lawyers assassinated.[32]

Critics have charged the current government with politicizing justice and judicializing politics. The first speaks to long-established practices inherited by the GANA. Prosecutors work under the auspices of the Public Ministry, and Congress selects the judges on appeals courts, the Supreme Court, and the Constitutional Court. Politicization of the selection process has a ripple effect, as the Supreme Court is responsible for overseeing judicial decisions as well as naming, transferring, and dismissing lower court judges. The Berger administration has refrained, however, from the blatant interference in the judicial process that characterized its predecessor. After a prolonged legal and political battle, the government accepted Constitutional Court decisions prohibiting direct financial payments to ex-PAC members and declaring the CICIACS unconstitutional.

The judicialization of politics is a more subtle charge. Critics argue that the government uses the courts to settle political disputes and to undermine its opponents. Even those who applaud investigations and trials of people accused of graft claim justice is biased, blind to abuses of power of governing party members and associates.[33]

Although all persons, irrespective of gender, ethnic origin, nationality, and sexual orientation, are entitled to equal protection under the law and are to be treated equally before the courts, the Latin American aphorism "justice is for the poor" remains as true as ever in Guatemala today. Despite the reopening of the Public Defenders Institute and efforts to provide more court interpreters and bilingual judges, the quality of public defenders remains poor, there has yet to develop a culture of *pro bono* defense, and the number of justice officials who speak a Mayan language lags far behind demand. As a result, convictions of the politically and economically powerful for crimes committed against indigenous and poor people remain the exception rather than the rule. The country's elite command resources enabling them to resort to legal devices, such as constitutional shelter, to halt proceedings or to prolong them indefinitely through appeals. They also tend to face sympathetic judges—whether as a result of bribes and threats or because of political affiliation. For instance, the continued presence of FRG-appointed justices may explain why so few former FRG officials charged with abuse of power have either been convicted or served prison terms; why former President Portillo, accused of embezzlement, remains a fugitive in Mexico; and why the establishment of the CICIACS was aborted.

In March 2004, the government announced its intention to demilitarize the Guatemalan state by enacting a military reform stipulating reductions in personnel and budget that surpassed targets set in the peace accords. These efforts resumed a process paralyzed by the assassination of Bishop Gerardi two days after the release of the church-based Truth Commission report in April 1998 (which Gerardi oversaw) and reversed during the FRG administration. The reform has yielded significant changes without destabilizing the democratic political process. The number of troops was slashed from 27,000 to 15,500 and the budget trimmed to 0.33 percent of GDP, half the amount allowed by the accords.[34] For the first time, the post of defense minister was occupied by an official with no connection to the civil war, and the current minister has proposed the creation of a new civilian position of vice minister.

In consultation with civil society organizations, the armed forces published a *White Book on National Defense* and followed it with the public presentation of a new military doctrine in July 2004. To be enacted over the next five years, the doctrine affirms institutional respect for human rights and the democratic process and pledges to engage in continued open dialogue with civil society. More specifically, the armed forces have committed themselves to rationalizing promotion procedures, reforming their educational curriculum, enhancing transparency with respect to military spending, and eradicating corruption within the institution.[35]

The Guatemalan legal system has also increasingly used its powers to investigate and hold military and police officers accountable for a series of crimes, including human rights violations, kidnappings for ransom, and corruption. The two most recent cases include the October 2005 confirmation by the Supreme Court of 40-year sentences against 14 military officers implicated in the massacre of returned refugees in Xaman a decade earlier, and a lower level tribunal's sentencing of a former police commissioner to a 37-year prison term for the kidnapping for ransom of the nephew of the president of the Bank of Guatemala.[36] Officers implicated in corruption scandals involving diversion of Ministry of Defense funds are also currently facing trial.

These are small advances. Much more remains to be done to address the continuing challenge of impunity and to ensure that the military's commitment to reform remains steadfast and deepens. The need to rein in security forces deeply implicated in the drug trafficking and organized crime that they are supposed to be fighting, the persistent abuse of human rights by members of the police force, the assertion of civilian control over the intelligence services, the increasing demand for justice in Guatemala by victims of the armed conflict, and the likely appearance of irrefutable evidence of crimes long denied in the cache of police documents discovered in the munitions depot this past July are but a sampling of the difficult challenges that lawmakers must confront. As evidence of the likely resistance, the armed forces have recently proposed changes to their code that would allow military trials for high-ranking and retired officers convicted of common crimes.

In terms of property rights, the challenge in Guatemala is not over the right to own property either alone or in association with others, which is constitutionally guaranteed, but rather over who has rights to which land. Issues of land tenure and access have provoked escalating conflict over the past several years, leading to squatting by peasants claiming titles to often disputed lands, frequently followed by forced evictions by landowners and members of the security forces. The communities, mainly indigenous, displaced by the armed conflict have been especially victimized and vocal, having lost land rights on the basis of improperly applied abandonment criteria, which assume that they voluntarily abandoned their holdings when in fact they had to flee advancing army or guerrilla forces.[37]

In June 2005, some nine years after the peace accords pledged to review land tenure, the government passed enabling legislation.[38] The law calls for the creation of a national land registry and the launching of a review of the status of idle lands and of lands illegally acquired during the armed internal conflict. It also provides for the creation of a system of agrarian tribunals and the training of experts to aid the process. As a complement to the seven envisioned agrarian courts, the government plans to increase the number of alternative dispute resolution centers dealing specifically with land issues above the 25 that currently exist.

Contracts and concessions awarded to foreign mining companies have caused persistent and at times violent clashes between the state and indigenous communities over the past year. Indigenous communities have publicly protested and held popular consultations and referendums in which they have signaled their massive opposition. They charge that the awarded contracts unduly favor foreign interests, are insufficiently tied to reinvestment in social development, and harm the environment. They also accuse the government of neglecting its legal obligation to consider indigenous rights as they pertain to natural, nonrenewable resources and are expressed in both a reformed municipal code, governing reconstituted local development councils, and in Covenant 169 of the International Labor Organization. In the few cases brought before the courts, judges ill trained to adjudicate on matters pertaining to customary law have tended to uphold the legality of the concessions.

Recommendations
- The government must dedicate itself to building a climate in which the rule of law prevails. This includes: upgrading the investigative and prosecutorial branches of the Public Ministry; building more courtrooms and training more personnel to address the backlog of cases and to confront the demands likely to arise from the recently approved Cadastral Law; improving security so as to protect judges and lawyers; purging the judiciary and the security forces of those with ties to organized crime and the clandestine security apparatus; ensuring that customary legal traditions are incorporated into judicial decision making.
- The government must stand firm in its commitment to modernize and reform the army. It must ensure that reforms introduced are sustained and should carefully consider proposals to create a regional security force and to replace the army and police with a national guard. It should also insist that officers charged with crimes continue to be tried in civilian courts.
- The Cadastral Law must be the first in a rapid series of steps taken to address land tenure conflicts, a key to sustained peace and the gradual eradication of extreme poverty.

ANTICORRUPTION AND TRANSPARENCY – 3.10

The Berger administration has refrained from excessive involvement in the economy to the extent that the World Bank estimates that only 5 percent of government revenue currently comes from state-owned enterprises and property. At the same time, bureaucratic regulations, ambiguous requirements, and widespread allegations of customs office corruption continue to hamper the establishment of private businesses.[39]

Early on in its tenure, the probusiness GANA signaled its commitment to eradicate corruption. The government has zealously pursued high-ranking former FRG officials and associates accused of graft. Until recently, less attention had been paid to lower-ranking and local office holders. Critics still charge that the Berger administration continues to practice its predecessors' custom of awarding contracts to businesses owned by relatives or friends.[40] Given the current degree of interpenetration of elite economic and political spheres, this is a particularly vexing problem.

Probity legislation has tended to get stuck in no-man's-land. A 2004 law introduced to enhance transparency through a monitoring system that oversees bids for state contracts, resulting concessions, and subsequent purchases, is now being extended to cover NGOs that receive public funds. As is, however, the law is routinely circumvented in all spheres of government. A package of proposed changes to the penal code designed to enhance integrity by insisting on public financial disclosure, penalizing bribery of public officials and other forms of influence peddling, as well as the use of privileged information, has been sent to Congress where, like so much other legislation, it now languishes.

The government has yet to tackle possible conflicts of interest in the private sector and has not intervened in an educational system perceived as only moderately less corrupt than most public sector institutions.[41] Nonetheless, GANA officials have conceded the need to reform other state institutions in ways that enhance their effectiveness and transparency and generate greater public trust. Toward these ends, it has established a special commission charged with modernizing the state sector that engages in dialogue with civil society organizations mandated to pursue similar objectives. It has also recently agreed to collaborate with USAID in eradicating corruption within the judiciary along lines contemplated in the Inter-American Anti-Corruption Convention, which Guatemala ratified in 2001.[42]

The six-year-old Superintendence of Tax Administration (SAT) receives mixed reviews. It has been criticized for failing to exercise its autonomy, and its customs office is seen as particularly riddled with corruption. At the same time, the SAT recently announced an 11.6 percent increase in tax revenue collected during the first six months of 2005, has begun to ferret out tax evaders (even pinpointing corporations employed by the public sector), has proposed a raffle designed to cultivate a tax-paying culture, and is working with the executive in pushing for legislation that would impose penalties for tax evasion.

The Comptroller General's Office is charged with overseeing the proper use of public resources. In the past, the office itself was a site of corruption, charged during the recent electoral campaign with channeling funds into political party coffers and with abuse of power as evidenced by the recent conviction of a former comptroller general for money laundering. In a promising sign of a newfound willingness to exercise oversight, the comptroller's investigation into expenditures for 2004 revealed some 500 anomalies involving 56 public institutions, ranging from the National Peace Fund to the Ministry of Defense and local development councils.[43] Perhaps as a stopgap move while reformist measures urged by the local NGOs and members of the international community are considered, the government has hired a foreign accounting firm to audit congressional spending.[44]

Allegations of corruption are given widespread media coverage, especially those pertaining to the FRG administration that had been at loggerheads with the press. At times media attention may hamper ongoing investigations by divulging names of suspects and sources. Allegations of corruption by government officials at the national and local levels, meanwhile, are poorly investigated, a function of inefficiencies and biases in the judicial system, as well as the absence of witness-protection programs. In addition, those presumed guilty of corruption are often linked to those charged with its prosecution. The police compete with political parties for highest billing in popular perceptions of the most corrupt institution in Guatemala, while the judiciary and the military follow close behind.[45] Given this environment, it is hardly surprising that journalists, prosecutors, and judges who investigate and prosecute graft frequently become the targets of threats and violence.[46] For their part, victims of corruption have few formal means of redress. They rely on a court system that rarely convicts and even more infrequently punishes. Nevertheless in certain high-profile cases, including the pillaging of the Social Security Institute and the SAT during FRG rule, the state has demanded and even retrieved a portion of the diverted funds.

The government engages in meaningful legislative review of the budgetary process, which receives ample media coverage, and does not intervene in the disbursement of foreign assistance. Access to information remains a source of tense debate. Some 65 percent of all requests for government information made between October 2002 and June 2004 were rejected, a rate that increased to 78 percent during the 2003 electoral campaign.[47] A law guaranteeing access is currently under consideration in Congress. In the interim, the government provides web-based information about its services and decisions, including budgets and expenditures. However welcome a step, it is also one that permits selective disclosures and restricts access to the literate with internet capabilities.

Recommendations

- The government must display the same resolve to weed out and prosecute corruption within its own administration and ranks as it has shown in its willingness to go after former FRG officials. This could be achieved in part by appointing an anticorruption czar.
- The government must pass conflict of interest and access to information legislation.
- A culture of greater trust in public institutions should be fostered by addressing concerns voiced by civil society watchdog organizations, publicizing work emerging from the government's comprehensive review of the state sector, and ensuring that legislation formulated is passed and enforced.
- Legislative efforts, which could include the naming of an anticorruption czar, should focus on addressing embedded institutional corruption, whether in the customs office, the police and military, or the judiciary.

NOTES

[1] "Guatemala" in *Political Database of the Americas* (Washington, D.C.: Georgetown University and the Organization of American States), http://www.georgetown.edu/pdba/Elecdata/Guate/guatemala03.html (accessed March 27, 2006).

[2] "Towards a new New Left?," *Inforpress: Central America Report,* vol. XXXII, no. 19 (20 May 2005) pp. 6–7.

[3] Ibid.; *Monografía de Partidos Politicos 2000–2004* (Guatemala: Asociacion de Investigacion y Estudios Sociales [ASIES], 2004); Diego Achard and Luis Gonzalez, *Political Par-*

ties in Central America, Panama and the Dominican Republic (Washington, D.C.: Inter-American Development Bank [IDB], 2004); Fredy Portillo, "En 17 meses hubo 36 'transfugos,'" *Siglo Veintiuno,* 14 July 2005, http://www.sigloxxi.com.

4 "Descalifican a Ministerios", *Prensa Libre,* 14 November 2005, http://www.prensalibre.com (accessed March 27, 2006).

5 *Monografía* (ASIES); "9th and Final Report on Fulfillment of the Peace Accords in Guatemala" (Guatemala City: U.N. Verification Mission in Guatemala [MINUGUA], 30 August 2004), http://www.nisgua.org/articles/minugua_Final_Report_Aug2004.htm.

6 Political violence that includes the assassination of an advisor to one opposition party, the Patrido Patriota, and of a Congressional deputy to the opposition, UNE, has increased again more recently as Guatemala looks forward to the next electoral campaign. See *Prensa Libre,* "Presagios de violencia en proceso electoral" April 8, 2006, (accessed April 8, 2006).

7 For a discussion of CICIACS, see The United Nations and the Government of Guatemala, "Agreement Between The United Nations and the Government of Guatemala for the Establishment of a Commission for the Investigation of Illegal Groups and Clandestine Security Organizations in Guatemala," January 7, 2004, http://www.tula.ca/health/guatemala_issues/ciciacs-eng.pdf (accessed April 5, 2006) and Amnesty International Press Release, "Guatemala: President Berger's political will to end impunity on the line," August 7, 2004, http://web.amnesty.org/library/index/engamr340152004 (accessed April 5, 2006).

8 See Laura Zuvanic and Mercedes Iacoviello, "El Rol de la Burocracia en America Latina" (IDB, 2005). Brazil trails Guatemala with 9.5%, followed by Bolivia with 9%. If these three countries are excluded the Latin American average dips to just 1%.

9 "9th and Final Report" (MINUGUA); "Guatemala Embarks on Judicial Reform," released August 30, 2004, http://www.nisgua.org/articles/minugua_Final_Report_Aug2004.htm and The World Bank, "Guatemala: the role of judicial modernization in post-conflict reconstruction and social reconciliation," *Social Development Notes: Conflict Prevention & Reconstruction* (Washington, D.C.: World Bank, February 2005) (accessed April 4, 2006). http://extsearch.worldbank.org/servlet/SiteSearchServlet?q Url=&qSubc=wbg&ed=&q=guatemala+administration+justice&submit.x=8&submit.y= 3, (accessed March 27, 2006).

10 Centro de Estudios de Guatemala [CEG], 6 April 2005), http://www.c.net.gt/ceg/ (accessed March 27, 2006).

11 Committee to Protect Journalists, "Guatemala," in *Attacks on the press 2004: Documented cases from the Americas for 2004* (New York: Committee to Protect Journalists [CPJ], no date), http://www.cpj.org/attacks04/americas04/guatemala.html; accessed March 27, 2006 International Freedom of Expression Exchange, "Guatemala: Top Court Rules Against Insult Laws" (Toronto: International Freedom of Expression Exchange [IFEX], no date), http://www.ifex.org/fr/content/view/full/67505/?PHPSESSID=b06cefb651 a5598a831329dfdf17e1b6 (accessed March 27, 2006).

12 "9th and Final Report" (MINUGUA).

[13] "Investigan a 25 policias denunciados por abuso contra mujeres" Centro de Estudios de Guatemala, 25 November 2005 and "mujeres organizadas densuran a autoridades del sistema por violencia contra ese sector," 26 November 2005, Centro de Estudios de Guatemala.

[14] "PDH denuncio poca investigacion a policias acusados de delitos" (CEG, 23 May 2005).

[15] Pablo Rodas Martini and Mariela Bautista, "Guatemala Integrity Assessment: Civil Society, Public Information and Media," The Center for Public Integrity, nd, http://www.publicintegrity.org/ga/country.aspx?cc=gt&act=ia; "PDH Critica Situacion de Carceles," *Centro de Estudios de Guatemala,* La Semana en Guatemala, del 22 al 28 de agosto de 2005.

[16] The most recent murders include two members of the national peasant union, CONIC. See *Prensa Libre,* "La Conic insiste en protestas," April 8, 2006 (accessed April 8, 2006).

[17] Guatemala Human Rights Commission – USA, Guatemala Human Rights Update, 18, 3 (Washington, DC: Guatemala Human Rights Commission – USA, February 2, 2006) http://www.americas.org/item_25369 (accessed March 26, 2006).

[18] *Guatemala: No protection, No Justice: Killings of Women in Guatemala* (London: Amnesty International [AI], 9 June 2005), http://web.amnesty.org/library/Index/ENGAMR3 40172005?open&of=ENG-GTM; Leonardo Cereser, "Feminicidos, en alza constante desde 2001," *Prensa Libre,* 12 July 2005, http://www.prensalibre.com/pl/2005/julio/12/118621.html (accessed July 14, 2005).

[19] Luz Mendez, "Enhancing the Role of Women in Electoral Processes in Post Conflict Countries: Guatemalan Case Study" (Cambridge, MA: The Initiative for Inclusive Security, January 2003), http://www.womenwagingpeace.net/content/conflict_areas/articles.asp#guatemala (accessed December 12, 2005).

[20] *Informe Sobre Desarrollo Humano 2005* [Human Development Report 2005] (New York: United Nations Development Programme [UNDP, 2005], http://hdr.undp.org/reports/global/2005 (accessed March 27, 2006).

[21] Laura A. Langberg, *Summary of Final Report on the Trafficking of Women and Children for Sexual Exploitation in the Americas* (Washington, D.C.: Organization of American States [OAS], Inter-American Commission of Women [CIM], 1 August 2002), http://www.oas.org/cim/English/Proy.Traf.SumFinalRep.htm (accessed July 15, 2005).

[22] The Protection Project, "Guatemala" (Baltimore, MD: Johns Hopkins University, Protection Project, 2005), http://www.protectionproject.org/guatemala.doc (accessed March 27, 2006).

[23] "Menchu case ends in a 'safe' sentence," *Central America Report,* 8 April 2005; "Guatemala politicians were racist," BBC News, 5 April 2005, http://news.bbc.co.uk/2/hi/americas/4411207.stm (accessed December 13, 2005).

[24] "9th and Final Report" (MINUGUA).

[25] *Indigenous Peoples, Poverty and Human Development in Latin America: 1994–2004: Guatemala – Highlights* (World Bank), http://web.worldbank.org/WBSITE/EXTERNAL/COUNTRIES/LACEXT/GUATEMALAEXTN/0,,contentMDK:20505837~menuPK:328123~pagePK:141137~piPK:141127~theSitePK:328117,00.html (accessed December 12, 2005).

26 *Guatemala: Rights of People With Disabilities* (Chicago: Center for International Rehabilitation [CIR], nd, http://www.cirnetwork.org/idrm/reports/guatemala.cfm.

27 *Issues of Family Unity, Identity and Culture: Guatemala* (Geneva: Internal Displacement Monitoring Centre [IDMC]/Internal Displacement Project [IDP], 26 August 2004, http://www.db.idpproject.org/Sites/IdpProjectDb/idpSurvey.nsf/wViewCountries/B8FAF FB7EB35B8D7C1256EFA005E7D31 (accessed December 12, 2005).

28 Journalists at CAFTA Protests Threatened," "Protests Against CAFTA continue," in *Guatemala Human Rights UPDATE* 17, 7 and "CAFTA Protests Continue," in *Guatemala Human Rights UPDATE* 17, 8 (1 and 15 April 2005) (Washington, D.C.: Guatemala Human Rights Commission [GHRC]/USA), http://www.ghrc-usa.org; Carol Pier, "DR-CAFTA Falls Short on Workers' Rights" (New York: Human Rights Watch [HRW], 27 July 2005, http://hrw.org/english/docs/2005/07/27/usint11493.htm (accessed December 12, 2005).

29 Guatemala Human Rights Update, "Government Attempts to Criminalize Demonstrations," 17, 8 (April 15, 2005) http://www.ghrc-usa.org/Publications/UpdateIndex.htm (accessed March 26, 2006).

30 "Stein pide depuracion en ministerio de justicia," *Prensa Libre,* 25 November 2005, http://www.prensalibre.com/pl/2005/noviembre/25/index.html (accessed March 26, 2006).

31 Graeme Thompson, "Putting Guatemala's Justice System on Trial," *IDRC Reports* (Ottawa: International Development Resource Centre), 3 December 2004, http://web .idrc.ca/en/ev-67553-201-1-DO_TOPIC.html#aaa.

32 For a discussion see "Matan a juez de Chiquimula," *Prensa Libre,* 26 April 2005, "piden seguridad para jueces y magistrados," 26 October 2005.

33 "Analisis de Situacion, 25" (Guatemala City: Fundacion Derechos, Economicos, Sociales y Culturales para America Latina [DESC], 16 August 2005) (accessed December 10, 2005).

34 See for instance, "Concluye reduccion militar," *Prensa Libre,* 30 June 2004 (accessed April 4, 2006)

35 "9th and Final Report" (MINUGUA).

36 "40 anos de carcel," *Prensa Libre,* 22 October 2005 http://www.prensalibre.com/pl/ 2005/octubre/22/126122.html and "Condenan a plagiario de Lizardo Sosa," *Prensa Libre,* 14 October 2005, http://www.prensalibre.com/pl/ 2004/octubre/14/99411.html (accessed April 5, 2006).

37 For a discussion of these topics see Refugees International, "Forgotten People: Internally Displaced Persons in Guatemala," http://www.refugeesinternational.org/content/article/ detail/6344/?PHPSESSID=5ce00f92779c166324e1d (accessed April 5, 2006), and Internal Displacement Monitoring Centre, "Lack of Progress in Implementing Peace Accords Leaves IDPs in Limbo," http://www.internal-displacement.org/8025708F004 CE90B/(httpCountries)/ADC95A48885DA5B3802570A7004CF4E3?opendocument& count=10000 (accessed April 6, 2006).

38 "Ley del Registro de Información Catastral" (Fundacion DESC, 2005), http://www .fundadesc.org/documentos.htm (accessed December 15, 2005).

39 "Guatemala," in *2005 Index of Economic Freedom* (Washington, D.C./New York: The Heritage Foundation/ *The Wall Street Journal,* nd, http://www.heritage.org/research/ features/index/country.cfm?id=Guatemala (accessed December 15, 2005).

40 *Global Integrity: An Investigative Report Tracking Corruption, Openness and Accountability in 25 Countries: Guatemala* (CPI, 2004), http://www.publicintegrity.org/docs/ga/2004Guatemala.pdf (accessed December 14, 2005).

41 *Global Corruption Barometer 2004* (Paris/Berlin: Transparency International [TI], 9 December 2004), http://www.transparency.org/pressreleases_archive/2004/2004.12.09.barometer_eng.html (accessed December 14, 2005).

42 "Hacia una nueva legislacion contra la corrupcion," *Alerta Legislativa* 10, 52 (April 2005) (Guatemala: Accion Ciudadana), http://www.accionciudadana.org.gt/file1/af%20abril%202005%202.pdf (accessed December 8, 2005).

43 See for instance, Prensa Libre, "anomalias millonarias," 30 May 2005, http://www.prensalibre.com/pl/2005/mayo/30/115461.html (accessed April 5, 2006).

44 "Coalicion por la Transparencia" (Accion Ciudadana, nd), http://www.accionciudadana.org.gt/servicedet.asp?id=118 (accessed December 15, 2005).

45 *Global Corruption Barometer 2004* (TI).

46 "Cerigua documenta ataques contra periodistas guatemaltecos" (IFEX), http://www.ifex.org/20fr/content/view/full/69300/?PHPSESSID=2602611d4c8d3be3cf70bcb965624639, (accessed December 10, 2005).

47 "Lider del Congreso apoya proyecto de ley de aceso a la informacion" (IFEX), http://www.ifex.org/20fr/content/view/full/68315/?PHPSESSID=2602611d4c8d3be3cf70bcb965624639; "Una evaluación anticorrupción revela que el secretismo todavía debe superarse en las Américas" (TI, 29 September 2005), http://www.transparency.org/pressreleases_archive/2005/2005.09.29.secrecy_es.html (accessed December 15, 2005).

GUYANA

CAPITAL: Georgetown
POPULATION: 0.8 million
GNI PER CAPITA: $990

SCORES	2004	2006
ACCOUNTABILITY AND PUBLIC VOICE:	N/A	4.53
CIVIL LIBERTIES:	N/A	4.76
RULE OF LAW:	N/A	4.79
ANTICORRUPTION AND TRANSPARENCY:	N/A	3.99

(scores are based on a scale of 0 to 7, with 0 representing weakest and 7 representing strongest performance)

Ivelaw L. Griffith

INTRODUCTION

Many people outside Guyana associate the country with "Jonestown," the murder-suicide of the 913 followers of the Reverend Jim Jones and his People's Temple in the jungles of Guyana on November 18, 1978. That sordid episode involved few Guyanese.[1] Yet, Jonestown was a morbid representation of the crossroads Guyana then faced as it grappled with challenges of authoritarian governance and socialist economics, among other things.

Much has changed in Guyana since that day. The political roost is no longer ruled by Forbes Burnham and the People's National Congress (PNC); Burnham died in 1985, and the PNC lost power in 1992 to Burnham's nemesis, Cheddie Jagan, and his People's Progressive Party (PPP). However, in 2006, Guyana finds itself again at a crossroads, due to a combination of political, economic, and other circumstances, as the nation grapples with democratic governance and liberal economics. The present situation has some new dimensions and implications for the current political order and the trajectory of change. For example, in contrast to 1978, overt racial hostility is building, partly because one racial

Ivelaw L. Griffith, a political scientist, is Provost and Vice President for Academic Affairs at Radford University in Virginia. An expert on Caribbean and Inter-American security, drugs, crime, and politics, his most recent book is *Caribbean Security in the Age of Terror* (2004).

group—the Indo-Guyanese—controls both the political and the economic levers of power. Moreover, the advent of democracy following the 1992 elections—which marked the first time in 28 years that all political parties and the international community agreed that the elections were relatively free and fair, although voting still occurred mainly along racial lines—has spawned rising political and economic expectations that, regrettably, the power elites have been unable to fulfill.[2]

Guyana is a South American country in geography, occupying 83,000 square miles (214,970 square kilometers) in northern South America, but a Caribbean country in political culture. For all its geographic size, its mid-2004 population was a mere 750,000, giving it one of the lowest population densities in the Americas. Indeed, the population has shrunk over the last few years, due mostly to emigration; it contracted by 0.1 percent in 2004.[3] About 90 percent of the population lives along the country's Atlantic coast which is some 270 miles long and up to six feet below sea level in some places. This habitation pattern leaves vast sections of the heavily forested country under-peopled and under-protected, a situation with considerable national security implications given the country's illegal drug transshipment problem and territorial disputes with Venezuela and Suriname. The country derives its name from an Amerindian word meaning "land of many waters." Its economy revolves around agriculture (mainly sugar and rice), mining (notably bauxite and gold), and services.

About 49 percent of the population is of Oriental Indian descent, or Indo-Guyanese, while 32 percent are of African descent, or Afro-Guyanese. Amerindians and people who self-identify as whites, Chinese, and mixed comprise the remainder. General life expectancy is 66 years, and functional literacy is 97 percent. However, the country's socioeconomic situation is bleak. According to the Caribbean Development Bank (CDB), its 2003 gross domestic product (GDP) per capita was US$986, one of the lowest in the Americas, and its rate of real GDP growth for the same year was a mere 0.7 percent. Despite debt relief from Trinidad and Tobago, Britain, the United States, Canada, and several international financial agencies, the country still carried a debt burden of US$1.08 billion in 2004.[4] Fully one-quarter of the population is below age 15, and infant mortality is 49 deaths per 1,000 live births.[5] More than 30 percent of the population live in poverty.[6] Thus, remittances are critical to the economic survival of thousands of families.

Remittances account for at least 10 percent of the GDP of Guyana.[7] Inter-American Development analysis in 2005 cites Guyana as one of 23 hemispheric countries where remittances in 2004 exceeded Official Development Assistance for that year. Remittances also accounted for at least 10 percent of the GDP of Guyana and five other Caribbean Basin countries. Total remittances to Guyana, coming mainly from the United States, Canada, and Britain, grew from US$119 million in 2002 to US$137 million in 2003 to US$143 million in 2004.[8]

In January 2005, Guyana experienced the highest recorded rainfall since 1888, resulting in a flood whose aftermath seriously tested the effectiveness of the government. According to one UN study, the flood affected some 84 percent of the country's population. The estimated damage and loss to the social sectors (housing, education, health), productive sectors (agriculture, commerce, tourism, manufacturing), and infrastructure (drainage and irrigation, water supply, road transport, electricity, telecommunications) totaled nearly US$500 million.[9] The disaster received little international attention, coming soon after the tsunami in Asia, but it killed 34 people and generated disease, ruined crops, polluted drinking water, battered the nation's already feeble economy, and strained race relations. There had been plenty of warnings that the 200-year-old drainage system had fallen into disrepair, but the government failed to grasp the scope of the problem until the torrential rains began on January 14.[10] Moreover, the emergency management team was initially in disarray, and the warehouse that stored dry rations, blankets, and medicines had been emptied when the government helped the island of Grenada after Hurricane Ivan.

While the flood was a natural disaster it also was a governmental effectiveness disaster. Astoundingly, the government dismissed calls for an investigation into the affair. It claimed to be interested in "going forward" and not "moving backwards," oblivious to the value of a comprehensive review for future planning and execution. Further, the politicization of some relief efforts resulted in the bypassing of some predominantly Afro-Guyanese areas as supplies were rushed to mostly Indo-Guyanese ones.[11]

Thus, while notable strides have been made toward democracy, there is cause for concern about political stability. Elections in 2006 mean governance in Guyana will command the attention of concerned local and foreign publics interested in electoral transparency specifically and democratic propriety generally. The expectation that Guyana will continue its democratic journey is both reasonable and realistic. But it is up to the people of that nation to adopt appropriate precepts and practices to move beyond the current crossroads.

ACCOUNTABILITY AND PUBLIC VOICE – 4.53

Guyana's 1980 constitution created a hybrid of parliamentary and presidential systems of rule, with a 65-member unicameral legislature called the National Assembly. The leader of the party with the largest parliamentary group becomes president, having earlier been designated the presidential candidate and the leader of the party list of candidates. Traditionally, each political party designates its political leader as the presidential candidate and leader of the party list of candidates. The present electoral system is the product of constitutional reform that followed the controversial elections of 1997 and 2001, which were marred by election-day violence prompted by voting irregularities.[12] One feature of the system is the Largest Remainder Hare (L-R Hare) method, which provides for geographic and gender representation.

Between the time of independence in 1966 and the 1980 constitutional change, the legislature comprised 53 members. With the adoption of the new constitution in 1980, only 53 of the 65 members of the legislature were elected directly, while the remaining 12 were indirectly elected from the Regional and National Council of Local Demographic Organs. Under the current system, adopted after considerable legislative action in 2000 and 2001, all members of the assembly are directly elected. Twenty-five members are elected from the ten geographic constituencies, and the remaining 40 are elected from a national list to guarantee a high degree of proportionality. Political parties that contest seats in the assembly must contest in at least six of the ten geographic constituencies and nominate candidates for 13 of the 25 constituency seats. Furthermore, at least one-third of the candidates on a party's geographical lists must be women.[13]

The last elections were held in March 2001. Both the local elections managers and the nearly 150 foreign observers declared them to be free and fair, although operations were marred in several places by some undesirable practices. For instance, the Carter Center's final report cited "post-election street violence and lingering doubts about the accuracy of the voters list and final results."[14] Moreover, it noted that "problems with the voters list and voter registration were the principal reasons for opposition party claims that GECOM [Guyana Elections Commission] was not ready for election day and that these greatly affected the level of confidence of the Guyanese people in GECOM and the electoral process. Although GECOM had extended pre-election deadlines and issued supplemental voter registration lists in an effort not to disenfranchise voters, the final OLE (Official List of Electors) still suffered from repeated but correctable errors."[15] The center also provided appraisals of several key aspects of the electoral system, including voter registration, party observers, election management systems, and media operations.

The elections returned President Bharrat Jagdeo and the People's Progressive Party/Civic (PPP/C) to power, with 34 seats in parliament. The People's National Congress/Reform (PNC/R), led then by the late former president Hugh Desmond Hoyte and now by Robert Corbin, secured 27 seats, while the Guyana Action Party/Working People's Alliance (GAP/WPA) won two seats, and Rise, Organize, and Rebuild (ROAR) and The United Force (TUF) each received one seat. Disenchanted leaders of three of the main parties—Rafael Trotman (PNC/R), Khemraj Ramjattan (PPP/C), and Sheila Holder (GAP/WPA)—repudiated their former parties and formed a new one, Alliance for Change, on October 29, 2005.[16]

Guyana holds regular elections with universal suffrage and secret ballot open to multiple parties. Indeed, the 1992 elections were contested by 11 parties and the 1997 elections by ten. In 2001, although 11 parties met the elections petition deadline, only eight were contesting in enough of the geographic regions to qualify to contest on the national list. Notwithstanding the multiparty contestation, Guyana's elections are complicated by the fact that the main political groups, the PPP/Civic and the PNC/Reform, are organized along racial lines, with mostly Indo-Guyanese supporting the former and mostly Afro-Guyanese supporting the latter. The Indo-Guyanese represent a greater share of the population, as well as commanding more economic resources than their Afro-Guyanese counterparts. The net effect is that it is very unlikely that the PNC/Reform will ever gain political ascendancy, although it is in theory possible that it could form a coalition with some of the smaller parties to straddle the ethnic divide.

The legal basis for the country's democratic governance is the constitution plus the National Registration Act (1967), the Representation of the People Act (1964), the Local Democratic Organs Act (1980), the National Assembly (Validity of Elections) Act (1964), and the Elections Laws (Amendment) Act (2000), among key legislation. The 2005 National Registration (Amendment) Bill was passed in July of that year to allow continuous registration in preparation for the next elections, due in 2006. The new law amends the 1967 National Registration Act, which provided for periodic registration at designated start and end dates.[17] Key to the dynamics of electoral accountability and voice is the Guyana Elections Commission (GECOM), which sets policy for voter registration, maintains the list of voters, and administers all national, regional, and local elections. GECOM comprises a chairman and six commissioners, supported by a secretariat. Under the Constitution (Amendment) Act No. 2 of 2000, the chairman is appointed by the president following consultation between him and the leader of the opposition, who is the parliamentarian heading the party with the largest bloc of votes after the ruling party. The same law specifies how the commissioners are to be named.

Despite a constitution, statutes, and organizational machinery that provide for electoral choice, Guyana gets low marks in practice for free and fair elections, implementation of the extant statutes, management of the organizational machinery, and the dynamics of party campaign financing, civil society engagement, and media operation. For example, the issue of campaign financing has long been a contentious matter. There is no public campaign financing for elections at any level. Instead, political parties and potential candidates raise funds from individuals and corporations inside the country and from the Guyanese diaspora, especially in New York, Toronto, London, and Port of Spain. Accordingly, the ruling party is able to use the power of incumbency in a way that undermines political fairness. As one study notes, there are few real constraints on the ruling party's use of government resources, including print and electronic media, for campaign purposes. In addition, there is "inequitable distribution of private financial resources to competing political parties as various interests groups seek to position themselves to benefit from government favors after the results of elections, and the scheduling of the commissioning of projects in such a manner as to permit 'official occasions' to be used as an excuse to showcase incumbents' successes while in office," among other things.[18]

The inherent unfairness of this situation is amplified by the nature of the sole legislation on the matter, the Representation of the People's Act, Part III, and how it is administered. The law limits personal campaign expenses for each party contesting elections. It also requires campaign expense reporting after elections and outlines penalties for such actions as illegal campaign payments and employment. But GECOM does not enforce these rules, and therefore no one adheres to them. As one appraisal notes, "Various explanations for the lack of compliance are offered, ranging from the suggestion that the parties themselves reached an informal agreement in 1992 not to comply, to others saying that when they approached GECOM for guidance on fulfilling the requirements, they were told 'don't worry yourselves with that.'"[19]

Besides the obvious implications of this situation for the perception and actuality of free and fair elections, there are larger implications for the nature and stability of a polity where illegal entrepreneurs or the wealthy few influence electoral choice and public policy. Analysts in *Money in Politics* recently declared: "The smaller political parties typically have one source of funds, either the party leader or a wealthy individual. There are no laws, regulations, or guidelines governing sources of political party contributions. Businesses donate funds to political parties with the expectation that once in power, party leaders will implement policies that work in the interest of businesses." They added: "'Drug money' is also becoming an increasing source of funding for political parties and political party leaders. Many respondents alleged that drug and other criminal barons have contributed large amounts of money to the ruling party."[20]

Generally, civil society groups are free to pursue their interests and are funded by individual, corporate, and international donors. The media independence and freedom of expression climate is fairly healthy. The regime does not dominate the media, owning just one of the two major daily newspapers, the *Guyana Chronicle*. The other, *Stabroek News,* is independent, as is the monthly news magazine *Guyana Review.* The government controls just one of the many television stations, Guyana Television, which was merged with the Guyana Broadcasting Corporation in March 2004 to create the National Communications

Network. However, the government does control media through other means. These include zero government advertising in some media outlets that criticize official policies, the peremptory closure of the stridently critical CNS Channel 6 TV in January 2005 for a month, and the periodic harassment of media workers. In August 2005, the Association of Caribbean Media Workers sounded the alarm about assaults against journalists and gunfire directed against a vehicle transporting journalists. The government does not attempt to control internet access.

A major point of contention relates to broadcast frequencies. The regime owns the only radio station, a monopoly that has generated local and foreign criticism. President Jagdeo had promised the monopoly would end in mid-2005 with parliamentary action on the long-awaited broadcast legislation. Previously, the government had argued that it could not grant frequencies to private stations, as there was no legislation to govern the action. The new scheme envisages a three-tiered system with public, commercial, and community broadcasting, managed by an independent National Broadcasting Authority.[21] But although a draft broadcasting bill has circulated since July 2003, legislative action has been stymied by disputes over its provisions.

Recommendations
- In the medium term, campaign financing should be regulated, with the provision of new ceilings for campaign spending and meaningful enforcement of all aspects of the legislation by the Guyana Elections Commission. In the long term, thought should be given to having forms of state support for all parties contesting national elections.
- The government should end the invidious discrimination and censorship inherent in the denial of government advertising to media outlets that are regular critics of its policies and practices.
- In order to enhance transparency and build confidence among political actors, all national print, radio, television, and electronic media outlets should be listed on all appropriate governmental web portals, with appropriate links provided.
- Negotiations on the broadcasting bill should be concluded promptly, with a view to ending the government monopoly on radio broadcasting.

CIVIL LIBERTIES – 4.76

Guyana does not have serious problems with state-sanctioned torture, nor are unjustified imprisonment or arbitrary arrest the norm. The government also is not known for deliberate long-term detention without trial. However, it is common for individuals to become victims of the inefficient and inadequate criminal justice system and be detained for years in police station lockups before trial, or to be imprisoned for lengthy periods as their cases work their way through the legal appeals process. Measures for seeking redress against a senior government official for an infraction are inadequate.

Guyana has five prisons, and most of the larger facilities are overcrowded, some to the point that the situation poses a threat to the safety and well-being of both inmates and guards.[22] Thus, even when rehabilitation is intended, it is not feasible. Beyond this, financial, manpower, training, and equipment constraints make for awful physical conditions, poor sanitary facilities, substandard meals, and very limited medical attention. Furthermore, security in some prisons is compromised, which leads to many prison breaks. Conditions at many pretrial detention facilities often are no better than at prisons. Inmates are known to die in detention. For instance, Kellowan Etwaroo's dead body was found by his wife in his cell at the La Grange police station on July 7, 2004. The autopsy revealed death to be the result of massive head injuries, apparently caused by knocking his head against the cell wall for several hours.[23]

Generally, Guyana's rulers score high marks on promises but low marks on delivery. Political elites seem to believe that delivering grand speeches or signing treaties ipso facto solves a problem at hand and that they can afford to pay scant attention to implementation and evaluation. Crime is one example that highlights the government's effectiveness challenge. The level of crime has created a climate of fear enveloping most of the nation.[24] In April 2003, Steve Lesniak, security chief at the U.S. embassy in Georgetown, was kidnapped; his family paid US$10,000 for his return.[25] Since then, the crime situation has improved in some areas but deteriorated in others. For instance, murders declined by 36 percent between 2003 and 2004—from 206 to 131. But in November 2005, Deputy Police Commissioner Henry Greene declared that although serious crimes, including murder, declined between January 1 and November 20, 2005, armed robbery rose by 50 percent for the same period.[26]

Yet the government has made some headway in combating crime, helped by private sector bodies, nations such as the United States and Britain, and international agencies such as the Inter-American Development Bank. Announced in June 2005, the national drug strategy proposes action in several fields: partnerships with the private sector and nongovernmental organizations (NGOs), establishment of a national commission on law and order and a community policing ministerial unit, tougher laws against racial incitement and violence, penal reform, gun control measures, improved law enforcement facilities, and acquisition of equipment and training, among other things.[27] Implementation of the strategy remains to be seen.

In addition, new anticrime legislation has been adopted, including the 2003 Criminal Law (Offenses) (Amendment) Act, the 2002 Prevention of Crimes (Amendment) Act, the 2002 Racial Hostility (Amendment) Act, and the 2003 Kidnapping Act. The police have also carried out special anticrime maneuvers jointly with the army. For instance, Operation Stiletto, conducted in October 2005 in the crime-prone village of Buxton, which involved 400 policemen and soldiers, aimed at flushing out criminals.[28] However, some of the laws and maneuvers have been criticized. In Operation Stiletto, for example, the Guyana Human Rights Association (GHRA) was alarmed about rule of law, free movement of citizens, and privacy related to data collection for a crime database. In 2003, Amnesty International raised concerns about the Criminal Law Offenses (Amendment) Act, the Prevention of Crime (Amendment) Act, and other laws, noting that "criminal legislation recently enacted could seriously jeopardize human rights and should be reformed in accordance with the country's international human rights obligations."[29]

In January 2004, a self-confessed informant publicly claimed knowledge of "death squads," with membership that included existing and former police officers. Amnesty International later acknowledged receiving a list of some 64 alleged victims. Local press reports alluded to telephone records purportedly showing that the minister of home affairs, whose portfolio includes the police, had communicated with members of the squad. The affair compelled the minister to take administrative leave, and it precipitated the creation of a presidential commission of inquiry (PCI), comprising Appeals Court Judge Ian Chang, former chancellor of the judiciary and attorney general Keith Massiah, and retired Guyana Defense Force chief of staff Major General Norman McLean. On June 24, 2004, just weeks before the PCI was formed, self-confessed death squad member George Bacchus was executed while sleeping at home, where his brother, Shafeek Bacchus, had also been murdered on January 4, 2004.

The PCI submitted its report to the president in April 2005. It stated that the crime wave had spawned the establishment of death squads, but it found no direct complicity by the minister. However, it cited so much evidence of ministerial irregularities that his suitability for the position was widely questioned. When President Jagdeo reinstated him, his action was rebuked by local political and civic activists and by the United States, Britain, Canada, and the European Union, with threats of aid suspension in some cases. The minister eventually resigned, effective May 31, 2005.

The constitution and several laws institute gender equity in several areas, and there have been noteworthy accomplishments over the years. For example, women workers are protected during pregnancy and after childbirth from discrimination, disciplinary action, or dismissal for their pregnancy or reasons connected with their pregnancy by the constitution, the Termination of Employment and Severance Pay Act, and the Prevention of Discrimination Act.[30] A persisting problem, however, is enforcement. For example, domestic violence cuts across racial and economic lines. The Domestic Violence Act does criminalize domestic violence and gives women the right to seek protection. But for several reasons—primarily lack of resources and training, and ingrained attitudes—the legislation is often not enforced. Thus, as the Canada-based Guyanese scholar Alissa Trotz asserts, "In contemporary Guyana a relatively progressive constitutional order and legal framework coexists with pervasive gender inequalities within the family and the workforce."[31]

The age of sexual consent garnered considerable attention during 2004 and 2005 after the escapades of a fairly prominent businessman and his 13-year-old child lover drew significant media and legal attention. This led to a change in October 2005 of the official age of sexual consent from 13 to 16.[32] In November 2005, the GHRA called the abuse of girls Guyana's "single most pressing human rights problem." In an indictment of government and society, it cited the actions of some judges and magistrates, who fail to protect female victims of physical

and sexual abuse from further trauma in court; failure of the legal profession to reform a culture hostile to sexual crime victims; failure of the
government to use the opportunity presented by the debate over the
age of sexual consent to effectively protect young women from sexual
predators; failure of the Ministry of Human Services to shelter vulnerable girls adequately; and failure of major religious bodies to confront
violence against women of all faiths.[33] Moreover, the ineffective response
to the upsurge in rapes is troubling. In 647 reported rape cases between
2000 and 2004, there were only 9 convictions; in 2004, only 40 percent of rape reports resulted in charges; and the number of girls below
age 13 who had had sexual relations rose 16-fold from 2000 to 2004.

Between 2003 and 2005, the issue of human trafficking also commanded national and international attention following the release of
scathing reports by the U.S. Department of State and Amnesty International, especially the trafficking for sexual purposes of Amerindian
(American Indian) girls. In response, in April 2005 President Jagdeo
signed the Combating Trafficking in Persons Act. The law criminalizes
human trafficking as well as actions that facilitate it and provides victims with immunity from prosecution. It also offers assistance and protection to victims of human trafficking, establishes a national task force
to implement measures for the prevention of trafficking, and makes trafficking an extraditable offense.[34]

Constitutional and statutory safeguards exist for most ethnic, religious, and other groups. However, there are credible claims of discrimination against Afro-Guyanese in housing and land distribution and in
employment. Moreover, notwithstanding many efforts to improve the
economic and social conditions of the Amerindians, their circumstances
lag those of the rest of the population. People with disabilities also face
discrimination. While a 2003 constitutional amendment does proscribe
discrimination against people with disabilities, no law specifically protects them. The National Policy on Rights of People with Disabilities
that does exist lacks enforceable legal standing.[35]

Freedom of conscience and freedom of religion are protected. The
major religions in Guyana are Christianity—notably Catholics, Angli-
cans, and Evangelicals—Hinduism, and Islam. Partly because of the
racial and religious diversity in Guyana and the desire of various governments to foster inclusiveness, since political independence in 1966
many religious observances have been institutionalized as national hol-

idays. Freedoms of association and assembly also are protected. Unionism is strong. Civil society activism through demonstrations and protests is permitted, and the police rarely use excessive force. Exceptions are places such as the crime-prone village of Buxton or the Tiger Bay section of the capital, Georgetown, where a civil protest could well be a cover for decidedly criminal intentions, requiring the use of force.

Recommendations
- The safety and well-being of inmates and prison guards in detention centers and prisons should command more attention on the part of the government, with greater accountability and better incentives to improve management at prisons and detention centers and working conditions for guards.
- Adequate and appropriate training should be provided to police and social service workers to facilitate better enforcement of the Domestic Violence Act. In order to make the training useful, personnel, equipment, and other resources also are needed to correct enforcement deficiencies.
- The government should focus attention on people with disabilities by conferring legal status to the National Policy on the Rights of People with Disabilities and granting adequate resources to the Ministry of Human Services and NGOs that foster the interests of people with disabilities.
- The government should go beyond rhetoric in relation to the national drug strategy and provide periodic parliamentary and public reports on the progress of the plan's implementation.
- The Guyana Police Force and the Guyana Defense Force should implement confidence-building measures to restore some of the public trust and confidence lost due to the death squad saga and the outcomes of some anticrime operations.

RULE OF LAW – 4.79

The primacy of the rule of law in civil and criminal matters is respected in Guyana. Judicial independence is the norm, although credible allegations have surfaced in recent years about executive branch intrusion into judicial business. Allegations of judicial misconduct are rare, and they create discomfort in the society when they occur.

Overall, the dispensation of justice is affected by a shortage of magistrates, court officers, and other personnel, and by low salaries, inadequate training, and poor facilities. In addition, the highest judicial post, chancellor of the judiciary, has been vacant since April 2005, when Chancellor Desiree Bernard resigned to become a founding judge of the new regional judiciary, the Caribbean Court of Justice (CCJ). Bernard's departure prompted discord over procedures to fill that vacancy. This was complicated by the government's attempt to conflate some of the duties of the chancellor, who heads the judiciary, and the chief justice, who heads the Supreme Court, through the introduction of the High Court Amendment Bill in 2005. The proposed law was viewed by some as a reflection of the government's desire to alter the legal and criminal justice architecture. The government eventually withdrew the draft in November 2005.[36]

Although citizens have the right to and access to independent counsel in criminal and civil matters and are presumed innocent until proven guilty, the net effect of the resource constraints and inefficiencies is that sometimes judgment takes place without justice, and often due process is undermined. For example, as described in a February 2005 letter to the editor, citizen Raymond Jaundoo waited 15 months for the judge's decision in his civil litigation against corporate giant Weiting and Richter.[37] The Guyana Police Force (GPF) and the Guyana Defense Force (GDF) high command respect and accept the principle of civilian control. Generally, senior security sector officials make efforts to remain outside the political fray. Nevertheless, as the ruling party is led predominantly by Indo-Guyanese, some ruling-party officials may well be uncomfortable that both the DPF and GDF heads are Afro-Guyanese, and thus suspect their loyalty to the government.

While property rights are protected by law, inefficiencies in the administration of justice frustrate property transactions. This serves as a disincentive to investment initiatives by local and foreign entrepreneurs.[38] For instance, securing clear title to land often is cumbersome and time-consuming, as is acquiring licenses and permits to operate businesses. This is aggravated by the slowness of court proceedings, the inefficiency of the registrar of courts in tracking cases accurately, and the perception of political influence–peddling in some large investment transactions, among other things.[39]

Recommendations

- The government and the relevant opposition parties should quickly resolve the issue of the appointment of the new chancellor of the judiciary to avoid the matter becoming a core campaign issue in the 2006 parliamentary and presidential elections.
- The government, with appropriate NGO and international partners, should address the incapacity of the police and other components of the criminal justice system and the social services system to address the upsurge in rapes.
- The government needs to address the inefficiencies of the justice system by improving training and salaries of all court employees.

ANTICORRUPTION AND TRANSPARENCY – 3.99

Clearly, the economic travails, institutional weaknesses, criminal justice inefficiencies, and nexus between politics and race cited earlier provide fertile ground for corruption, which exists through acts of commission and omission in government ministries and other executive branch agencies, in the police force, and elsewhere. It is therefore not surprising that Guyana's score in Transparency International's 2005 Corruption Perceptions Index was 2.5 on a scale of 1 to 10, the same as Bolivia and Guatemala, and lower than Cuba and Suriname. Several different laws deal with various aspects of corruption and other malpractice: the Integrity Commission Act, the Procurement Act, the Criminal Law Enforcement Act, the Fair Trading Bill, and others. Thus, the corruption challenge relates less to the absence of laws and more to their poor implementation, the socioeconomic and sociopolitical environment, and political interference with due process when senior government officials or high-level party apparatchiks are involved.

For instance, in July 2004 it became apparent that McNeal Enterprises, a company owned by the presidential adviser on empowerment, which was not a licensed wildlife exporter, had been involved in efforts to export 25 dolphins valued at US$500,000. No one was charged. A review by the auditor general of the operations of the Wildlife Division in January 2005 highlighted fraud possibly exceeding G$50 million (US $263,850). It is noteworthy that the auditor general complained about political interference in his investigation, the results of which have yet to be published. In addition, G$14 million (US$73,880) was stolen from the old-age pension fund in 2003. About G$3.1 million (US $16,360) was repaid, but no one was prosecuted. Thirteen postal officials were dismissed, but 14 others allegedly involved in the printing and cashing of counterfeit pension vouchers kept their jobs.

Also, an illegal migration scheme was uncovered in 2004 that involved falsification of documents granting entitlement to import vehicles free of duty. About 52 files were involved. Two junior officers of the ministries of Finance and Foreign Affairs were charged, but the outcome of their cases remains a mystery. In the case of Guyoil, in October 2005 the head of fuel marketing, a former army major, was dismissed for complicity in fraud that included the disappearance of G$85 million (US $448,550), among other things. The probe was still under way at the end of November 2005.[40] However, despite the instances of corruption and other malpractice, all government workers are not corrupt; most are law-abiding, working under tough conditions, and guided by a sense of propriety.

Much hope had been placed in the Integrity Commission created in 1997 to help curb corruption. However, as a review by the Guyana Fiduciary Oversight Project found, the commission is underfunded, unfocused, and ignored by many officials. Among other things, the Fiduciary Oversight Project suggested publication annually of only personal interest information and not the financial details of assets, liabilities, and income. Moreover, it recommended that the declaration of public interests could cover sources of income, directorships held, bank accounts possessed, state contracts, family trusts, real estate owned, overseas travel undertaken, and gifts received. Transparency received a boost in December 2004 with the passage of amendments to the Parliamentary Standing Order, allowing meetings of the parliamentary Sectoral and Public Accounts committees—which examine the auditor general's reports and Public Accounts—to be opened to the public. However, deliberations of the recently constituted Parliamentary Management Committee, which considers and decides on the key aspects of the running of National Assembly, will remain secret.[41]

The budget process is open to legislative review, but government contracts and the management of foreign aid lack transparency and efficiency. There is some access to governmental information through access to the parliamentary chambers, although the number of citizens able to gain information is severely limited by physical and bureaucratic constraints. However, the government information agency, the office of the president, GECOM, and other agencies maintain websites to which many government documents are uploaded. Many of the sites also are kept fairly up-to-date, although the National Assembly's website, which has some useful information as well, is less so. Notwithstanding all the information available on the web, Guyana is still far from having a political culture that supports freedom of information.

Recommendations

- The government should consider allowing public participation in additional parliamentary committees as a way to increase transparency and foster greater citizen involvement in the business of democratic governance.
- The Speaker of the National Assembly should organize special orientation sessions for journalists and civil society leaders so they can better understand parliament's structure and operation and, thus, be better able to take advantage of transparency opportunities such as public access to committee meetings.
- The government should implement recommendations of the Fiduciary Oversight Project on a phased basis, with pursuit of appropriate technical and financial assistance from interested international partners.

NOTES

[1] For examination of the Jonestown drama, see Linden Lewis, "The Jonestown Affair: Towards a Sociological Analysis," *Transition*, Vol. 3, No. 1, 1980: 42–56; U.S. Congress. House. Committee on Foreign Affairs, *The Assassination of Representative Leo J. Ryan and the Jonestown, Guyana, Tragedy*, Report of the Staff Investigative Group. 96th Cong., 1st Sess., May 15, 1979; and David Chidester, *Salvation and Suicide: Jim Jones, the People's Temple, and Jonestown*, 3rd edition (Bloomington: Indiana University Press, 2003).

[2] See Gary Brana-Shute, "Guyana 1992: It's about time," *Hemisphere* 5 (1993), 40–44; Ralph Premdas, "Guyana: the Critical Elections of 1992 and a Regime Change," *Caribbean Affairs* 6 (1993), 111–40; *Observing Guyana's Electoral Process, 1990–1992* (Atlanta, GA: Council of Freely Elected Heads of Government, 1993); and Ivelaw L. Griffith, "Political Change, Democracy, and Human Rights in Guyana," *Third World Quarterly* 18, No. 2 (1997), 270–71.

3 *2004 Social and Economic Indicators of Borrowing Member Countries* (Bridgetown, Barbados: Caribbean Development Bank, April 2005), 9.

4 Ibid., 10, 68, 72.

5 "Background Notes" (Washington, D.C.: U.S. Department of State, Bureau of Public Affairs, August 2005).

6 "Executive Summary," in *2005 Poverty Reduction Strategy Progress Report* (Georgetown: Government of Guyana, June 2005), ii, http://www.povertyreduction.gov.gy/iprsp.htm.

7 "Remittances to Select LAC Countries in 2004" (Washington, D.C.: Inter-American Development Bank [IDB], 2005), http://www.iadb.org/mif/remittances/index.cfm. The five other high-remittance countries are Haiti, Nicaragua, El Salvador, Jamaica, and the Dominican Republic.

8 Ibid.

9 *Guyana: A Macro-Social Economic Assessment of the Damage and Losses Caused by the January–February 2005 Flooding* (Santiago/New York: Economic Commission for Latin America and the Caribbean [ECLAC]/United Nations Development Program [UNDP]), esp. Slides 13, 14, 24, 25, http://www.undp.org.gy/docs.html.

10 Joe Mozingo, "In Guyana, Water is the Enemy," *Miami Herald,* February 21, 2005, 1A.

11 For example, see "Victoria Villagers meet President over flood Relief," *Stabroek News,* February 14, 2005, available at http://www.stabroeknews.com/index.pl/article?id=11098817; and "Ethnic Relations body calls for Equal access to Flood Assistance," *Stabroek News,* February 12, 2005, available at http://www.stabroeknews.com/index.pl/article?id=10958155.

12 "General Elections Declaration of Results," *Official Gazette,* Legal Supplement B, 30 January 1998, http://www.guyana.org/special/1997.html; "Herdmanston Accord" (Georgetown: Caribbean Community [CARICOM], 17 January 1998), http://www.sdnp.org.gy/elections/pdf_laws/Herdmanston%20Accord.pdf; and "Electoral Observation in Guyana 1997," in Electoral Observations in the Americas Series, No. 11 (Washington, D.C.: Organization of American States [OAS], 8 April 1998), http://www.upd.oas.org/lab/Documents/publications/electoral_observation/1997/pbl_11_1997_eng.pdf.

13 See Douglas Rae, *The Political Consequences of Electoral Laws* (New Haven: Yale University Press, 1967); and Enid Lakeman, *How Democracies Vote* (London: Faber, 1970); Rudolph James and Harold Lutchman, *Law and the Political Environment in Guyana* (Turkeyen: University of Guyana, 1984), 75–87; Guyana Elections Commission (GECOM), http://www.sdnp.org.gy/elections.

14 See *Observing the 2001 Guyana Elections: Final Report* (Atlanta, GA: The Carter Center, The Democracy Program, February 2002), http://www.cartercenter.org/documents/1036.pdf.

15 Ibid, especially 46–49.

16 See Miranda La Rose, "Alliance For Change Launched—Ramjattan Leader and Chairman, Trotman Presidential Candidate," *Stabroek News,* 30 October 2005, http://www.stabroeknews.com/index.pl/article?id=34554695.

[17] "Revised Registration Bill Passed after Long Debate," *Stabroek News,* 15 July 2005, http://www.stabroeknews.com/index.pl/article?id=24284541.

[18] Sheila V. Holder, "Political Party and Campaign Financing in Guyana," in Steven Griner and Daniel Zarotta, eds., *From Rhetoric to Best Practices: The Challenge of Political Financing in the Americas* (Washington, D.C.: OAS Department for Democratic and Political Affairs, 2004), 8. Interestingly, the Guyana dollar exchange in 1990 was around G$45 = US$1. In early 2006, it was about G$190 = US$1.

[19] Shari Bryan and Denise Baer, eds., *Money in Politics: A Study of Party Financing Practices in 22 Countries* (Washington, D.C.: National Democratic Institute for International Affairs, 2005), 65. The relevant sections of the campaign financing legislation are available at http://www.sdnp.org.gy/elections.

[20] *Money in Politics,* Ibid, 66. For a discussion of some larger implications, see Ivelaw L. Griffith and Tevor Munroe, "Drugs and Democracy in the Caribbean," *Journal of Commonwealth and Comparative Politics* Vol. 33 (November) 1995: 357–76; and Ivelaw L. Griffith, "Caribbean Security in the Age of Terror: Challenges of Intrusion and Governance," in Denis Benn and Kenneth O. Hall, eds., *Governance in the Age of Globalization* (Kingston, Jamaica: Ian Randle Publishers, 2003), 383–415.

[21] "2004 World Press Freedom Review" (Vienna: International Press Institute [IPI], 2005), http://www.freemedia.at/wpfr/Americas/guyana.htm. For a copy of the draft bill, visit Guyana's Government Information Agency (GINA), http://www.gina.gov.gy/docreports index.html.

[22] Ibid.

[23] For example, see "Guyana Jailbreak Prisoners Held," BBC Caribbean.com, 14 November 2005, http://www.bbc.co.uk/caribbean/news/story/2005/11/printable/051114_prisonescape.shtml+director+of+prisons+guyana&hl=en; and "US Slams Guyana on Police Abuse, Shoddy Prisons," *Stabroek News,* 1 March 2005, http://www.stabroeknews.com/index.pl/article?id=12532033.

[24] "Public Safety: A Shameful Situation," *Guyana Review* 13 (August 2005), 19–21; and Michael Lettieri, "Justice and Democracy in Guyana fly Limply in the Breeze" (Washington, D.C.: Council on Hemispheric Affairs [COHA], Memorandum to the Press, 8 September 2005), http://www.coha.org/NEW_PRESS_RELEASES/New_Press_Releases_2005/05.101_Justice_Democracy_Guyana.html+guyana+crime+legislation+2005&hl=en.

[25] Rickey Singh, "U.S. Special Forces Probing Kidnapping Saga," *Caribbean Style,* 13 April 2003, http://www.caribbeanstyle.com/ubb/Forum1/HTML/003337.html+lesniak+kidnapping+2003&hl=en; "Following early Morning Kidnapping US Diplomat Released," *Guyana Chronicle,* 13 April 2003, 1.

[26] "Robbery under arms up 50% – most of the guns used come from Brazil," *Stabroek News,* 27 November 2005, http://www.stabroeknews.com/index.pl/article?id=37272129.

[27] "Update on the Drug Strategy Master Plan" (GINA, 31 October 2005), http://www.gina.gov.gy/crimeindex.html; "Law and Order Commission to Review Previous Crime Reports," *Stabroek News,* 1 December 2005, http://www.stabroeknews.com/

index.pl/article?id=37646994; "Closed Circuit TV Cameras to be in place by year end –Teixeira," Stabroek News, 13 November 2005, http://www.stabroeknews.com/index.pl/article?id=35976045.

28 "Operation Stiletto," *Stabroek News,* 31 October 2005, http://www.stabroeknews.com/index.pl/article?id=34629674.

29 " 'Stiletto' raises rule of law concerns—human rights group says in reply to criticisms," *Stabroek News,* 4 November 2005, http://www.stabroeknews.com/index.pl/article?id=35094766; "Guyana: Human Rights and Crime Control Not Mutually Exclusive" (London: Amnesty International [AI], Report No 35/003/2003, 13 January 2003), http://web.amnesty.org/library/Index/ENGAMR350032003?open&of=ENG-GUY.

30 See, "National Labor Law Profile: Guyana" (Geneva: International Labor Organization, June 2004), http://www.ilo.org/public/english/dialogue/ifpdial/ll/observatory/profiles/guy.htm.

31 D. Alissa Trotz, ""Between Despair and Hope: Women and Violence in Contemporary Guyana," *Small Axe* 15 (March 2004), 5.

32 Edlyn Benfield, "Businessman Grabs 13-year-old Sweetheart from Aunt," *Stabroek News,* 22 May 2004; Andre Haynes, "National Assembly Fixes age of Consent at 16," *Stabroek News,* 25 October 2005, http://www.stabroeknews.com/index.pl/article?id=34378209.

33 "Abuse of Girls Single Most Pressing Human Rights Problem —GHRA," *Stabroek News,* 25 November 2005, http://www.stabroeknews.com/index.pl/article_local_news%3Fid%3 D37129811+stabroek+news+abuse+of+girls&hl=en.

34 "Public Safety: A Shameful Situation," *Guyana Review* 13 (August 2005), 21.; Martin Patt, "Human Trafficking and Modern-day Slavery" (University of Massachusetts, 2004), http://gvnet.com/humantrafficking/.

35 "Human Rights: Persons with Disabilities," *Guyana Review* 12 (December 2004), 43–45; "Guyana: Rights of People with Disabilities" (Chicago and Washington, D.C.: Center for International Rehabilitation [CIR], 2004), http://www.cirnetwork.org/idrm/reports/guyana.cfm.

36 "Chancellor Bernard named to Caribbean Court," Stabroek News, 20 November 2004, 1; "Jagdeo, Corbin begin Consultations on Chancellor," Stabroek News, 21 April 2005, http://www.stabroeknews.com/index.pl/article?id=17348026; "CJ Bill put off – after Strenuous Opposition Protest," *Stabroek News,* 25 November 2005, http://www.stabroeknews.com/index.pl/article?id=37129814.

37 "Waiting Fifteen months for Judge's Decision," Stabroek News, 23 February 2005, http://www.stabroeknews.com/index.pl/article?id=11921516; "US Ambassador urges Reform to Backlogged Court System," *Stabroek News,* 12 March 2005, http://www.stabroeknews.com/index.pl/article?id=13602897.

38 See Anthony Interlandi, "Property Rights and the Rule of Law" (Georgetown, Guyana: U.S. Embassy, speech, 24 August 2004), http://georgetown.usembassy.gov/guyana/lions_remarks_082004.html; "Guyana to Grapple with Intellectual Property Rights," *Stabroek News,* 23 April 2005, http://www.stabroeknews.com/index.pl/article?id=17525844; "2005 Index of Economic Freedom" (Washington, D.C./New York: Heritage Foundation /The Wall Street Journal [WSJ], 2005), http://www.heritage.org/research/features/index/indexoffreedom.cfm..

[39] Ibid.

[40] See "Auditor General Probing Fraud at Guyoil," *Stabroek News,* 9 September 2005, http://www.stabroeknews.com/index.pl/article?id=29376092; "President orders Probe into Corruption Allegations at Parika Marketing Center," Stabroek News, 11 September 2005, http://www.stabroeknews.com/index.pl/article?id=29544910; "Fuel Marker on the Street—two GEA Workers to be fired," *Stabroek News,* 8 October 2005, http://www.stabroeknews.com/index.pl/article?id=32257308; "Corruption Revisited," *Stabroek News,* 8 November 2005, http://www.stabroeknews.com/index.pl/article?id= 35470912; Jeune Bailey Van-Keric, "Seven Man C'ttee to look into Rogue Cops," *Guyana Chronicle,* 29 November 2005, www.guyanachronicle.com/topstory.html\l.

[41] "Some Parliament Committees to be open to the Public," *Stabroek News,* 17 December 2004, http://www.stabroeknews.com/index.pl/article?id=8670938

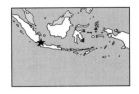

INDONESIA

CAPITAL: Jakarta

POPULATION: 221.9 million

GNI PER CAPITA: $810

SCORES	2004	2006
ACCOUNTABILITY AND PUBLIC VOICE:	4.03	4.70
CIVIL LIBERTIES:	3.32	3.70
RULE OF LAW:	2.95	2.97
ANTICORRUPTION AND TRANSPARENCY:	2.46	2.45

(scores are based on a scale of 0 to 7, with 0 representing weakest and 7 representing strongest performance)

Edward Aspinall [1]

INTRODUCTION

Indonesia has been dramatically transformed since President Suharto's government collapsed in 1998. From being a society in which an authoritarian regime severely constrained political expression and organization, in little over a year Indonesia became a vigorous multiparty democracy with a vibrant media and civic life. However, the democratic transition was marred by a series of violent communal and separatist conflicts. Corruption scandals rocked successive governments. Government institutions often proved ineffective as they struggled to respond to the many challenges of Indonesia's political transition and the severe economic crisis that began in 1997 and from which the country has still not fully recovered.

Since late 2003, political reform has continued, albeit not at the dizzying pace of the immediate post-Suharto years. In April 2004, the second post-Suharto legislative elections were held, producing a national parliament dominated by seven major parties. Following a fourth round of constitutional amendments in 2003 (the first round was in 1999), the first direct election by voters of the president and vice-president also

Edward Aspinall is a Fellow in the Department of Political and Social Change, Research School of Pacific and Asian Studies, Australian National University. He is the author of *Opposing Suharto: Compromise, Resistance and Regime Change in Indonesia* (Stanford University Press, 2005).

189

took place in 2004 (previously they had been chosen by members of the People's Consultative Assembly, or MPR). The successful candidates, winning with 61 percent of the popular vote in a second round of voting in October 2004, were the former general Susilo Bambang Yudhoyono and his running mate, Jusuf Kalla, who campaigned on a platform of combating corruption, restoring economic growth, and improving government services. The principle of direct popular elections was also applied for the first time for choosing heads of regional governments in provinces and districts. About 200 such elections were held in 2005, with more to follow in coming years.

Other new bodies mandated by the reform process have come into being, including a Constitutional Court (established in August 2003), an Anticorruption Commission (December 2003), and a Regional Representative Council (DPD), a kind of upper house for Indonesia's parliament, albeit one without strong powers (its members were elected in the April 2004 elections).

Indonesia is no longer ruled by an authoritarian government that systematically restricts political participation and resists efforts to make it accountable, as was the case in the Suharto years. Instead, the political system is open and democratic in its basic structures, and multiple actors compete to assert influence. Despite the restructuring of the political architecture, however, less progress has been made in transforming the modalities of political behavior or the inequalities and attitudes that underpin them. Many of the country's democratic institutions function poorly or are sanctuaries of undemocratic and abusive behavior. Abuse of public office for private gain remains endemic. There is no longer a systemic authoritarian blockage to reform at the top, as in the past, but corrupt relationships between powerful private actors, government bureaucrats, politicians, and security officials infuse the political system and undermine it from within. The Yudhoyono government has promised to pursue political reform and tackle corruption, but given this context, even the most determined government would face enormous challenges in pursuing these goals.

Moreover, the political challenges are unevenly distributed across the country. A far-reaching process of decentralization, implemented after 1999, has transformed the country into a political mosaic in which pockets of more accountable and effective governance coexist with regions in which corruption and abuse of power are virtually unchecked. The problems have been especially great in areas that have experienced civil conflict. In the years following the collapse of the Suharto regime in 1998, previous separatist conflicts erupted with renewed strength in Papua and Aceh, and communal conflicts occurred in, among other places, Maluku (the Moluccas islands) and Poso, Central Sulawesi. In these areas, governance problems of all kinds have been amplified, and security forces have committed egregious human rights abuses. In the period covered by this survey, conflict in Maluku and Poso declined in intensity. In Aceh, conflict first dramatically peaked with the declaration of a military emergency by the government in May 2003, but then sharply declined following the December 26, 2004, Indian Ocean tsunami and successful peace talks between the government and the Free Aceh Movement.[2] In Papua, amid imperfectly implemented central government political concessions, popular distrust of Jakarta remains high, and there are intermittent violent incidents, but large-scale violence has not erupted.

ACCOUNTABILITY AND PUBLIC VOICE – 4.70

The most dramatic change in Indonesian politics has been the rapid and successful institutionalization of elections as the means of appointing governments. The year 2004 witnessed several further milestones in this regard: the second democratic legislative election since the fall of Suharto; the ending of reserved military and police seats in legislatures, meaning that legislative bodies are now entirely elected; and amendments to the Law on Regional Government, paving the way for the first elections of heads of regional governments in 2005. Under Indonesia's electoral laws, legislative and executive elections are held on a five-year cycle, all citizens over 17 years of age may vote, and elections are supervised by an independent General Elections Commission.

Reports of irregularities were common in the various national and regional elections in 2004 and 2005, including intimidation of voters, attempted vote buying and, especially, fraud in vote counting. However, the level of such irregularities appears low compared to other post-authoritarian countries in Southeast Asia such as Thailand and the Philippines. Electoral authorities moved to punish those responsible and, in several cases, ordered recounts or repeat votes. Many domestic and international independent electoral monitoring groups observed the polls and declared them free and fair.

Nonparty candidates are not allowed to run in legislative elections (except for the less important DPD). Registration requirements for political parties are relatively stringent; as a result, of 237 parties listed with the government in February 2003, only 24 eventually passed verification.[3] The most onerous requirement is that parties must show they have branches in at least half the districts in half the provinces, a rule designed to exclude local parties perceived as threatening to national unity. The registration rules are applied fairly, however, and once parties have successfully registered, they have equal campaigning opportunities.

Institutionalization of open elections offers the opportunity for effective rotation of power. To a large degree that opportunity has been exercised. There was considerable turnover in legislatures in the 2004 elections (for instance, representation of former President Megawati Soekarnoputri's PDI-P party fell from 154 seats to 109 seats in the national legislature), and new players were elected to executive posts. However, a combination of highly fragmented party representation in legislative bodies, few substantial policy differences between parties, a pervasive culture of money politics, and a tendency for de facto grand coalitions when dividing up executive power, has tended to limit voters' choice in practice. Political parties competed during elections, but at the national level they colluded and formed party cartels once in power.[4] At the local level, the parties were often so weak that they allowed independent figures, often with only minimal links to the parties, to dominate executive office.[5]

These trends were especially visible prior to 2004, when heads of the executive were elected by party representatives in legislatures rather than directly by citizens. Instead of leading to competition between candidates with clearly delineated policy alternatives, this system frequently produced opportunistic horse-trading, alliances of convenience, and vote selling for corrupt payments. Winning candidates for executive positions often did not represent the largest parties but were those with the most money and strongest bureaucratic networks. The election of Susilo Bambang Yudhoyono, and of many new regional heads, suggests that direct popular elections provide better avenues for dissatisfied voters to replace their governments. However, there are still elements of continuity. For instance, Yudhoyono's cabinet includes representation of almost all major parties, continuing the party cartel approach. A requirement that candidates in direct elections at the local level be nominated by parties with a minimum representation in the relevant legislative body has produced a tendency among parties to auction nominations to the highest bidders.[6] Overall, the pervasiveness of corruption means that oligarchic business interests exercise a preponderant influence on parties, legislatures, and the executive.

The influence of money politics has been a matter of considerable public concern in Indonesia, and regulations limit funds that individuals and companies may provide to political parties and candidates, as well as require parties to disclose their finances in a timely and transparent manner. However, members of corruption watchdog organizations and the General Election Commission itself have strongly criticized these regulations for containing loopholes and lacking sufficiently tough sanctions.[7] The result is that political parties often remain beholden to powerful donors.

There have also been efforts to improve government accountability, although they have been less successful than the reforms to the electoral system. Since 1999, Indonesian lawmakers have entrenched the separation of powers principle in the constitution and designed mechanisms to enable the executive, legislative, and judicial branches of government to oversee and hold each other accountable. A major step in this regard was the establishment of the Constitutional Court in August 2003, which among its several powers has the authority to determine the constitutionality of laws and declare them invalid. The court has thus far struck out provisions of several laws, including an attempt to limit the court's own authority to review laws to only those passed since 1999, as well as a prohibition on former members of the Communist Party running in elections and another allowing retroactive punishment of terrorism offenses. Previously, no effective mechanism had existed for determining whether the legislature, in passing laws, was submitting to the limits on its power set out in the constitution. By providing such a mechanism, the Constitutional Court has the potential to become a foundation for the rule of law.[8]

The record of legislative bodies in scrutinizing the executive at national and regional levels is mixed. Democratization has invigorated the legislatures and, on some issues, legislators have been fierce critics of government on all manner of topics, ranging from privatization of government assets to instances of high-level corruption. On the whole, however, the dominant trend has been rent-seeking rather than monitoring, with legislators using legislative review to extort bribes from government officials.[9]

In principle, members of the civil service are selected, promoted, and dismissed on the basis of open competition and merit. In practice, corrupt payments and connections are often crucial in recruitment and career advancement. The local press has reported on the role of brokers who charge fees to secure places for applicants during civil service recruitment drives, even detailing the prices for admission to more lucrative departments.[10] The new government has recognized the problem and encouraged the public to report bribery cases. However, the practice remains widespread.

Although the political influence of well-connected business and bureaucratic groups remains dominant, Indonesia's democratic transition has also seen a dramatic widening of space for political engagement and monitoring by civil society. A broad range of groups can testify and comment on pending government policy or legislation, and civil society groups beyond Jakarta have especially flourished. However, their influence varies greatly, depending on the nature of the interests arrayed against them. There have been notable successes. For example, a law on domestic violence passed in September 2004 was the culmination of years of lobbying by women's organizations. Yet, when they confront powerful vested interests (for instance, when lobbying on bills dealing with defense and security), civil society groups are less influential.

To a large degree, nongovernmental organizations (NGOs) are free from legal impediments and onerous requirements for registration. Under Indonesian law it is relatively simple to establish a *yayasan* (foundation), which is the legal form taken by most NGOs. Funders of civic organizations and policy institutes are likewise mostly free of pressure, although the government intermittently circumscribes foreign funding agencies and NGOs in conflict areas such as Papua and Aceh.

Another sphere that has seen dramatic progress is media independence and freedom of expression. The Suharto government's onerous licensing procedures for media outlets were abolished, as was direct censorship of media content. The principle of press freedom is now enshrined in law, and the country is home to an array of vigorous media outlets, even in regional areas. Generally, the state no longer engages in direct or indirect forms of censorship, nor does it as a matter of policy use funding or other indirect measures to elicit favorable reporting. Private citizens have unrestricted internet access.

However, there are exceptions to the generally favorable climate. For instance, government media intervention persists in conflict areas. When the government declared a military emergency in Aceh in May 2003 (which continued until May 2004, when it was replaced by a civil emergency until May 2005), it imposed extensive controls on journalists.[11] Another cause for concern has been government efforts to exert control over the broadcast media. On the basis of a controversial 2002 law on broadcasting, in late 2005 the government issued four regulations that, inter alia, granted the government the power to issue and revoke licenses and blocked local media from directly relaying news programs from foreign providers (a staple of many local radio stations), prompting protests from associations of private television and radio broadcasters.[12]

While official censorship has become exceptional, major threats to press freedoms derive from the corrupt nexus between private interests and state officials, especially at the local level. There are frequent reports of journalists suffering violence and intimidation by security officials or private actors (especially *preman,* or gangsters) when they cover corruption, land disputes, or similar issues that involve major financial interests; such reports are rarely followed by criminal investigations or prosecutions.[13] Another cause for concern is the recourse by powerful interests to civil and criminal defamation laws. In one such case, the politically well-connected businessman Tomy Winata took the respected newsmagazine *Tempo,* and its sister organization, the *Koran Tempo* newspaper, to court for articles implying he was involved in a fire in Jakarta's Tanah Abang district and gambling in South Sulawesi; the publications were ordered to pay punitively high damages (US$1 million in the case against *Koran Tempo*) while *Tempo's* editor was sentenced to 12 months' imprisonment. One obstacle to press freedom is that the judicial system is so corrupt that it cannot be relied on to investigate or decide on such cases impartially. Of equal concern is corruption in the media itself, with envelope journalism (by which journalists are handed envelopes containing cash to encourage favorable reporting) widely practiced by state officials and businesses. Reflecting both progress and significant continuing difficulties, Reporters sans Frontieres places Indonesia 102nd out of 167 in its 2005 Worldwide Press Freedom Index, a considerable slide since the country ranked 57th in the organization's first index in 2002.[14]

Restrictions on cultural expression, such as literature and cultural productions, which were a feature of the Suharto era, have largely disappeared (in theory, some literary works by left-wing authors like the famous novelist Pramoedya Ananta Toer remain banned, but the ban is not enforced). However, creative artists, television producers, and filmmakers complain of unpredictable but increasing censorship of images deemed sexually provocative (including dance movements and on-screen kissing) due to pressure from religious groups.

Recommendations

- There is continuing need for election campaign finance reform in order to reduce incentives for corruption and to increase the ability of electoral bodies and monitoring organizations to scrutinize party accounts.
- Anticorruption agencies should be empowered to investigate reports of corrupt payments being made to political parties to secure nominations in legislative and executive elections.
- Criminal libel laws should not be used to control the media, and the authorities should prioritize investigation of instances of physical violence and intimidation against journalists.
- The government should revise the broadcasting law and associated regulations to ensure full independence from government control of electronic media.

CIVIL LIBERTIES – 3.70

Indonesia has made substantial progress in protection of civil liberties. A remarkably open political climate has replaced the authoritarian restrictions of the Suharto years. In general, the state recognizes the rights of civic, business, and political associations to organize, mobilize, and advocate for peaceful purposes. The constitution establishes freedom of association and assembly, and the state no longer compels citizens to join any association, as it did during the Suharto era. This liberalization has produced a proliferation of civic, political, and religious organizations, most of which would attest to much-improved civil liberties. The government has also liberalized rules concerning trade unions, although intimidatory methods are sometimes used by management, hired thugs, or security forces against labor activists.

Nevertheless, restrictions on political expression remain. Marxism-Leninism is still banned, and it is illegal to "insult the head of state" (a charge under which 14 persons were tried and imprisoned during the Megawati Soekarnoputri presidency). Above all, *makar* (treason) provisions are used extensively against persons peacefully advocating secession in Aceh, Papua, and Maluku. In July 2004, for example, the regional police chief in Maluku announced that arrest warrants had been issued for 300 members of the Maluku Sovereignty Front (FKM), and several of its leaders were subsequently tried and given long prison sentences.

It will be immediately apparent from this and the following discussion that human rights abuses by security forces have been especially severe in conflict areas during the period covered by this report, especially in Aceh and Papua, where separatist sentiment has been strongest. It should also be noted, however, that the human rights situation in Aceh improved dramatically after the signing of the peace agreement between the government and Free Aceh Movement rebels in mid-2005.[15] In Papua, by contrast, the central government often appears indifferent or even hostile to local aspirations and has interpreted key elements of its own Special Autonomy Law very narrowly. This dynamic has fostered a climate in which political tensions, violent demonstrations, and abuses by security officers remained a feature in Papua, while the peace process achieved remarkable success in Aceh.[16] An important conclusion is that two of the most important steps the government can take to improve civil liberties protection in Indonesia are keeping the peace process on track in Aceh and engaging in serious dialogue with local leaders in Papua, with a view to responding positively to local aspirations for greater autonomy.

In addition to harassment of groups espousing secession, there are reports of less systematic maltreatment of other political activists, especially when they threaten the interests of well-connected business or bureaucratic groups in the regions. Physical attacks by thugs hired by such groups or individuals have occurred, with targets including human rights groups critical of military abuses, labor activists, and peasants involved in land disputes.[17] In September 2004, a noted human rights activist, Munir, was murdered by arsenic poisoning while on a flight to the Netherlands. A court in December 2005 found a Garuda airlines pilot guilty of the crime; the presiding judge implied the killing was part of a conspiracy involving the State Intelligence Agency, BIN. More generally, the state sometimes fails to protect citizens from abuse by private actors; for example, some police and security officials collaborate with criminal elements involved in extortion and protection rackets.

The picture is similarly mixed with respect to public protests, which have become a regular feature of political life. Citizens are required by law to notify police when they seek to protest; authorities in most cases merely authorize and monitor them. However, in some instances, especially in locations distant from the capital, police have responded brutally. Among the more significant cases in 2004–2005 were a protest by farmers in Ruteng, Flores, at which police shot dead six participants, and a violent rampage by police through a university campus in Makassar, South Sulawesi, in May 2004 that left more than 350 persons injured. Police officers are rarely punished in such instances, although the commanding officer in Ruteng was removed from his post and given a written reprimand, and 20 officers in Makassar were removed from their posts or jailed for up to 21 days.[18]

There are widespread accusations that officers of the state commit torture, especially in Aceh and Papua and during interrogations of individuals accused of terrorism offenses. Reports are also frequent of violent methods being used during interrogation of ordinary criminal suspects. Prison conditions are generally poor, with overcrowding common. Prisoners commonly must rely on relatives or friends to provide good quality food and other amenities; corruption is rife so that wealthy prisoners are often able to purchase special privileges.[19] However, reports of systematic violence or other vindictive behavior by prison authorities are rare.

Indonesia's criminal procedures code provides protection against arbitrary arrest, and these protections are partially observed, again with the notable exception of conflict areas like Aceh (before the peace process) and Papua, although efforts to improve police practice have even been made in Papua.[20] Long-term detention without trial is also unusual. Even during the crackdown in Aceh in 2003–2004, the authorities generally moved quickly to try most of the hundreds of people they arrested (the quality of these trials, however, fell far short of international standards of fairness). In recent years there have been efforts to reform the police, including by improving policing practices and institutional accountability. Serious problems remain, including poor capacity, inadequate numbers, and low salaries that encourage police officers "to seek additional income from other sources, both legitimate and illegitimate."[21] At best, progress in police reform has been uneven.

When they experience abuses by public officials, citizens have several avenues for petition and redress, including a National Human Rights Commission. However, these avenues are often inaccessible for ordinary citizens (the commission has offices in only two provinces outside Jakarta and is poorly resourced), and collusion and ineffectiveness in the police, prosecutors, and courts often mean effective follow-up is minimal. On the other hand, the new climate of media freedom means that some victims of abuses are able to publicize their cases widely.

The constitution guarantees all persons freedom from discrimination and grants both men and women equal civil and political rights. The Ministry of Women's Empowerment aims to promote gender mainstreaming, affirmative action, and laws and regulations favoring women.[22] However, numerous areas of gender discrimination persist, and the state's record in reviewing laws and practices discriminating against women has been mixed. Some substantive progress has been made in recent times, including the 2004 law on domestic violence. On the other hand, when an interdepartmental working group drafted revisions to Islamic civil laws to promote gender equity in marriage, inheritance, and divorce (including by banning polygamy), an outcry from conservative Islamic groups caused the minister of religion to shelve the plan. A draft law on pornography and porno-action being considered by the national legislature as this article goes to press includes provisions that have been widely condemned by women's and other groups for criminalizing women's bodies (for example, one section makes it illegal to "display certain sensual parts of the body," including the navel, waist, breasts, and thighs, in whole or in part).[23] In Indonesia's newly plural political system, groups favoring women's equality, visibility, and free expression have been empowered, but so too have groups that would restrict them. It is not yet clear which will be stronger in the long run, although so far those favoring greater equality have had more victories.

However, there is substantial regional variation. In the context of decentralization of political power to the regions, conservative Islamic forces have been able to influence local governments in several regions to introduce regulations that restrict women's autonomy. In the province of Aceh, which has begun to implement elements of Sharia as part of special autonomy arrangements, Muslim women are obliged to wear Islamic dress in public. Several district governments in other parts of Indonesia likewise require female public servants to wear Islamic dress. An especially controversial example of this trend was the introduction of an anti-prostitution regulation in the district of Tangerang, West Java, that prohibited any person whose "attitude or behavior is suspicious and gives rise to the opinion that s/he is a prostitute" from being in public places; this regulation led to the arrest of large numbers of women.[24] Even in areas where such requirements are not embodied in law, the state rarely intervenes to protect women from pressures from conservative groups.

The state has begun to take measures to prevent trafficking of women and children, although they are not yet sufficient to address the massive scale of the problem (UNICEF estimates that 100,000 women and children are trafficked in Indonesia each year).[25] Some persons involved in this trade have been prosecuted successfully, although they often receive relatively light sentences, averaging just over three years.[26] A law on child protection was passed in 2002 under which some involved in trafficking have been prosecuted. Human rights groups have campaigned on the need for a law on human trafficking, and one is being prepared.

No single ethnic group dominates in Indonesia, meaning that discussion of discrimination on ethnic, linguistic, and cultural grounds must be highly contextualized. The state motto is "unity in diversity," and pride in Indonesia's multiethnic makeup runs deep in official circles and the wider public. Active state discrimination against minority ethnic groups has been minimal. One exception has been ethnic Chinese, who under Suharto were subject to a range of discriminatory rules. Post-Suharto governments have removed several legal impediments to their full equality, but discrimination continues in practice.

During the Suharto era, the central government also frequently rode roughshod over minority indigenous groups, especially in resource-rich areas. Decentralization has enhanced the ability of such groups to assert their interests but has also given rise to official discrimination against minorities (especially migrants from other parts of Indonesia) in some districts. For example, non-indigenous residents in Bali are required to have special Migrant Resident Identity Cards, are charged special fees, and complain about harassment by village officials.[27] The special autonomy law for Papua requires that candidates for governor be indigenous Papuans, leading to the disqualification of two candidates in elections in early 2006.[28] In many districts, complaints are more frequent about less formal discrimination against migrants, for instance, in recruitment of civil servants or the awarding of contracts for construction work.

Although the state engages in little overtly discriminatory behavior, it also takes little positive action to prevent discrimination in such areas as employment. Members of ethnic and religious minorities sometimes complain of discrimination in employment, and gender is often specified in job advertisements. The government has ratified international conventions prohibiting racial and gender discrimination, but there is no readily available legal recourse for people who feel they have suffered discrimination. Prosecution for discrimination is unknown, and the country lacks an antidiscrimination law. Similarly, although a 1997 law prohibits discrimination against persons with disabilities, the state has taken virtually no action to enforce that prohibition. The state makes almost no effort to provide information about government services and decisions in ways that are accessible to people with disabilities.

Most Indonesians, including those in public life, value religious pluralism. The constitution guarantees freedom of religion, but it also enshrines the principle of "belief in one supreme God." This has translated into official recognition of only five faiths (Islam, Protestantism, Catholicism, Buddhism, and Hinduism).[29] The state generally does not interfere in private religious practices of citizens, including those outside the five officially recognized faiths. However, members of religious groups other than the main five (a small proportion of the overall population) can face discrimination. For example, they may experience difficulties in obtaining national identity cards or official permission to establish houses of worship. Every person is expected to have a religion, and promotion of atheism is formally banned by the criminal code.

There are also instances of state suppression of minority religious practice. The government reserves the power to ban groups it labels deviant sects, usually accusing them of endangering religious harmony, but effectively in order to enforce orthodoxy in the five main religions. In 2005, police failed to protect followers of the Ahmadiyah group when their headquarters in Bogor, West Java, were attacked by a mob of 10,000 who believed the group contravened Islamic teachings. Ahmadiyah, founded by a nineteenth-century Pakistani prophet, has about 200,000 adherents in Indonesia.[30] A 1984 Ministry of Religion decree bans dissemination of the group's teachings, and following the attack, local officials in some districts closed Ahmadiyah offices and banned its activities. Physical attacks by mobs on Ahmadiyah premises have continued in some areas.

Advocates of unorthodox practice or belief are occasionally placed on trial and imprisoned, usually under "insulting religion" provisions of the criminal code. For instance, in 2005 a preacher in East Java was jailed for using the Indonesian language in Islamic prayers. Another form of enforcement of orthodoxy occurs in those (relatively few) regions where elements of Sharia are being introduced by regional governments. As noted above, a feature of many such regulations is enforcement of Islamic dress codes for women (especially public servants), but such regulations also sometimes include other elements restricting individual religious autonomy. In Aceh, for example, the tasks of the new Sharia police include ensuring that all Muslims attend Friday prayers and that businesses are closed during prayer times.

There are also various informal restrictions amounting to religious discrimination. Members of religious minorities (especially Christians) have long complained that a 1969 government decree restricted their ability to establish new houses of worship because it required government permits and local community consent, which are not always forthcoming. In 2005, several instances were reported of Muslim mobs closing down irregular Christian churches that lacked authorization. In 2006, the government revised the decree, but a requirement that any new house of worship would have to be supported (in writing) by at least 60 local residents and have at least 90 registered users was criticized by spokespersons of some minority religions as entrenching the restrictions in the 1969 decree. However, the government does not intervene in the appointment of religious or spiritual leaders or in the internal activities of faith-related organizations.

Recommendations

- Articles of the criminal code on treason, hatred-spreading, insulting the president, and insulting religion should be amended or removed to ensure they cannot be used to persecute persons for peacefully expressing political views or practicing their own religious faiths.

- The government should pass an antidiscrimination law providing avenues of legal redress for persons who have suffered from discrimination.
- Laws should be amended to provide equal status to all religious beliefs, not just the five currently recognized; the government should cease all restrictions on unorthodox and minority religious views and groups and provide them protection from harassment and violent attacks.
- Allegations of torture as well as violence by authorities when responding to peaceful protests should be investigated promptly and followed by criminal prosecution and punishment.
- The National Human Rights Commission should be funded to open offices in all provinces and provided with expanded investigatory powers.
- The government should take all steps to ensure successful implementation of the peace process in Aceh and improve implementation of the 2001 Papuan Special Autonomy law, engaging in genuine dialogue with Papuan leaders.

RULE OF LAW – 2.97

A major challenge confronting implementation of the rule of law in Indonesia is the extreme corruption that pervades the judiciary and other law enforcement agencies. Indonesian commentators speak of a court mafia in which brokers arrange for plaintiffs and defendants to pay bribes to judges, defense lawyers, prosecutors, and police in order to fix the outcomes of trials. The effect is that judicial decisions are routinely bought and sold or otherwise determined by collusion and connections rather than according to legal principles. This results in a system of law enforcement that is both inconsistent and inequitable and lacks the confidence of much of the population.

Undeniably, significant efforts have been made to strengthen the rule of law, including strengthening judicial independence and improving the professionalism of law enforcement agencies. In early 2004, the Supreme Court launched a new blueprint for judicial reform, while the new

Constitutional Court has the potential to become an exemplar of judicial professionalism. Numerous individual judges and other officials have struggled to uphold rule of law principles in difficult circumstances.

Indonesia's judiciary is increasingly independent politically. Full responsibility over the administrative and financial affairs of the judiciary was transferred to the Supreme Court from the Ministry of Justice in 2004. Although political intervention is still possible at the highest levels, overall it appears that judges are appointed, promoted, and dismissed in a relatively unbiased manner. Government authorities generally (though not always) comply with judicial decisions. In contrast, training for judges is often perfunctory and poorly resourced, so that "judges do not receive training matching the needs."[31] The skills of judges, and their ability to administer justice fairly, vary widely between courts and from individual to individual; in many, perhaps most, cases they are inadequate, especially in lower courts.

The law stipulates that every person charged with a criminal offense is presumed innocent until proven guilty. In practice, however, many judges have not shaken off Suharto-era habits of viewing themselves as partners of police and prosecutors, to the great disadvantage of the accused.[32] Although hearings are generally public and timely, they are thus often neither fair nor impartial. Judicial monitoring organizations note frequent and often glaring deviations from prescribed procedures in court cases.[33] The criminal procedures code provides that all persons accused of crimes have the right to access to independent legal counsel, and persons able to afford such counsel usually receive access. The code also requires the state to provide free independent counsel to all persons without means who are charged with a crime punishable by a custodial sentence of five years or more; in practice such assistance is rarely provided.

Indonesian corruption and judiciary watchdog bodies have accused prosecutors of being highly politicized and also corrupt and of refusing, avoiding, sabotaging, or prematurely ending corruption investigations into prominent political figures, military officers, and businesspeople. The new attorney general has promised sweeping reform, and the government has achieved some dramatic successes in anticorruption prosecutions (see below). However, there is no evidence that the promised thorough reform among prosecutors has taken place.

Enforcement of property rights and contracts is dependent on the vagaries of the legal system and is thus often inadequate and inconsistent. Theft of intellectual property is widespread. Businesses (especially foreign investors) frequently complain about poor enforcement of contracts and violations of property rights (for instance, illegal mining on company leaseholds) that go unpunished because of official collusion. In fact, the people whose property and contractual rights are least secure are the poor. For example, poor landowners and indigenous communities are vulnerable to land expropriation by developers and/or state authorities, while employers frequently violate workers' employment contracts with impunity.

In sum, although the Indonesian constitution provides equal status before the law, effective access to justice is often determined by wealth and political connections. A World Bank study on access to justice for village people found that "Formal justice institutions—the police, prosecutors and courts—are [viewed as being] biased and remote. As a result, many choose to bury their grievances instead of seeking redress."[34] Public officials are rarely prosecuted for abuses of power or other wrongdoings.

Although they espouse human rights principles, security forces are generally not respectful of these rights. Some police and military personnel have been punished by military courts and other tribunals for using violence against civilians. However, those punished are usually junior, their crimes are often relatively minor, and their punishments are invariably light. Notably, all senior military officers who were tried by ad hoc human rights courts for abuses committed during the Suharto era or during East Timor's transition to independence in 1999 have been acquitted, either in the first instance or on appeal. Thus, while the security forces no longer enjoy complete impunity for human rights abuses, they have something close to that status.

Like past post-Suharto governments, Susilo Bambang Yudhoyono's government has promised sweeping military reform. In some areas there has been progress (e.g., winning military agreement to the Aceh peace process), but no substantive new reforms have yet been implemented. Somewhat more progress has been made in reforming the police force, for example, by the introduction of a new community police program, supported by international donors.[35]

In theory, security forces, including both the military and the police, are now subject to civilian control. Certainly, they do not exercise direct influence in politics as they did under Suharto. Active military officers have been removed from government posts and legislatures. Other measures have been taken to reform the security sector, including separating the police from the military and thus in theory reducing the military's role in internal security. In practice, however, it has proved difficult for the legislative and executive branches to carry out meaningful oversight of the armed forces (the police are marginally less problematic). Civilian legislators and bureaucrats lack the skills, inclination, and confidence to scrutinize military budgets and behavior. As a result, the military has almost complete autonomy in organizing its internal affairs and is virtually unchallenged when determining security policy.

Ineffectiveness of civilian control is based on two deep foundations. The first is continuation of the military's territorial structure, by which military forces are distributed throughout the country in a system of commands that shadow civilian administrative structures at every level. This arrangement provides military officers with extensive opportunities to become involved in local political and economic affairs. Attempts to reform this structure, which began in the early post-Suharto period, have stalled.

Second is inadequate state funding of the security forces. Only an estimated 30 percent of security force funds are provided by the state budget.[36] Security officers raise the remainder through a variety of legal, semi-legal and illegal business activities, ranging from providing security services to large multinational companies in the mining sector to involvement in protection rackets, smuggling, prostitution, drug-dealing, and gambling. With security forces responsible for raising much of their own funds, the line between public and private interests in the forces becomes blurred, security officers are drawn into criminal activities (so much so that violent turf wars between police and army units sometimes occur), and government loses its ability to engage in effective oversight. The product is a security force that is still largely a law unto itself whose members are rarely held accountable for abusing office for personal gain. The 2004 Armed Forces Law requires military businesses to be transferred to the government within five years. The new defense minister, Juwono Sudarsono, has tried to implement this provision; senior officers, however, insist that the military should keep control of cooperatives and other bodies primarily concerned with soldiers' welfare, which could amount to as many as 197 of the military's 219 businesses.[37]

Recommendations

- The government should accelerate efforts to take control of all military businesses, criminalize direct payments by companies and other private actors to the security forces, and eventually provide full funding of all security force activities from transparent budgetary sources.
- Stalled plans to reform the military's territorial structure should be restarted, with a view to its eventual abolition.
- Priority should be placed on continuing police reform, especially improving police accountability and introducing community policing programs.
- Using the Supreme Court reform blueprint as its basis, the government should support efforts to reform the judiciary and eliminate the court mafia that subverts the justice system. Training of judges should be improved and expanded.

ANTICORRUPTION AND TRANSPARENCY – 2.45

Corruption has been the bane of Indonesia's political transition. In 2005, Transparency International in its annual Corruption Perceptions Index ranked Indonesia as one of the most corrupt countries in the world, at 147th out of 159 countries surveyed.[38] A survey of 1,000 expatriate businesspeople in 2004 conducted by the Hong Kong–based Political and Economic Risk Consultancy (PERC) rated Indonesia as the most corrupt country in Asia.[39] However, although corruption is endemic, it is also universally and publicly condemned. Combating corruption is the theme par excellence of investigative media reporting; it was central to the platforms of most parties and candidates in the 2004 elections and is a major public preoccupation of the Yudhoyono presidency. A plethora of initiatives has been announced to overcome corruption as well as some high-profile prosecutions. Still, the magnitude of the challenge is enormous, because corruption is woven into the very fabric of political and economic life.

Arguably, the sociopolitical environment has become less conducive to corruption. Under the triple blows of the Asian economic crisis of

1997–98, a six-year IMF economic rescue package (1997–2003), and low investor interest in subsequent years, successive governments have pursued privatization polices, reduced direct state involvement in the economy, and cut back on bureaucratic regulations and other controls that increase scope for corruption. However, investors and economic commentators still complain about excessive government regulation. Decentralization has increased the scope for new regional players to intervene in economic decision making and extract corrupt payments. The most serious structural problems relate to the internal organization of the bureaucracy and require thorough civil service reform.[40]

Corruption is so deeply entrenched in politics and the bureaucracy that public office is rarely separated from the personal interests of office-holders. No adequate rules govern how public officials should manage their business interests while in office, and no rules require divestment.[41] The government has promised to issue new rules to regulate how businesses owned by officials and their family members participate in state-funded projects and to prevent state officials' misusing confidential information during tender processes, but no concrete progress had been made by the time this report was finalized.

Since the fall of Suharto, successive governments have introduced a battery of new regulations, investigative bodies, and procedures to promote integrity and prevent, detect, and punish official corruption. These include, most importantly, the Corruption Eradication Commission (KPK) established in late 2003, an Ombudsman's Commission, and specialist anticorruption courts. In addition, numerous auditing bodies monitor government expenditure. The Supreme National Audit Agency (BPK) regularly releases estimates of state funds lost to corruption. However, in the words of a World Bank report, "While there is no shortage of auditing, the audit process is flawed, reflecting poor funding of the Supreme Audit Agency, the lack of a modern state audit law, lack of systematic follow up on audit findings, and the inability of audit agencies to successfully prosecute cases of corruption."[42]

During the first few years of the post-Suharto political transition, frequent accusations arose that political interference and corruption itself were impeding corruption investigations. In recent years, while such accusations still surface, it is generally acknowledged that some progress has occurred, especially in pursuing a handful of high-profile cases.[43] For instance, in 2005 two provincial governors (Abdullah Puteh of Aceh and Djoko Munandar of Banten) were convicted of corruption. A supportive public climate persists, with the print media in particular devoting considerable energy to exposing corruption scandals. However, the new investigatory bodies have only begun to scratch the surface, and their work is seriously hampered by lack of resources.[44]

In the private sector, the KPPU (Commission for the Supervision of Business Competition) is empowered to monitor and prevent monopolistic practices and anticompetitive behavior, including bid rigging and other conflicts of interest; however, such conflicts are rife in practice. The organization is widely viewed as ineffective, and many of the cases it has brought to court have failed on appeal, with its investigators blaming judicial corruption.

While some corruption in higher education has been reported, graft appears not to be so pervasive as to seriously corrode academic standards in admissions and awarding of grades. A more problematic area is tax collection. Although a system of internal audits exists, tax collection is widely recognized to be deeply corrupt. Tax officials frequently extort money from businesses in exchange for reducing their tax bills, and millions avoid income tax altogether, with catastrophic effects on state revenues.[45]

Victims of corruption can now pursue their rights through several anticorruption institutions, and the political context is broadly supportive. However, the legal environment is still insufficiently robust to allow anticorruption activists, investigators, and, especially, whistle-blowers to feel secure about reporting cases of bribery and corruption. The law that establishes the KPK requires the body to "provide protection" for witnesses and whistle-blowers. However, anticorruption campaigners argue that this and similar provisions in the criminal procedures code are inadequate, and a long-awaited bill on witness protection is yet to be passed into law.

One of the major challenges in effectively combating corruption is poor government transparency. While legal, regulatory, and judicial transparency has certainly improved since the Suharto era, citizens still face substantial difficulties in gaining access to information about decisions that affect them. Some parts of government at the national and local level have attempted to rectify this problem (for instance, the municipality of Gorontalo has introduced its own freedom of information regulations), but officials still routinely refuse to divulge even basic information by claiming that they are protecting state secrets. A long-awaited bill on freedom of information may rectify this problem, but although it has been in preparation since 2001, it has not yet become law.

The government has made some progress in providing public access to information about the financial assets of public officials. The KPK inherited responsibility for compiling reports on the wealth of state officials from an earlier body. After initially stating it would not provide public access, the KPK decided to continue publishing the reports, and they have been circulated in the media. Critics, however, suggest the KPK in this area lacks powers of compulsion, provides insufficient detail, does not distribute the reports sufficiently widely (for instance, via the internet), and does not investigate when officials on low salaries seem suspiciously wealthy.[46]

The budget-making process has become much more open since the fall of Suharto. The legislature now reviews the process extensively, although legislators lack resources and expertise, and some at least use the review process for extortion. The government is far less adept at publishing detailed, timely, and accurate accounting of expenditures.

A major source of corruption is the awarding of government contracts. The World Bank has called the public procurement system "the principal source of leakage from the budget," citing the existence of "collusive rings" involving bidders and government officials.[47] In recent years, some marginal improvements have been made in tendering processes, which are generally somewhat more competitive than in the past. Overall, however, the problem is severe in the central government and even more so in the regions, where local government officials, legislators, and private contractors routinely subvert open bidding processes and apportion government contracts on the basis of corrupt payments.

The government does generally enable the fair and legal administration and distribution of foreign assistance. However, bureaucratic impediments can be substantial, notably the requirement that donors must find partner government agencies. In some places, such as Papua, the extent of intervention by local government and security officials can be so great that some donors choose not to become involved (after the December 2004 tsunami, by contrast, conditions for donors became very open in Aceh). Most donors also recognize that significant leakages occur from programs that are channeled through the state bureaucracy.

Recommendations

- The long-delayed bills on witness protection and freedom of information should be passed into law swiftly. A proposed new state secret law should not be so restrictive as to prevent public scrutiny of government expenditure, policies, and performance.
- The government should increase the resources available to anti-corruption and probity agencies.
- Reform to the public procurement system to increase transparency and reduce opportunities for collusion is needed.
- A thorough process of civil service reform is required, beginning with review and restructuring of mechanisms for civil service remuneration, recruitment, and promotion in order to reduce incentives for corruption, as well as provision of adequate funding for core government services.

NOTES

1   The author would like to thank Ross McLeod and Marcus Mietzner for their helpful comments on an earlier draft, and Bima Arya Sugiarto for research assistance.
2   See Edward Aspinall, *The Helsinki Agreement: A More Promising Basis for Peace in Aceh?* (Washington, D.C.: East-West Center, 2005).
3   Ramlan Surbakti, "Peserta Pemilu 2004" *Kompas* (Jakarta), 18 February 2003.
4   For an elaboration of this theme concerning national politics prior to direct presidential elections, see Dan Slater, "Indonesia's Accountability Trap: Party Cartels and Presidential Power after Democratic Transition," *Indonesia* 78 (2004): 61–92.
5   Vedi R. Hadiz, "Power and politics in North Sumatra: the uncompleted reformasi," in Edward Aspinall and Greg Fealy, eds, *Local Power and Politics in Indonesia: Decentralisation and Democratisation* (Singapore: Institute of Southeast Asian Studies, 2003), 119–31.
6   Marcus Mietzner, "Local Democracy," *Inside Indonesia* 17 (January–March 2006): 17–18.
7   See comments by Hidayat Komaruddin, head of the official body providing oversight of the election (Panwaslu), in *Tempo*, 18 July 2004, 54.
8   Selina Wrighter, "Questions of judgement: the new Constitutional Court combines law and politics," *Inside Indonesia* 81 (January–March 2005).
9   Ross H. McLeod, "The Struggle to Regain Effective Government under Democracy in Indonesia," *Bulletin of Indonesian Economic Studies* 41, 3 (2005): 367–86
10 Humphrey R. Djemat, "Sorotan Hukum: Bayang-bayang KKN pada Seleksi CPNS," *Sinar Harapan*, 25 November 2004.

[11] *Muzzling the Messengers: Attacks and Restrictions on the Media* (New York: Human Rights Watch [HRW], 2003).

[12] See, for example, "Broadcast rules feared to turn back the clock," *Jakarta Post,* 3 December 2005; Arie Rukmantara, "Controversial broadcasting regulations to be revised," *Jakarta Post,* 25 February 2006.

[13] In one case, a journalist who was covering corruption in a local election in Nias, North Sumatra, was reportedly abducted by thugs and disappeared: "Police told to act on missing journo," *Jakarta Post,* 17 October 2005.

[14] *Worldwide Press Freedom Index, 2005* (Paris: Reporters sans frontieres [RSF], 2005), http://www.rsf.org/rubrique.php3?id_rubrique=554.

[15] *Aceh: So Far, So Good* (Brussels: International Crisis Group [ICG], 2005).

[16] *Papua: The Dangers of Shutting Down Dialogue* (ICG, 2006), 8.

[17] On human rights violations in land expropriation, see *Tutup Buku dengan "Transitional Justice"? Menutup Lembaran Hak Asasi Manusia 1999–2004 dan Membuka Lembaran Baru 2005,* (Jakarta: Lembaga Studi dan Advokasi Masyarakat [ELSAM], 2005), 41–52.

[18] *Praktik Brutalitas Polisi di Masa Transisi Indonesia: Sebuah analisis kebijakan di Indonesia* (Jakarta: Tim Imparsial, 2005).

[19] See Hasanudin Abdurakhman, "Penjara, Wajah Reformasi Kita," *Kompas,* 25 February 2006.

[20] For example, after a violent protest in Abepura, Papua, in March 2006, in which attacks by demonstrators resulted in the deaths of five members of the security forces, commanders took weapons from some members of the police mobile brigade (brimob) and moved quickly to replace them with another unit in order to prevent reprisal attacks against local people (nevertheless, violent reprisals did in fact take place).

[21] *Indonesia: Rethinking Internal Security Strategy* (ICG Asia, 2004), 7.

[22] See the ministry's website: http://www.menegpp.go.id.

[23] In fact, the restrictions in the draft bill would not only limit women. For example, one passage proposed banning "kissing on the lips" in public.

[24] "Perda Kota Tangerang Tak Sesuai KUHP," *Kompas,* 3 March 2006.

[25] "At a glance: Indonesia" (New York: UNICEF, 2005), http://www.unicef.org/infoby country/indonesia_23650.html.

[26] "Indonesia" (Washington, D.C.: Human Trafficking.org, 2006), http://www.human trafficking.org/countries/eap/indonesia/index.html.

[27] "Kegelisahan Para Pendatang di Bali," *Kompas,* 7 January 2003.

[28] *Papua: The Dangers of Shutting Down Dialogue* (ICG, 2006), 8.

[29] Legal ambiguity surrounds the status of Confucianism. Practitioners of this faith complain about extensive discrimination. However, recent presidents have successively assured them that their faith is recognized: Tony Hotland, "Don't target Chinese, SBY tells officials," *Jakarta Post,* 5 February 2006.

[30] Theresia Sufa, "Thousands besiege Ahmadiyah complex," *Jakarta Post,* 16 July 2005.

[31] *Country Governance Assessment Report: Republic of Indonesia* (Manila: Asian Development Bank, 2004), 112.

[32] One judge in a high-profile case involving an Australian citizen accused of drug trafficking in Bali in 2005 told an Australian newspaper that in eight years of sitting on the

bench he had never acquitted a defendant in 500 drug cases: "Corby judge never acquitted drug case," TVNZ.co.nz, 25 May 2005, http://tvnz.co.nz/view/news_world_story_skin/567953?format=html.

33 See the series of reports of monitoring of court cases by the Masyarakat Pemantau Peradilan Indonesia (Indonesian Judicial Monitoring Community) at http://www.pemantau peradilan.com/pantau.php.

34 *Village Justice in Indonesia: Case studies on access to justice, village democracy and governance* (World Bank, 2004), 2.

35 "A new concept of community policing," *The Jakarta Post*, 18 March 2006.

36 Indonesia Corruption Watch has reported that negligible sums are provided to police officers to cover expenses when investigating cases (Rp. 7.500 for minor cases and Rp. 250.000 for major cases), thus "legitimizing accepting money from outside": *Laporan Akhir Tahun 2004 Indonesia Corruption Watch: Hukum dan Peradilan di Indonesia: Masih Berpihak Kepada Koruptor* (Jakarta: Indonesia Corruption Watch, 2004), 3.

37 Marcus Mietzner, *The Politics of Military Reform in Indonesia: Elite Conflict, Nationalism and Institutional Resistance* (Washington, D.C.: East-West Center, forthcoming).

38 *Corruption Perceptions Index, 2005* (Berlin: Transparency International, 2005).

39 "Indonesia Masih Negara Terkorup di Asia," *Kompas*, 3 March 2004.

40 According to the World Bank, problems in the civil service include a "highly opaque and non-transparent system of compensation" for public servants in which "only a small proportion of an official's income comes from his salary" and the consistent underfunding of state budgets, with the result that "government agencies are implicitly expected to find other means of meeting their needs, thus blurring the line between public and private expenditures and encouraging rent-seeking behavior": *Combating Corruption in Indonesia: Enhancing Accountability for Development* (Washington, D.C.: World Bank, East Asia Poverty Reduction and Economic Management Unit, 2003), vii, 19; see also Ross H. McLeod, "The Struggle to Regain Effective Government under Democracy in Indonesia," *Bulletin of Indonesian Economic Studies* 41, 3 (2005): 367–86.

41 This phenomenon has become a particular cause of public concern during the government of Susilo Bambang Yudhoyono, as 13 members of the cabinet have backgrounds in business, and their business interests have appeared to benefit from their owners' holding public office. For example, the Bakrie Brothers company, part-owned by the then coordinating minister for economic affairs, Aburizal Bakrie, recorded an extraordinary increase in profits during the government's first year, with 55 percent of its income coming from the government-dependent infrastructure sector: Metta Dharmasaputra and Efri Ritonga, "Berbagai Usaha dengan Kuasa," *Tempo*, 28 November–4 December 2005.

42 *Combating Corruption in Indonesia* (World Bank), 19.

43 In his first year in office, President Yudhoyono approved the investigation and/or detention of 67 senior officials on corruption charges: "Presiden Setujui 3 Pejabat ditahan," *Kompas*, 29 December 2005.

44 In early 2005 it was reported that underfunding meant that members of the Ombudsman's Commission had not been paid their salaries for four months: "Komisi Ombudsman Berutang Rp 400 Juta," Kompas, 9 April 2004. The KPK itself had only about 150 staff members in late 2005. See also Stephen Sherlock, "Combating Corruption in

Indonesia? The Ombudsman and the Assets Auditing Commission," *Bulletin of Indonesian Economic Studies* 38, 3 (2002): 367–383.

[45] See "Graft methods uncovered" and other articles in *Jakarta Post,* 19 January 2006.

[46] See, for example, "Ada Usaha Memandulkan Upaya Pemberantasan Korupsi," *Kompas,* 25 August 2004; "Asal-usul Kekayaan Menteri Perlu Diusut," *Kompas,* 27 November 2004; "KPK Akan Umumkan Kekayaan Pejabat di Tiap Instansi," *Koran Tempo,* 22 January 2005.

[47] *Combating Corruption in Indonesia* (World Bank), 31, 32.

JORDAN

CAPITAL: Amman
POPULATION: 5.8 million
GNI PER CAPITA: $1,850

SCORES	2004	2006
ACCOUNTABILITY AND PUBLIC VOICE:	2.94	2.83
CIVIL LIBERTIES:	3.57	3.12
RULE OF LAW:	2.75	3.12
ANTICORRUPTION AND TRANSPARENCY:	2.92	2.28

(scores are based on a scale of 0 to 7, with 0 representing weakest and 7 representing strongest performance)

Pete W. Moore

INTRODUCTION

In 1989, the Hashemite Kingdom of Jordan launched the Arab World's most promising experiment in political liberalization and reform. A well-educated professional class, a history of political participation, and a cooperative Islamist movement all gave Jordan a comparative advantage in expanding rights and inclusion. Today, unfortunately, the country has reversed course, and the actions of recent years no longer demonstrate a clear commitment to democratization. Freedoms of assembly and expression have been restricted, the electoral system remains unrepresentative, and years of economic liberalization policies have failed to decentralize economic power. In a 2005 opinion poll, 77 percent of Jordanian respondents reported that they fear criticizing their government.[1] Dissidents, observers, and scholars agree that the source of this de-liberalization is the quest by the monarchy to maintain centralized power in the face of domestic opposition and regional instability. While capital flight from the violence in Iraq and violence between Palestinians and Israelis has benefited the political and economic elite of the

Pete W. Moore is assistant professor of Political Science at Case Western Reserve University and a Senior Research Fellow at the Interuniversity Consortium for Arab and Middle Eastern Studies, Montreal. He is the author of *Doing Business in the Middle East: Politics and Economic Crisis in Jordan and Kuwait* (Cambridge University Press, 2004).

country, the risks of instability were never distant. Tragically, those risks were realized by Iraqi insurgent bombings of three Amman hotels on November 9, 2005. As a result, King Abdullah quickly replaced the government of Prime Minister Adnan Badran to make way for a government headed by former general Marouf al-Bakhit.

When he ascended to the throne in 1999 after the death of his father, King Hussein, Abdullah II bin Hussein inherited a country that had already begun backsliding on political reforms. The logic for this is straightforward. As a general rule, monarchies cultivate the image of an umpire above politics, yet in reality, their survival depends very much on politics, specifically, formal constitutional powers over all branches of government and informal cultivation of support from a narrow segment of society and manipulation of opposition from the wider segments. Thus, the liberalizations initiated in 1989 and the end of martial law in 1991 can be seen as controlled measures to cope with a previous decade of economic decline and decreasing patronage from the state. In the 1990s, the Jordanian monarchy began to realize new funding and political support through its relationships with Washington and Tel Aviv, as well as its involvement in the Oslo Peace Process. When Jordanians began to utilize their new liberties to voice disagreement with these policies, the monarchy was forced to choose between détente with Washington and democratization for Jordanians. The choice was clear. In the last years of his life, King Hussein moved aggressively to deny professional associations the right of political expression, curtail press freedoms, and jail a number of opposition leaders and journalists. The rhetoric of democratization endured while the rollback of political liberties moved forward. From 1994 until 2005, American financial and military aid to Amman reached a total of US$5 billion.[2] In 2000, Jordan became only the second Middle Eastern country, after Israel, to conclude a Free Trade Agreement (FTA) with the United States. The FTA has been hailed as proof of Jordan's reform progress, yet government restrictions on the freedom of association in 2004 and 2005 directly contravened commitments to labor rights in the trade agreement.[3]

After assuming the throne, King Abdullah delivered speeches suggesting democratic change was coming; however, the decline in rights and participation has continued. In 2001, the king suspended Parliament and over the next two years ruled by decree, enacting some 250 temporary laws. Continued violence in the West Bank and Iraq has generated capital flight, making Jordan "a hub for activities in Iraq."[4]

Such investment to Jordan has primarily benefited the country's political and economic elites, who dominate the real estate and service sectors that have absorbed the capital. Consumer prices, particularly for fuel and housing, have increased significantly, while overall per capita income has remained close to what it was in the mid-1980s.[5] Violence between street demonstrators and police took place in 1996 in Marj al-Hammam and in 1997 in Kerak, while the most extensive clashes took place in November 2002 in the city of Ma'an. Government officials were quick to blame this and other unrest on outside criminal influence, yet subsequent analysis suggests the unrest was related to domestic political de-liberalization and economic pressure.[6] In 2002, the government launched a public relations campaign titled "Jordan First," ostensibly to counter the vision of a divided Jordan. However, popular opinion came to see the campaign as a clever means to paint any opposition to government policies as anti-Jordanian. The return to parliamentary elections in 2003 was welcome, but biased electoral rules resulted in the election of a progovernment Parliament.

In 2004, the government's campaign against the nation's professional associations—the country's largest civil society organizations—led to a crisis as the Interior Ministry and security officials attempted to deny the associations the freedoms of assembly and expression. Peaceful street demonstrations were met with security force deployments and arrests. King Abdullah eventually broke the standoff by calling for the resignation of then prime minister Faisal al-Fayez and appointing a new government under Adnan Badran.

Throughout this period, the Jordanian government's role in Washington's war on terrorism and support of U.S. policy has been tied to mounting reports of torture, secret detention centers, public/private corruption, and press intimidation, all of which have damaged Jordan's international standing. In response, King Abdullah launched a National Agenda Committee to create a 10-year reform strategy for the country. Hints of the agenda's reform proposals have leaked, yet as of November 2005 no document had been publicly offered. More broadly, the National Human Rights Center (NCHR) in Jordan concluded that "no substantial change or positive development in legislation or procedure related to civil and political rights took place during 2005."[7]

ACCOUNTABILITY AND PUBLIC VOICE – 2.83

Since institutionalization by British mandate authorities in the 1920s, a hereditary monarchy (the Hashemite family) has ruled Jordan. The selection of the monarch and a crown prince are internal family matters with no public participation (Article 28 of the constitution). Jordan's constitution vests all executive power with the monarch, including the power to appoint a prime minister, the cabinet, and a 55-person Senate. Along with the Senate, an elected 110-member Chamber of Deputies (or Lower House) comprises the legislative branch of government; however, Article 91 of the constitution directs the prime minister and his cabinet to submit draft laws, leaving the Chamber of Deputies the power only to amend and to approve. With few exceptions, draft laws are crafted and introduced by the cabinet with little if any participation by outside societal or interest groups. The monarch has sole purview to call Parliament into session and to disband it. The constitution also allows for the monarch to dictate temporary laws when Parliament is not in session. Through formal and informal means, the monarch rules by decree and manipulates the electoral process.

Few avenues exist for informing citizens and political parties about government activities. Formally, Article 96 of the constitution allows parliamentarians to pose questions to ministers on public issues. In practice, few such inquiries are made, and better connected parliamentarians simply rely on informal means to gather information. Parliamentarians and civic associations regularly complain of the lack of knowledge about draft bills in preparation or temporary laws. For example, upon the return of the elected Parliament in 2003, members were surprised to find that instead of an expected 100 to 150 temporary laws, the number presented to Parliament actually approached 250.[8]

Since the late 1990s, civil society activists and opposition candidates have increasingly complained that the Government Intelligence Directorate (GID) regularly intervenes in parliamentary votes as well as electoral campaigns. In the 2003 election, for example, one parliamentary candidate reported receiving a warning from the head of the GID about his campaign platform: "If your sons want to work in Jordan in the future, it might affect them."[9] In 2005, the NCHR reported that members of several political parties were summoned by security officials on charges of distributing criticisms of government economic policies.[10]

Political parties are legal in Jordan, yet historically very weak. Of the two dozen or so political parties, only the Islamic Action Front (IAF) is viable and effective. In part, this general weakness is due to the simple fact that political power is centralized within the monarchy, and thus parties are not competing for genuine political power or participation. More specifically, this weakness is tied to the lack of electoral representation in Jordan.

In 1993, a controversial one-person, one-vote electoral law came into force on the heels of a rezoning of the country's 20 electoral districts (now 45 districts). The rezoning created a system that underrepresents opposition-minded Palestinian urban areas and overrepresents rural, regime-loyal East Bank areas. For example, the second district of Amman (location of the Wihdat refugee camp) has over 73,000 registered voters and is allotted three seats, whereas the Governorate of Ma'an, with 23,000 registered voters is allotted five seats. In combination with one-person, one-vote, the incentive is for the voter to support "the candidate you might know personally and of whom you may expect direct assistance should you need it, rather than voting on issues or ideology."[11] The result has been the consistent electoral dominance of tribal and pro-monarchy candidates.

This law was only slightly modified for the June 17, 2003, elections. While the modifications set aside quotas to increase representation for women and continue quotas for minorities—nine seats for Christians, three each for Circassians and Chechens, and six for women—the systematic underrepresentation endured. The 2003 election thus returned a Parliament with 62 seats going to pro-regime loyalists and the IAF accounting for 17. Turnout was 57 percent with few complaints of voter fraud. All political parties participated, although the IAF boycotted the earlier municipal elections in response to a temporary law that allowed the government to appoint all mayors and half of all municipal council members.

Potentially, the most important development on the electoral horizon concerns hints of reform coming from the still-evolving National Agenda. In September and October 2005, elements of these reform recommendations began appearing in the local media. Most notable was the idea of moving away from a one-person, one-vote system to proportional representation or split-ticket voting, something the opposition has called for since 1993. On the other hand, the leaked recommendations made little progress in establishing a truly independent electoral commission, advising instead that the judiciary be tasked with oversight.[12] It is important to emphasize these are only recommendations and drafts and therefore far from constituting actual change in Jordan's unrepresentative electoral system.

All nongovernmental associations require approval from the government to operate. This gate-keeping function has allowed government officials to block formation of associations for political reasons. This was precisely the claim by Jordanian human rights activists in response to the continued government refusal to allow registration of the Jordan Citizen's Rights Association in 2004.[13] It does not appear that laws restrict foreign funding of nongovernmental organizations.

The Jordanian government and King Abdullah consistently proclaim commitment to press freedom and free speech. Indeed, independent-minded publications do emerge, such as *Al-Arab Al-Yawm* in 1998 and *Al-Ghad* in 2004, but within a few years informal and formal regime restrictions push them into line. In December 2003, the government ended its monopoly over broadcast media, allowing registration of private entities. However, rules for approval are vague and licensing fees quite high—even higher if the outlet wishes to have political content. Out of 14 radio stations licensed to broadcast, only 10 are currently on the air, and in 2005 only one FM station, AmmanNet, carried news and limited political content. In 2003, the government amended a 2001 temporary law that had allowed prosecution of media persons in state security courts; instead, trials would take place in civil courts. However, legislative approval is still pending.

In point of fact, Jordanian officials regularly impose both direct and indirect restrictions on press freedom. The state funds a number of media outlets, including prominent daily newspapers such as *Al-Rai*. Hence, the press engages in a great deal of self-censorship, particularly regarding information about the U.S. military in Jordan, relations with Israel, public corruption, or criticism of the monarchy. Human rights observers and journalists consistently report that GID officials intimidate editors and employ a network of informants among the press. For example, on September 19, 2005, GID officials stopped print runs of the weekly *Al-Wahda* as a means of censoring an article in that edition.[14]

Officials also take advantage of Jordan's vaguely worded penal code (Article 191) regarding "slander" and "defamation" of government officials (foreign and domestic) to jail journalists and writers. In 2004, security officials detained Fahd al-Rimawi, editor in chief of the private weekly *Al-Majd,* for a story about Jordanian military cooperation with the United States in Iraq.[16]

These laws are also used to discourage poetic expression. Poets Haider Mahmoud in early 2005 and Sameer Al-Qudah in 2004 were summoned by GID officials after publishing work that was viewed as criticizing the monarchy and public corruption.[17] In response to the unfavorable international reaction, King Abdullah issued decrees in April 2005 prohibiting the arrest and detention of journalists. However, just four months later in a national address he warned: "We should refrain from joining these newspapers in promoting whatever rumors, accusations, and slander they circulate."[18] The implication is that there are a number of ways to curb press freedom short of physical detention. To whit, a new survey of journalists in 2005 revealed the use of 12 additional means including official and unofficial threats, summons by security agencies, suspension from work, arbitrary transfer, and bodily harm.[19]

The National Agenda is also reported to be considering media reforms. Among the recommendations to surface is an end to mandatory membership in the Jordanian Press Association for all journalists. International human rights organizations have praised the recommendation as supporting worker freedom and choice.[20] Journalists in Amman protested the idea as threatening their collective action by weakening the association.[21]

In regional comparison, Jordanians' access to the internet is relatively free. All internet service providers, however, are routed through government firms. Censorship does occur, especially regarding news sites. As of 2004, at least two outside news sites were banned within Jordan, and one domestic news site has been harassed.[22]

Recommendations

- The Hashemite monarchy should initiate a political process to detach itself from all executive power and place the institution and its individuals under the law within a constitutional framework. Such a process would entail a number of sizable reforms, but simple announcement of the intent to constitutionalize the monarchy would represent the foundation for the ability of Jordanians to become citizens and not subjects.

- The Government Intelligence Directorate should be expressly barred from involvement in domestic political issues, and past offenses by its officials should be brought to public light.
- Reforms considered under the National Agenda need to abolish the current voting system in favor of a proportional or mixed voting system. An independent and transparent electoral commission should be established.
- The government should remove itself from the media by liquidating or privatizing its holdings in those firms.
- Penal code laws that allow prosecution of speech acts should be revoked. Intimidation and censorship of the media should be criminalized.

CIVIL LIBERTIES – 3.12

Jordan's constitution and penal code expressly outlaw torture, detention without trial, and arbitrary arrest. In practice, however, state enforcement has been weak and citizen complaints of mistreatment by state officials rarely prosecuted. Human rights observers and opposition leaders consistently highlight patterns of violations of individual rights. While the penal code calls for prosecutorial notification within 24 hours after a suspect's arrest and the filing of formal charges within 14 days, delays and extensions can significantly postpone trials and lengthen pretrial imprisonment.

Reports of torture and extralegal detention are common, particularly in connection with the government's support for Washington's "war on terrorism." International human rights organizations have documented the testimony of several Jordanian citizens arrested abroad and in-country who accuse GID officials of beatings, sexual violations, and psychological torture.[23] There is no accountability for torture perpetrators. It is widely assumed that Jordan is one center for the U.S. rendition program, a program in which U.S. authorities covertly turn individuals over to foreign governments for interrogation that likely involves torture. Additionally, Jordan is reported to be the location for a detention and interrogation center run by Central Intelligence Agency officials.[24] Though the existence of these highly classified American centers has been detailed through investigative reporting in the United States,[25] Jordanian officials pointedly denied their involvement in October 2004.[26] For 2004, the country's NCHR reported that it received 56 complaints of torture in the period from June 2003 to December 31, 2004. In its 2005 report, the NCHR stated that it received 54 similar complaints.

NCHR was established by royal decree in December 2002, but its independence and power to pursue violations are highly suspect. The head of the NCHR is former prime minister Ahmed Obeidat, who prior to becoming prime minister in the 1980s was the long-time head of the GID, the state agency most associated with rights violations and de-liberalization. Of the 56 torture complaints in 2004, the center report-edly closed only 10 cases with "satisfactory results."[27] The 2005 report was less specific, stating only that security officials had adopted specific measures in 74 percent "of the beating complaints." The most notable and positive aspect of the NCHR's first report was its investigation into conditions at nine of the country's prisons. Although investigators in 2004 were not allowed to visit facilities run by the GID or the military, findings on the prisons that were visited highlighted inmate over-crowding, complaints of torture by guards, and "the lack of judicial monitoring of prisons and detention facilities." In 2005, the NCHR was allowed to tour a GID detention facility and a military run Reform and Rehabilitation Center, yet the representative nature of these sites was unclear as was the status of prisoners interviewed.

In the last several years, women's rights have shown signs of formal advancement in some areas (appointment of women to prominent gov-ernment offices and fulfillment of the quota for Parliament), yet disap-pointing implementation in other areas (honor killings and employment). Women do not have full equality under the law, and where laws stipulate equal treatment (in pay, for instance), enforcement is rare. Female em-ployment has generally been concentrated in the civil service, but in the last several years, government officials have funded programs to encour-age greater female employment in private garment industries operating in the country's Qualifying Industrial Zones (QIZ). Zone managers and government officials contend that these factories succeed in employing and training rural women, a demographic traditionally lacking extra-household income. Labor activists and studies have criticized some of the factory working conditions and questioned the high percentage of foreign workers.[28] The NCHR conducted its own survey in 2005 and found QIZ working conditions below acceptable standards in terms of health, safety, environment, and wages. Government officials have responded with anecdotal evidence of fair practices, but as yet no systematic information about the conditions of QIZ employment or the benefits to female employment has appeared.

The government has also failed to follow up regarding the issue of honor killings, a crime in which a male family member kills a female member for perceived harm to family honor. Often perpetrators are able to go free by exploiting loopholes in the penal code. Reliable government data on violence against women is scarce. A little-known government agency, the Department of Family Protection, affiliated with the GID, released a 2005 study indicating that between 1998 and 2005, 1,761 crimes were reported against women, including rape, kidnapping, and honor killings.[29] The National Institute for Forensic Medicine reported in 2004 that in Amman alone, 750 women a year visit their medical clinics suffering from the effects of domestic violence. According to human rights reports, 17 women were victims of honor crimes in 2003 and 22 in 2002. In cases of abuse and death, activists believe the real numbers are higher. Police officials commonly employ the tactic of jailing potential victims of honor crimes for protection.

The government announced in September 2004 its intent to create women's shelters in 2005, but it was unclear if potential victims of honor killings would be welcome. Activists have praised the king and queen for their roles in championing reform in this area, yet since 2002, progress has halted. Among the temporary laws passed between 2001 and 2003 were two important revisions: the loophole was closed in Article 340 (though Article 98 has been used similarly) of the penal code that had allowed perpetrators of honor killings to go free, and the Personal Status Law was passed, giving women the right to divorce and the right to monetary compensation. Parliament has yet to take up the revisions to the penal code, and in June 2004, the Lower House rejected the proposed personal status law. Given the monarchy's previous vocal support for the new law and the rights of women, the lack of executive action or government response puzzled observers. In contrast, in the same session of Parliament, after deputies amended a law to stop all cooperation with Israeli human rights groups, the government swiftly forced a re-vote that killed the amendment.

Women have the right to vote. In the 2003 elections, 54 female candidates competed, yet owing to the electoral rules, none of the six reserved seats were filled by women from the largest urban area, Amman. Four of the six won in the more progovernment southern parts of the country,[30] and the largest vote-getter proved to be the Islamic Action Front's first elected female to Parliament.[31] Meanwhile, Jordan's first ever elected female parliamentarian, Tojan al-Faysal, was convicted in 2003 of slandering the prime minister (she published a letter criticizing some of the temporary laws). Although her prison sentence was suspended by the king after a month, the conviction in state court made al-Faysal ineligible to run for public office.

The status of children from the marriage of a Jordanian woman to a foreign man remains unresolved. There are an estimated 40,000 to 150,000 such marriages. Children born in these marriages are unable to receive Jordanian citizenship. Increasingly, the non-Jordanian spouse is simply deported.[32] In June 2004, it was reported that the government was considering several amendments to these laws, including allowing all children born to Jordanians (male and female) to be considered citizens wherever they are born (a positive step forward if passed) as well as less positive amendments in which children from marriages involving Palestinians would not be granted citizenship.[33] Inheritance laws still favor males.

Although accurate census data is lacking, it is generally believed that Jordanians of Palestinian origin are a majority, based mainly in urban areas in the middle and northern parts of the country. In September 1970, King Hussein and Jordanians loyal to the monarchy prevailed in a short but bloody civil war with Yasser Arafat's PLO commandos. Thus, the Palestinian–East Bank divide is an important yet complex issue in Jordanian society and politics. Jordanians of Palestinian origin are not a monolithic group but have traditionally been identified with various forms of political opposition. Supporters of the monarchy and the rank and file of the security forces are generally East Bank tribes and elites. As a result, Palestinians are discriminated against in government employment.

Sunni Muslims comprise 92 percent of the population, with smaller percentages of Christians, Druze, Shia Muslims, and Baha'is. The constitution establishes Islam as the state religion but provides for freedom of worship. Complaints of government interference in minority religious affairs are rare. However, the Ministry of Religious Affairs oversees and controls all of the country's Islamic institutions. Imams and their sermons are monitored, and unapproved political commentary is punishable. In September 2004, local government officials detained several imams for giving Friday sermons without prior approval.[34] Human Rights Watch reported that since the beginning of 2004, about 40 imams have been barred from preaching.

The Jordanian constitution says little about the rights of disabled persons. Since the 1990s there have been laws for the protection of disabled persons and a national registry; however, these initiatives either diverge from World Health Organization standards or are simply not implemented. Nationally, there are just two public facilities for sheltering the mentally disabled, and in 2005 only 253 out of 1,073 applications for exempting customs duties on car purchases for the disabled were approved.[35]

Government authorities have severely curtailed the right to assemble and associate. The weakness of political parties and political representation has led Jordanians to turn to their 13 professional associations (or syndicates, al-niqabat)—with more than 130,000 members in fields such as law, engineering, and medicine, but excluding business associations—as avenues of political expression. Membership in these professional associations is mandatory for practice in one's given field. Labor unions (limited to 17) are controlled by the Ministry of Labor, and public sector employees and teachers are not permitted to organize. Mandatory membership is controversial. Union and association leaders (domestic and international) argue obligatory membership is the only means to guarantee a profession's collective action capacities (membership density and financial resources from dues). International human rights agencies tend to argue that obligatory membership restricts individual choice.

Indeed, since the 1990s government officials have sought a number of ways to weaken associational autonomy and independence of expression. In 2004 and 2005, Interior Minister Samir Habashneh launched a campaign to vilify the activities of all 13 syndicates as political and anti-Jordanian. He demanded the associations "completely halt" all activities deemed political. The governor of Amman followed by announcing that "any kind of event, gathering or meeting, save for weddings, should obtain prior approval."[36] In December 2004, Ali Hattar, a member of the Jordanian Engineers Association, gave a speech at the Professional Associations headquarters in Amman entitled, "Why we boycott America." Hattar was subsequently detained by security officials, charged with slandering government officials, and ultimately fined for his speech.[37]

In March 2005, the prime minister presented a controversial draft law for the professional associations. Among the draft's provisions were rules allowing government oversight of association elections, a banning of political activities, pre-approval from the Interior Ministry for any public gathering, and creation of disciplinary committees to punish members. Leaders of the associations supported by opposition activists universally rejected the changes proposed in the draft law for professional associations as well as those in a draft law on political parties— the provisions of which would criminalize any coordination among professional associations, political parties, human rights groups, and mosques. Association members peacefully attempted to protest the proposals. On four occasions, security officials physically intimidated protesters, shut down sit-ins, and even tore down posters at the associations' headquarters.[38] Consequently, a majority of Jordanians believe that the right to demonstrate and protest is not guaranteed.[39] Further standoffs were avoided with the replacement of Al-Fayez's government with Adnan Badran in April 2005. The draft laws are still pending.

Recommendations

- The Jordanian government should respond to accusations of torture with transparency. International human rights groups should receive access to prison facilities. Accusations of torture should be publicly adjudicated in civilian courts of law.
- The recently created National Human Rights Center should be detached from its connection to the government in all respects. An independent NCHR could then investigate abuses impartially.
- Legislation pertaining to the Personal Status Law should be reintroduced to the Lower House for approval. All loopholes in the penal code that allow perpetrators of honor killings to claim self-defense or fits of passion need to be closed.
- The state's repression of civil society, especially the country's professional associations, should end. Laws and regulations that control freedom of association and the rights of professional associations to expression should be revoked. Associations and the government

should enter a national dialogue to establish new legal parameters for the relationship between the state and associations, including the issues of mandatory membership and the extent of state involvement in associational activities.

RULE OF LAW – 3.12

Jordan has three court types: civil courts, which adjudicate civil and criminal cases; Sharia and other religious courts, which adjudicate personal status and family issues; and the state security court, which in theory rules only on threats to national security (which include defamation of the monarchy, drug trafficking, armed insurrection, and financial crimes).

The security court was established in 1991 after the end of martial law. Though state authorities have avoided a return to formal martial law, the judicial mechanisms of martial law and their repressive effects have been reintroduced through the increased use of the security court and the manipulation of civilian courts. The security court is comprised of a three-judge panel, whose members can be military or civilian and are appointed by the prime minister. The acceptance of testimony under duress, limited pretrial access to a lawyer, and the secret military character of the security court intimidate defendants and compromise judicial independence.[40]

The security court is a key element in Jordan's de-liberalization as it has been used to supplant and bypass civil courts to punish journalists and opposition figures on misdemeanor charges. Two examples are prominent. First, in December 2004, Jamil Abu Bakr, a member of the IAF and editor of its website, published criticisms of favoritism and corruption by public officials. He was subsequently charged with slandering public officials under the vague wording of the penal code. In early 2005, a civilian court dismissed these charges. In early 2006, however, prosecutors at the security court charged Abu Bakr with "belittling the dignity of the Jordanian state."[41] The NCHR's 2005 report suggested this pattern of extrajudicial punishment was regularized with 513 persons reportedly detained by security officials.[42] Second, a part of the civilian appeals court, the Court of Cassation, has ruled that the state security court cannot issue death sentences based solely on confessions under duress. Human rights observers argue this ruling is often ignored by the security courts. In particular, two men convicted for involvement in the killing of an American diplomat in 2002 received death sentences from the security court despite claims that their confessions were products of torture. In January 2005, the security court upheld the death penalties despite appeals to the Court of Cassation.[43]

In addition to interference, the autonomous operation of civil courts is impaired by internal factors. The Higher Judicial Council is tasked with the appointment and transfer of judges. However, the council, which consists of judges and senior ministry officials, greatly lacks independence and is accountable to the king, not Parliament. Judicial appointments are consistently criticized as reflecting particularistic interests, not professional merit or judicial philosophy.

Defendants are presumed innocent until proven guilty and have the right to counsel. The state provides counsel for defendants in capital cases. Though Article 100 of the Law of Penal Procedures stipulates that a defendant be given judicial review after 24 hours of arrest, the NCHR's 2004 report estimated that more than 5,000 individuals were held beyond this period in 2004. The 2005 report concluded that there has been no progress on curbing these violations. In addition, defendants are often denied timely access to legal counsel. The length of trials and delays are common complaints, along with denial of counsel during interrogation.

Increasing court costs are of concern, as it was argued in the NCHR's report that many citizens do not avail themselves of judicial avenues because of the cost. Strict guidelines on fines and sentencing and the lack of judicial independence are blamed for the inability of judges to show flexibility in reducing fees or streamlining court procedures to fit circumstances.[44] Reports that the Higher Judicial Council adopted a code of ethics in late 2005 to address some of these issues may improve the situation. However, absent a capable bureaucratic agency to implement and investigate the new guidelines, observers believe the reforms will falter. Beyond these anticipated reforms, there appears to be no centralized effort to ensure the training or qualifications of judges to carry out justice. The increasing use of the security court and the continued control of the executive over the appointments of judges have resulted in widely varying levels of judicial competency and skill at the local level. High-ranking government officials are rarely prosecuted for wrongdoing, and there were no major cases in 2004 and 2005.

The principal intelligence and security arm of the government, the GID, is not under civilian control but reports directly to the king.

Observers in and out of Jordan agree that the GID and affiliated military/ security agencies regularly violate human rights. The GID operates both internationally and domestically, maintains a number of secret detention facilities outside public scrutiny, and is generally judged to be one of the government's largest bureaucracies. The sole event in which a high-ranking GID official was held accountable for his actions was the July 2003 conviction (by the state security court) of former GID head Samih Batikhi on fraud and embezzlement charges. This was the first time a head of the GID was put on trial, but observers suggested that Batikhi's crimes were much more extensive and politically sensitive than those for which he was convicted. Moreover, the lack of investigations or indictments since suggests the Batikhi trial was extraordinary and not likely to be repeated.

In May 2005, King Abdullah named General Samih Asfura, a long-time assistant to Batikhi, to head the agency. The king also created a new National Security Agency, but its functions are unknown.[45] In the wake of the November 2005 bombings, dissidents and opposition figures expressed fear that the interference of the GID in domestic political issues would continue to expand. In particular, the role of the GID in manipulating and intimidating the political opposition and civil associations is expected to increase. Also, given the power and independence of GID officials, speculation has increased in the private sector community that some officials operate businesses that profit from public works contracts and trade monopolies.

Jordan has long identified itself as a free market economy. Private property rights are guaranteed in the constitution, and public expropriations are rare. Still, land wealth and political patronage have historically been closely related in Jordan. In the last several years, significant real estate booms and property speculations have occurred in Amman and the port city of Aqaba. At the same time, rumors have increased of royal land grabs by redefining state or municipal land as crown land.[46]

Recommendations

- The use of the State Security Court should be ended altogether. In all cases, testimony resulting from torture or intimidation should be expressly outlawed.
- The GID should be made accountable to elected officials, not to the monarchy.

- The Higher Judicial Council should be enhanced so that regular monitoring of judicial ethics and standards can take place. Greater transparency in the appointment of judges is needed through publication of lists of candidates under consideration and their qualifications.
- Judges should be given greater discretion in determining court fees and increasing the speed of trials.

ANTICORRUPTION AND TRANSPARENCY – 2.28

Corruption and patronage are integral elements of Jordan's monarchical system, not aberrations. The issue is not the presence of these informal mechanisms (which exist in all societies) but who controls them and what they are used for. Historically condemning corruption and patronage, the monarchy has long utilized private goods (land grants and jobs) and public monopolies (such as state-owned enterprises, protocol trade agreements, and public works) to reward political allies and punish rivals. Though public officials acknowledge the need to address corruption in order to attract foreign investment, the political rationale for corruption is likely stronger.

In 2005 the Council of Ministers completed a draft anticorruption law that would include formation of an anticorruption committee.[47] The level of the committee's independence and powers was not clear, and the law has not been submitted to Parliament for approval. Despite the perception of Jordan as a free market system (among Arab states, Jordan ranked fourth in terms of economic freedom in the Heritage Foundation's 2005 index),[48] the Jordanian economy is defined by extensive state involvement yet weak regulation. State-controlled shareholding companies combined with the government employ roughly 50 percent of Jordan's labor force.

The state's budget relies heavily on external revenue in the forms of foreign economic and military aid, government-owned mineral exports, and oil trade agreements. It is difficult to provide an accurate measurement of these resources as not all forms of aid (particularly military and security) are reported, and revenue/expenditure statistics are highly suspect. By the government's own calculation for the 2005 budget, foreign aid accounted for 15 percent of gross domestic product. It is not known, for instance, how much revenue the Jordanian government earns from its sale of oil (provided by Kuwait and Saudi Arabia at preferential prices), a curious omission given that Central Bank statistics released in 2004 show Jordanian export of oil products increased 46 times from 2002 to 2003.[49] The political weight of this issue is clear, given that while the Jordanian government is exporting oil products, its citizens have had to absorb significant increases in the price of domestic gas since 2004.

There is little transparency in how such externally derived resources are spent. It is not known how much foreign aid, specifically U.S. financial assistance, has been spent on the GID or whether those funds support the agency's role in domestic abuse and denial of rights.[50] Public access to government budgets and expenditures is correspondingly low. Formal presentation of the budget through Parliament offers only a limited view. On the one hand, the information-gathering capacities of the Jordanian government are underdeveloped, so that economic and budgetary data is uneven. In the late 1990s, for example, the Jordanian government twice misreported its gross domestic product to the World Bank. On the other hand, economic and budgetary information that is deemed politically sensitive is manipulated. For example, as of 2005 the government would report the number of businesses that opened in a given year, but not the number that failed.

Measuring direct foreign investment (FDI) is likewise manipulated with the pledged investment reported as FDI rather than actual investment. Since the late 1990s, Jordan's tax system has been undergoing fitful reform to increase tax collection through a national sales tax. Parliamentary efforts to craft a direct income tax faltered in 2004 and 2005. Effective internal tax auditing lags as does uniform implementation of the sales tax. In higher education, it is widely believed that bribery and personal connections are used to secure entrance, guarantee better grades, and win scholarships. Given that some of the violence in the 1990s and 2000 took place on university campuses, it is also believed that the GID has increased its presence at universities.

The process and selection of awarding public work contracts and private-public initiatives is determined less by merit and more by ascriptive concerns (East Bank versus Palestinian) and political necessities. In an act of rare public criticism, outgoing U.S. Ambassador to Jordan, Edward Gnehm, said in a June 2004 speech before American and Jordanian businesspersons: "We also continue to press for full transparency in the awarding of government contracts. . . . We must all work together to ensure that fairness and openness in contracting and procurement is pre-eminent."[51] While a centralized tenders office exists and tenders are publicized, the process of deliberation and criteria lacks transparency.

The sale and privatization of government assets, a program first introduced in the mid-1980s, likewise lacks transparency. There is a Higher Privatization Council, but since public investment can be held by different ministries, the process of privatizing a given enterprise is decentralized and without transparency. Just as political necessity to maintain power shapes electoral laws, what is privatized and who does the buying is driven not so much by economic goals or competition but by political necessity.

Bribery of public officials, while outlawed, is irregularly punished and quite difficult to track (kickbacks to a minister's family member, for example). When bribery charges are brought against public officials, the evidence remains secret, as was the case with former GID head Samih Batikhi. No major corruption trials took place in 2004 or 2005. The high turnover of ministry officials, combined with few regulations to prevent private-public conflicts of interest, means that public service regularly yields private gain. The Lower House of Parliament did complete a draft financial disclosures law, which would require high-ranking public servants to reveal their family assets (in a sealed document) prior to holding office. Unfortunately, Upper House consideration of the draft was tabled in 2004 and 2005.

Reports of public-private corruption are numerous. Some of the more prominent and sensitive issues involve the QIZ, particularly accusations of public corruption in the Aqaba Special Economic Zone; Jordan's oil supply agreements (first with preinvasion Iraq and now with Kuwait and Saudi Arabia) in which the Jordanian sale of the oil goes to private accounts of government ministers; misappropriation of funds in the Ministry of Religious Affairs; and the growing economic roles of GID officials and their family members.

As with other reform issues, King Abdullah has consistently spoken out against corruption. A number of economic committees and reform agendas have followed his edicts. One of the first efforts was the creation in 2000 of the Economic Consultative Council (ECC), staffed with private sector representatives and chaired by the king. Tasked with charting economic reform and tackling corruption, the ECC eventually fell out of public favor amid reports of committee members' benefiting from public contracts and monopolies.[52] The fate of the ECC is emblematic of a larger problem: the lack of a centralized auditor independent from the very subjects of investigation.

Most ministries maintain their own anticorruption units, resulting in narrow purviews and little bureaucratic incentive to investigate seriously. In 2003, the prime minister announced the creation of another anticorruption unit to operate out of the GID. Given the role of the GID in previous corruption scandals and the highly political character of corruption, it is no surprise that major corruption indictments were absent in 2004 and 2005. Additionally, there remains no legal protection for whistle-blowers.

Recommendations

- A comprehensive and enforceable financial disclosure law should be acted on by the Upper House.
- Ministry-level anticorruption offices, especially the recent unit created within the GID, need to be centralized under an independent public accounting office.
- The government's annual revenue and expenditure data should be standardized and made more transparent. In particular, all forms and applications of foreign aid assistance should be made public.
- Wide-ranging reform and disclosure is needed in how public works contracts are awarded as well as the process of privatizing public entities.

NOTES

1 *Democracy in Jordan* (Amman: University of Jordan, Center for Strategic Studies [CSS], 2005).

2 Alfred B. Prados, "Jordan: US Relations and Bilateral Issues" (Washington, D.C.: U.S. Congress, Congressional Research Report, 19 May 2005), 16.

3 "Justice for All: The Struggle for Workers Rights in Jordan" (Washington, D.C.: American Center for International Labor Solidarity), 48–50.

4 "Jordan: Post-Program Monitoring Discussion," IMF Country Reports No. 05/100, March 2005, p. 11.

5 Marwan A. Kardoosh, "Jordan's Economy from a Western Perspective," *Daily Star* (Beirut), 26 November 2002.

6 "The Challenge of Political Reform: Jordanian Democratisation and Regional Instability" (Brussels: International Crisis Group [ICG], Middle East Briefing No. 10, 8 October 2003).

7 "Status Report of Human Rights, The Hashemite Kingdom of Jordan, 2005," (Amman: The National Centre for Human Rights [NCHR], 2005), p. 5.

8 Curtis R. Ryan and Jillian Schwedler, "Return to Democratization or New Hybrid Regime?: The 2003 Elections in Jordan," *Middle East Policy* XI, 2 (Summer 2004): 143.

9 Neil MacFarquhar, "Heavy Hand of the Secret Police Impeding Reform in the Arab World," *The New York Times,* 14 November 2005.

10 "Status Report of Human Rights, The Hashemite Kingdom of Jordan, 2005," (Amman: The National Centre for Human Rights [NCHR], 2005), p. 29.

11 Schirin Fathi, "Jordanian Survival Strategy: The Election Law as a Safety Valve," *Middle Eastern Studies* 41, 6 (November 2005): 892.

12 Admad Barakat, "Thirteen Recommendations on Elections Law Forwarded to the King," *Jordan Times,* 4 October 2005.

13 "Jordan's Rights Activists Seek King's Help," United Press International, 8 May 2005.

14 "Overview of Human Rights Issues in Jordan," Human Rights Watch, 18 January 2006.

15 "Jordan: Slander Charge Signals Chill" (New York: Human Rights Watch, 23 December 2003).

16 *Annual Jordan Report, 2004* (CPJ).

17 Stephen Glain, "Letter from Jordan," *The Nation,* 30 May 2005; MacFarquhar, "Heavy Hand."

18 Speech full text: http://www.kingabdullah.jo/main.php?main_page=0&lang_hmka1=1.

19 "Status Report of Human Rights, The Hashemite Kingdom of Jordan, 2005" (Amman: The National Centre for Human Rights [NCHR], 2005), p. 26.

20 "Jordan: Reform Proposal Would Expand Press Freedom" (HRW, 23 November 2005).

21 Barakat, "Thirteen recommendations."

22 "Internet Under Surveillance Reports Online 2004" (Paris: Reporters Without Borders [RSF], 2004.

23 "Jordan Report" (London: Amnesty International [AI], 2004 and 2005).

24 "USA/Jordan/Yemen: Secret Detention Centers," Amnesty International Press Release, August 4, 2005.

25 James Risen, *State of War: The Secret History of the CIA and the Bush Administration* (New York: Free Press, 2006), pp.30–31.

26 "Jordan," Amnesty International Annual Report, 2005.

27 "State of Human Rights in Jordan 2004" (Amman: The National Centre for Human Rights [NCHR], 2004 http://www.nchr.org.jo/pages.php?menu_id=20&local_type=0&local_id=0&local_details=0&local_details1=0&localsite_branchname=NCHR#annex1

28 "The Struggle for Workers Rights in Jordan," pp. 40–41.

29 "Women's Rights Violations Rise in Jordan," United Press International, 21 June 2005.

30 Fathi, "Jordanian Survival Strategy: The Election Law as a Safety Valve," 896.

31 Ryan and Schwedler, "Return to Democratization . . . ?," 146.

32 "Status Report of Human Rights, The Hashemite Kingdom of Jordan, 2005," (Amman: NCHR, 2005), pp. 22–23.

33 Jumana Tamimi, "Jordanian Women Married to Foreigners Still Wait for nationality Rights," Agence France Presse, July 7, 2004.

34 "State of Human Rights in Jordan 2004" (NCHR).

35 "Status Report of Human Rights, The Hashemite Kingdom of Jordan, 2005," (Amman: NCHR, 2005), pp. 56–57.

36 Shadi Hamid, "Jordan: Democracy at a Dead End," *Arab Reform Bulletin* (Washington, D.C.: Carnegie Endowment for International Peace, May 2005).

37 "HRW Concerns Regarding Jordan's Draft Law on Professional Associations" (HRW, 30 March 2005).

38 Glain, "Letter from Jordan."

39 *Democracy in Jordan* (CSS).

40 "Jordan: Attacks on Justice 2000," International Commission of Jurists, http://www.icj .org/news.php3?id_article=2577&lang=en

41 "Jordan: Editor Prosecuted for Posting Articles by MPs," HRW, January 26, 2006.

42 "Status Report of Human Rights, The Hashemite Kingdom of Jordan, 2005," (Amman: NCHR, 2005), p. 10.

43 "Jordan: Stop Executions and Investigate all Allegations of Torture Made by Detainees," AI, 14 March 2006.

44 "State of Human Rights in Jordan 2004" (NCHR).

45 "Jordan Gets New Intelligence Chief," *Al-Jazeera.net,* 5 May 2005. http://english.aljazeera .net/NR/exeres/872BA63F-E2BB-4E56-AA3A-D340E73FD8D1.htm

46 Glain, "Letter from Jordan."

47 "Status Report of Human Rights, The Hashemite Kingdom of Jordan, 2005," (Amman: NCHR, 2005), p. 21.

48 *2005 Index of Economic Freedom* (Washington, D.C./New York: Heritage Foundation/ *Wall Street Journal,* 2005.

49 *The Monthly Statistical Bulletin,* Central Bank of Jordan, May 2004.

50 Silverstein, "US-Jordan."

51 "US-Jordanian Economic Relations," Embassy of the United States, Amman, Jordan, July 30, 2004.

52 Oliver Schlumberger and Andre Bank, "Succession, Legitimacy, and Regime Stability in Jordan," *Arab Studies Journal* (Fall 2001/Spring 2002).

KAZAKHSTAN

CAPITAL: Astana

POPULATION: 15.1 million

GNI PER CAPITA: $1,780

SCORES	2004	2006
ACCOUNTABILITY AND PUBLIC VOICE:	1.94	2.51
CIVIL LIBERTIES:	3.61	4.01
RULE OF LAW:	1.90	2.62
ANTICORRUPTION AND TRANSPARENCY:	1.58	2.04

(scores are based on a scale of 0 to 7, with 0 representing weakest and 7 representing strongest performance)

Martha Brill Olcott

INTRODUCTION

Kazakhstan's constitution provides for a highly centralized political system with a strong president who dominates the executive branch, shapes the judiciary, and influences the legislature. The political system is largely the creation of one man, Nursultan Nazarbayev, who first assumed power as Kazakhstan's Communist Party leader in 1989 and one year later became the country's president. He has held the post ever since, modifying the constitution in 1998 to enable himself to serve two additional seven-year terms.

Nazarbayev has often urged that Kazakhstan be viewed as a bridge between Asia and Europe. Politically, though, the leadership in Kazakhstan has been unwilling to commit to European norms for democratic governance. For example, the country has signed and ratified the International Covenant on Civil and Political Rights (ICCPR), but has yet to abide by the treaty's obligations. Kazakhstan is not a member of the Council of Europe, so it is neither bound by the European Convention on Human Rights nor subject to the jurisdiction of the European Court of Human Rights in Strasbourg.

Even more tellingly, Kazakhstan has campaigned hard for the 2009 chairmanship of the Organization for Security and Cooperation in

---

Dr. Martha Brill Olcott is a Senior Associate at the Carnegie Endowment for International Peace, and most recently author of *Central Asia's Second Chance.*

Europe (OSCE), which will be awarded in 2006, but it has been willing to accept only limited OSCE guidance in reforming its legal and electoral systems. Consequently, Kazakhstan has yet to hold a major election that has met OSCE norms of freedom and fairness. Moreover, the state's media and nongovernmental organizations (NGOs) lack the legal protection expected in leading OSCE nations. Kazakhstan will, however, be one of the top ten oil and gas producers within a decade, and it seems as if President Nazarbayev believes the country's economic potential is sufficient to ensure its prominent place in the international community.

Kazakhstan has been Central Asia's strongest economic performer and one of the strongest performers of any of the Soviet successor states (excluding the three Baltic countries). Fueled by unexpectedly high oil prices, Kazakhstan's gross domestic product (GDP) reached $40.7 billion in 2004, with the World Bank projecting 8.2 percent annual growth for 2004 to 2008. The country has a favorable balance of trade; fuel and oil products made up just over half the country's total exports in 2004.[1] The Kazakh government has an ambitious program, outlined by President Nazarbayev in his 1998 "Kazakhstan—2030" address and in a February 2005 message to the population, to develop other sectors of the economy over the next quarter century.[2] But it is far from clear that the government will have the skill and discipline necessary to translate these rather vague goals into well-executed policies.

Kazakhstan's small and medium enterprises are flourishing, but economic transparency is a major problem among the country's partially privatized large enterprises, which the government continues to favor disproportionately. Pervasive corruption and a weak judiciary have further slowed the country's growth and hampered investment, both domestic and foreign.

Despite these problems, some sectors have done very well in the transition period. Kazakhstan, for instance, has a strong banking sector, especially given how recently it was established. The country's principal banks all have international investment grade ratings and growing personal loan sectors, which cover both housing and auto loans. The country also has a National Fund, modeled after the Norwegian national oil fund, to invest a share of oil and other extractive industry income. It will grow to well over ten billion dollars in the next decade.[3] The fund is intended to help the government cope with cyclical trends in the value of exported resources and should help mitigate some of the negative impact of continuing corruption in the extractive sectors.

Corruption notwithstanding, the government of Kazakhstan has done a comparatively good job of helping its citizens meet their basic human needs while simultaneously adapting its pension, education, and health-care systems to market conditions. The key objective of the Nazarbayev regime in working to achieve this result has been to prevent a "color" revolution. To this end, the regime has sought to channel public political activity in ways that strengthen the control of existing power holders while preserving the semblance of regime accountability. However, the regime has also sought to increase its popularity by addressing or making a show of addressing the bread-and-butter issues with which most Kazakhs are concerned, such as salaries, pensions, education, and health care.

ACCOUNTABILITY AND PUBLIC VOICE – 2.51

Despite some minor improvements, elections in Kazakhstan fall short of OSCE norms. Opposition political groups continue to experience difficulty in registration, both as movements and as political parties, and the leadership and their families have been victims of more than a typical share of "random" violence. In early 2005, a split in the opposition party, Ak Zhol, led to the formation of Naghuz (the true) Ak Zhol, which failed to gain registration as a political party. Another opposition party, Democratic Choice of Kazakhstan (DVK), was ordered to disband in December 2004, formally because it breached the country's national security laws, but effectively because it was so critical of the president and the government. In January 2005, implementation of this decision led to a public protest during which seven party leaders were arrested for holding the unsanctioned demonstration and fined or sentenced to short prison terms.

Election administration in Kazakhstan is transparent but biased and flawed. The country has a four-tiered system of election commissions: one national, 16 regional, 204 district, and 9,580 precinct. Each has seven members, who serve five-year terms. The Majlis selects members of the national commission based on nominations by the president. Local Maslikhats (councils) select the members of local commissions based on nominations by political parties. Some 55 percent of precinct election commission members work directly for the state or for state enterprises.

The legislative elections for 77 seats in the Majlis (lower house)—67 seats in single-mandate districts and ten seats chosen from party lists—took place in September 2004 with the propresidential parties winning nearly every seat. Otan (Fatherland) took 42 seats, the Agrarian-Industrial Union of Workers took 11, Dariga Nazarbayeva's Asar took four, and the Democratic Party of Kazakhstan took one. Opposition Ak Zhol won one seat, but the candidate refused to accept it, protesting the conduct of the elections. The remaining 18 seats went to independent candidates, but most of these were de facto affiliated with Otan.[4]

The OSCE/ODIHR election mission strongly criticized the Central Election Commission (CEC) for their actual conduct of the election, including some very confusing last-minute instructions regarding the country's experimental electronic voting system. The nonrepresentative makeup of local election commissions and their actions were also condemned. The results were tabulated with little transparency and much room for alterations.[5] In fact, the process was so flawed that only a small observation team was sent to the second round, which was held on October 3.

The OSCE report praised the initial registration of parties and candidates but remarked that subsequent de-registrations were politically motivated. In most cases de-registered candidates received notice of the CEC's decision only after the legal deadline for reinstatement had already expired. The report also criticized the CEC and local election commissions for their handling of voter lists, which created the opportunity for widespread fraud. According to the OSCE, opposition parties faced "a pattern of interference" during the campaign. Police detained opposition activists, and the CEC attempted to pull opposition advertisements from television just before the election. The decisions of local officials consistently favored propresidential parties.[6]

The opposition tried to raise public ire over the results of the parliamentary poll but was unsuccessful, arguably due to public apathy and improving living conditions in the country's most important and populous cities. In November 2004, the opposition began a petition campaign to call for a referendum to invalidate the results of the election, but the CEC denied registration for the campaign and the Constitutional Council upheld this decision.

On December 4, 2005, Nursultan Nazarbayev was reelected president of Kazakhstan with 91 percent of the vote.[7] Zharmakhan Tuyakbai, head of the For a Just Kazakhstan movement finished second at 6.6 percent.[8] An International Republican Institute (IRI) exit poll had predicted 83.2 percent for Nazarbayev and 9.9 percent for Tuyakbai.[9] The OSCE concluded that the 2005 ballot "did not meet a number of OSCE commitments and other international standards for democratic elections."[10] Problems included: bans on public demonstrations during the election period; restrictions on opposition candidates' campaign events; harassment and, in some cases, beating of opposition activists; use of legislative restrictions to limit press criticism of the incumbent president, resulting in the confiscation of newspapers on three occasions; and underrepresentation of opposition parties on election commissions.[11] These criticisms notwithstanding, OSCE cited several positive developments, including a live, televised debate between the country's principal candidates. President Nazarbayev did not participate in the debate, however. The CEC, which met in regular open session, took steps to improve the election process and promote voter education. Lower-level electoral commissions also improved their performance, and voter lists were somewhat more accurate than they had been in 2004.[12]

Nazarbayev's use of administrative resources dominated the campaign from its beginning on October 25, 2005. While the president did not officially campaign, he dominated media coverage and billboards throughout the country. Meanwhile, private companies and local officials told opposition candidates that there was no advertising space available, presumably as a result of government pressure. The Tuyakbai campaign complained that out of 51 requests for public meetings only 5 were granted. Nazarbayev's team was quick to find and report violations by other candidates, and courts sometimes imposed administrative penalties against them. In several cases the authorities intimidated opposition parties by videotaping their rallies.[13] The OSCE confirmed reports of Tuyakbai's campaign representatives being beaten. On the positive side of the ledger, formal complaints from two candidates resulted in the provision of larger venues for meetings, though these were usually situated far from city centers.[14]

The media environment similarly favored the incumbent, Nazarbayev. Tuyakbai's campaign complained to the CEC that three channels on TV had established restrictive requirements relating to the minimum length of paid spots and their placement. Under Kazakhstan's election law each candidate was guaranteed 15 minutes of free airtime on television and 10 on radio, plus two free articles in print media, during the campaign. State media largely met these obligations, but opposition candidates alleged they were required to modify the content of their segments and articles. More damaging were legal restrictions on freedom of expression and dissemination of information, which prevented the electorate from making fully informed choices.[15]

The media remain heavily influenced by the government and pro-regime interests, and it can be quite lucrative for journalists to agree to write pieces that support various political or economic interest groups. Very few media outlets in the country are economically viable without government support.

President Nazarbayev's family still has extensive media holdings through the Khabar network.[16] Independent media are subject to police harassment, especially when they violate legal and constitutional provisions against impugning the dignity of the president, thereby infringing Article 46 of the constitution. In October 2005, in the middle of the presidential election campaign, police seized 30,000 copies of an issue of the newspaper *Svoboda Slova* because it contained an article about the business activities of Nazarbayev's youngest daughter, Aliya. Just weeks before, in late September, editors of *Svoboda Slova, Epokha, apta.kz, Zhuma-Times,* and *Azat* held a hunger strike to protest the refusal of the Daur printing house to publish their newspapers. Daur relented three days later.

Systematic intimidation of opposition journalists has somewhat decreased; however, journalists suffer more than their share of street violence and traffic accidents, which have led to the death or injury of both progovernment and opposition journalists. The most suspicious incident of violence was against the editor of the provocative internet journal *Navigator,* Ashkat Sharipjanov. Sharipjanov was hit by a car while crossing a street late at night in July 2004 and died of his injuries. The incident occurred shortly after Sharipjanov had completed an interview with Zamanbek Nurkadilov, former mayor of Almaty. Nurkadilov had allegedly given Sharipjanov compromising material about Nazarbayev for publication. The material was never found on Sharipjanov's computer.[17] Nurkadilov died of what was ruled a suicide in November 2005, shortly before the date on which he had promised to release the same material.

In early 2004, Nazarbayev's government seemed intent to curtail press freedom even further. The president introduced a bill that would have given the state broad power to fire journalists or close opposition media outlets for insulting "the honor and dignity of a citizen, state organ, or other bodies."[18] Following criticism of the bill from the West and the Kazakh opposition, Nazarbayev sent it to the constitutional court for review. The court found the bill violated Kazakhstan's basic law, and Nazarbayev later vetoed it.[19]

At the moment, the regime seems content with existing means of press control and resigned to relatively uncontrolled internet journalism. Self-censorship remains a more serious problem than formal censorship, and both the progovernment and opposition press are very uneven with regard to their degree of professionalism; they are often more concerned with political advocacy than reporting, as understood in the Western context. Distribution networks for print media remain under heavy state control. Restrictions on defaming the honor of the president affect coverage of events within and outside the election cycle. Just before the election, some opposition newspapers disappeared along with some websites, and opposition websites such as Navigator have felt the need to move their operations out of the country.[20] The government applies little or no pressure on other forms of cultural expression. Music, art, and cinema, for example, all seem to be going through a revival.

Under strong international pressure, the government backed off legislation that would have severely limited the rights of independent nongovernmental groups when the Constitutional Council vetoed two laws on NGOs on August 23, 2005.[21] But the position of foreign-supported nongovernmental groups remains potentially precarious, particularly for those with explicitly political agendas. The prodemocracy youth group Kahar was raided by the police in October 2005, allegedly because they were receiving unreported foreign financing.[22] This raid was facilitated by changes in the law on national security passed in June 2005. There is also an implicit threat that the government may introduce restrictive legislation that would force the re-registration of NGOs under a more onerous registration process, and restrict foreign funding and participation.

Kazakhstan does have two very active international human rights groups, the Almaty Helsinki Committee (a member of the International Helsinki Federation for Human Rights) and the Kazakhstan International Bureau on Human Rights and Rule of Law. Their respective leaders, Ninel Fokina and Evgeny Zhovtis, are accepted figures in Kazakhstan's political landscape, able to meet foreigners at home and abroad fairly freely, but relegated to a marginal status in Kazakhstan.

Recommendations
- The government should provide enhanced legislative protection to ensure the freedom of nongovernmental organizations, including streamlined registration procedures. Timely legislation would allow these groups a meaningful role in national political debate in advance of the next national legislative cycle.
- The government should enact legislation that creates real legal protection of independent media, providing juridical protection for constitutional provisions.
- Kazakhstan should work to improve the electoral system. The central and local electoral commissions should be more balanced and diverse in their composition, and more attention should be given to the integrity of the vote-counting process.

CIVIL LIBERTIES – 4.01

Despite some reform efforts, the penal system in Kazakhstan falls short of offering conditions respectful of human dignity. Although Kazakhstan has a large per capita prison population, prisons are filled to just 61.9 percent of capacity.[23] This is a legacy of Kazakhstan's large Soviet-era prison system, which once housed inmates convicted of crimes committed throughout the USSR. The Kazakhs have long-term plans for building new facilities and modernizing old ones, but the complexity of the plans outstrips the capacity of the government to execute them. Some were developed as the result of a three-year project on prison reform, run in cooperation with the International Centre for Prison Studies of King's College London. This project also included a prison health program designed to help address the spread of tuberculosis, HIV/AIDS, and illegal drug use among Kazakhstan's prison population.[24] But conditions in the prisons remain harsh, and in October 2004, a Russian press report revealed that 15 prisoners in Taraz had sliced their stomachs to protest inhumane treatment by prison officials.[25]

The Kazakh government has not used torture or made frequent use of long-term detention as a tool of political control; however, pretrial detainees do account for 15.8 percent of the prison population. The question of torture in Kazakhstan has largely focused on the government's willingness to hand over people in custody who are at risk of torture in neighboring states. Kazakh behavior has been inconsistent, yielding to both Western and Russian, Uzbek, or Chinese influence on a case-by-case basis.

Kazakhstan's legal system offers little legal guarantee to political opponents of the ruling party that their peaceful protests will not result in arrest and detention. Leading opposition politicians remain targets of the regime. Bolat Abilov, a leader of For a Just Kazakhstan, was arrested for slander during the 2004 election campaign, which effectively disqualified him from running in the September 2004 elections.[26] Sergei Duvanov, who was arrested on rape charges after publishing compromising materials about President Nazarbayev's involvement in corruption, was released in January 2004 after serving one year of a three- and-a-half-year prison sentence.[27] The conviction, though, was not overturned. As of November 2005, Galymzhan Zhakiyanov is the country's only high-profile political prisoner. Zhakiyanov, the former governor of the northern Pavlodar region, became a prominent figure in Democratic Choice of Kazakhstan (DCK) in 2001. He attracted the support of entrepreneurs and staged a successful rally in Almaty. Alarmed by the DCK's gathering momentum, the Nazarbayev government cracked down on the group and its allies. Zhakiyanov and another important DCK politician, former energy minister Mukhtar Ablyazov, were arrested. While Zhakiyanov's arrest was clearly political, the corruption charges levied against him may well have had some substance. In recent years, Kazakh authorities have done little to improve protection of citizens from abuse by private and nonstate actors or to enhance their capacity to petition effectively for redress when their rights have been violated.

Women and ethnic minorities still encounter various degrees of discrimination, yet they remain reluctant to seek legal redress. Traditional cultural values continue to reinforce the perception of many women that they are not entitled to the same jobs as men, while members of ethnic minority communities remain nervous about putting forward claims because they believe the system is biased against them.

Women remain underrepresented in public life. There is only one woman in the cabinet, the minister of justice, and there are no female *akims* (governors). One of the president's daughters, Dariga Nazarbayeva, is the only female head of a political party. Women hold six of 67 single-mandate seats and three out of every 10 in the list system in the Majlis, the lower house of parliament; the latter figure reflects the government's effort to compensate for their underrepresentation and show its commitment to gender equality. Ethnic minorities are also underrepresented, although the country's largest minority, the Russians, remains very visible in public life. Only one current member of government, the minister of energy, and two akims are ethnic Russians. The chairman of the Constitutional Council is also ethnic Russian.[29]

In recent years, Kazakhstan has made some progressive efforts toward combating trafficking in women. In 2003, the country's assessment in the U.S. State Department's Trafficking in Persons Report improved, moving from a Tier 3 to Tier 2, due to measures including the adoption of anti-trafficking legislation and the establishment of anti-trafficking law enforcement. However, the government still does not meet minimum standards for elimination of trafficking, and Kazakhstan is considered a "source, transit, and destination country for people trafficked for the purposes of sexual exploitation and forced labor."[30]

The constitution of Kazakhstan upholds freedom of conscience (Article 22). To date, the changing legal environment has not led to the deterioration of conditions for religious believers. The government continues to make its purported support for religious tolerance a tool in foreign policy toward the United States, Israel, and India, among others. If anything, the government has been more tolerant than in previous years, allowing a group of Jehovah's Witnesses in Northern Kazakhstan previously denied registration to register. Legislation introduced in 2004 simplified the process of registration for religious groups but also essentially made registration mandatory. Despite this change, a number of unregistered groups (mostly Christian sects) continue to operate freely in the country.[31]

While disabled persons are nominally a protected group under the Kazakh constitution and the 1991 law "On Social Protection of Disabled Persons in the Republic of Kazakhstan," their needs are typically not accommodated in practice.[32] One reporter called the disabled "the most disadvantaged stratum of society."[33]

The state does not meet its constitutional obligations to ensure freedom of association and assembly. The April 2005 amendment to the elections law bans all public rallies following elections until the results are announced. The Law on National Security prohibits any unauthorized assemblies, protests, or public meetings that might affect political stability. The state has threatened and occasionally used force to break up demonstrations without permits. Further, in several instances, organizers of such rallies were fined. The government has also hampered the development of independent trade union movements.

The regime has continued its efforts to compete with the independent NGO sector by sponsoring progovernment organizations. Many of the progovernment NGOs lack large numbers of active members, although President Nazarbayev has promised increased state funding to help them become better rivals of independent groups.[34] In some areas, such as women's issues, health, and ecology, the NGO sector seems to function harmoniously, with regime-allied groups working well alongside independent groups. The government is relatively supportive of organizations designed to advance the interests of ethnic minority groups, save those with overly political or potentially secessionist agendas. Political parties cannot be organized explicitly along ethnic or religious lines, and nongovernmental groups cannot incite ethnic or religious hatred.

Recommendations
- The Kazakh government should increase its efforts to eliminate torture and promote prison reform generally.
- The Kazakh government should expand its educational efforts in support of gender equality. It should also increase outreach efforts to educate adults about their legal right to use the courts to redress grievances of gender or ethnic discrimination.
- The Kazakhs need to do a better job of addressing informal patterns of ethnic prejudice that remain prevalent in the state sector. The

government should also consider offering probationary periods of employment for otherwise qualified candidates who lack adequate Kazakh (or Russian) language skills.

- The Kazakh government should repeal all restrictions on freedom of assembly.

RULE OF LAW – 2.62

Kazakhstan lacks an independent judiciary, and the executive branch continues to dominate the courts. Although plans to move toward a jury system are regularly discussed, the Kazakhs have been slow to employ them. There is a moratorium on the death penalty, but it has not yet been permanently banned. Legislative and executive authorities generally comply with judicial decisions, but control of the procuracy and legal appeals allows the government significant influence over the judicial process. Local governments tend to exploit appeals more than the regional or federal governments. The president sets the number of judges and their salaries. He appoints all judges, save for members of the Supreme Court, who are appointed by the Senate based on presidential nomination. The president receives recommendations from the Higher Judicial Council for the 48 Supreme Court judges and 572 *oblast* (provincial) judges; the Ministry of Justice recommends the 1,851 *rayon* (local) judges. All appointments are quasi-competitive, with anywhere from a few to 25 candidates per post.

The president can discipline judges, but this procedure is nontransparent. At lower levels disciplinary panels enforce norms of judicial behavior and their proceedings are published. Judges can face punishment for having too many of their decisions overturned, but not all of the criteria for judicial censure are clearly elaborated. The Union of Judges of Kazakhstan has an ethics committee that holds hearings, runs training sessions, and sets ethical norms. Judicial oversight is increasing, and an attempt is being made through both government and private publications to create legal debate on the Kazakh court system.[35]

Judicial incompetence is one of the main obstacles preventing citizens from receiving a fair hearing before an impartial tribunal. By law, defendants are presumed innocent, but this protection often means little in practice. All verdicts, and the vast majority of trial proceedings, must be conducted in public.[36] However, judges have violated this law in the past and have occasionally excluded the public or the press from judicial proceedings. While the constitution provides for a right to counsel, Kazakhstan has yet to implement a competent and universally accessible public defender system. Defense lawyers are generally at a disadvantage relative to prosecutors and need greater authority to collect evidence.[37]

The primary law governing the judiciary is Constitutional Law No. 132 of December 25, 2000. It does not establish an independent judiciary, but it moves Kazakhstan away from the Soviet judicial system toward a more Western-style system in several respects: by reducing the power of the procuracy, reforming the system of court funding, giving judges tenure, and establishing minimum qualifications and ethical standards for judges. The 2004 Central European and Eurasian Law Initiative (CEELI) study, the most comprehensive evaluation of Kazakhstan's judiciary available, criticized the Kazakh system for lack of accountability and transparency but praised its level of funding and efficiency.[38]

Kazakhstan is modernizing its courts by adding professional staff and introducing computers. Judges receive high salaries by the standards of the Kazakh civil service. All new judges now must complete a two-year training program, run by the Judicial Academy, which graduates 45 judges annually. The number of law schools is increasing rapidly, but the number of qualified instructors is not increasing apace. Kazakhstan has approximately 150 schools offering legal training (as compared to a mere two during Soviet times), with some 65,000 law students. In July 2004, a mandatory exam for state certification was introduced; however, insufficient attention has been paid to the development of an *advocatura* (defense bar).[39]

Courts are divided into civil, criminal, and supervisory (administrative) sections. The seven-member Constitutional Council, which replaced the constitutional court in 1995, decides the constitutionality of legislation and decrees. Decisions of the Constitutional Council can be vetoed by the president, but the council can override a veto with a two-thirds vote and generally finds in favor of the president's public positions, as when it ruled in favor of Nazarbayev on whether the constitution permitted him to set the election date in December 2005.[40]

It avoids controversial issues and has no direct right to rule on presidential decrees. The president, the heads of the two houses of parliament, and the prime minister can bring cases to the council. The parliament may also bring a case if at least one-fifth of deputies vote in favor.[41]

Much of the legal system is still a hybrid from Soviet times. Private citizens may prosecute not only minor assaults and batteries (similar to tort cases in the United State) but also rape, a serious crime that should clearly be of direct interest to the state. As the CEELI study notes, "the procuracy seems to be intervening in cases where the state may not have a real interest, but where it may be able to solicit bribes, while at the same time failing to provide protection to citizens whose cases seem less important to the local authorities. . . ."[42]

Kazakhstan has reformed the procuracy far less than the judiciary. Prosecutors can still intervene in any civil or commercial matter and routinely appeal when judgments go in favor of the defendant. Prosecutors, rather than judges, issue arrest, search, and detention warrants, and the acquittal rate is very low (1 to 2 percent).[43] Reform has already created tension between judges and procurators because the latter feel the former are impinging on their traditional prerogatives.

While all Kazakh citizens enjoy equal protection under the law, the biggest problem is that courts are subject to undue influence from state powers and private economic interests. There is no difficulty in finding a judge willing to deliver a "proper" verdict for a high-profile case. No real mechanism exists through which the public can register complaints of judicial misconduct. There is a national ombudsman, who has successfully remedied civil rights violations, enforced provision of pensions and social benefits, and obtained recognition of previously ignored court decisions.[44] However, there is little public expectation that he can render independent judgments in high-profile cases.

Still, judicial oversight of administrative practice is improving. The CEELI study reported that one administrative judge overturned the judgments of tax authorities in 90 percent of cases, and in 80 percent of these cases, they accepted his judgment.[45]

The Kazakhs have made little progress toward effective civilian and democratic control of the police or organs of internal security. Military reform is proceeding on a separate and faster track. The police, military, and security services are fully subject to the president and do not serve as an independent political force. While these groups have never been systematically held accountable for corruption or other abuses of power, the state frequently singles out individuals for punishment to maintain legitimacy. The Kazakh security services do not flagrantly ignore human rights, but their practices do not meet OSCE standards.

The Zhakiyanov case mentioned above epitomizes the pattern of anticorruption prosecutions in Kazakhstan. The targets of such prosecutions have in some cases engaged in corruption, but the impetus behind the cases is invariably political. While all trial information in Kazakhstan is public, scarcely any discussion of corruption cases occurs at the local level.

While the legal system gives everyone the right to own individual property (with the exception that foreigners cannot own agricultural land), the courts do an inadequate job of protecting property rights. The biases in the legal system work to the advantage of the indigenous Kazakhs and against the minority populations that entered the country during the Soviet period, as only the Kazakhs enjoy the right to be repatriated and resettled with property awards.[46] The state sometimes violates property rights to pursue a political agenda, as in the cases against Abilov and Zhakiyanov. However, the government is currently trying to create a legislative and juridical environment friendlier to private property, albeit one that is likely to continue to privilege those with close ties to government officials.

Recommendations
- Kazakhstan should expand its legal retraining program for sitting judges; particular attention should be paid to the training in property rights.
- The government should develop a timetable for shifting responsibilities away from the procuracy, which currently investigates and prosecutes crimes, in order to strengthen the courts.
- The Kazakhs need to improve the role and quality of the defense counsel. In particular, greater effort needs to be made to improve the training of lawyers who work in remote regions. The Kazakh government should be encouraged in its effort to develop a strong public defender system.
- The Kazakh government should develop a jury system.
- The role of the ombudsman should be strengthened, in particular to make it a more effective check on legislative power.

ANTICORRUPTION AND TRANSPARENCY – 2.04

The government of Kazakhstan is unlikely to take decisive steps to eliminate corruption as long as Nursultan Nazarbayev remains president of the country. Most outside observers see him as part of the problem. It is hard to imagine that he will support a complete overhaul of the existing system, which has brought significant wealth to his family. Transparency International's 2005 Corruption Perceptions Index gives Kazakhstan a 2.6, placing the country in a 10-way tie for 107th place with nations such as Zimbabwe and Belarus. Nonetheless, this is a marked improvement for Kazakhstan, which ranked 122nd in 2004, with a score of 2.2.

The state does not systematically enforce existing legislation designed to promote integrity and punish corrupt public officials. Although the necessary laws are on the books, to date, the state has used them primarily to remove incompetent judges and local officials. Victims of corruption have little effective recourse. They can turn to the ombudsman, but the power of this office is limited. President Nazarbayev continues to issue anticorruption decrees and create anticorruption agencies, such as the Disciplinary Committee and the Agency for Fighting Corruption; however, these institutions lack real teeth and remain subject to political pressure.[49]

The press is biased in its coverage of corruption scandals, although the coverage does reflect a diversity of biases. The media is restrained by laws preventing it from impugning the dignity of the president. There is no environment of protection for anticorruption activists. At the same time, there have been positive developments. Dariga Nazarbayeva has formally relinquished control of the Khabar media network while serving as a deputy in the Majlis, although she still remains involved with the outlet. In addition, the president's son-in-law, Timur Kulibayev, stepped down as the number-two person at KazMunaiGaz, the state oil and gas company, in October 2005, nominally to pursue personal business interests.[50] Candidates for elected posts must file assets declarations, but other state officials rarely make financial disclosures.

Corruption in higher education remains widespread. In a 2002 World Bank study, one in four households containing a university student reported paying bribes. Of these bribes, 69 percent were for admission and 10 percent for better grades.[51] Despite this problem, talented young people still have many resources and opportunities open to them.

The U.S. State Department's 2005 Investment Climate Statement on Kazakhstan noted, "tax experts consider Kazakhstan's tax laws to be among the most comprehensive in the former Soviet Union," but also pointed out that foreign firms operating in the country frequently complain of unannounced inspections and other forms of harassment by the tax police. Kazakh entrepreneurs make similar complaints. The government has planned further reductions and rationalization of the tax structure; however, more work needs to be done to improve internal auditing and accountability.

The Kazakhs are making concerted, albeit slow, efforts to streamline bureaucratic regulatory processes. In some key sectors of the economy these efforts are leading to rules and regulations that provide for first arbitration in Kazakh courts rather than foreign or international ones. The state remains heavily involved in the economy, particularly the vital energy sector, where KazMunaiGaz dominates.

Some signs of progress in the effort to increase government transparency have appeared. Kazakhstan's government has remained committed to diverting a large portion of its income from extractive industries to the National Fund. However, the Open Society Institute has charged that the fund is insufficiently transparent, unaccountable, subject to excessive presidential control, and governed by unclear rules.[53]

The executive budget process is still less transparent than the National Fund, largely escaping legislative scrutiny. The government publishes some accounting information, but it is often incomplete or difficult to interpret. Government contracting remains nontransparent. On the other hand, the government has made considerable progress in introducing international auditing mechanisms for programs funded by foreign aid.

In general, the Kazakhs are making strides in using the internet to improve government accountability. All the major state agencies and ministries maintain bilingual websites. Several, including the Ministry of Internal Affairs,[54] have active, regularly maintained question-and-answer sections. These sites demonstrate the pressure exerted on the government from a very active internet sector, which draws growing participation and lively debate.[55] The Kazakh government has also maintained the legacy of feedback mechanisms from the Soviet era—reception time and telephone complaints. The government publicizes the telephone numbers of officials and the hours when they are available, which is not to suggest public satisfaction with these interactions. Citizens have a legal right to obtain information, but finding out about how to do this is typically difficult, and the procedures are cumbersome. The state has made no effort to make information accessible to citizens with disabilities.

Recommendations

- The government should increase the pace of civil service reform, with special emphasis on increasing the transparency of government operations and educating citizens on their legal rights.
- The Kazakhstan government needs to hold corrupt officials accountable with stiff fines and jail terms imposed for infractions of the law.
- Kazakhs should continue their efforts to develop e-government and increase the transparency of government activities through the effective use of the internet.
- The taxation and tax collection system should be further improved.
- Kazakh authorities need to streamline official registration procedures and bureaucratic oversight at all levels of the economy and society.

NOTES

[1] *Kazakhstan at a Glance* (Washington, D.C.: World Bank, 20 September 2005), http://devdata.worldbank.org/AAG/kaz_aag.pdf.

[2] Nursultan Nazarbayev, "Message of the President of the Country to the People of Kazakhstan," Kazakhstan–2030 (London: Embassy of the Republic of Kazakhstan, 1998), http://www.kazakhstanembassy.org.uk/cgi-bin/index/145; Nursultan Nazarbayev, "Kazakhstan on the Road to Accelerated Economic, Social, and Political Modernization" (London: Embassy of the Republic of Kazakhstan, 18 February 2005), http://www.kazakhstan embassy.org.uk/cgi-bin/index/176. In general the website of the Embassy of Kazakhstan in the U.K. is a very useful source for up-to-date links to all branches of the Kazakh government.

[3] It was valued at 902,180,696,000 tenge (~US$7.5 bn) on 1 December 2005; http://www.nationalfund.kz/index.php?uin=1120635107&chapter=1133927392&lang=rus.

[4] *OSCE/ODIHR Election Observation Mission Report, Republic of Kazakhstan, Parliamentary Elections, 19 September and 3 October 2004* (Warsaw: Organization for Security and Co-operation in Europe [OSCE], 2004), 24, http://www.osce.org/documents/odihr/2004/12/3990_en.pdf.

5 Ibid., 2.

6 Ibid., 10–12.

7 Gulnoza Saidazimova, "Kazakhstan: Officials Declare Nazarbayev Winner of Presidential Election" (Prague and Washington, D.C.: Radio Free Europe/Radio Liberty [RFE/RL], 5 December 2005), http://www.rferl.org/featuresarticle/2005/12/8db051d7-0afd-4ad0-b243-3c1eaac119f6.html.

8 Ibid.

9 "IRI-Gallup Poll Predicts 83.2% Win for Nazarbayev" (Washington, D.C.: International Republican Institute [IRI], 5 December 2005), http://www.iri.org/12-05-05-KazakhstanEO.asp.

10 Ibid., 1.

11 Ibid., 2–3.

12 *International Election Observation Mission, Presidential Election, Republic of Kazakhstan – 4 December 2005, Statement of Preliminary Findings and Conclusions* (Astana: OSCE, 5 December 2005), 2, www.osce.org/documents/odihr/2005/12/17232_en.pdf.

13 The opposition candidates were: Zharmakhan Tuyakbai (For a Just Kazakhstan), Alikhan Baimenov (Ak Zhol/"Bright Path"), Yerasyl Abylkasymov (Communist People's Party of Kazakhstan), and Mels Eleusizov, (Tabighat/"Nature").

14 Ibid., 8–9.

15 Ibid., 9–10.

16 See IREX Media Guide for Kazakhstan, issued in 2004, for details, as well as a thorough introduction to the development of independent and government media and their penetration throughout the country. *Media Sustainability Index 2004* (Washington, D.C.: International Research & Exchanges Board [IREX], 2004), 230, http://www.irex.org/msi/2004/MSI-2004-Kazakhstan.pdf.

17 "Attacks on the Press 2004: Kazakhstan" (New York: Committee to Protect Journalists, 2005), http://www.cpj.org/attacks04/europe04/kazak.html.

18 Bruce Pannier, "Kazakhstan: Journalists Concerned About Effects of Draft Media Law," RFE/RL, 16 January 2004, http://www.rferl.org/featuresarticle/2004/01/59608d31-d3ef-484c-9ad7-0f6efab3facd.html.

19 Erica Flynn, "Kazakhstan's Constitutional Council due to Rule on NGO-Related Legislation," *Eurasia Insight* (New York: EurasiaNet.org), 11 August 2005, http://www.eurasianet.org/departments/insight/articles/eav081105.shtml.

20 For instance, Eurasianet.org is occasionally blocked [IREX, 2005 Media Sustainability Index: 9]. The Navigator website, navi.kz, reported in May that it was being blocked by Kaztelecom, a state-owned Internet provider [Human Rights News, Human Rights Watch, Oct. 12, 2005].

21 "Kazakh Constitutional Council Pronounces NGO Laws 'Unconstitutional,'" *Kazakhstan Daily Digest* (EurasiaNet), 24 August 2005, http://www.eurasianet.org/resource/kazakhstan/hypermail/200508/0030.shtml.

22 Ibragim Alibekov, "Kazakhstan's President Shifts Tactics During Presidential Election Campaign," EurasiaNet, 2 November 2005, http://www.eurasianet.org/departments/civilsociety/articles/eav110205.shtml.

23 "Prison Brief for Kazakhstan" (London: Kings College London, International Centre for Prison Studies [ICPS], 14 December 2005), http://www.kcl.ac.uk/depsta/rel/icps/worldbrief/continental_asia_records.php?code=98.

24 *Prison Reform in Kazakhstan* (ICPS, 10 December 2005), http://www.kcl.ac.uk/depsta/rel/icps/kazakhstan.html.

25 "15 Kazakhskikh zakliuchennykh razrezali sebe zhivoty [15 Kazakh Inmates Slash Own Stomachs]," RusPortal.net, 10 April 2005, http://news.rusportal.net/rus/21529.html.

26 "Kazakhstan Votes," RFE/RL, http://www.rferl.org/specials/kazakh_votes/parties.aspx.

27 *Kazakhstan 2004 Annual Report* (Paris: Reporters Without Borders, 2005), http://www.rsf.org/article.php3?id_article=9963.

28 Aldar Kusainov, "Domestic Crackdown in Kazakhstan Could Have Economic Conse- quences," *EurasiaNet Business & Economics,* 6 August 2002, http://www.eurasianet.org/departments/business/articles/eav080602.shtml.

29 See http://www.government.kz for the full makeup of the government, photos, and bios.

30 "Kazakhstan" in *Trafficking in Persons Report* (Washington, D.C.: U.S. Department of State, 3 June 2005), http://www.state.gov/g/tip/rls/tiprpt/2005/46614.htm.

31 "Kazakhstan" in *International Religious Freedom Report 2005* (U.S. Department of State, 8 November 2005), http://www.state.gov/g/drl/rls/irf/2005/51561.htm.

32 Zhanat Zakiyeva, "Disability Rights: The View from Kazakhstan," *Disability World,* Issue 21, November–December 2003.

33 Marat Yermukanov, "Bibi-Ana: NGO for Disabled Single Mothers in Kazakhstan," *Central Asia-Caucasus Analyst,* February 16, 2000, http://www.cacianalyst.org/view_ article.php?articleid=371&SMSESSION=NO.

34 1 billion tenge—approximately US$7.5 million—has been promised: "Kazakh Presi- dent Encourages, Warns NGOs," *Kazakhstan Daily Digest* (EurasiaNet), 13 September 2005, http://www.eurasianet.org/resource/kazakhstan/hypermail/200509/0006.shtml.

35 See http://www.supcourt.kz for the range of publications, bulletins, and journals that are being supported in Russian and Kazakh. The content of this site is identical in Russ- ian and Kazakh, but as is true of most Kazakh government sites, it is very incomplete in English.

36 For a comprehensive discussion on this, and details on judicial reform in Kazakhstan, see: *Judicial Reform Index [JRI] for Kazakhstan* (Chicago: American Bar Association, Cen- tral European and Eurasian Law Inititiative [ABA/CEELI], February 2004), 38, http://www.abanet.org/ceeli/publications/jri/jri_kazakhstan.pdf.

37 Ibid., 2.

38 Ibid., 5.

39 Ibid., 2.

40 "Postanovlenie Konstitutsionnovo Soveta RK ot 19 avgusta 2005 g. No 5 [Resolution of the Constitutional Council of the Republic of Kazakhstan, 19 August 2005, No. 5]" (Astana: Constitutional Council of the Republic of Kazakhstan), http://www.constcouncil.kz/rus/decisions/constitution/index.shtml?id_new=82. The English-lan- guage version of this website is very incomplete, while the Kazakh and Russian versions appear to be identical.

41 *Constitution of Kazakhstan,* Section VI, Article 72, http://www.kazakhstanembassy
    .org.uk/cgi-bin/index/227.

42 *JRI* (ABA), 2.

43 Ibid., 18.

44 Ina Iankulova, "Kazakhstan's Ombudsman Reports on First Six Months," *Kazakhstan
    Daily Digest* (EurasiaNet), 8 April 2003, http://www.eurasianet.org/resource/kazakh-
    stan/ hypermail/200304/0021.shtml.

45 Ibid., 13.

46 There is one exceptional minority, the Uzbeks, who are also indigenous to the country
    and enjoy legal protections virtually identical to those of the Kazakhs in fact, not just in
    law.

47 *Corruption Perceptions Index 2004 and Corruption Perceptions Index 2005* (Berlin: Trans-
    parency International [TI], 2004–5). The 2005 score has a 90 percent confidence inter-
    val of 2.2–3.2 and is based on six different surveys. The 2004 score has a 90 percent
    confidence interval of 1.8–2.7, based on seven different surveys: http://www.transparency
    .org/policy_and_research/surveys_indices/cpi/2005; http://www.transparency.org/
    policy_and_research/surveys_indices/cpi/2004.

48 *JRI* (ABA), 30.

49 Marat Yermukanov, "Nazarbayev's Anti-corruption Campaign: Honest Effort or One-
    man Show?," *Eurasia Daily Monitor* (Washington, D.C.: Jamestown Foundation), 25
    April 2005, http://www.jamestown.org/publications_details.php?volume_id=407&issue
    _id=3309&article_id=2369643.

50 Kulibayev was subsequently appointed deputy head of Samruk, a new state holding com-
    pany. Arkady Dubnov, "Politics: President Nazabayev Brought His Son-in-law Timur
    Kulibayev to Moscow," *Vremya novostei,* 4 April 2006, http://enews.ferghana.ru/
    4printer.php?id=1353. "Kazakh President Orders Creation of Holding Company for
    State Assets," *Kazakhstan Daily Digest* (EurasiaNet), 3 February 2006, http://www
    .eurasianet.org/resource/kazakhstan/hypermail/200602/0003.shtml.

51 Nataliya Rumyantseva, "Higher Education in Kazakhstan: The Issue of Corruption"
    (Boston: Boston College, Center for International Higher Education, Fall 2004),
    http://www.bc.edu/bc_org/avp/soe/cihe/newsletter/News37/text013.htm.

52 *2005 Investment Climate Statement—Kazakhstan* (U.S. Department of State, February
    2005), http://www.state.gov/e/eb/ifd/2005/42065.htm.

53 Svetlana Tsalik, *Caspian Oil Windfalls: Who Will Benefit?* (New York: Open Society Insti-
    tute, 2003), 146–49, 155–57, http://www.eurasianet.org/caspian.oil.windfalls/full_
    report.pdf.

54 Ministry of Internal Affairs of the Republic of Kazakhstan, http://www.mvd.kz.

55 For examples, see "Navigator," http://www.mizinov.net, and "Kub," http://www.kub.kz.

KENYA

CAPITAL: Nairobi

POPULATION: 33.8 million

GNI PER CAPITA: $400

SCORES	2004	2006
ACCOUNTABILITY AND PUBLIC VOICE:	4.22	5.16
CIVIL LIBERTIES:	4.59	4.58
RULE OF LAW:	3.97	3.90
ANTICORRUPTION AND TRANSPARENCY:	3.80	3.24

(scores are based on a scale of 0 to 7, with 0 representing weakest and 7 representing strongest performance)

Edward R. McMahon

INTRODUCTION

In December 2002, Mwai Kibaki was elected president of Kenya. He defeated Uhuru Kenyatta, the son of Kenya's first president and chosen successor of Daniel arap Moi, Kenya's autocratic president since 1978. For the first time, power passed from the hands of the Kenyan African National Union (KANU) to the Kibaki-led National Rainbow Coalition (NARC), a broad-based grouping of ethnically diverse parties opposed to KANU's corrupt and authoritarian rule. The election raised hopes that Kenya's move toward democratic consolidation and respect for the rule of law was meaningful and that consequential political and economic reform would take place.

Kenya is now a more democratic country than it was under the KANU regime. Nonetheless, the high expectations that accompanied Kibaki's victory have been tempered by a more measured recognition of the complexities and constraints regarding democratization in the Kenyan context. Kenya is in the process of defining the limits and boundaries of democratic conduct as well as the relationship among various components of a democratic system. There are numerous layers and

Edward R. McMahon holds a joint appointment as Research Associate Professor in the Department of Community Development and Applied Economics, and the Department of Political Science at University of Vermont.

sectors in this kaleidescope, some of which are moving more certainly in a democratic direction than others.

The Kibaki government has undertaken many initiatives designed to promote democratic governance, and political space has increased in some important respects. The media, parliament, political parties, and nongovernmental organizations (NGOs) function with considerable freedom. Yet political tensions, entrenched corruption, lack of specific reform results, and questions regarding the depth of the government's commitment to reform raise serious concerns about the state of Kenya's democratic experiment. The record is replete with expressions of good intent and stalled reform initiatives. The government's base of support has narrowed, lessening its appetite for ambitious reform measures. In particular, its inability to address corruption in a sustained and meaningful manner remains a critical challenge.

Characterized by openness, competitiveness, and an energetic civil society, Kenya has a strong political culture. However, its performance in effective law enforcement and public morality is weaker. Kenya's faults, especially regarding corruption, threaten to trump the positives in its nascent democratic opening.

Civil society has weakened as its members have entered government, and the initial euphoria of change has somewhat dissipated. In addition, parties united in opposition to KANU have had to redefine their relationships with each other, and some have left the governing coalition. The threat of terrorism and at-times strained relations with donor countries also present complicating factors.

A proposed revised constitution was soundly defeated, approximately 58 percent to 42 percent, in a November 2005 referendum. The lengthy constitutional-revision process had raised hopes that the result would further strengthen democracy. An initial draft known as the Bomas version reflected considerable popular support and input, but the final government-edited draft contained a number of controversial provisions. In addition, many key actors and commentators characterized the vote more as a referendum on President Kibaki's rule than on the relative merits of the draft constitution.

ACCOUNTABILITY AND PUBLIC VOICE – 5.16

With the 2002 elections, for the first time, Kenyans were able to choose their leaders in genuinely open and competitive polling. The result was a successful alteration in power. Prior elections, uniformly won by KANU, were characterized by poor election administration, electoral manipulation, and alleged vote rigging and voter intimidation. By contrast, the 2002 elections displayed low levels of coercion and violence. According to the Commonwealth observer delegation, "By common consensus, it was the best General Election the country had ever had, and the most peaceful: despite the intense interest it provoked, the atmosphere was less violent and more tolerant than in either 1992 or 1997."[1] Nonetheless, the Commonwealth delegation criticized the pro-government bias of the Kenya Broadcasting Corporation (KBC) coverage, the ruling party's use of state resources during the election campaign, and problems with voter registry. These incidences were not of a sufficient magnitude to deny NARC a victory, but could potentially arise in subsequent elections. Another criticism targeted the liberal use of new provisions regarding voter assistance in the polling place.

Concerns also arose about inappropriate use of government resources and incidents of violence and campaign intimidation surrounding the 2005 constitutional referendum; however, no significant complaints were recorded about administration of the referendum. Both referendum supporters and detractors accepted the clear-cut result.

In recent years, the electoral commission has become more professional and more adequately funded, except in the area of voter education. It currently enjoys significant independence from the government, although this issue may resurface in the run-up to the 2007 national elections as some commissioners' terms end. Several stakeholders, such as human rights and election-observation groups, have emphasized the need for the government to continue to make inclusive and broad electoral commission appointments.

Despite the fact that the two national polls since 2002 have been viewed as legitimate, they are nevertheless the first of their kind. Areas of continuing concern include candidate nomination processes and campaign financing, electoral gerrymandering, inappropriate use of government resources for electoral purposes, levels of violence surrounding elections, and the marginalization of disadvantaged sectors of society. The country thus has a long way to go to consolidate its nascent and fragile electoral processes.

Although the NARC coalition entered office with a mandate for political reform, including the introduction of transparency into political party finances, no progress on this issue has been made. Draft legislation containing provisions for public funding of political parties has not been introduced into parliament. This legislation would provide public funding to political parties with parliamentary representation. The question of political party funding also featured prominently in the constitutional reform process. There is concern about the current potential for the Registrar of Societies, under whose regulatory purview political parties fall, to make decisions about party registration on a partisan basis. The draft Political Parties Bill would provide a new regulatory and legal framework for parties.

While Kenyans' political choices are not dominated by the military, foreign powers, or totalitarian parties, and although NARC has been a multiethnic movement, voting patterns continue to fall largely along ethnic lines.[2] Despite increased parliamentary influence, power remains heavily concentrated in the executive branch under the Kibaki government. The ministers and ministries within this branch tend to champion the narrow interests of President Kibaki's largely Kikuyu and central Kenya–based political constituency and are known colloquially as the Mt. Kenya mafia. The NARC coalition has, over time, lost support from parties other than Kibaki's Democratic Party.

Although in theory the executive, legislative, and judicial branches of government oversee one another's actions and seek to hold each other accountable, the power of the presidency takes precedence in practice. This question of parliamentary versus presidential power was probably the single most contentious issue addressed in the constitutional reform debate. The penultimate Bomas draft provided for a significantly heightened parliamentary role. However, the final draft, prepared under the close supervision of Attorney General Amos Wako, weakened the powers of the proposed prime minister.

Members of parliament are entitled to propose legislation, but in practice the attorney general usually introduces government-drafted laws. Over the past couple of years, parliament has demonstrated some independence from the executive, for example in passing the Forest Act over President Kibaki's objections. It has also tabled or significantly altered government-introduced legislation, such as privatization and anti-terrorism bills. Parliamentarians have also aided anticorruption and transparency efforts through commission investigations. For example, the Anglo-Leasing government contracting scandal, in which several leading cabinet ministers have been implicated, was first exposed in parliament in early 2004.

The civil service is administered by a Public Service Commission. Kenya's public administration has some roots in the British administrative tradition, in which the civil service is supposed to be highly qualified and politically neutral. A 2003 UN Development Program study found that, overall, the civil service did not meet these standards. It identified poor dissemination of codes and regulations to civil servants, declining professionalism, and widespread nepotism and corruption as key problem areas.[3] The government has established an 11-person team to monitor the performance of civil servants and instituted a job-review policy before reappointment for many civil servants, but significant problems remain.

Traditional attitudes circumscribe the role of women in politics. Only nine female members (four elected and five nominated) sat in the National Assembly prior to the 2002 general elections; the cabinet included only one female member. The December 2002 elections increased the number of women in the 224-member parliament to eight elected and seven nominated.[4] Three women served in the cabinet prior to its dismissal by President Kibaki in November 2005. The defeated constitution included a mandatory provision that women comprise one-third of representatives at the national and district legislative levels.

Kenya's energetic and robust civil society has been one of the core strengths of its political culture. The success of the 2002 elections was largely due the ability of the country's NGOs to push for open political space and greater freedom. In recent years, public-policy NGOs in Kenya have achieved significant elements of transparency, especially when compared to those in many other countries wrestling with the legacy of decades of authoritarian rule. Most NGOs are generally free from legal impediments from the state and able to function openly. Civic organizations and public policy groups have had considerable access to the media and have been able to convey their views to the public, especially in major urban areas. The drawn-out constitutional review process involved a wide range of civic groups and associations.

Some NGOs have been able to influence public policy in the Kibaki administration. For example, the Kenyan Section of the International Commission of Jurists has influenced judicial reform, and the Federation of Women Lawyers has had an impact on legal and gender issues).[5]

Further, the Sexual Offences Bill, Criminal Law Amendment Act, and bills on refugees as well as children's welfare and trafficking are some examples of actual or draft legislation influenced by civil society advocacy efforts. A number of women and men in senior government positions have made gender issues a priority, but they often encounter bureaucratic inertia and/or resistance, especially as the NARC's base of political support has narrowed.

The government has at times responded defensively to NGO criticism. In addition, some civil society organizations' credibility has suffered from a lack of distance from the Kibaki administration. For example, the Board of Trustees of Transparency International Kenya (the chair of which openly acknowledged his closeness to President Kibaki) forced Gladwell Otieno, the organization's executive director, to resign from her job in April 2005, after she criticized the government's stand on corruption.[6]

The constitution provides for freedom of speech and of the press, and Kenya's press traditionally has been lively, especially when compared to that of many other African countries. The media includes 4 major daily newspapers, 25 FM radio stations, and 4 main television stations. In the latter years of Moi's rule, the electronic media also began to demonstrate signs of independence. This trend has continued in the Kibaki administration, which came to power promising further media liberalization. In late 2003, however, the government cracked down on unregistered "alternative" newspapers, using a controversial law passed by the previous government. The government, though, does not restrict access to the internet.

The media has called for the overhaul of parts of certain laws that hamper press freedom, including the Official Secrets Act, Section 194 of the penal code, the Books and Newspapers Act, the Defamation Act, the Judicature Act, the Kenya Broadcasting Corporation Act, and the Communication Commission of Kenya Act. The issues of media licensing and cross-ownership of newspaper and electronic media remain controversial, as they have the potential to reduce the breadth of views expressed by the press. According to the director of the independent, Nairobi-based Media Institute, the country's political transition has allowed the press to publish freely and created an atmosphere that does not directly threaten journalists' physical safety. Concerns exist, however, that no institutional or legal context actually protects these freedoms. The government is developing a media bill in consultation with relevant stakeholders, designed to emphasize self-regulation. The bill also contains provisions for a minimum wage for journalists and a new code of conduct.[7]

In the past, public officials have used libel laws to attack publications directly critical of actions by government officials. While in office, for example, one of President Moi's chief lieutenants, Nicholas Biwott, won a large libel suit, provoking criticism that the rulings were politically motivated and intended to protect senior government officials.

Recommendations

- The constitutional review process should be renewed, with the Bomas draft used as a point of reference.
- Parliament should give expeditious consideration to the drafts of political party and media bills.
- Appointments to the Electoral Commission should be made in consultation with the broad range of stakeholders.

CIVIL LIBERTIES – 4.58

The Kibaki government has placed considerable emphasis on the protection of human rights. Civil and political rights are more respected in Kenya today than at any time in the country's history. In its "State of Human Rights Report, 2003–2004," the Kenya National Human Rights Commission (KNHRC) suggested that the Kibaki government's record on human rights has been a vast improvement from that of the previous regime. The report indicated that problems such as detention without trial, tribal clashes, and extrajudicial killings had diminished considerably and that living conditions in prisons had greatly improved.

Much remains to be done, however. Actions such as police abuse and violence by security forces during the constitutional referendum campaign period raise considerable questions about the protection of civil liberties.[8] A survey commissioned by the KNHRC suggests continued reluctance on the part of citizens to report incidents of alleged torture. In February 2005, Kenyan human rights groups presented a report to the UN Committee on Human Rights alleging torture by government authorities. One example cited were the deaths of 14 prisoners in eastern Kenya.[9]

Although checks against arbitrary arrest exist in the legal system, they are not uniformly observed. In addition, the Kibaki government ostensibly continues to support revised draft legislation on antiterrorism, which, although improved from an earlier version, would give police sweeping arrest and search powers without authority from the courts.[10]

The constitution provides that persons arrested or detained be brought before a court within 24 hours in the case of noncapital offenses and within 14 days in capital cases. The law, though, does not stipulate the period within which the trial of a charged suspect must begin. Indicted suspects have often been imprisoned for months or years before trial begins. The law provides that families and attorneys of persons arrested and charged be allowed access, although this right is often ignored.

The Kibaki government has sought to improve prison conditions. Vice President Moody Awori has led a high-profile effort on this topic. Specific actions and initiatives include the community service order program, which aims at decongesting prisons. More than 200,000 petty offenders have been released from jail to undertake community service in recent years.[11] Police have resisted plans to give parole to minor offenders, arguing that this would increase crime. Some efforts have been made to improve health and living conditions in prisons.

No instances of politically motivated assassination have been proven over the past two years, although previous high-profile, politics-related killings suggest that such events are not alien to Kenya. For example, three men arrested for the September 2003 murder of Dr. Crispin Mbai, a key player in the constitutional review commission considering limiting executive branch powers, were acquitted due to lack of evidence in April 2005. No other suspects have been arrested.

The state's ability to protect citizens from abuse by private and non-state actors remains limited for some sectors of the population, especially in poor and rural areas. Intimidation has been common in some parts of the country. The rule of law is very weak in the sparsely populated northeastern region bordering Somalia. These disadvantaged groups are also relatively less able to petition effectively for redress when their rights are violated by state authorities.[12]

To date, the state's ability to ensure and enforce the equality of all citizens regarding civil and political rights has also been limited. Evidence suggests that there is widespread violence against women; according to the Kenya Demographic Health Survey, in 2003, 44 percent of women aged between 15 and 49 had been physically or sexually violated by a husband or parent.[13] Many of these cases go unpunished, despite repeated complaints by women's groups that Kenyan laws remain too lenient in sentencing offenders in cases of violence against women.

The constitution was only amended in 1997 to include a specific prohibition of discrimination on grounds of gender. Kenya ratified the Convention on the Elimination of All Forms of Discrimination Against Women in 1984. The Kibaki government initially targeted improved women's rights as a key policy goal. This issue was also the focus of considerable attention and discussion in the constitutional review process. The government promised that gender units would be established in all government ministries, and a domestic violence bill was passed. A sexual offenses bill under consideration by parliament as of late 2005 would carry strong sanctions against individuals or spouses who infected partners or victims with HIV or engaged in gang rape, defilement, child trafficking, child prostitution, child sex tourism, incest, or sexual harassment.

Overall, however, the government's record has not matched its intentions in this realm. In 2002, a draft Gender Equity Bill was withdrawn after it created considerable public controversy, with some Muslims protesting that its scope was too sweeping. The government announced in 2004 that a revised bill would be introduced in parliament, but this has not occurred. In 2004, parliament passed the National Commission on Gender and Development Bill, but the commission lacks a budget and has maintained a low profile. A number of human rights organizations have expressed concern about the state of women's property rights. They highlight problems regarding women's ability to inherit from deceased husbands or family members, traditional practices such as "wife inheritance" by male members of a deceased husband's family, and loss of property as a result of divorce or separation. Ineffective courts and unresponsive government authorities are singled out as significant contributing factors.[14]

The constitution prohibits slavery, and the penal code outlaws forced detention of women for prostitution and labor as well as the sexual exploitation of children. Despite these provisions, trafficking in women and children is a problem, although it is difficult to determine its exact magnitude. According to the U.S. Department of State's 2005 Trafficking in Persons Report, "Kenya is a source, transit, and destination country for men, women, and children trafficked for the purposes of forced labor and sexual exploitation." The report determined that while the Kenyan government does not fully comply with the minimum standards for the elimination of trafficking, it has expanded its efforts in this area. In mid-2004, for example, the Kenyan Police Service launched a 10-person Human Trafficking Unit to undertake investigations.

The constitution prohibits discrimination on the basis of a person's "race, tribe, place of origin or residence or other local connection, political opinions, color, or creed." Yet the country's population is divided into more than 40 ethnic groups, and, not surprisingly, the challenge of governing such a disparate population has been complicated by frequent and credible allegations of discrimination as well as sporadic interethnic violence.[15]

In the public sector, it is common for members of most ethnic groups to grant preferential treatment to other members of the same group. Political cleavages have tended to correlate with ethnic cleavages. For example, concerns have been expressed especially about favoritism toward the Kikuyu ethnic group in government personnel appointments.[16]

The government has singled out the overwhelmingly Muslim ethnic Somalis as the only group whose members are required to carry an additional form of identification to prove their citizenship. The continued presence and at times criminal activities of Somali refugees have exacerbated the problems faced by citizens of Somali ethnicity. Some groups suffer from inadequate protection and security. In July 2005, for example, at least 19 people, many of them children, were killed and dozens wounded in a raid on a remote village in eastern Kenya in what residents said was an inter-clan attack spurred by long-running disputes over water and pasture rights.[17]

Within a context of limited resources and higher priority issues, the Kibaki administration has made a modest effort to improve the status of people with disabilities. For example, President Kibaki began 2004 by signing into law the Persons with Disabilities Act, designed to improve the rights and rehabilitation of people with disabilities.[18] It established the National Council for Persons with Disability with

27 members, of whom 20 have disabilities. The council's role is to formulate policies regarding the disabled and advise the government on how to avoid discrimination. Employers are required to allocate a certain percentage of available jobs to disabled persons, and duties on imported tools and equipment for those with disabilities are waived. The extent of compliance with these provisions is not yet clear.

In general, the government has a good track record in respecting freedom of religion. According to the 2004 U.S. State Department Report on International Religious Freedom, "there is generally a great level of tolerance among religious groups." The report concluded that Kenya was one of the least repressive African states in this regard. The state has not tended to intrude on the appointment of religious or spiritual leaders or on the internal organizational life of faith-related organizations, nor has it placed restrictions on religious observance, ceremony, or education. However, as terrorist acts associated with Islamic fundamentalism have been committed on Kenyan soil in recent years—including a car bomb that blew up the U.S. embassy in Nairobi in 1998 and a bomb blast in an Israeli-owned hotel in Mombasa in 2002—religion-based tensions have risen.

Religion-based tension also arose over the draft constitution. The Federation of Churches in Kenya, which represents 41 Christian congregations across the country, spearheaded opposition to the draft constitution provisions concerning the role of Islamic "Kadhi" courts, a potential for easing abortion restrictions, and the legalization of gay marriage. In the draft constitution, religious courts were defined in an open-ended manner, allowing for the reintroduction of customary courts to mediate matters of family and personal law.

Violence has broken out occasionally between Muslims and those of other faiths. Many Muslims believe, with some justification, that the government is hostile toward them, poses additional bureaucratic requirements for their access to government services, and discriminates against them in law enforcement. Muslims have specifically complained about government repression in the name of the war against terror; they have pointed to the draft Protection Against Terrorism Bill, arrests of Muslims on suspicion of terrorism, and the banning of Muslim charity organizations, such as the African Muslim Agency.[19]

Demonstrations and public protests in Kenya are generally permitted; however, in November 2005, government banned demonstrations calling for new elections following the constitutional referendum's defeat, claiming that such demonstrations would present a "threat to national security."[20] Further, several credible reports brought to public attention the use of excessive force to deal with demonstrations and public protests. Amnesty International's Kenya 2004 annual report stated, "Law enforcement officials continued to use excessive force in dispersing demonstrations, and during the arrest of criminal and 'terrorist' suspects." For example, one person was killed and 33 injured in July 2005 protests against parliament's revision of the draft constitution. At least eight people subsequently died in referendum campaign violence.[21] The state does not force citizens to join associations or political parties; it also does not place registration or legal impediments on NGOs.

All workers other than members of the police and military are legally free to join unions of their choice. The government may deregister a union, but the registrar of trade unions is required to give that union 60 days to challenge the deregistration notice. While not having the force of law, the Industrial Relations Charter—executed by the government, the Central Organization of Trade Unions, and the Federation of Kenya Employers—gives workers the right to engage in legitimate trade union organizational activities. Both the Trade Disputes Act and the charter authorize collective bargaining between unions and employers. A civil service union strike in 2005 met strong government resistance and resulted in a change in union leadership.

Recommendations
- Greater emphasis should be placed on reforming police structure and operations to reduce human rights violations and improve the quality of cases prosecuted.
- Renewed emphasis should be placed on developing and implementing initiatives designed to promote the rights of women through increased education, stricter enforcement of existing laws against discrimination, and greater women's representation at all levels of government.
- The state needs to address the problems of human trafficking through tightening controls over cross-border movements, putting greater emphasis on trafficking-specific public education and awareness campaigns in trafficking-prone communities, and

expanding programs that provide direct protective assistance to children in prostitution.

RULE OF LAW – 3.90

Although Kenya's judicial system is based on the British model, its actions have reflected the primacy of the executive branch for much of the independence period. In 2002, for example, when a panel of Commonwealth judicial experts from Africa and Canada examined the court system, they concluded that it was among the most incompetent and inefficient in Africa, with judges subject to political pressure and often accepting bribes to influence their decisions.[22] A 2005 report by the International Commission of Jurists determined that corruption in the administration of justice as well as in the judiciary remains a serious impediment to the rule of law in Kenya. The report emphasized that while some attempts had been made to reform the judiciary, substantive and far-reaching administrative and institutional measures had never been taken. It also noted that more emphasis has been placed on purging the judiciary of perceived corrupt officers than on addressing the fundamental and underlying institutional causes of poor judicial functioning.[23] Another report has concluded that "Independence of the judiciary is still a far off dream, and incompetent and corrupt judges remain on the bench."[24]

Kenya lacks a tradition of effective judicial review over legislative and executive actions. The Constitutional and Judicial Review Division of the High Court was created in 2004, but its actions have been very limited. In addition, the government has at times demonstrated an attitude of being above the law, for example, ignoring judicial decisions in the Amboseli and Kenyatta International Convention Center cases. The attorney general's docket mandate is also extremely broad, making it virtually impossible for him to function effectively in all areas of his jurisdiction.

The president has extensive powers over appointments, including those of the attorney general, chief justice, as well as appellate and High Court judges. He appoints judges on the advice of the Judicial Service Commission—a body lacking independent status itself as it is comprised of the chief justice, attorney general, chair of the Public Service

Commission, and two High Court or Court of Appeals judges. The chief justice is a member of the Court of Appeals and the High Court, thus undercutting the principle of judicial review. Although most judges have life tenure, the president has extensive authority over transfers. In addition, Philip Murgor, the director of public prosecutions, was fired in 2005 in the wake of his energetic probing of politically sensitive drug and corruption cases. This episode points to the need for a politically independent Public Prosecutor's office, which has been frequently subjected to political influence and control.

In recent years, criticism of the judiciary has been aired more freely, and a public policy debate about its shortcomings has ensued. The Kibaki government entered office promising that the rule of law would be upheld and judicial independence strengthened. It has created the Ministry of Justice and Constitutional Affairs, although some in the legal community believe that the ministry's existence has, at least in part, undermined rather than promoted the independence of the judiciary.[25]

President Kibaki criticized the extent of corruption in the judiciary and instructed the minister of justice to establish a process for the immediate identification of corrupt judges.[26] In 2003, in what some have dubbed "radical surgery," President Kibaki oversaw the firing of 24 judges and 87 magistrates accused of corruption. While these actions were generally viewed favorably, they did not reflect a sustained, institutional effort to strengthen judicial independence. Courts do not receive adequate resources from the state to fulfill their responsibilities in a timely and effective manner, although there are few direct examples of state funding for the judiciary being used as an instrument of control or political pressure.

Civilians are tried publicly, although some testimonies may be given in closed session. The law provides for a presumption of innocence and for defendants to have the right to attend trial, confront witnesses, and present witnesses and evidence. But, delays in the administration of justice are common. Legal provisions that allow courts to release suspects on bail or bond pending the hearing and determination of their case are not fully utilized, which has led to overcrowding in detention facilities. Frequent adjournment has also been cited as a cause for delays in the completion of cases. Prosecutors further lack the staff and resources to prosecute criminal cases expeditiously. The breadth of legal provisions for criminal offenses not subject to bail is another cause of prison congestion.[27]

Defendants have the right to government-provided legal counsel only in capital cases. For lesser charges, free legal aid is rarely available, and then only in Nairobi and other major cities. Defense lawyers do not always have access to government-held evidence. The government can cite the State Security Secrets Act as justification to withhold evidence, and local officials sometimes classify documents to hide the guilt of government officials. Court fees for filing and hearing cases are costly for the average Kenyan.[28]

The government has undertaken a number of reforms, including outlawing the holding of suspects in custody for more than 14 days and the abolition of legal validity of confessions made to police, in the Criminal Law (Amendment) Act of 2003. Some reports suggest, however, that such reforms have adversely affected investigators and prosecutors' ability to do their jobs. As of late 2005, the government was considering legislation to roll back some of these reforms.[29]

The issue of whether to establish a Truth, Justice, and Reconciliation Commission to investigate the Moi presidency's abuses of power drew considerable interest and support early in the Kibaki presidency. Many argued that such a commission was necessary to properly assess previous governments' records and provide grounds for further democratic consolidation. A Task Force on the Establishment of a Truth, Justice and Reconciliation Commission recommended immediate establishment of a commission in October 2003. The political sensitivity of the issue, however, has resulted in no action taken.

The Kenyan economy has long been oriented along capitalist lines. The government, especially in contrast to many other African regimes, has traditionally had a fairly good record of respecting property rights. According to the Heritage Foundation 2006 Index of Economic Freedom, however, problems exist. "Property and contractual rights are enforceable, but long delays in resolving commercial cases are common."[30]

A tradition of civilian control over security forces persists. At times, however, some security forces have acted with relative impunity. The Kibaki government has stated its intent to introduce effective control and accountability over the security forces. President Kibaki has appointed new army and police commanders, but the record of specific reforms in the security sector remains limited to date. Sufficient executive or parliamentary oversight of military and intelligence service functions, including budget development and expenditure, is lacking.

Recommendations

- The Judicial Service Commission should be expanded with input from consumers of justice. Furthermore, the commission's independence should be enhanced.
- The state needs to institute more transparent and qualitatively improved judicial appointment procedures.
- In order to heighten confidence in the justice system, increased resources should be devoted to resolving murders with political implications.
- The currently wide mandate of the attorney general should be reduced and better focused.
- Greater emphasis should be placed on judicial training.

ANTICORRUPTION AND TRANSPARENCY – 3.24

Kenya has embraced capitalism since independence, yet the state has traditionally been involved in the economy. The Heritage Foundation's 2006 Index of Economic Freedom states that government intervention has increased compared to previous years.[31] State intervention has taken place officially and through corrupt practices. In fact, corruption has long been a serious problem; Kenya has consistently ranked in the bottom 10 percent on Transparency International's (TI) Corruption Perceptions Index.[32] According to the TI 2005 Bribery Index, while the overall incidence of corruption has dropped as compared with that of 2002, the average size of bribes has increased significantly. The study suggests that the Kenyan police force is the most corrupt institution in the country; the Teachers Service Commission, a government agency that manages teachers' affairs, was identified as the second-most corrupt state institution. The report also cited widespread corruption among local government authorities.

The Kibaki administration has made some efforts to curb corruption, including the 2003 passage of the Anti-Corruption and Economic Crimes Act, changes in the judiciary, the formation of the Kenya Anti-Corruption Commission (KACC), legislation requiring public servants to declare their wealth, and increases in government salaries.[33] In addition, President Kibaki signed into law the Procurement and Disposal Bill, designed to raise standards in the government procurement process in 2005.[34] A Serious Crimes Unit has been established within the Department of Public Prosecution, and the government is engaged in the Governance, Justice, Law and Order Sector project, an ambitious donor-supported effort to improve transparency and governance throughout the bureaucracy. The KACC has recommended prosecution of a number of government officials.

Overall, however, results have been very disappointing. The Kibaki administration has come under increasing and considerable criticism for its lack of progress in curbing corruption. This is exacerbated by the fragility of the governing coalition, President Kibaki's detached governing style, the sheer magnitude of the problem, limited resources available to address it, and underlying structural, economic, and cultural issues. These factors have all combined to significantly deflate initial reform initiatives.

In the 2004–2005 parliament, NGOs, the press, and indeed some official bodies unearthed examples of government corruption and malfeasance. These included alleged fraud in the procurement of naval vessels from Spain, a new system of passports, and the printing of national currency. Numerous official commissions are investigating particular scandals, but former high-ranking officials have yet to be prosecuted. The results to date have been meager, as exemplified by investigations such as the Goldenberg foreign exchange scandal, which highlight the magnitude of the challenge of reducing corruption in Kenya. In addition, President Kibaki's increasing reliance on the Mount Kenya mafia—a small group of trusted aides—some of whom are believed to be highly corrupt, has further heightened concerns. In early 2005, the British High Commissioner made public a list of 20 cases alleging official corruption that have either been dismissed or remain under investigation by the KACC.[35] In 2005, Transport Minister Chris Murungaru was denied visas by the U.K. and U.S. governments on grounds of suspected corruption. In addition, the military and intelligence services remain closed institutions; the scandal involving the alleged purchase of Spanish naval vessels has emphasized the lack of adequate security services' budgetary and expenditure oversight.

The Kibaki administration does not commonly take action against senior political appointees suspected of corrupt activities. However, in an isolated case, the government charged six former senior civil servants with "abuse of office" for awarding millions of dollars in irregular contracts in February 2005 to supply equipment to Kenya's immigration department and build a police forensic laboratory.[36]

The KACC has investigated more than 3,000 cases of alleged corruption since its inception in 2003, but its track record of initiating successful prosecutions has been very modest. It has investigatory, but no prosecutorial powers. One of President Kibaki's early appointments was John Githongo, the widely respected head of the TI–Kenya chapter, to head the government's Office of Ethics and Governance. Frustrated by continued corruption and the Kibaki administration's failure to enact meaningful reforms, Githongo resigned in early 2005.

In an attempt to separate public office from personal interests, the Public Officer Ethics Act requires government officials to file annual declarations of wealth. However, the fact that these reports are not made public has called the transparency of this process into question. Draft legislation to remedy this issue is under consideration.

Under significant international pressure, in February 2005, President Kibaki ordered an audit report on high-level corruption in the awarding of security contracts to be forwarded to the KACC for action; the next day, he carried out a cabinet reshuffle. However, the director of the KACC, Aaron Ringera, told the BBC that the commission was not prepared to prosecute any cabinet ministers because it is "usually very difficult to pin any documentary evidence against a minister."[37]

Currently, no legal protection exists for government whistle-blowers who expose corruption cases, although draft legislation to remedy this has been introduced. The Official Secrets Act has been cited by senior government officials (including Francis Muthaura, head of the civil service and secretary to the cabinet) as a deterrent against civil servants providing classified information to the press. Muthaura specifically warned civil servants in 2004 against leaking information after the media highlighted corruption implicating government ministers.[38]

In 2004, President Kibaki signed into law the Public Audit Bill, which provides for a more systematic audit of state corporations. The legislation reorganized the office of controller and auditor general through the establishment of the Kenya National Audit office. It is still too early to determine the effectiveness of this initiative. Other legislation passed to address corruption includes the investment code and the Finance Management Act.

While citizens have the legal right to obtain information about government conduct, public access to government information has been limited. In 2005, the Kenya Human Rights Commission issued a report rating various government ministries and offices on their openness to the public. The military and the presidency were judged the "most opaque," while the Ministry of Environment and National Assembly were given the highest marks for responsiveness. Other top performers were the ministries of sports, agriculture, finance, and justice.[39]

Calls to codify the public's right to information were made in the context of the constitutional review process. In theory, the executive budget-making should enjoy a degree of transparency; however, in reality, the budget has been closely managed by the office of the president without much opportunity for review and input. However, the Kibaki government has opened up the process to an extent, and parliament has increasingly sought to exercise meaningful legislative scrutiny. Draft freedom-of-information legislation is in parliament, although it has been critiqued by advocacy groups for being overly legalistic and narrow in scope.[40]

In 2005, the government commissioned Deloitte South Africa to audit several projects, including those funded by the World Bank. Finance Minister David Mwiraria indicated that this decision was made after fraud was detected in the Kenya Urban Transport Improvement Project. The National Audit Office has improved its audit compliance of government projects. The government has promised to expeditiously release audits regarding cases of alleged embezzlement of state funds.

Recommendations

- The KACC should be embedded in the constitution and should either be given prosecutorial powers or develop a more effective and productive relationship with the director of public prosecutions.
- Legislation should be enacted requiring government-official wealth declarations to be made public.
- The state needs to ensure adequate legal protection for whistleblowers.
- The government should adopt freedom-of-information legislation.

NOTES

1   *Report of the Commonwealth Observer Group* (London: The Commonwealth, 27 December 2002), http://www.thecommonwealth.org/Templates/Internal.asp?NodeID=35148.

2   Stephen Ndegwa, "Kenya: Third Time Lucky?," *Journal of Democracy* 14, 3 (July 2003).

3   *Public Service Ethics in Africa* 2 (New York: UN Development Program (UNDP), 2001), 41.

4   "Review of 2002 Election Result" (Nairobi: UN Integrated News and Information Networks [IRIN], 21 January 2003).

5   *East Africa Democracy Report* (Nairobi: East African Human Rights Institute [EAHRI], December 2004), 14.

6   "Anti-Graft Watchdog Boss to Mediate Between Kenya, Berlin Chapters," *The Nation,* 24 April 2005.

7   "Talks Begin on Improved Media Bill," *The Nation,* 16 November 2005.

8   "Rolling Back Torture" (Nairobi: Independent Medico-Legal Unit, 2005).

9   "Keeping Torture Under Wraps," *IPS-Inter Press Service,* 25 April 2005.

10   Joyce Mulama, "Anti-Terror Bill Pushed by U.S. Worries Many," *IPS-Inter Press Service,* 6 September, 2005.

11   "Magistrates to Hold Sessions in Prisons Soon," *The East African Standard,* 7 October 2005.

12   See *Kenya: Minorities, Indigenous Peoples and Ethnic Diversity* (London: Minority Rights Group International [MRGI], 2005).

13   *Kenya Demographic and Health Survey 2003: Preliminary Report* (Nairobi: Ministry of Health, 2003), 32.

14   "Review of Kenya's Compliance with the ICCPR," *Human Rights Watch Letter to Human Rights Committee, United Nations* (New York: Human Rights Watch [HRW], 10 March 2005).

15   See *Kenya: Minorities* (MRGI).

16   Adrian Bloomfield, "President Goes to Bed as Kenya Declines," *Daily Telegraph,* 16 February 2005, 15.

17   "Kenya deploys security forces as bloody clan attack kills at least 19," Agence France-Presse (AFP), 12 July 2005.

18   "Kibaki Signs Six Crucial Bills Into Law," *The Nation,* 1 January 2004, 5.

19   "Muslims Denounce Harassment By State," *The East African Standard,* 29 October 2005.

20   "Kenya Bans Opposition Rallies, Rejects Calls for Snap Polls," AFP, 27 November 2005.

21   "Nobel Peace Laureate Out to Calm Stormy Post-Referendum Kenya," AFP, 29 November 2005.

22   David Mugonyi, "New Reforms Plan to Curb Corrupt Judges," *The Nation,* 18 May 2002, 1.

23   Wilfred Ngunjiri Nderitu and Samuel Mbithi, "Press Statement on Corruption in Government" (Nairobi: International Commission of Jurists–Kenya), http://www.icj-kenya.org/news.asp.

24   *East Africa Democracy Report* (EAHRI), 9.

[25] Tony Kago and Wahome Thuku, "Ministry Encroaching CJ's Docket, Says Lawyers' Lobby," *The Nation,* 22 September 2005, 5.

[26] David Mugonyi, "Kibaki's Warning to Lawyers," *The Nation,* 1 August 2003.

[27] Cyrus Kinyungu, "Judiciary Blamed for Jail Woes," *The Nation,* 11 August 2005, 4.

[28] Emmanuel Wetangula, "Try Non-Legal Ways to Settle Most Disputes," *The Nation,* 15 August 2005, 12.

[29] Gitonga Munuki, "All Are to Blame for Flaws in Criminal Law," *The Nation,* 29 August 2005, 14.

[30] "2006 Index of Economic Freedom" (Washington, D.C./New York: Heritage Foundation/The *Wall Street Journal*), http://www.heritage.org/research/features/index/country .cfm?id=Kenya.

[31] Ibid.

[32] *Corruption Perceptions Index 2005* (Berlin and London: Transparency International [TI], 2005), http://www.transparency.org/cpi/2005/cpi2005_infocus.html.

[33] Eric Shimoli, "New Cabinet Expected to Focus on Promises," *The Nation,* 25 November 2005, 3.

[34] Benson Kathuri, "State Simplifies Tendering Procedure," *East Africa Standard,* 28 July 2005, 11.

[35] "The Corruption is Sickening," *The Economist,* 13 August 2005, 38.

[36] "Under fire, Kenya charges six former government officials with graft," AFP, 16 February 2005.

[37] "Kenya's Anti-Graft 'Not Ready' to Sue Ministers Over Corruption," BBC Monitoring of Kenya FM Radio, 24 February 2005.

[38] Mwalimu Mati, "Will Kibaki Fall on His Own Sword?," *The East African Standard,* 25 July 2004, 15.

[39] Tony Kago, "State Is Rated Most Secret," *The Nation,* 30 September 2005, 6.

[40] Priscilla Nyokabi, "Introduction of Access to Information Legal Regime in Kenya," *The Media Observer* 3 (December 2005): 16.

KYRGYZSTAN

CAPITAL: Bishkek
POPULATION: 5.2 million
GNI PER CAPITA: $340

SCORES	2004	2006
ACCOUNTABILITY AND PUBLIC VOICE:	1.84	4.17
CIVIL LIBERTIES:	3.17	4.17
RULE OF LAW:	2.62	3.38
ANTICORRUPTION AND TRANSPARENCY:	2.34	2.54

(scores are based on a scale of 0 to 7, with 0 representing weakest
and 7 representing strongest performance)

Adam Smith Albion

INTRODUCTION

The Tulip Revolution of March 2005 brought 14 years of increasingly
authoritarian and kleptocratic rule under President Askar Akaev to a
swift and ignominious end. In the 1990s, Kyrgyzstan won plaudits as
the most democratic, progressive country in Central Asia thanks to
Akaev's comparative tolerance of opposition parties and free media, and
his openness to market reforms. His credentials as a liberal reformer were
severely tarnished by the 2000 presidential election, which was characterized by fraud and repression of the opposition, including the jailing
of his foremost political challenger, former national security minister
Feliks Kulov. During the last five years of his rule, Akaev steadily consolidated power and misused it to neutralize rivals, intimidate independent media, and manipulate the judiciary. As the international spotlight
moved to Central Asia in the aftermath of September 11, 2001, both
the United States and Russia established airbases in Kyrgyzstan as responses to the war on terrorism. These developments raised Akaev's profile on the world stage and emboldened him to clamp down on his
domestic opponents still further. Meanwhile corruption, nepotism, and
graft flourished, blurring the boundaries between government and organized crime. The president's family and allies took control of many of

Adam Smith Albion is Director of Critical Areas Research for World Monitors, Inc., and
Director of the Central Eurasia Leadership Academy (CELA).

281

the country's prime economic resources, hiding assets through dozens of shell companies, but their rapacity was growing blatant and their support was dwindling. Rigged elections, in which two of Akaev's children won seats in parliament, hinting at the possibility of a dynastic succession, were the last straw.

Akaev's regime collapsed in a matter of hours, but his legacy is taking longer to overcome. Opposition leader Kurmanbek Bakiev won an impressive mandate in a new presidential election, promising to accelerate democratic reforms, tackle poverty, and crack down on corruption. However, his administration faces numerous obstacles to implementing such an ambitious program, some of its own making. The parliament was chosen in fraudulent elections, meaning that Kyrgyzstan has a hybrid government of a fairly elected executive and an Akaev-era legislature. Many of the deputies are believed to have links with mafia groups. Powerful and prevalent, organized crime has emerged from the shadows as one of the country's most troubling issues.

Civil liberties have improved after the revolution, yet the new authorities have occasionally revealed instinctual tendencies, reminiscent of the old regime, to try to rein in critical journalists or limit protests. At the same time, the revolution, with its heady whiff of "people power," has unleashed forces of its own that menace social order and the stability of the state. Street demonstrations, the storming or blockading of government buildings, appointments of officials by popular acclamation—techniques all employed to good effect to topple Akaev's authoritarian rule—have outlasted their time and are now employed to lobby or defy Bakiev's democratically elected government. His weak administration is still struggling to bring the country under its control against a backdrop of low-level violence and outbreaks of anarchy in which organized crime, partnered by corrupt security forces, are playing an increasingly visible role.

ACCOUNTABILITY AND PUBLIC VOICE – 4.17

Kyrgyzstan's March 2005 revolution was precipitated by street protests against fraudulent parliamentary elections held the previous month.[1] The authorities had interfered in election campaigns and systematically rigged results to produce wins for political allies and family members of President Askar Akaev. Akaev fled the country on March 24 after demonstrators stormed the White House (main government building) in the capital, Bishkek. Opposition figures, led by Kurmanbek Bakiev, a former prime minister who had turned against the regime, took control of government. They faced the conundrum of all revolutionary leaders professing to stand for democratic governance and the rule of law: Their elevation to power was extraconstitutional and thus strictly speaking illegal.[2] To their credit, they recognized the problem and the importance of observing legal niceties if the country was to be steered onto a more democratic course. Consequently, three key decisions were taken with a view to shoring up the new order's political legitimacy and preserving, as much as possible, the constitutional forms. First, Akaev was induced to sign an official letter of resignation, which he did on April 4; it was formally accepted by the legislature the following week. Second, a new presidential election was scheduled within three months of Akaev's resignation, as required by law; it was duly held on July 10. Third, and most controversially, fresh parliamentary elections were not called; the flawed results of the February/March balloting were allowed to stand. This meant overlooking the violations that had sparked the revolution in the first place. Yet the alternative—annulling the results, dissolving the new parliament, reinstating the old one, and extending its mandate on an ad hoc basis—would have been a political improvisation, taking government ever farther outside the constitutional framework. Accepting the legitimacy of the compromised parliament was seen as a devil's bargain, but it signaled a commitment not to change the system arbitrarily and to abide by law and precedent. As such, it brought the revolutionary phase of the political transition to a swift close.

Bakiev won the presidential election with 88.6 percent of the vote. Official voter turnout was 75 percent. The scale of Bakiev's victory owed much to the decision by his strongest potential opponent, leader of the Ar-Namys (Dignity) party and former dissident Feliks Kulov, not to run against him. Instead they campaigned as a tandem on the understanding, duly honored, that Kulov would become prime minister. While noting a small number of serious irregularities, especially in the counting and tabulation stages, international monitors declared the election free and mostly fair, and did not question the legitimacy of the result. The Organization for Security and Cooperation in Europe (OSCE) said Kyrgyzstan had made "tangible progress" in meeting its democratic commitments.

A paradox of the revolution was that, while it breathed new life into the political system, the sweeping scale of Bakiev's victory temporarily sucked the air out of multiparty democracy. With Akaev gone and the opposition in power, there was no one to contest policies of the new government. However, opponents have now started to fractionate out of the pro-Bakiev camp. Two of his former top lieutenants—Roza Otunbaeva, interim foreign minister, and Azimbek Beknazarov, ex-prosecutor general—have now broken with him and declared themselves in political opposition. At present, though, beyond their personal disgruntlement it is unclear where they (or, for that matter, any of the political parties) fundamentally disagree with the government on a policy level and whether they have an alternative vision to offer. Of the 65 political parties in Kyrgyzstan, 23 came into being after the revolution. However, multiparty democracy is less developed or vibrant than those numbers imply. Instead of coalescing around a set of definable policies, most parties hover around a charismatic or wealthy leader and exist as a ragtag vehicle to promote his (rarely her) political ambitions. Campaign finance laws are nonfunctional: candidates reportedly secure many votes by simple handouts of cash or clannish promises of patronage. Parties are fragmented and disorganized. Even the anti-Akaev opposition forces, riven by competing strong personalities, could barely muster a united front in February and March 2005 and often seemed to have no particular platform beyond ousting the president.

Moreover, in February 2003, Akaev pushed through certain constitutional amendments tailor-made to weaken the role of parties. In place of a two-chamber legislature with a total of 105 deputies, the new system created a new unicameral body with 75 seats. In previous parliamentary elections, a quarter of the seats were determined on the basis of party lists, and the rest were single-mandate constituencies. Under the new rules, party lists were abolished and all the races took place in single-seat constituencies. Consequently, parties played almost no role in the February 2005 parliamentary elections, nominating a mere 18 percent of the candidates.[4] However, in November 2005, the Constitutional Council (a body established after the revolution to draft constitutional amendments for public debate) proposed a return to a version of the pre-2003 system. A significant but currently unspecified number of seats in the legislature would again be awarded through party lists, on the basis of proportional representation. The rest of the seats would be competed for in single-mandate constituencies on the basis of a first-past-the-post system.[5] The changes, which would be implemented in the next parliamentary elections in 2010, could vivify multiparty democracy by encouraging coalition-building and sharper definition of political programs. Meanwhile, parties need to build up national bases for politics to move beyond the excessive clannishness and narrow regionalism that currently hold sway, promoted by the single-mandate system.

While the constitution provides for checks and balances between the executive, the legislature, and the judiciary, Akaev steadily concentrated power in the presidency and controlled patronage to the point where his initiatives were rarely thwarted. The Constitutional Court was responsible for some decisions that mildly curtailed the government's freedom of action, as when it struck down certain restrictions on freedom of assembly in October 2004. The parliament was mostly supine before Akaev. The new parliament is feistier and flexed its muscles at once by turning down six out of Bakiev's original 16 cabinet nominations. Nonetheless, the president's power makes the office excessively strong. An original goal of the postrevolution Constitutional Council was to craft suggestions for trimming back the presidential powers; however, Bakiev seemed at times to be manipulating the Constitutional Council to grab more power for his office rather than give any up.[6]

Civil society in Kyrgyzstan is lively. Even under Akaev there was never a concerted crackdown on nongovernmental organizations (NGOs), although some human rights activists suffered intimidation and arbitrary curtailments of their activities. Particular pressure was brought on the Kyrgyz Committee on Human Rights (KCHR): Its president was driven to self-imposed exile in Europe, his daughter in Bishkek was beaten up by unknown men in July 2004, and a car allegedly tried to run her over later that year.[7] Civil society actors played a prominent public role during the revolution and have continued to do so. NGOs must register with the Ministry of Justice, but the process is not arduous (a group requires only three members to register, for example). In fact, no indigenous NGO is reported to have been denied registration in 2004–2005. Today an estimated 7,000 to 10,000 NGOs are registered in the country, although a mere fraction of that number are active and perhaps only 100 of them are financially self-sustaining.[8] Organizations such as the Coalition for Democracy and Civil Society, an umbrella for some 170 NGOs nationwide, regularly offer vigorous and critical assessments of the government's actions and public affairs generally. The public has also been able to comment on pending legislation through the Constitutional Council, which was opened to suggestions on constitutional amendments from civic groups and individual citizens. In November 2005, Bakiev ordered the government to disseminate information on the draft changes and to conduct local-level public discussion about them until the end of the year. The amendments are due to be put to a national referendum in 2006.[9]

Media freedom has improved greatly since the revolution, but significant problems remain. Akaev's regime harassed critical journalists through various means: politically motivated tax inspections, defamation lawsuits (manipulating the courts to award penalties), or sudden power outages at the printing presses. Meanwhile, the improbabe frequency with which journalists were attacked by anonymous street thugs strongly suggested the authorities were behind the incidents. Important sections of the media were controlled by Akaev family members, notably Akaev's son-in-law Adil Toigonbaev, whose business empire included Kyrgyz Public Educational Radio and Television (KOORT) and the newspaper *Vechernii Bishkek.* The president also appoints the director general of the state-owned National Television and Radio Company (NTRK).[10]

Bakiev came to power vowing to rein in government influence over the media, but the record is mixed. Crude forms of intimidation by the government have ended: According to an IREX report on media freedoms, "[n]ot a single crime was committed against journalists in 2005."[11] There is no censorship of the internet. Yet many journalists still practice self-censorship because they are not confident of state protections, and the fact that there is no statute of limitations on libel in the criminal code is a potent source of worry. There are indications that Bakiev's government is becoming less tolerant of criticism. *Vechernii Bishkek,* which was predictably hostile to the new order and continued to promote Akaev's interests, was wrested from Toigonbaev's control and put under the management of Aleksandr Kim, a Bakiev stalwart. KOORT also provided critical coverage of the government after the revolution. It too was prised from Toigonbaev; an October 2005 shareholders' meeting elected Kim to be KOORT chairman. A subsequent attempt to install a fresh management team consisting of government loyalists provoked a revolt by KOORT employees. In an open letter they complained that the new managers had ordered them to praise top officials in an analytical program.[12] The popular independent station Piramida TV has also complained of government pressure.

Perhaps surprisingly, the government channel NTRK maintained the most unbiased editorial line throughout the year. In November 2005, the parliament considered a draft bill to transform NTRK into a public service broadcaster. Observers lauded the plan in principle as a way to expand freedom of information and expression, yet there were concerns that the bill, as written, did not contain guarantees against political and commercial interference. Because the president would appoint the director general and nominate all the advisory board members, NTRK's independence could clearly be in jeopardy.[13] Other laws on media freedom drafted by parliamentary working groups have also disturbed international watchdog organizations, which have noted that "some restrictions are so vague that they could mean almost anything. The prohibition on printing 'unprintable expressions' is probably the best example of such restrictions."[14]

Recommendations

- The people must be permitted to express their will about draft amendments to the constitution through a free and fair national referendum, following a sufficient period of informed public debate.
- The president should cooperate on legislative reforms to reduce the power of the executive in relation to other branches of government.
- The government must stop interfering, either directly or by proxy, in the workings of KOORT, Piramida, or other independent media to compel favorable coverage or suppress unfavorable coverage.
- The charter of NTRK as a public service broadcaster and the accompanying legislation must ensure the station's independence from pressure by political and commercial interests.

CIVIL LIBERTIES – 4.17

Akaev's final year in power was characterized by growing autocracy and a commensurate erosion of civil liberties in Kyrgyzstan. The Ministry of Internal Affairs (MVD) and the National Security Service (SNB) were seen increasingly as instruments of state repression. Members of the opposition Ar-Namys (Dignity) party were persecuted and harassed or driven to quit the party under threat of losing their jobs. Human rights defenders were also subject to intimidation and surveillance by security agents. Such overt use of law enforcement to suppress political opponents has ceased under the Bakiev government. There have been no political prisoners in Kyrgyzstan since the release, during the revolution, of the Ar-Namys leader (now prime minister), Feliks Kulov. However, democratic slogans and personnel changes at the top (including reshuffles in the Ministry of Internal Affairs and a new Bishkek police chief) have not eliminated overnight the culture of abuse and brutality that seeped through the police and security organs during Akaev's lengthy rule.

Arbitrary arrest and detention without trial are forbidden by the Kyrgyz constitution (Article 18).[15] However, numerous opponents of Akaev's regime were illegally jailed for short periods of time or underwent unwarranted hospitalization in retaliation for criticism or to prevent them from making public appearances. In November 2004, Tursunbek Akunov, the head of the Human Rights Movement of Kyrgyzstan and leader of a campaign for Akaev's impeachment, was summoned to a meeting with the police and vanished. He reappeared at a Bishkek hospital two weeks later, asserting that he had been abducted and kept in a basement during that period by SNB and MVD members.[16] Opportunistic police officers have also been known to arrest citizens on false charges and then—in a form of state-sponsored kidnapping—offer to let them go in exchange for money.

In November 2003, the criminal code was amended specifically to prohibit torture (already outlawed by Article 18 of the constitution). Nevertheless, its use remained widespread, although not systematic, in both pretrial detention facilities and prisons. The MVD, taking its cue from a high-profile but brief anticorruption drive launched by Akaev in February 2004, reported that it had opened criminal cases against scores of police officers and disciplined many more in response to citizens' complaints. Yet notwithstanding some cosmetic changes and half-hearted measures, police corruption and impunity have remained serious problems. Officials have yet "to acknowledge the extent and gravity of Kyrgyzstan's torture problem or to formulate a plan to resolve it."[17]

The harsh and degrading conditions in Kyrgyzstan's prisons became a national scandal in 2005. The first attempts at penal reform came in 2002 with a decision to transfer authority over the prisons from the

MVD to the Ministry of Justice. Despite some improvements since then, three waves of bloody prison riots swept the country in late 2005 as inmates protested against chronic overcrowding, starvation rations, and epidemics of hepatitis, tuberculosis, HIV, and other infectious diseases. The resulting publicity also threw a spotlight on entrenched corruption in the penitentiary system—a world where jailed criminal bosses lived in luxury with access to weapons and money and colluded with prison officials in running drugs.[18] Bakiev vowed to restore order and improve conditions, but little money has been allocated to back up his promises.[19]

Freedom of assembly is guaranteed by the constitution. Under Akaev, the authorities were relatively tolerant of rallies and protests (quite a common sight even outside the White House and the parliament) except when they were deemed to pose an unacceptable political threat. In such cases, the state could exploit ambiguities in the law—which required advance written notification and permission to hold public assemblies but did not spell out how to meet those requirements—to prohibit or disband gatherings. In April 2004, police forcefully intervened to stop dozens of demonstrators marching in support of (then) jailed oppositionist Feliks Kulov. The use of excessive force against rallies has been a long-standing concern, most notoriously on display in the town of Aksy in March 2003 when police fired into a crowd of antigovernment protesters, killing five. Bakiev, incidentally, was prime minister at the time and initially backed the police, although he eventually resigned over the incident. As president, too, he has already courted controversy by deploying special forces, carrying large-caliber automatic weapons and grenade launchers, to crush a prison rebellion in November 2005. Amid the ensuing uproar, human rights ombudsman Tursunbai Bakir-uulu promised an investigation into the incident, in which least four inmates were killed and many more were said to be seriously injured.[20]

However, such strong-arm tactics against public unrest and demonstrations have been the exception rather than the rule under Bakiev. For the most part, his weak government has been permissive to the point of helpless surrender in the face of protests and other manifestations of "people power" unleashed by the revolution. The question for Kyrgyzstan is not whether the state permits demonstrations and protests—they have continued almost nonstop around the country throughout the year—but whether it can possibly stop them. In November 2005, the new prosecutor general, Kambaraly Kongantiev, told the National

Security Council there had been at least 1,200 unauthorized protests and 2,286 illegal public meetings since January. He echoed warnings by other officials that the ongoing chaos and anarchy could bring Kyrgyzstan to the brink of collapse. Thus a civil liberties issue, freedom of association and assembly, has blurred dangerously into a public-security issue. In October 2005, Kongrantiev (then a parliamentarian) floated a draconian proposal to impose a year-long ban on demonstrations, marches, and any public activity involving "calls for subversive action designed to destabilize the situation and hinder the work of government and law-enforcement bodies."[22] The proposal was shelved after it provoked outrage among many rights activists and legislators.

Kyrgyz law accords equal status to men and women, and gender discrimination is prohibited by the constitution (Article 15). However, in February 2004, Akaev tacitly recognized that there were violations on paper and in practice when he decreed an analysis of all legislation from the standpoint of gender equity. This was followed by a government action plan, implemented in November 2004, to eradicate all forms of discrimination against women. While creditable as first steps, these measures have made limited headway against a real and growing problem. On the one hand, Kyrgyz women are well represented in the labor force and the white-collar professions. They comprise approximately one-third of the country's judges and are prominent as attorneys.[23] The chief justice of the Constitutional Court, Cholpon Baekova, is female, and there were women ministers (and one vice prime minister) under Akaev. On the other hand, there is currently not a single female deputy in the parliament, and only one woman with a senior post in Bakiev's government—Aigul Ryskulova, who chairs the State Committee for Migration and Employment. Of the country's 65 political parties, only two are headed by women.[24]

Kyrgyzstan's failing economy poses perhaps the greatest threat to women's equality. Paid less on average than their male counterparts, they are more likely to be unemployed and first to be laid off—even though more Kyrgyz women than men have higher education degrees. Women are particularly disadvantaged in the countryside, where poverty is rife and scarce socioeconomic resources such as jobs and educational opportunities are preferentially given to males.[25] Moreover, many rural women must contend with traditional patriarchal attitudes that regard their proper place as the kitchen and the bedroom. The customary practice of bride-stealing—kidnapping and, in some cases, raping girls for forced marriage—has enjoyed something of a popular revival in rural areas since the collapse of the USSR. Although the practice is outlawed, local authorities have tended to turn a blind eye. Abuses have grown sufficiently widespread that, in December 2004, the government backed an NGO-sponsored Campaign Against Violence and Bride Kidnapping to educate young people, officials, and the police about the wrongs of the matter and sensitize them to domestic violence. Trafficking of women is another problem to which the state has belatedly awakened. An estimated 2,500 Kyrgyz women have been trafficked abroad for the purpose of sexual exploitation, 80 percent of them ending up in the United Arab Emirates. The U.S. State Department has listed Kyrgyzstan as a Tier 2 country, meaning that the government does not fully comply with the minimum standards of the Trafficking Victims Protection Act but, following the adoption of a new comprehensive anti-trafficking law in January 2005, is making significant efforts to do so.[26]

The rights and needs of people with disabilities, recognized on paper, are usually neglected by the state, citing scarce resources. Wheelchair ramps are a rarity; mental hospitals are in shambles; discrimination against people with disabilities is common in the job market. Numerous NGOs have stepped into the vacuum left by the government and work to train and support people with disabilities, particularly children. However, their work inevitably reaches only a small proportion of the disabled population, about whose numbers no reliable statistics exist.

Kyrgyzstan is a multiethnic state of 5.1 million people, of whom ethnic Kyrgyz comprise 67.4 percent. Ethnic Russians (10.3 percent) are concentrated in the north of the country, while ethnic Uzbeks (14.2 percent) have their stronghold in the south. Although the law proscribes discrimination on the basis of race or ethnicity, non-Kyrgyz have been consistently underrepresented in government posts. Russians in particular allege they are treated unfairly in the private sector as well. This perception of a glass ceiling has contributed to their mass emigration (Russians made up a fifth of the country's population in 1990). To encourage them to stay, Akaev's government had Russian designated in the constitution, beside Kyrgyz, as the official state language; still, the status of Russian has been periodically challenged by nationalist groups keen to promote wider use of Kyrgyz. When another public row erupted over the issue in November 2005, Bakiev (whose wife is Russian) had to intervene in support of retaining Russian's official status.

By contrast, a petition in 2002 by the Uzbek community to have their language upgraded to a state language was ignored. Many Uzbeks supported Akaev nonetheless as a bulwark against Kyrgyz nationalism and were correspondingly tepid in their support for the revolution. Uzbeks have warmed to Bakiev's administration since its handling of the refugee crisis in spring–summer 2005, when hundreds of Uzbek citizens sought asylum in Kyrgyzstan after the bloody suppression of a demonstration in the Uzbek town of Andijon. The government upheld, for the most part, its obligations under international law not to repatriate them and eventually allowed 450 Uzbek citizens (many of whom had family ties to ethnic Uzbeks in Kyrgyzstan) to be airlifted to third countries.[28]

Kyrgyzstan is a secular state in which freedom of religion is legally guaranteed and mostly respected in practice. About 80 percent of the inhabitants (essentially, the Kyrgyz and Uzbeks) are Sunni Muslims. Russians tend to follow the Russian Orthodox faith, at least nominally, although a small number have been attracted by a diverse group of Protestant denominations whose missionaries operate with minimal state inference. All religious organizations must register first with the State Commission on Religious Affairs (SCRA) and then with the Ministry of Justice; the process is cumbersome and can take over a month but is basically pro forma only, as almost all unregistered groups report that they can function freely.[29] The exceptions to this pattern of tolerance are restrictions on radical Islamic groups regarded by the state as threatening to security and stability. Foremost among them is Hizb ut-Tahrir, banned in 2003, which agitates for the establishment of Islamic rule and has an estimated 3,000 clandestine followers in the south of the country. Its members, arrested typically for distributing propaganda leaflets and literature, have sometimes been fined or let off with a warning, but the trend now is toward less tolerance and more imprisonments. The charges are usually inciting religious, ethnic, or racial hatred. In the first half of 2005, prosecutors opened 34 criminal cases and held 36 individuals on charges of extremism.[30] Meanwhile the government, acting through the muftiate (the official Islamic spiritual leadership), has started taking steps to monitor the preaching of itinerant Muslim preachers.[31]

The very first law signed by Bakiev as president in August 2005 was "On Combating Extremist Activity," whereby merely "to assert" certain views may be punishable.[32]

Recommendations

- The penal system must be reformed to humanize conditions for ordinary prisoners and provide for their welfare, eliminate the privileges accorded to criminal bosses, and punish corrupt prison officials.
- Allegations of state torture must be investigated promptly, impartially, and fully, and the government should ensure appropriate prosecution and punishment.
- The president should demonstrate his commitment to combat discrimination by promoting more women and minorities, particularly ethnic Uzbeks, to senior offices.
- The government should bring its new anti-trafficking legislation into force and expand efforts to clamp down on the trafficking in persons.

RULE OF LAW – 3.38

Akaev dominated the judiciary to consolidate his rule. Two especially notorious decisions set the tone. In 1998, the Constitutional Court held that Akaev could run for a third term, notwithstanding the two-term limitation spelled out in the constitution. In January 2001, his chief political rival, Feliks Kulov, was found guilty of abuse of power, although the same charges against him had been dismissed the previous year; a further prosecution for embezzlement left him with a 10-year sentence. The judge who had initially dismissed the case was reassigned to a remote regional court.[33] Kulov remained in prison until freed during the revolution, when he was cleared of all charges.

The justices on both of Kyrgyzstan's upper courts, the Supreme Court and the Constitutional Court, and all lower court judges are appointed by the president—a system ripe for compromising the independence of the judiciary, although judges must now also be confirmed by the parliament pursuant to constitutional amendments introduced in February 2003. Candidates are screened in a nontransparent fashion by qualification collegiums whose political independence is dubious. Judges must have a law degree and at least five years' experience in the legal profession (10 years to sit on the Supreme Court and Constitutional Court). The level of training available for judges has been evaluated as mostly adequate,[34] although the complexities of the appointment process mean it is not always the best-qualified candidates who make it to the bench. All in all, the process has reportedly been plagued by corruption, with candidates often purchasing their judgeships or being chosen on political considerations. The participation of the parliament has had some effect as a check on the presidency (a few of whose judicial nominees have been rejected) but is not an unmitigated good, considering how frequently deputies themselves are litigants and how many of the present incumbents are believed to have ties to shady businesses and organized crime. Thus, the fear is that the judiciary, previously corrupted by only one branch of government, the executive, could now be actively subverted by two—"that bribes would now be paid to members of Parliament or that the members would 'call in favors' of those judges whom they had supported."[35] The poor salaries of most judges (less than $200 a month) contribute to their susceptibility to improper influence.

Under Bakiev's chairmanship, the Constitutional Council has drafted a raft of constitutional amendments that would affect the judiciary. While they are intended ostensibly to improve and democratize Kyrgyzstan's legislation and institutions, some seem designed to remove curbs on the presidency by weakening the courts, especially a plan to abolish the Constitutional Court and make it a special chamber of the Supreme Court. The Constitutional Court decides the constitutionality of laws, determines the validity of presidential elections, and umpires jurisdiction between the institutions of state. Proponents of its abolition say the move would eliminate the danger that the two upper courts might contradict one another. Another draft amendment would make it easier to dismiss Supreme Court justices.[36]

Defendants have the right to legal representation. Those who cannot afford an attorney are provided one at public expense. However, clients do not always gain access to their lawyers immediately and are sometimes interrogated in the absence of counsel. The criminal code was revised in March 2004 to render any statements made without an attorney present inadmissible in court.[37] The law mandates the presumption of an accused person's innocence until proven guilty, yet in practice the judicial system frequently acts as if the opposite were true. Verdicts of not guilty are exceptionally rare: According to official statistics for 1998 to 2002, 98.7 percent of defendants were found guilty.[38] Judges almost always defer to the powerful prosecutors who are in charge of criminal proceedings; it is the latter (not judges) who currently have the right to issue arrest warrants, order searches, or approve wiretaps.[39] So-called telephone justice—late-night calls to the judge's home from the president's or the prosecutor general's office, telling him what verdict to hand down the next morning—frequently determined important political and financial cases under Akaev's regime. It is unclear how widespread political interference in the judiciary is nowadays. Even if cleaner government under Bakiev has put a lid on the practice, there is a range of nonstate actors, from oligarchs to mafia bosses, who probably know what telephone calls to place to make their influence felt.

During Akaev's rule, senior state officials and their allies were effectively above the law. After the revolution, however, the new prosecutor general, Azimbek Beknazarov, launched aggressive investigations into the alleged corruption and criminal activities of the Akaev clan and its entourage. Criminal charges were brought against Akaev's son-in-law (and prepared against his son) as well as numerous ex-officials including the former prime minister, presidential chief of staff, head of the national bank, and Central Electoral Commission chief. Beknazarov was also credited with efforts to turn the prosecutor general's office into a more independent body by distancing it from the executive branch. In September 2005, Bakiev abruptly fired him, supposedly for mishandling an investigation. An uproar ensued: Beknazarov supporters claimed the real reason for his dismissal was that his anticorruption crusade was getting too close to uncovering shady dealings of the current administration. Beknazarov announced to journalists that corruption was rampant at the highest level of government under Bakiev.[40] The truth remains murky, but the incident has raised concerns about Bakiev's commitment to judicial independence and government accountability.

Although the law guarantees property rights, the state has struggled at times to assert and protect them. Efforts by Beknazarov to renationalize factories and enterprises whose shares, he said, had been improperly acquired put him in conflict with powerful business interests and may have contributed to his ouster. Meanwhile the judiciary was sidelined in 2005 as two business rivals, Bayaman Erkinbaev (a member of parliament) and Abdalim Junusov, struggled to assert ownership of the Karasuu town bazaar. A local court confirmed Erkinbaev's ownership. Nonetheless, factions clashed on the streets, property was attacked, and eventually both men were shot dead in contract killings. In September 2005, a Karasuu court ruled that Erkinbaev's purchase of part of the bazaar had actually been illegal and ordered that it become state property. This ruling has not been complied with. The authorities have also been impotent in the seizure of the five Karakeche coal mines, four of which were privately owned. These were taken over in June 2005 by a local firebrand, Nurlan Motuev, saying their privatization had been illegal. Motuev is now producing and selling the coal himself.[41]

Since 1998, citizens have had the right to own land. The authorities fueled land hunger by promising, perhaps unrealistically, to distribute plots to whoever needed them most. Available land in Kyrgyzstan is scarce (especially in the densely populated Ferghana Valley region in the south) and arable land even scarcer in a largely mountainous country. Distribution schemes under Akaev were loaded with bureaucracy and shot through with corruption and cronyism. Weeks after the revolution, in April 2005, at least 30,000 people took advantage of the authorities' impotence and the atmosphere of anarchy by beginning to seize land outside Bishkek.[42] Bakiev's government promised to build apartment buildings and to seek legal solutions, but unlawful seizures continued with impunity through the summer and autumn. Meanwhile, the land's owners were deprived of their property; farmers in particular complained they had lost the year's crops. Not until October 2005 did the government unequivocally invoke the inviolability of private property and say that no land already established as private property would be redistributed.[43] The standoff with squatters, unimpressed by legal technicalities and calling for social justice, was still unresolved in November 2005.

The Ministry of Internal Affairs (MVD) controls the police and a 4,000-strong paramilitary force for riot control and counterinsurgency operations. These forces have demonstrated brutality and indifference to human rights on multiple occasions, most notably in the March 2002 assault on peaceful demonstrators in Aksy. Yet when the revolution came, the interior forces were mostly bystanders and abandoned Akaev; crucially, they did not fire on the crowds. The Organization for Security and Cooperation in Europe (OSCE) subsequently took partial credit for their peaceable response, referencing a training project launched in

2003 to educate Kyrgyz police about human rights, community policing, and democratic accountability: "The value of the OSCE police assistance programme in Kyrgyzstan was clearly demonstrated by the
restraint shown by the police in Bishkek in March 2005, despite the real
threat of violence. This was in marked contrast to the behaviour of some
police units during previous incidents in the country."[44] This vision of
conscientious policing in Kyrgyzstan may be too optimistic and is certainly premature. Prime Minister Kulov (who himself served as minister of national security under Akaev) struggled inconclusively through
the autumn to bring the law enforcement bodies under tighter government control.

Recommendations

- The process by which judges are screened and appointed should be
  reformed to guarantee their independence; the powers of the courts
  should be strengthened in relation to those of state prosecutors.
- The presumption of innocence until proven guilty must be upheld
  and respected at all times by prosecutors, judges, and other parties
  (e.g., politicians).
- The government should act more forcefully and unequivocally to
  protect property rights and work to ensure that disputes are decided
  through the courts, not on the streets.

ANTICORRUPTION AND TRANSPARENCY – 2.54

Corruption pervaded the state under Akaev. He and his family set the
pace, seeking to monopolize political and economic opportunities to
enrich themselves. Government officials followed their example. In February 2004, Akaev launched a Good Governance Council to implement
a high-profile government anticorruption program, but it was widely
viewed as an exercise in hypocrisy. Whistle-blowing journalists who uncovered instances of corruption were persecuted, not thanked. In the
same month that the Good Governance Council was formed, an official
inquiry into the death of Ernis Nazalov—a journalist who had been
investigating government corruption until his corpse was found in a river
covered in bruises and stab wounds—concluded that he had drowned
accidentally after a drunken party. Akaev's fall was hastened by the graft
and greed that he exemplified. A February 2005 exposé in an opposition

newspaper, shedding light on his personal wealth and family's business interests, has been seen as one of the detonators of the revolution.[45]

Bakiev promised measures to advance clean and transparent government significantly. He has fallen short of his promises. From the moment he assumed power, he squandered popular trust and sowed doubts about his integrity as he brought his own friends and relatives into the government to replace Akaev's. The media reported that some posts were being bought and sold as before. The interim finance minister, Akylbek Japarov, filled key positions in the customs service and financial police with his family members.[46] Bakiev himself went on to appoint his three brothers, Marat, Adyl, and Jusupbek, to become, respectively, ambassador to Germany, trade representative in China, and deputy director of the Agency for Community Development and Investment.

In April, a commission headed by Deputy Prime Minister Daniyar Usenov was created to track down assets of dozens of companies apparently belonging to Akaev and his inner circle. Entities allegedly under their control included many of the country's major economic assets, including media outlets, shopping centers, restaurants, vacation resorts, factories, and an airport. However, it is discouraging that the Akaev investigation has been conducted without independent oversight. As the International Crisis Group has pointed out, the inquiries "are not by independent auditors so there is a possibility they will simply lead to a transfer of control to other political players."[47]

Among the monies apparently stolen by the Akaev family were funds that might have been earmarked for foreign assistance or investment to the country. Alam Service, a company that supplied fuel to American warplanes at Manas airport, belonged to Akaev's son-in-law, Toigonbaev, who apparently siphoned off at least $16.5 million from the contract with the U.S. government—cash that should have been paid into the state treasury. Another fuel supplier, Manas International Service, belonged to Akaev's son Aydar, who may have stolen $30 million per year.[48] Competition for government contracts or other lucrative ventures was neither fair nor open in Akaev's Kyrgyzstan, where the best opportunities were steered towards family members and allies. It is of special concern to know what safeguards the Bakiev government intends to put in place against such diversions of funds in the future, now that the foreign donor community is ramping up financial assistance to

Kyrgyzstan. In November 2005, Kyrgyzstan entered the threshold program of the Millennium Challenge Corporation for fiscal year 2006: a waiting-room for countries that have not yet qualified for Millennium Challenge Account (MCA) funding assistance but have demonstrated a significant commitment to improve their performance on the MCA eligibility criteria, which include a democratic political system and strong anticorruption credentials.

However, with its corruption-fighting energies focused on malfeasance under Akaev, the government has made no systematic effort to tackle corruption as it continues to exist on a day-to-day basis. There have been a few piecemeal measures. In November 2005, a new Financial Police Service was established to combat economic crimes and tax evasion. The Ministry of Finance is pursuing certain companies that were sheltered by Akaev's regime to force them to pay back taxes; the ministry also has claimed some successes in stanching the flow of illegal funds. The government has approved a program to root out corruption among the traffic police, a notoriously crooked institution despised by motorists.[49] Yet these measures are merely chipping around the edges of a monolith of entrenched corruption. The Transparency International 2005 Corruption Perceptions Index ranked Kyrgyzstan 130 out of 159 countries, with a score of 2.3 on a scale from 0 ("highly corrupt") to 10 ("highly clean").[50] This is a meager improvement on the previous year's score of 2.2. Judges, doctors, civil servants, police officers, customs officers, teachers, university examiners and administrators, vendors of airline tickets, and tax inspectors—practically any state employee who controls the dispensation of goods or services regularly—require a bribe to do their job in a timely manner yielding a favorable result. Miserable state salaries impel, and to their mind justify, officials' rent-seeking behavior.

Probably nowhere is the conflict between public duty and private interest as obvious (and as unresolved) as in the legislature. Since March 2004, government officials have been required by law to disclose all sources of income. Yet in the current parliament sit numerous individuals whose enterprises are shady at best. Some are generally known to be connected with gangsters and have become deputies to protect their businesses better and because the status offers immunity from prosecution. Bakiev openly accused MPs of subverting the police and cooperating with organized crime in a speech in September 2005.[51] Three MPs

were murdered in 2005—two in contract killings, one in a prison riot—
for reasons believed to have to do with their business interests or criminal relations.

Economic growth is stymied by corruption; the bribes are frequently
required during licensing procedures, dispute settlements, government
procurement, regulatory activity, and taxation. It takes an average of 21
days to register a business,[52] and business owners often need licenses
from 20 different state agencies. The customs and tax inspectorate are
reckoned to be the most corrupt institutions in the land. Formally,
though, government involvement in the economy is relatively low (4.65
percent of revenues came from state-owned enterprises and government
ownership of property in 2004) and diminishing. The Heritage Foundation rated the Kyrgyz economy in 2005 as "mostly free."[53]

Citizens have the right to request information about government
operations, and such requests are generally honored although state organs may take a long time to comply. The government's annual budgets
are published in state newspapers, but statistics tend to lack the fine
detail needed to make them very meaningful; actual tax expenditures
are not given, for example. Under Akaev, annual budgets were crafted
in the president's office through a nontransparent process, passed by the
parliament with minimum dissension, and then routinely ignored by all
the state institutions called on to implement them. Bakiev will not be
able to push his first budget through so easily. It is sure to come in for
sharp scrutiny from freshly empowered civic groups and is likely to face
strong challenges in the parliament. This process is likely to further the
cause of transparent, accountable government in Kyrgyzstan.

Recommendations
- The government must take measures to attack nepotism and
  cronyism in public life.
- The president and his colleagues must publicly declare their
  sources of income, as required by the disclosure laws for state
  officials, and should compel members of parliament to do the same,
  making the relevant documentation available for public scrutiny.
- The commission investigating assets allegedly belonging to Akaev
  and his allies should publicize its results, and the subsequent process
  of property redistribution should be conducted in a transparent
  fashion under the supervision of independent auditors.

- The state budget should be formulated openly and debated publicly; government expenditures should be declassified to the maximum extent possible and be published for public review.

NOTES

1   The first round of voting was on February 27. Runoffs between the two leading candidates in a constituency if neither received a first-round majority were held on 13 March.

2   In the political vacuum left by Akaev's flight, the new interim authorities were recognized by the chief justice of the Constitutional Court, Cholpon Baekova, who gave the transfer of power her imprimatur. This was good politics, but it is disputable whether she actually had the legal authority to do so.

3   Leila Saralaeva, "Landslide Win for New Kyrgyz Leader" (London: Institute of War and Peace Reporting [IWPR], 11 July 2005), http://iwpr.net/?p=rca&s=f&o=255942& apc_state=henirca5f60e2cb70738c66e029962d2dbed3c4.

4   *Kyrgyzstan: After the Revolution* (Bishkek/Brussels: International Crisis Group [ICG], Asia Report No. 97, 4 May 2005), 1, http://www.crisisgroup.org/library/documents/ asia/central_asia/097_kyrgyzstan_after_the_revolution.pdf.

5   Aziza Turdueva, "Kyrgyz Parties Join Forces" (IWPR, 3 December 2005), http://www .iwpr.net/?p=rca&s=f&o=258414&apc_state=henh.

6   Saralaeva and Cholpon Orozobekova, "Kyrgyz Leader Pushes for More Power" (IWPR, 15 Nov 2005), http://iwpr.net/?p=rca&s=f&o=257784&apc_state=henircaa499a 109fb0f9795d1b2bcc8f504dd15; "Kyrgyzstan: Is the President Losing Interest in Constitutional Reform?" (New York: Eurasianet, 25 August 2005), http://www.eurasianet .org/departments/insight/articles/eav082505.shtml.

7   "Kyrgyzstan," in *Human Rights Watch World Report 2005: Events of 2004* (New York: Human Rights Watch [HRW], 2005), 395–96, http://www.hrw.org/wr2k5.

8   Celia Chauffour, "Kyrghyzstan [sic] and its 8,000 NGOs: a strange laboratory of democracy in Central Asia," *Caucaz europenews* (Tbilisi), 27 November 2005, http://www .caucaz.com/home_eng/breve_contenu.php?id=212.

9   "Kyrgyz President Starts Nationwide Discussion of Constitutional Reform" in *Newsline* (Prague and Washington, D.C.: Radio Free Europe/ Radio Liberty [RFE/RL], 15 November 2005), http://www.rferl.org/newsline/2005/11/2-TCA/tca-151105.asp. Visiting Kyrgyzstan in October 2005, U.S. Secretary of State Condoleezza Rice said, "I want to urge the constitutional council to complete the reform process by the end of 2005, forming a new constitution in open partnership with parliament and the full range of society": "Rice Lauds Kyrgyzstan's Democratic Progress" (RFE/RL, 11 October 2005), http://www.rferl.org/featuresarticle/2005/10/17a9ae41-bc7a-47c4-b460-ad991f1ef2e9.html.

10   "Kyrgyzstan," in *Attacks on the Press 2004* (New York: Committee to Protect Journalists [CPJ] 2005), http://www.cpj.org/attacks04/europe04/kyrgyz.html; "Authorities harass independent media ahead of legislative elections" (Paris: Reporters Without Borders [RSF], 25 February 2005), http://www.rsf.org/article.php3?id_article=12671.

11   *IREX Media Sustainability Index 2005* (Washington, D.C.: International Research and Exchanges Board), 228, http://www.irex.org/msi/2005/MSI05-Kyrgyzstan.pdf.

12   "Kyrgyz Television Employees Protest Management Change," in Newsline (RFE/RL, 19 October 2005), http://www.rferl.org/newsline/2005/10/2-TCA/tca-191005.asp.

13   "Re. Establishment of Public Service Broadcasting in Kyrgyzstan" (London: Article 19, 9 November 2005), http://www.article19.org/pdfs/letters/kyrgyzstan-psb.pdf.

14   "Promoting Media Freedom in Kyrgyzstan Proving More Difficult Than Originally Anticipated" (Eurasianet, 9 November 2005), http://www.eurasianet.org/departments/insight/articles/eav110905.shtml.

15   For an English text of the Constitution of the Kyrgyz Republic (adopted 5 May 1993, last amended 2 February 2003), see http://www.legislationline.org/view.php?document=62326.

16   *HRW World Report 2005*, 394 ff.; "Human Rights Watch Submission to the EBRD" (HRW, 23 June 2004), http://www.hrw.org/english/docs/2004/06/23/kyrgyz8962_txt.htm; "Kyrgyzstan," in *Europe and Central Asia: Summary of Amnesty International's Concerns in the Region, July–December 2004* (London and New York: Amnesty International [AI], 1 September 2005), http://web.amnesty.org/library/Index/ENGEUR010022005?open&of=ENG-KGZ.

17   *HRW World Report 2005*, 398.

18   Gulnoza Saidazimova, "Kyrgyzstan: Prisons Hell for most, But Comfortable for Criminal Kingpins" (RFE/RL, 4 November 2005), http://www.rferl.org/featuresarticle/2005/11/017fd703-abce-4bb9-9d87-90d780942ccc.html.

19   "Kyrgyz President Asks New Head of Penal System to Establish Order," in *Newsline* (RFE/RL, 1 November 2005), http://www.rferl.org/newsline/2005/11/2-TCA/tca-011105.asp.

20   Saralaeva, "Kyrgyzstan: Furore Over Crushing of Prison Revolt" (IWPR, 5 November 2005), http://iwpr.net/?p=rca&s=f&o=257797&apc_state=henircad445b657370b5c19016669510335d47f.

21   "Official Says Kyrgyzstan Sliding Toward Anarchy" (RFE/RL, 21 November 2005), http://www.rferl.org/featuresarticle/2005/11/BA844CAA-D858-4289-9544-EA634B6D1153.html; ". . . But No Ban On Demonstrations Is Planned," in *Newsline* (RFE/RL, about 22 Nov), http://www.rferl.org/newsline/2005/11/2-TCA/tca-221105 .asp.

22   Saralaeva, "Plans to Curb Protests Under Fire in Kyrgyzstan" (IWPR, 15 October 2005), http://iwpr.net/?p=rca&s=f&o=257336&apc_state=henircac2fc5b45b317b15a83133a65e5661215.

23   *Judicial Reform Index for Kyrgyzstan (JRI)* (Washington, D.C.: American Bar Association, Central European and Eurasian Law Initiative [ABA/CEELI], June 2003), 10, http://www.abanet.org/ceeli/publications/jri/jri_kyrgyzstan.pdf; *Legal Profession Reform Index for Kyrgyzstan (LPRI)* (Washington DC: ABA/CEELI, October 2004), 30, http://www.abanet.org/ceeli/publications/lpri/lpri_kyrgyzstan.pdf.

24   Bakiev presented three female nominees for ministerial positions—Roza Otunbaeva (foreign affairs), Alevtina Pronenko (social security) and Toktokan Borombaeva (culture)—but all three failed to win parliamentary confirmation. The two parties headed by

women are Borombaeva's Elmuras (People's Heritage), and the Jany Kuch (New Force) led by Tokon Shailieva. Both have largely female memberships.

25 "OSCE conference raises awareness of women's access to economic and social resources in Kyrgyzstan" (Bishkek: Organization for Security and Cooperation in Europe [OSCE], press release, 9 October 2005), http://osce.org/item/16552.html.

26 "Kyrgyz Republic," in *Trafficking in Persons Report* (Washington, D.C.: U.S. Department of State, 3 June 2005), http://www.state.gov/g/tip/rls/tiprpt/2005/46614.htm.

27 *CIA World Factbook* (Washington, D.C.: U.S. Central Intelligence Agency), http://www.odci.gov/cia/publications/factbook/geos/kg.html.

28 Kyrgyzstan repatriated only four Uzbek citizens, despite heavy pressure from Uzbekistan. The international legal principle of non-refoulement bars all states from returning individuals to a country where their lives are at risk or where they are likely to be subjected to torture: *Kyrgyzstan: Refugees in Need of a Safe Haven* (AI, 28 June 2005), http://web.amnesty.org/library/Index/ENGEUR580082005?open&of=ENG-KGZ; *Amnesty International's concerns at the 56th session of the Executive Committee of the United Nations High Commissioner for Refugees* (AI, October 2005), section 1.2, http://web .amnesty.org/library/Index/ENGIOR410602005?open&of=ENG-KGZ.

29 "Kyrgyzstan," in *International Religious Freedom Report 2005* (Washington, D.C.: U.S. Department of State, 8 November 2005), http://www.state.gov/g/drl/rls/irf/2005/51562.htm; Igor Rotar, "Kyrgyzstan: Religious freedom survey, January 2004" (Oslo: Forum 18 News Service [Forum 18], 7 January 2004), http://www.forum18.org/Archive.php?article_id=222.

30 "Kyrgyz Police Open 34 Extremism Cases in 2005," in *Newsline* (RFE/RL, 10 August 2005), http://www.rferl.org/newsline/2005/08/2-TCA/tca-100805.asp.

31 Rotar, "Kyrgyzstan: Official claims government control of Islam" (Forum 18, 16 June 2005), http://www.forum18.org/Archive.php?article_id=587.

32 As defined by the law, one type of extremism is "to assert the exclusivity, superiority or inferiority of citizens on the basis of their attitude to religion or their social, racial, national, religious or linguistic group": Rotar, "Kyrgyzstan: Wide-ranging extremism law not seen as threat" (Forum 18, 19 October 2005), http://www.forum18.org/Archive .php?article_id=673. For Hizb-ut-Tahir's policy and beliefs, see their website, http://www.hizb-ut-tahrir.org; also, Rotar, "Central Asia: Hizb-ut-Tahrir wants worldwide Sharia law" (Forum 18, 29 October 2003), http://www.forum18.org/Archive .php?article_id=170.

33 *JRI,* 11, 24.

34 *JRI,* 6

35 *JRI,* 8.

36 Saralaeva, "Kyrgyzstan: Saving the Constitutional Court" (IWPR, 29 November 2005), http://iwpr.net/?p=rca&s=f&o=258356&apc_state=henirca6816caa92dcc69ac41bdcabe 6212ba2a; Saralaeva and Orozobekova, "Kyrgyz Leader Pushes for More Power" (IWPR).

37 *LPRI,* 8.

38 *JRI,* 25.

39 Among the Constitutional Council's draft amendments are proposals to transfer the right to issue such warrants from prosecutors to the courts.

40 *Kyrgyzstan: A Faltering State* (Bishkek/Brussels: International Crisis Group [ICG], Asia Report No. 109, 16 December 2005), 4–6, 10–11, http://www.crisisgroup.org/home/index.cfm?id=3838&l=1; Saralaeva and Turdueva, "Kyrgyzstan Reels at Prosecutor's Fall" (IWPR, 21 September 2005), http://iwpr.net/?p=rca&s=f&o=255816&apc_state=henircab94b8e9c1cfc8c7893292c6479096307; "Kyrgyzstan's Revolution at Risk" (Eurasianet, 26 September 2005), http://www.eurasianet.org/departments/insight/articles/eav092605.shtml.

41 *Kyrgyzstan: A Faltering State* (ICG), 4–9.

42 *Kyrgyzstan: After the Revolution* (ICG), 12–13. Land seizures have also been reported in the south of the country: Hamid Toursunof, "Kyrgyzstan: Land Fever" (Transitions Online, republished on Eurasianet, 15 August 2005), http://www.eurasianet.org/departments/insight/articles/pp081505.shtml.

43 *Kyrgyzstan: A Faltering State* (ICG), 9–10; Saralaeva, "Land Rights and Wrongs in Kyrgyzstan" (IWPR, 11 November 2005), http://iwpr.net/?p=rca&s=f&o=257787&apc_state=henircaa8c10c6fe3da973188a1e852 80ec4f8.

44 "OSCE Chairman welcomes pledges of 670,000 Euro for police assistance programme in Kyrgyzstan" (Vienna: OSCE, press release, 16 June 2005), http://osce.org/item/15206.html.

45 David Gullette, "Akayev's Legacy in Kyrgyzstan Proving Difficult to Overcome" (Eurasianet, 10 May 2005), http://www.eurasianet.org/departments/insight/articles/eav051005a.shtml.

46 *Kyrgyzstan: After the Revolution* (ICG), 10.

47 *Kyrgyzstan: After the Revolution* (ICG), 13–14.

48 David S. Cloud, "Pentagon's fuel deal with Kyrgyzstan is a big lesson" (*Wall Street Journal,* 15 November 2005, republished on Alexander's Gas & Oil Connections, 8 December 2005), http://www.gasandoil.com/goc/news/ntn54966.htm; Orozobekova, "Kyrgyzstan Tells US to Pay Up for Air Base" (IWPR, 10 November 2005), http://iwpr.net/?p=rca&s=f&o=257790&apc_state=henircaa8c10c6fe3da973188a1e852180ec4f8.

49 The United States has agreed to fund a $1.5 million reform program to combat corruption within the Kyrgyz State Traffic Inspectorate, but only on the condition that all of the Inspectorate's 995 employees be sacked: "U.S. Extends Aid to Revamp Kyrgyz Traffic Police," in Newsline (RFE/RL, 6 October 2005), http://www.rferl.org/newsline/2005/10/2-TCA/tca-061005.asp.

50 *Corruption Perceptions Index 2005* (Berlin and London: Transparency International [TI], December 2005), http://www.transparency.org/policy_and_research/surveys_indices/cpi/2005.

51 "Everyone knows well who is tied up with whom. There are businessmen among you who, unfortunately, are not always in alignment with the law, starting with tax evasion. I know that many of you bribe the law-enforcement agencies, and that they take bribes from you. The agencies and the gangsters work hand in hand. I know this for a fact": Saralaeva and Aida Kasymalieva, "Politician's Murder Rocks Kyrgyzstan" (IWPR, 24

September 2005), http://www.iwpr.net/?p=rca&s=f&o=255809&apc_state=henircafb 34135dc9b040d1559de56156e796b6.

52 *Kyrgyz Republic FY 06 Country Indicator Rankings – Low Income Category (LIC)* (Washington, D.C.: Millennium Challenge Corporation, 2005), http://www.mca.gov/countries/rankings/FY06/index.shtml.

53 *Index of Economic Freedom* (Washington, D.C./New York: Heritage Foundation/ *The Wall Street Journal,* 2006), http://www.heritage.org/research/features/index/country .cfm?id= KyrgyzRepublic.

MALAWI

CAPITAL: Lilongwe

POPULATION: 12.3 million

GNI PER CAPITA: $160

SCORES	2004	2006
ACCOUNTABILITY AND PUBLIC VOICE:	N/A	4.75
CIVIL LIBERTIES:	N/A	4.58
RULE OF LAW:	N/A	4.37
ANTICORRUPTION AND TRANSPARENCY:	N/A	3.50

(scores are based on a scale of 0 to 7, with 0 representing weakest and 7 representing strongest performance)

Stanley Khaila and Thomas Lansner

INTRODUCTION

Just over a decade after a national referendum ended 30 years of dictatorship under former President-for-life Hastings Kamuzu Banda, commitment to multiparty democracy, human rights, and the market economy appears, at least in principle, embedded in Malawi's political culture and embraced by the country's major political parties.

Yet Malawi's political system is characterized less by competing policies or ideologies than it is by personality- and patronage-driven rivalries in the framework of ethnoregional party loyalties.[1] This reality was reflected in events of 2004–2005, including the failed attempt to extend presidential term limits, the contentious third multiparty elections in 2004, victorious President Bingu wa Mutharika's resignation from the United Democratic Front (UDF) and creation of the Democratic Progressive Party (DPP), and subsequent UDF attempts to impeach the president. All contributed to political turmoil that inhibited effective government response to Malawi's deepening food crisis and persistent criminality. Even President Mutharika's sorely needed and much-heralded anticorruption campaign, which has netted many prominent suspects, appears now to be focusing primarily on his political rivals.

Dr. Stanley Khaila is Director of the Center for Agricultural Research and Development at Bunda College, University of Malawi. **Thomas Lansner** is Adjunct Assistant Professor of International Affairs at the School of International and Public Affairs, Columbia University.

Malawi's 1993 national referendum, in which 63 percent of the voting population opted for multiparty democracy, brought an end to the centralized, one-party, one-man dictatorship that had ruled the country since it gained independence in 1964. The referendum was the climax of a prodemocracy movement that included strikes, student demonstrations, and riots in opposition to the country's vast economic inequalities and political repression under President Banda and his Malawi Congress Party (MCP). Mounting domestic opposition, coupled with the pressure of foreign donors' suspension of nonhumanitarian aid, forced the dictator to accept a national referendum on the adoption of a multiparty political system.

Bakili Muluzi of the United Democratic Front (UDF) defeated Banda in the country's first multiparty elections in 1994, launching a decade of UDF political domination. The main parties during the first two terms of multiparty rule reflected the country's regional/ethnic voting patterns, which largely persist today. The ruling UDF gained overwhelming support in the country's heavily populated southern region, the MCP dominated the central region, and the Alliance for Democracy (AFORD) drew backing largely in the northern region. Personality battles rather than substantive debates over policy or ideology prompted an MCP-AFORD alliance prior to the 1999 elections, the rise of the National Democratic Alliance (NDA) in 2003, and an internal division in the MCP that aligned the majority with the UDF under John Tembo and left the rest aligned with AFORD under Gwanda Chakuamba. A narrow presidential win for Muluzi and parliamentary victory for the UDF in the 1999 elections was followed by violent protests, particularly in the AFORD-dominated north.[2]

UDF attempts to gain parliamentary approval for a constitutional amendment to allow Muluzi to seek a third presidential term dominated the political landscape in 2003 in the run-up to the 2004 elections. A host of civil society organizations, particularly religious coalitions, vigorously opposed Muluzi's efforts to change the constitution. A narrow parliamentary defeat decided the third-term debate, ending Muluzi's bid to retain power and marking a clear victory for the checks and balances of constitutional democracy in Malawi.

The 2004 elections ultimately ushered in what appears a new era for multiparty rule. The UDF's loss of its parliamentary majority to the MCP and Bingu wa Mutharika's ascent to the presidency have prompted an array of new political alignments while raising anticorruption to a national priority. After being handpicked by Muluzi as the UDF candidate, Mutharika broke from the party in February 2005 to form his own Democratic Progressive Party (DPP). Malawi politics have been dominated by a bitter personal and partisan dispute between Mutharika and Muluzi ever since. The dismissal of the vice president and enforcement of a constitutional ban on elected members of Parliament switching parties during a parliamentary session have become contentious and politicized issues.

Severe drought in 2005 devastated small-scale agriculture, which is the backbone of an economy based largely on subsistence farming, especially maize production.[3] This has seriously threatened food security for millions of Malawians, who are now dependent on external food aid. Widespread and dire poverty continues to afflict the populace, with an estimated 55 percent of the population falling below the poverty line in 2004.[4] The country's per capita income today (US$170) is a mere 10 dollars higher than it was in 1994,[5] and from 2003 to 2005, economic growth averaged below 5 percent, far less than the 6 percent that the International Monetary Fund's (IMF's) Malawi Poverty Reduction Strategy Paper projects as necessary to significantly ameliorate the country's grinding poverty.[6] Expansionary monetary policies have contributed to rapid inflation, which jumped from 8.5 percent in June 2003 to 11.6 percent in June 2004 and reached 14 percent in March 2005.[7] Depreciation of Malawi's currency, the kwacha, has driven fuel import and retail prices higher and further raised the cost of living.[8]

ACCOUNTABILITY AND PUBLIC VOICE – 4.75

Section 40 of the Malawi constitution guarantees the rights to form, join, and participate in the activities of political parties; to vote and campaign for political office or a political cause; and to freely make political choices.[9] However, the electoral process, as currently practiced, makes genuine realization of these rights problematic.

Parliamentary and presidential elections were held at the mandated five-year intervals, in 1994, 1999, and 2004, in accordance with Section 83 (3) of Malawi's constitution. Although the president is constitutionally limited to two five-year terms, three years in advance of the 2004 election, the UDF launched a campaign to scrap the term limit.

Active lobbying by civil society and faith-based organizations helped secure a narrow parliamentary defeat that prevented Muluzi from seeking a third term. Consequently, Bingu wa Mutharika was handpicked by Muluzi as the UDF candidate; it was believed that his older age and lack of political experience would allow Muluzi to continue to exercise real power in his role as national chairperson of the UDF.[10]

Although the May 2004 elections were conducted by secret ballot, numerous controversies and irregularities were documented before and during the voting. Several local election-monitoring groups, including the Public Affairs Committee (PAC) and the Malawi Electoral Support Network (MESN), rated the elections as less than free and fair.[11] Voter registration, unequal access to campaign resources, state media bias, and lack of transparency in vote tabulation were identified as the most problematic areas. The Malawi Election Commission (MEC), institutionalized by the constitution to ensure free and fair elections, exhibited a clear bias toward the UDF throughout the election process. The election was postponed for two days when a coalition of opposition parties, collectively known as Mgwirizano, took the MEC to court on the basis of a near–two-million discrepancy between the number of registered voters and the number of MEC-printed ballots.[12]

The constitution guarantees universal suffrage (except for serving members of the military) as well as opportunities for the rotation of power among a range of political parties. Five candidates from different parties competed in the 2004 presidential election, and 14 parties were represented in the parliamentary vote.[13] The UDF's surprising loss of its majority in the 2004 parliamentary elections (winning 49 of the National Assembly's 193 seats as opposed to the MCP's 59 seats) indicates that despite electoral manipulation, power can change hands.[14] Government efforts to bar the NDA (consisting mainly of disaffected UDF members) from registering for the presidential elections were eventually blocked by the High Court but consumed the opposition's valuable time and resources. And not all parties shared equal campaigning opportunities. The ruling party candidate enjoyed extensive use of state resources during frequent presidential rallies, as well as de facto support from the state-run electronic media. The Malawi Broadcasting Corporation (MBC) Television gave the UDF and its allies, AFORD and the New Congress for Democracy, nearly 90 percent of election coverage airtime and mostly positive coverage. The scant coverage of other parties and candidates was largely negative.[15]

Police frequently refrained from preventing election-related violence by the UDF's militant youth group, the Young Democrats, and failed to arrest alleged perpetrators due to political pressures and allegiances.[16] There were numerous reports of candidate intimidation.[17] Disputes marred the tabulation of the vote; the MEC was accused of prematurely announcing results, prompting suspicion that the vote counts were manipulated.

The Malawian constitution (Section 40[2]) includes several clauses on political financing, which stipulate that funding is to be allocated to parties proportionally, and any party that acquires a minimum of 10 percent of the national vote is eligible for funding. The country has no regulations regarding how state funding is spent, no limits on total election spending or spending disclosure laws, no laws prohibiting political party ownership of businesses, and no regulations regarding additional sources of funding.[18] The International Institute for Democracy and Electoral Assistance (IDEA) identifies the "national electoral management body" (i.e., the MEC) as responsible for the administration and enforcement of constitutional financing regulations.[19] Reports of widespread and open distribution of money to voters and abuse of state resources by the ruling party, as well as several allegations that the MEC failed to fulfill its responsibility under the constitution and the Parliamentary and Presidential Elections Act to address these violations, are indications that campaign finance regulations are not enforced.[20]

The Malawi constitution calls for the separation of powers and equal authority among the executive, legislative, and judicial branches of government. The presence of official oversight institutions (among them the Human Rights Commission, Ombudsman, National Compensation Tribunal, Law Commission, and the Anti-Corruption Bureau) and several instances in which one branch of government attempted to check another in the last few years indicate an operative, if not fully effective, system of checks and balances. Examples include Parliament's defeat of President Muzuli's push for a third term and the successful challenge of President Mutharika's appointment of an inspector general of police without parliamentary approval as required by the constitution. When Parliament accused two of its members of committing crimes and expelled them, a court review found the offenses did not meet the threshold of "moral turpitude" required for expulsion and ordered them reinstated. Further, the United States Agency for International Development has identified the vigorous response of the Anti-Corruption Bureau (ACB) and Parliamentary Committee on Agriculture to the 2005 "maize scandal" as a sign of the healthy emergence of checks and balances and accountability mechanisms.[21]

However, lack of funding and competent personnel continues to limit effective oversight and each branch's ability to effectively check another's actions. Resources and infrastructure in the judicial branch are especially poor, contributing to a large backlog of cases and prolonged delays in the administration of justice.[22] Overall, the executive branch, especially the presidency, still dominates. The head of state retains the right to refer any constitutional dispute to the Constitutional Court for interpretation. In October 2005, as part of the continuing dispute between the Muluzi-led UDF and Mutharika's breakaway DPP, the Constitutional Court twice declared portions of the opposition-led Parliament's procedures to impeach the president illegal.[23]

The civil service was a prime target of donor efforts to promote good governance in the 1990s following the political transition to multipartyism. However, reforms were largely resisted by long-serving civil service members, who perceived a direct threat to privileged positions they had gained under the Banda regime, stifling badly needed reform and blocking the rise of competent and committed officials.[24] While the Civil Service Commission is constitutionally mandated to handle recruitment and promotion in the civil service, reports suggest that appointments and dismissals at the highest levels are not made on a merit basis. The Ministry of Education failed to provide an explanation for not renewing the contract of Zangazanga Chikhosi, a principal secretary in the ministry, at the end of 2004 and rehired him in November 2005, only to fire him less than a week later. Many speculate that those decisions were motivated by a fear that the fact the minister of education and Chikhosi's were both from the central region would create an impression of regional imbalance that could promote political tensions.

The state has made an effort to address the specific interests of women, who, despite constitutional protections, remain unequal citizens in Malawi. Based on government findings that marriage and divorce practices are not constitutional and violate international standards regulating gender equality, a Special Law Commission on Review of Gender-Related Laws was established in late 2005 to "set uniform standards" for marriage and divorce in the country. Notable gaps between standards and traditional norms exist.[25] In the cabinet, women hold key appointments, including minister of education and gender. Mary Nangwale was appointed the first female inspector general of police in Africa, although Parliament rejected her appointment in what seemed to be a show of political defiance against the president rather than a rejection of her as an individual or a woman.

Malawi has public and privately owned schools, training centers, and businesses run by and for people with disabilities, and Section 13 of the constitution commits the government to support disabled people through greater access to public places, fair employment opportunities, and full participation in all spheres of Malawi society. The Ministry of Social Development and Persons with Disabilities was created in 1998, and some official programs and international assistance is coordinated through the official Malawi Council of Disability Affairs (MACODA). Yet the government has not mandated accessibility to buildings and services for the disabled, and the majority of Malawi's disabled population lacks equal access to public places. Three deaf students were turned away from the University of Malawi in 2003, for example, because of a lack of interpreters.[26] The greater challenge for the government is in changing societal attitudes. For example, the popular belief that HIV/ AIDS can be cured through sexual intercourse with disabled persons has led to incidents of abuse of women and girls with disabilities.[27]

Malawi has a vibrant civic society. Hundreds of civic groups comment on government policy and legislation, although they are largely concentrated in urban centers. Many civic groups were particularly active during the third-term debate.[28] The Public Affairs Committee, a coalition of religious groups, has played a strong role in promoting Malawi's democratic development since 1992, bringing charges against the state-run MBC, for example, for its bias toward the UDF during the 2004 elections. In the run-up to the June 2005 national budget session of Parliament, civic groups held several meetings specifically to address this issue, and the Malawi Economic Justice Network delivered a thorough position report to Parliament.[29] Some civic groups have been effectively using

FM radio for live debates on impending legislation or an issue being discussed in Parliament. These debates are popular and have evoked responses from government officials. Key watchdog groups include the Civil Liberties Committee, the Public Affairs Committee, and official but to varying degrees largely autonomous offices including the Ombudsman, Anti-Corruption Bureau, Law Commission, and Malawi Human Rights Commission.

Nongovernmental organizations (NGOs) require official registration, but to date this has apparently not been used to limit their activities.[30] NGO activities and membership are restricted by the 2002 Non-Governmental Organizations Act, which established a 10-member board appointed by government in consultation with the Council for Non-Governmental Organizations in Malawi (CONGOMA) to register and regulate NGO operations. To qualify, an NGO must: have at least two Malawi citizens as directors/ trustees, provide a plan of activities and sources of funding (they are permitted to engage in public and other forms of fundraising), and pledge not to engage in "partisan politics including electioneering and politicking."[31] Also affecting NGO membership and influence is the 2003 amendment of Section 65 of the constitution barring members of Parliament from associating with any organization political in nature—which appears to be in violation of Section 40(1) of the constitution, guaranteeing all persons the right to "form, join, and participate in the activities of, and recruit members for a political party."[32] This amendment, however, has been applied extremely selectively.

Donors and funders of civic organizations are free from state pressures. Lack of coordination among both state and nonstate funders, however, has helped create funding imbalances in some development sectors.

Malawians' rights to freedom of expression and freedom of the press were clearly violated in the last few years, especially during the May 2004 elections, despite constitutional guarantees of each in sections 35 and 36, respectively. The state's failure to prevent police from, or later prosecute them for, arresting or attacking political dissenters indicates a general failure to support these constitutional protections during this time period. During the third-term debate, the 2004 campaign period, and just prior to and after the May 2004 elections, newspapers reported numerous cases in which individuals and journalists were harassed or physically attacked, especially by UDF militants, for expressing their opinions.[33] Three days after the contested presidential elections, police shuttered the community radio station MIJ 90.3 in the commercial capital of Blantyre, arrested four of its journalists, and accused two of them of inciting violence.

Media harassment has generally declined since the elections. In October 2004, Director of Public Prosecutions Fahad Assani ordered police to discontinue the arbitrary arrest of journalists and protect them from intimidation, warning that such acts are unconstitutional.[34] The Centre for Human Rights and Rehabilitation reported a remarkable improvement in various groups' access to the Malawi Broadcasting Corporation and Television Malawi in the first few weeks of Mutharika's administration. In 2005, it reported, "Today it is possible to hear news critical of government as well as views from the opposition."[35] In March 2005, however, two journalists from *The Nation* were arrested for reporting that President Mutharika had moved out of the presidential palace because he feared it was haunted. They were charged with "publishing a false story likely to cause public fear" and "causing ridicule to the high office of the President."[36] The Mutharika government has used libel and similar laws to pressure other journalists, and a number of government critics have been arrested during his tenure, including Malawi's former parliamentary Speaker Sam Mpasu and other UDF legislators.[37] Media watchdog groups are pressing for revisions of restrictive legislation.[38] However, the dangers of incitement by an immature or irresponsible media must be noted. A recent report has noted that the Catholic-owned Radio Maria and Radio Islam have engaged in what it describes as "vitriolic radio wars."[39] There is no evidence to suggest that the state directly censors print or broadcast media, despite occasional harassment and brief detentions of journalists. Government does not hinder access to the internet, although limited availability reflects a general lack of infrastructure.

Recommendations

- The system for political party funding should include enforceable laws to govern private funding to political parties with full disclosure that is transparent and accountable to the public.
- The government should ensure that sufficient funding is provided for local elections to be held as constitutionally scheduled.

- State media should serve as a nonpartisan outlet for news and civic and voter education, especially during campaign periods, and offer unbiased analysis of important campaign issues.
- The government should refrain from using libel or other laws to inhibit legitimate media expression and vigorously prosecute party militants or officials involved in assault, harassment, or illegal detention of media workers as well as other citizens.
- Media training focusing on covering corruption, development, human rights, and elections should be offered in addition to general journalism training that instills ethical approaches in media.

CIVIL LIBERTIES – 4.58

Malawi's constitution and the Convention Against Torture (CAT), to which Malawi is a signatory, prohibit torture. Yet, according to the Malawi Inspectorate of Prisons and other reports, police continue to beat and physically assault prisoners to intimidate them and force confessions. Prison conditions are extremely dehumanizing, harsh, and often life-threatening due to overcrowding, inadequate nutrition, substandard sanitation, and poor health facilities. From January 2003 to June 2004, 259 prisoners died; the rate of 12 deaths in every 10,000 prisoners surpasses the International Committee of the Red Cross (ICRC) maximum acceptable death rates.[40] NGOs are permitted prison visits, and efforts to build new prisons and refurbish existing facilities are under way.[41] Yet conditions remain dire, and prisoners sometimes suffer food shortages that reflect deteriorating conditions among the general population. In November 2005, the *New York Times* reported: "This is life in Malawi's high-security prisons, Dickens in the tropics, places of cruel, but hardly unusual punishment. Prosecutors, judges, even prison wardens agree that conditions are unbearable, confinements intolerably long, justice scandalously uneven."[42]

Chapter IV, Section 42 of the constitution protects against arbitrary arrest and unlawful detention and guarantees Malawians a fair and public trial. The Human Rights Commission reported that it registered a total of 663 cases during 2004, most concerning overstay on remand, denial of bail, and unheard appeals.[43]

No cases of deliberate denial of fair trial were officially admitted in the 2003 and 2004 reports of the Malawi Inspectorate of Prisons, although very long delays in bringing detainees to trial often mean that justice is effectively denied. As of September 2004, many of the 763 detainees remanded on homicide charges had been held without trial for over a decade.

Section 129 of the Malawi constitution makes provisions to protect and promote human rights in Malawi in the broadest sense possible. Furthermore, Section 5 of the Ombudsman Act empowers the ombudsman to investigate any alleged instance or matter of abuse or manifest injustice or oppressive or unfair conduct by any employee in any part of the government. The constitutionally mandated offices of the ombudsman and the Human Rights Commission have been moderately effective in protecting and promoting human rights, but these agencies are unable to address many relevant issues because of staff and budget shortages.

General societal discrimination and violence against women remain serious problems in Malawi, as traditional norms continue to constrain women's inheritance rights and full participation in the country's economic and political life. In some areas, initiation rites that include genital cutting, which is not illegal, still prevail.[44] Malawi signed the Convention on the Elimination of all Forms of Discrimination against Women (CEDAW) in 1979, which came into force in 1981. The right to equal treatment is provided for in Section 20 of the constitution. In line with these provisions, the Human Rights Commission initiated the formulation and adoption of a policy on sexual harassment in the workplace. The Law Commission finalized and submitted to the Ministry of Justice a bill on wills and inheritance and a domestic violence bill and is currently finalizing a bill on marriage and divorce. These bills are intended to modify or replace existing laws, regulations, customs, and practices that constitute discrimination against women and promote relevant provisions in the constitution and the international conventions.

The state has stiffened punishments for those involved in trafficking of women. It has also increased awareness campaigns on trafficking, which has resulted in increased arrests, including at least two in 2005. While the government has moved to protect women's rights in specific instances, its broader ability to promote them remains constrained by a lack of capacity and resources in both autonomous constitutionally mandated groups such as the Malawi Human Rights Commission and the police, prosecutorial, and judiciary services. The Industrial Relations

Court is the prime instrument for resolving violations of workers' rights, including sexual harassment at the workplace.[45]

In general, no serious cases of religious or ethnic discrimination have been reported; members of the country's approximately 20 percent Muslim minority have been active participants in several political parties and serve at the highest levels of government. There are concerns among Malawians of Asian origin over the new land policy that reserves the right to freehold only to citizens. Asians fear this policy could discriminate against them because many of them maintain dual citizenship.

Freedom of conscience, thought, religion, and belief, guaranteed in Section 33 of the constitution, is widely respected. A requirement for religious groups to register with the government has not been used to limit religious expression, and the government and larger society have promoted a tradition of religious tolerance and peaceful integration. People of different religious persuasions generally live in relative harmony. Occasional clashes have taken place between Muslims and adherents of Nyau, a traditional religious group, in the Central Region, and isolated instances of violence between Muslims and Christians have occurred. However, such disputes have largely been related to local grievances and usually quickly resolved.

There are no reports of religious or other distinct groups receiving favorable government treatment or being denied opportunities to exercise their rights on the basis of group identity. Homosexuality is illegal, but no prosecutions have been reported recently. People with disabilities have legal rights to fair employment opportunities and are offered some public support, although access to buildings and services is not guaranteed by law and remains constrained by the lack of funding.[46] A 2004 report observed, "Hotels and banks are accessible to less than ten percent of individuals with disabilities. Places of worship, health care clinics, hospitals, shops and public transport are on the other hand reported to be accessible by over two-thirds majority of those with disabilities. The most notable shortcomings are schools, accessible to only 20 percent and the workplace, accessible to only 26 percent of the disabled population."[47] Societal discrimination against people with HIV/AIDS remains prevalent despite public education campaigns. A June 2005 industrial relations court ruling that awarded compensation to persons fired because they were HIV positive might set a useful precedent in protecting such workers.[48]

The constitution guarantees the rights of freedom of expression and assembly. In 2004, the government barred many peaceful demonstrations or marches by opposition political parties. Attempts to suppress freedom to assemble provoked riots that included the burning of offices of the ruling UDF in Blantyre in April 2004. There is no compulsory membership in state or party organizations. Freedom of assembly and expression have been threatened by actions of party militants, especially from the UDF, that were often neither prevented nor prosecuted by government authorities, although such abuses have been curbed since the election of President Mutharika. Despite these problems, Malawians have exercised their right to political debate vigorously.

Workers' rights are protected in Section 38 of the Malawi constitution, under which the Labor Relations and the Employment Acts have codified the rights of workers into substantial protective laws. In 2004, of 451 cases of alleged workplace malpractice that were taken to the Industrial Relations Court, only 56 were resolved. The International Labour Organisation reports that the Ministry of Labor lacks resources to enforce labor laws efficiently or to facilitate improvements in working conditions effectively.[49] Reports of child labor are numerous, especially on tobacco plantations.[50] Conditions in garment factories are described as very difficult, with long hours at extremely low wages and "scant regard for workers[sic] health and safety."[51]

Mandatory union registration with the Registrar of Trade Unions and Employers' Organizations under the Ministry of Labour and Vocational Training is routinely approved. Unions may organize and operate freely in most circumstances but have faced harassment and occasional violence during strikes. Workers in essential services cannot strike, however, and unions say they have little access to the country's export processing zones.

Recommendations
- Funding for the Ombudsman and the Human Rights Commission should be increased to allow sufficient staffing and resources to expand and improve promotion, monitoring, and enforcement of human rights.
- Parliament should debate and enact all human rights–related bills (jointly reviewed by the Human Rights Commission and the Law Commission) as a matter of urgency.

- Legislation to improve gender equality should be expanded and enforced.
- Greater efforts to protect Malawians with disabilities, and to make public spaces accessible to them, should be pursued.
- Labor laws should be strictly enforced, particularly those concerning children, and closer monitoring of worker safety and health regulations undertaken, especially on sugar and tea plantations and in export-processing zones.[52]

RULE OF LAW – 4.37

Section 103 of the Malawi constitution establishes an independent judiciary. Despite many limitations, some observers see Malawi's judiciary as its "most credible branch of government."[53] Other groups, including Transparency International, have noted political pressure on the courts and perceived prevalence of bribe taking in the justice system.[54] Malawi's judicial system is based on the British model, comprising magistrate's courts, lower courts, a high court, and a Supreme Court of Appeal. The chief justice appointed by the president must be confirmed by the Parliament with a two-thirds majority of members present and voting. The president on recommendation of the Judicial Service Commission appoints all the other judges. Magistrates and persons appointed to other judicial offices are appointed by the chief justice on recommendation of the Judicial Service Commission (Section 111). Judicial independence is enhanced by Section 119 of the constitution, which protects judicial tenure. All justices are appointed until the age of 65 and may be removed only for reasons of incompetence or misbehavior, as determined by the president and a majority of the Parliament.[55]

In general, higher courts have in recent years demonstrated substantial independence, ruling against the government in several cases that were considered politically sensitive. For example, the court ruled in favor of opposition leader Gwanda Chakwamba when the government charged him with forgery. In addition, the constitutional review court ruled against the government's challenge to Parliament's rejection of the appointment of Mary Nangwale as inspector general of police.

Section 42 (2) of the constitution states that every person arrested for, or accused of, the alleged commission of an offense shall, in addition to the rights he or she has as a detained person, "have the right to . . . be presumed innocent and to remain silent during plea proceedings or trial and not to testify during trial . . . to be represented by a legal practitioner of his or her choice or, where it is required in the interest of justice, to be provided with legal representation at the expense of the state, and to be informed of these rights." However, accused persons are very often not brought to court and charged or informed of the reason for their arrest within the constitutionally required 48 hours.[56] Once cases come to court, suspects are generally given fair and public hearings by impartial courts. In felony cases, the state provides accused persons with legal counsel.

Judicial performance is hampered by dependence on the executive branch for resources as well as a lack of qualified staff and legal officers. From the senior resident magistrate level to the justices of the Supreme Court of Appeal, court officials are generally competent and appropriately trained. Their tenure is legally protected, and as noted earlier, efforts at blatant political interference have been rebuffed by a combination of political and civic opposition. However, low salaries hinder the courts in recruiting and retaining qualified personnel and provide fertile ground for corruption. The Office of the Director of Public Prosecutions (DPP) holds power to prosecute all criminal cases in the country (Section 99 of the Malawi constitution) but is severely limited by lack of resources and competent staff. Currently, there are only four prosecutors instead of the 20 or more that the DPP requires to be effective. Consequently, the DPP very often relies on ill-trained police to prosecute cases.

Magistrate courts (e.g., 4th grade, 3rd grade, 2nd grade, and 1st grade magistrate courts) handle the majority of cases in the country. However, the lower courts have few competent staff. Only senior resident magistrates are lawyers. Reliance on the police as prosecutors results in the mishandling of many cases. Furthermore, lack of legal expertise in the lower courts causes higher courts to reverse many lower-court decisions. Military cases are handled by the civilian judiciary and receive a similar level of fairness and impartiality but are also subject to similar problems.

By and large, both parliament and the executive comply with court decisions. However, there have been cases in which convicts have been pardoned by the executive on apparently dubious grounds.

Section 153(3) of the Malawi constitution subjects the powers of the police force to the direction and orders of the courts. Furthermore, the political responsibility of the police is vested in the minister of the government, and the appointment of police personnel is through an independent Police Service Commission. The Malawi Army has generally refrained from overt engagement in the political process. The police have on occasion acted with apparent political bias, especially in 2003–2004, in not protecting members of the opposition from militants of the then-ruling UDF party.

Overall, the police are generally regarded as poorly trained, inefficient, and corrupt, and it is reported that confidence in the police has plummeted.[57] The government has sought to curb police excesses over the past year and continued to seek external support for police training programs, some of which are described as successful in raising police standards.[58]

Unfortunately, the level of education among the police is very low. In the history of the Malawi police, no university graduate has held the position of inspector general. Officers who make arrests assess the case and decide on the charge. Inadequate training means that most officers do not know which law to use to charge a suspect, and many cases are dropped or delayed because of lack of proper police procedure in formulating charges or collecting evidence.

People are sometimes detained in jails or prisons without warrants. This is often because of incompetence rather than flouting of the law. Most prison wardens are poorly educated, are ill-trained in proper procedures, and have difficulties in understanding remand warrants.

The powers of the Malawi Defense Force are vested in the president subject to the recommendation of the Army Council. Furthermore, the powers of the Malawi Defense Force are under the scrutiny of the Defense and Security Committee of Parliament. There is effective and democratic civilian control of the Malawi Defense Force.

The rights to own property and engage in economic activity are provided for in sections 8 through 30 of the constitution. In this connection, the government has formulated a new land policy that aims to provide secure land tenure to all citizens without regard to gender, age, marital status, ethnic origin, or religion. When the draft bill is enacted, customary land transfers will be transacted within this legal framework. Generally, the government has not subjected citizens to arbitrary or unjust deprivation of their property. Compensation has been paid when land is needed for public utility. Furthermore, in the draft bill, compensation will now be at market price and the government will not have the final say on the compensation value.

Recommendations

- Adequate resources should be provided to the Office of the Director of Public Prosecutions to recruit and maintain qualified prosecutors and minimize the role of junior police in legal matters.
- To limit the executive branch's use of the budget to restrict or influence other arms of government, the judiciary and Parliament should be funded to their full budget allocations and allowed to control their own resources.
- The government should increase the judiciary's capacity to clear the large backlog of homicide cases. International recruitment of judges to cover short-term needs should be complemented by expanding the intake of the law school at the University of Malawi to provide trained Malawians for judicial service.
- To alleviate extreme congestion in prisons, more community service sentences should be introduced for minor offenses, and the government should expand prison space to accommodate those inmates who are considered to be a menace to the public.

ANTICORRUPTION AND TRANSPARENCY – 3.50

President Bingu wa Mutharika has made a strong commitment to fight corruption and widespread graft. In line with his tough anticorruption stance, many arrests have occurred. The mayor of Blantyre was arrested, tried, and sentenced to prison for the crime of theft by public servant. In May 2005, the former minister of education was dismissed from the cabinet post and charged with misappropriation of public funds. Further, the secretary of the treasury was arrested over allegations of financial malfeasance.

The ACB arrested a former finance minister on allegations that he built a hotel using public finances. Moreover, the ACB is investigating the former head of state, Bakili Muluzi, on several allegations, including diverting large amounts of public funds to private accounts.

These investigations and arrests seemed to indicate President Mutharika's seriousness in fighting corruption. However, slow progress in prosecuting many cases has raised public doubts about the new government's credibility in this area. A recent report argues that many institutions are politically constrained and ineffective, whistle-blower protection is insufficient, and perceptions of the current anticorruption effort hold that it is "selective, favours the rich and the ruling party, and is quick to penalise the poor."[59] Media reports of graft at senior levels of the new administration are rising. As well, corruption investigations now seem to be focusing on President Mutharika's political rivals. In November 2005, three UDF parliamentarians who were instrumental in moving impeachment proceedings against President Mutharika were arrested on various charges, including forging a school certificate, and Vice President Cassim Chilumpha was detained on corruption charges shortly afterward.

The Chronicle newspaper in November 2005 reported that "Civil society organisations in the country have accused the Anti-Corruption Bureau (ACB) of bias in the way it is investigating and prosecuting corruption cases, charging that it is only targeting opposition politicians."[60] President Mutharika has also failed to enforce full compliance with the requirement of disclosure of assets by appointees to senior public offices, and a number of ministers and members of parliament have failed to disclose their assets.

At the beginning of his term of office, President Mutharika promised Malawians a clean and accountable government and that he would appoint civil servants based on merit through open and equitable competition. He trimmed the cabinet from more than 40 ministers to about 28. He dissolved the parastatal business corporation boards and replaced a number of top officials in the civil service. But it took the president more than a year in office to appoint new boards for the parastatals. The CHRR 2005 editorial suggests that in his appointments, Mutharika prefers individuals from certain geographic areas for key public positions. He has also apparently exceeded his official powers by creating the position of chief secretary for the public services without parliamentary approval as well as improperly dismissing senior officials.[61]

Several incidents have caused the public and Parliament to question the government's commitment to good governance. Both the World Bank and the IMF have lauded the new government for holding down public expenditure. However, the CHRR reports several controversies over government fiscal management. The president's many international trips, averaging one per month during his first year in office, and the functions of some members of the presidential entourage have been questioned. President Mutharika has also been criticized for poor prioritization of expenditures, including official purchases of luxury vehicles. Third, the executive decision to create a Malawi Rural Development Fund (MARDEF) worth MK1 billion without parliamentary approval was seen as ignoring fiscal procedures and regulations.[62]

The Public Finance Management Act provides for management and control of public finances and specifies offenses for overexpenditure, misuse, mismanagement, or misallocation of public monies. Sections 25A–D of the Corrupt Practices (Amended) Act, 2003, create offenses for several types of abuse of office. However, allegations of serious corruption continued to surface in the media.[63]

Yet the very basics of public finance are in question, a recent report claims, because the "budget process is a theatre that masks the real distribution and spending. All the actors, civil society, government, and donors seem aware that many of their statements and actions have little bearing on actual distribution of resources."[64] Despite this, some civil society groups are improving their capacity to monitor government spending and use this as a tool for advocacy.[65]

Many abuses reported by the auditor general have not been prosecuted despite the existence of these laws. A lack of resources clearly hinders prosecutorial capacity, but failure to pursue government officials may also reflect the DPP's status as an appointee, whom, under Section 102 of the constitution, the president may dismiss without parliamentary approval.

During the one-party rule of Kamuzu Banda, most companies in the country were state owned. Since the transition to democratic rule, a market economy has taken root. A Privatization Commission divested many state assets, including Malawi Railways, Malawi Lake Services Limited, and Malawi Telecommunications Limited (MTL). While it is clear that the government is serious about privatizing government companies, the divestment process has not always been transparent.

The president, cabinet ministers, parliamentarians, and other public officers are required to declare their assets on taking office. The law also requires the president to appoint an independent manager to oversee any personal businesses he/she may own during his/her term of office. Public officers and parliamentarians are required under penalty of law to disclose circumstances where they have a direct or indirect material interest in a matter being handled by their office and are prohibited from participating in any decision on the matter.

Legally, separation of public office from the personal interests of public officeholders is sufficient, but enforcement is deficient. Not all cabinet members or parliamentarians declare their assets. Numerous reports in the news point to cases of ministers interfering with contracts for public projects, and one cabinet member has been tried and convicted for abuse of office.[66] There have also been persistent charges of localized abuses of donor food aid on the basis of nepotism or other affiliations. The governance dimension of food security and food aid is a crucial consideration in how Malawi meets continuing challenges of drought and potential famine.[67]

Allegations of corruption are reported extensively in the independent media, although the very influential state-controlled broadcaster, while more open than in previous years, remains far more cautious in its reporting. While legal mechanisms to implement the access to information guaranteed in the constitution are under consideration,[68] there are complaints that the de facto situation is deteriorating.[69]

For the past 10 years, higher education has suffered from rampant corruption and graft, involving cases of cheating in examinations, manipulation of grades, and stealing of certificates.[70] Several official efforts have helped curb such abuses. The Malawi National Examination Board has strengthened its oversight in the sector. A new law criminalizes many such behaviors, and fines have been enhanced. In addition, the University of Malawi has set up its own university entrance examination to assess applicants independently of the sometimes questionable credentials they offer.

Recommendations
- A robust, easily enforceable freedom of information act should be adopted as soon as possible.
- The current anticorruption campaign should be pursued on a demonstrably nonpartisan basis, with sufficient resources assigned to the ombudsman and the Anti-Corruption Bureau to allow them to operate effectively and without political interference. Protections for whistle-blowers should be enhanced.
- Government should strive to publish accurate budgets that are subject to full public scrutiny.

- Financial disclosure requirements for elected officials should be rigorously enforced.
- Government should strive to assure fair and equitable distribution of food aid and development assistance.

NOTES

[1] Useful background on this divide may be found in Wiseman Chijere Chirwa, "Elections in Malawi: The Perils of Regionalism," *Southern Africa Report Archive* 10, 2, http://www.africafiles.org/article.asp?ID=3967, accessed 26 April 2006. A very useful analysis that includes reference to Malawi's "neopatrimonialism" and "presidentialism" is included in David Booth and Diana Cammack, "Drivers of Change and Development in Malawi" (London: Overseas Development Institute [ODI], Working Paper 261, January 2006), http://www.odi.org.uk/Publications/working_papers/wp261.pdf.

[2] Chris Maroleng, "Malawi General Election 2004: Democracy in the Firing Line," *Africa Security Review* 13, 2 (2004), http://www.iss.co.za/pubs/ASR/13No2/AWMaroleng.htm.

[3] Mustafa Hussein, "Combating Corruption in Malawi: An Assessment of the Enforcement Mechanisms," *African Security Review* 14, 4 (2005), 94.

[4] "Malawi Country Profile," *CIA World Factbook* (Washington, D.C.: United States Central Intelligence Agency [CIA], 2006), http://www.cia.gov/cia/publications/factbook/geos/mi.html#Econ.

[5] "Doing Business in Malawi" (Washington, D.C.: World Bank Group, 2006), http://www.doingbusiness.org/ExploreEconomies/Default.aspx?economyid=118.

[6] "Malawi: Poverty Reduction Strategy Report Progress Report" (Washington, D.C.: International Monetary Fund [IMF], Country Report 05/209, June 2005), 5.

[7] Ibid.; "Press Statement by IMF Staff Mission to Malawi" (IMF, Press Release 05/50, 3 March 2005), http://www.imf.org/external/np/sec/pr/2005/pr0550.htm.

[8] "Currency Depreciation to Hurt Malawi Consumers," afrol News/ *The Chronicle,* 20 February 2006, http://www.afrol.com/articles/18207.

[9] Constitution of the Republic of Malawi, http://www.sdnp.org.mw/constitut/chapter4.html#40.

[10] Maroleng, "Malawi General Election 2004," 78–79.

[11] "Statement on 2004 Parliamentary and Presidential Elections" (Malawi: Public Affairs Committee [PAC], 25 May 2004), http://www.sdnp.org.mw/~solomon/mec/pac.htm; "Republic of Malawi 2004 Parliamentary and Presidential Elections, 20 May" (The Malawi Electoral Support Network [MESN]), http://www.sdnp.org.mw/~solomon/mec/mesn.htm.

[12] Maroleng, "Malawi General Election 2004," 78.

[13] "Republic of Malawi Presidential and Parliamentary Elections, May 20, 2004, Final Report" (Brussels: European Union [EU] Election Observation Mission), http://europa.eu.int/comm/external_relations/human_rights/eu_election_ass_observ/malawi/eu_eom_malawi_fin_rep_04.pdf, 14.

[14] Maroleng, "Malawi General Election 2004," 79.

15 "Statement," (PAC), http://www.sdnp.org.mw/~solomon/mec/pac.htm; "Republic of Malawi 2004" (MESN).

16 Also see "Malawi Human Rights Report 2003–04" (Lilongwe, Malawi: Centre for Human Rights and Rehabilitation [CHRR], 2005), http://www.chrr.org.mw/downloads/malawi_human_rights_report_2003_04.pdf.

17 *The Nation* (Blantyre), 24 June 2003.

18 Andile Sokomani, "Money in Southern African Politics: the Party Funding Challenge in Southern Africa," *African Security Review* 14, 4 (2005), http://www.iss.co.za/pubs/ASR/14No4/ESokomani.htm.

19 "Matrix on Political Finance Laws and Regulations" (Stockholm: International Institute for Democracy and Electoral Assistance [IDEA], Political Finance Database), http://www.idea.int/publications/funding_parties/upload/matrix.pdf.

20 "European Union Election Observation Mission to Malawi 2004 Elections" (EU, 22 May 2004), http://www.sdnp.org.mw/~solomon/mec/EU_statement.htm.

21 Caroline Sahley, Bob Groelsema, Tom Marchione, and David Nelson, "The Governance Dimensions of Food Security in Malawi" (Washington, D.C.: United States Agency for International Development [USAID], 20 September 2005), http://www.sarpn.org.za/documents/d0001649/index.php.

22 Hussein, "Combating Corruption," 99.

23 "Malawi Constitutional Court Imposes Another Ban on Presidential Impeachment," *The People's Daily Online* (Beijing) 27 October 2005, http://english.people.com.cn/200510/27/eng20051027_217136.html.

24 Gerhard Anders, "Civil Servants in Malawi: Mundane Acts of Appropriation and Resistance in the Shadow of Good Governance" (Leiden: African Studies Center), http://www.ascleiden.nl/Pdf/paper08092005-anders.pdf.

25 Hopkins Mundango Nyirenda, "Malawi reviews marriage, divorce laws," *The Chronicle,* 29 November 2005, http://www.afrol.com/articles/17477.

26 "Malawi Human Rights Report 2003-04" (CHRR), http://www.chrr.org.mw/downloads/malawi_human_rights_report_2003_04.pdf.

27 Ibid.

28 "Bertelsmann Transformation Index" (Munich: Center for Applied Policy Research and Bertelsmann Foundation), http://www.bertelsmann-transformation-index.de/72.0.html?L=1.

29 "Comments on the Proposed Malawi Budget 2001–2002, Report for Members of Parliament" (Lilongwe, Malawi: Malawi Economic Justice Network, 18 February 2002), http://www.sarpn.org.za/CountryPovertyPapers/Malawi/Feb02/MalawiBudget2002.pdf.

30 "NGO Laws: Malawi, Mozambique, Namibia, South Africa and Tanzania" (New York: Human Rights Watch [HRW], Backgrounders, 2004), http://hrw.org/backgrounder/africa/zimbabwe/2004/12/6.htm.

31 Ibid.

32 "Malawi Human Rights Report 2003–04" (CHRR), http://www.chrr.org.mw/downloads/malawi_human_rights_report_2003_04.pdf.

33 "Malawi – 2004 Annual Report" (Paris: Reporters Without Borders [RSF], 3 May 2004), http://www.rsf.org/print.php3?id_article=10180.

34 "Malawian Police Ordered to Protect Journalists," afrol News, 7 November 2004, http://www.afrol.com/articles/10616.

35 "Human Rights Report 2003–04" (CHRR).

36 "Attacks on the Press in 2005, Africa: Snapshots" (New York: Committee to Protect Journalists [CPJ]), http://www.cpj.org/attacks05/africa05/snaps_africa_05.html#mala.

37 "Malawi's Former Speaker Arrested," *People's Daily Online,* 5 November 2005, http://english.people.com.cn/200511/05/eng20051105_219189.html.

38 "2005 World Press Freedom Review" (Vienna: International Press Institute [IPI]), http://service.cms.apa.at/cms/ipi/freedom_detail-new.html?country=/KW0001/KW0006/KW0164/.

39 Booth and Cammack, "Drivers of Change" (ODI), 59, http://www.odi.org.uk/Publications/working_papers/wp261.pdf.

40 "Malawi Human Rights Report 2003–04" (CHRR), http://www.chrr.org.mw/downloads/malawi_human_rights_report_2003_04.pdf.

41 "Malawi," in Country Reports on Human Rights Practices – 2005 (Washington, D.C.: U.S. Department of State, Bureau of Democracy, Human Rights, and Labor, 8 March 2006), http://www.state.gov/g/drl/rls/hrrpt/2005/61579.htm.

42 Michael Wines, "The Forgotten of Africa, Wasting Away in Jails Without Trial," *New York Times,* 6 November 2005, http://www.nytimes.com/2005/11/06/international/africa/06prisons.html?ex=1288933200&en=7036e8fea197e295&ei=5088&partner=rssnyt&emc=rss.

43 "Annual Report of the Malawi Human Rights Commission for the Year 2004" (Lilongwe, Malawi: Malawi Human Rights Commission [MHRC], March 2005), http://www.malawihumanrightscommission.org/doclinks.asp?group=ANNUAL%20REPORTS.

44 See *Mfulu,* The Malawi Human Rights Commission Bulletin, www.malawihumanrightscommission.org/docs/mfulu_march2006.pdf.

45 For instance, Alice Nazombe, a personal secretary to the chief elections officer, was dismissed due to "relationship breakdown" with her boss. On February 2004, the court ruled in her favor and asked that she be reinstated (CHRR, 2004).

46 "Malawi Human Rights Report 2003–2004" (CHRR, 5 April 2005), http://www.chrr.org.mw/downloads/malawi_human_rights_report_2003_04.pdf.

47 "Surveys on Living Conditions among People with Activity Limitations in Southern Africa" (Trondheim: Norwegian Insititute of Technology, Foundation for Scientific and Industrial Research [SINTEF], 2005), http://www.sintef.no/content/page1__1561.aspx.

48 "Malawi," in *Country Reports* (U.S. Department of State), http://www.state.gov/g/drl/rls/hrrpt/2005/61579.htm.

49 "Botswana, Lesotho, Malawi and Zambia: Strengthening Labour Administration in Southern Africa" (Geneva: International Labour Organization, Projects, February 2002–February 2005), http://www.ilo.org/dyn/declaris/DECLARATIONWEB.ProjectDetails?var_Language=EN&var_ID=200, accessed 15 April 2006.

50 Chikondi Chiyembekeza, "Malawi's tobacco tenants 'suffer horrible abuses,'" *The Chronicle,* 8 March 2005, http://www.afrol.com/articles/15855, accessed 16 April 2006.

51 *Garment Production in Malawi* (Amsterdam: Clean Clothes Campaign [CCC] and Centre for Research on Multinational Corporations [SOMO], September 2003), http://www.cleanclothes.org/publications/03-09-malawi.htm, accessed 16 April 2006.

52 "Malawi" in *Country Reports* (U.S. Department of State), http://www.state.gov/g/drl/rls/hrrpt/2005/61579.htm, accessed 16 April 2006.

53 *State of the Judiciary Report: Malawi 2003* (Washington, D.C.: International Foundation for Election Systems [IFES], April 2004), http://www.ifes.org/files/rule-of-law/SOJ/SOJ_Malawi_Final.pdf.

54 "Malawi 2004," in National Integrity Systems (Berlin: Transparency International [TI], Country Study Report), http://www.transparency.org/policy_research/nis/regional/africa_middle_east, accessed 16 April 2006.

55 Please see "Malawi," in *Crime and Society, A Comparative Criminology Tour of the World,* http://www-rohan.sdsu.edu/faculty/rwinslow/africa/malawi.html.

56 "Malawi" in *Country Reports* (U.S. Department of State), http://www.state.gov/g/drl/rls/hrrpt/2005/61579.htm, accessed 16 April 2006. http://www.state.gov/g/drl/rls/hrrpt/2005/61579.htm, accessed 16 April 2006

57 "Malawi 2004," in *National Integrity Systems* (TI), http://www.transparency.org/policy_research/nis/regional/africa_middle_east, accessed 16 April 2006.

58 Christopher Stone, Joel Miller, Monica Thornton, and Jennifer Trone, *Supporting Security, Justice, and Development: Lessons for a New Era* (New York: Vera Institute of Justice, June 2005), http://www.vera.org/publications/publications_5.asp?publication_id=298.

59 Hussein, "Combating Corruption," http://www.iss.org.za/pubs/ASR/14No4/EHussein.htm.

60 "Civil Society Accuse Anti-Corruption Bureau of Bias," *The Chronicle,* 21 November 2005.

61 "Statement on the Termination of Contracts for Principle [*sic*] Secretaries" (CHRR, press release, 25 January 2005), http://www.chrr.org.mw/press_room/pr_principle_secretaries.php.

62 "Defiant Mutharika's Loan Scheme Provokes Opposition," *IRIN News,* 1 September 2005, http://www.irinnews.org/report.asp?ReportID=48869.

63 *Weekend Nation,* 7–8, 14–15, and 21–22 January 2006. The Malawi Kwacha exchange rate was US$1 = MK130.

64 Lisa Rakner, L. Mukubwu, N. Ngwira, and K. Smiddy, "The Budget as Theatre—the Formal and Informal Institutional Makings of the Budget Process in Malawi" (London: Overseas Development Institute [ODI]), http://www.odi.org.uk/pppg/cape/seminars/may04papers/Schneider_Political_Economy_Malawi.pdf.

65 "Malawi: NGOs Monitor Budget Spending on Education," *IRIN News,* 14 December 2004, http://www.irinnews.org/report.asp?ReportID=44662.

66 Pilirani Phiri, "Malawi Loses US$ 40 Million in Corruption," *The Chronicle,* 21 November 2005, http://www.afrol.com/articles/17342.

67 Sahley, Groelsema, Marchione, and Nelson, "The Governance Dimensions of Food Security in Malawi" (USAID), http://www.sarpn.org.za/documents/d0001649/index.php.

68 Frank Namangale, "Access to Info Bill Operation Set for Next March . . . NGOs support the Bill," *The Daily Times* (Malawi), 27 April 2006, http://www.dailytimes.bppmw.com/ article.asp?ArticleID=1529.

69 "Malawi: Access to Information Threatened," *The Chronicle,* 10 April 2006, http://www.allafrica.com/stories/200604101126.html.

70 See, for example, Raphael Tenthani, "Heads Roll after Malawi Exam Fraud," *BBC News,* 18 October 2000, http://news.bbc.co.uk/2/hi/africa/978389.stm, accessed 01 May 2006.

MALAYSIA

CAPITAL: Kuala Lumpur
POPULATION: 26.1 million
GNI PER CAPITA: $3,880

SCORES	2004	2006
ACCOUNTABILITY AND PUBLIC VOICE:	3.11	3.04
CIVIL LIBERTIES:	3.50	2.97
RULE OF LAW:	3.52	4.01
ANTICORRUPTION AND TRANSPARENCY:	2.31	2.87

(scores are based on a scale of 0 to 7, with 0 representing weakest and 7 representing strongest performance)

William Case

INTRODUCTION

Malaysia's patterns of politics and governance, combining authoritarian controls with democratic procedures, have cumulated in what can broadly be understood as a hybrid regime. During 2004–2005, limits on freedom of communication and assembly persisted. Arrests also took place during this period under the country's Internal Security Act, legislation that permits preventive detention without trial. Despite these controls, electoral contests remain competitive enough that when the government won reelection by wide margins in March 2004, analysts regarded its victory as convincing.

Malaysia's judiciary, though sophisticated by regional standards in its infrastructure and form, lost much of its independence during the 22-year tenure of Mahathir Mohamad, the former prime minister. However, since Abdullah Badawi became prime minister in November 2003, the courts have recovered some of their earlier standing, signaled most clearly by the release from prison of Mahathir's one-time rival, Anwar

---

William Case is Associate Professor in the Department of International Business and Asian Studies, Griffith University, Australia. He has held teaching or visiting research positions at the University of Malaya, National University of Malaysia, MARA University of Technology in Shah Alam, Malaysia, the Centre for Strategic and International Studies in Jakarta, and the Institute of Asian Studies at Chulalongkorn University in Bangkok. His most recent book is *Politics in Southeast Asia: Democracy or Less.*

Ibrahim, the former deputy prime minister, although he has not been fully exonerated.

The government's record on gender equity has been reasonably sound, with little evidence of official discrimination against women in civil service appointments. The record on minority rights has been less equitable, however, with Malays systematically advantaged over ethnic Chinese and Indians through the New Economic Policy (NEP) and various successor programs. Indeed, during 2005, pressure mounted within the United Malays National Organization (UMNO), the country's dominant political party, for the revival of NEP quotas and redistributive measures. Religious groups judged deviationist by the government were harassed during 2003–2005. Developers and logging companies continued to trample on the customary land rights of indigenous groups.

Public accountability is a serious problem in Malaysia, with collusion between government politicians and favored business people. During 2004–2005, however, Abdullah terminated or reviewed several dubious state contracts, then called for open-tender bidding. Moreover, the country's Anti-Corruption Agency began to conduct investigations more seriously. A few top officials were arrested and committed to trial, an unprecedented action in Malaysia. A commission was also established to review police performance, and it released a midterm report in 2005 that proposed unexpectedly rigorous reforms. On the other hand, despite much rhetoric on anticorruption and transparency, the government's campaign against corrupt practices remained sporadic. Suspended state contracts were in some cases restored, investigations grew infrequent, and police behavior appears so far to have remained unchanged.

ACCOUNTABILITY AND PUBLIC VOICE – 3.04

In Malaysia, elections are held regularly as provided for in the constitution. They have been meaningful in the sense that an elected prime minister wields state power, the voting is inclusive, enough opposition parties are registered that a multiparty system exists, and vote counting and reporting are promptly carried out. However, closer inspection reveals some distortions. The campaign period is kept brief, usually less than two weeks. Opposition candidates receive little access to mainstream media outlets. And while limits on campaign contributions and spending are formally codified, the government mostly ignores them in its own campaigning, and it appears not to have scrutinized opposition finances closely either.[1]

Furthermore, although the voting franchise is inclusive, electoral rolls are frequently manipulated though unannounced transfers of voters across constituencies. Ballots contain numbered counterfoils, posing a subtle form of intimidation because individual preferences could conceivably be discovered. Counting centers are small, dealing with perhaps six hundred votes across "streams," broadly revealing local preferences. Opposition parties are not permitted to oversee the counting of postal ballots cast by members of the military and police, nor do they gain equal access to polling station data. The Election Commission that supervises electoral procedures is partisan.

Municipal- and district-level elections have been suspended since the mid-1960s. At the parliamentary level, a plurality system based on single-member districts magnifies the thin margins that the government sometimes obtains into extraordinary parliamentary majorities. Partisan redistricting, last organized by the Election Commission in 2003,[2] then ratified by parliament, further ensures the government's dominance. Districts are thus heavily distorted through malapportionment and gerrymandering.

Under these conditions, opposition parties can gain significant numbers of parliamentary seats and win some state-level assemblies outright, but they are prevented from winning enough seats to form their own federal government. Still, when Malaysia's last general election was held in March 2004, the popularity of the new prime minister, Abdullah Badawi, and heightened suspicions about the Islamist-led opposition, contributed to a government victory so overwhelming that it could hardly be attributed to electoral manipulations. Indeed, the government's share of the popular vote reached 65 percent, an increase of roughly 10 percent over the previous election in 1999—an outcome widely attributed to Abdullah's comparative popularity over Mahathir.

Despite Malaysia's federalist and parliamentary arrangements, state power remains tightly centralized in the hands of the executive. Institutional checks, horizontal accountability, and local autonomy thus remain very limited. Indeed, in an address in mid-2004, the minister of parliamentary affairs in the Prime Minister's Department, Nazri Aziz, dismissed the notion of separation of powers as "too idealist" for Malaysia.[3] But while the concentration of power has many negative effects, it has ensured that people's political choices are rarely overruled by other kinds of organized interests, including the military, economic oligarchies, regional hierarchies, or foreign powers.

Under the NEP and its successor programs, ethnicity-based reverse discrimination has long ensured that civil service recruitment has been heavily tilted toward Malays. In addition, during Mahathir's tenure civil service careers lost much of their prestige relative to corporate and entrepreneurial pursuits. As a result, despite the retention of merit-based examinations and promotion criteria, bureaucratic performance appears to have declined. Abdullah has signaled his commitment to restoring good governance in the public sector. Thus, in public enterprises, top positions appear now to be filled with more regard for professionalism.

While nongovernmental organizations (NGOs) in Malaysia must gain official registration, requirements are not usually onerous. The government is responsive to civic groups that it regards as oriented toward problem-solving, especially those geared to governance and consumer issues. By contrast, the government generally ignores NGOs committed to stronger advocacy and more systemic reforms. Fearful of being tarred by the government as being in the pay of foreigners, these latter groups have usually forgone contributions from overseas, leaving them to subsist on membership dues and subscriptions. They are also denied access to mainstream media outlets and frequently to commercial printing firms, remaining confined to an internet presence. Suhakam, a human rights commission set up by the government, has on occasion investigated restrictions placed on civic organizations, although it is weakened by the partisanship of some appointees.[4] In any event, its recommendations are often unheeded by the government.

Article 10 of Malaysia's constitution guarantees rights of free expression. Article 149, however, enables parliament to restrict expression when it believes the national interest to be threatened. The most important piece of such legislation is the Printing Press and Publications Act, requiring all print media to obtain annual licenses from the Internal Security Ministry. If the ministry finds that a publisher has maliciously published what is deemed to be false news, it may revoke or refuse to renew its license. The publisher can also face charges that, if upheld in court, incur fines and prison terms.

Several other laws also restrict press freedoms, including the Sedition Act, the Official Secrets Act (OSA), the Control of Imported Publications Act (which enables the government to ban the circulation of foreign publications in Malaysia when they are viewed as prejudicial to national security or public morality), and the Broadcast Act (which empowers the minister of information to monitor radio and television broadcasts and to revoke licenses).[5] These laws deaden the political reporting of the mainstream media in Malaysia.

A government-controlled news agency, Bernama, set up in the late 1960s but vastly strengthened in 1990, has exclusive rights to distribute economic data, news photographs, and other material through the print media. Patterns of media ownership extend government control even more deeply. All major newspapers—whether Malay, Chinese, or English language—and all broadcast outlets are owned either directly by the government or by companies linked to political parties in the ruling coalition, enabling them to be used for partisan purposes. The government and top business people aligned with it have also resorted to libel suits, especially against the international press, in response to critical analysis.

Even so, during 2004–2005, the courts sometimes ruled against the government or its allies in libel cases. In this situation, the mainstream print media grew more willing to provide analysis critical of the government, while giving more extensive coverage to the internal dealings of opposition parties, especially general assemblies and party elections. *Malaysiakini,* an internet-based news daily, was also permitted to start up a Chinese-language version during 2005. And most surprisingly, the *People's Daily,* often regarded as the mouthpiece of the Communist Party of China, received a publishing and printing permit, enabling it to produce its inaugural tabloid in Malaysia on January 1, 2005.[6] Probably owing to self-censorship, there were no reports during the period under review of journalists being intimidated or coerced by state authorities. Nor, in contrast to 2003, were there reports during this period of journalists investigating local triads being victimized by nonstate actors, though this is probably more attributable to journalists' increasing caution than any serious reduction in criminal activities.

Recommendations

- Malaysia's Election Commission should be made independent, a first step toward which might involve removing it from the prime minister's department. Commissioners should also be selected through transparent procedures from among qualified personnel, rather than simply hiring trusted civil servants nearing retirement.
- Restrictions on campaign financing and expenditures should be more rigorously enforced.
- Civil service recruitment should gradually be widened to non-Malay applicants, providing a larger pool of candidates in order to restore bureaucratic quality and merit.
- The licensing system associated with the Printing Presses and Publication Act should be abolished in order to encourage greater media scrutiny of the government and business dealings. Safeguards should be put in place to reduce the partisanship of libel cases.

CIVIL LIBERTIES – 2.97

Malaysian law prohibits arbitrary arrest. However, two pieces of legislation, the Internal Security Act (ISA) and the Emergency (Public Order and Prevention of Crime) Ordinance, empower the minister of internal security and the police to detain persons indefinitely without trial if reasonable suspicion is said to exist. Further, the Dangerous Drug Act has been amended in ways that also permit preventive detention by the police, though only for 39 days.

The ISA, in place since 1960, is used primarily against opposition politicians, dissidents, alleged terrorists, and criminals whose activities are deemed to affect national security. Detainees are held in undisclosed places, they remain uninformed about the reasons for their arrest, and they are denied access to legal counsel or family visits. Given the absence of judicial oversight, suspicions persist that detainees are regularly subjected to harsh treatment, amounting to psychological and sometimes physical torture. After the initial period of interrogation under the ISA, the minister of internal security may issue a two-year detention order, under which detainees are generally transferred to a central facility. Conditions then usually improve, with detainees able to gain legal counsel and have limited family visits. However, detainees have no protection against consecutive detention orders, amounting to indefinite detention. Still, there are no documented instances of the government's going so far as to kill its political opponents.

In its annual report for 2004, Suhakam recorded that the number of ISA detainees had increased from 97 in 2003 to 113 in 2004. The majority were held for alleged terrorist activities. But forgers were also detained even though they, in the view of Suhakam, should instead have been dealt with through the normal penal system.[7] In December 2004, 20 detainees accused prison security personnel of beating them during a spot check. The Abolish ISA movement (AIM) took up their case, calling for Suhakam to mount a public inquiry. A parliamentary caucus also pledged to investigate. In July 2005, the habeas corpus applications of nine detainees from the opposition Parti Islam SeMalaysia (PAS), including the son of the chief minister of the state of Kelantan, were dismissed by the federal court, leading to public protests in Kuala Lumpur. In addition, five students deported from Pakistan while studying at a local madrassa were detained on their return to Malaysia in 2003 (the "Karachi 5"). Though finally released in March 2005, they were placed under restricted residence orders, limiting their freedom of movement.

In criminal cases, police have invoked the Emergency Ordinance, enabling them to detain local gangsters and drug lords for an initial 60-day investigation period without a remand order. The minister of internal security can afterward order two-year periods of detention in a centralized facility or impose restrictions on movement. The Dangerous Drug Act permits detention for 39 days without a remand order. Ill-treatment of ordinary criminals detained under the Emergency Ordinance and Dangerous Drug Act results in frequent deaths in police custody. Abdullah's taking office as prime minister has not been accompanied by relaxation of any of this legislation. On the contrary, in an address to the Asia Media Summit conference held in April 2004, Abdullah stated that "we have in place tough laws and some of them are preventive in nature. . . . [W]e do not apologize for them."[8]

Turning to issues of gender discrimination, in 2005 three women held full ministerial posts in Malaysia's government, including the minister of trade and industry. Women also held top positions in the state apparatus: Zeti Akhtar Aziz is governor of the central bank, while Siti Norma Yaakob was appointed in 2005 as Chief Judge of Malaya, one of the country's four top judicial positions.[9] Moreover, throughout the civil service, women are reasonably well represented. On the other hand, while women are nominated as electoral candidates by UMNO and its main coalition partner, the Malaysian Chinese Association, the proportion of candidacies they gain remains quite small, especially at the state level. They face even greater discrimination in PAS.

Further, although the constitution's recently amended Article 8(2) appears to protect women's interests in economic life, the government's overall responsiveness to women's issues—often forcefully articulated by a few small but prominent women's organizations—has been inconsistent. By UN standards, Malaysia's Sharia courts, whose jurisdiction for Muslims is compulsory in some areas, have discriminated grossly against women, especially in family law cases. But women have also faced discrimination in the country's secular court system. For example, in May 2005, the Federal Court rejected an appeal by a former flight attendant, Beatrice Fernandez, against an earlier judgment that favored her employer, Malaysia Airlines. Fernandez had been forced to resign in 1991 after becoming pregnant, prompting her to mount a 14-year legal battle to declare her termination as void. Responding to the federal court's ruling, academic Andrew Aeria characterized the Malaysian judiciary as "stuck in the Dark Ages and in dire need of enlightenment as far as the views of gender-based discrimination are concerned."[10]

Malaysia does not comply fully with even minimum standards for eliminating human trafficking. Suhakam has drafted a national action plan for containing trafficking, but it has not yet been approved by the government. Without comprehensive legislation, victims are deemed illegal migrants and can be arrested under immigration laws. Trafficked victims are also recruited into prostitution, sometimes with the connivance of local officials. In February 2005, some home ministry officials in the National Registration Department were detained under the ISA for issuing forged permanent resident identity cards to human trafficking groups.[11] The government appears to be trying to improve its record, however. In December 2004, the Ministry for Women, Family and Community Development announced that it would set up a shelter for foreign trafficking victims.

Politics in Malaysia—where approximately 60 percent of the population is Malay/Muslim, 26 percent ethnic Chinese, and 7 percent ethnic Indians—have long been dominated by leaders of the Malay/Muslim community. The constitution grants the Malay special rights, manifested in the NEP's ethnic quotas on state hiring, contracts, credit, business licensing, corporate employment, and equity ownership. A National Culture Policy has also privileged Malay ethnicity and Islam as the symbols of state and national identity. Over the past decade and a half, the NEP has been replaced by milder programs. But at the UMNO general assembly held in mid-2005, the party's youth organization demanded that a "New National Agenda" be introduced as a precursor to the program's full revival, a call duly taken up by the information minister, Abdul Kadir. Ethnic Chinese and Indian leaders have expressed fears that freedoms of communication and assembly could be further constrained to facilitate a stronger imposition of quotas.

At the same time, the requirements of industrialization and changing electoral dynamics have encouraged some new government responsiveness to social minorities. Thus, the government has ceded to the Chinese community greater freedoms in cultural pursuits and education, with the quotas on university admissions that had strongly favored the Malay/Muslim community now officially removed. Further, the country's National Service Program, which during 2004 drafted some 85,000 17-year-olds, was designed by the government explicitly to encourage deeper community integration, with participants "assigned to camps . . . according to a complex formula designed to maximize diversity."[12] In contrast, people with disabilities receive no particular attention, not even in the form of information provided in formats accessible to them. The government does warn periodically, if tepidly, that persons with HIV should not be discriminated against. Malaysia is also one of the few countries in Asia where local funding is made available to advocacy groups. People living with AIDS still complain, however, that they are heavily stigmatized.

While Islam is Malaysia's official religion, the constitution protects religious freedoms. However, to convert from Islam to another religion requires sanction from the court, which is rarely granted. In addition, the government monitors Islamic activities closely, banning Muslim groups that it labels deviant. In mid-2005, the government deemed 22 sects deviant. It moved most forcefully against Sky Kingdom, a group of some 200 followers of the self-styled spiritualist Ariffin Mohammad ("Ayah Pin"), based in Terengganu.[13] Shortly after Christian groups were invited to the Sky Kingdom's compound for faith-sharing, the Terengganu

Islamic Affairs Department demolished the compound's structures, arrested many followers, and drove Ariffin into hiding.

Followers of Christianity, Hinduism, Buddhism, and Sikhism in Malaysia, while permitted to practice their faiths, are barred from proselytizing among Muslims. They can officially establish their own places of worship, although they often encounter strong bureaucratic obstruction over zoning and building approvals. Otherwise, there appears to be little government interference with minority religions.

The Malaysian constitution guarantees freedom of assembly, though with restrictions "in the interest of security and public order." Thus, amendments to the Police Act (1967) require that a permit be obtained 14 days before any political meeting is held. Nonetheless, a reasonably well-developed civil society has emerged in Malaysia, at least in urban areas. Trade unions are permitted to form, with the Malaysian Trades Union Congress (MTUC) serving as an umbrella organization. However, only in-house unions can normally be organized in the country's free-trade zones, where foreign-invested manufacturing facilities geared toward vital exports predominate. Strike actions are tightly regulated and street protests prohibited. Public rallies during electoral campaigns were banned in 1978. The Election Commission announced in 2003 that it would lift the ban, but it still requires organizers to obtain police permits before holding rallies. During electoral campaigning in 2004, the reform was revealed as nearly meaningless, as police rarely granted permits to the opposition. In addition, university students remain barred under the University and University Colleges Act from engaging in any activities that the attorney-general deems political.

Recommendations

- The Internal Security Act and the Emergency Ordinance should be repealed. The governments should encourage better police work and development of new methods for evidence gathering so that open trial proceedings can be conducted.
- Political parties should be encouraged to nominate more women candidates, and the secular and Sharia court systems should be encouraged to make rulings that avoid gender discrimination.
- The government should adopt comprehensive legislation against human trafficking while also instituting a sheltering program.

- The Police Act and the University and University Colleges Act should be repealed, allowing scope for peaceful social activism.

RULE OF LAW – 4.01

Malaysia possesses a large judicial apparatus that is sophisticated in its formal appearance and functioning. Appointments of judges have been skewed, however, by constitutional requirements that they be made formally by the king on the advice of the prime minister, triggering criticisms from Suhakam and the Malaysian Bar Council over a lack of fairness and transparency. Such interference has distorted judicial rulings in political cases, especially during Mahathir's prime ministership. The attorney-general's chambers, which is not obliged to state publicly its reasons for commencing or terminating cases, appears to be equally dominated by the executive. There is no judicial review of legislation.

However, since Abdullah became prime minister, the judiciary appears to have regained some of the independence that it had enjoyed prior to Mahathir's tenure. For example, in April 2004, the high court in Shah Alam overturned the conviction of Ezam Nor, leader of the opposition Keadilan (Justice) party's youth wing. Ezam had been convicted under the OSA of having circulated classified reports about corrupt practices. The high court ruled that the documents had been classified only after Ezam had been charged.[14]

More striking, in August 2004, the federal court overturned the conviction of former Deputy Prime Minister Anwar Ibrahim on sexual misconduct charges. Anwar, after having challenged then–Prime Minister Mahathir at a party meeting in 1998, was purged from the government and charged with corruption and sexual misconduct. Amid controversial proceedings, he was found guilty by the courts and sentenced to a lengthy prison term.[15] The latest federal court ruling, however, found that the testimony against Anwar was not credible, leading to his immediate release.[16] Still, while Anwar was found innocent of sexual misconduct, his conviction for having tried corruptly to conceal this misconduct was left to stand, hence barring him from running for office for a period of five years. Commenting publicly on this outcome, Abdullah denied that any deal with the judiciary had been struck. But the contradiction in logic between these rulings, alongside the clear benefits for

Abdullah and UMNO—muting local and international criticisms over unjust treatment, yet blunting Anwar's political effectiveness—made it difficult to believe that executive approval had not been tacitly granted for the judiciary's new display of independence.

Two months later, the high court in Penang issued yet another ruling favorable to Keadilan. In the general election, Anwar's wife, Wan Azizah, had been the only Keadilan candidate reelected to parliament. The UMNO candidate against whom she had run petitioned the courts for a recount. Opposition leaders anticipated that this petition would be successful, and they prepared for a by-election that they feared they would lose. But the high court found the allegations baseless, thereby affirming Wan Azizah's place in parliament.[17]

In ordinary criminal cases, citizens in Malaysia receive a reasonably fair and public hearing by an independent and impartial tribunal established by law, and prosecutors are independent of political control.[18] An assumption of innocence prevails. Indigent suspects can qualify for free legal aid through the Legal Aid Center, operated by the Malaysian Bar Council, or through the initiatives of individual lawyers. Through the Legal Aid Bureau the government also provides assistance for civil cases. However, as noted above, before suspects appear in court, they are often interrogated harshly by police, with forced confessions and deaths occurring in custody. Before Abdullah became prime minister, very few high-level officials were prosecuted for wrongdoing unless they had fallen from favor.

The security forces of Malaysia, in contrast to many of their counterparts in the region, are fully subject to civilian control. However, the executive has regularly deployed police agencies for political purposes, with the Special Branch, Federal Reserve Unit, and Police Field Force gathering information on dissidents and suppressing opposition activities.[19] As in previous years, family members of ISA detainees who mounted protest actions during 2004–2005 reported that they were systematically harassed and threatened by Special Branch agents.

The sundry ethnic quotas imposed through the NEP and successor programs (see "Civil Liberties") raise questions about equal treatment and respect for property rights. Thus, while Malaysia's economy is in important ways market-based, state interventions force redistribution according to ethnicity, especially in connection with equity ownership. For example, firms owned by non-Malays have been required by law to allocate 30 percent of their equity to Malay recipients, usually at discounted rates, lest their operating licenses be withdrawn. Accordingly, the country's minority Chinese and Indian communities, confronted also by the government's Islamization policies, lament their second-class citizenship. This inequity does not carry over, however, into ordinary judicial proceedings. To be sure, the judiciary is made up mainly of ethnic Malays, while lawyers are mostly Chinese and Indian. But rulings in most criminal and civil cases are handed down without regard for ethnic or religious affiliation. In contrast, by UN standards the country's Sharia courts discriminate unfairly against women over matters of family law and inheritance (see "Civil Liberties").

The land rights of indigenous non-Malay groups remain for the most part unprotected in areas targeted for development. Clashes have occurred between indigenous groups and logging interests over land use, especially in East Malaysia. In 2005, Iban communities in Sarawak protested against logging in areas that had been recognized as "native customary rights land." But as the logging had been licensed by the state forestry department, the protest leader, village chief Ajan Wen, was threatened with arrest.[20] Similar disputes over logging on customary lands and in national parks led to lawsuits and appeals to Suhakam throughout 2004–2005.

On the other hand, in September 2005, the court of appeal upheld a high court decision in a case first brought by seven Orang Asli (indigenous persons) a decade earlier against the government and a well-connected construction company. Lands belonging to the Orang Asli had been seized for construction of the Nilai-Banting highway, with minimal compensation. The high court determined that the Orang Asli held native title under common law and that they should be paid compensation and damages.[21]

Recommendations

- The independence of the judiciary should be fully recognized by the executive. The executive should refrain from openly criticizing judges and the Bar Council as well as making statements about cases before rulings have been made.
- Judicial appointments should be made with greater transparency and independence. To this end, a judicial services commission should be set up to make recommendations about appointments.

Appointments at the federal court level should also be approved by parliament.

- The attorney-general's chambers should strengthen its independence from the executive by declaring publicly the criteria by which it institutes, conducts, or discontinues hearings.

ANTICORRUPTION AND TRANSPARENCY – 2.87

The role of the state bureaucracy in affirmative action and business expansion help account for the substantial corruption in Malaysia. As resources are often politically allocated rather than driven by the needs of the market, a nexus has emerged between government and business that has systematically bred conflicts of interest.

In 2003, Abdullah Badawi called for "people power" as a means to oppose corrupt practices.[22] After he became prime minister and preparations began for the general election in 2004, a number of sitting UMNO parliamentarians and state assemblymen suspected of corruption were denied renomination. A month later, Abdullah led a two-day ethics seminar for the government's 198 members of parliament (MPs), then presented a new code of ethics that stressed professional norms and honesty. He also announced that henceforth, MPs would have to declare their assets in full.[23] The rigorously specified terms of disclosure required that MPs list their corporate interests, the types of business activities in which they were involved, and the value of their investments. These terms extended also to family members and any other persons who might function as trustees or proxies. A deadline of May 31, 2004, was imposed.

In extending his drive against corruption from UMNO to the bureaucracy, Abdullah formed the Malaysian Institute of Public Ethics, backed by a National Integrity Plan in 2004.[24] He ordered that spot checks be carried out in targeted government departments, namely immigration and customs, transport, land registration offices, and the police force.[25] Indeed, with the police "suffer[ing] an 'image crisis,' due to corruption, brutality, and poor service,"[26] Abdullah ordered a formal review of the police force. To this end, he set up the Special Commission to Enhance the Operations and Management of the Royal Malaysian Police. This commission was led by a former federal court chief justice, Mohamed Dzaiddin Abdullah, widely regarded as realistic but reformist. Among its members were several lawyers and NGO activists (including Tunku Abdul Aziz, then head of Malaysia's Transparency International chapter) and a range of former high-level political, corporate, and police figures. Six months later the commission delivered an interim report whose findings were unexpectedly critical and, contrary to earlier government pronouncements, publicly disclosed. Final recommendations were to be made at the end of 2005; however, by the end of November, there was no indication that the police had begun to act seriously on the interim report.

The main body through which the government seeks to investigate corrupt practices is the Anti-Corruption Agency (ACA). The ACA appears to possess significant capacity for investigation, and it operates a website where informants can report instances of corruption anonymously. As mentioned above, prior to Abdullah's gaining power, corruption was not rigorously prosecuted. Shortly after he became prime minister, however, several notables were committed to trial for corruption. The minister for land cooperative development, Kasitah Gaddam, was arrested in early 2004, allegedly for having been involved in an illegal sale of shares in a state-owned enterprise. Eric Chia, a former managing director of the state-owned steel company, was also arrested, allegedly for having approved an illicit payment to a Japanese partner. Shaharin Shaharudin, a former chief executive of a state investment company, Pernas (Perbadan Nasional), was charged with illicit dealings. Furthermore, in mid-2005, UMNO's disciplinary board purged the party of some top officials against whom claims of having engaged in money politics (i.e., vote-buying) at the previous year's general assembly were found to have been substantiated. Surprisingly, UMNO's topmost vice-president, Isa Samad, was suspended, resulting in his removal as minister of federal territories.

However, after the government won a landslide in the March 2004 general election, its drive against corrupt practices began to wane. Although public attention focused intently on four allegedly corrupt ministers, Abdullah did little to shake up his cabinet, leaving two of these ministers in their posts, while the remaining pair was merely shifted to other portfolios.[27] Nazri Aziz was viewed as most vulnerable to dismissal; while minister of entrepreneur development, he had undergone much-publicized questioning by the ACA over his issuance of taxi licenses. However, after the election he was transferred to the Prime Minister's Department, whose capacity Abdullah had expanded from four to six ministers. Indeed, the proportion of ministers, deputy ministers, and parliamentary secretaries swelled to nearly one-third of the government's ranks of parliamentarians, thus procuring overall "a strong sense of continuity from a prime minister who had appeared bent on differentiating his administration from Mahathir's."[28] At the same time, in Malaysia's universities, procedures for appointment, promotion, and removal grew highly politicized, leading to forced resignations and termination of contracts.

The code of ethics that Abdullah had earlier introduced for members of the governing coalition was only laxly administered, requiring that MPs make self-assessments, then electronically submit their "report cards" on a quarterly basis. Further, their asset declarations were not disclosed publicly, while the penalties for failing to make them at all were left unclear. The May deadline was thus roundly ignored, prompting Abdullah to offer an extension.[29] In addition, under Abdullah victims of corruption were given no additional mechanisms through which to seek redress.

Malaysia received a score of 5.0 in Transparency International's 2004 Corruption Perceptions Index, in which 10 represents the least corrupt. This constituted an overall drop from the previous year's score of 5.2.[30] Similarly, a World Bank study portrayed Malaysia as trending steadily downward in five areas of governance between 1998 and 2004, improving during the last two years only in terms of political stability.[31] Nonetheless, the Malaysian public seemed untroubled. A survey conducted by Merdeka Centre for Opinion Research in mid-2004 revealed the "overall concern for corruption in the public sector had subsided since the March general election."[32]

In terms of institutional safeguards for transparency, Malaysia has an auditor-general's office and a public complaints bureau. But like the ACA, these agencies are neither effective nor nonpartisan. A parliamentary public accounts committee also exists, and, under the chairmanship of an independent-minded government MP and his opposition deputy, it has succeeded lately in contributing meaningfully to public debate. The Malaysian Integrity Institute (IIM) has been tasked with assisting the ACA while implementing the National Integrity Plan. To this end, it has recently partnered with the United Nations Development Program. However, it is too soon to evaluate the IIM's effectiveness in exposing bureaucratic corruption. A recently introduced system of parliamentary select committees remains rudimentary.

As nearly all mainstream newspapers and television stations are either owned by the government or aligned with it, they undertake little independent investigation. Whistle-blowers, anticorruption activists, and investigators who seek to present government documents as evidence of corruption risk severe penalties under the OSA. Attempts by opposition politicians to meet with top officers in such agencies as the ACA are usually rebuffed. Most of the government's many websites offer little substantive information, and there is no freedom of information act.

Nonetheless, Abdullah has tried intermittently to increase the transparency of some government decision making, even if institutions remain weak. First, seeking to reduce the deal-making between government and business, he cancelled several large infrastructure projects, most famously an electrified double-track railway that was to have run the length of peninsular Malaysia's west coast. He also scaled back plans for a new customs facility and elevated bridge link between Malaysia's southern state of Johor and Singapore, the folly of which had been ensured by Singapore's withdrawal from the project. On the other hand, although Abdullah ordered a review of the massive Bakun Dam hydroelectric project in Sarawak, the project continues unabated.[33] And while he has advised that any additional government contracts will be awarded not through opaque and personal dealings but instead through open-tender bidding, there was little indication of improvement by November 2005.[34]

In another positive step, many of the Malay entrepreneurs whose interests had been favored by the government during boom times, only to be brought low by the currency crisis, were finally forced to relinquish their holdings. Their assets were mostly acquired by the government's investment vehicle, Khazanah Nasional. Although analysts typically dismiss increases in state ownership as worsening distortions, in the Malaysian context of highly politicized privatization these transfers promised to raise transparency and share prices.[35] Efficiencies also accrued when other vehicles such as Ministry of Finance Inc. sold the equity stakes that they held either to Khazanah, to the state-owned petroleum company (Petronas), or to the national superannuation scheme (the Employees' Provident Fund).[36] At the same time, in order to bolster further Khazanah and key government-linked corporations such as Telekoms Malaysia and Tenaga Nasional, the national power utility, new cohorts of professionally trained Malays and even foreign executives were recruited as corporate leaders.[37]

Most dramatically, a furor erupted over the distribution by the ministry of international trade and industry of import licenses for automobiles. Known locally as "approved permits" (APs), these licenses were initially introduced in 1970 as a way for Malay businesspeople to get a footing in the automobile industry, which was dominated locally by Chinese. However, after Mahathir, upon his retirement as prime minister, was appointed as an advisor to the national car company, Proton, he denounced the AP system as undercutting the company's competitiveness. Opposition leaders took up the cry, demanding that the system be made transparent. The government responded by reversing its long-standing policy of not revealing the names of recipients, publishing lists of persons who together had been awarded more than 67,000 APs.

The government's commitment to effective macroeconomic management remains strong, with the budget-making process taken seriously. The budgets proposed during Abdullah's tenure have been widely assessed as prudent, targeting the deficits that had mounted during Mahathir's last years in office.[38] To this end, Abdullah also bolstered the state's extractive capacity, with Inland Revenue raiding 10 of the country's largest construction firms over tax evasion during his first year in office.

Just as the government's fight against corruption fluctuated during this period, so did its commitments to transparency. The budget's great length and complexity are beyond the capacity of an underresourced opposition to oversee properly. In addition, significant amounts of government revenue and expenditure remain off budget. For example, Petronas, the national petroleum company, is housed within the Prime Minister's Department, leaving it almost entirely unaccountable to parliament. The government thus remains quite silent on many of its expenditures, while disclosing many others in an impenetrable aggregate form.

After the 2004 general election, some of the state contracts that had been placed under review were quietly restored, with Abdullah insisting that the government was bound by the letters of intent that his predecessor had signed.[39] Indeed, some of Abdullah's own family members appear to have benefited from these contracts. Attention focused on the dealings of his brother, Ibrahim Badawi, whose company, Gubahan Saujana, won deals with a catering subsidiary of Malaysia Airlines. Through an opaque privatization process, Gubahan Saujana secured a revenue guarantee of 80 percent over a nine-year period.[40]

Analysts also observed the meteoric rise of a newly listed oil and gas company, Scomi Group, in which Abdullah's son Kamaluddin held a majority interest. When the government announced plans to develop smaller oil fields, expectations mounted that Scomi would be the chief beneficiary of state contracts, driving up the firm's share price by an incredible 588 percent over its listing price four months earlier.[41] A company subsidiary, Scomi Precision Engineering, was also cleared hastily in early 2004 by the Foreign Ministry and police after becoming embroiled in a scandal for exporting centrifuge parts to Libya, allegedly through a black market in nuclear equipment.[42] In the view of Wan Azizah Wan Hamzah, wife of Anwar Ibrahim and president of Keadilan, such "abus[e] [of] diplomatic machinery and resources to defend a private company owned by the son of the prime minister is clear poof of how cronyism and nepotism [have] been shamefully institutionalized . . . in Malaysia."[43]

Recommendations

- Malaysia's anticorruption agency should be removed from the Prime Minister's Department, leaving it freer to investigate cases of corruption in nonpartisan ways. The Integrity Management Committee should be given enforcement powers.
- Officials and politicians should be made to declare their assets publicly, and government contracts should be awarded through open bidding.
- Whistle-blowers should not be threatened with prosecution under the OSA or other laws.
- The recommendations of the Special Commission to Enhance the Operations and Management of the Royal Malaysian Police contained in the mid-term report should be adopted in full.
- The revenues and expenditures of Petronas and other government-linked corporations and agencies operating with off-budget accounts should be specified in the federal budget and scrutinized by parliament.

NOTES

[1] See Mavis Putucheary and Noraini Othman, eds., *Elections and Democracy in Malaysia* (Bangi, Malaysia: Penerbit UKM, 2005).

[2] Lim Hong Hai, "New Rules and Constituencies for New Challenges?" *Aliran Monthly,* n.d., http://www.aliran.com/monthly/2003/6j (accessed 28 August 2003).

[3] Beh Lih Yi, "Separation of Powers Too 'Idealistic,' Says Nazri," *Malaysiakini,* 3 June 2004.

[4] See *Assessment of the National Human Rights Commission (Suhakam)* (Kuala Lumpur: Suara Rakyat Malaysia [Suaram], April 2002), http://www.Suaram.org/suHakam-evaluation-2002.htm.

[5] "Civil and Political Rights Including the Question of: Freedom of Expression; . . . Report on the Mission to Malaysia" (New York: UN Economic and Social Council, Commission on Human Rights, 23 December 1998), http://www.hri.ca/fortherecord1999/documentation/commission/e-cn4-1999-64-add1.htm.

[6] Pauline Puah, "M'sia Approves Permit for Chinese Communist Party Organ," *Malaysiakini,* 10 January 2005, http://www.malaysiakini.com/news/32720.

[7] Beh Lih Yi, "Suhakam: ISA Detentions Increased Last Year," *Malaysiakini,* 20 June 2005, http://www.malaysiakini.com/news/37147.

[8] "Pak Lah: Tough Laws Needed to Preserve Racial Ties," *Malaysiakini,* 19 April 2004.

[9] "Siti Norma, First Woman in Top Judicial Post," *Malaysiakini,* 9 February 2005, http://www.malaysiakini.com/news/33516.

[10] Quoted in Tony Thien, "Federal Court Reasoning Described as 'Archaic,'" *Malaysiakini,* 30 May 2005, http://www.malaysiakini.com/news/36535.

[11] "Malaysia Detains Officials on Human Trafficking Allegations," Agence France Presse, 12 February 2005, http://www.channelnewsasia.com/stories/afp_asiapacific/view/132194/1/.html.

[12] "Forging a Nation," *The Economist,* 21 October 2004, web edition, http://www.economist.com/displayStory.cfm?story_id=3321010.

[13] "Malaysia: Protect Freedom of Belief for Sky Kingdom" (New York: Human Rights Watch [HRW], 21 July 2005), http://hrw.org/english/docs/2005/07/21/malays11397_txt.htm.

[14] Arfa'eza A Aziz, "'Classified' Documents in Doubt: Ezam Freed," *Malaysiakini,* 17 April 2004, http://www.malaysiakini.com/news/2004041500115153.php.

[15] See William Case, "The Anwar Trial and its Wider Implications," in Colin Barlow and Francis Loh Kok Wah, eds., *Malaysian Economics and Politics in the New Century* (Cheltenham, UK: Edward Elgar, 2003), 119–31.

[16] S. Jayasankaran, "A Leader Returns," *Far Eastern Economic Review,* 16 September 2004, 12–13.

[17] Beh Lih Yi, "Wan Azizah Keeps PKR's Sole Seat," *Malaysikini,* 28 October 2004.

[18] International Commission of Jurists Legal Resource Center, "Malaysia—International Legal Community Denounces Government Interference in the Rule of Law in Malaysia," 5 April 2005, http://www.icj.org/news.php3?id_article=2521&lang=en.

19 Harold Crouch, *Government and Society in Malaysia* (Ithaca: Cornell University Press, 1996), 137.

20 Tony Thien, "Longhouse Folks See Red Over Logging," *Malaysiakini,* 18 July 2005, http://www.malaysiakini.com/news/37977.

21 Colin Nicholas, "Orang Asli Land Rights Upheld," *Aliran Monthly* 25, no. 8 (2005), http://www.aliran.com/monthly/2005b/8e.html.

22 Lim Kit Siang, media statement (Selangor, Malaysia: Democratic Action Party [DAP], 8 August 2003), http://dapmalaysia.org/english/lks/aug03/lks2505.html.

23 Claudia Theophilus, "PM: Asset Declaration Includes Immediate, Extended Families," *Malaysiakini,* 19 April 2004, http://www.malaysiakini.com/news/2004041900115212 .php.

24 Kimina Lyall, "PM's Graft War Right on Money," *The Weekend Australian,* 14–15 February 2004, 12.

25 Leslie Lopez, "He's No Mahathir, and That's OK," *Far Eastern Economic Review,* 25 December 2003–1 January 2004, 13.

26 "Ex-CJ Dzaiddin to Head Royal Police Commission," *Malaysiakini,* 4 February 2004, http://www.malaysiakini.com/new/2004020400113898.php.

27 S. Jayasankaran, "Not So Fast," *Far Eastern Economic Review,* 8 April 2004, 20.

28 "Malaysia PM Faithful to Old Guard in New Cabinet," *New York Times* on-line edition/ Reuters, 27 March 2004, http://www.nytimes.com/reuters/international/international- malaysia-cabinet-html.

29 "Asset Declaration: Extension, Not Exemption," *Malaysiakini,* 4 June 2004, http://www .malaysiakini.com/news/2004060400115900.php.

30 Corruption Perceptions Index (Berlin: Transparency International [TI]), http://www .infoplease.com/ipa/A0781359.html.

31 Claudia Theophilus, "Malaysia's Governance Standards Drop," *Malaysiakini,* 11 May 2005, http://www.malaysiakini.com/print.php?id=36047.

32 Pauline Puah, "Graft-riddled image of Gov't Persists, Shows Survey," *Malaysiakini,* 17 September 2004, http://www.malaysiakini.com/news/30125.

33 "Aluminium Intrigue," *The Edge,* 19 December 2005, 70–74.

34 "Not Yet Out of Mahathir's Shadow," *The Economist,* 31 January 2004, 25.

35 "The Malay Way of Business Change," *The Economist,* 20 August 2005, 46.

36 S. Jayasankaran, "Behind the Politics, A Pressing Deficit," *Far Eastern Economic Review,* 4 March 2004, 14–15.

37 "Young Professionals to Head Two Top Utility Firms in Revamp," *Malaysiakini,* 20 May 2004, http://www.malaysiakini.com/news/200405200015653.php.

38 "Govt Confident It Can Rein in Budget Deficit," *Malaysiakini,* 12 September 2005, http://www.malaysiakini.com/news/40286.

39 Michael Vatikiotis and S. Jayasankaran, "Softly, Softly Go Reforms," *Far Eastern Economic Review,* 3 June 2004, 23.

40 "Pak Lah faces question for 'Meteoric Rise' of Son's Company," *Malaysiakini,* 20 September 2003, http://www.malaysiakini.com/news/2003092000112211.php.

41 Ibid.

42 "Bush: M'sia Says Scope No Longer Makes Centrifuge Parts," *Malaysiakini,* 12 February 2004, http://www.malaysiakini.com/news/2004021200114019.php.

43 "Malaysian Opposition Accuses Prime Minister of Nepotism," *Los Angeles Times,* 24 February 2004.

MOROCCO

CAPITAL: Rabat
POPULATION: 30.7 million
GNI PER CAPITA: $1,310

SCORES	2004	2006
ACCOUNTABILITY AND PUBLIC VOICE:	2.42	3.30
CIVIL LIBERTIES:	2.66	3.67
RULE OF LAW:	2.42	3.04
ANTICORRUPTION AND TRANSPARENCY:	1.54	2.14

(scores are based on a scale of 0 to 7, with 0 representing weakest and 7 representing strongest performance)

John Damis

INTRODUCTION

Morocco has made notable progress toward democracy since 1990, although this progress lacks a permanent institutional foundation. Despite constitutional reforms to improve accountability and political representation, ultimate authority continues to rest with the king, who occupies the unique position of all-powerful political actor and arbitrator. Legislative and municipal elections have become more transparent and regular, but they serve more to provide spoils for elites than to promote genuine political representation.

Morocco is a monarchy with a constitution, a bicameral parliament, and an independent judiciary. In practice, however, the king's power has virtually no effective constraints. He is head of state and of the armed forces, he represents both temporal and spiritual authority, and he is above the law. Following legislative elections, the king appoints the prime minister and members of the government. He presides over the Council of Ministers and has the power to dissolve parliament, call for new elections, or rule by decree. King Mohammed VI assumed the throne in July 1999 following the death of his father, Hassan II, who had ruled for 38 years.

John Damis is Professor of Political Science and Director of the Middle East Studies Center at Portland State University. He is the author of numerous publications on the politics and international relations of North Africa, including the Western Sahara.

Important political reforms took place in the 1990s. With constitutional revisions in 1992 and 1996, the powers of the two-chamber parliament were expanded. The parliament now votes on the government and reviews its general policies. It can also investigate the government's actions through commissions of inquiry and dissolve a government through a motion of censure or a vote of no confidence. In 1998, the king named a coalition government headed by an opposition socialist leader who called for political and economic change. The left-of-center coalition made rule of law, transparency, and social reforms their major priorities. However, the government's performance fell far short of public expectations. After the 2002 legislative elections, rather than appointing a prime minister from the party with the largest number of parliamentary seats, the king appointed Driss Jettou, a palace loyalist with no party affiliation.

Despite the public commitment of the monarch to democratization, these modest reforms have had little impact on the political process or the daily life of Moroccans. Civil and political rights ultimately depend on the king's goodwill and political expediency. When the king acts decisively, as he did with the reform of the family code in 2003–2004, personal rights are substantially enhanced. However, even though Morocco adheres to major international conventions, civil and human rights violations have increased since the Casablanca terrorist bombings in May 2003, which killed 45 people. The legal system remains vulnerable to corruption and political pressure, though the king and government have worked since 1999 to make the rule of law a major priority. Corruption remains endemic at several levels of Moroccan society, from communal and district courts to the top level of large public enterprises. High-profile investigations of embezzlement by senior figures in the public sector rarely lead to indictments. Moreover, politically charged cases—including those involving terrorism, corruption of public officials, and offenses against the monarchy, Islam, or territorial integrity—are subject to extrajudicial pressure. Territorial integrity, for the king, government, and virtually all Moroccans, includes the Western Sahara, a large former Spanish territory claimed by Morocco and occupied and administered by the kingdom since 1976.

ACCOUNTABILITY AND PUBLIC VOICE – 3.30

The Moroccan constitution provides the basis for representative government and stipulates that "sovereignty shall be that of the People who shall exercise it directly, by means of referendum, or indirectly, through the constitutional institutions." Despite this commitment to representative government, Article 19 vests ultimate power in the king, who "shall be the Supreme Representative of the Nation and the Symbol of the unity thereof."

Elections in Morocco have historically been infrequent but have become increasingly regular since the 1990s. Constitutional reforms in 1992 and 1996 have improved the validity of elections, and successive elections have become freer of accusations of manipulation, lower-level corruption, and vote buying. By most accounts, Morocco's most recent votes—parliamentary elections in 2002 and municipal elections in 2003—were free, fair, and transparent.

Morocco has had a multiparty political system since independence in 1956, and citizens are now free to affiliate with any of 29 legal political parties registered with the Ministry of Interior. Morocco has made improvements in allowing equal campaigning opportunities for political parties. This is evidenced in the acceptance of participation of strong Islamist candidates in parliamentary elections. In 1996, the Islamist party Unity and Reform was allowed to enter mainstream politics by joining an existing party, the Popular Democratic and Constitutional Movement (MPDC). Under this party, Unity and Reform members secured nine parliamentary seats in the November 1997 elections. As Unity and Reform members gained control of MPDC, they continued to campaign under the party's new name, the Party of Justice and Development (PJD). In the September 27, 2002, elections, the PJD won 42 seats in the 325-seat parliament, securing the third-largest bloc.

Among the parties banned by the authorities is the most important, popular, and largest Islamist-oriented political party—the Justice and Charity Association. With considerable popular support, Justice and Charity would easily win a plurality if not a majority of votes if the monarchy allowed its legal operation—and if the party was willing to participate in the political process.

The government is taking steps toward improving the Moroccan people's ability to create political parties. On October 30, 2005, the interior commission in the Chamber of Deputies approved new legislation to reform the process involved in the formation of political parties and the campaign finance law, including providing parties with an annual subsidy. Proposed revisions of the electoral code are also scheduled to be addressed before upcoming elections in 2007. However, the government maintains the right to block some parties from full participation, and by banning the Justice and Charity Association it is excluding the country's most popular party from the political process. The July 2005 political parties law forbids the establishment of parties on the basis of religion, race, or tribe. Furthermore, the government does not provide adequate regulations to prevent economically privileged interests from exercising undue influence on political parties.

The executive, legislative, and judicial branches of the Moroccan government can neither oversee one another's actions nor hold each other accountable for excessive exercise of power. This is in large part due to the manner in which the authority of the monarchy over the legislative and judicial branches is formally institutionalized. Although members of parliament are selected by a popular vote based on universal suffrage, the king reserves the right to appoint and dismiss the prime minister and dissolve parliament at his discretion. The king must also approve any changes in the constitution. The legislature and judiciary suffer from corruption and have been unsuccessful in gaining the trust and support of the Moroccan people. The parliament remains weak, disorganized, and in need of institutional reforms to improve its legislative, regulatory, and inquiry capacities.

In April 2004, parliament signed a Memo of Understanding with USAID to pursue two programs. The parliamentary program sought "to bridge the gap between members of parliament (MPs), civil society leaders, and constituents, and to improve the efficiency and effectiveness of MPs and party caucuses."[1] The political party program sought to help parties "to overcome the gap dividing parties from citizens, to build the capacity of women and youth to participate fully in political parties, and to improve political party members' access to skills and resources and communication within and between their parties."[2] With the relative success of these efforts, international donors have undertaken similar programs to improve the effectiveness of parliament and Morocco's individual political parties.

The civil service is legally accessible to all who qualify, based on open competition and on merit. However, in reality selection is often based on connections. The government currently employs some 80,000 "ghost employees" who continue to receive salaries and pensions for no work. Dismissal is rare in the civil service, as employment is often for life.[3]

In comparison to other Arab nations, Morocco practices liberal control over the establishment and activities of civil associations, and in many circumstances such groups are able to testify, comment on, and influence pending government policy or legislation. For example, liberal civic associations and women's rights groups were instrumental in procuring the January 2004 passage of the new Family Code. The government has also been increasingly supportive of nongovernmental organizations (NGOs), which have become an important fixture in Moroccan politics and generally enjoy the cooperation of the Moroccan government. Three officially recognized nongovernmental human rights groups operate in Morocco: the Moroccan Human Rights Organization (OMDH), the Moroccan Association of Human Rights (AMDH), and the Moroccan Defense League of Human Rights (LMDDH). The OMDH and LMDDH receive support from the government in the form of subsidies. Other important groups include the Moroccan Forum for Truth and Justice (FVJ) and the Moroccan Observatory of Prisons (OMP). The FVJ has been active in urging the government to acknowledge past practices of disappearances and arbitrary arrests. The government is passively, and sometimes actively, supportive of organizations dedicated to improving civil and political rights. NGOs work with the government and receive state subsidies, and a number of local and national independent organizations specifically advocate women's rights. The government often overlooks the legal requirements to establish a civic association, though it sometimes cites these requirements to constrain persons or organizations that advocate sensitive causes. The Ministry of Interior has the authority to dissolve associations and prevent any unwanted organization from operating. Thus, some Berber activists, Islamic associations, and leftist human rights and political parties are denied approval.

Although Article 9 of the Moroccan constitution guarantees "freedom of opinion" and "of expression in all its forms," historically, the monarchy has maintained tight control of the press. With the ascent of King Mohammed VI to the throne, the government has made a few promising gestures that suggest a commitment to liberalization of the media. In March 2002, the Commission on Foreign Affairs and National Defense in the parliament unanimously approved a revised press code. On January 7, 2004, seven journalists were released by royal pardon along with 24 other prisoners. Included in this official pardon was the well-known dissident Ali Lmrabet, who was imprisoned in June 2003 for publishing a cartoon criticizing the royal family. The king also pardoned three journalists who had been imprisoned for printing an article discussing the history of the Islamist movement in Morocco and its alleged relationship to Morocco's intelligence services.

Despite these improvements, the Moroccan government continues to utilize repressive means to curtail media independence and freedom of expression. The revised press code of 2002 only slightly reduced the penalty for defaming the royal family or public officials, and the government retained the right to revoke publication licenses and directly confiscate materials viewed as threatening to the public. The government often makes onerous libel claims against journalists who scrutinize government officials or policies. For example, on August 15, 2005, Ahmed Reda Benchemsi, managing editor of the independent weekly *Tel Quel*, and Karim Boukhari, his editor, were each given a two-month suspended prison term, charged 1 million dirhams ($100,000) in damages, and fined an additional 2,500 dirhams ($250). The suit was in response to a fictional story titled "A Brunette's Secret," featuring a dancer named "Asmaa" who becomes a legislator. A parliamentarian named Hlima Assali assumed she was the target of the satire, and charges of libel were brought on her behalf. Upon appeal by Benchemsi, the fine was reduced slightly to 800,000 dirhams ($80,000). In April 2005, the Directory of Royal Protocol sent a warning to the newsweekly *Al Jarida Aloukhra* for publishing a series of articles on the king's wife, threatening interdiction, suspension, and arrests.

The government continues to censor and harass journalists who attempt to cover the Western Sahara issue. For example, on May 24, 2005, Munir al-Ktawi of the weekly *Bidawi* attempted to cover a meeting of Sahrawi officials. When the officials realized he was a member of the press, he was kicked, punched, and thrown out of the building and had his equipment broken by his assailants. On May 25, 2005, Salam

Zoukani, a television technician, was beaten by security forces while covering demonstrations in Laayoune, the major city in the Western Sahara. On June 16, 2004, Tor Dagfinn Dommersnes and Fredrik Refvem of the Norwegian daily *Stavanger Aftenbladet* were expelled from Morocco for meeting with Ali Salem Tamek, a well-known Western Sahara activist.

The Moroccan government does not restrict access to the internet, with the exception of two Western Sahara websites. The government does, however, influence the media through direct ownership of numerous television and radio stations throughout the country. The Moroccan government owns the country's largest broadcasting outlet, Moroccan Radio-Television (RTM). Morocco's next largest broadcaster is the French-backed MEDI-1, which, although independent, practices self-censorship.

Recommendations

- Constitutional reforms should be undertaken to remove the monarchy's supreme authority over the legislature and judiciary, and to improve oversight among these three branches of government.
- Senior officials appointed by the king to key public positions should be equally accountable to the government.
- Press and judicial codes should be reformed to prevent the harassment and censure of Moroccan journalists.
- Parliamentary and political party reforms should continue in order to increase public confidence in the political process.

CIVIL LIBERTIES – 3.67

Major reforms of the Moroccan constitution in 1992 and 1996 were intended to bring Moroccan law into conformity with international human rights conventions. The constitution now guarantees "the rights and liberties of citizens," "political equality between men and women," "freedom of worship," and "freedom of opinion, expression, association, and public gathering." In 1996, the penal code was revised to proscribe torture, establish legal provisions for arrest and due process, and set limits on preventive detention. By June 2005, the UN Committee against Torture noted the positive development in the overall human rights situation in Morocco.

On January 7, 2004, King Mohammed VI inaugurated the Equity and Reconciliation Commission (IEC) to "close the file on past human rights abuses." The 17-member commission was composed of former political prisoners and human rights activists and was chaired by a former long-time political detainee. The IEC, inspired by the panel that spotlighted crimes in apartheid South Africa, was intended to complete the work of the Royal Consultative Council on Human Rights (CCDH) established by King Hassan II in 1990, with the added roles of issuing findings and providing compensation to the victims. In 1998, the CCDH had compiled a list of 112 cases of forcible disappearance, thereby officially recognizing state responsibility for human rights violations. To provide compensation to victims of past abuses, King Mohammed VI established the Arbitration Commission on Compensation in 1999, and by 2003 some 4,750 claimants against the state had received a total of over $100 million in indemnities for past violations.

The IEC received a mandate to look into cases of "enforced disappearance and arbitrary detention" that occurred between Morocco's independence in 1956 and the end of King Hassan's reign in 1999, a long period of government suppression of political and religious dissent that Moroccans call "the years of lead." The IEC's hearings began on December 21, 2004, in Rabat. Unprecedented in the Arab world, the hearings were public, open to national and foreign journalists and NGOs, and broadcast to wide audiences on national radio and television. The IEC's hearings gave victims and their relatives the opportunity to present vivid testimonies of disappearance, arbitrary detention, and torture.

The IEC's statutes, however, did not allow victims to identify their abusers or torturers. Moroccan human rights groups complained that the perpetrators of abuse could not be prosecuted and that testimony was not allowed on abuses that continued after 1999. IEC members argued it was necessary to protect the legal rights of both perpetrators and victims and to prevent retribution. To bypass the IEC's rules, the AMDH led a parallel series of public hearings beginning in February 2005 in which post-1999 victims could testify and abusers could be named. It then published a list of alleged torturers it thought should face trial, including members of Morocco's current administration.[4]

[*Editor's note:* On December 1, 2005, the IEC submitted the final report of its 18-month investigation to the king, who ordered its publication on December 16. The commission found that 322 people had been shot dead by government troops during protests and 174 people had died in arbitrary detention. The AMDH maintained the true figures were much higher.]

Despite these highly publicized efforts to expose past infractions, allegations of post-1999 human rights abuses and acts of torture continue. The Moroccan parliament passed a new antiterrorist law within 10 days of the May 2003 terrorist attacks in Casablanca. The law gives police and security forces the right to hold suspects without access to a lawyer, to intercept telephone calls, internet communication, and mail, and to search private dwellings and businesses without a warrant. More importantly, the law extends the time limit for incommunicado detention from three to 12 days, which greatly increases the risk of mistreatment and torture of detainees. By many accounts, in the months following the May 2003 attacks, some 2,100 persons were detained under the provisions of the 2003 antiterrorism law. Many were held in prolonged incommunicado custody and denied access to a defense lawyer.[5] In November 2003, the UN Committee against Torture expressed its concern about reports of the increased number of detainees, including political prisoners, and increased allegations of torture and cruel, inhuman, or degrading treatment or punishment. Many allegations of mistreatment of detainees focused on the detention center at Témara, ten miles south of Rabat, where detainees were said to be held in secret, sometimes for months, without access to their families or the outside world. Amnesty International (AI) reported in June 2005 that alleged Islamists were systematically exposed to torture and ill treatment at the Témara center, which was operated by Morocco's internal intelligence service, the Directorate for the Surveillance of the Territory (DST), which reports directly to the palace. According to the AI report, DST personnel "are neither agents nor officers of the judicial police and are not authorized under Moroccan law to arrest, detain or question suspects."[6] As of November 2005, of the 2,100 people who had been arrested in 2003, several hundred remained in detention. Conditions in Morocco's 46 prisons remain extremely poor, with serious problems of overcrowding, corruption, maltreatment, lack of hygiene, sexual abuse, drug abuse, and violence. Human rights groups and the press reported that several detainees died in police custody, with little or no serious investigation by the authorities.

Harsh treatment of Sahrawi militants in the disputed Western Sahara territory continues. Beginning in May 2005 and continuing the rest of the year, the Western Sahara was rocked by frequent demonstrations, especially in the one major urban center, Laayoune. Demonstrators expressed support for the Polisario Front or called for independence from Morocco. In responding to these demonstrations, local police and special urban security units used forceful measures, violence sometimes ensued, and dozens of demonstrators were arrested. Of those arrested, 14 went on trial in late fall. [*Editor's note:* On December 14, all 14 were convicted and given sentences ranging from six months to three years in prison.] Human rights groups alleged that some of the detainees had been tortured, none of them was allowed to call witnesses in his own defense, and seven were human rights activists who were unfairly convicted for their political views.

To provide greater protection, the Moroccan parliament passed two laws on October 20, 2005, that criminalize torture. The new laws call for a prison term of five to ten years for any civil servant who practices torture against an individual as defined by the law and sentences of 30 years to life if torture is practiced against civil servants, judges, security agents, witnesses, minors, victims, or pregnant women.

Efforts since 1990 by women's groups and liberal political forces to change the *Mudawana* (personal status code), which governs family and estate cases, were strongly resisted by conservative and Islamic forces. In a speech to parliament on October 10, 2003, the king tipped the balance in favor of change by presenting a plan for a new, "modern Family Law" that was "meant to free women from the injustices they endure" and that was grounded in Islamic values. Parliament ratified the new law in January 2004 with numerous amendments.[7] The new Family Law eliminates language degrading to women, raises women's status as full partners with men, and upholds equality between husband and wife. Among the law's main improvements, the age of marriage for women was increased from 15 to 18, equal to that of men; the family is now under the joint responsibility of both spouses; the wife is no longer obliged to obey her husband; a woman can marry without the presence of a guardian; divorce laws now apply equally to men and women and can be exercised by either; polygamy is made virtually impossible; alimony payments are enforceable by the courts; and husband and wife now share property attained during marriage.[8] The implementation of the reforms will depend on the establishment of 70 family courts and the training of judges to implement the reforms. Although citizenship still passes through the father, King Mohammed VI instructed parliament on July 30, 2005, to reform the citizenship code to allow Moroccan women to transmit their citizenship to their children.[9] As a result, the Ministry of Justice established a commission to draw up proposals to amend the current legislation and present them to parliament.

However, even in cases in which the law provides for equal status, cultural norms often prevent a woman from exercising her rights. Moreover, the law does not ban domestic violence against women. Although sexual assault and rape outside of marriage are severely punished, most sexual crimes are unreported because of the stigma of the loss of female virginity outside of marriage. Within marriage, spousal rape is not a criminal offense.

The government has revised labor, commercial, and administrative texts to eliminate various forms of discrimination against women, including discrimination in employment and occupation. For example, a wife no longer needs her husband's permission to sign a contract, engage in business, or obtain a passport. Although women seldom hold top positions in the civil sector, they often find positions in such key sectors as public health and education, the state administration, and public companies. The new electoral code of 2002 reserved 30 seats for female candidates in the legislative elections, and there are currently 35 women in the Moroccan lower house (the Chamber of Deputies) out of 325 members, compared to only two in each of the previous two parliaments. However, there is no legislation against sexual harassment, and due to social and workplace taboos and laws heavily favoring employers, citizens rarely take action when they are victims of prejudice.

Morocco's geographic location makes it convenient as a transit center for international human trafficking. Morocco fully complies with the minimum standards for the elimination of trafficking. The government made progress in its prosecution efforts in 2004 when it dismantled 423 trafficking rings and arrested 262 traffickers.[10] In addition, Moroccan police arrested 70 Nigerian traffickers and rescued 1,460 Nigerian victims hidden by traffickers. In 2004, Morocco introduced severe punishment for promoting prostitution, pornography, sex tourism, child pornography, and child sexual abuse. Despite these efforts, some young Moroccan women are trafficked to Saudi Arabia, Syria, and the United Arab Emirates for the purpose of sexual exploitation.

While the constitution calls for equality among all citizens, priority is given to Arab culture. Modern standard Arabic (as distinct from the Moroccan Arabic dialect) is the sole official language. While French is still used, Arabic is the primary language of national government, local administration, public media, and education. To give greater recognition to the Berber heritage of 60 percent of Morocco's population (including the royal family), the king established the publicly funded Royal Institute for Amazigh Culture (IRCAM) in 2002. Teaching of the Berber language began in primary schools in September 2003. A year later, the teaching of Berber had expanded to 1,278 primary schools, and the government pledged to teach Berber in all public schools by 2008. These initiatives did not satisfy Berber activists, who complained that press coverage of Berber culture and official media broadcasts in Berber were too limited. Berber associations maintained that the government refused to register births for children with traditional Berber names, limited the activities of their associations, and continued to arabize the names of towns and villages.[11]

Freedom of religion is protected by the constitution. Islam is the official state religion, and the king is designated as "Commander of the Faithful," with a responsibility to protect Islam and guarantee freedom of worship. A few thousand Moroccan Jews and 25,000 mostly expatriate Christians practice their faiths openly. However, Baha'is are not allowed to hold services, and the government restricts the distribution of Christian religious materials. Proselytizing is illegal, and the penal code allows a sentence of up to three years for attempting to convert a Muslim to another faith. Foreign missionaries are investigated, and Moroccan Muslims who convert to other religions are subject to prosecution and detention. Since the May 2003 Casablanca bombings, the Ministry of Islamic Affairs and Endowments monitors the activities of mosques and provides religious training for imams, and the government strictly controls the construction of new mosques. Following the attacks, some employees in the private sector who displayed a more religious appearance were laid off from their positions. They had little legal recourse in a country experiencing fear and grief, where the perpetrators of the attacks wore the same religious garb.

Government estimates of persons with disabilities (especially polio victims) are 2.2 million, or 7 percent of the population. The government has established institutions to improve access for disabled people to various services. The Ministry of Social Affairs attempts to integrate persons with disabilities into society. For example, the Ministry of Islamic Affairs and Endowments in 1999 published 4,000 copies of the Quran in Braille. The government has built five acoustic libraries, while seven others are to be built as part of a program to provide universities with infrastructures for blind and amblyopic people. However, their integration is left largely to private charities, and most people with disabilities are supported by their families. Morocco has no laws to assist those with disabilities; access to buildings for the disabled is not mandated.

The constitution guarantees the rights of association, organization, and representation. Workers and professionals have a choice of membership in 19 labor unions, though only 6 percent of the country's 10 million workers belong to a union, and unions are sometimes subject to government interference. Most labor unions joined with government and business to draft a new labor code that went into effect in June 2004. The new law prohibits antiunion discrimination but also denies such public employees as members of the military, the police, and the judiciary the right to form unions. Most strikes are relatively brief; in 2004, strikes involving the teachers' union, Royal Air Maroc employees, bank officers, and healthcare professionals lasted only one to two days.

For security reasons, public gatherings and demonstrations require authorization from the Ministry of Interior, which can deny permits to prevent critics of government policies from holding meetings or peaceful sit-ins. Security police occasionally use excessive force to disperse demonstrators, as they did in Laayoune in the Western Sahara in May 2005; generally, however, the police monitor but do not hinder demonstrations.

Recommendations

- The government should establish an independent body to ensure full implementation of the two 2005 laws that criminalize torture.
- The government should establish a high-level commission to investigate human rights abuses since 1999 and to fully compensate and rehabilitate victims.

- The government should take the necessary steps to ensure full implementation of all provisions of the 2004 Family Code.
- A law should be adopted to protect the rights of peaceful demonstrators against the excessive use of force by the police and security police officers who violate those rights should be prosecuted without delay.
- The government should create an environment in which women who have been assaulted and other victims can feel comfortable pressing charges against their assailants. This would include training security forces to act in a professional manner in dealing with cases of physical assault. In addition, the government should continue its efforts to fight domestic violence, expanding efforts to build outreach programs to educate men and women on the subject.

RULE OF LAW – 3.04

The Moroccan constitution guarantees the independence, impartiality, and fairness of the judicial system. However, Article 86 of the constitution stipulates, "the king shall preside over the Supreme Council of the Judiciary." Verdicts are pronounced in the name of the king, and public prosecution is the domain of the executive branch, not the judicial branch. In April 2004, King Mohammed VI delivered a speech in which he emphasized the necessity of shielding the magistracy from any form of influence or interference in application of the constitution, whether from the executive and legislative branches or other forms of power.[12] Yet such measures have not been implemented, and Moroccan judges are known to give in to various forms of corruption or meddling.[13]

Given the absence of independence in the Moroccan judicial system and the political role of the minister of justice, who has broad judicial authority enabling him to intervene, many court decisions take political factors into consideration, hence rendering the appeal process rigid and artificial. In fact, in terror-related cases and cases dealing with threats to public order, detainees are forced to turn to unconventional methods, such as hunger strikes, after conventional appeals are rejected. In turn, prosecutors, deterred by widespread corruption, continue to be reluctant about exercising their duties, despite changes in the political climate.

Article 84 of the constitution allows the king to appoint all judges by royal decree at the proposal of the Supreme Council, itself presided over by the monarch. Judges receive instruction at the National Institute of Judicial Studies, which focuses on providing them with initial training prior to their joining the corps of magistrates as well as professional development during their tenure.

In 1999, Morocco introduced the concept of an accused person's being innocent until proven guilty, along with due process principles.[14] The presumption of innocence was first applied in 2003.[15] However, the judicial system has been widely criticized by various Moroccan and international human rights groups for failing to "fulfill their role as a bulwark against abuse" by accepting evidence obtained through torture or coercion and allowing fabricated testimonies, arbitrary procedures, absence of witnesses, lack of proof, and other due process violations.[16] Magistrates have been known to reject a plaintiff's grievances and allegations of torture or fabricated statements, as well as hinder the defense process, if defense lawyers are at all present.[17] As the example of the 2004–2005 Equity and Reconciliation Commission shows, perpetrators of past abuses have not been held accountable. While the constitution clearly stipulates that all Moroccan citizens are equal and the laws guarantee the protection of all citizens, in practice preferential treatment is given to the well connected, the very wealthy, and members of the governing and business elites.

The king, who is the supreme commander of the Royal Armed Forces, appoints civil and military personnel, who report directly to him. The king retains direct control of all security-related institutions, control that is never challenged.

The Moroccan state has been reinforcing private ownership in certain sectors previously controlled and run by the state. Private ownership is legally permitted to all, whether alone or in association with others. Individuals or other entities, including foreigners, are allowed to purchase or sell their property as they see fit. The state enforces property rights of individuals or groups holding titles or written contracts. However, access to certain sectors of the economy is limited to a few families directly connected to the palace.

The state has been known to confiscate ancestral tribal land or provide little compensation for its seizure. Moreover, when disagreements arise between powerful entities and a citizen or group, the state is less likely to defend the rights of the less powerful.

Recommendations

- The Moroccan judicial system should be reformed and made truly independent from interference from government circles, the royal court, and other political influences. Judges must be able to act independently and provide fair and impartial rulings, regardless of any political interest that may exist.
- A law should be adopted to protect the rights of citizens to appeal court decisions and to prevent the intervention of the minister of justice in the appeal process.
- The government should train security forces to act in a professional manner when dealing with cases of physical assault.

ANTICORRUPTION AND TRANSPARENCY – 2.14

During the nearly four decades of authoritarian rule under King Hassan II, corruption became enmeshed in the political, economic, judicial, and administrative systems—to such a degree that by his death in 1999, it was normalized and institutionalized.[18] Corruption can be found in virtually every aspect of public life, from elections to the regulation of business to taxes.

The severity of this problem is reflected in the findings of international reporting and watchdog groups. The Economist Intelligence Unit reported in 2005 that corruption is widespread throughout the bureaucracy. Morocco's corruption ranking in Transparency International's annual reports went from the 41st percentile of 90 countries surveyed in 2000 down to the 49th percentile of 158 countries surveyed in 2005, and its score fell from 4.7 to 3.2 on a 0–10 scale from 2000 to 2005 in Transparency International's Corruption Perceptions Index.[19] The overwhelming majority of Moroccan entrepreneurs consider corruption the main obstacle to investment and economic development, and widespread corruption has seriously eroded public confidence in authority.

To confront the significant level of corruption, the government of Prime Minister Abderrahmane Youssoufi (1998–2002) gave the issue a high public priority and in 1999 made the fight against corruption official policy. The NGO Transparency Morocco, a branch of Transparency International, was allowed to raise the issue of corruption and to make public its findings for the first time. In a July 2004 report, this NGO described the bribery of officials, including the judiciary, as a serious obstacle to human progress. Since 1999, corruption has been routinely and explicitly discussed and denounced in the press and in various conferences and workshops. In reporting that would previously have been censored, the press now writes critical articles about government corruption.[20]

Nevertheless, legal protections are lacking for whistle-blowers, anti-corruption activists, and investigators who report on cases of bribery and corruption. Despite the existence of anticorruption laws, persons who dig too deep into off-limits topics—Islam, the monarchy, territorial integrity (namely, the Western Sahara issue), trafficking by senior officials—are arrested and prosecuted. This was the fate of Hamid Naimi, editor of the weekly *Kawaliss Rif* (Stories of the Rif), who was convicted in March 2005 on several libel counts in cases dating back to 1998. These closed cases were reactivated after Naimi published an article in November 2004 about the embezzlement of public funds by officials in Nador on Morocco's Mediterranean coast. A Nador court sentenced him to three years in prison and a fine of approximately $50,000.[21]

Corruption is widespread in higher education. The state has not implemented protection for higher education against corruption. University professors are hired primarily through personal connections rather than on merit, and it is not uncommon for some professors to share exams with, or give good grades to, family members or favorite students.

Morocco lacks an effective internal audit system to ensure accountability of tax collection. While taxes are withheld from all salaried employees, the many Moroccans who work professionally in the private sector or operate in the vast informal or underground economy routinely conceal part or all of their income without fear of audit.

No adequate financial disclosure procedures are in place to prevent conflicts of interest among public officials. The public and the media do not have ready access to information about the assets of public officials. Morocco has no freedom-of-information law, and access to information continues to be limited. An International Research & Exchanges Board (IREX) report of November 2005 revealed the existence of an array of laws and administrative procedures that obstruct access to legitimate information and data.[22] Various government ministries have broadened the scope of information available on their websites for public access and are providing capacity to allow complaints to be filed, including corruption charges. The Ministry of Modernization of the Public Sector was charged with developing a plan to fight corruption, and in May 2005 it issued a draft of "The Plan of Action to Fight Corruption." This ambitious 38-page plan outlines many areas of action to fight corruption, including placing online government services and information for citizens to use in order to lodge complaints of corruption. It also provides links to a database of laws and decrees, of civil administration personnel information, statutes, and the like to which the public can have access.[23]

New anticorruption laws have been enacted and existing codes have been upgraded since 1998. In the last few years, the government has disciplined and prosecuted hundreds of magistrates and police agents accused of corruption. In August 2004, for example, the Supreme Council of the Judiciary began disciplinary proceedings against 14 judges and eventually dismissed two of them and retired four more.[24] For the most part, however, the anticorruption measures and efforts at prosecution have targeted petty corruption. Investigations into corruption generally do not go beyond a certain level in the state hierarchy. An exception was the prosecution in July 2004 of two senior local government officials in Casablanca; they were charged with diverting funds for public housing while they were working within the powerful Ministry of Interior in the 1990s.[25] The first case in which magistrates were prosecuted for corruption was that of Abdelkader Younsi and Mohamed Farid Benazzouz in Tetuan in March 2005;[26] as of November 2005, their case was still pending.

Drug trafficking in the north of Morocco along the Mediterranean coast remains a major source of corruption. In response to high demand for drugs in Europe, drug lords engage in smuggling and the bribery of judges, magistrates, and high security and customs officials, amassing power and influence. Despite government efforts to act against smuggling rings and police corruption in the northern provinces in 2004, drug trafficking, with its elaborate production, distribution, and protection networks, continues to thrive and is an important component of a vibrant multibillion-dollar underground economy.

It is illegal in Morocco to offer or accept bribes. In April 2005, the Government Council adopted the UN Convention against Corruption, which Morocco had signed in 2003. Notwithstanding these legal strictures, the problem of major corruption in Morocco has yet to be seriously confronted. The problem has deep political roots and involves powerful entrenched interests, including the armed forces and big business. From the 1970s through the 1990s, prominent urban families with close ties to the monarchy used their high position in government and the public sector to amass huge private fortunes. Morocco's best public companies were exploited for private gains, and billions of dollars were embezzled in the public sector. These families established and maintain a monopoly over key sectors of the economy, and the legacy of corruption from the period of King Hassan II continues to plague Morocco.

Recommendations

- The government should expand the present focus on the prosecution of petty corruption to include the prosecution of major corruption.
- The judiciary should be empowered to fight corruption at all levels, regardless of a person's position of power.
- The government must allow full public access to official information.
- The government should establish legal protections for whistleblowers, anticorruption activists, and investigators who report on cases of bribery and corruption.

NOTES

[1] Morocco: Party Strengthening and Parliament Reform (Washington, D.C.: Consortium for Elections and Political Process Strengthening [CEPPS]/National Democratic Institute [NDI], *Quarterly Report,* 1 April–30 June 2005), 1.

[2] Ibid., 1–2.

[3] Al-Amin Andalusi, "Moroccans Skeptical About Anti-Corruption Plan," IslamOnline.net, 26 April 2005.

[4] Susan Slymovics, "Morocco's Justice and Reconciliation Commission," *Middle East Report* (4 April 2005), 1–2, 4, http://www.merip.org/mero/mero040405.html; Craig Whitlock and Steve Coll, "Terrorism Tempers Shift to Openness," *Washington Post,* 18 April 2005, A1; "Morocco/Western Sahara: Amnesty International welcomes public hearings into past violations" (London: Amnesty International [AI], News Service No. 320, 14 December 2004), 1–2; "Morocco Truth Panel Details Abuse," BBC News, 17 December 2005, 1, http://news.bbc.co.uk/go/pr/fr/-/1/hi/world/africa/4536258.stm.

The government made no attempt to interfere with the AMDH hearings; for details on the hearings, see the AMDH website, http://www.amdh.org.ma.

5 "Morocco: Human Rights at a Crossroads" (New York: Human Rights Watch [HRW], October 2004), 59, http://hrw.org/reports/2004/morocco1004/morocco1004.pdf.

6 "Torture in the 'Anti-Terrorism' Campaign: The Case of Témara Detention Centre," *Amnesty International,* 24 June 2005, 2, http://web.amnesty.org/library/Index/ENG MDE290042004?open&of=ENG-MAR, 4.

7 Bruce Maddy-Weitzman, "Women, Islam, and the Moroccan State: The Struggle over the Personal Status Law," *Middle East Journal* (Summer 2005), 393, 404–06.

8 See *Code de la Famille* (Mohammedia: Ministry of Justice, 2005). For an unofficial English translation of the Family Code, go to http://www/hrea.org/moudawana.html.

9 "Royal Speech: King Announces Key Decisions," *Morocco Times,* July 30, 2005, 1, http://www.moroccotimes.com/paper/article.asp?idr=2&id=8515.

10 "Morocco (Tier I)," in Trafficking in Persons Report (Washington, D.C.: U.S. Department of State, June 2005), 1, http://www.gvnet.com/humantrafficking/Morocco-2.htm.

11 "Morocco," in Country Reports on Human Rights Practices – 2004 (Washington, D.C.: U.S. Department of State, Bureau of Democracy, Human Rights, and Labor, 28 February 2005), 14.

12 "Judges Must Be Protected from Any Influence or Interference, King Mohammed VI," in "Morocco, Judicial," ArabicNews.com, 13 April 2004, 1, http://www.arabicnews.com/ansub/Daily/Day/040413/2004041315.html.

13 Haizam Amirah Fernández, "Morocco is Failing to Take Off" (Madrid: Real Instituto Elcano de Estudios Internacionales y Estratégicos, 27 September 2004), 2, http://www .realinstitutoelcano.org/analisis/609.asp.

14 "Morocco proposes novell[sic] concepts in law: Innocent till proven guilty, and due process principles," in "Morocco, Judicial," ArabicNews.com, 18 August 1999, http:// www.arabicnews.com/ansub/Daily/Day/990818/1999081844.html.

15 "Moroccan Court May Set Historic Precedent on Innocent till Proven Guilty Concept," in "Morocco, Judicial," ArabicNews.com, 19 December 2003, http://www.arabic news.com/ansub/Daily/Day/031219/FP.html.

16 "Torture Reintroduced by Morocco's Terrorism Fight," Afro News, 21 October 2004, http://www.afrol.com/articles/14609.

17 "Two Newspaper Journalists Get 'Disproportionate' Sentences for Libelling a Parliamentarian" (Paris: Reporters sans frontieres [RSF], 17 August 2003), http://www.rsf .org/article.php3?id_article=14706.

18 Abdeslam Maghraoui, "Political Authority in Crisis: Mohammed VI's Morocco," *Middle East Report* (Spring 2001), 13–14.

19 "Corruption Perceptions Index" (Berlin: Transparency International [TI], 2000–2005), http://www.transparency.org/publications/gcr.

20 Guilain Denoeux, "The Politics of Morocco's 'Fight against Corruption,'" *Middle East Policy* (February 2000), 4–5; "Morocco," in Country Reports on Human Rights Practices – 2004 (U.S. Department of State), 5, 7.

21 "Western Sahara, Government Corruption and Palace Life Are All Off-Limits for the Press" (RSF, 13 April 2005), 1, http://www.rsf.org/article.php3?id_article=13197.

22 "Access to Information in Morocco: Centre for Media Freedom Report Recommends Steps towards Reform" (Washington, D.C.: International Research and Exchanges Board [IREX], November 2005), http://www.irex.org/newsroom/news/2005/1111_media.asp.

23 *Plan d'actions de lutte contre la corruption* (Rabat: Ministry of Modernization of the Public Sector, 2005), http://www.mmsp.gov.ma.

24 "Morocco," in Country Reports – 2004 (U.S. Department of State), 5.

25 Eileen Byrne, "Yesterday's Men," *Middle East International,* July 9, 2004, 18.

26 Aboubakr Jamai, "Morocco's Choice: Openness or Terror," CNN.com, 31 May 2003, http://www.cnn.com/2003/US/05/31/nyt.jamai/.

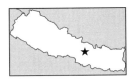

NEPAL

CAPITAL: Kathmandu
POPULATION: 25.4 million
GNI PER CAPITA: $240

SCORES	2004	2006
ACCOUNTABILITY AND PUBLIC VOICE:	3.84	2.23
CIVIL LIBERTIES:	3.93	2.80
RULE OF LAW:	3.96	2.73
ANTICORRUPTION AND TRANSPARENCY:	3.81	2.30

(scores are based on a scale of 0 to 7, with 0 representing weakest and 7 representing strongest performance)

Ravi Bhatia

INTRODUCTION

Nepal is facing one of the biggest political crises in its history. A civil war between radical agrarian Maoist rebels and King Gyanendra (backed by the army) has affected vast parts of the civilian population and damaged relations with India and the West. The violent insurgency led by the rebels first emerged in 1996 and has grown large enough to threaten Nepal's constitutional monarchy. The civil war has led to the deaths of more than 11,000 people.[1]

Using the civil war as an excuse, through a series of creeping coups culminating in an overt coup in February 2005, King Gyanendra has suspended Nepal's entire democracy, dismissed parliament, and appointed a handpicked prime minister and cabinet. The rule of law has been subverted through the creation of a number of extrajudicial bodies, and human rights have been profoundly compromised. The army, security forces, and the Maoists have all committed grave human rights violations including summary executions, torture, and detention without trial.

It is estimated that Maoists control up to two-thirds of the country. They espouse an extreme left-wing ideology and partly model themselves

Ravi Bhatia is the South Asia Editor/Economist at the Economist Intelligence Unit in London. He regularly comments on Nepalese and South Asian affairs in leading journals and on leading news channels.

on the Peruvian Shining Path guerrillas with the ultimate aim, in theory, of establishing a peasant-led revolutionary Communist regime. In practice, they want Nepal to have a new constitution, written by members of a newly established constitutional assembly, which will "abolish the monarchy" and establish some form of republic.[2]

The Maoist insurgency has been strengthened by the lack of a unified front to tackle it, the result of severe tensions between the king and Nepal's political parties. Even prior to the Maoist insurgency, Nepalese politics had traditionally been unstable, with coalition governments collapsing frequently. Arguing that he was faced with perpetual political instability, on the one hand, and a strengthening Maoist threat on the other, in October 2002 the king suspended Nepal's normal democratic procedures and began appointing prime ministers by royal decree. Between October 2002 and February 2005, the king appointed (and dismissed) four prime ministers. However, during that time parliament remained active. Going one step further, in what was widely referred to by the media as a "royal coup," on February 1, 2005, the king dismissed the prime minister and government, adjourned parliament completely, placed leading politicians, including the prime minister, under house arrest, and declared a state of emergency.[3]

Since February 2005, King Gyanendra has ruled as chairman of a self-appointed council of ministers. He has, however, stated that he intends to restore multiparty democracy. Crucially, he continues to be strongly supported by the army (although the army chief has said that he remains loyal to whichever government is in power). The February 1 coup angered the politicians and a large part of the urban and rural public and led to widespread demonstrations and protests in several towns across Nepal. It also led the politicians to consider closer ties with the Maoists, something that in the past they had refused to do.

The triangular, tense, and unstable relationship between the king, the politicians, and the Maoists makes the future of Nepal highly uncertain. In mid-November 2005, at secret meetings held in New Delhi, India, Nepal reached a turning point when seven main political parties arrived at an understanding with the Maoist movement. Both the political parties and the Maoists agreed to oppose "autocratic" or absolute monarchy and press for the election of a new constituent assembly (one of the Maoists' key demands).[4] In a 12-point statement released by the political parties and the Maoists on November 22, the Maoists stated that they were ready to disarm and take part in elections if the United Nations oversaw them.[5] In return, the political parties would support the Maoist campaign to set up a new constituent assembly, which would draft a new constitution. The joint announcement by the Maoists and the parties asserted that they would oppose "autocratic" monarchy, leading several politicians to argue that perhaps a "ceremonial" monarchy with limited powers might be acceptable to the Maoists.

The November 2005 developments make it more difficult for the king to maintain the current direct royal rule, as he now faces an alliance of the main political parties and the Maoists. The developments mean that Nepal has reached a turning point in its political crisis. The understanding between the Maoists and the political parties sharpened the lines of the political struggle, with the Maoists and the political parties on one side and the king and the army on the other.

In October, preempting his opponents' November 22 announcement, the king ordered the Election Commission to hold a general election before mid-April 2007. He also called for lower-level municipal polls scheduled for early 2006 to proceed (however, the political parties have stated they will boycott these as they view them as a back-door attempt by the king to legitimize his rule). In November 2005, Gyanendra softened his stance further by stating that his February 1 actions were not designed to curb democracy but rather to save Nepal from becoming a failed state without clear leadership.

However, the situation could also go the other way and provide the king with an excuse to crack down on *both* the Maoists and the political parties. The king has already asked the political parties to clarify their positions on terrorism (existing laws bar any form of association with Maoist rebels, who have been declared terrorists, and this includes drafting joint declarations with the Maoist leadership) while the police and army have been heavy-handed with politicians and prodemocracy activists.

What is clear is that a polarization has taken place, with the king backed by the army on one side and the political parties and the Maoists on the other. Essentially a deadlock and somewhat of a balance of power has been reached. The deadlock should be viewed as an opportunity to negotiate a compromise that both the king and the Maoists can accept, one in which the king gives up most of his powers, the Maoists give up arms and join the mainstream political process, and democracy is restored. The best basis for the improvement of Nepal's human rights situation and the freedom of Nepalis is the cessation of violence and the restoration of some form of full democracy.

ACCOUNTABILITY AND PUBLIC VOICE – 2.23

Since 1990, Nepal has, in theory, been a democracy; however, normal democratic procedures have been suspended since October 2002. Between October 2002 and February 2005, the king appointed four prime ministers by royal decree. On February 1, 2005, the king dismissed Prime Minister Sher Bahadur Dueba (whom he had selected), placed him under house arrest, and appointed himself chairman of a new, handpicked council of ministers, without consulting any of Nepal's main political parties.[6] Subsequently, several other leading politicians have been placed under house arrest, and the king has suspended civil rights and the independent media. The army, loyal to the king, began patrolling the streets to maintain law and order. The king made a rare television broadcast in which he said that he had dismissed the government for failing to quell an ever-growing Maoist insurgency.[7] On February 18, political parties protested the February 1 action; several demonstrators were detained that day.

In sum, the authority of the government in Nepal is not based on the will of the people as expressed by regular, free, and fair elections and universal and equal suffrage. Since February 2005, the situation has become even worse, with participants in prodemocracy campaigns and protests subject to summary detention by the state administration and political parties not being permitted to campaign.[8] However, the current royal administration does seem to treat all political parties with equal disdain.

The executive, legislative, and judicial branches of government in Nepal are not able to hold each other accountable. Despite protests, the legislature was unable to stop the king from suspending democracy. The judiciary has also largely remained mute on the subject. Distribution of power among the king, political parties, and judiciary has always been troubled. The royal household has traditionally wrestled with politicians since limited democracy was first introduced in Nepal in 1959.

The civil service is widely viewed as being politicized, inefficient, and corrupt. Promotions and dismissals remain highly politicized, and merit is only one of a gamut of considerations. The civil service is dominated by Bhramins (the highest Hindu caste) and Kshatriyas, despite the fact that they represent only around 40 percent of the country's population.

Since 1990, when restrictions on nongovernmental activity were lifted, civil society groups and nongovernmental organizations (NGOs), most of which are reliant on foreign aid, have expanded swiftly. By 2005, Nepal had over 30,000 vocal NGOs commenting on government policy, legislation, and the democratic process. However, since the royal coup of February 1, 2005, a clampdown on civil society groups and NGOs has been in effect.

On November 10, 2005, the government issued a 15-point code of conduct to regulate NGOs. The new code requires NGOs to operate in accordance with government priorities and seek approval before obtaining foreign assistance. Further, the Social Welfare Council (SWC) has the power to suspend or dissolve NGOs that violate the new NGO code, and all employees of the SWC are government officials. NGOs have also been threatened by the Maoists, who have accused NGO workers of acting as government informers in remote districts.

The new government code of conduct upset several NGOs, and when the NGO Federation of Nepal met on November 18, they stated that they would not abide by it.[9] The code is also being challenged in the Supreme Court. On November 23, in an interim order, the Supreme Court requested that the government not implement the code pending its analysis of the case.

NGOs have not been the only casualties of the current political climate. The state is also actively involved in direct and indirect censorship of the print and broadcast media. From 1990 on, Nepal had managed to establish a prolific media and radio presence that was respected all across South Asia. After February 1, 2005, the government went to the extent of stationing military officers in newspaper, radio, and television stations to control activity. Prominent editors have been summoned to government offices to be reprimanded for "objectionable" material. Private radio stations were no longer permitted to broadcast the news. (Radio remains the largest news source in a poor country where vast numbers of the population remain illiterate and too poor to afford a television set.) The government also stopped publishing public notices in private newspapers, leading to a sharp fall in advertising revenue.

In May 2005, the government ordered the closure of a radio production company, Communications Corner, arguing that it was operating illegally. Later in the year, the authorities raided the offices of a major radio station, Kantipur FM, attacked journalists, and confiscated transmission equipment. The radio station was then ordered to stop relaying news. In October 2005, the government promulgated a Media Ordinance that amended six separate statutes regarding the media. It strengthened restrictive provisions contained in those acts and introduced new restrictions on the right to seek and impart information. The ordinance made defamation a criminal offense and gave the government-controlled Press Council the ability to cancel journalists' licenses.

The United Nations expressed concern that the restrictions went beyond those permitted by the International Covenant on Civil and Political Rights. In October 2005, under the ordinance, FM stations were banned from broadcasting anything other than entertainment programs. In late 2005, Nepali police forced the closure of another radio station, Sagarmatha Radio, for attempting to broadcast a BBC interview with a Maoist leader. Protests by journalists have led to immediate arrests. In November 2005, more than 2,000 people staged demonstrations against the controversial new media law. In other demonstrations, over a dozen journalists were arrested for protesting. The state funds its own media channels and is aggressively attempting to promote an official point of view.

The new and controversial media law as well as action taken against journalists in the wake of the February 1, 2005, events, demonstrates that the state does not oppose the use of onerous libel, security, and other laws to punish those who scrutinize government officials and policies. The government has not protected journalists from extrajudicial intimidation and arbitrary arrests and detention at the hands of state authorities or other actors. Nor have there been fair and expeditious investigations and prosecutions when cases do occur.

The state continues to monitor the internet as an information source. On February 1, 2005, the government cut all international telephone lines and internet connections but reestablished them shortly thereafter.

Recommendations

- As part of a negotiated settlement between the king, the political parties, and the Maoists, the current ceasefire must be maintained and extended indefinitely. A prolonged ceasefire must then be transformed into a negotiation process and a peaceful settlement whereby democracy is restored and the Maoists are encouraged to enter the mainstream political process.
- The king should restore parliament, with full freedom for political parties, and restore the independence of state institutions.
- NGOs must be permitted to operate without intimidation. To achieve this, an independent NGO regulator, with domestic and international representation, should be established with the freedom to publicize and probe intimidatory acts. Further, the new code monitoring NGO activity should be repealed.
- Journalists must be permitted to operate without intimidation. To achieve this, an independent media regulator, with international representation, should be established with the freedom to publicize and probe intimidatory acts.
- The new media ordinance must be repealed.

CIVIL LIBERTIES – 2.80

According to a human rights group, Informal Sector Service Centre (INSEC), the conflict between the Maoists and the government has led to more than 12,690 deaths since 1996. INSEC states that while the Maoists have killed 4,530 people, the state has killed 8,163 people. Going by these and similar statistics, Nepal remains far from a free society where civil liberties are upheld. Nepalese civilians have been victims of rising tension between the Maoists and the state. Prison conditions remain poor, and the state has taken little action when attacks have led to the deaths of political activists. Several citizens have been held for long periods without trial.

Nepal has faced condemnation at the United Nations for its poor human rights record. In March 2005, the United Nations warned that Nepal was facing a humanitarian crisis. In a subsequent report, the United Nations listed, in strong language, the difficulties faced by individuals caught up in fighting in Nepal.[10] It stated that Nepalis are denied access to humanitarian and medical supplies.[11] In May 2005, the UN Office of the High Commissioner for Human Rights (OHCHR) opened a branch in Nepal. It presented its first report to the UN General Assembly on September 16, 2005. The report stated that it was investigating reports of a number of human rights violations by the state, including extrajudicial executions, killing of civilians, disappearances, arbitrary arrests, detention, torture, threats, and violations of the rights to freedom of expression, assembly, and association.[12] The UN body was also looking into violations by groups that receive direct or indirect support from the security forces as well as violations by Maoists. The report further stated that in July 2005, 187 detainees were being housed in army barracks, and 1,200 others were being held under the Terrorism and Disruptive Activities (Control and Punishment) Ordinance (TADO). The OHCHR declared that it would inform the UN Department of Peacekeeping Operations (DPO) about Royal Nepalese Army (RNA) personnel and units implicated in the violations so that DPO could review their suitability for deployment under the UN flag.

In practice, Nepalese citizens do not have the means of effective petition and redress when human rights violations occur. Articles 11 to 23 of Nepal's 1990 constitution provide a number of fundamental rights, including freedom of expression and due process of law. The prohibition of torture is defined in Article 14 (4) of the constitution and states that no person who is detained during investigation or for trial shall be subjected to physical or mental torture or cruel, inhuman, or degrading treatment. In addition the 1996 Compensation Relating to Torture Act (CRT) permits a victim to file a claim for compensation in the courts; the alleged perpetrator of torture is defended by the attorney general. Several other legal safeguards exist. However, in practice, these safeguards are not implemented, and human rights violations occur regularly.

From September 10 to 16, 2005, the United Nations dispatched a special rapporteur, Manfred Nowak, to Nepal on a fact-finding visit at the invitation of the Government of Nepal. On September 15, Nowak accused the security forces of systematic torture. In his later report, he concluded that "torture is systematically practiced by the armed police and Royal Nepalese Army. Legal safeguards are routinely ignored and effectively meaningless. Impunity for acts of torture is the rule, and consequently victims of torture and their families are left without recourse to adequate justice, compensation or rehabilitation."[13] Nowak also stated that only one person had been compensated for torture since the Torture Compensation Act took effect in 1996. The report's appendix highlights several individual cases of human rights violations. Nevertheless, the Royal Nepal Army continues to deny systematic torture.

Women especially been victims of the civil war. In theory, Nepalese law does not actively discriminate against women but, in practice, women do not enjoy the same rights as men.[14] For instance, women hold less than 10 percent of civil service positions, and violence against women is a major problem. Nepal is also one of the few countries in which female life expectancy is lower than that of males. The overall adult literacy rate in Nepal is 57 percent, but among women it is only 30 percent. In November 2005, the Supreme Court ordered the government to issue passports to women under the age of 35 without the (previously required) consent of their guardians after a writ challenged a 1995 decision. However, the government has yet to address the right to citizenship by descent through the mother or the existence of discriminatory inheritance and property laws. The Nepalese government has recognized that gender inequality is a problem and has therefore included gender equality programs in Nepal's Tenth Five-Year Plan. The plan identifies women as vital to achieving poverty reduction and development. Nevertheless, the Tenth Five-Year Plan does not specifically address gender discrimination in employment in either the public or the private sector.

In the current political climate of intimidation and fear, domestic violence against women has also risen. The police have sent out directives stating that domestic violence is a criminal offense. However, this has been hard to enforce due to entrenched ideas. In a survey conducted by a local NGO, Saathi, 42 percent of respondents stated that medical personnel were uncooperative in cases of violence against women. The Human Trafficking Control Act prohibits the sale of persons within Nepal or abroad, and Nepalese law prescribes strict jail sentences of up to 20 years for persons who traffic women. However, antitrafficking enforcement is weak and convictions are rare.

Ethnic minorities have also suffered since the suspension of democratic freedoms. Although the government and the laws do not overtly discriminate against the country's 75 ethnic and religious minority groups, in practice it is commonplace. Nepal is a Hindu-dominated society, and caste discrimination remains widely prevalent. Furthermore, freedom of conscience and belief was shaken when in 1990 Nepal's new constitution declared Nepal to be a Hindu state. Tibeto-Burman ethnic groups questioned this as they did not consider themselves Hindus. As a result of the caste system, several ethnic minority groups are often treated quite like lower-caste Hindus. The domination of upper castes however, preceded the 1990 constitution.

The Maoists have been sympathetic toward the demands of ethnic minorities and have been urging that ethnic minorities should gain autonomy over areas in which they are in a majority. Despite the tensions associated with the Maoist action and the February 1, 2005, action, the situation has not grown much worse than it was previously. Religious freedom has largely been maintained, and the state continues to refrain from involving itself in the appointment of religious and spiritual leaders and generally steers clear of the internal activities of faith-related organizations.

Nevertheless, ethnic minorities continue to face traditional discrimination. Brahmins and Kshatriyas dominate politics and the senior military and civil service ranks. Members of low-caste groups face active discrimination in competition for both senior and junior posts. The state has made few efforts to lessen ethnic and caste discrimination, and in practice terms of employment and occupation have not changed. The state has no formal policy on maintaining interfaith understanding. In addition, reacting to Chinese pressure, the state has restricted public celebrations by the Tibetan community. In January 2005, the government closed two offices associated with the Tibetan leader, the Dalai Lama. While in principle there is no discrimination against people with disabilities, in practice little has been done to further their rights.

Since February 1, 2005, a state of emergency has been in effect, and the state has suspended the right to freedom of association and assembly. Rallies have been banned, and several public meetings have been curtailed or forcefully disbanded. Several reports of police tear-gassing demonstrators, as well as arresting demonstrators on unclear legal grounds, have surfaced. There has also been a failure to provide medical care for injured demonstrators. In September 2005 a senior UN human rights official and representative of the OHCHR, Ian Martin, voiced concern at the alleged use of excessive force against prodemocracy demonstrators in Nepal. Martin referred to beatings and abuse and stated that they constituted torture. Citizens are not protected from being directly or indirectly compelled to belong to certain associations. In particular, vast numbers have been unwillingly inducted into the Maoist movement under threat of violence. Maoists have a policy of forcibly recruiting one family member per rural household into their movement.

Recommendations

- The Royal Nepal Army (and the Maoists) must, as part of the cease-fire, stop killing, torturing, and harassing members of the public. In particular the RNA must stop attacking "potential Maoists" and Maoists must stop attacking "royal sympathizers."
- The government must improve human rights training for the army and the police. In particular, the government must work with the United Nations to improve the army's trigger-happy engagement tactics.
- Indefinite and arbitrary detention of Maoists and others must cease.
- Human rights violations on both sides must not go unpunished. Domestic and international NGOs and international official bodies must be permitted by the government to engage Maoists to set up oversight systems to document and punish cadres for excessive use of force in combat operations as well as force used against civilians. An internal Maoist human rights watchdog should be established with the power (granted by the Maoist leadership) to liaise with NGOs and UN officials and monitor Maoist operations from a human rights standpoint.

RULE OF LAW – 2.73

Nepal's legal system is based on the British legal system and legal principles, and judges are required to have earned a recognized law degree. They are reasonably well trained to carry out justice in a fair and unbiased manner. Unfortunately, in practice Nepal's judiciary has failed to deliver timely and equitable justice, and judges are not always appointed, promoted, or dismissed in a fair and unbiased manner. Because the king is involved in their appointment, many judges' loyalty resides with him. Lower courts are viewed as slow and corrupt. Cases can, in some circumstances, take over 20 years to be resolved. The judiciary is also severely underfunded.

In principle, everyone charged with a criminal offense is presumed innocent until proven guilty. In theory, citizens are also given a fair and public hearing by a competent tribunal. Citizens also have the right and access to independent counsel, and the state does provide citizens charged with serious felonies with access to independent counsel when it is beyond their means, although in practice this rarely happens.

Since 1990 the judiciary has often been called upon to interpret the constitution. The judiciary has traditionally remained outside the political fray, although there have been some corruption allegations against the institution. Under existing law, only parliament can impeach Supreme Court judges. The judiciary comprises 75 district courts and 16 appeals courts of general jurisdiction, one special court, four revenue tribunals, one administrative court, a labor court, one loan-recovery tribunal, a loan-recovery appeals tribunal, and the Supreme Court.

Since the state of emergency was declared in February 2005, the judicial system has been severely altered. On February 16, the king created a powerful anticorruption body with questionable legal status.[15] It comprises ex-government administrators, a general, and an intelligence officer. The six-member Royal Commission on Corruption Control (RCCC) has powers to investigate and indict suspects, to hear cases, and to order sentences in relation to smuggling, revenue-related crimes, irregular contracting procedures, and other acts. It is also authorized to investigate charges against the heads of constitutional agencies and to recommend necessary action to the king. Under rules approved on March 14, 2005, the RCCC can initiate investigations at its own discretion and order suspects to present themselves at its offices within 24 hours. It can also detain subjects up to 30 days. Individuals can be held in contempt by the RCCC and can also be jailed for six months.

The RCCC affects the entire structure of the legal system and has undermined the relative independence of the judiciary, as it reports directly to the king. Prosecutors within the RCCC are not independent of political direction or control. Very controversially, the RCCC has the power to investigate even Supreme Court judges. Critics also argue that it has an unusual structure, combining the roles of prosecutor and judge into one role. Nepal's most influential group of lawyers, the Nepal Bar Association, has stated that it will boycott the commission.

Given the developments since February 2005, Nepalese courts can no longer be viewed as being protected from interference from the executive. Traditionally, the legislative, executive, and other government authorities have complied with judicial decisions. However, this may change in the near future. A contest between the RCCC and the Supreme Court is a possibility. Judges in the normal courts (not the RCCC) have been appointed, promoted, and dismissed in an arbitrary manner. However, the possibility that the king will begin actively interfering in the judicial appointment process cannot be ruled out.

Apart from the differences between the RCCC and the Supreme Court, ruling party actors or public officials have rarely been prosecuted for abuse of power and wrongdoing. The military has been a crucial element in the overall political equation and has largely remained unchecked by law. Charged with thwarting a Maoist advance, especially into the Kathmandu Valley area, it has been given a relatively free rein. Nepal's army is commanded by the king. This strengthens the hand of the king in all political negotiations and provides him with leverage. The constitution states that the king is the supreme commander of all the armed forces and gives him the power to appoint the commander in chief of the army, upon the recommendation of the prime minister. In an unclear check on the king's powers, Article 18 of the constitution puts the army under the control of a National Defense Council chaired by the prime minister and including the royally appointed commander in chief. The king also commissions officers, thereby keeping the officer corps loyal to him. Senior officers are traditionally promonarchy loyalists.

In addition, the police and armed forces are rarely held accountable for abuses of power for personal gain and have little regard for human rights. The army has been excessively brutal with protesters and prison inmates. The UNHCHR's report to the General Assembly "raised serious concerns . . . regarding alleged violations by security forces."[16] When queried by the United Nations, the army stated that when human rights violations by military personnel occur, a board of inquiry is ordered and, on the recommendations of the board, the violator is sentenced by a military court. However the UN report states that "punishment in cases of grave violations remains light."[17]

The Nepalese legal system also suffers from more mundane problems. Nepalese law recognizes citizens' rights to private property and the sale of private property both as individuals and in association with others. However, more than half of the backlog of legal cases in the courts relate to property matters. Owing to the lack of a tamper-proof registration procedure, disputes over title are commonplace. Courts are slow to provide judgments in property matters, and loss or expropriation of property in many cases goes uncompensated. In theory, all persons, apart from the king and the royal family (who remain above the law in several respects), are entitled to equality before the courts and tribunals.

Recommendations
- The Supreme Court should take a more proactive stance in highlighting democratic and human rights breaches since February 1, 2005. Courts must penalize infringements of human rights. Judicial salaries should be raised, and funding for the judiciary must be increased.
- The Royal Nepal Army must take immediate steps to punish gross human rights violations within its own ranks.
- A computerized tamper-proof, corruption-free private property register must be created.

ANTICORRUPTION AND TRANSPARENCY – 2.30

Corruption appears to be widespread in Nepal. This is despite the country's several legal provisions designed to fight corruption. For example, a Prevention of Corruption Act is backed by several regulatory bodies, including the Auditor General's Office, the Public Service Commission, and the Election Commission. The constitution guarantees the Auditor General's Office total legal and professional independence. There is also a Special Police Department (SPD), a Commission for the Investigation of Abuse of Authority (CIAA), and a Public Accounts Committee. At the district level, Chief District Officers (CDO) are responsible for anticorruption efforts. In 2005, Nepal was ranked 117 on Transparency International's Corruption Perceptions Index alongside Afghanistan, Guyana, Ecuador, Bolivia, Guatemala, Libya, the Philippines, and Uganda.[18]

Although Nepal has an impressive array of antigraft bodies, enforcement remains a severe problem. In addition, the anticorruption bodies do not always act impartially. Corruption is also viewed as a problem that affects all levels of society. In fact, it is widely perceived that corruption is institutionalized, with it almost accepted that embezzlement of public funds is the norm. In addition, a large bureaucracy, extensive red tape, and an ongoing civil war with the Maoists increase opportunities for corruption. Despite strong anticorruption legislation, part of the problem of enforcement stems from the fact that the Nepalese government's remit remains weak. This weak remit has permitted not only the growth of graft but the emergence of the Maoist movement and a new rural culture of corruption, lack of transparency, and extortion. Maoists have begun to run parallel administrations as well as quasi-legal systems in the areas they control. Corruption has worsened against the backdrop of the Maoist campaign—Maoists "extort money in 'revolutionary taxes' and ha[ve] a policy of forcefully recruiting one family member per household."[19]

One of the biggest problems facing business is the threat of extortion from Maoist groups. In several parts of the country, a culture of extortion has developed with businesses and petty trade held to ransom. The International Crisis Group reports that "using extortion and coercion, the Maoists are imposing an authoritarian regime on steadily increasing swathes of rural Nepal."[20] Maoists have staged blockades of Kathmandu Valley and imposed strikes that have paralyzed the entire economy. As the state has begun to fail in its job of protecting businesses, opportunities for graft have grown. That the Maoists' systematic extortion of the countryside is possible is also due to the fact that Nepal is essentially an agrarian economy. Around two-thirds of Nepal's economically active population works in agriculture, and agriculture contributes approximately 39 percent of the gross domestic product. This agrarian, often subsistence economy has historically been (and continues to be) largely free of government controls. It is this lack of government control that has let the Maoists fill the void. In the countryside they operate in an atmosphere of complete impunity.

The state does enforce legislation or administrative procedures designed to prevent, detect, and punish the corruption of public officials, but it does so in an arbitrary and biased manner. This bias is highlighted by the focused way the new RCCC is being misused.[21] In what is widely viewed as a political trial, the RCCC charged former prime minister Sher Bhahadur Dueba with corruption. However, Dueba refused to recognize the commission, arguing that the institution is corrupt and charges against him are politically motivated. The trial related to a contract for the construction of an access road to the Melamchi Water Supply Project, which was funded by donor agencies including the Asian

Development Bank. The Asian Development Bank, which launched its own investigation into the project, concluded that all business was aboveboard and ruled out corruption. Nevertheless, the RCCC claimed that Dueba and Prakash Man Singh, the former minister of works and transport, influenced contractor selection. On July 26, 2005, Dueba was sentenced to two years in jail and fined NRs 90 million (US$1.3 million).[22] The commission ordered a similar sentence for Singh. Four other people were also sentenced.

Both Dueba and Singh refused to testify before the RCCC, arguing that it was an unconstitutional and opaque body. They also had no lawyers representing them. Dueba has appealed to the Supreme Court to declare the rulings null and void. The legality of the RCCC remains an issue that the Supreme Court has begun investigating. A writ filed on August 10, 2005, argues that the RCCC is an illegal body. In September 2005, the Supreme Court asked the RCCC to explain why it jailed the former prime minister, sparking rumors of friction between the RCCC and the Supreme Court. As of November 30, 2005, the RCCC had not yet responded.

The entire RCCC matter highlights the fact that allegations of corruption are not investigated without prejudice. The state does not enforce effective legislation, nor is the administrative process designed to promote integrity and to prevent, detect, and punish the corruption of public officials. In addition, the state does not provide victims of corruption, or those accused of corruption, with adequate, clear, or transparent mechanisms to pursue their rights. Corruption investigations in Nepal are a selective and politically motivated issue—politicians out of favor become the target of anticorruption investigations. Anticorruption investigations are used as a tool to threaten individuals into remaining loyal to the king. Dueba is not the first politician to fall afoul of the selective investigation process. In May 2003, the CIAA, a constitutionally appointed body designed to deal with corruption, summoned 40 people, including another former prime minister, Girija Koirala, for questioning on corruption allegations. Critics at the time argued that the entire investigation was designed to discredit Koirala.

The state makes no adequate provision against conflicts of interest in the private sector. Nor does it ensure transparency, open bidding, or effective competition in the awarding of government contracts. Economically privileged interests have historically commanded undue influence in manufacturing and industry and won government contracts with regularity. Nepalese industry is dominated by the overarching influence of the monarchy (and a small palace elite), a political elite, and the civil service (beset by inefficiency and corruption) in nexus with a few chosen industrialists. This coterie defends their privileges at the expense of the populace at large. Industry has been constrained by the small domestic market, Indian competition, and the lack of sea access, providing industrialists with a ready excuse for a lack of transparency. Fear of Indian competition has also provided local industry with high tariff protection. Consequently, smuggling from India has become rampant.

One of the by-products of this is that industrialists in favor have received loans at low interest rates and despite a track record of default have continued to receive funds. Government contracts are also not always awarded on merit. The privileges of the few industrialists were highlighted yet again in 2005. In May, the government announced that it would take tough action against major loan defaulters by blacklisting them, confiscating their passports, barring them from public office, and preventing them from disposing of assets other than to repay debts. However, the blacklisting was not implemented, owing to the fact that several defaulters allegedly included cabinet ministers, large industrialists, and relatives of the royal family. The state also does not protect higher education from graft, and corruption is therefore endemic at the university level. Anecdotal evidence suggests that bribes are a requirement for admission to universities and even to secondary schools.

Financial disclosure procedures that prevent conflicts of interest among public officials remain inadequate. The constitution guarantees the auditor general complete legal and professional independence; unfortunately, implementation remains a huge problem. The 1999 Financial Procedures Act and the 1999 Financial Administration Regulations contain detailed provisions for the reporting of government and budget expenditure and the production of financial statements. The Audit Act 1991 stipulates that the auditor general should examine whether the accounts and revenue and all other incomes are correct and that the rules relating to assessment, realization, and methods of bookkeeping are adequate and followed. Nevertheless, budgets are almost never monitored, and penalties authorized by these procedures are almost never imposed. State auditors generally lack sufficient expertise in accounting and finance, and internal auditing and management accounting remain poor.

As a consequence, government tax administrators do not adequately implement effective internal audit systems to ensure the accountability of tax collection. In addition, the executive budget-making process is not subject to meaningful review and scrutiny. Nor does the government publish detailed and accurate accounting of expenditures in a timely fashion.

The Office of the Auditor General (OAG) in theory sends auditors for field audits to two-thirds of the most important (from a gross volume of revenue basis) districts. For the remaining districts, district treasury controller officers are told to complete the audit according to the requirements set by the OAG. However, in practice, Maoist control of the countryside has led to a new rural culture in which revenue owed to the government is diverted to the Maoists.

As anticorruption activists, whistle-blowers, and investigators do not have a legal environment that protects them, they do not feel secure about reporting cases of bribery and corruption. Government bodies in Nepal act with very little transparency, which facilitates corruption and makes it hard for the public to gain access to government information. In theory, Nepali citizens do have a right to obtain information about government operations. The constitution states that every citizen shall have the right to demand and receive information on any matter of public importance. However, in practice there is no mechanism to legally bind the government to provide this information nor is there a practical mechanism to petition government agencies for it. There is no right to information act (as was recently passed in India, for example), although several groups have been lobbying for one and several drafts have been presented. The state makes no special provisions in order to provide information in formats and settings that are accessible to people with disabilities. Several government offices are not even designed to provide wheelchair access. Foreign aid is closely monitored by donors, including the World Bank, and as a consequence these funds are more equitably distributed and monitored than government tax proceeds.

Recommendations

- Foreign auditors should monitor key revenue and expenditure items of the government.
- A right to information act should be passed that forces access to key financial statements and documents to any member of the public.

- Civil servants should be protected from intimidation and their salaries should be increased.

NOTES

[1] Ray Marcelo, "Foreign Allies Express Anger," *Financial Times,* 2 February 2005.

[2] Rabindra Mishra, "Maoist Rethink on Nepal Monarchy," *BBC News,* 27 November 2005, http://news.bbc.co.uk/1/hi/world/south_asia/4475510.stm.

[3] Binod Bhattarai and Ray Marcelo, "Monarch of Nepal Takes over Power in Coup," *Financial Times,* 2 February 2005.

[4] Bishnu Budhathoki, "Parties, Maoists Announce 12-pt Agreement," eKantipur.com, 22 November 2005, http://www.kantipuronline.com/kolnews.php?&nid=57919.

[5] Mishra, "Nepal Awaits the King's Move," *BBC News,* 24 November 2005, http://news.bbc.co.uk/1/hi/world/south_asia/4467408.stm.

[6] Bhattarai and Marcelo, "Monarch of Nepal," *Financial Times,* 2 February 2005.

[7] Nepal Television Corporation, 1 February 2005.

[8] Marcelo, "Rights Groups Plan Nepal Rally," *Financial Times,* 8 February 2005.

[9] "Nepal Donors in NGO Code Protest," *BBC News,* 17 November 2005, http://news.bbc.co.uk/2/hi/south_asia/4444674.stm.

[10] *Report of the United Nations High Commissioner for Human Rights on the Situation of Human Rights and the Activities of Her Office, Including Technical Cooperation, Nepal* (New York: United Nations Commission on Human Rights [UNCHR], 16 February 2006).

[11] Ibid.

[12] *Report of the United Nations High Commissioner for Human Rights on the Human Rights Situation and the Activities of Her Office, Including Technical Cooperation, in Nepal* (New York: United Nations General Assembly, 16 September 2005).

[13] Manfred Nowak, *Report by the Special Rapporteur on Torture and Other Cruel, Inhuman or Degrading Treatment or Punishment* (New York: United Nations Economic and Social Council, Mission to Nepal, 9 January 2006).

[14] "Court Victory for Nepal's Women," BBC News, 29 November 2005, http://news.bbc.co.uk/1/hi/world/south_asia/4481392.stm.

[15] S. Chandrasekharan, *Nepal: King Pushing the Democrats into the Arms of the Maoists?* (Noida, India: South Asia Analysis Group [SAAG], 1 August, 2005), http://www.saag.org/%5Cnotes3%5Cnote270.html.

[16] *Report . . . , in Nepal* (UN General Assembly).

[17] Ibid.

[18] *Corruption Perceptions Index 2005* (Berlin: Transparency International, 2005).

[19] Jo Johnson, "Insurgency in India—How the Maoists Threat Reaches beyond Nepal," *Financial Times,* 26 April 2006.

[20] *Nepal: Dealing with a Human Rights Crisis* (Brussels, International Crisis Group [ICG], Asia Report No. 94, 24 March 2005), http://www.crisisgroup.org/home/index.cfm?l=1&id=3337.

[21] See Rule of Law, above.

[22] "Nepal Jails Ex-PM for Corruption," *BBC News,* 26 July 2005, http://news.bbc.co.uk/2/hi/south_asia/4717605.stm.

NICARAGUA

CAPITAL: Managua

POPULATION: 5.8 million

GNI PER CAPITA: $740

SCORES	2004	2006
ACCOUNTABILITY AND PUBLIC VOICE:	4.56	4.49
CIVIL LIBERTIES:	4.42	4.20
RULE OF LAW:	3.95	3.61
ANTICORRUPTION AND TRANSPARENCY:	2.69	3.40

(scores are based on a scale of 0 to 7, with 0 representing weakest and 7 representing strongest performance)

David R. Dye

INTRODUCTION

Nicaragua has evolved within an outwardly democratic framework during the 16 years since Violeta Chamorro ousted the revolutionary Sandinistas from their grip on power in 1990. During this time a climate of respect for civil liberties has generally prevailed. But attempts to root out historically entrenched corruption and make government responsive to citizens have foundered, while the rule of law is perilously weak, and the fairness of the electoral system is fraying at the edges. What explains this pattern is the failure of the dominant elites of the Sandinista National Liberation Front (FSLN) and the Liberal Constitutionalist Party (PLC) to assimilate the ethos that must permeate a consolidated system of democratic rule. While Sandinista leader Daniel Ortega remains committed to a basically socialist political vision, former president Arnoldo Alemán, who has been convicted of money laundering but still holds sway over the PLC, strives to recreate a variant of the strongman rule of the Somoza family era.

Making matters worse, stalemate between these parties and their leaders (locally called *caudillos*) has twice, in 2000 and 2004, led them into power-sharing pacts at the expense of other forces, making the

David R. Dye is a political consultant who lives in Nicaragua. He has worked as the correspondent for the London–based Economist Intelligence Unit in Nicaragua since 1994 and is currently consulting for the Carter Center mission observing the 2006 elections.

development of democratic institutions even more difficult.[1] In these pacts, which involved reforms to the constitution, the two *caudillos* divided up power in the Supreme Court, the electoral branch, and the Office of the Comptrollers General, providing them with impunity from prosecution. The first of the two arrangements also restricted the elections law in order to limit the formation of rival parties. Not surprisingly, faith in the institutions affected by these pacts has withered.

The persistence of authoritarianism has likewise impeded the nation's economic advance. Nicaragua remains the Western hemisphere's second poorest country, with a per capita income of just over $800 a year.[2] Though the proportion of the population who are poor may be declining in percentage terms, their absolute numbers are rising, and the distribution of national income has become severely unequal. Poverty coupled with political weaknesses means that most people, though conscious of certain rights, lack effective political resources with which to use their rights. One consequence is that in comparison with the rest of Latin America, political protest and demonstration are surprisingly timid. Another is that (non-business) civil society, though slowly gathering strength, is still too weak to pressure the government in most policy areas or force lawmakers to pass legislation beneficial to its interests.

Convinced that Nicaragua's long-term viability is threatened, current president Enrique Bolaños Geyer, elected in November 2001 on the PLC ticket, has tried finally to get development under way and has crafted a national development plan to take advantage of the growth opportunities offered by the Central America–US Free Trade Agreement (CAFTA).[3] But the policy continuity needed to reap the fruits of these efforts after a new administration takes office in January 2007 is doubtful given Bolaños' lack of a political heir. Similarly, government under Bolaños has gone some way toward controlling ordinary corruption. In mid-2002, Bolaños also began pursuing his predecessor (he had been Alemán's vice president) in the courts for malfeasance, but his government's efforts to prosecute officials of the previous Liberal administration have run up against a deeply politicized and increasingly corrupt judiciary, whose integrity was vitiated by the pacts. The Bolaños administration has likewise sought to promote institutional reform in the judicial and electoral branches of state but has seen its efforts in this regard stymied by a very weak legislative base. The PLC bench in the assembly went into opposition to Bolaños in 2003, and most of the lawmakers have remained staunchly loyal to Alemán.

As a result, gridlock among the powers of state has increasingly set in. This gave rise to a 10-month-long crisis after Bolaños refused in December 2004 to accept constitutional reforms voted by the majority Sandinista and Liberal parties that stripped the executive branch of certain prerogatives. The crisis was resolved in October 2005 through a political agreement facilitated by the Organization of American States to postpone the changes until January 2007.

ACCOUNTABILITY AND PUBLIC VOICE – 4.49

Fairness and public confidence in the electoral system have slowly declined since the 2000 political pact and ensuing reform of the election law. This pact completely politicized the Supreme Electoral Council, which is under the firm control of the major party leaders. Doubts about its ability to conduct fair elections grew in 2004 in the wake of a flagrant fraud apparently committed in the city of Granada during municipal voting, in which the arbitrary annulment of a single vote board's tally threw victory to the FSLN.[4] The case demonstrated that the dominant parties could be relied on to count each other's ballots fairly but not necessarily those of third-party rivals.

In a similar vein, the electoral law (Law 331) spawned by the 2000 pact imposes stiffer requirements for the registration of political parties than anywhere else in Latin America. This law clearly aimed to restrict electoral competition to the advantage of the Liberal and Sandinista parties. Only one other party contested the 2001 elections. As the 2006 election approaches, fear is widespread that the major party leaders will use their control over the electoral and judicial branches of government to arbitrarily prohibit potential challengers from entering the race.[5] However, Nicaraguan elections since 1990 have not been characterized by intimidation of or violence against voters, nor are restrictions placed on the campaign activities of any party. No incidents of this kind were reported in the 2004 municipal voting.

Political finance laws and regulations are weak, allowing economically powerful actors wide latitude to exert undue influence and tainted money to contaminate campaigns. Although the law provides significant public funding for party campaigns, it imposes no restrictions on campaign media spending. Rules for the disclosure of campaign financing sources are unspecific, and enforcement is lax and subject to political manipulation. In November 2002, charges arose that monies pilfered from the state by ex-president Alemán had filtered into the campaign coffers of the new president, Enrique Bolaños. Instead of investigating promptly and fairly, the major party leaders held the charges over Bolaños' head as a political club for the following three years. The harassment only ended in December 2005 when a Sandinista judge dropped the charges against Bolaños and his ministers.

The branches of state do not check one another as liberal-democratic governance requires. Since 2000, the dominant Sandinista and Liberal parties have used their control over the National Assembly to colonize and subordinate other branches and agencies of government, with the current exception of the executive. In 2005, these parties continued to control the elections council, judiciary, comptroller's office, attorney general's office, and ombudsman's office, politicizing each and vitiating the independence of and separation among the powers of government, thereby fostering corruption.

The iron personal grip of Daniel Ortega and Arnoldo Alemán over their parties' nominations for deputies also gives them very strong leverage over their party benches in the assembly, often relegating the political concerns of ordinary citizens to the sidelines when laws are debated. At the same time, domestic banking groups exercise excessive influence over some economic policies through direct lobbying of the president. In addition, fully a third of the national budget is financed by foreign aid, giving multilateral institutions and foreign donors strong influence over government policy. Still, by steering clear of gross corruption, the Bolaños government has regained the confidence of donors and achieved some degree of freedom to launch independent policy initiatives such as the national development plan, which guided much public investment during 2003–2005.

According to a 2003 civil service law, the recruitment and promotion of public servants must be based on merit. However, procedures for applying the law have not been developed, and it has not been implemented.

Civil society organizations engage in considerable lobbying and a certain amount of demonstrating to influence public policies and the national budget. Most groups lack much depth of representation or capacity to mobilize their supporters to the streets, however, so their influence over policy or legislation, though at times tangible, is usually limited. Certain groups, notably the Consumer Defense Network, have learned to use the judicial system to block initiatives of the executive or legislative branches. As opposed to the Alemán administration, which was widely accused of harassing national and even foreign nongovernmental organizations (NGOs), the Bolaños administration has not been accused of restricting the organization of any civil society group or exerting pressure on such groups' funding sources.

Alone among the three post-1990 governments, the Bolaños administration has accorded the constitutionally mandated national economic and social planning council (*Conpes*) a modest, although intermittent consultative role. *Conpes*, which was originally comprised of representatives from business groups, unions, professional associations, and NGOs, has provided the government with recommendations on fighting poverty, the national development plan, and the annual budget. Along with select civil society actors, the government furthermore drafted the Citizen Participation Law, which passed the assembly in late 2003. In 2004–2005, it created department-level development councils intended to provide input into the national development plan. Also in 2005, Conpes was reorganized on a territorial basis ostensibly to provide the interior of the country with representation.[6] As NGOs headquartered in the capital that address social issues were shunted aside in the process, it is not clear whether this change was an improvement.

The Bolaños administration generally respects freedom of the press and media. Its only recent lapse was a three-day closing in June 2005, allegedly for tax evasion, of *La Trinchera,* a political news bulletin published by supporters of former President Alemán.[7] The government owns the official Radio Nicaragua and a semi-defunct TV station but does not control any media distribution networks or printing facilities other than the official gazette. Nor does it directly fund any private media or impose restrictive requirements for their registration. Of considerable weight in the total advertising market, government advertisements were allocated mainly in proportion to the audience reached by each media outlet, but with some minimum doled out to the smaller players. The administration does not interfere with access to or communications over the internet. Similarly, it does nothing to limit freedom of cultural expression but little either to promote national culture.

Rather than the executive branch, the national assembly and the political parties controlling it are among the important threats to press and media freedom. In late 2004, the FSLN and PLC voted a constitutional reform that abrogated the media's right to import equipment and supplies duty free, and an ordinary law subsequently limited customs exemptions for these goods. Media owners denounced the limits as an attack on their freedom, some seeing them as a political reprisal by the major parties against sharp criticism of their political pact, especially from the daily newspaper *La Prensa* and TV Channel 2.[8] Other institutions have posed occasional threats. In a few instances, the police or the courts have attempted to force journalists to reveal sources of information under an outdated law. The affected journalists all refused to comply, however, and the spotlight of publicity thrown by the media themselves induced the offending institutions to draw back.

A still latent threat is the College of Journalists, a professional association approved by the assembly in 2003, in which membership is supposedly required. *La Prensa* and Channel 2 have appealed the law in the Supreme Court as unconstitutional, and its implementation is currently stalled. It is feared that the college could fall under political control and infringe upon journalistic freedom.

Organs of government have also failed to protect journalists from violent attacks or fully investigate them. Three murders of journalists occurred in 2003–2005, a signal departure from prior years in which no cases were recorded. The investigations into the January 2004 slaying of radio station owner Carlos Guadamuz, a Sandinista dissident, and the killing of *La Prensa* reporter María José Bravo by a former PLC mayor after the November 2004 municipal elections, resulted in the apprehension and eventual conviction of suspects. But the inquiry into the Guadamz murder failed to convince the family of the deceased that the attorney general and police had the will to uncover the identity of those ultimately responsible for the killing.[9] In the case of the August 2005 murder of *La Prensa* reporter Adolfo Olivas, justice was apparently done but suspicion has lingered, as the reporter was investigating drug trafficking in his home area of Estelí. In addition, during the period other *La Prensa* journalists reportedly received death threats from both drug traffickers and local police officials for publishing exposés of the traffic on the Atlantic Coast.

Recommendations

- Restoring credibility to elections in Nicaragua requires the wholesale depoliticization of the election system. This must start with the naming of magistrates to the Supreme Electoral Council on a strictly professional and nonpartisan basis.
- Political finance regulations in the 2000 elections law need to be revised to limit campaign media spending and greatly strengthen disclosure rules for contributions.
- The relevant authorities should deepen their investigations into the killings of Carlos Guadamuz and Adolfo Olivas.
- The national assembly should reconsider its decision to create the College of Journalists in light of criticism from international media watchdogs.

CIVIL LIBERTIES – 4.20

No state-sponsored murders or politically motivated disappearances have been recorded since the early 1990s. Similarly, there have been no arbitrary arrests by security forces of political opponents of the government. However, the arrest of mayoral candidate Alejandro Fiallos in August 2004 on corruption charges was widely viewed as a political act orchestrated by the PLC. Running in Managua under the APRE party flag, Fiallos threatened to take votes from the PLC's candidate.[10]

In 2004, 20 allegations of unlawful killings were lodged against members of the national police; seven of the accused were exonerated and 11 received an administrative punishment; none of the cases were sent to court.[11] Denunciations of physical abuse by police officers were numerous in relation to the size of the body. In a force of only 6,600, in 2004, 1,336 abuse charges were reported to the police general inspectorate, of which 528 were found to have merit. Beatings to obtain confessions and excessive force when detaining suspects were common complaints. Some investigation of the cases by the inspector general clearly took place, and a large number of officers, some 728, were sanctioned in some fashion.[12] In addition, 77 accusations of arbitrary detention by police were brought before the human rights ombudsman in 2003, the last year the body published a report.[13] However, few officers were remanded to the courts for processing, and fewer court verdicts have been forthcoming, suggesting a significant level of impunity.

In addition to the police's general inspectorate, until recently the human rights defense procurator or ombudsman served as a barrier against certain rights abuses. In 2003, the last year for which data have been published, the ombudsman investigated 263 denunciations against the national police, mostly allegations of physical mistreatment, psychological abuse, and illegal detention. The body judged that the police authorities complied with some 40 percent of the 75 resolutions with recommendations for action it had made after processing the cases.[14] Unfortunately, the national assembly elected new authorities for this body in December 2004 who were drawn from the FSLN and PLC parties. This action deeply politicized the institution, and top officials responsible for the rights of women, children, and indigenous minorities resigned in protest during 2005. The body has consequently lost much of its credibility and now receives many fewer complaints.

Now that application of the 2002 criminal procedure code has been extended to all new cases, instances of long-term detention without trial, frequent under the former code of criminal instruction, have noticeably waned from 26 percent of all prisoners in the penitentiary system in 2002 to 14.7 percent in 2004 and should eventually disappear.[15] Police holding cells, where short-term detainees are routinely held during the course of their trials, are grossly overcrowded and conditions wretched. With 5,601 inmates, the prison system itself is running slightly above its capacity of 5,358.[16] Severe resource limitations lead to harsh conditions—food rations are clearly inadequate for even minimum nutrition, and medical care and drugs are sorely lacking. Prison guards, who receive human rights training from international donors and the Nicaraguan Human Rights Center (Cenidh), are judged to have treated prisoners well. The government regularly permits independent human rights groups access to prisons to monitor conditions. One of these, Cenidh, has detected the emergence of prison gangs that in recent years have challenged the penitentiary authorities for control of some institutions.[17]

Protection against abuse by nonstate actors is extremely weak on the Atlantic coast, where drug traffickers appear to have penetrated the police and are able to intimidate judicial system personnel and the population at large without being checked by an effective state response. In May 2004, armed men reportedly linked to the traffic attacked the police headquarters in the South Atlantic port of Bluefields, slaying four officers; the crime has not been solved. Though far less developed than in other Central American countries, juvenile gangs (*pandillas*) cause pervasive insecurity in poor neighborhoods in Managua, where they are linked to drug distribution; in one survey, one-third of urban residents reported being affected somewhat or a lot by gangs.[18] Since 2003, efforts by the police to organize vigilance by local residents and work by civil society activists with youthful offenders have curbed the gangs in certain areas of the capital.

Women and children are very poorly protected against sexual abuse and intra-family violence, which is endemic. In 2004, 17,281 complaints of such abuse were lodged before the women's commissariats of the national police, which have been expanded and are playing an increasing role as the first instance in processing cases.[19] Government does little beyond this initial point, however, referring victims to civil society organizations for further help. As in the past, prosecutions for domestic and sexual abuse remain rare. The Cenidh has roundly criticized the attorney general for failing to take rape and family violence cases to court.[20]

Although the 1987 constitution bans almost all forms of discrimination, the state is not committed or working to eradicate discrimination against women. A draft equal rights and opportunities law that would give teeth to constitutional provisions has languished in the legislature since late 2003. The Bolaños government has given minimal attention to women's issues, and the budget of the official Nicaraguan Institute for Women (INIM), which should be at the forefront of efforts to combat discrimination, is meager. Protection against discrimination in hiring and wages is especially weak. Sexual harassment is also a frequent and serious problem in the workplace, where little is done to stop it.

Although the extent of the phenomenon is unclear, cases of trafficking of young Nicaraguan women to work as prostitutes in Guatemala and Mexico continued to be reported and for the first time have elicited some government response. Migration authorities have begun questioning young women crossing border points unaccompanied by family and turned back some 1,500 between December 2004 and September 2005, suspecting they were being trafficked.[21] Although the trafficking is not formally illegal, the women's commissariats have done educational work in high schools about the danger from the trade.

The human and civil rights of minority religious groups, mainly evangelical Protestants, are respected without limitation. But the full exercise of rights by the ethnic minorities of the Atlantic Coast (Miskito, Mayangna, Garifuna, and Rama) is a distant prospect, in particular given the very weak fiscal base of the regional governments. With the overall coast population increasingly mestizo, the political representation of ethnic minorities in the regional councils has weakened, contradicting the spirit of the 1987 Autonomy Statute, which reserves a certain number of candidate slots in regional council elections for the indigenous.[22] Unfairly excluded from the 2000 municipal elections, the Miskito political party Yátama had to appeal to the Inter-American Court of Human Rights, which issued a ruling in its favor in June 2005.[23] On the positive side, indigenous children receive education in their native tongues through the third grade. Although court proceedings are conducted in Spanish, bilingual personnel are currently being trained for an alternative dispute resolution program.

A 1998 law enjoins the government to take positive steps to assist people with disabilities, estimated in this post–civil war country to number more than 500,000. But there are no government programs in this area, and civil society provides the little help that is available.[24] A civil service law passed in 2003 effectively reserves employment in the public sector for the physically able. As is the case with women and indigenous people, protection for people with disabilities against discrimination in hiring and wages is basically nonexistent.

Although 75 percent of Nicaraguans are Roman Catholics, there is no state religion, and government has consistently respected the right of citizens to hold and freely express their religious beliefs.[25] The state places no restrictions on religious observance or education, though only Catholic schools receive subsidies. The government also refrains from interference in the appointment of religious leaders or the internal affairs of churches. In a possible exception to this rule, the Bolaños government was alleged in 2004 to have tried to persuade Pope John Paul II to retire Cardinal Miguel Obando y Bravo, the leader of the Catholic Church in Nicaragua, for political reasons.

The constitution guarantees the freedoms of association and assembly, with the usual exceptions for military and police personnel. The national assembly continues to routinely grant legal status to all new civil associations requesting it, including churches. The Nicaraguan government has ratified ILO Conventions 87 and 88 on freedom of union organization. However, the 1996 labor code makes union organization difficult, as employers can legally fire organizers providing they are willing to pay extensive severance pay. During the report period, credible allegations surfaced of labor ministry collusion with employers to prevent the formation of new unions.[26] The Sandinista Workers Central (CST), the victim in most instances, lodged a 2004 suit before the ILO, but no action has been taken. The restrictive labor code mandates complicated and cumbersome procedures for going on strike, making legal strikes rare and dampening the incentive to unionize.

The labor code forbids compulsory membership in unions, and the result is that many workplaces have more than one union representing the workers. In many instances, this is a result of the post-1990 organization of progovernment unions to counter those affiliated with the FSLN. No laws mandate obligatory membership in business and professional organizations, with the exception of the College of Journalists (see "Accountability and Public Voice").

As protest demonstrations normally draw few people, the need to control them is slight. Police regularly grant permits for rallies. Far from using excessive force against demonstrators, the national police have arguably been lax in their treatment of student and other protesters who employ tactics including low-level violence and intimidation. In May 2005, a policeman was killed in one such clash with students. Judicial system favoritism toward FSLN-linked students and other protesters means that charges are never brought against demonstrators for violent behavior, fostering impunity.[27]

Recommendations
- The National Assembly should revise and approve the equal opportunities law submitted in late 2003 to provide a legal basis for discrimination suits.
- Reform of the penal code is urgently needed to make child prostitution and trafficking of women illegal.[28]
- The 2003 civil service law should also be reformed to eliminate bias against people with disabilities.

- The 1996 labor code should be changed to prevent employers from firing union leaders through the awarding of severance pay and recognize the right of union federations and confederations (not just individual unions) to strike.
- The assembly should amend the 2003 law on municipal budget transfers to include mandatory funding for the Atlantic coast regional governments.

RULE OF LAW – 3.61

The lack of judicial independence from political influence is one of Nicaragua's most severe problems. The two FSLN-PLC pacts have put the Supreme Court under tight political control by the big party *caudillos,* Ortega and Alemán, who choose the magistrates through the assembly. The assembly then appoints all lower-level personnel. The independence of the lower-court justices is therefore minimal, as the upper ranks interfere ever more pervasively in decisions.[29] A judicial career law passed in October 2004 ostensibly aims to provide a nonpolitical merit system for the hiring, promotion, and disciplining of lower court justices, but it has not been implemented; in practice clientelism still dominates the selection of judges. Both judicial training and general legal education are weak; for example, there is no bar exam for lawyers.[30]

Political interference was notorious in a number of high-profile civil suits involving businessmen in 2004.[31] These cases sparked serious tension between the executive and judicial branches, with President Bolaños protesting several key decisions publicly and accusing the Supreme Court of corruption. In the past two years, with increasing frequency, the executive branch has simply ignored judicial decisions it regards as political. The most serious conflict of this kind occurred over constitutional reforms passed by the legislature in late 2004 and ratified by the Supreme Court that the Bolaños government refused to accept. Instead, Bolaños obtained a ruling supporting his position from the Central American Court of Justice, which he argued had legal precedence over his nation's Supreme Court.

According to the constitution, everyone charged with a crime is presumed innocent until proven guilty. A new penal procedure code, introduced in December 2002 and expanded in late 2004 to apply to all new cases, has established an oral accusatory system for criminal proceedings. Trials are now public, justice is more prompt, and the proceedings have arguably become fairer. In 2004, few prisoners were held beyond the 48-hour time limit to be brought before a judge, and the average time to arrive at a verdict has been reduced to less than 15 days. A drawback, however, is that the politicized attorney general now has most of the say over which cases are taken to court. As in the past, the jury system has also proven subject to bribery or pressure from the judges. The code of civil procedure has not been reformed and would benefit from oral procedures to reduce the time in which suits are decided.[32] Courts are lacking altogether in outlying rural areas, where alternative dispute resolution is run by an OAS-sponsored system of judicial volunteers.

Since 2002, the state has made the services of public defenders available on a limited basis to those unable to pay lawyers. In 2005, however, there were still only 78 throughout the country, meeting a third of the demand at most.[33] Judges may compel private attorneys to fill this role, but most pay a fine to avoid service. With the new procedure code, a new crop of public prosecutors has also been recruited and trained by foreign assistance missions. But the public ministry remains politicized, and informed sources reveal that prosecutors at all levels continue to be pressured by their superiors as to how to investigate certain cases.

Under Article 27 of the constitution, all persons are equal under the law and entitled to the same protection. Nevertheless the belief that people without means bear the full brunt of the law while the well-to-do buy their way out of trouble is pervasive. Serious judicial system corruption, combined with the lack of prosecution of police misbehavior (see "Civil Liberties"), suggests that this belief is justified in very large part. The constitution likewise bans discrimination on grounds of gender, ethnic origin, and nationality, though not sexual orientation. But specific legislation that might allow discrimination cases to be brought before the courts is lacking, and of six observers of the Nicaraguan justice system, none was able to recall a single case of prosecution for discrimination of any kind.[34]

The civilian branches of state do not exercise full and effective control over the military, security, and police forces. Presidential authority is limited to the naming of the three top-ranking officers in the army. While the legislature exercises pro forma vigilance over the military budget, there is little outward sign of deputies being informed of the details, or questioning military budget requests. Control over the police was until recently somewhat firmer, but after President Bolaños removed the PN's second-in-command in May 2005, the national assembly passed legislation in November stripping him of this power.[36] Supervision by the finance ministry and comptrollers general over the assets held in the army's pension fund institute is similarly superficial, so that control over possible cases of illicit enrichment is lacking.

Despite this de facto autonomy, the armed forces have refrained from interfering in the political process. They have actively resisted calls from civilians to become involved in the power struggles among political groups, notably during the 2005 conflict over constitutional reform, and occasionally acted behind the scenes to dampen these conflicts. Both the army and the police receive extensive human rights training from donor groups and civil society organizations. Few army officers have been accused of human rights violations in recent years.

The right to individual private property is recognized in the constitution, while cooperative and indigenous communal holdings are covered by ordinary law. The executive branch has not committed acts of unjust expropriation (defined as without fair and prior compensation) in many years. The judicial branch is a different story. Influenced by corruption, lower-level judges revoke property titles, many of them provisional, held by peasant smallholders and cooperative members frequently, leading to periodic evictions of scores of poor families by the police. This usually occurs in response to efforts by former property holders to recover their holdings, but other parties may also be involved. However, property rights are not fully protected even for the well-to-do, and 60 percent of the respondents in a recent World Bank survey of the business climate expressed a lack of confidence in the judicial system in this respect.[36] The manipulation of outdated property registers, which are managed by the Supreme Court and staffed largely by Sandinista-nominated officials, magnifies the problem. The passage in late 2003 of a law to demarcate and provide title for indigenous communal land-holdings is an important advance, but its implementation has barely begun.[37]

The pervasive influence of the Sandinista and Liberal parties and a poorly trained, ill-equipped judiciary also make contract enforcement fragile. On procedural complexity in contract enforcement, Nicaragua ranks above the Latin American average, which in turn is far above the OECD average.[39]

Recommendations

- Significant improvement in the rule of law in Nicaragua is impossible without depoliticizing the judicial system. Ideally, the choice of Supreme Court justices should be made professional and non-partisan, but the likelihood of Nicaragua taking this step in the medium term is low. Absent such a change, the 2004 Judicial Career Law should at least be revised to transfer control of the hiring, promotion, and disciplining of judges from the magistrates of the Supreme Court to an independent body.
- The system of property registers should likewise be transferred from the ambit of the Supreme Court and placed under the governance ministry.
- Complex contract enforcement procedures should be simplified through reform of the appropriate codes.
- Reform of the National Police Organic Law should be considered to strengthen the president's appointment and dismissal powers.

ANTICORRUPTION AND TRANSPARENCY – 3.40

As is traditional in Latin America, Nicaraguan public administration is beset by excessive regulations and red tape. In a recent survey, senior executives in medium and large firms reported spending upwards of 20 percent of their time dealing with regulations.[40] Although the current government lacks a program for overhauling the system in its entirety, it has eliminated unnecessary regulations in areas of importance to major economic agents, opening so-called one-stop windows for exporters and foreign investors and greatly reducing the time needed to open a business. Starting under the Alemán government, customs procedures were notably streamlined through a so-called self-dispatch system.

Government interference in the economy is minimal. With very few exceptions, the vast system of state enterprises inherited from the Sandinista period has long since been liquidated, many public utilities have been privatized, and few prices are controlled.

The separation of public functions from the private interests of officeholders is established in Article 130 of the constitution. Conflicts of interest are dealt with in the Probity Law for public servants approved in mid-2002.[41] The Probity Law lacks clarity regarding enforcement agents as well as coercive power. Despite these flaws, the observance of the law by the current executive branch has been reasonably good, while that of other powers of state has been poor. In October 2005, the Supreme Court came under intense media scrutiny after one of its magistrates permitted $600,000 to be returned to a suspect convicted for money-laundering through an elaborate judicial ruse.[42]

The law also provides rules for asset declarations by public officials. However, declarations are made only upon officials' entering and leaving office and not on a yearly basis. More important, the law does not enjoin the comptrollers' office to publish the officials' statements, greatly reducing transparency. Bolaños administration officials have generally filed asset declarations upon taking and leaving their posts.

An office of public ethics established in 2003 has conducted extensive training seminars for public officials concerning the above-mentioned laws and developed manuals for their conduct. However, the government has not focused on ways to curb corruption in the private sector, leaving that task to business groups. Citizens aggrieved by corrupt acts may denounce these to the state attorney (procurator general, an executive branch official), the public ministry (attorney general, elected by the national assembly), or the police. In theory, a citizen could also seek an injunction known as a writ of *amparo* and bring suit before the administrative law chamber of the Supreme Court, but this undertaking is very complex and the chances of success given the court's politicization are minimal. Up to half of the cases taken to court by the state attorney's office originate in private denunciations.[43] However, denunciations are relatively rare due to fear of reprisals and the lack of any way to protect whistleblowers against them.

Until recently, a university autonomy law passed by the outgoing FSLN government in 1990 has shielded public universities from scrutiny of how they spend a constitutionally mandated 6 percent share of all government revenue. This lack of transparency led rectors to be questioned sharply, as clientelism plays a major role in their election. A revised budget law passed in 2005 will henceforth oblige them to render an accounting. Control over all government revenue could also be bolstered, as the revenue branch of the finance ministry lacks proper internal audits (although in 2005 it began to review systematically the collection performance of its department offices).

Formally speaking, both the general comptrollers of the republic (CGR) and the human rights defense procurator (PDDH and ombudsman) are independent organs of state whose leaders are elected by the national assembly. In practice, both have become highly politicized, and their effectiveness is severely compromised. Corruption investigations by the public ministry are highly selective and distinctly lacking in vigor, especially when the fate of Alemán-era officials is at stake. Although the state attorney may take corruption cases to court, the new criminal procedure code requires the public ministry to desist from a case before the government attorney can take it up.

Coupled with judicial system malfeasance, these limitations mean that most corruption allegations are never properly investigated and courts issue few convictions. Instead, a string of high-ranking Alemán-era officials has been acquitted in recent years, or charges have been dropped after deliberate delays allowed the application of the statute of limitations.[44] Although President Alemán himself was sentenced to 20 years imprisonment for fraud and money laundering in December 2003, the appeal of his conviction has been converted into a political bargaining chip between Alemán and Daniel Ortega. As the appeal dragged on, Ortega used his control over the judicial process to extract concessions from Alemán and enhance his power quotas in the institutions under the pact.

Starting in the Alemán years, the newspapers and television became the most vigorous investigators of official abuses, and they have won public confidence. Press exposés of corruption regularly spark at least some response on the part of relevant state organs.[45]

In the absence of specifying legislation for Article 66 of the constitution, which guarantees citizens the right to "true information," Nicaraguans still lack the legal tools to demand information from their government. A draft access to information law was submitted to the assembly in late 2003 but has not been approved. Although President Bolaños is strongly committed to the law, access to government information in practice is spotty and subject to the discretion of ministers and lower-ranking officials. In the face of legislative paralysis, the Bolaños administration has begun a pilot project to place official information online in six ministries.

Though still inadequate, the budget process has become more open and comprehensive. A state financial administration law approved in

2005 has unified public investment with other spending and imposed reporting requirements on autonomous state agencies, municipalities, and public universities for the funds they receive from the public budget. However, the ministry of finance and public credit posts a review of expenditure execution on its website only on a quarterly basis, and the data are neither complete nor presented in as prompt or detailed a fashion as would be helpful to professional users.[46] Previous law allows the deputies to raise the budget ceiling provided they specify matching revenues, and legislative scrutiny of the budget in recent years has been consistent.[47] However, the deputies mainly transfer money among spending categories without raising the ceiling.

In contrast to the previous Alemán administration, in which corruption was rife, under Bolaños an IDB-funded efficiency and transparency program has improved transparency in public bidding. Scandals involving bidding have been few, and the number of bids subject to challenge by the losing parties has dropped. But the stagnation in Transparency International's index of corruption perceptions (2.6 in 2005, down from 2.7 in 2004[48]), as well as anecdotal evidence from businesspeople, suggest that the government has not succeeded in decisively curbing unfair manipulation of bidding terms and procedures by public officials.[49]

Until recently, most foreign assistance was monitored directly by donors to ensure probity and efficacy. In May 2005, major European donors together with the World Bank agreed to begin converting their project assistance into undifferentiated budget support for the central government, signaling confidence in the Bolaños administration's management of their aid monies. However, the transport and infrastructure ministry has failed to exercise proper oversight over several major road projects tendered to foreign construction companies.

Recommendations
- The executive branch should finalize a general anticorruption strategy and implement a comprehensive plan to eliminate needless regulations from government at all levels.
- The Probity Law should be revised to make asset declarations by government officials public.
- The state financial administration law needs to be reformed to include absolutely all agencies of government in the national budget

and more clearly specify procedures for public reporting of budget execution.

- The National Assembly should stop delaying and approve the pending access to information law forthwith.

NOTES

[1] For details of the 2000 pact, see David R. Dye, *Patchwork Democracy* (Brookline, MA: Hemisphere Initiatives, November 2000), passim, http://www.hemisphereinitiatives.org.

[2] *Informe Anual* (Managua: Banco Central de Nicaragua, 2004), i, http://www.bcn.gob.ni.

[3] *Propuesta de Plan Nacional de Desarrollo* (Managua: Gobierno de Nicaragua, September 2003), 5–40.

[4] "Elecciones Municipales 2004: Informe Final," Managua: Grupo Civico Etica y Transparencia [EYT], 2004), 3–5, http://www.eyt.org.ni/novedades/INFOfinal04.pdf.

[5] "Tercer Informe de Observación Electoral de las Elecciones 2006" (EYT, 25 August 2005), 6–8, http://www.eyt.org.ni/novedades/3erinfo2006.pdf.

[6] Amparo Aguilera ("Quiero hacer el Conpes del pueblo," *La Prensa* [Managua], 9 November 2005, 7) treats the reorganization.

[7] "Nicaragua," *Report of the 61st General Assembly* (Miami: InterAmerican Press Association [SIP/IAPA], 7–11 October 2005), 2, http://www.sipiapa.com/publications/informe_nicaragua2005o.cfm.

[8] Ibid.

[9] *2004 World Press Freedom Review* (Vienna: International Press Institute [IPI], 2004), 1–2, http://www.freemedia.at/wpfr/Americas/nicaragu.htm. For some, suspicion points to Daniel Ortega in the murder of Guadamuz, and to drug traffickers in that of Olivas.

[10] The former government official was jailed for eight days, and eventually scored poorly in the voting. See Lizbeth García, "Bola recia a Fiallos," *El Nuevo Diario* (Managua), 18 August 2004, http://www.elnuevodiario.com.ni.

[11] "Informe de Denuncias Interpuestas en la Dirección General de la Policía Nacional y Sus Dependencias" (Managua: Policía Nacional de Nicaragua, January–December 2004), 34.

[12] Ibid., 7, for all figures on cases of mistreatment.

[13] *Informe Anual 2003* (Managua: Procuraduría para la Defensa de los Derechos Humanos, May 2004), 79.

[14] Ibid.

[15] "Informe estadístico de internos que se encuentran en el Sistema Penitenciario Nacional" (Managua): Sistema Penitenciario Nacional, 30 November 2004), n.p.

[16] Ibid.

[17] Personal communication, Bayardo Izabá, executive director, Centro Nicaragüense de Derechos Humanos (Cenidh), Managua, 18 November 2005.

[18] Luis Serra Vázquez, Pedro López Ruíz, Mitchell A. Seligson, *The Political Culture of Democracy in Nicaragua* (Nashville, TN: Latin American Public Opinion Project [LAPOP], 2004), 80, http://www.lapopsurveys.org; Elizabeth Romero ("Hialeah vigila

con técnicas militares," *La Prensa,* 8 April 2005, 10–11) describes how one Managua barrio has organized itself in self-defense.

19 "Resultados del Trabajo de las Comisarías de la Mujer" (Policia Nacional, Comisarías de la Mujer, 2004), 1.

20 "Aplicación del Código Procesal Penal y el Derecho de Acceso a la Justicia en la Región del Pacífico" (Managua: Cenidh, 2004), 3–4, http://www.cenidh.org/files/Doc.CPP .Pacifico.pdf.

21 Data from ministry of governance (Gobernación), reported on TV Channel 2, 9 November 2005.

22 "Las Regiones Autónomas de la Costa Caribe" in Informe sobre Desarrollo Humano 2005 (New York: Programa de las Naciones Unidas para el Desarrollo [UNDP], 2005), 226–27, http://www.idhnicaribe.org/pef/7_capitulo_v.pdf.

23 The court's ruling (*Corte Interamericana de Derechos Humanos, Caso Yátama vs. Nicaragua, Sentencia de 23 de junio de 2005*) is found at http://www.corteidh.org.cr/ seriecpdf/seriec_127_esp.pdf. It enjoins the state of Nicaragua to reform the elections law to specify the procedures whereby the Supreme Electoral Council decides whether party registration requirements have been fulfilled, among other points.

24 Sabrina Quezada, "Discapacitados exigen cumplir sus derechos," *La Prensa* [Managua], 13 January 2005.

25 "Nicaragua," *International Religious Freedom Report* (Washington, D.C.: U.S. Department of State, Bureau of Democracy, Human Rights and Labor, 15 September 2004), 2, http://www.state.gov/g/drl/rls/irf/2004/35548.htm.

26 A notable example occurred in the Arnecom factory in the city of León. See "Auto Parts Workers in Nicaragua Denied their rights & Paid just 41 cents an hour" (New York: National Labor Committee [NLC]/Leon: Arnecom Nicaragua, July 2005), http://www .nlcnet.org/countries/arnecomreportcomplete.pdf.

27 For an example, see Silvia Carrillo and Eloisa Ibarra, "Fiscalía no ve delitos en violencia callejera," *El Nuevo Diario* [Managua], 27 April 2005, 14, http://www.elnuevodiario .com.ni.

28 Idalia Gutiérrez ("Legislar para castigar los delitos sexuales," *El Nuevo Diario* [Managua], 18 October 2005, 1) discusses the lacunae in the code at present.

29 For judicial developments through 2004, see David R. Dye, *Democracy Adrift* (Managua: Prodeni, November 2004), 45–52, http://www.hemisphereinitiatives.org.

30 Booz Allen Hamilton, *Trade and Commercial Law Assessment–Nicaragua* (Washington, D.C.: U.S. Department of State, Agency for International Development [USAID], December 2004), IV–1, http://pdf.dec.org/pdf_docs/PNADE088.pdf.

31 See Dye, "Democracy Adrift," 50–52, for discussion of the *Zamora vs. Montealegre* and *Agroinsa vs. Iniser* cases.

32 Trade and Commercial Law Assessment, (USAID), IV–6.

33 Data supplied by USAID official, 15 November 2005.

34 Author interviews.

35 Luis Felipe Palacios, "Diputados sugieren restar facultades a Bolaños," *La Prensa* [Managua],10 November 2005, 1.

[36] "Table 1A: Investment Climate Indicators" in *World Development Report* (Washington, D.C.: World Bank, 2005), http://www.worldbank.org.

[37] "Las Regiones Autónomas de la Costa Caribe" in *Informe sobre Desarrollo Humano 2005* (UNDP), 255–58.

[38] Trade and Commercial Law Assessment (USAID), II–1.

[39] Ibid, IV–3. Nicaragua's score was 79 versus a regional average of 70. The OECD average was 43.

[40] "Investment Climate Snapshot: Nicaragua" in *Enterprise Surveys* (World Bank, 2003), http://rru.worldbank.org/InvestmentClimate?ExploreEconomies/Snapshot.aspx?economyid=.

[41] For basic background on the 2002 Probity Law see Prodeca, *Perfil del Sistema Nacional de Integridad de Nicaragua* (Berlin: Transparency International [TI], 2003), 29–32, http://www.transparency.org/activities/nat_integ_systems/dnld/sni_nicaragua.pdf.

[42] Eloísa Ibarra, "Secuencia del atraco que estremece a la CSJ," *El Nuevo Diario* [Managua], 31 October 2005, 8-9.

[43] Personal communication, state criminal attorney Iván Lara, Managua, 18 November 2005.

[44] See Dye, *Democracy Adrift,* 45–46.

[45] A leader in this regard is the weekly review *Confidencial,* which has recently published an in-depth investigation of the bidding process involved in a government highway project. See Oliver Bodán, "Guasaule: pruebas de irregularidades," Confidencial, 6–12 November 2005, http://www.confidencial.com.ni.

[46] "El presupuesto: una herramienta para construir ciudadanía, no sólo un tema de economía," *Indice Latinoamericano de Transparencia Presupuestaria,* November 2003, 12–13. An update of this survey for 2005 can be found at http://www.fundar.org.mx/indicetransparencia2005.

[47] Ibid., 20 [Index for 2003]. But the depth and quality of the debate are judged to be low.

[48] *Corruption Perceptions Index* (TI, 2005), http://www.transparency.org/policy_and_research/surveys_indices/cpi/2005.

[49] Although TI's measurements have remained stable, they may well mask contrasting trends in different institutional arenas, with lower scores for judicial system performance offsetting higher scores for the executive branch.

NIGERIA

CAPITAL: Abuja

POPULATION: 131.5 million

GNI PER CAPITA: $350

SCORES	2004	2006
ACCOUNTABILITY AND PUBLIC VOICE:	4.02	3.51
CIVIL LIBERTIES:	4.37	3.34
RULE OF LAW:	3.60	2.90
ANTICORRUPTION AND TRANSPARENCY:	3.00	2.51

(scores are based on a scale of 0 to 7, with 0 representing weakest and 7 representing strongest performance)

Darren Kew

INTRODUCTION

As Nigeria enters the seventh year of its latest effort to build democratic rule, the country remains trapped at the political crossroads, vacillating between democratic consolidation and the slow road to decay and dissolution. With an estimated population of 130 million growing at nearly 3 percent annually, and an oil output of 2.5 million barrels per day increasing to 4 million by the end of the decade, Nigeria should be taking its rightful place as the giant of Africa. Instead, the giant was brought to its knees by 20 years of brutal and corrupt military rule, which left a legacy of executive dominance and political corruption in the hands of Nigeria's so-called godfathers—powerful political bosses sitting atop vast patronage networks who view the government primarily through the lens of their own personal enrichment. Since President Olusegun Obasanjo was elected in 1999, he has undertaken a number of marginal reforms seeking to reverse this situation. At the same time, however, he has increased his personal hold over the ruling Peoples Democratic Party (PDP) and refused or been unable to promote the most important reforms to secure democratic consolidation, such as ensuring the independence and probity of the electoral commission or

Darren Kew is Assistant Professor of Dispute Resolution at the University of Massachusetts, Boston. He is the author of numerous articles on Nigerian political matters and a forthcoming book, *Civil Society, Conflict Resolution, and Building Democracy in Nigeria.*

419

respecting the independence of the legislature through the budgetary process.

Freedom in Nigeria remains protected more by the nation's immense size and massive diversity than by the actions of its government. The lifting of military rule in 1999 opened the public arena to a host of nonstate actors, producing a renaissance in civil society and the media. Labor unions regained their place as the leading public advocate amid an explosion in the number of civic associations and nongovernmental organizations. Journalists, meanwhile, grew increasingly bold in their political coverage, forcing the removal of two Speakers of the House and a Senate president after exposing their corrupt practices. Moreover, with some 250 ethnic groups speaking myriad languages and split evenly across the Muslim-Christian divide, Nigeria's sheer cultural complexity evokes an environment of constantly shifting alliances and ready balances that tend to check the authoritarian inclinations of the country's political elite.

Yet the Nigerian government remains distant from serving the interests of its people. Politics at the federal, state, and local levels of the Nigerian federation are dominated by the powerful mandarins who built vast patronage networks during the military days and who now use political office to expand these networks and their personal fortunes. Moreover, many of these so-called godfathers have been cultivating personal militias to secure their positions, prompting a local arms race in some regions, particularly in the oil-producing Niger Delta.[1] Even though several governors are under indictment for money laundering abroad and others are being investigated at home, the bonanza continues at public coffers for these power holders, while basic public infrastructure in many parts of the country remains as dilapidated as it was under military rule. Electricity, for instance, is available to less than half of the population and is on for as little as two hours per day in some areas, while many major roads are nearly impassable, and health clinics face a severe shortage of trained staff and supplies.[2]

To his credit, President Obasanjo has kept the military loyal under civilian control and has undertaken a number of key macroeconomic reforms—including some privatization and paying down the nation's exorbitant foreign debts—that have fostered moderate gross domestic product (GDP) growth. He has also set up anticorruption machinery at the federal level. Yet the president has been unable or unwilling to attack the heart of the corruption empires of Nigeria's godfathers through the government-controlled oil industry, their monopolization and exploitation of government contracts, or their subversion of the nation's electoral system. Indeed, the president has shown a growing willingness to play their game. He appears inclined to build such a network himself to ensure his tenure beyond his constitutionally limited second term, which ends in 2007. While politicians wrestle endlessly for control, most Nigerians suffer from declining health, poor education, and a lack of employment standards. In fact, the British government has declared that "Nigeria has some of the worst social indicators in the world."[3]

For freedom and democracy to continue to grow in Nigeria, the government will have to make some tough decisions that work against the interests of many of the powerful men who dominate the nation's political landscape. These reforms will become even more difficult as the potentially explosive 2007 elections loom near and virtually impossible if the president's supporters are successful in amending the constitution to extend his time in office, which is likely to require the cooperation and heighten the influence of the godfathers.

ACCOUNTABILITY AND PUBLIC VOICE – 3.51

The bitter fruits of Nigeria's flawed 2003 elections came to harvest throughout 2004 and 2005. The drama of the July 2003 coup in Anambra state, where the governor was arrested by what seem to have been rogue police on behalf of an estranged godfather, continued with a string of stunning revelations regarding the extent of election fraud in 2003. While mediating between the governor and the godfather, President Obasanjo (who has close ties to the godfather) told the media that both men admitted to rigging elections in their state.[4] They were both subsequently suspended from the ruling party, and in 2005, an election tribunal overturned the governor's election. As of late 2005, however, the governor remains in office awaiting an appellate court decision on his case, and the former godfather in question has been readmitted to the ruling party.

A similar drama played out between the governor of Plateau state and his political opponents. Community anger over reportedly rigged elections followed by inflammatory actions and corruption by the governor ignited Muslim-Christian tensions in the state, leading to religious riots in several cities across Nigeria and prompting the president to impose six months of emergency rule in Plateau starting in May 2004.

Worryingly, the president himself appeared to grow less interested in accountability and free elections in 2005. Early in the year he packed the leadership of the ruling party, the PDP, with his supporters, who then ensured that backers of the president's main rival, the vice president, were unable to vote in the PDP party congresses from October to December 2005.[5] This move has ensured that the president's supporters will have a lock on determining who can run in the PDP primaries in late 2006.

Meanwhile, the Independent National Electoral Commission (INEC) shows little interest in addressing its vulnerability to rigging. Despite stating that the outcome of the 2003 elections was primarily the result of "how much money exchanged hands," the new INEC chairman later announced that international monitors will not be permitted for the 2007 elections.[6] He also said that the commission intended to introduce electronic voting, but opposition parties voiced concern that the machinery would be even less transparent and prone to more centralized rigging. In addition, because campaign finance laws are minimal and largely not enforced,[7] the president's supporters will hold an overwhelming advantage as the 2007 elections approach, having both access to state funds and the power of the presidency. INEC also remains chronically underfunded, receiving only 13 percent of its budget appropriation in 2005.[8]

Opposition parties control 8 of the 36 states of the federation, but are too divided to pose much of a challenge to PDP governance. The opposition is generally free to campaign on the pages of newspapers and to some extent in the private televised media, but the government has grown increasingly willing to prevent them from holding rallies in the capital and major cities across the country.[9] In some states and in the rural areas more generally, opposition parties face formal and informal harassment when they organize and campaign. The states of the Niger Delta have proven particularly inhospitable to opposition events; a major opposition figure, Marshall Harry, was assassinated there in 2003. Televised media, especially the public stations, generally carry positive news about the government, although opposing views are occasionally aired. Hostility to opposition within the PDP over 2004 and 2005, however, grew far worse among the factions jostling for control, particularly between those loyal to the president and those connected to the vice president.

Rotation of political offices among Nigeria's ethnic groups and geographic regions has become a firmly entrenched principle of politics. The leading political parties are widely multiethnic, due in part to progressive election laws, and they typically rotate elected offices and party positions among members of their own party across the main regions of the country. Cabinet offices and leadership positions in the National Assembly are also distributed to mirror the 36 states of the federation, and state-level offices are similarly distributed across intrastate divides. Critics of President Obasanjo's purported third-term bid, however, have argued that it would violate the rotation principle and jeopardize the fragile stability that this principle has afforded.

The legislatures and judiciaries at the federal and state levels remain largely beholden to the executives, although important pockets of independence have grown. The National Assembly mounted an impeachment effort in 2004 that fizzled after several months, and both the National Assembly and state assemblies contain a number of members truly dedicated to reform who have launched investigations into a number of allegedly corrupt practices. The Supreme Court for its part has shown a dogged determination to protect its independence and to defend the rule of law in Nigeria.

The key source of the executives' institutional dominance remains their monopoly of public funds. The presidency collects the revenues first (particularly from oil), and even though the National Assembly passes a budget to allocate the funds, the president has refused to release the budgeted amounts every year and instead has released funds as he has seen fit. Governors in turn receive their states' portions of the oil revenues first; they have used this control as leverage against their assemblies and judicial branches. Within this context, the civil service remains troubled by political patronage and advancement by personal loyalties rather than through objective standards of merit, although some state and federal bureaucracies have improved their performances, as has the military in this regard.

Civil society has grown vibrant in recent years, managing to make its voice heard on a number of important issues, such as fuel price hikes, and some minor legislation. The National Assembly has proven increasingly open to civil society involvement. Perhaps the most important civil society–led legislation is the Freedom of Information Act (see "Anticorruption and Transparency"). Politics overall, however, remain dominated by the Big Men, and civil society groups have to continue to clamor for respect and recognition from many government actors. Moreover, President Obasanjo's bid for a third term is prompting many civil society groups to return to organized opposition, a move that will close some of the doors in government that have opened to civil society in recent years.

Nigeria's fabled independent media remain largely vibrant, particularly on the internet, which is awash in competing political visions and investigative journalism. The print media, however, have increasingly fallen prey to bribery, especially as media houses often refuse to pay field reporters under the expectation that they will raise their own funds. Government harassment of journalists, which was largely absent in Obasanjo's first term, has reappeared in the last two years.[10] The State Security Service's (SSS) closing of the *Insider Weekly* magazine and arrest of its production manager in 2004 for releasing several articles critical of the president was particularly telling, in that the issue that prompted the arrival of the SSS and the seizure of 15,000 copies alleged that the president was planning to amend the constitution to allow himself a third term in office.[11] In addition, the Bayelsa Broadcasting Corporation and African Independent Television were both closed for periods of 2005 for televising stories on subjects that were deemed politically sensitive.[12] Many journalists feel increasing pressure for self-censorship.

Recommendations

- Proper checks and balances should be restored to Nigerian democracy by giving the legislatures control of revenue collection, appropriation, and allocation agencies and processes so that the assemblies truly have the power of the purse.
- The independence of the INEC must be assured. This can be achieved in part by giving the INEC direct access to a guaranteed minimum percentage of the federal budget, extending the tenure of the chair to an 8- to 10-year term (subject to impeachment), giving opposition parties significant oversight of the election process, and allowing domestic and international election monitors substantive watchdog roles. State electoral commissions, now often heavily manipulated by local politicians, should be absorbed into INEC.

- The party primary process should be reformed so that candidates must win their nominations through competitive, open elections sanctioned by the INEC, which should monitor and regulate party finances and election expenditures.
- Political opposition and opposition parties should be allowed to organize and hold peaceful public rallies and events without unreasonable government interference or prohibition. Opposition parties should be given formal oversight roles in the legislatures, including substantial voice in the anticorruption oversight committees.
- Government harassment and detention of journalists should stop, and the media houses should be encouraged to institute standards and oversight practices to expunge bribery from Nigerian journalism. Civil society groups should be given the government access and oversight privileges that are expected in a free society.

CIVIL LIBERTIES – 3.34

Use of torture by Nigerian police and security services remains rampant, despite condemnation of these practices from the upper echelons of the government and spirited efforts by civil society groups to alter entrenched patterns.[13] Police and military brutality also remain standard practice, particularly in the militarized Niger Delta region, where peaceful, women-led protests against multinational oil corporations' lack of investment in their communities were met with gunfire on several occasions in 2004 and 2005.[14] Security forces frequently fire indiscriminately when in hot pursuit of suspects. The government occasionally prosecutes unjust police behavior, such as the four police officers who fired at Abuja market traders over nonpayment of bribes in 2005; however, the prominence given to this case by the media underscores the infrequency of such prosecutions.

Ethnic and religious militias, sometimes supported by state actors, also engage in an array of torture and violent practices. State-sponsored enforcers of the Sharia criminal code, known as the Hisbah, are notorious for practicing summary justice that typically involves corporal punishment. Ethnic militias associated with oil smuggling networks are particularly violent and known to murder opponents both within and outside their ranks. The president spearheaded a successful disarmament and amnesty program in the Niger Delta in late 2004, but the program was allowed to lapse and the participating militias had largely rearmed with more modern equipment by late 2005.

Prison conditions across Nigeria remain abysmal. Most inmates do not come to trial for 10 years on average, and police evidence is often poor or fabricated. Policemen are frequently open to hire for a range of noble and ignoble activities, including political skullduggery and criminal gang dealings. Consequently, arrests are often arbitrary and financially motivated, and judicial redress, much less appeals, can often take years unless the individual has powerful political connections. In response to these concerns and to overcrowding in the prisons, the Obasanjo administration announced in January 2006 that it would release 25,000 prisoners, roughly half the entire prison population, who had already served longer terms than they would have received through sentencing had they been brought to trial, or who were too old or sick to be public security concerns.[15] Amnesty International hailed the move as an important step forward, but the structural problems in the justice system remain largely unaddressed.

With regard to women's rights, Nigeria remains a firmly male-dominated society. Only 24 of the 469 members of the National Assembly are women, and women face significant discrimination in the workplace. President Obasanjo has made some effort to reduce this trend by naming an increasing number of women to high-level positions in his government, including four ministerial positions, most notably the powerful position of finance minister. Women's organizations across the country have also increased their political advocacy, winning important legal battles that expand women's protections under the Sharia code, such as the internationally covered case of Amina Lawal, who would have been stoned to death for adultery had she been convicted. At home, however, women face regular brutality; the *New York Times* reported that one-third of Nigerian women surveyed had responded that they have been beaten by their husbands.[16] In addition, women's legal rights to property, particularly land, are denied on occasion.

International news coverage over the last two years of Nigerian prostitute-smuggling rings to Europe has brought increasing attention to the scope of this problem. Most of the women are fooled into thinking that they are joining guestworker or exchange programs and then forced into prostitution once they arrive in Europe. The federal government has declared its intention to eradicate the smuggling rings. State and local authorities, however, have been far less willing to become involved, and the police remain on both sides of the issue.

Ethnic-based discrimination is a perpetual problem in a society as diverse as Nigeria's. Political elites have enshrined ethnic balancing as a political principle, but Nigerians outside the political arena face a more difficult picture. Officially, the constitution condemns ethnic discrimination, but individuals typically derive their citizenship based on the state of origin of their parents or grandparents. Nigerians living outside their home states are, therefore, typically deprived of a range of citizenship privileges, such as running for political office, even if they have lived most of their lives outside their states of origin.

The Nigerian constitution also calls for a principle known as federal character, which is generally applied as ethnic quotas in government hiring. Private companies that do business with the government must also feature ethnically balanced employee profiles in line with federal character standards, and government contracts account for a significant portion of all Nigerian economic activity. Federal character practices have generally led to a more ethnically diverse profile in government hiring and, to some extent, among corporate leadership. Southern Nigerians, however, have historically enjoyed higher income and education levels, and some have complained that federal character has been used primarily to give northerners preference in key positions in business and government; in response, northerners point to southern dominance of the civil service.[17]

Religious freedoms are also a controversial subject in Nigeria. From one perspective, Nigeria allows a level of religious self-determination that is rivaled by few nations of the world, in the sense that each state of the federation is allowed to implement its own religious and traditional legal codes and public policies. Muslim majority states in northern Nigeria have implemented their own interpretations of the Islamic Sharia code and promulgated religious-inspired policies such as banning alcohol, while Christian majority states in the south have passed Christian-inspired policies as well, such as providing public funds for Christian festivals or events. The federal constitution prohibits a state religion, but the federal government provides funds for a range of religious activities such as pilgrimages to Mecca for the Hajj and to Jerusalem for Easter.

The appropriate limits of self-determination of the states, however, are deeply disputed across the federation. The most notable problem has been the case of Christian minorities residing in Muslim-majority states who have argued that they face religious discrimination and persecution. The 12 state governments that have implemented the Sharia criminal code (in addition to the civil code that has been in force since 1979 in most Muslim-majority states) officially claim that most provisions of the code are not applied to Christians, who have recourse to the secular courts, but policies such as alcohol bans have universal effect. Moreover, the Hisbah militias have enforced their interpretations of the Sharia on Christians as well as Muslims, and instances of Hisbah-led violence against Christians in the Sharia states have been reported. Overall, however, rights abuses by the Hisbah appear to have declined since 2003.[18] Muslims living in Christian-majority states have also been targeted for reprisal killings after minor disputes have ignited inter-communal clashes elsewhere in the federation.

Civic associations are generally allowed to form and function freely, and by and large most Nigerians belong to several such groups, including community associations, religious organizations, and a range of trade and professional associations. Trade unions are heavily regulated by the government, but union leaders have been at the forefront of opposition to a number of Obasanjo administration policies, most notably fuel price hikes. In response to union activism, the Obasanjo administration pushed the National Assembly to introduce legislation in 2005 to break up the umbrella union of all Nigerian trade unions, the Nigerian Labour Congress, but the assembly has yet to pass it.

Union and other public demonstrations are generally allowed, but the government has prohibited or blocked them on occasion. Several unionists and opposition figures have been arrested at these protests, including Nobel laureate and opposition leader Wole Soyinka briefly in May 2004.[19] Security forces fired on peaceful protesters on several occasions over the period of this report, as noted in the case of women's movements in the Niger Delta, or in the case of ethnic-interest rallies in the Igbo, Yoruba, or other regions. Most worrisome, however, was the government's de facto admission in 2005 that the machinery for the notorious death squads active under General Sani Abacha in the 1990s has apparently not been dismantled, and that hitmen from these squads—some awaiting trial—have been returned to duty at the Directorate of Military Intelligence and other state security services.[20]

Recommendations

- The federal government should undertake a sweeping reform of the police, the security services, and the prison system; torture in particular should not be tolerated, while perpetrators of torture should be investigated and punished.
- The federal government should investigate the persistence of Abacha-era death squad machinery in the security services, dismantle any that are discovered, and dismiss officers who are known to have taken part in these units.
- Federal and state governments should undertake comprehensive efforts to disarm, demobilize, and reintegrate militias across the country, focusing on those in the Niger Delta in particular, while dismantling the oil-bunkering networks and prosecuting the political kingpins who benefit from them.
- The government should respect the rights of Nigerian unionists to organize, peacefully protest, and strike, and should refrain from dismantling the Nigerian Labour Congress.
- Implementation of constitutional and legal provisions must be improved, especially regarding women's rights.

RULE OF LAW – 2.90

Nigeria's judiciary continues to be vulnerable to compromise through bribery and political influence. Starved of funds and intimidated by the executive for decades, many judges have lost their independence. The national body charged with administering to the judiciary, the National Judicial Council (NJC), has made some efforts to crack down on these practices, and the national bar association continues to be an important critic of and advocate for judicial development. The appointment and promotion processes in particular have seen some improvement through NJC action, and several judges have been dismissed for impropriety. Notably, the NJC suspended the two judges who gave initial legal backing to the Anambra coup (see above), in which a political godfather paid an assistant inspector general of the police to arrest the Anambra governor in an effort to force him to resign.[21]

Yet the Anambra fiasco underscores the fact that only the most high-profile and brazen breaches of the rule of law typically get remedial attention, while the bulk of the system remains deeply susceptible to compromise. Moreover, both the federal and state executives have shown an increasing selectivity in enforcing court judgments over the past two years, as well as a willingness to overstep their constitutional authority. The president set the tone in this regard when, in May 2004, he declared a state of emergency in Plateau state and suspended the governor, deputy governor, and state assembly for six months, placing the state under a military-style sole administrator in the interim. The National Assembly quickly moved to authorize the president's declaration after the fact, but the Nigerian Bar Association argued that these dismissals far exceeded the president's constitutional emergency powers and that the attorney general admitted that they had been made under a defunct 1961 law.[22]

The Supreme Court remains the most trusted judicial body in the federation, after several landmark rulings in the early part of the decade. Because of this trust, however, it has been overburdened with a crush of appeals cases. Thus, the court ruled on the suit brought by the losing candidate for the 2003 presidential election only in July 2005, although part of this delay was attributed to the election tribunals themselves. Supreme Court analysts have also been waiting to see if the four new justices appointed to the court in mid-2005 by President Obasanjo will continue in the path-breaking role of their predecessors.

Under Nigerian law, citizens are presumed innocent until proven guilty, although some Nigerian interpretations of the Sharia criminal code place differential burdens of proof on men and women in certain circumstances. Once an accused person has entered the system, he or she is rarely afforded legal representation. A number of human rights organizations across the country try to offer legal assistance, but they are capable of reaching only a small percentage of the total number of cases in the country. Moreover, persons can remain in detention for more than a decade before coming to trial (see "Civil Liberties").

Presidential control of the military and internal security forces has remained fairly constant over the past several years, but legislative oversight and civilian defense capacity have grown slowly. In the field, the security services remain unpredictable, using deadly force unnecessarily on occasion and harassing the public by demanding bribes at security checkpoints. In a particularly egregious incident of indiscipline, army and police officers leveled their guns at each other over an interpersonal dispute, turning a Lagos neighborhood into a war zone for two days in October 2005.

The Nigerian constitution clearly states that all Nigerians have the right to own property. An important exception is property that sits upon mineral, oil, or gas deposits, which is owned by the federal government.[23] Moreover, the 1978 Land Use Act effectively placed all land under state control, creating a difficult network of government licensing astride traditional communal approaches to land tenure, which together remain in practice across the federation. This arrangement allows the federal and state governments to revoke property rights with relative ease and without engaging in a deliberative legal process. This has been most evident in disputes over control of oil-producing lands, but housing contracts awarded under military regimes or other instances have also been arbitrarily revoked without judicial decisions.[24]

Recommendations
- The president and the National Assembly should work with the NJC and the Supreme Court to undertake a sweeping reform of the Nigerian judicial system. Particular attention should be paid to giving the judiciary direct access to its portion of the budget, with a minimum guaranteed percentage, and control over all logistics necessary for its proper functioning.
- All Nigerians should have access to free legal counsel in the secular, Sharia, and customary courts when they have been accused of criminal offenses. The government should sponsor an extensive public education program, particularly in the rural areas, that alerts Nigerians to their fundamental rights.
- The federal government should undertake a comprehensive review of land ownership in Nigeria and reform the system in a manner that better protects individual property rights and that protects poorer, traditional, and communal landowners.

ANTICORRUPTION AND TRANSPARENCY – 2.51

President Obasanjo has made anticorruption a central priority for his administration. In 2000, he established the Independent and Corrupt Practices Commission (ICPC), which has sweeping powers to investigate and prosecute public corruption. The ICPC, however, has made only a handful of arrests of prominent individuals, primarily in connection with a bribery case involving several state high court justices.[25] Consequently, the president in 2003 created a second anticorruption commission, the Economic and Financial Crimes Commission (EFCC), which was originally tasked with tracking down the many "419" or financial fraud networks and other scams that had become Nigeria's fifth-largest foreign exchange earners by 2004. The EFCC soon gained tremendous credibility with the public, such that it was tasked with a wider array of anticorruption responsibilities. In early 2005, the EFCC even arrested the inspector general of police for stealing public funds and leveled charges against two governors. The education minister and the Senate president were also forced to resign in mid-2005 over corruption allegations—raised by the president himself on national television—although neither individual has so far been prosecuted.

Since 2003, the federal government has been publishing the revenues and budget allocations of the federal, state, and local governments on the internet,[26] which has improved overall transparency in budgetary matters. The president's Due Process Unit also received international recognition of its work to improve the quality and transparency of government contracts issued under capital projects, which account for roughly 15 percent of the total federal budget. In addition, Nigeria signed the Extractive Industries Transparency Initiative (EITI) in 2003, under which the government promised to undertake elaborate auditing and publication of oil revenues over the course of 2005 with civil society and media oversight. This information is to be released in early 2006; Shell—the largest petroleum corporation active in Nigeria—is working with the government through EITI and has been releasing data on its oil earnings and payments to the federal government.[27]

These laudable efforts have begun to chip away at the edges of corruption in Nigeria, but the overall system remains deeply compromised. Federal government contracts are routinely inflated to provide kickbacks for officeholders, and contractors frequently provide substandard or nonexistent services. State- and local-level corruption has been far more brazen. The British government in 2005 accused two Nigerian governors of money laundering, jailing one of them while in London for surgery (yet who somehow managed to escape Britain while on bail). The EFCC investigated both cases and arrested one governor after he was impeached. Details of many of the 36 governors' foreign assets have begun to circulate in the media, including lavish properties in Britain and the United States.

Nigerian media reports allege that powerful politicians own an array of front companies, particularly in the oil industry, that receive preferential treatment in access to buying and selling control of oil prospecting zones and other profitable enterprises. Moreover, roughly 10 percent of Nigeria's oil is being bunkered—stolen from pipes by rogue militias and criminal gangs in the Niger Delta region and resold on the black market. Many observers of Nigerian politics, Human Rights Watch among them, indicate that these bunkering empires have connections to some of the nation's most powerful figures, as well as allies within the military and oil corporations themselves.[28] Such grand corruption filters down throughout the system, such that Nigeria stood as the sixth most corrupt nation in the world on Transparency International's 2005 Corruption Perceptions Index.[29]

Officeholders are required to submit declarations of assets to the Code of Conduct Bureau, but these declarations are not made public. The bureau, which has a wide mandate to probe the ethics of public officers, has been largely dormant. Moreover, public officeholders are not required to retire from their corporate positions, and their businesses regularly contract with the government despite the obvious conflicts of interest. The president himself remains owner of Obasanjo Farms, which has done business with the government and for which he reported $250,000 in monthly earnings in 2004.[30]

Worryingly, some of the gains made in building anticorruption machinery were in danger of politicization by late 2005. The EFCC in particular was showing a disturbing tendency to investigate prominent political figures who were opponents of the president. Other important transparency mechanisms have been restrained. The auditor general's office has been largely quiet since early 2003, when the auditor general was removed after he released a report decrying fiscal irregularities at all three tiers of government. Private accounting practices, for their part, also remain problematic.

A new Freedom of Information Act passed the House in 2004 and is likely to pass the Senate in 2006, which would provide citizens and public advocacy organizations outlets for requesting government documents and information. Whistle-blowers will also gain some protections under the Freedom of Information Act, but at present they enjoy no formal legal cover. Government agencies in general retain a culture of secrecy, and officers are often reluctant to share even mundane information.

Recommendations

- The National Assembly should develop Nigeria's conflict-of-interest laws so that public officeholders must resign all other positions of employment before taking office; the assembly should conduct an independent review of the privatization process to date.
- To assure increased balance and depoliticizing of Nigeria's anti-corruption efforts, the ICPC should be moved to the control of the National Assembly, while the EFCC should endeavor to refocus its activities to its original mandate, perhaps by moving the higher profile political cases to office of the attorney general. The Code of Conduct Bureau should be reformed and should publicize the declarations of assets of all public officers. Independent state-level anticorruption machinery should also be established as required in the original ICPC law.
- The president should expand the Due Process Unit and give it authority to review all procurements under government contracts across the budget. Civil society groups should continue their participation in the unit's review process.
- The office of the auditor general should be moved to report directly to the National Assembly, with an extended term of office and a guaranteed budget to help ensure its independence.
- The Nigerian government should fulfill all its obligations under the EITI in a timely fashion and require that any corporation, foreign or domestic, that does business in the oil and gas industry in Nigeria be a signatory to the EITI.

NOTES

[1] Nicolas Florquin and Eric Berman, eds., *Armed and Aimless: Armed Groups, Guns, and Human Security in the ECOWAS Region* (Geneva: Small Arms Survey, 2005), ch. 1, 328–57.

[2] Nike Sotade, "A Nation in the Grip of Darkness," *The Guardian* (Nigeria), 9 January 2006.

[3] "Nigeria," in *Country Profiles: Africa* (London: Department for International Development (DFID), 4 January 2006), http://www.dfid.gov.uk/countries/africa/nigeria.asp.

[4] "Obasanjo Tackles Ogbeh over State of Nation," *Vanguard* (Nigeria), 19 January 2005.

5 "Disquiet over Proposed PDP Convention," *The Guardian,* 12 September 2005.

6 "Iwu to Tackle Polls Fraud," *The Guardian,* 13 July 2005; "CDD Statement on Expressed Intention to Bar Foreign Monitors from Nigeria's 2007 Elections" (London/Lagos/Abuja: Center for Democracy and Development [CDD], 28 September 2005).

7 Ndubisi Obiorah, ed., *Political Finance and Democracy in Nigeria: Prospects and Strategies for Reform* (Lagos: Heinrich Boll Foundation, January 2004).

8 "2007 Elections Shaky—INEC Boss," *The Tribune* (Nigeria), 7 September 2005.

9 Reuben Abati, "Kano, Plateau, and the Agents of Violence," *The Guardian,* 14 May 2004.

10 See, for instance, incidents reported by the Committee to Protect Journalists (CPJ); "Nigeria" in *Attacks on the Press in 2004* (New York: CPJ, 2005), http://www.cpj.org /regions_06/africa_06/africa_06.html#nigeria.

11 "SSS Defends Raid on Magazine, Rights Group Disagrees," *The Guardian,* 7 September 2004.

12 "The Closure of Bayelsa State," *The Guardian,* 12 December 2005.

13 "Nigeria: Despite Reforms, Police Routinely Practice Torture" (New York: Human Rights Watch [HRW], 27 July 2005.

14 "One feared dead as soldiers quell women's protest in Isoko Local Council of Delta State," *The Guardian,* 18 February 2005.

15 "Nigeria to free half its inmates," BBC Online, 5 January 2006, http://news.bbc.co.uk/2 /hi/africa/4583282.stm.

16 Sharon LaFraniere, "Entrenched Epidemic: Wife-Beatings in Africa," *The New York Times,* 11 August 2005.

17 Jibrin Ibrahim, "Affirmative Action in Nigeria" (London: Overseas Development Institute, Inter-Regional Inequality Facility, 11 July 2005), http://www.odi.org.uk/inter-regional _inequality/papers/Policy%20Brief%2015%20-%20Nigeria.pdf.

18 "Political Shari'a? Human Rights and Islamic Law in Northern Nigeria" (HRW, 4 September 2004), http://www.hrw.org/reports/2004/Nigeria0904.

19 "Court Remands NLC Leaders in Prison," *ThisDay* (Nigeria), 15 October 2003; "Wole Soyinka Detained by Police," BBC Online, 15 May 2004.

20 "News in Brief," Nigeria Today Online, 14 November 2005.

21 "NJC Suspends Nnaji over Order on Ngige," *The Guardian,* 25 March 2004.

22 Nigerian Bar Association, "To Save Democracy," *The Guardian,* 9 June 2004. See also Constitution of Nigeria, Section 305, for president's power to declare a state of emergency.

23 See the Constitution of Nigeria, Section 44 (3).

24 "Rivers Communities Shut Shell Facilities," *The Guardian,* 17 August 2005.

25 "ICPC Arrests Akwa Ibom Chief Judge," *The Guardian,* 21 April 2004.

26 See "Federal Allocation Account" (Lagos: Federal Government of Nigeria, Ministry of Finance, 10 January 2006), http://www.fmf.gov.ng/detail.php?link=faac.

27 "2004 People and the Environment Annual Report" (Lagos: Shell Petroleum Development Company of Nigeria, 27 May 2005), http://www.shell.com/static/nigeria/downloads /about_shell/2004_rpt.pdf.

28 *The Warri Crisis: Fueling the Violence* (HRW, November 2003), http://www.hrw.org/ reports/2003/nigeria1103/5.htm.

29 "Corruption Perceptions Index, 2005" (Berlin: Transparency International, 2005). www.transparency.org.

30 "Obasanjo admits huge farm wealth," BBC News, 24 November 2004, http://news.bbc .co.uk/2/hi/africa/4037633.stm.

PAKISTAN

CAPITAL: Islamabad

POPULATION: 162.4 million

GNI PER CAPITA: $520

SCORES	2004	2006
ACCOUNTABILITY AND PUBLIC VOICE:	1.89	2.15
CIVIL LIBERTIES:	2.57	1.76
RULE OF LAW:	2.03	1.83
ANTICORRUPTION AND TRANSPARENCY:	2.12	2.14

(scores are based on a scale of 0 to 7, with 0 representing weakest and 7 representing strongest performance)

Husain Haqqani

INTRODUCTION

Weak civil society and ineffective political institutions operate in Pakistan under the shadow of a dominant national security establishment. The military has ruled Pakistan, directly or indirectly, for most of the 58 years since the country's independence. Even during periods of supposed constitutional rule, a compliant judiciary and a legislature that has rarely been allowed to function independently have allowed the overpowerful executive to ignore or sidestep fundamental rights.

Pakistan's military and security agencies have managed to retain power and influence over the country's government even during civilian rule. This is best exemplified by the 10 years of democracy, 1988 to 1999, when successive weak and corrupt civilian governments alternated in power while the military and its security arm, Inter-Services Intelligence (ISI), set Pakistan's ideological and international agenda. In October 1999, the civilian government of Prime Minister Nawaz Sharif was overthrown in a military coup led by General Pervez Musharraf. Accusing the preceding civilian governments of corruption and bad governance, General Musharraf declared the creation of "true democracy"[1] as

Husain Haqqani is Director of Boston University's Center for International Relations and author of *Pakistan Between Mosque and Military* (Carnegie Endowment, 2005). He has served as an adviser to former Pakistani prime ministers and as ambassador to Sri Lanka.

his objective. Pakistan's latest military regime has mixed political and economic reforms with expansion of the military's role in government, thereby consolidating Pakistan's status as a semiauthoritarian state.

Through a referendum in April 2002—widely described as massively rigged—General Musharraf extended his presidency by five years. Parliamentary elections, viewed as deeply flawed by human rights organizations and independent observers, were held in October 2002 under a package of constitutional amendments known as the Legal Framework Order (LFO).[2][3] The LFO comprised 29 amendments to the constitution and was introduced by presidential decree. The constitution as amended by the LFO gave the president the power to dismiss the prime minister and dissolve the legislature. It also created a military-dominated National Security Council (NSC) as a constitutional body.

For several months after the convening of parliament, the government failed to secure parliamentary ratification of the LFO. In order to secure parliament's approval of his arbitrary constitutional amendments, General Musharraf had promised to give up his military uniform by December 31, 2004, as part of an agreement to secure support of the religious parties for the LFO. But a few days before that deadline, Musharraf claimed that he was "indispensable"[4] to the country, especially with respect to Pakistan's fight against terrorism and religious extremism. Musharraf extended his dual office as army chief and president by three years, until 2007. Local government elections were held in Pakistan in August 2005 on a purportedly nonparty basis in an effort to create a tier of local officials supporting the ruling party, the Pakistan Muslim League (Q). The (Q) signifies Quaid-e-Azam, the title of Pakistan's founder Muhammad Ali Jinnah, and is used by the pro-Musharraf faction of the PML to distinguish itself from the mainstream of the party headed by former prime minister Nawaz Sharif. Nonparty local elections helped the official party because individuals elected due to tribal and clan factors were coerced into declaring their affiliation with PML (Q) after the fact of their election. Distribution of local patronage and extension of local services was made conditional to elected officials joining the government party.

The Pakistani military regime's cooperation with the United States in the war on terrorism, coupled with successful propaganda against its civilian predecessors, has resulted in limited international criticism of its lack of progress in returning Pakistan to full democracy. Western governments, notably the United States, have been reluctant to criticize the Musharraf regime's record publicly.

ACCOUNTABILITY AND PUBLIC VOICE – 2.15

Pakistan is currently governed by the military, with some civilian participation in government following the parliamentary elections of October 2002. Prior to the elections, the Legal Framework Order (LFO), comprising 29 amendments to the constitution, was promulgated by executive fiat. LFO enhanced the president's powers at the expense of the legislature and changed the constitutional scheme of parliamentary democracy by making the president, as opposed to parliament or the prime minister, the center of executive and legislative authority. The LFO assured General Musharraf a five-year term as president without a contested election as required by the constitution. Article 58(2)(b) to the constitution was restored, giving the president the unilateral authority to dismiss the government and the national and provincial legislative assemblies. The LFO also validated all decisions of General Musharraf and those serving in his military regime without recourse to judicial review.

The right of individuals to stand for elected office in the 2002 parliamentary election and subsequent by-elections for the current parliament has been limited by the requirement that only those with a bachelor's degree could run. Thus, while several career politicians were disqualified, retired military officers and clerics were allowed to run, as graduation from the military academy and Islamic seminaries was equated with a university degree.[5] Criminal convicts, defaulters on bank loans or utility bills, and absconders from court proceedings were also disqualified from elections. Some of these restrictions were arguably aimed at excluding exiled former prime ministers Benazir Bhutto and Nawaz Sharif, as well as several of their loyalists, from the electoral process.[6] The government has moved further with its strategy to marginalize the two former prime ministers and their parties with the holding of local elections.

The military regime considers political parties, especially secular ones, as a direct threat. Thus various means—legal, judicial, administrative—are often employed to discredit them and to bar them from holding office or rallies. Pakistan's political parties have been barred from holding public meetings or rallies since the 1999 coup d'etat.

In addition to limiting opposition parties' ability to reach out to the people, the military regime propped up a splinter group of former Prime Minister Nawaz Sharif's Pakistan Muslim League (PML), known as the Pakistan Muslim League – Quaid-e-Azam (PML-Q). Widely nicknamed the "king's party,"[7] the PML-Q emerged as the single largest party from the restricted elections of 2002 and was able to form the government with the help of smaller parties and a splinter group from former prime minister Benazir Bhutto's Pakistan Peoples Party (PPP). The ISI openly pressured individual legislators to support the king's party, denying them their right to vote their consciences.

On the more positive side, the LFO eliminated separate electorates for religious minorities, thereby enabling them to vote alongside Muslims and paving the way for their full political and civic participation. In addition, seats were reserved in the National Assembly, the lower house of parliament, for both women and religious minorities.

An alliance of Islamic parties, the Muttahida Majlis-e-Amal (MMA), dominated the provincial assembly in the Northwest Frontier Province and has run the provincial government until now. From the day the National Assembly was convened in 2002 the mainstream opposition parties (the PPP and the PML) as well as the MMA demanded the restoration of the constitution and parliament's right to review the LFO. The government's rejection of their demand led to boycotts and disruption of parliamentary proceedings.

The government initiated negotiations with the MMA, but the PPP and PML, now united in the Alliance for Restoration of Democracy (ARD), opted not to negotiate unless persecution of their parties and exiled leaders ends. The ARD also protested against the interference of the ISI in the political process. The proceedings of parliament have, since its inception, been marred by the government's generally ignoring the opposition and the opposition's periodically disrupting the legislature's functions.

There are no effective means for citizens to obtain information about the conduct of government in Pakistan. Legislation by decree or ordinance precludes the possibility of open debate prior to enactment of laws, although groups do selectively comment on government policies in the media. According to Pakistan's minister for parliamentary affairs, the National Assembly held seven sessions during 2005 that were spread over

132 working days, barely fulfilling the 130-day minimum constitutional requirement for the lower house of parliament's meeting days. During this period only nine laws were enacted through parliament, and the bulk of legislation continued to be pursued through presidential ordinances.[8]

Local government elections were held in three phases during 2005 under the Local Government Ordinance 2001, promulgated by General Musharraf. As in the past, local government elections were held on a non-party basis, but candidates openly identified themselves to the voters by party affiliation. By keeping party affiliation unofficial, the government enabled itself to coerce local officials elected with the support of other parties into declaring their affiliation with the official PML-Q after the election. The International Crisis Group declared the local elections "rigged" and asserted that they were designed to "weaken further the mainstream opposition parties and lay the ground for [the military government's] supporters to dominate forthcoming parliamentary elections."[9]

Pakistan's civil service is selected through competitive exams, but recruitment is carried out on the basis of provincial quotas, which does not always ensure equal opportunities on merit for all candidates. In addition, 10 percent of civil service positions continue to be reserved for the military. Currently, the head of the Federal Public Service Commission, which recruits civil servants, is a retired lieutenant general. Retired military officers are included in all provincial public service commissions as well, ensuring the military's institutional influence over the civil services.

The military and security services dominate the governing process with a veneer of constitutional-democratic rule, to the detriment of political parties and civil society. The authority of General Musharraf's government is not based on the will of the people; there is no opportunity for rotation of power, and the military's influence, exercised through the intelligence services, over the political process is quite extensive. This has not changed despite the election of the federal and provincial legislatures and the appointment of civilian prime ministers.

Pakistan has a very vibrant civil society, with around 70,000 nongovernmental organizations (NGOs),[10] a large majority of which are Islamist in nature. However, as the military regime is wary of NGOs, they continue to face legal impediments. Registration is used selectively to influence both NGO work and the areas in which they may operate. The government periodically attempts to interfere in the flow of assistance to NGOs. Another, more subtle, method of control has been the Pakistan Center for Philanthropy—an NGO that is ultimately controlled by the government and has been set up to govern other NGOs. The Edhi foundation, the largest nonprofit relief organization in Pakistan and one that takes positions on social issues independent of the government, received anonymous letters threatening to blow up its office buildings in 2005. Officials, including General Musharraf, periodically accuse NGOs receiving foreign donations of undermining Pakistan's international prestige by highlighting human rights violations.

Article 19 of the Pakistani constitution guarantees freedom of the press, circumscribed partly by several laws. The government has relaxed some of the controls over broadcasting and television since 2002, and private satellite television channels in Urdu operating from outside the country have expanded the choices available to Pakistani households. Pakistan's print media remain diverse and considerably independent. There are around 500 dailies, 1,236 weeklies, 270 fortnightlies, and 2,182 monthlies.[11] The military regime uses different means to control this aspect of freedom, ranging from harsh legislation to curb free expression to the outright ban of publications that are too critical.

A major issue during 2005 was the government's attempt to limit reporting on the Pakistani military's actions in the U.S.-led military effort along Pakistan's border with Afghanistan. According to Reporters Sans Frontieres, "The authorities regularly targeted journalists deemed to be harming the country's interests. Armed forces spokesman Gen. Shaukat Sultan in September accused the Pakistani media of 'selling the national interest in return for a few hundred dollars.' He said a ban on journalists circulating in South Waziristan was justified because some had acted unethically and 'helped the foreign media to discredit Pakistan.' Reporters Without Borders registered more than 25 cases of journalists being arrested, or prevented from circulating freely, or having their equipment confiscated in this area."[12]

The pattern of intimidation of critical journalists by military intelligence services, especially the ISI, also continued. Beginning in November 2004, the deputy editor of the monthly *The Herald,* Amir Mir, was harassed by ISI officials through visits to his home, phone calls, and interception of his e-mail.[13] The government withdrew advertising by state-sector corporations in an effort to punish the conservative newspaper group Nawa-i-Waqt Publications in February and again from the Urdu-language daily *Jinnah* in July. RSF reported that Sarwar Mujahid, the correspondent of the Urdu-language daily *Nawa-i-Waqt* in the eastern Okara district of Punjab province, "was detained for several months for writing about a dispute between tenant farmers and paramilitaries."[14]

There were other instances of direct and indirect pressures on the media. The government exerted considerable pressure in an effort to dissuade the privately owned station ARY Digital TV from covering the return to Pakistan of Shahbaz Sharif, an opposition member and brother of former Prime Minister Nawaz Sharif. When Mr. Sharif arrived at Lahore airport, a CNN producer, Syed Mohsin Naqvi, was arrested and about 10 journalists were manhandled by police.

After the October 8 earthquake, military authorities became particularly sensitive to "negative media coverage of Pakistan's response to the earthquake."[15] General Musharraf expressed displeasure over "excessive criticism" at a press conference in October. In November, Pakistan's government-run electronic media regulatory authority, Pakistan Electronic Media Regulatory Authority (PEMRA), stopped three local partners of the BBC from broadcasting two daily 30-minute special features on the earthquake. PEMRA officials and armed policemen shut down the offices of one of BBC's local radio partners in Karachi, seizing electronic equipment. The government also ordered two satellite television partners to stop running news content from the BBC.

The government's subtle and not so subtle pressures have made the press "less and less inclined to tackle subjects likely to cause irritation such as military corruption," says RSF in its 2005 Annual Report. It goes on to say that a number of journalists in the state and privately owned media cooperate with the authorities in disparaging "such eternal enemies as the Indians, or enemies of the moment such as the foreign press."[16]

Recommendations

- General Musharraf should adhere to his roadmap for democracy and genuinely transfer power to the elected parliament and government. He should set a date for giving up his position as army chief and adhere to it.

- The degree of military intervention, which has disrupted constitutional governance in Pakistan and undermined popular political participation, must be reduced. The ISI's internal wing should not be allowed to interfere in the affairs of political parties or civil society organizations. Clear demarcation of functions between military and civil authorities must be introduced and the encroachment of serving or retired military officials on civil service positions must be phased out.
- The legal and practical restrictions on major political parties should be withdrawn.
- The political parties should reach agreement on a political code of conduct that prevents the winner-take-all politics of the past that has facilitated military intervention.
- The government should introduce laws to protect journalists and punish officials intimidating them or otherwise interfering with the constitutional guarantees of freedom of the press. The Council of Pakistan Newspaper Editors (CPNE) and the All Pakistan Newspapers Society (APNS) should be involved in any new legislation related to the media.

CIVIL LIBERTIES – 1.76

Pakistan's 1973 constitution envisaged a parliamentary democracy, with legal protections for civil liberties and political rights and against arbitrary arrest, detention without trial, and torture. Though articles 16 and 17 of the constitution guarantee freedom of association and of assembly, the misuse of the term "reasonable restriction" or of the need for "national security" have resulted in an overpowerful executive's systemically and routinely violating these constitutional protections. The judiciary is either helpless or, in some cases, complicit in allowing the executive to get its way.

The absence of judicial enforceability of constitutional protections enables the Pakistani state to arrest and detain citizens indefinitely. In August 2004 brothers Zain Afzal and Kashan Afzal, U.S. citizens of Pakistani origin, were abducted from their home in Karachi, kept in illegal detention, tortured by security personnel, and finally released in April 2005.[17] In some cases, opponents and critics of the regime are charged with other offenses, such as corruption or terrorism, and then denied bail. When former prime minister Nawaz Sharif, who is in exile in Saudi Arabia, requested permission to travel to Pakistan to bury his father, the government denied the request.[18] Mr. Sharif's request for issuance of a fresh Pakistani passport in lieu of his expired travel document was similarly not honored for several months. He was finally issued a passport in November 2005 to enable him to seek medical treatment in England.

Pakistan's police and other law enforcement agencies are known to use torture against prisoners, sometimes resulting in death. According to Amnesty International, at least 100 people die in Pakistan from police torture every year.[19] Extrajudicial killings are also widely reported and documented, although precise numbers remain unavailable. Security force personnel continue to torture persons in custody throughout the country. Prison conditions are extremely poor, except those of wealthy or influential prisoners. Overcrowding in prisons is widespread. In a significant ruling and in contravention of international norms, on December 5, 2004, the Lahore High Court struck down the Juvenile Justice System Ordinance, designed to protect the rights of children, on the grounds that it was unconstitutionally vague.

Since the days of the anti-Soviet Mujahideen resistance in Afghanistan, Pakistan has been home to several Islamist militant groups. Pakistani authorities have been known to encourage the militants, especially in their efforts to wage a low-intensity war against India in the disputed territory of Jammu and Kashmir. Some of these groups have also engaged in sectarian terrorism within Pakistan. The government banned five religious militant groups in January 2002, but they reconstituted themselves under new names. Sectarian attacks by members of these groups against Shia Muslims, members of the Ahmadiyya sect, and Christians continued throughout 2005.[20]

The state has generally failed to provide for the free practice of religion by all citizens, despite constitutional and legal guarantees. Members of the Ahmadi sect, which has been designated a non-Muslim minority under the constitution since 1974, continue to face discrimination. Pakistani laws forbid Ahmadis (who consider themselves a sect of Islam) from using Islamic religious symbols or rituals, and they are discriminated against in education and employment. Other religious minorities, such as Hindus, Sikhs, and Christians, do not face such explicit legal restrictions. However, the Blasphemy Law is often used by low-level officials to threaten or persecute these minority religious communities.

Gender equity and minority rights have not improved significantly in the past two years, despite the government's efforts to reform existing laws. Pakistan's constitution prohibits discrimination based on race, religion, caste, residence, or place of birth. However, systemic discrimination endures, as does widespread abuse and violence directed at women and minorities. Given the government's wide-ranging executive power, this reflects a failure and/or unwillingness to enforce the rights of its citizens.

The present government created the National Commission on the Status of Women (NCSW), expanded women's representation in senior government positions, and amended some of the laws considered discriminatory. However, the NCSW has only an advisory role, and its independence is hampered by its being wholly dependent on the government for financial aid. On May 14, 2005, a peaceful rally of men and women, organized by the nongovernmental Human Rights Commission of Pakistan was stopped by the police; participants were arrested and subjected to verbal abuse and beaten in public.[21] On April 3, 900 activists of the Islamist alliance, the Mutahhida Majlis-e-Amal (MMA), armed with batons and firearms, attacked the participants of a race in the town of Gujranwala in which men and women were to run together. The attackers' message was that gender integration was unacceptable and that women should remain excluded from sports events.

In July, religious political parties in the North West Frontier Province (NWFP) barred women from contesting or casting votes in the local government elections. Other political parties agreed to enforce the ban. One woman, Zubaida Begum, was gunned down in August for defying this edict. The NWFP, which had adopted the Sharia Act in 2002 to declare the supremacy of Islamic law in the province, tried to expand Islamization through the Hisba (public morals) bill. This law was aimed at creating a religious police to enforce Islamic morals and preventing indecent behavior in public places. The NWFP legislature passed the bill but, under a presidential reference, the Supreme Court turned down the bill as unconstitutional in August.

One of the most significant sources of legal discrimination and oppression against women is the Hudood Ordinance, a law introduced in 1979 during the Islamization drive under previous military ruler General Zia-ul Haq. It equates rape with consensual sex, demands that rape victims support their charge with four male Muslim witnesses, excludes the testimony of non-Muslim and women witnesses in certain cases, and treats a 10-year-old female child as an adult on the basis of her reaching puberty. Human Rights Watch cited "informed estimates" to suggest that over 200,000 cases under the Hudood laws are under process at various levels in Pakistan's legal system.[22] Although two government-appointed women's commissions have recommended its abolition, most recently in September 2003, the law has not been abolished or changed.

Rape, domestic violence, and honor killings (the practice of killing a female relative for marrying against the will of the family or engaging in premarital or extramarital sex) remain pervasive problems. In 2004, the Human Rights Commission of Pakistan (HRCP) estimated that there were more than 700 cases of rape that year and more than 1,000 cases of kidnapping of women for sexual exploitation.[23] According to Pakistan's Interior Ministry, more than 4,000 honor killings have taken place in the last six years. Proposed legislation on honor killings drafted in consultation with NGOs and the Human Rights Commission of Pakistan was sidelined by the government in favor of a far weaker bill.[24]

The authorities have failed to successfully prosecute an overwhelming majority of the killers involved in honor killings and the practice continues to be widely condoned. Conviction rates for most violent crimes against women remain low, indicating a systemic bias against the victims. The case that attracted most attention during 2005 was that of Mukhtar Mai, who was raped on the orders of a tribal council in retaliation for a supposed misdemeanor by her brother, which later turned out to be false. The attackers were first sentenced to death by the Anti-terrorist Court in August 2002, but in March 2005, five of the six were acquitted on appeal by the Lahore High Court. The victim refused to be intimidated and accepted support from women's rights groups in taking her case to the public. The Supreme Court overturned the High Court judgment two weeks later and ordered a retrial. In doing so, the court was clearly responding to the public outcry and adverse international publicity about the widespread use of rape and gang rape as a weapon against women and as a form of revenge or retaliation to defend family honor in certain parts of Pakistan. Mukhtar Mai was invited to the United States by women's groups but was barred from travel abroad by the government. The result was a major controversy that exposed the government's attitude toward women's rights and highlighted the arbitrary nature of governance in Pakistan. On June 17, General Musharraf acknowledged that he ordered a travel ban on Mukhtar Mai "to protect Pakistan's image abroad." Musharraf said that Mai was being taken to the United States by foreign NGOs "to bad-mouth Pakistan" over the "terrible state" of the nation's women. He said local NGOs are "Westernized fringe elements," which "are as bad as the Islamic extremists."[25]

In an interview with *The Washington Post* in September 2005, General Musharraf said, "You must understand the environment in Pakistan. This has become a money-making concern. A lot of people say if you want to go abroad and get a visa for Canada or citizenship and be a millionaire, get yourself raped."[26] After being widely condemned, Musharraf denied making the statement but the *Post* released the tape-recording of his remarks, which reflected a callous disregard for Pakistani rape victims.

Although Pakistani law forbids trafficking in women and children, the practice continues. The women, mainly from Bangladesh and Burma, are kidnapped or married to agents by parents in their home countries. They are sold to brothel owners or for forced marriage upon arrival in Pakistan. According to the U.S. State Department's Trafficking in Persons Report 2005, "The Government of Pakistan does not fully comply with the minimum standards for the elimination of trafficking; however, it is making significant efforts to do so."[27]

Underage Pakistani children continue to be sold to Gulf Arab sheikdoms for use as camel jockeys. Between April and August, at least 500 Pakistani "camel kids" were rescued from appalling living conditions in the Gulf and brought back home.[28] Corrupt police officials receive commissions and bribes from traffickers in return for ignoring the law. Political authorities have failed consistently to prioritize the prevention of trafficking in women and children among improvements in law enforcement.

Among the amendments passed under the LFO was one that circumscribed freedom of association by allowing the government to proscribe organizations it deems detrimental to public order. Pakistani governments in the past have routinely used the Maintenance of Public Order Ordinance to detain political opponents without trial. This new provision under the LFO has enabled the state to further circumscribe this freedom, which is also hampered by a preexisting ban on student unions and organizations as well as limitations on trade union activity. Periodically the government cracks down on student movements or trade unions to keep them under control.

The government also continues to use the National Accountability Bureau (NAB) and a host of anticorruption and sedition laws in a discriminatory manner against political opponents, who were either jailed or blackmailed into joining the ruling party or desisting from criticizing the military authorities.

On December 21, 2004, the police cracked down violently on PPP activists, who had assembled at the Islamabad airport to welcome Asif Ali Zardari, the husband of former prime minister Benazir Bhutto, on his first visit to Islamabad after he was released on bail in November. He had been imprisoned for eight years on corruption charges without being convicted on any count. Several dozen party members were arrested at the airport, and police beat up the welcoming crowd.

In April 2005, thousands of PPP supporters were again arbitrarily arrested in a countrywide crackdown aimed at preventing them from greeting Mr. Zardari on his return from a trip to Dubai to meet his family. The detainees were released in a phased manner over the next few days, but the crackdown impaired the opposition's ability to mobilize its supporters for peaceful meetings, rallies, or demonstrations.

Recommendations
- The Pakistani government should implement the recommendations of the National Commission on the Status of Women. The government should seek the cooperation of major political parties and women's organizations to repeal the Hudood ordinance.
- The role of security agencies, such as the ISI, in supporting Islamic militant groups should be brought to an end so as to progressively eliminate sectarian and religious militancy.
- Provisions discriminating against minorities, especially the Ahmadis, should be repealed. The government should seek the cooperation of major political parties and women's organizations to amend the blasphemy laws.
- The broad powers of the National Accountability Bureau should be restricted in accordance with the normal penal and criminal procedure codes.

- The ban on student unions and the limitations on political parties and trade unions should be lifted.

RULE OF LAW – 1.83

Pakistan's constitution provides for an independent judiciary; however, in practice, the judiciary is far from independent.[29] Judges are appointed by the executive on recommendations from the Ministry of Law, without any checks or balances. After General Musharraf's military coup in 1999 the judges of the higher judiciary were ordered by the new military government to take fresh oaths of allegiance to the Provisional Constitution Order—the military chief's proclamation suspending the constitution. When the chief justice of the Supreme Court and five other justices refused, they were replaced. The new Supreme Court then provided legal cover to the military takeover on grounds of the doctrine of necessity. The pliant judiciary subsequently rejected all legal challenges to military rule, including those against arbitrary constitutional amendments. The courts have consistently ruled in favor of the government on issues relating to civil liberties and fundamental rights, often ignoring the letter and intent of the law as well as their own prior rulings. In addition, widespread corruption prevails at all levels of the judiciary, which influences criminal and civil proceedings.

Sharia courts established in 1979 continue to exist, but the government has stopped referring cases to them and, in the case of the federal Sharia court, vacancies remained unfilled as of November 2005. However, informal traditional systems of adjudication continue to pose a threat to fundamental human rights. In the tribal areas of NWFP, Baluchistan, and even in parts of Sindh, *jirgas* (tribal councils) decide feuds and impose penalties. In the Pashtun areas the Pathan tribal code is the way of life, with its high premium on maintaining family honor and taking revenge for wrongs (either real or perceived).

In the absence of judicial independence at the highest level, there is little prospect of independence of prosecutors from political direction as they can be appointed and removed from office by the executive at will without protection of tenure by law or by the judiciary. Nor is there any provision, in law or in practice, of state-provided attorneys for citizens charged with serious felonies. In some cases political parties and individuals have been targeted for arrest based on their political affiliation.

In July 2002, the government issued a draconian Contempt of Court Ordinance,[30] which made contempt of court punishable with imprisonment for six months or a fine up to US$1,700, or both. On May 15, 2005, the chief editor of the weekly *Nawa-i-Hurriyat,* Khawar Nawaz Raja, was served a contempt-of-court notice, arrested, and sent to jail pending trial for publishing a story about the corruption of judges in Pakistan-controlled Kashmir.[31] Criticism of the conduct of a judge in parliament has also been declared a punishable offense thus reducing the prospect of parliamentary oversight.

The government has delayed filling several vacancies for judges in the high courts, the Federal Services Tribunal, banking courts, labor courts, and other courts of law, slowing down the administration of justice. In the absence of fully manned courts, the executive branch gains advantage in prioritizing the cases that will be heard. The Human Rights Commission of Pakistan also notes the scarcity of women judges.[31] Pakistan's law enforcement and judicial system suffers from inadequate resources and insufficient training. According to a Pakistani human rights expert, "The investigative capacity of the police is virtually non-existent and the lower-level judiciary simply lacks the training, means, and awareness to adjudicate within the framework of the law."[32] In contrast to the elaborate training facilities available for military officers and civil servants, starting with the initial two years at the military or civil service academy, Pakistan's district judges receive less than a fortnight of orientation.

Despite attempts by the military regime to control lawyers, especially the bar councils, Pakistan's lawyers continue to fight for their independence. In March 2005, the Pakistan Bar Council opposed the government's decision to establish federal courts for settling monetary disputes, calling it an attempt to establish a parallel judiciary. The dispute reflects a growing concern among lawyers about the judiciary's independence.

Concepts such as equal treatment under the law and accountability of security forces and military to civilian authorities are mentioned in Pakistan's constitution but are not, in effect, practiced. Pakistan has used its status as a frontline ally in the "war on terrorism" to openly flout any rules calling for accountability of military and security forces to civilian authorities. Since March 2004, the army has been engaged in an operation in the Federally Administered Tribal Areas (FATA). By terming this an antiterrorism operation, it has not only prevented independent bodies or journalists from covering the operation but also justified the use of draconian methods like collective punishment and economic blockades.[34]

Soon after assuming power, General Musharraf's military regime created army monitoring teams made up of military officers to oversee the functioning of all civilian officials, including law enforcement personnel. The National Accountability Bureau, which prosecutes corruption cases, is headed and largely manned by military officers. Special courts created to deal with terrorism and corruption cases also operate in close cooperation with military authorities. The LFO allows General Musharraf to combine the offices of president and chief of army staff for an indefinite period, thereby entrenching the military's institutional domination of Pakistan's political life. An overly powerful executive, with virtually no check on its authority, is the principal source of abuses in Pakistan.

The state's respect for and enforcement of property rights is also selective. From 2002 onward the Pakistani army has brutally repressed a farmers' movement in the Okara district of Punjab. When tens of thousands of tenant farmers opposed the military's attempt to take over their land, they were subjected to arbitrary detention and torture and their villages were besieged for weeks. The conflict between the army and the farmers continues.[35]

Recommendations

- The executive should not interfere in the working of the judiciary. In addition, an attempt should be made to restore the independence of Pakistan's judiciary, starting with the higher echelons, via appointment of judges of good repute. The process of appointments to the superior judiciary should be made more transparent, possibly involving the Pakistan Bar Council and open hearings before a parliamentary committee. Funding and training for the judiciary should be increased.
- The military's interference with law enforcement and judicial proceedings should be rolled back, along with the abolition of parallel courts and prosecution bodies. There is, for example, no justification for military officers' serving as prosecutors in the NAB nor is there a need for special courts for specific offenses, as is the case with terrorism and corruption-related offenses.
- Security and intelligence services should not be allowed to remain above the law.

- More judges should be appointed to clear the extensive backlog in lower courts.

ANTICORRUPTION AND TRANSPARENCY – 2.14

Corruption persists at almost all levels of government in Pakistan. Protections against conflict of interest are inadequate and even less adequately enforced. Separation of public office from the personal interests of public officeholders is not always maintained. Bribes are common in the higher education system, both for admission and for good grades. General Pervez Musharraf, however, claims credit for introducing "corruption free governance"[36] in view of the government's efforts at eliminating kickbacks and no-bid contracts at higher levels. Prime Minister Shaukat Aziz also believes that though Pakistan was "rated as one of the most corrupt countries" three years ago, today "no one talks about [corruption]."[37]

Although government regulation of the economy has progressively declined over the last several years, lack of transparency in government decision making still provides opportunities for corruption. Corruption is rampant at lower levels, where government officials demand bribes and gratuities for performing even routine functions. Low salaries and minimal compensation for government employees is often a major factor in perpetuating the graft. Pakistan's score in Transparency International's Corruption Perceptions Index for 2005 stood at 2.1 on a scale of 0 (highly corrupt) to 10 (highly clean), the same as that for the previous year.[38]

The recent earthquake has brought all of these factors into view. Most NGOs and experts believe that endemic and systemic corruption in the awarding of contracts for government construction projects was one of the reasons for the large-scale, devastating losses. Around 8,000 schools collapsed in the NWFP and 2,000 in Azad Kashmir, the area of Kashmir controlled by Pakistan.[39]

The NAB spearheads the government's anticorruption drive. It operates under the National Accountability Ordinance of 1999. The ordinance was re-promulgated in September 2002 with some modifications, such that it will remain in force after the election of a new parliament. The NAB has, so far, selectively targeted politicians and civil servants from preceding civilian governments in a politically motivated campaign aimed at discrediting civilian administrators. Judges and military officers and political allies of the government have been virtually exempt from any accountability.

From the beginning of the current military government in 1999 through March 2005, the NAB prosecuted 368 cases of high-level corruption.[40] Of these prosecutions, 173 cases involved politicians and only 13 involved former armed forces personnel, even though serving and retired military officers head several public sector enterprises and hold more than 1,000 positions in the civil service. Pakistani civilians resent the suggestion that only civilians are corrupt and that the large number of military officers serving in lucrative civilian jobs, and often living beyond their means, are untainted by corruption.

The politicized nature of the NAB's prosecutions came to light when in February 2005, Pakistan's Supreme Court refused the government's request to withdraw a corruption case against an incumbent minister. The NAB had filed a case of bank default of 690m rupees ($11m) against the minister, Faisal Saleh Hayat, when he was a member of the opposition PPP. The NAB's request to end the prosecution against Hayat followed his defection from the opposition to the government. The Supreme Court bench hearing the case accused the NAB "of trying to use the Supreme Court for its own purposes."[41] The case reflected the judiciary's frustration with the NAB's selective prosecutions and was a rare attempt by the court to assert independence.

The combination of draconian provisions and the facts that the burden of proof lies with the accused, the jurisdiction of the NAB is unfettered, the president appoints the NAB chairman, and all three chairmen of the NAB since 1999 have been serving army generals has ensured that the accountability process in Pakistan is biased against civilian politicians and civil servants. The NAB claims that its efforts have eliminated high-level corruption, improving transparency in the award of major government contracts and financial dealings. It is true that there have been hardly any reports of massive kickbacks on large projects similar to the widely reported instances of such corruption under civilian rule. But this could well be a reflection of greater control over the flow of information within the military government.

At the time of parliamentary elections in October 2002, the government required all candidates for elective office to file declarations of their assets. Although cabinet members, civil servants, and military officers are required by law to file asset declarations as well, enforcement of these laws has been weak and selective at best; there was no visible improvement during 2005. The *nazim* (mayor) structure set up under the Local Government System 2001 was aimed at reducing corruption by ensuring that the nazims were more accountable to the people. However, corruption is so endemic at the local government level that graft as well as the accountability effort to keep graft in check has delayed the delivery of basic services to the citizens.[42]

Pakistani laws provide for open and competitive bidding in awarding government contracts, but information on government expenditures as well as about governmental decision making are not always public. A Freedom of Information Ordinance was promulgated in September 2002,[43] but it has not significantly improved the availability of government records to the public.

Administration and distribution of foreign assistance through government bodies is not always transparent, particularly as most donors no longer station large numbers of personnel on the ground due to the security situation.

Recommendations

- Pakistan's efforts against corruption are unlikely to bear fruit unless the military and the judiciary are also held accountable.
- Appointment of the NAB's personnel should be subjected to checks and balances and its jurisdiction should be extended to the military and the judiciary. The NAB should not be used for the political purpose of discrediting politicians and civilian administrators.
- Improvements in pay scales for civil servants and judges are necessary to inhibit the environment for corruption.
- The scope of the Freedom of Information Ordinance must be expanded and an enforcement mechanism provided. Secrecy in government should be minimized.

NOTES

1 "I Want a True Democracy," interview with General Pervez Musharraf, *Time* Magazine, 6 December 1999, http://www.time.com/time/asia/magazine/99/1206/pakistan.musharraf.html.

2 "Pakistan: Entire Election Process Deeply Flawed" (New York: Human Rights Watch [HRW], Press Release, 9 October 2002), http://www.hrw.org/press/2002/10/pakistan-bck1009.htm.

3 "Legal Framework Order," Chief Executive's Order of August 21, 2002, *Gazette of Pakistan Extraordinary* (Islamabad, 21 August 2002).

4 Robin Wright and Peter Baker, "Musharraf: Bin Laden's Location is Unknown," *The Washington Post,* 5 December 2004.

5 "The Nazimate of Chakwal," Dawn (Karachi), 30 September 2005, http://www.dawn.com/weekly/ayaz/20050930.htm.

6 Ian Talbot, "General Pervez Musharraf: Savior or Destroyer of Pakistan's Democracy?" *Contemporary South Asia* 11, 3 (2002): 311–28.

7 "Jamaat Accuses Govt. of Backing King's Party," *Dawn,* 8 September 2002; "Pakistan: Entire Election Process Deeply Flawed" (HRW); Susannah Price, "Pakistan's Democracy Test," British Broadcasting Corporation (BBC), 9 October 2003, http://news.bbc.co.uk/2/hi/south_asia/2310527.stm.

8 "NA Passes 18 Bills in Third Parliamentary Year," *Daily Times* (Lahore), 27 November 2005.

9 "Pakistan's Local Polls: Shoring Up Military Rule" (Islamabad/Brussels: International Crisis Group, Update Briefing, 22 November 2005), http://www.crisisgroup.org/library/documents/asia/south_asia/b043_pakistan_s_local_polls_shoring_up_military_rule.pdf.

10 "Freedoms, Association and Assembly in Pakistan," in *FIDH Report, 2005* (Paris: International Federation for Human Rights [FIDH]), 47.

11 Ibid., 37.

12 "Pakistan – Annual Report 2005" (Paris: Reporters San Frontieres [RSF], 2005), http://www.rsf.org/article.php3?id_article=13435.

13 Ibid.

14 Ibid.

15 "Pakistan: Donors Need Accountability on Human Rights" (HRW, 16 November 2005), http://hrw.org/english/docs/2005/11/16/pakist12045.htm.

16 "Pakistan – Annual Report 2005" (RSF).

17 Brad Adams, "The Other Face of the War on Terror," *Dawn,* 2 June 2005.

18 Muhammad Najeeb, "Senate Nod for Musharraf's two offices," *South Asia Monitor,* November 2004, http://www.southasiamonitor.org/pak/2004/nov/1pak1.shtml.

19 "Pakistan" in *AI Report 2005* (London: Amnesty International [AI], 2005), http://web.amnesty.org/report2005/pak-summary-eng.

20 "Sectarian Violence in Pakistan" (New Delhi: Institute for Conflict Mangement, South Asia Terrorism Portal [SATP], 2005), http://www.satp.org/satporgtp/countries/pakistan/database/sect-killing.htm.

21 Ali Dayan Hasan, "Pakistan's moderates are beaten in public," *International Herald Tribune,* 15 June 2005, http://www.iht.com/articles/2005/06/14/news/edhasan.php.

22 "Human Rights Overview, Pakistan" in *World Report 2005* (HRW, 2005), http://hrw.org/english/docs/2004/12/14/pakist9852.htm.

23 "Current Human Rights Information – Women" (Lahore: Human Rights Commission of Pakistan [HRCP], 2005), http://www.hrcp.cjb.net.

24 *World Report 2005* (HRW).

25 "I stopped Mai from going abroad: President," *Daily Times,* 18 June 2005, http://www.dailytimes.com.pk/default.asp?page=story_18-6-2005_pg1_3.

26 "General Musharraf's Lies," *The Washington Post,* 1 October 2005.

27 "Trafficking in Persons Report 2005" (Washington, D.C.: U.S. Department of State, 3 June 2005), http://www.state.gov/g/tip/rls/tiprpt/2005/46614.htm.

28 "HRCP Welcomes Return of Camel Kids" (HRCP, 29 August 2005), http://www.hrcpweb.org/P_releases.cfm#HRCP%20welcomes%20return%20of%20camel%20kids.

29 For background see Paula R. Newberg, *Judging the State: Courts and Constitutional Politics in Pakistan* (New York: Cambridge University Press, 1995).

30 "Contempt of Court Ordinance," Ordinance IV of 2003, *Gazette of Pakistan,* 10 July 2003.

31 *FIDH Report,* 2005 (FIDH), 28.

32 "Increasing regimentation depriving citizens of fundamental rights" (HRCP, 12 September 2005, http://www.hrcp-web.org/P_releases.cfm#Increasing%20regimentation%20depriving%20citizens%20of%20fundamental%20rights.

33 Ali Dayan Hasan, "The Jurisdiction Dilemma," *Dawn,* 21 March 2005, http://hrw.org/english/docs/2005/03/21/pakist10356.htm.

34 "Human Rights Overview, Pakistan" (HRW, 2005), http://hrw.org/english/docs/2004/12/14/pakist9852.htm.

35 "Pakistan, Military torturing farmers in Punjab" in *Human Rights News* (HRW, 21 July 2004), http://hrw.org/english/docs/2004/07/21/pakist9102.htm.

36 Pervez Musharraf, "Pakistan: U.S. Ally at the Crossroads of Central, South and Southwest Asia" (Los Angeles World Affairs Council, speech, 10 January 2003), http://www.lawac.org/speech/pre%20sept%2004%20speeches/musharraf%202003.htm.

37 Shaukat Aziz, interview in Asia Source, 20 April 2004, http://www.asiasource.org/news/special_reports/aziz.cfm.

38 "Corruption Perceptions Index 2005" (London/Berlin: Transparency International, 18 October 2005), http://www.transparency.org/surveys/index.html#cpi.

39 David Montero, "The Pakistan quake," *Christian Science Monitor,* 8 November 2005, http://www.csmonitor.com/2005/1108/p01s03-wosc.htm.

40 "Prosecutions" and "Investigations" figures (Islamabad: National Accountability Bureau [NAB], 2005), http://www.nab.gov.pk.

41 Zaffar Abbas, "Court Blow for Pakistan Minister," BBC News, 22 February 2005, http://news.bbc.co.uk/2/hi/south_asia/4287327.stm.

42 "Corruption hinders uplift: tehsil nazim," *Dawn,* 10 May 2005, http://www.dawn.com/2005/05/10/nat25.htm.

43 "Freedom of Information Ordinance," Ordinance XCVI of 2002, *Gazette of Pakistan,* 26 October 2002.

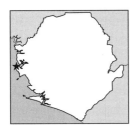

SIERRA LEONE

CAPITAL: Freetown

POPULATION: 5.5 million

GNI PER CAPITA: $150

SCORES	2004	2006
ACCOUNTABILITY AND PUBLIC VOICE:	4.13	4.65
CIVIL LIBERTIES:	3.81	4.15
RULE OF LAW:	3.76	3.78
ANTICORRUPTION AND TRANSPARENCY:	3.01	3.17

(scores are based on a scale of 0 to 7, with 0 representing weakest and 7 representing strongest performance)

William Reno

INTRODUCTION

The record of Sierra Leone's government in providing basic personal security and guaranteeing the predictable operation of state institutions has improved since the end of an 11-year war fought primarily against the Revolutionary United Front (RUF) between 1991 and 2002. Officially the government guarantees a wide range of civil rights; however, a considerable gap remains between legal and administrative frameworks and performance. State agencies suffer from insufficient resources and difficulties of coordination, reflecting a lack of capacity after decades of corruption and mismanagement and the near collapse of the government administration during the war. The government remains heavily dependent on security guarantees associated with a British military training contingent and foreign financial aid to provide even basic services. Societal groups that fought the central government during the war potentially hinder the exercise of state authority in some areas, especially outside the capital.

Sierra Leone's 1991–2002 war followed more than two decades of grievous mismanagement of the economy, and the subordination of government institutions to a deeply corrupt system of rule through the

William Reno is an Associate Professor of Political Science at Northwestern University. He is the author of many publications concerning Sierra Leone, including *Corruption and State Politics in Sierra Leone* and *Warlord Politics and African States*.

manipulation of patronage. Government officials, including past presidents, participated in the illicit mining and smuggling of diamonds. This undermined state capacity to the extent that internal sources of government revenues by 2003 stood at about a third of their peak in the mid-1970s. By 2004, gross domestic product per person was $130, about 40 percent of the 1985 figure.[1]

State officials and foreign aid donors recognize the urgent need for judicial reform. Progress in this sector remains limited, reflecting the state's extremely weak capacity overall. The joint Government of Sierra Leone and United Nations Special Court for Sierra Leone commenced hearing cases in 2004 for those charged with greatest responsibility for human rights violations during the war. The court targets leaders from all sides in the war to demonstrate an intention to promote the rule of law. It is not universally popular, however, as it also prosecutes leaders of armed groups that protected some local communities. Such prosecutions risk aggravating security threats from supporters of those armed groups.

Corruption undermines the legitimacy of government policies. The government created an anticorruption commission in 2000 to address administrative corruption and conflict of interest among officials, but the weakness of the judicial sector and pervasive informal influence of politicians undermines this commission's work. The continuation of illicit diamond mining challenges the authority of the government. The influx of outsiders into mining areas causes members of some communities to defy licensing and tax regulations, although progress has been made in rebuilding government institutions in this area.

Citizens in Sierra Leone elect high state officials in regularly scheduled competitive multiparty elections. The current government, under the leadership of Ahmed Tejan Kabbah of the Sierra Leone People's Party (SLPP), was first elected in 1996 in the country's first competitive multiparty election since 1967. International observers pronounced national elections in 1996 and 2002 to be free and fair, as well as the 2004 local elections. However, in 2004, local officials and traditional authorities were alleged to have interfered in the electoral process in many wards. These and other irregularities were brought before the National Electoral Commission, where most complaints were dismissed.

The country's radio and newspapers partially compensate for the lack of official transparency. Sierra Leone's democratic transition benefits from a political culture that values critique, considerable international engagement and financial resources, and a leadership interested in reform in principle. Nevertheless, formidable obstacles remain, including extremely weak government institutions, poverty, and continuing fears of future insecurity. Solving these problems will require continued significant international engagement to provide security and finance and oversee the implementation of reforms.

Sierra Leone's record of sustaining a relatively nonauthoritarian government is a remarkable achievement in light of the serious nature of human rights abuses during the internal war and the nearly complete collapse of state institutions by the late 1990s. This is due in part to the government's very weak bureaucratic capacity—it cannot organize effective repressive measures—and its extreme dependence on Western military and financial aid to remain in office. Under these conditions, the most democratic and conciliatory elements of Sierra Leone's political culture can exercise important influence. The country's best hope for a democratic future is to consolidate the influence of these domestic forces in an environment of relative political stability. In doing so, it must confront the problem of extreme reliance on donors. Many of the formal legal protections and new government agencies that promote human rights and accountability are heavily dependent on donor funding and personnel to an extent that rivals the efforts of the Sierra Leone government itself.

ACCOUNTABILITY AND PUBLIC VOICE – 4.65

Sierra Leone has a directly elected president and unicameral parliament. The conduct of national elections adheres to constitutional form. The first multiparty national election since the 1978 declaration of a one-party state took place in 1996, in the middle of the war. In national presidential and parliamentary elections on May 14, 2002, 10 parties participated, including the political arm of the RUF. All parties had opportunities to campaign, although many complained that the incumbent SLPP had privileged access to information and that some local officials intimidated opposition party candidates. The incumbent president, Ahmed Tejan Kabbah of the SLPP, was reelected with 70 percent of the popular vote. Many international monitors pronounced the election to be free and fair, although confusion in registration and organization of voting stations was observed.[2]

The 1991 constitution provides for the revival of elected local governments abolished in 1972. Local elections were originally scheduled for 1999 but did not take place until May 2004. The electoral process was highly dependent on donor financial support and UN logistical and technical assistance.[3] A widening gap between revenue-generating capabilities and capacities to meet popular demands for services sparked the reemergence of historic antagonisms over financial resources between newly elected district councils and chieftaincy authorities.[4] Such conflict was a source of serious political instability in local government in the 1950s and 1960s. Paramount chiefs continue to be the most durable (and not popularly elected) basis for local governance.

Campaign finance regulations are weakly enforced. Campaign resources usually come from the personal fortunes of candidates. It is widely believed that many candidates acquire these resources through corrupt means. However, despite the intrusion of these interests, recent elections were conducted without significant interference from particular political parties or armed forces. Some groups with links to wartime militias continue to exercise considerable authority, but the presence of UN and other foreign peacekeepers limits their influence in elections. Conversely, private and group interests intrude into the selection of civil servants, where weak monitoring capacity and low pay encourage corruption. Applicants must occasionally make informal payments to gain civil service positions.

The power of the president overshadows the power of the legislature and courts. This reflects the paucity of resources available to legislative representatives, who work with very little staff support. Furthermore, the tendency of weakly institutionalized parties to focus on personal and factional quarrels undermines the legislature's capacity to exercise a check on executive power.

Sierra Leone possesses a vigorous civic culture, with numerous nongovernmental organizations (NGOs) supporting popular causes. The state protects the rights of this sector to the extent its weak capacity allows, although it is less enthusiastic about allowing civic groups to comment on or influence policy making. Activists complain of the remoteness of some officials and about the slow transmission of government information; the appearance of television and radio talk shows and discussions has brought improvements in communication. Civil society organizations freely collect donations from within Sierra Leone and from abroad. Women, minorities, and people with disabilities are prominent in this sector, reflecting both the failure of the government to take account of their interests in formulating policy, and the support for these groups by foreign NGOs and official aid programs. The post-conflict Truth and Reconciliation Commission's report, released in 2005, repeats many of the recommendations offered by these NGOs, and legitimates the monitoring role that these organizations play.

Sierra Leone's constitution guarantees freedom of expression. The government regulates media through the Independent Media Commission (IMC), created by parliament in 2000. Dynamic media outlets reflect social norms that support free speech. Conditions for journalists greatly improved after the war. Since 1998, when the West African expeditionary force restored the civilian government with British diplomatic and military assistance, media outlets have proliferated. Dozens of newspapers are published, many openly critical of the government. Numerous private radio stations offer a wide array of views and information. The Sierra Leone Broadcasting Service (SLBS) operates a television station in Freetown with considerable civil society input in the production of some shows.[5]

Persecution of journalists has occurred; officials continue to charge critical journalists with libel, low professional standards, and threats to public order.[6] Critical stances of some of the more established newspapers have attracted retaliation by those officials facing criticism. Seditious libel cases are often brought under the 1965 Public Order Act, long a target of criticism from journalists in Sierra Leone and abroad. The IMC banned the daily newspaper *For Di People* for six months in late 2004 in connection with a seditious libel case against its editor, Paul Kamara. Kamara was convicted in October 2004 and sentenced to two years in prison for his publication of a series of articles that provided excerpts of a 1967 corruption investigation into a government agency that the current president helped to oversee. He was released in November 2005 after the Freetown appellate court overturned his conviction. In February 2005, the editor of the satirical newspaper *The Peep* was held in connection with an article concerning official corruption. He was charged with seditious libel but released after three days. In May 2005, criminal charges of seditious libel were brought against the editor and a reporter for *The Trumpet*. Both were released two weeks later.[7]

Harry Yansaneh, acting editor of *For Di People,* alleged in May 2005 that a violent attack on him was ordered by a member of parliament

(MP). A magistrate ordered the arrest of the legislator in connection with the case, but she was later released. Yansaneh died on July 28, 2005, from complications following the beating. It was unclear whether the attack was related to the content of the journalist's reports or to a dispute arising from the MP's efforts to evict *For Di People* and five other newspapers from the offices that they rented from her and her late husband.

Some journalists allegedly accept bribes in return for favorable coverage or for promises to halt investigative reporting. Others are accused of using their newspapers to settle personal scores. Politicians continue to act as shadow proprietors for some newspapers to ensure favorable coverage. Inaccurate or false reports undermine the credibility of the press.

In spite of these problems, the coverage of the 2004 elections demonstrated the considerable value of Sierra Leone's media for enhancing public voice and ensuring accountability. Media provided access for all political parties, including the political leadership of the RUF. In the opinion of several newspaper editors, the reporting of the government-owned SLBS helped promote equal access for political candidates to newspaper coverage.[8] SLBS television and radio gave airtime access to all 10 presidential candidates for the 2002 election on a quota basis to avoid favoring any one candidate.

The country's poverty hampers efforts to improve the quality of media. While many editors adhere to high professional standards, some are school dropouts who have discovered that setting up a newspaper and then selling favorable coverage or blackmailing targets of exposés can provide an alternative to a professional career. Low levels of investigative and editorial capacity reflect poor economic conditions. But the tumult of Sierra Leone's media, particularly newspapers, also reflects a long history of vigorous press participation in political debates stretching back to the earliest days of nationalist ferment. The University of Sierra Leone started a degree course in journalism in 2003, which may lay the foundations for a more professionalized sector.

Recommendations
- Improvements in electoral accountability will require continued focus on local government reforms. This will entail difficult political negotiations with paramount chiefs.

- The government of Sierra Leone should repeal its seditious libel law under the 1965 Public Order Act, as recommended by the Truth and Reconciliation Commission (TRC).
- The government of Sierra Leone should take a minimalist approach to monitoring professional standards of journalists. It should leave this task as much as possible to the SLAJ, whose efforts to establish professional standards will be more successful and less contentious than direct government regulation of the media.

CIVIL LIBERTIES – 4.15

The 1991 Constitution Act provides for freedom of assembly, freedom of movement, freedom of conscience, and equal access for women to political and civil rights. Nonetheless, weak state capacity dilutes official guarantees of civil rights.

Sierra Leone's 1991 constitution prohibits "any form of torture or any punishment or other form of treatment which is inhuman or degrading" (Section III, 21[1]). Torture is a punishable offense. Alleged violations of civil and political rights have been investigated and prosecuted,[9] although the weak capacity of the judicial system (see "Rule of Law") limits the consistency of this practice. No serious allegations of extrajudicial killings of state opponents have appeared since 2000. State agencies generally do not persecute political opponents or peaceful activists as a matter of policy, although individual officials may use prerogatives of their office to pursue critics or rivals for personal interest. Protections against arbitrary arrest and access to legal counsel are rights that exist in law, but poor pay for police and a dearth of legal professionals seriously inhibit state enforcement of these rights. Police are rarely disciplined for abuse of citizens. Citizens do not have means to redress inconsistent enforcement of rights.

Citizens have a constitutional right to written charges within 24 hours of detention, but this is rarely observed. Suspects often suffer long-term detention in very harsh prison conditions. Prolonged detention reflects the inability of the judicial system to process cases promptly and the failure of police and prison authorities to maintain accurate and timely records. Citizens have statutory rights of redress when state authorities violate their rights, and the Special Court for Sierra Leone, hearing cases since 2003, extends the right of redress against officials who violated rights during the 1991–2002 war. However, in practice, citizens' complaints confront incapacity and disorganization in government institutions, regardless of official policy or intent.[10]

It is current state policy to protect citizens from abuse by private and nonstate actors. State capacity to do this is limited by serious logistical and financial constraints, especially outside the capital. Changes in popular perceptions of security since the end of the war in 2002 reflect the presence of UN peacekeepers, the success of the disarmament process, and the restoration of government administration throughout the country; however, the estimate that more than 50 percent of diamond-mining activities in the country remain unlicensed indicates the limits of control in mining areas.[11] In September 2004, over 75 percent of those surveyed across Sierra Leone reported that they felt "safe or very safe," with more than half of those who were adults before the war began reporting that they felt safer than they did before the war. A majority of respondents, however, anticipate that low police and army salaries will translate into threats to personal security after the UN peacekeepers' scheduled departure in December 2005.[12]

Sierra Leone is a party to the African Charter on Human and People's Rights, which guarantees "elimination of every discrimination against women." This right is incorporated in Sierra Leone's constitution (Section III, 19[1]). However, in practice, scarce resources and social custom limit women's access to education, health care, and economic opportunities. Many existing statutes reinforce gender discrimination, including those in customary and family law that are exempt (Section I, 27[4]) from the constitutional guarantee.[13] This exemption extends to the widespread practice of female genital mutilation. Outside of discussion of this problem in capital-based NGOs, government officials have had very little impact on this practice. State policy prohibits trafficking in women. Government officials now participate in the Coordinating Committee on Sexual Exploitation and Abuse, and the Sierra Leone police operate a Family Support Unit. Both efforts are heavily dependent on donor funding and coordination. Some prosecutions for human trafficking have occurred since 2004.

Rural women play a major role in subsistence agriculture, with limited chance for outside employment or education. Women in urban areas have found greater opportunities for political involvement since the end of the war, primarily within the NGO sector in Freetown. Historically, women have participated in government; Constance Cummings-John became Freetown's first woman mayor soon after independence in 1961, and Ella Koblo Gulama distinguished herself as the country's first female cabinet minister in 1962. Today, women find a dearth of opportunities in government. About 10 percent of the more than 1,100 candidates in the May 2004 local elections were women, and women account for 16 percent of the current parliament's members.

Most minorities do not suffer systematic discrimination with regard to the enforcement of rights and freedoms and enjoy full equality before the law, within the serious limits of state capacity to provide it. The only significant exception concerns treatment of ethnic Lebanese residents, many of whom are from families resident in the country for generations. The Sierra Leone Citizenship Act of 1973 limits citizenship to persons who are of "Negro African descent" and whose father or grandfather was born in Sierra Leone.[14] In principle, this means that those of Lebanese descent cannot be citizens, although many individuals have been able to use personal connections and persuasion to procure citizenship. This precarious legal status historically left people of Lebanese descent vulnerable to extortion by corrupt officials wielding threats of deportation, but the civilian government has not enforced this practice since it came to power in 1996.

Freedom of religious observance is constitutionally guaranteed and widely respected in practice. Nonbelievers and adherents of minority religious faiths enjoy official protections. State officials refrain from interfering in the appointment of spiritual leaders. The government does not have requirements for recognizing, registering, or regulating religious groups.

The state has a strong record of adhering to constitutional provisions recognizing every person's right of association. The state respects citizens' rights to form and join trade unions, although police abuses have occurred during strikes as a result of inadequate institutional control of police officers. The state effectively protects the rights of citizen organizations to mobilize and advocate for peaceful purposes insofar as the government is able to control its own agents in a particular territory. Police were able to control rioters in Kenema and Bo in October 2005 without excessive use of force. Citizens are not compelled to belong to any association. Some NGOs complain about registration fees, but there is no evidence of systematic discrimination. Political organizations with ties to the RUF have been allowed to organize and register. Demonstrations in support of opposition candidates for the 2004 elections were tolerated, and authorities have not banned any of several large demonstrations by groups critical of government policies.

Recommendations

- The greatest threats to civil and political rights in Sierra Leone come from unauthorized actions of individual government agents and the lack of coordination of official policy due to continuing weakness of government institutions. Overall strengthening of administrative capacity and oversight are the most basic measures needed to remedy this problem.
- Continued police training and more vigorous prosecution of police abuse of citizens are basic measures necessary to improve the government's record for protecting existing rights.
- Rehabilitation of the country's court system will be necessary to provide citizens with means to redress inconsistent enforcement of rights. This measure will require a mechanism to ensure the country's impoverished majority gains access to these institutions.
- Promotion of gender equality depends on continued development of civil society coordinating and watchdog groups, along with an increased capacity of the administration to implement and courts to enforce existing laws.
- Constitutional provisions that limit citizenship on the basis of ancestry must be modified to address legal vulnerabilities of ethnic Lebanese Sierra Leoneans.

RULE OF LAW – 3.78

The decay of state institutions, economic collapse, and the 1991–2002 war had deeply negative consequences for the security of Sierra Leone citizens and seriously undermined the rule of law in civil and criminal matters. In a nationwide poll conducted in November 2002, 82 percent of respondents reported that they were forced to leave their homes at some point during the war.[15] RUF fighters and renegade elements of the Sierra Leone Army occupied large portions of the country from 1993 to 2001, holding the capital for over eight months in 1997–1998 until a West African force expelled them. During that time, and again during their invasion of Freetown in January 1999, RUF forces systematically targeted judicial institutions and employees.

More than a decade of war left the judiciary and law enforcement institutions in tatters. Although Sierra Leone's legal and judicial sectors benefit from international assistance, concerns remain over the capacity of the government to sustain this progress in the event of a decrease in foreign assistance. Nonetheless, the country's judiciary demonstrates some independence in the administration of justice when it is able to function, such as the reversal of the conviction for Paul Kamara (see "Civil Liberties").

Judges enjoy considerable constitutional protection from governmental interference. A judge can be removed only if incapacitated or found to have engaged in serious misconduct. Since approval of the 1991 constitution, removal can occur only with the authorization of the president on a recommendation from a special tribunal and approval from parliament. Salaries and pensions are paid from the Consolidated Fund, which is staffed with civil servants who are not political appointees, insulating judicial remuneration from direct political interference. Judges are subject to laws and the constitution and do not receive direction from any state official. However, legislative, executive, and other governmental authorities only sporadically comply with judicial rulings.

Judicial appointments reflect professional experience and merit. By law, Supreme Court judges must have practiced or sat on the bench for at least 20 years, court of appeals judges for 15, and high court judges for 10. However, the exigencies of rebuilding judicial institutions after the war have necessitated relaxing some of those requirements. The paucity of state resources means that magistrates receive no training or continuing education.

By April 2005, at least one magistrates' court operated in each of the country's 12 administrative districts. Only five magistrates staffed these courts, leaving local justices of the peace to hear many cases.[16] As more than 80 percent of cases in Sierra Leone are heard in magistrate courts, staff shortages cause serious delays in hearing cases and burden underpaid court officials. Low pay has been identified as a source of corruption in the judiciary. In 2002, Sierra Leone's 15 presiding magistrates earned annual salaries of only $900. High court judges were paid $8,000, and court of appeals judges received only $9,000.[17]

The office of the director of public prosecutions undertakes proceedings against any person charged before all but local courts. Prosecutors are relatively independent of political direction, although this agency suffers the same institutional deficiencies that afflict other branches of the judicial services. The attorney general's office, however, which is fused with duties of the old office of minister of justice, lacks the independence of the public prosecutions office. In high-profile cases, it is conceivable that an attorney general can act as liaison between the judiciary and other branches of government, while simultaneously appearing in court as counsel for the state.

Those charged with criminal offenses are presumed innocent before proven guilty. However, defendants are often held for long periods without charge and are not offered reasonable prospects for bail, reflecting the scarcity of resources and the inability of state agencies to keep records and monitor defendants. In principle, citizens are promised fair hearings in competent, independent, impartial tribunals. However, the public perception is that corruption often determines the outcome of court proceedings. Courts lack adequate translation services to render hearings and documents comprehensible in Krio or other indigenous languages. This situation leaves at least three-quarters of the country's population without judicial services in a language they understand. All of these problems are related to the abysmal conditions of service in the judiciary, its crushing caseload, low pay, and poor physical facilities.

The constitution promises all defendants "access to a legal practitioner or any person of his choice" (Section XVII, 2 [b]). The cost of hiring a lawyer, however, exceeds the means of the vast majority of citizens. The state guarantees provision of independent counsel only to those accused of capital crimes, but the capacity of the government of Sierra Leone to provide legal assistance is practically nonexistent. Instead, civic organizations are the main source of legal aid for those able to receive it at all. In practice, most defendants appear before tribunals without assistance of a lawyer and face court proceedings in a language they do not understand.[18]

Insecurity, poverty, and the consequences of the 1991–2002 war reduce official capacity to afford all citizens in Sierra Leone access to equal treatment under the law without distinction of condition or circumstance. Nonetheless, the extent to which these rights are exercised within the constraints noted above is remarkable. This includes judicial enforcement of property rights, which receives strong backing in law but is subject to constraints of resources and corruption. Rebuilding state institutions and addressing related problems of corruption remain the primary challenges to enforcing legal rights.

In a pattern reflecting the distribution of government authority in Sierra Leone, court decisions carry more weight in the capital. Government agents, especially police, exercise more ad hoc power outside the capital to deal with directives in their own fashion. This is due in part to the absence of resources to publish and communicate court decisions to relevant agencies. It also indicates that the war struck the country's national police force particularly hard. RUF fighters deliberately targeted police officers as part of a campaign to undermine state capacity; during one week of fighting in Freetown in 1999, RUF fighters killed about 250 police officers.[19] The UN Civilian Police program had trained almost 1,800 police recruits by late 2004 out of a force of 8,000 for the entire country. Low pay continued to hamper the recruitment of qualified candidates.[20]

Legal bifurcation is a controversial element of the Sierra Leone judicial system. This practice is part of the UN's and international donors' efforts to decentralize the country's government administration. In practical terms, it means that Sierra Leone's formal legal system coexists with customary legal practices inherited from traditional methods of adjudication. The current arrangement places adjudication under customary law, which affects the majority of the country's citizens, in the hands of court chairmen appointed by unelected local paramount chiefs. These courts are administered under the jurisdiction of the ministry of the interior and not the ministry of justice.

Court chairmen often are not independent of the interests of the paramount chiefs who appoint them. Because officials receive fees from fines that they impose, local complaints that this power is used unfairly are rife. Disputes over fines are widely considered to have been an underlying grievance that motivated some youth to fight against the government as the war spread in the 1990s.[21] The chronic abuse of this authority has figured in every major instance of armed conflict from the 1950s to the present. Yet the government of Sierra Leone and its international donors lack the resources to extend formal legal institutions to all local adjudication. Recognition of these problems of legitimacy remains largely absent from government and UN documents concerning legal and administrative reform.

Customary law is not adequately codified. In instances such as the rights of women in family law, it contradicts official guarantees of human rights. In practice there is scant opportunity for appeal, owing to the poverty of most rural people and the weak capacity of formal legal institutions.

UN reports prior to 2004 expressed concern that the operation of the Special Court for Sierra Leone would provoke unrest among supporters of the leaders of armed groups who were being tried there. These concerns especially focused on indictments of Chief Sam Hinga Norman, former Civil Defense Forces national coordinator and minister of internal affairs, and two associates, all of whom still have considerable numbers of supporters in Sierra Leone's society. To date, no significant incidents have occurred, though UN reports refer to the necessity of providing protection from attack to court employees.[22] The Special Court draws criticism from some government officials and local newspapers for financial aspects of its operation. The court now operates on a budget of $65 million from 2002 to 2005, vastly exceeding the total payroll of the Sierra Leone judiciary.

UN efforts to reinstate the rule of law include support for a Truth and Reconciliation Commission, which heard testimony of wartime victims and perpetrators between April and August 2003. The TRC submitted its final report to President Kabbah in October 2004, and the report has been publicly available since August 2005.[23] The paucity of donor support for the commission contributed to the relatively short duration of hearings. Of an initial budget of $4.5 million, only $2.3 million was received from donors.[24] The TRC heard testimony while the Special Court for Sierra Leone was issuing indictments against suspected war criminals. Some suspected that testimony that they gave to the TRC might be used in the Special Court's proceedings, but this did not occur.

The international community has been slow to recognize the extent to which Sierra Leone's security and rule of law depend on regional developments. As late as 2000, UN Secretary-General Kofi Annan thanked Liberia's president Charles Taylor for helping to release UN peacekeepers taken hostage,[25] despite widespread evidence that Taylor personally aided the groups responsible for the hostage taking. Taylor, who now lives in exile in Nigeria, was indicted before the Special Court on March 7, 2003. UN officials have now developed mechanisms to exchange information between missions in Sierra Leone and Liberia and with officials in Côte d'Ivoire. These include discussions about mutual threats to the rule of law from outside Sierra Leone, particularly the problem of the movement of fighters across international borders from the current conflict in Côte d'Ivoire. In June 2005, for example, UN Secretary-General Kofi Annan pointed out the continued capacity of Charles Taylor to promote insecurity in the region.[26]

Members of the military and police refrain from interference in politics and remain under civilian control. The presence of British military trainers reduces the chance that any coup attempt would succeed.

Recommendations

- Competitive salaries must be provided for court officials, police, and military to attract competent people and to combat corruption.
- The movement of fighters across international borders in the region remains a threat to Sierra Leone. The end of the UN peacekeeping mission in December 2005 requires that the Sierra Leone government devote greater attention to meeting the costs of operations and improving the living conditions of security service members.
- The members of the Special Court continue to require protection, given their prosecution of individuals who still enjoy high standing among some groups in the country's population.
- Bringing Charles Taylor before the Special Court would increase the legitimacy of this body before the Sierra Leone public.
- The bifurcation of the country's legal system must be reformed, despite serious, possibly violent opposition from those who have benefited from the arrangement. It should not be entrenched in current decentralization efforts.

ANTICORRUPTION AND TRANSPARENCY – 3.17

Official corruption lay at the heart of the collapse of state authority and legitimacy in the decades prior to the 1991 start of the war, and it remains pervasive today. Corruption regularly features in citizens' complaints about their government, despite the advent of civilian rule and regular elections. High government officials make frequent pronouncements recognizing the seriousness of the situation, and it is widely acknowledged as a problem in the society, with over 95 percent of the population citing corruption as a major concern.[27] Corruption is also a concern for international donors and businesses and is regarded as a primary obstacle to sustained recovery of an autonomous national authority capable of surviving without massive international aid. Sierra Leone scores 2.4 out of a possible 10 (where 10 indicates no corruption) on Transparency International's 2005 Corruption Perceptions Index.[28]

Corruption in Sierra Leone stems in part from excessive bureaucratic regulations and registration requirements. Low-paid civil servants have a vested interest in maintaining these rules as opportunities to solicit bribes, which remain common.[29] The pervasiveness of corruption hinders state efforts to protect against conflicts of interest; periodic requirements for officials to declare personal assets are ignored. The slow process of divestment of state-owned companies, begun in the early 1990s, has helped mitigate corruption, but the decrepit condition of many of these enterprises hinders the process. Moreover, state officials have a history of involvement in illicit commercial pursuits and therefore have a personal interest in manipulating the application of official regulations and law enforcement.

State enforcement of anticorruption measures is weak, despite institutional remedies. For example, the Anti-Corruption Commission (ACC), created in 2001, is charged with investigating allegations of corruption in government agencies and publishing regular reports of its activities. Its annual summaries do not contain reports of successful prosecutions of wrongdoing. The ACC received 897 reports of official corruption in its first four months of existence.[30] It proceeded with only 22 cases that year, one of which resulted in prosecution. Of 43 cases in 2002, 10 were prosecuted, as were 11 of 43 in 2003.[31] Subsequent annual reports are not yet available. The failure to coordinate the ACC's activities with effective enforcement of asset declaration requirements for public officials hinders prosecution. Strengthening audit capabilities is crucial for the success of the ACC. Almost all quasi-governmental organizations, such as the University of Sierra Leone and state-run companies, go without audits for years, and even decades.

The president appoints the auditor general, who is confirmed by the parliament. The auditor general produces outspoken and critical reports. Her audits, however, suffer due to the failure of ministries to report accounts. Records of previous expenditures are extremely difficult to review, in part because the voucher archive room at the ministry of finance is poorly organized. A current World Bank–sponsored program is attempting to redress this problem.

Sierra Leone's attorney general cites lost files and insufficient evidence as reasons for the failure to prosecute the bulk of cases brought before his office. The attorney general is a political appointee, and it is plausible that concern not to weaken the president's political base may motivate decisions on whether to prosecute cases.[32]

Corruption in the diamond-mining industry is a national problem. UN Security Council Resolution 1306 of September 2000 requires Sierra Leone's government to institute a certification scheme to guarantee the legality of exported stones. As much as 50 percent of the country's diamond mining still occurs clandestinely, with most of the production smuggled out of the country.[33] Under these circumstances, it has the potential to help finance conflict in Sierra Leone and elsewhere. Nonetheless, great progress has been made in regulating this industry. Official diamond exports of $126 million in 2004, versus $10 million in 2000, reflect the growing capacity of the government to manage this important source of economic opportunity and state revenue.[34]

Formal regulations, including restrictions on foreigners entering mining areas and enforcement of anti-smuggling measures, remain weakly implemented.[35] Because politicians based in Freetown have been involved in illicit diamond mining, often in collusion with customs and police officials, investigations of corruption, much less its prosecution, remain bound up in problems of institutional capacity and conflicts of interest among officials. Investigations also confront risks and challenges from armed gangs that benefit from illicit mining, local popular suspicion of central authorities, and the arrival of migrants in mining areas.

Citizens have the right to obtain information about the conduct of government. In terms of transparency, government efforts to provide public access to information are limited. The lack of organization of many offices means that mandated information is not made available to the public. Efforts have been made to put information on internet sites, but some sites do not post more politically sensitive information such as prosecutions for corruption or records of official expenditures. The budget material and details of the budget process that are available are beyond the reach of the great majority of citizens, who are without internet access. The failure of the government to publish comprehensive accounts of expenditures contributes to perceptions of corruption, although for those motivated to visit government offices in Freetown, hard-copy versions of more extensive accounts are occasionally available. Local newspapers are an important vehicle for dissemination of this information, as many journalists reprint material from websites as feature articles. However, often more extensive information is found in World Bank and International Monetary Fund internal documents on Sierra Leone than in official government open-source documents.

Budgets are subject to legislative review, but actual expenditures, especially cost overruns, receive cursory legislative attention. This may be because individual legislators occasionally derive personal benefit from these practices. The country's news media publish regular accounts of insider influence in the awarding of government contracts. Foreign assistance provides vital support to administrative functions, and foreign experts play an important role in monitoring and assisting in the distribution of aid.

The office of ombudsman was created in April 2000 to work closely with the ACC and assist in handling citizen complaints and petitions to government. However, the ombudsman's powers are not judicial and at present are more oriented to acknowledging inquiries than to addressing them.

Recommendations
- The prosecutorial weakness of the attorney general's office with respect to corruption is related to the general weakness and understaffing of the country's judiciary, and will have to be addressed in the context of overall reform of that governmental sector.
- The government must provide greater political support for oversight and investigative agencies.
- The government needs to provide better information to the public about its programs.

NOTES

[1] *Sierra Leone: Selected Issues and Statistical Appendix,* (Washington, D.C.: International Monetary Fund, 29 October 2004), 3, 13.

[2] *Observing the 2002 Sierra Leone Elections: Final Report* (Atlanta: Carter Center, May 2003).

[3] *Twenty-second Report of the Secretary-General on the United Nations Mission in Sierra Leone* (New York: UN Security Council, 6 July 2004), para. 12.

[4] Author's discussions with local government informants in the Kenema area, July 2005.

[5] Center for Media, Education and Technology (Freetown, 2004), http://www.cmetfree town.org.

[6] *Sierra Leone: 2004 Annual Report* (Paris: Reporters without Borders, 2005), http://www.rsf.org/country-36.php3?id_mot=521&Valider=OK.

[7] *Cases 2005: Sierra Leone* (New York: Committee to Protect Journalists, 2005), http://www.cpj.org/cases05/africa_cases05/sierra.html.

[8] Personal communication.

[9] *Twenty-sixth Report of the Secretary-General on the United Nations Mission in Sierra Leone* (New York: UN Security Council, 20 September 2005), para. 28.

[10] Personal communications and author's observations in Sierra Leone.

[11] *Twenty-seventh Report of the Secretary-General on the United Nations Mission in Sierra Leone* (New York: 12 December 2005), para. 37.

[12] *People's Perceptions of UNAMSIL Withdrawal in Sierra Leone* (Freetown: Post-Conflict Reintegration Initiatives for Development and Empowerment [PRIDE], with support from Military Observers/UNAMSIL and United Nations Development Programme [UNDP], March 2005), 21–23, 32.

[13] *Unequal Rights: Discriminatory Laws against Women in Sierra Leone* (Freetown: Lawyers Centre for Legal Assistance, 2005).

[14] *Sierra Leone Citizenship Act 1973,* http://www.unhcr.ch/cgi-bin/texis/vtx/rsd/rsddocview .html?tbl=RSDLEGAL&id=3ae6b50610.

[15] Campaign for Good Governance (Freetown) poll conducted November 2002, results in possession of the author.

[16] *Twenty-fifth Report of the Secretary-General on the United Nations Mission in Sierra Leone* (New York: UN Security Council, 26 April 2005), para. 20.

[17] Minneh Kane et al., *Sierra Leone: Legal and Judicial Sector Assessment* (Washington, D.C.: World Bank Legal Vice Presidency, May 2004), 13.

[18] Personal communication, Freetown, July 2005.

[19] *In Pursuit of Justice: A Report on the Judiciary in Sierra Leone* (Freetown: Commonwealth Human Rights Initiative, 2002), 28.

[20] *Liberia and Sierra Leone: Rebuilding Failed States* (Brussels: International Crisis Group, 8 Dec. 2004), 17.

[21] *No Rights, No Justice, More War* (Freetown: CARE draft document, June 2004) and the research of Paul Richards and Steve Archibald.

[22] *Twenty-fifth Report,* para. 45.

[23] *The Final Report of the Truth and Reconciliation Commission of Sierra Leone,* http:// www.trcsierraleone.org/drwebsite/publish/index.shtml.

[24] *Eighteenth Report of the Secretary-General on the United Nations Mission in Sierra Leone* (New York: UN Security Council, 23 June 2003), para. 47.

[25] *Fourth Report of the Secretary-General on the United Nations Mission in Sierra Leone* (New York: UN Security Council, 19 May 2000), para 67.

[26] *Report of the Secretary-General Pursuant to Security Council Resolution 1579 (2004) Regarding Liberia* (New York: Security Council, 7 June 2005), para. 39.

[27] *National Anti-Corruption Strategy* (Freetown: National Anti-Corruption Strategy Secretariat, February 2005), 13.

[28] *Corruption Perceptions Index,* 2005 (Berlin: Transparency International, 2005), http:// www.transparency.org/cpi/2005/cpi2005_infocus.html#cpi.

[29] The author observed numerous efforts of traffic police to collect bribes.

[30] *Sierra Leone: Diagnostic Study of the Investment Climate and Investment Code* (Washington, D.C.: Foreign Investment Advisory Service [International Finance Corporation and The World Bank], May 2004), 13.

[31] *Analysis of Annual Report* (Freetown: Anti-Corruption Commission, 2001, 2002, 2003).

[32] *National Anti-Corruption Strategy,* 25.

[33] *Twenty-fifth Report,* para. 25.

[34] *Diamond Industry Annual Review: Sierra Leone 2005* (Ottawa: Partnership Africa Canada, February 2005), 6.

[35] Personal observations during visit in July 2005.

SOUTH AFRICA

CAPITAL: Pretoria

POPULATION: 46.9 million

GNI PER CAPITA: $2750

SCORES	2004	2006
ACCOUNTABILITY AND PUBLIC VOICE:	N/A	5.06
CIVIL LIBERTIES:	N/A	4.98
RULE OF LAW:	N/A	4.44
ANTICORRUPTION AND TRANSPARENCY:	N/A	3.91

(scores are based on a scale of 0 to 7, with 0 representing weakest and 7 representing strongest performance)

Mark Yaron Rosenberg

INTRODUCTION

South Africa celebrated its first decade of universal democracy in 2004, an achievement punctuated by the holding in April of the country's third free and fair general election. That election demonstrated the continuing political dominance of the African National Congress (ANC), popularly considered to be the major force behind the transition to nonracial democratic rule and the party of South Africa's most revered public figure, former president Nelson Mandela. The ANC won just under 70 percent of the national vote, securing a governing majority in parliament and the reelection of President Thabo Mbeki, who succeeded Mandela in 1999.

In 1910, the Union of South Africa—including the British colonies of the Cape and Natal and the two Afrikaner republics, Transvaal and Orange Free State—was created as a self-governing dominion of the British Empire. All political and most civil rights were limited to South Africa's minority white population; the majority black population, as well as the colored (mixed-race) and Asian (primarily Indian) minorities, were effectively disenfranchised. In 1948, the Afrikaner-dominated National Party (NP) came to power on a platform of comprehensive,

Mark Yaron Rosenberg is researcher at Freedom House and assistant editor of *Freedom in the World*. He serves as the Southern Africa analyst for *Freedom in the World* and *Freedom of the Press*.

institutionalized racial separation, or "apartheid." Partly as a result, South
Africa declared formal independence in 1961 and withdrew from the
British Commonwealth. The NP governed South Africa under the
apartheid system—a new constitution promulgated in 1984 granted
only limited political power to coloreds and Asians—until the first nonracial general elections in 1994. Four years earlier, mounting domestic
and international pressure prompted then-president F. W. de Klerk to
legalize the previously banned ANC and Pan-African Congress and
release ANC leader Nelson Mandela from prison. The intervening years
saw almost all apartheid-related legislation abolished and an interim,
democratic constitution negotiated and enacted.

The April 1994 elections—judged free and fair by international observers despite significant political violence—resulted in a landslide victory for the ANC and the election of Nelson Mandela as president. As
required by the interim constitution, a national unity government was
formed, including the ANC, the NP, and the Zulu-nationalist Inkatha
Freedom Party (IFP). Negotiations within a Constitutional Assembly
produced a permanent constitution that was signed into law by Mandela
in December 1996. In 1999, general elections saw the ANC claim
almost two-thirds of the national vote; Thabo Mbeki, Mandela's successor as head of the ANC, won the presidency.

The ANC's rise to power has been accompanied by increasing tensions within the party's governing alliance—including the South African
Communist Party (SACP) and the Congress of South African Trade
Unions (COSATU)—as well as with independent media, opposition
parties, traditional leaders, and the white minority. Vociferous debates
surround the government's approach to poverty, economic inequality,
land reform and housing, basic service delivery, corruption, the ongoing
crisis in Zimbabwe, and HIV/AIDS. The last of these issues is particularly crucial, as an estimated 6 million South Africans are infected with
HIV/ AIDS, making South Africa home to the world's largest such population. Mbeki's government, arguing that the HIV virus does not necessarily cause AIDS, has resisted making antiretroviral drugs available to
the public health system. In 2003, the government yielded to substantial
international and domestic pressure to provide universal antiretroviral
drug treatment, a process that began in 2004. Shortly thereafter, however, Mbeki reappointed controversial health minister Manto Tshanalala-
Msimang, who has publicly recommended traditional remedies such as

garlic, lemon, olive oil, and beetroot as superior to antiretrovirals in combating HIV/AIDS.

ACCOUNTABILITY AND PUBLIC VOICE – 5.06

South Africa has emerged from decades of minority racialist rule as a parliamentary democracy under the 1996 Constitution of the Republic of South Africa. National authority is shared by the executive and parliament and checked by an independent judiciary; executive and legislative powers also exist on the provincial and local levels. Extensive political rights are guaranteed by the constitution, which provides for universal adult suffrage,[1] a national common voters' roll, regular elections contested by multiple parties and determined by a proportionally representative system, and the establishment of an Independent Electoral Commission (IEC) and an Electoral Court. In addition, a constitutionally incorporated Bill of Rights assures South African citizens of the rights to form and campaign for a political party and stand for public office.

National general elections held on April 14, 2004, demonstrated the practical fortitude of the South African electoral system, as well as its overwhelming domination by the ruling ANC. Despite concerns about voter apathy, 76.7 percent of almost 21 million registered voters turned out to cast ballots on behalf of 39 political parties. The contest saw the ANC garner 69.7 percent of the vote, the party's largest majority since coming to power, leading to the unanimous reelection of ANC party leader Thabo Mbeki as president and head of state by the National Assembly (NA). The ANC also secured outright majorities in seven of the nine South African provincial legislatures. The liberal (and primarily white-based) Democratic Alliance (DA) won 12.4 percent of the vote (50 seats in the NA), while the IFP won almost 7 percent (28 seats). Several small opposition parties captured the remaining votes.[2]

The polling was declared free and fair and reflective of the people's will by more than 218 observers from 14 international observer groups and some 4,000 domestic observers representing 101 civil society organizations.[3] Overall, the election was conducted in a peaceful, efficient, and orderly manner; however, minor problems were reported, including the use of insufficiently distinct national and provincial ballots and ballot boxes, inconsistency in the layout of polling stations, and the lack of monitors at some polling stations. Citing a list of 46 incidents of election irregularities it reported to the electoral commission—including an inaccurate voters' roll and minor instances of intimidation—the IFP challenged the election results for KwaZulu-Natal at the Electoral Court;[4] the challenge was later withdrawn.

During the campaign period preceding the elections, the IEC successfully conducted two voter registration drives and a voter education campaign, all of which included substantial participation by political parties, civil society, and the media. Widespread concerns about political violence during the preelection campaign period—focused primarily on potential clashes between ANC and IFP supporters in KwaZulu-Natal—proved mostly unfounded. Nevertheless, several people were killed as a result of campaign violence, and rallies led by Mbeki and DA leader Tony Leon were both marred by acts of violence and intimidation. Allegations of pro-ANC bias at the state-owned South African Broadcasting Corporation (SABC) gathered steam after it broadcast live Mbeki's speech launching the ANC's reelection campaign; the SABC denied similar coverage to opposition parties.

These opposition parties, while stringent critics of the government and the ANC, have not been able to pose a significant challenge to the ruling party since 1994. The lackluster performance in the 2004 elections of a preelection alliance between the two major (but ideologically distinct) opposition parties—the DA and the IFP—spoke to the lack of a realistic political alternative in South Africa. The New National Party (NNP), descendant of the NP that created and ruled the South African apartheid state, has seen its share of the national vote shrink by 90 percent in 10 years; allied with the ANC in the April 2004 elections, the NNP announced in August it was officially merging with the ANC and disbanded in April 2005. The strength of opposition politics is further diluted—and the dominant status of the ANC further entrenched—by the country's proportionally representative national electoral system and wide allowances for legislative floor crossing.[5]

While public funding of political parties through the Represented Political Parties' Fund is governed by the IEC, private contributions to political parties are completely unregulated. This system has elicited criticism from both elected officials and civil society as a major source of political corruption. In 2003, the Institute for Democracy in South Africa (Idasa) embarked on litigation to require all 13 parties represented in the NA to reveal the identities, amounts given, and dates of donations of all private donors since 1994. Although the Cape High Court noted that Idasa had "made out a compelling case," that court dismissed Idasa's application in April 2005;[6] during the trial, the ANC (and other parties) expressed cautious support for new legislation to regulate private donations.

South Africa's constitution mandates a robust system of checks and balances among the executive, legislative, and judicial branches of government. Executive power is held by a legislatively elected president, who serves as head of state; the president's appointed cabinet consists of the deputy president and ministers and deputy ministers for 27 ministries. The national legislature, including the NA and the 90-seat National Council of Provinces (NCOP),[7] has significant oversight and approval powers vis-à-vis the executive. Every executive or legislative act, in turn, is subject to review and scrutiny by the judiciary, headed by the Constitutional Court and the Supreme Court of Appeals.

In practice, the ANC's overwhelming control of the executive and the legislature (at both national and provincial levels) has undermined the efficacy of South Africa's accountability mechanisms. Parliamentary committees charged with overseeing executive ministries are often led by ANC loyalists and have been accused of approving executive decisions without sufficient debate. NA deputy speaker and ANC member Gwen Mahlangu has publicly derided her fellow legislators for sounding like *imbongis* (praise singers) for the government by speaking from texts prepared by executive departments for whose oversight members of parliament are responsible.[8] The ongoing corruption scandal over the 1999–2000 Strategic Defense Procurement Package (also known as the "arms deal," see "Anticorruption and Transparency") is the most notable failure of parliament's oversight function and at least partially the result of political pressure. The judiciary has demonstrated significant independence in hearing constitutional challenges to executive and legislative acts and in prosecuting abuses of power; nevertheless, political influence, a lack of resources, and the lack of an effective oversight mechanism for judicial conduct and ethics compromise this independence.

The Public Service Act (PSA) provides for a civil service in which posts must be filled on the basis of "equality and other democratic values and principles enshrined in the Constitution."[9] However, merit and open competition are often subordinated to political affiliation and nepotism, as well as to both explicit and implicit quotas based on race, gender, and disability.[10] The professionalism of the civil service varies widely by province, with the administration of the Eastern Cape considered the most problematic.

Thousands of civic groups and nongovernmental organizations (NGOs) operate freely throughout South Africa, including a vibrant and politically active trade union movement led by COSATU. A recent study found that most of these civil society organizations deal with democracy-related issues, transparency and governance, land reform, and housing.[11] Civil society organizations regularly testify before and submit presentations to legislative committees regarding pending legislation. While their close relationships with the ANC (stemming from the anti-apartheid movement) have discouraged many civil society organizations from pursuing public advocacy campaigns aimed at affecting legislation, this dynamic is changing. For example, the Treatment Action Campaign (TAC) has successfully pressured the government, through both the use and the threat of legal action, to reverse executive policy and begin distributing free antiretroviral drugs to HIV/AIDS patients in public hospitals in 2004. In 2005, COSATU—a governing ally of the ANC— organized the Western Province Coalition for Jobs and Against Poverty, an alliance of more than 70 religious and civic groups aimed at challenging the Mbeki administration's liberal economic development policies.[12]

Freedom of expression and the press, protected in the constitution, is generally respected. Nevertheless, several apartheid-era laws remain in effect that permit authorities to restrict the publication of information about the police, national defense forces, prisons, and mental institutions and to compel journalists to reveal sources. In November 2004, the parliament passed the controversial Law on Antiterrorism, which had been vigorously opposed by press freedom advocacy organizations and other elements of civil society. While this opposition forced the government to shelve the legislation earlier in the year, it reintroduced the law after its resounding victory in the April 2004 general election.

A number of private newspapers and magazines are sharply critical of the government; in particular, the *Mail & Guardian* and the *Sunday Times* have aggressively pursued reports about government corruption and other abuses of power. Elements within the ANC—including President Mbeki—have become increasingly sensitive to media criticism and investigations of corruption. Journalists who report on these issues have been accused of racism and have reportedly been blacklisted by the ruling party, leading to significant self-censorship. In 2005, the *Mail & Guardian* was issued a gag order and made to turn over documents related to its coverage of the ANC-related "Oilgate" corruption scandal. The SABC controls a majority of radio outlets, the medium by which most South Africans receive the news; the state broadcaster also dominates the television market. While editorially independent from the government, the SABC has come under increasing fire for displaying a pro-ANC bias and for practicing self-censorship; such criticism increased after former government spokesman Snuki Zikalala was appointed head of news. In addition, independent community radio stations feel pressure from ANC officials to produce positive coverage at the risk of licensing and advertising sanctions.[13] While journalists are rarely arrested or detained by state authorities, they continue to be subject to pressure—including instances of threats and harassment—from both state and nonstate actors. South Africans enjoy unhindered access to the internet, and there are no restrictions on setting up internet-based media.

Recommendations

- Given the ANC's dominant-party status, at least a portion of national legislators should be chosen on a constituency basis and not by proportional representation.
- Legislation mandating transparency in private contributions to political parties should be pursued, including the required disclosure of the source and amount of political contributions.
- A member of an opposition party that is not in coalition with the ANC should be selected to head parliamentary committees charged with overseeing executive actions.
- Steps should be taken to increase the independence of the SABC, including the appointment of a more independent head of news and prominent members of opposition political parties to the board of the SABC.

CIVIL LIBERTIES – 4.98

The constitution and the Bill of Rights provide South Africans with a comprehensive set of civil liberties that are generally enjoyed in practice.

Nonderogable rights included in the Bill of Rights are: equality, human dignity, life, freedom from torture and inhuman and cruel treatment, freedom from slavery and servitude, freedom from child abuse, and a series of procedural rights for arrested, detained, and accused persons.

The South Africa Police Service (SAPS) is under the civilian control of the Department of Safety and Security, and is primarily responsible for maintaining internal security and law and order. South Africans may report alleged rights violations by the SAPS to the Independent Complaints Directorate (ICD); between April 2004 and March 2005, the ICD received 5,790 complaints.[14] Citing resource constraints, the ICD fully investigated 63 percent of death cases (by police action or in police custody), 41 percent of criminal cases, and 44 percent of misconduct cases. Police remain badly underpaid, and corruption in the SAPS is a significant problem. Public confidence in the police forces to effectively combat South Africa's high rates of violent and petty crime is very low; partly as a result, private security forces outnumber police by a 5-to-1 ratio.[15]

Despite constitutional prohibitions, there were reports of torture and the use of excessive force by SAPS members during interrogation, arrest, and detention. In 2004, three activists of the Landless People's Movement were assaulted and subjected to torture after being arrested at an election-day demonstration. ICD investigators recommended charges of assault and intimidation be brought against a police superintendent; the trial began in April 2005.

Prison conditions in South Africa often do not meet domestic or international standards. According to the Department of Correctional Services, the country's 243 prisons suffer from an overcrowding rate of almost 136 percent,[16] a problem that will most likely be exacerbated by the April 2005 extension of mandatory sentencing laws passed by parliament.[17] There were reports of prisoners being physically and sexually abused by both fellow prisoners and prison employees, and corruption among prison guards is a problem. Over 40 percent of inmates are infected with HIV, and health services, while improving, are inadequate. Excessive pretrial detention and negligent conditions for pretrial detainees were cited by a UN Working Group in 2005 as major shortcomings of the South African penal system; while most prisoners wait an average of three months before trial, some must wait up to two years.

Gender equity is provided for in the constitution, which prohibits both state and private discrimination on the basis of "gender, sex, pregnancy [or] marital status"[18] and imbues the state with a positive duty to prevent discrimination via national legislation—a duty that has been confirmed by the Constitutional Court. While the constitution allows the option and practice of customary law, it—along with the Recognition of Customary Marriages Act of 1998—does not allow such law to supercede the constitutional rights assured to women as South African citizens. Nevertheless, women suffer de facto discrimination with regard to marriage, divorce, inheritance, and proprietary rights.[19] Women are also subject to sexual harassment and wage discrimination in the workplace and are not well represented in top management positions. Women hold 131 seats in the NA and head 12 (of 28) ministries and four provinces; in June 2005, Mbeki appointed Minerals and Energy Minister Phumzile Mlambo-Ngcuka as deputy president.

Domestic violence and rape, both criminal offenses, are serious problems: South Africa has one of the world's highest rates of sexual abuse.[20] The country's high rate of HIV infection makes incidents of rape particularly worrisome; a traditional belief that HIV can be cured by sexual intercourse with a female virgin has contributed to a rash of child rapes. Despite the government's operation of women's shelters and sexual offense courts, reporting and investigation of these crimes are hampered by a lack of resources and societal attitudes.

As of October 2005, no law specifically prohibits trafficking in women (or any person), and South Africa serves as a destination, source, and transit point for trafficked women. However, the government prosecuted traffickers—mostly in sexual offense courts—under a number of existing laws and cooperated with NGOs engaged in the issue.

As with gender discrimination, the constitution prohibits discrimination based on "race . . . ethnic or social origin, colour, sexual orientation,[21] age, disability . . . and birth."[22] State entities such as the South African Human Rights Commission (SAHRC) and the Office of the Public Prosecutor (OPP) are empowered to investigate and, with respect to the OPP, prosecute violations of antidiscrimination laws. Citing the legacy of the apartheid system, a significant amount of legislation has been passed mandating affirmative action for previously disadvantaged groups (defined as "Africans," "Coloureds," and "Asians") in both public and private employment as well as education. However, racial imbalances in the workforce persist. The 2003 Department of Labor Employment Equity Report notes the "higher proportions of Indian and White employees in higher-skilled occupations compared to African and Coloured employees that dominate the lower-skilled occupations."[23] The government has also focused policy (with very mixed results) on reforming racial inequities in housing, health care, and land ownership.

The indigenous Khoikhoi and Khomani San peoples suffer from social and legal discrimination. In a March 2005 report, the SAHRC found ample evidence of police abuse of members of the Khomani San community, including police culpability in the widely publicized killing of community leader Optel Rooi. The report also faulted the government for failing to provide the San with basic services after agreeing to a land-restitution program with the community in 1999.[24] In October 2003, the Constitutional Court ruled in favor of the Khoikhoi Richtersveld community in its land-restitution battle with the state mining company Alexkor.[25]

Increased illegal immigration, particularly from Zimbabwe and Mozambique, has led to a rise in xenophobia and occasional attacks perpetrated by both police and nonstate actors. Enacted in June 2005, the Immigration Amendment Act is intended to promote "a human rights-based culture of [immigration] enforcement" by establishing a Counter-xenophobia Directorate, tightening requirements for asylum seekers, and improving benefits for foreign workers.[26]

Freedom of religion is constitutionally guaranteed and actively protected by the government in practice. By law, there is no official state religion, though the majority of South Africans are Christians. The state is not involved in the appointment of religious leaders or the internal workings of religious organizations; in fact, the government does not require religious groups to be licensed or registered.[27]

Freedom of association and peaceful assembly is secured by the Bill of Rights, and South Africa has a vibrant civil society (see "Accountability and Public Voice"). Citizens are easily able to form civic organizations and obtain the required certificate of registration; tax-exempt status is awarded to civic organizations registered as nonprofit organizations or companies. South Africans are free to form, join, and participate in independent trade unions. Unions have been active since the early twentieth century and played a critical role in the antiapartheid movement; as a result, the country has a politically engaged and influential trade union movement. COSATU—which claims over 2 million affiliate members—is a member of a tripartite governing alliance with the ANC and the SACP. In September 2004, hundreds of thousands of public sector workers went on strike in the largest industrial action in the last decade. A number of strikes involving workers in the mining and textile sectors were peacefully conducted and resolved in the period under review.

The state generally protects the right of civil society groups to organize, mobilize, and advocate for peaceful purposes; however, security services have allegedly monitored the activities of the Landless People's Movement, TAC, and civil society organizations involved in a series of recent protests over poor service delivery.[28] In addition, police have used force to break up several of these protests, as well as other demonstrations over disease and housing issues. In September 2004, a teenager participating in a service protest was shot dead by a police officer, prompting an ICD investigation. In July 2005, some 40 people protesting the slow rollout of antiretroviral drugs in the Eastern Cape were injured after police used rubber bullets and tear gas to disperse the demonstration; two months later, police fired rubber bullets at protesting residents of the typhoid-stricken town of Delmas in Mpumalanga Province.

Recommendations

- Prison overcrowding should be addressed by reforming mandatory and minimum sentencing requirements and the construction of more modern prison facilities. Pretrial detainees should be housed separately from convicted criminals.
- The DCS must commit more resources to providing prisoners with adequate health care, particularly access to antiretroviral drugs for HIV-positive patients.
- The NA should pass and the president should sign the Criminal Law (Sexual Offences) Amendment bill, which expands the current definition of rape and creates several new criminal sexual offenses.
- Stronger mechanisms to ensure the compliance of customary laws with the constitution on the rights of women should be pursued, including the fortification of weak legal enforcement and a more robust public education campaign.

RULE OF LAW – 4.44

The independence of the South African judiciary is guaranteed by the constitution, and the courts have operated with substantial autonomy in the postapartheid era. The chief justice and deputy chief justice of the Constitutional Court are appointed by the president after consultation with the Judicial Service Commission and the leaders of parties represented in the NA. Constitutionally, the "racial and gender composition of South Africa"[29] must be considered in the selection of judges. Judges may be removed from office only by impeachment by the NA. Despite the political dominance of the ANC, the upper courts have resisted political interference, a fact confirmed by the high-profile trial of then-deputy president Jacob Zuma's financial adviser and ANC stalwart Schabir Shaik in 2005. Shaik was found guilty by the Durban high court of corruption and fraud charges related to the arms-deal scandal and sentenced to 15 years in prison. Zuma himself has been charged with corruption and appeared in court in October 2005 (see "Anticorruption and Transparency").[30] The lower (magistrate) courts are reported to be more susceptible to political influences.

Criminal defendants are presumed innocent until proven guilty, and the constitution provides for a litany of procedural rights—including the right to a fair, public trial conducted "without unreasonable delay," the right of appeal to a higher court, and the right to independent legal counsel (accused persons unable to afford such counsel have the right to a state-funded legal practitioner "if substantial injustice would otherwise result").[31] In practice, a lack of capacity—particularly staff and resource shortages—undermine South Africans' rights to a timely trial and legal counsel. As a result, poor and geographically isolated South Africans do not enjoy wide access to the justice system and often rely on customary courts. Capacity issues have also produced a significant backlog of cases, resulting in excessive pretrial detention and prison overcrowding (see "Civil Liberties"). While corruption in the upper courts is not a major concern, the magistrates' courts have proven more susceptible. In addition, there have been reports of violent intimidation directed at judges and magistrates.[32]

The National Prosecuting Authority (NPA), South Africa's centralized prosecuting authority, is ensured independence by the constitution and the NPA Act of 1998. The presidentially appointed National Director of Public Prosecutions (NDPP) is the head of the NPA, reports to parliament, and is accountable to the Minister of Justice. The arms deal criminal investigations—conducted by the Directorate of Special Operations (DSO, or the "Scorpions"), a unit of the NPA focused on tackling organized crime and corruption—underscored the NPA's independence. The scandal was marked by a substantial amount of political pressure directed at the NPA, particularly NDPP Bulelani Mgcuka and the DSO. In 2003, former transport minister Mac Maharaj (also under investigation for corruption) and former ANC intelligence operative Mo Shaik (Schabir's brother) accused Mgcuka of being a spy for the apartheid government, compelling Mbeki to appoint a special commission (the so-called Hefer Commission) to investigate the charges. Despite being cleared of these charges, Mgucka resigned in July 2004; he later stated that a politically independent NDPP was "wishful thinking" and that the position in fact "straddles the line between the Executive and the judicial."[33]

The South African National Defense Force (SANDF) is under effective civilian control; under the constitution, the president is commander in chief of the force, which is overseen by the Department of Defence (headed by a civilian defense minister) and subject to significant parliamentary oversight—most notably by the Joint Standing Committee on Defence and the Portfolio Committee on Defence.[34] Tasked mostly with maintaining external security, the SANDF also has some domestic obligations. Military personnel generally respect human rights, and soldiers are exposed to human rights training programs; however, abuses have been reported. In August 2004, five soldiers accused of assaulting and robbing illegal immigrants from Zimbabwe were arrested and tried after a nine-month investigation into the crimes.[35]

The protection of property rights is a subject of much controversy in postapartheid South Africa, the consequence of tensions between maintaining the rule of law, promoting economic growth, and remedying the country's gross inequities in land ownership. Some 80 percent of farmland is owned by white South Africans, who make up 14 percent of the population.[36] As a result, thousands of black and colored farmworkers suffer from insecure tenure rights, and illegal squatting on white-owned farms is a serious problem. In addition, a majority of the country's business assets remain in the hands of white-owned enterprises. The Mbeki administration has attempted to transform this reality by instituting a Black Economic Empowerment (BEE) program that aims to bring about, mostly through aggressive preferences in employment and government tenders, "significant increases in the numbers of black people that manage, own and control the country's economy, as well as significant decreases in income inequalities."[37]

Section 25 of the 1996 constitution states that "no one may be deprived of property except in terms of law of general application," which allows for property to be expropriated for a public purpose or in the public interest, subject to negotiated or court-mandated compensation according to market principles. Notably, the "public interest" includes "the nation's commitment to land reform, and to reforms to bring about equitable access to all South Africa's natural resources; and property is not limited to land." The constitution also provides that South Africans affected by past racially discriminatory laws are entitled to restitution, redress (including redistribution), or secured land tenure rights.[38] These provisions have guided the government's oft-criticized "willing buyer, willing seller" land reform program.

Despite being supported by a series of legislative acts and much political rhetoric, land reform has proceeded slowly. During Mandela's presidency (1994–1999), the process was hindered by bureaucratic obstacles, competing interests, complex land tenure legislation, and evictions of farmworkers—as well as an overarching effort to pursue racial reconciliation following the end of apartheid. As a result, by June 2000, less than 2 percent of the country's land had been transferred.[39] The Mbeki administration has made its mark on all three tenets—restitution, redistribution, and securing tenure rights—of the land reform program. The government has sped up the settlement of land restitution claims by shifting the process from judicial to administrative control and has opted to target land redistribution not at the rural poor but at promoting black commercial farmers.[40] Regarding land tenure rights, the government has supported the controversial Communal Land Rights Bill, which grants tribal chiefs control over the allotment of most unsecured land in the former homelands.

South African land reform efforts have been impacted by violence both within and outside country borders. The widespread state-backed seizures of white-owned farms in neighboring Zimbabwe that began in 2000 were initially backed by the ANC; however, the government quickly assured domestic and international business communities that such seizures would not occur in South Africa. In addition, attacks on white farm owners by black farmworkers—connected to a wave of informal land invasions—increased significantly after 2000. In 2001, the government established the Committee of Inquiry into Farm Attacks, which investigated attacks on both farm owners and farmworkers; the committee concluded that the attacks could be interpreted as motivated by both criminal and political agendas.[41]

Most of the pressure on the government to accelerate its land reform program has come from civil society organizations such as the Landless People's Movement and the National Land Committee. Civic opposition to the Communal Lands Rights Bill was vigorous, and in late July 2005, delegates to a state-sponsored national land summit advised the government to revise the "willing buyer, willing seller" land redistribution program in favor a quicker, less market-based approach.[42] New deputy president Phumzile Mlambo-Ngcuka, who attended the summit and supported the move away from market-friendly land reform, caused a major stir when she later stated that South Africa should "learn lessons" from and employ "the skills" of Zimbabwe in pursuing more rapid land reform. Conversely, farmers' groups led by the South African Agricultural Union (Agri-SA) have cautioned against too-rapid reform.

Despite these pressures, the state generally protects citizens from arbitrary deprivation of their property. However, in a landmark development in October 2005, the government issued the country's first expropriation order, forcing a white farmer to sell his land for redistribution after negotiations on a compensation price failed. The order was made possible by a January 2004 amendment to the 1994 Restitution of Land Rights Act, allowing the state to expropriate land through administrative rather than judicial means if the land fits the conditions laid out in the constitution (see above).[43] In addition, the government announced in January 2005 its intention to remove the country's informal settlements on the outskirts of cities and replace them with low-cost housing; about 9.5 million people live in these settlements. In July 2005, human rights groups protested a string of forced removals of residents from officially condemned buildings in Johannesburg, where the central business district is undergoing major renovations.[44]

Recommendations

- More prosecutors and magistrates should be trained to reduce the large backlog of pending criminal trials.
- The Department of Justice should reconcile its financial records and effectively record transactions in order to combat corruption in the judiciary, particularly at the magistrate level.
- The DSO, that is, the Scorpions, should continue to function under the umbrella of the NPA (and not be made a part of the SAPS) in order to maintain itsindependence, effectiveness, and constitutionality.
- Efforts to accelerate the pace of land reform must be conducted within the existing legal framework; land restitution, redistribution, and tenure remedies must always be carried out under the constitution and the rule of law.

ANTICORRUPTION AND TRANSPARENCY – 3.91

South Africa has a wide-ranging anticorruption framework, with several agencies and special bodies claiming a legal mandate to prevent, detect, and combat corruption among public officials. However, enforcement of these laws is a major problem.

Chapter 9 of the constitution established three so-called Chapter 9 Institutions that deal with corruption: the Office of the Auditor-General of South Africa (AGSA), the Public Protector, and the IEC. The Office of the AGSA, South Africa's supreme audit institution, is responsible for auditing and reporting to parliament on the accounts, financial statements, and financial management of any agency receiving public monies. These reports are accessible to the public free of charge. While the AGSA's independence is constitutionally guaranteed, the extent of this independence was called into question by the auditor-general's conduct vis-à-vis the arms deal (see below). In addition, incomplete reporting by public agencies, particularly at the provincial and municipal levels, hampers the institution's efforts, as does the lack of a positive obligation on the part of parliament to act on AGSA resolutions.[45]

The public protector, or national ombudsman, is empowered to investigate a litany of improprieties in public administration; citizens may report a matter directly to the public protector.[46] In addition, a public protector is appointed in every province. Ostensibly independent, the current public protector, Leonard Mushwana, a former ANC member of parliament (MP), has been accused of inhibiting investigations of senior ANC members. A lack of capacity, insufficient funding, and the fact that the public protector's recommendations are often ignored by parliament also dilute the ombudsman's effectiveness.[47] As with the AGSA, the public can access the public protector's reports promptly and free of charge.

Besides the Chapter 9 institutions, several other agencies and legislative instruments contribute to South Africa's anticorruption efforts—with varying degrees of success. Within the executive and legislative branches of government, the separation of public office from personal interests is superficially achieved by the Executive Members Ethics Act, the Code of Conduct for Assembly and Permanent Council Members, and the deliberations of the Joint Committee on Ethics and Members Interests, respectively. While these mechanisms mandate that relevant officials disclose private financial assets and interests, the extent of disclosures is inconsistent among national, provincial, and local governments, and none have credible oversight or enforcement mechanisms. Moreover, none have adequate postemployment restrictions.[48] Notably, while both executive and legislative officials' financial disclosures are legally available to the public, those of executive officials—particularly the president—are reported to be substantially more difficult to access.[49]

The South African media have vigorously investigated allegations of conflicts of interest and nondisclosure among members of the executive and the legislature. After the DSO announced it was investigating more than 20 MPs for illegally inflating their travel expenses to pay for luxury items, newspapers such as the *Sunday Times,* the *Cape Times,* and *This Day* played a major role in further investigating and exposing the corrupt members of parliament. However, while some 136 MPs were investigated, only five MPs were convicted of corruption in March 2005 (another 21 MPs were charged with travel-related fraud in June of that year). Despite this vigor, the media's ability to investigate political corruption is limited by a general lack of investigative reporting resources.[50]

The Public Service Commission (PSC) oversees the Department of Public Service & Administration (DPSA) and is "responsible for monitoring and evaluating the public sector," including cases of public corruption.[51] Senior public officials and members of the PSC are required to submit disclosure forms; however, adherence to these regulations is not only weak but has been worsening over time, and sanctions for failing to submit the requisite forms are virtually nonexistent.[52] The civil service also has no restrictions on post–public service employment. Petty corruption is a significant problem in the civil service.[53]

By law, the Protected Disclosures Act (PDA) protects whistle-blowers from various forms of retribution and recrimination; in practice, whistle-blowers are rarely protected from occupational detriment and other negative consequences. Moreover, internal mechanisms for acting on reports of corruption are unclear, ineffective, and inconsistent across provinces and municipalities. Efforts are being made to improve performance in this area: The PSC and the DPSA have recently established a national hotline for civil servants to report instances of corruption within their ranks, and the South African Law Commission is undertaking a review of the efficacy of the PDA. In 2002, the executive cabinet approved the Public Sector National Anti-Corruption Strategy, intended to provide "a holistic and integrated approach to fighting corruption."[54] A DPSA Anti-Corruption Unit was created to implement this strategy; its successful execution is still to be determined.[55]

Chapter 10 of the constitution states that "transparency [in public administration] must be fostered by providing the public with timely, accessible and accurate information." In addition, the Bill of Rights grants "everyone" the right of access to "any information held by the state" (with exceptions such as national security) and mandates that national legislation be enacted to this effect. This legislation, the 2000 Promotion of Access to Information Act, guarantees citizens' access to government information. However, enforcement of the act suffers from a tedious application process and slow responses to requests: A 2004 study by the Open Society Institute found that South Africa—particularly the executive branch—was the least responsive to information requests among a group of five transitional democracies.[56] It is estimated that 60–70 percent of access to information requests are met with "mute refusal" through purposeful delay or inaction.[57] The executive dominates the budget-making process. While the legislature must approve the budget, effective legislative oversight is greatly hampered by a lack of either formal amendment powers or preapproval of executive contracts. The independence and efficacy of the Standing Committee on Public Accounts (SCOPA), parliament's primary public funds oversight body, has been substantially weakened by its role in the arms deal scandal (see below) and a more general unwillingness to challenge executive actions.[58] The 1999 Public Finance Management Act (PFMA) and the 2003 Municipal Finance Management Act provide for a substantial degree of transparency in the use of national, provincial, and local government funds. Both acts mandate regular expenditure reports from departments and public enterprises to treasuries, the annual submission of audited financial statements to parliament, and the submission by all departments of an anticorruption strategy to the national treasury.[59] In addition, the AGSA must monitor government spending and adherence to relevant regulations. Critics of the PFMA's efficacy, however, point to the AGSA's questionable independence and inadequate capacity, as well as "the absence of a legal requirement for the publication of contingent liabilities and extra-budgetary activities."[60] Accurate and timely information on regular budgets and expenditures is easily available to the public.

In general, procurement processes are transparent and require competitive bidding and limited sole sourcing. In December 2003, the treasury introduced the Supply Chain Management Framework, devolving procurement responsibilities to accounting officers in government departments (excepting strategic procurements such as arms). The framework is also designed to meet the requirements of the PFMA by "ensuring more comprehensive oversight over the entire procurement and disposal of assets process."[61] A major legal exception to competitive bidding is the BEE program (see "Rule of Law"). The BEE has come under increasing scrutiny from the media and civic groups for enriching only small groups of politically connected blacks.

In April 2004, after extensive consultation with civic organizations and almost two years of parliamentary debate, President Mbeki signed into law the Prevention and Combating of Corruption Activities Act. This act—intended to remedy many of the legal ambiguities and enforcement issues of the previous Corruption Act of 1992—establishes more workable definitions of illegal corruption and extortion, reinstates the common law criminality of bribery, extends the presumption of prima facie evidence to facilitate prosecution, and expands the scope of the law to include all public officials and private citizens.[62] The act mandates very tough sanctions, including a maximum penalty of life imprisonment.[63] Significantly, the act places a positive duty on senior officials to report instances of corruption to the authorities, removing the whistle-blowing onus from junior officials. In addition, it established a Register of Tender Defaulters that excludes persons and companies convicted of corruption from government business for set periods of time; according to Transparency International, "South Africa appears to be the first country to establish such comprehensive legislation at a national level."[64] Nevertheless, up until October 2005, only a few prosecutions under the act had been carried out.

To a large extent, the act can be viewed as the state's reaction to the corruption scandals surrounding the country's controversial 1999 US$4.8 billion Strategic Defense Procurement Package (the arms deal). Democratic South Africa's largest-ever procurement package, the arms deal included five contracts between the executive and several international arms companies. The AGSA investigated the deal and produced a report summarizing its findings in September 2000; while the report "identified areas of concern," it found no evidence of corruption.[65] However, the AGSA allegedly bypassed SCOPA when submitting its report to the executive. SCOPA's own report called for an investigation into the arms deal, prompting an ANC-driven reshuffling of the committee's members and public criticism of the committee by prominent cabinet members—including then-deputy president Jacob Zuma. In 2001, SCOPA created a Joint Investigations Team (JIT)—comprising the AGSA, the NPA, and the PP—to investigate the arms deal. The exclusion of the Special Investigations Unit (SIU), the only state agency dedicated to combating corruption, from the JIT was a major source of controversy; Zuma had personally requested the SIU's exclusion.[66] Although the JIT's November 2001 report identified several improprieties in the transaction and made several recommendations aimed at strengthening parliament's oversight powers with respect to executive procurements, it found no evidence of "improper or unlawful conduct by the government."[67]

Nevertheless, the arms deal's unprecedented expense, the involvement of several senior ANC figures in the securing of contracts and subcontracts, and the very public crisis undergone by SCOPA (including the resignation of chairman Gavin Woods in protest of executive interference), sparked the attention of civic watchdogs and the media. In addition, the Scorpions carried out criminal investigations of numerous public officials involved in the deal. Most notable were the investigations (and eventual prosecution) of Schabir Shaik and former deputy president Jacob Zuma (see "Rule of Law"). Two weeks after Shaik's June 2005 conviction on charges of paying Zuma a series of bribes, Mbeki sacked Zuma as deputy president; the following week, Zuma himself was charged with corruption by the NPA. The Zuma investigation, including a much-publicized raid on his home, led to condemnations of the Scorpions[68] and Mbeki by the large segment of the governing alliance loyal to Zuma. In November 2005, Zuma appeared before a Durban magistrate's court; his corruption trial will begin in 2006.

Recommendations

- The government should initiate and sustain a major public education campaign to inform citizens about what constitutes public corruption, how to report it to the proper authorities, and the rights available to them as victims of corruption.
- The country's array of anticorruption legislation should be applied and enforced with vigor to close a substantial lacuna between law and practice. In particular, the new Prevention and Combating of Corruption Activities Act should be fully implemented and fortified by regular and consistent enforcement.
- Restrictions on post–public service employment in the private sector should be introduced and enforced, either as amendments to existing legislation or as new laws.
- The Protected Disclosures Act should be strengthened by establishing guidelines that distinguish between whistle-blowing and witness protection, encouraging government departments to establish and publicize specific whistle-blowing procedures, and engaging with civic organizations focused on fighting corruption.
- Oversight of executive decisions—including the budget-making process and budgetary and extrabudgetary procurements—should be enhanced through the strengthening of ostensibly independent bodies such as SCOPA and the AGSA and the effective implementation of the Supply Chain Management Framework.

NOTES

[1] Citizens aged 18 or over, including prisoners. The Electoral Act was amended in 2004 to allow for government officials, students, and vacationers living abroad (but not those working abroad) to vote in South African elections, including the 2004 general election.

2   *EISA Election Observer Mission Report: South Africa National and Provincial Elections 12–14 April 2004* (Johannesburg: Electoral Institute of Southern Africa [EISA], EOR 14, 2004), 23, http://www.eisa.org.za/PDF/sa04eomr.pdf. Notable among the electoral results for other opposition parties is the mere 1.7 percent of the vote (seven seats in the National Assembly) won by the New National Party, the descendant of the National Party that ruled South Africa during the apartheid era.

3   Ibid., 27.

4   "Challenge to polls in the offing" (Nairobi: UN Integrated Regional Information Networks [IRIN], 19 April 2004), http://www.irinnews.org/report.asp?ReportID=40646.

5   Interview with Dr. Khabele Matlosa and Grant Masterson of the Electoral Institute of Southern Africa (EISA)

6   *Democracy and Party Political Funding: Pursuing the Public's Right to Know* (Cape Town: Institute for Democracy in South Africa [Idasa], May 2005), http://www.idasa.org.za/index.asp?page=outputs.asp%3FTID%3D1%26OTID%3D18.

7   The NCOP consists of 10 members from each province, 6 "permanent delegates" appointed by the provincial legislature to five-year terms and 4 "special delegates" appointed by the legislature in consultation with the premier on a temporary basis.

8   H. van Vuuren, *National Integrity Systems Country Study Report: South Africa 2005* (Berlin: Transparency International [TI], March 2005), 36, http://ww1.transparency.org/activities/nat_integ_systems/dnld/draft_s_africa_18.03.05.pdf.

9   Public Service Act, No. 103 of 1994, Chapter IV (11), http://www.psc.gov.za/docs/legislation/public_service_act/publicserviceact.pdf.

10   Ibid.

11   *The State of Civil Society in South Africa* (Johannesburg: Idasa/Co-operative for Research and Education, December 2001), http://www.idasa.org.za/index.asp?page=outputs.asp%3FTID%3D4%26OTID%3D2.

12   Nick Miles, "South Africa's poor to tackle ANC," BBC News, 22 August 2005, http://news.bbc.co.uk/1/hi/world/africa/4173284.stm.

13   "FXI expresses concerns over state of media freedom in the world as well as in South Africa" (Toronto: International Freedom of Expression Exchange [IFEX], Action Alert, 3 May 2004), http://www.ifex.org/en/content/view/full/58640/.

14   *Annual Report of the Independent Complaints Directorate 2004/2005* (Pretoria: Ministry of Safety and Security, 2004), http://www.icd.gov.za/reports/2004/annualreport05.pdf. This represents a 2 percent decrease from the 2003–2004 financial year.

15   Interview with Boyane Tshehla of the Institute for Security Studies

16   "Basic Information" (Pretoria: Department of Correctional Services, 2005), http://www.dcs.gov.za/WebStatistics, "Incarceration Levels." In an attempt to decrease such overcrowding, the DCS released more than 7,000 prisoners in June 2005 under a special clemency program for nonviolent and petty criminals.

17   J. Sloth-Nielsen and L. Ehlers, *A Pyrrhic victory? Mandatory and minimum sentences in South Africa* (Pretoria: Institute for Security Studies [ISS], Occasional Paper 111, July 2005), http://www.iss.co.za/pubs/papers/111/Paper111.htm.

18   *Constitution of the Republic of South Africa 1996,* Chapter II (9).

[19] *An Overview of Women's Rights in African Customary Law* (Johannesburg: Legal Resources Centre, Women's Rights Project, 2004), http://www.lrc.org.za/Publications/Academic Papers.asp.

[20] "Campaign to create awareness on sexual offences law," *IRIN News,* 6 August 2004, http://www.irinnews.org/report.asp?ReportID=42560.

[21] South Africa's is one of the world's most liberal legal environments for homosexuals. In February 2004, the Supreme Court of Appeals ruled that the country's Marriage Act should include same-sex marriage. The Home Affairs department appealed to the Constitutional Court to overturn the ruling in May 2005; that body's decision is expected in December 2005. In 2002, the Constitutional Court ruled that homosexual couples should be allowed to adopt children.

[22] *Constitution of the Republic of South Africa 1996,* Chapter II (9).

[23] *Commission for Employment Equity Annual Report 2002-2003* (Pretoria: Department of Labor, 2003), http://www.labour.gov.za/download/9960/Useful%20documents%20E EA%20-%20Employment%20Equity%20Analysis%20Report%20-%202003.doc.

[24] *Report on the Inquiry into Human Rights Violations in the Khomani San Community* (Johannesburg: South African Human Rights Commission, November 2004).

[25] "SA herders win back diamond land," BBC News, 14 October 2003, http://news.bbc.co .uk/2/hi/africa/3192000.stm.

[26] "Govt plans to counter xenophobia," *IRIN News,* 30 June 2005, http://www.irinnews .org/report.asp?ReportID=47906.

[27] While the government allows public schools to include general religious education in age-appropriate curriculums, it is not required; preaching the tenets of a specific faith (religious instruction) is not permitted in public schools: *International Religious Freedom Report 2004: South Africa* (Washington, D.C.: U.S. Department of State, September 2004), http://www.state.gov/g/drl/rls/irf/2004/35383.htm.

[28] *Global Integrity Report: South Africa* (Washington, D.C.: The Center for Public Integrity [CPI], 2003), http://www.publicintegrity.org/docs/ga/2004South_Africa.pdf.

[29] *Constitution of the Republic of South Africa 1996,* Chapter XIII (177).

[30] Former ANC chief whip Tony Yenegeni was also charged with fraud and corruption in the arms-deal scandal; he was granted a plea bargain on the lesser charge of fraud in 2003.

[31] *Constitution of the Republic of South Africa 1996, Chapter II* (35).

[32] Edwin Lombard, "Criminals target judiciary," *Sunday Times,* 12 September 2004.

[33] Peter Bruce, "The end of an era," *Financial Mail,* 30 July 2004.

[34] James Ngculu, "Parliament and Defence Oversight: The South African Perspective," *African Security Review* 10, No. 1 (2001), http://www.iss.co.za/pubs/ASR/10No1/Ngculu.html.

[35] "SA soldiers 'robbed immigrants,'" BBC News, 18 August 2004, http://news.bbc.co.uk/ 2/hi/africa/3578172.stm.

[36] "SA proposes quicker land reform," BBC News, 27 July 2005, http://news.bbc.co.uk/1/ hi/world/africa/4720023.stm.

[37] *South Africa's Economic Transformation: A Strategy for Broad-Based Black Economic Empowerment* (Pretoria: Department of Trade and Industry, 2003), 12, http://www.dti.gov .za/bee/complete.pdf.

[38] *Constitution of the Republic of South Africa 1996,* Chapter II (25).

[39] *Blood and Soil: Land, Politics and Conflict Prevention in Zimbabwe and South Africa* (Brussels: International Crisis Group [ICG], September 2004), 139–50, http://www.crisis group.org/library/documents/africa/southern_africa/land_reform/blood_and_soil_ complete.pdf.

[40] Ibid., 162–68.

[41] *Report of the Committee of Inquiry into Farm Attacks* (Pretoria: South African Police Service, 2003), http://www.saps.gov.za/statistics/reports/farmattacks/_doc/summary.doc.

[42] "Govt ponders new land policy," IRIN News, 1 August 2005, http://www.irinnews.org/ report.asp?ReportID=48388.

[43] *Blood and Soil* (ICG), 165.

[44] "Evictions worsen low-cost housing crisis," *IRIN News,* 27 July 2005, http://www .irinnews.org/report.asp?ReportID=48330.

[45] *Global Integrity Report: South Africa* (CPI), Indicator No. 56.

[46] Public Protector Act, No.23 of 1994.

[47] *Global Integrity Report: South Africa* (CPI), Indicator No.53.

[48] It should be noted that provincial arrangements for some postemployment restrictions are in place in Guateng and the Western Cape.

[49] *Ethics in Post-Apartheid South Africa* (Idasa, 2003), 29–31, www.idasa.org.za.

[50] Interview with Hennie Van Vuuren and Andile Sokomani of the Institute for Security Studies' Corruption and Governance Programme.

[51] Van Vuuren, *National Integrity Systems* (TI), 52.

[52] Ibid., 56.

[53] H. van Vuuren, "Small Bribes, Big Challenge: Extent and nature of petty corruption in South Africa" *Crime Quarterly* (ISS), No. 9 (2004).

[54] *Public Sector Anti-Corruption Strategy* (Pretoria: Department of Public Service and Administration, January 2002).

[55] The strategy includes nine considerations: review and consolidation of the legislative framework; increased institutional capacity; improved access and protection for whistle-blowers; prohibition of corrupt individuals and businesses; improved management; partnerships with stakeholders; social analysis and policy advocacy; and awareness, training, and education.

[56] Armenia, Bulgaria, Macedonia, Peru, and South Africa. Access to Information Tool 2003: South Africa (New York, Open Society Institute, 2003)

[57] Interview with Alison Tilley of the Open Democracy Advice Centre (ODAC)

[58] *Global Integrity Report: South Africa* (CPI), 2.

[59] A. Folscher, W. Krafchik, and I. Shapiro, *Transparency and Participation in the Budget Process: South Africa* (Idasa, December 2000), 13.

[60] *Budget Brief no. 109: How transparent is the budget process in South Africa* (Idasa, October 2002), 2.

[61] Van Vuuren, *National Integrity Systems* (TI), 108.

[62] Ibid., 104.

[63] Only a high court may impose this extreme sanction. Regional courts can impose a fine or up to 18 years' imprisonment. Magistrate's courts can impose a fine or up to five years' imprisonment.

64 Van Vuuren, *National Integrity Systems* (TI), 106.

65 J. February, *Commissioned Case Study: South Africa—Democracy & the South Africa Arms Deal* (ISS, March 2004), 2, http://www.issafrica.org/SEMINARS/2004/1503graft/rsa.pdf.

66 This controversy contributed a great deal to the resignation of both Judge Willem Heath, the then-head of the SIU, and Gavin Woods, the then-chair of SCOPA.

67 *Joint Investigations Report into the Strategic Defense Procurement Packages* (Cape Town: Public Protector of SA/AGSA/NPA, November 2001), 373, http://www.info.gov.za/other docs/2001/investigationreport.htm.

68 Much of this condemnation focused on former NDPP Bulelani Ngcuka, who announced in 2003 there was "prima facie" evidence to suspect Zuma of corruption, but not enough to prosecute. Many Zuma supporters believed Ngucka's statement was politically biased, a charge that gained traction when Ngucka's wife was selected to replace Zuma as deputy president.

SRI LANKA

CAPITAL: Colombo

POPULATION: 19.7 million

GNI PER CAPITA: $930

SCORES	2004	2006
ACCOUNTABILITY AND PUBLIC VOICE:	4.45	4.27
CIVIL LIBERTIES:	4.47	4.45
RULE OF LAW:	4.49	4.15
ANTICORRUPTION AND TRANSPARENCY:	3.97	3.71

(scores are based on a scale of 0 to 7, with 0 representing weakest and 7 representing strongest performance)

Robert C. Oberst

INTRODUCTION

For a small island nation, Sri Lanka has a remarkable amount of ethnic diversity and conflict. The Sinhalese are the largest ethnic group on the island. They comprise 74 percent of the population and are concentrated in the central and southwestern areas of the country.[1] They claim to be the original civilized inhabitants of the island and speak the Sinhala language. Although there are some Christians among them, most profess the Buddhist religion. The Sri Lanka Tamils are the second-largest group, with about 12.7 percent of the population. They are descendants of early settlers in the island, speak Tamil, and are mostly Hindus. Although some live in large cities, they represent a majority in most of the northern and eastern parts of the island. Comprising 7.1 percent of the population, Muslims are descendants of early traders who settled and established commercial communities in coastal areas. Most speak Tamil. They live in strong concentrations along the eastern coast and in parts of the Sinhalese areas, especially in the larger cities. The final large ethnic group are the Indian Tamils who live primarily in the hill country of central Sri Lanka. They speak Tamil and most are Hindus. They differ from the Sri Lanka Tamils by their later arrival on the island, and they consider themselves culturally distinct. They are the descendants

Robert C. Oberst is Professor of Political Science at Nebraska Wesleyan University. He has written many books and scholarly articles on Sri Lanka and South Asia.

of workers brought from India by the British to work the tea and coffee estates in the nineteenth and early twentieth centuries. They comprise 5.5 percent of the population.

At independence, the dominant pre-independence political movement became the United National Party (UNP), which appealed primarily to the Sinhalese ethnic majority. The Tamils, who had been part of the independence movement with the founders of the UNP, formed their own party, the Tamil Congress. Both parties split in the 1950s, with a faction of the UNP, led by S.W.R.D. Bandaranaike, creating the Sri Lanka Freedom Party (SLFP). Growing unemployment among the youth and the failure of the government to resolve economic and social problems resulted in the development of youth movements among both the Sinhalese and the Tamils in the 1960s and 1970s. The Janatha Vimukthi Peramuna (JVP), among the Sinhalese, and the Liberation Tigers of Tamil Eelam (LTTE), among the Tamil youths, challenged the traditional political parties. The JVP, a Maoist party, led two bloody insurrections against the government, in 1971 and again in 1988–1989. The LTTE began attacking the government in the 1970s and militarily established their dominance among the other Tamil militant groups in the 1980s.[2]

A series of Tamil grievances ultimately led to the LTTE insurrection against the government. These complaints included allegations of ethnic bias in university admissions, high unemployment among Tamil youths, allegations of a Sinhalese bias in the awarding of jobs and government programs, and a series of anti-Tamil riots from 1977 to 1983 that many Tamils believed the government allowed to happen. In 1984, the simmering conflict developed into open warfare between the LTTE and the government. Over the nearly 20 years of warfare, there were very few high level contacts between the warring sides. During the height of the conflict from 1985 until 2001, both sides freely attacked civilian targets. These abuses peaked in the period from 1990 to 1994, when thousands of Tamil civilians died or disappeared in eastern Sri Lanka alone. In response to international pressure, both sides reduced their attacks against civilians after the mid-1990s. In 2002, a ceasefire was achieved through Norwegian intervention. The ceasefire continued through 2005, in spite of distrust from both sides and the breakdown of negotiations for a permanent peace in early 2004.

Despite the war, Sri Lanka has been able to maintain a constitutional democracy. The current constitution, the third since independence from Great Britain in 1948, was created in 1978. It formed a quasi-presidential system in which the president's executive power rests on the consent of the parliament. As a result, the otherwise strong executive steps back from the head-of-government role during periods of cohabitation.

The 2001 general elections gave the UNP a small majority in parliament. Accordingly, President Chandrika Kumaratunga assumed the role of figurehead president after seven years as the head of government. Nevertheless, using constitutionally legal if questionable means, she took control of the Defense, Interior, and Mass Communication ministries on November 4, 2003, and ultimately called new elections in April 2004. The April elections resulted in a closely divided parliament, which allowed her alliance, as the largest winner of seats, to form a minority government. In September 2005, the government obtained a parliamentary majority when the Sri Lanka Muslim Congress joined the government.

ACCOUNTABILITY AND PUBLIC VOICE – 4.27

The February 2002 ceasefire agreement between the government of Sri Lanka and the LTTE ended 18 years of war between the two sides; the agreement also divided Sri Lanka into two administrative areas—one controlled by the government of Sri Lanka and guided by the Sri Lankan constitution and one under the control of the rebel LTTE. Despite continuous problems with the democratic institutions of the north and east, the current situation is an improvement over the war years, when democracy barely functioned.

Fair electoral laws with universal and equal suffrage have survived the civil war; the country successfully held national parliamentary elections in April 2004 and a presidential election in November 2005. Despite continuing electoral violence, the 2004 parliamentary elections were not only relatively free and fair, but also the most peaceful since before the war began in the 1980s. The 2005 presidential elections, which resulted in a small victory for SLFP leader Mahinda Rajapakse over UNP candidate Ranil Wickremasinghe, were marred by an electoral boycott enforced by the LTTE in the north and east, but were otherwise relatively violence free.

While electoral violence declined in 2004, electoral fraud appeared to be a more serious concern. Sri Lankan voters are not required to produce their national identification cards in order to vote. In the absence of such verification, most major parties handed out polling cards of dead or missing voters to their supporters so that they could vote several times. This practice, particularly prevalent in the Muslim areas of Ampara, Batticaloa, and Trincomalee, has raised questions about the validity of election outcomes.[3] The large number of displaced voters and polling stations clustered at border crossings helped make this easier in the former war zone areas of the north and east.

Moreover, evidence surfaced of LTTE intimidation of Tamil party candidates opposed to the LTTE in the north and east. Prior to the election, several attacks occurred resulting in the deaths of candidates and their supporters. Although the level of violence was lower than that in the Sinhalese areas of the country in the 2001 parliamentary elections, it nevertheless intimidated candidates and limited their freedom to campaign.[4] In addition, many Muslim leaders in the 2004 elections established their residences and offices in the Sinhalese town of Ampara, which is outside the Muslim-populated areas of the district, because they feared violence from other Muslim parties.

Sri Lankan electoral laws prevent elections in areas that are not under the control of the Sri Lankan police. As a result, residents of areas under the control of the LTTE must travel to government territory to vote. Polling stations for these voters are placed at the border crossings between LTTE- and government-held territory. In the 2001 elections, the army at the border checkpoints refused to allow voters to cross over to vote. In the 2004 and 2005 elections, Tamil voters were allowed to pass through the border crossing.

Sri Lanka's quasi-presidential system does not separate powers between the three branches of government. The judiciary is largely controlled by the president, while the parliament, when it is controlled by the president's party, is a rubber stamp for the president. When it is controlled by a party other than that of the president, the parliament dominates the government and the prime minister becomes the executive power. Despite yielding much of her executive power, President Kumaratunga, when faced with a UNP parliamentary victory in the 2001 elections, retained control of the Defense Ministry and later asserted her authority to take control of several more ministries.

While Sri Lankan government functions reasonably well, the once-independent civil service of Sri Lanka has descended into a battleground of partisanship. Government politicians interfere with the appointment, transfer, and firing of public servants, and many bureaucrats avoid any action that might anger the governing party or supporters of opposition members who may ultimately come to power. Punishment for actions of which politicians disapprove is transfer to offices in unfavorable locations. During the civil war, this could mean being sent to government offices in the war zone.

Nongovernmental organizations (NGOs) in Sri Lanka have usually had ties to one of the political parties. This has resulted in a tense relationship between the government and NGOs associated with the opposition. The tension between domestic NGOs and the government has carried over to international NGOs, which are viewed with suspicion by many party leaders. Since the election of the UPFA government in 2004, the JVP and other Sinhalese nationalist supporters of the government have increased their efforts to limit and restrict NGOs. The nationalists fear that international and domestic NGOs with non-Buddhist ties are working to further Christianity or international forces and thus need to be controlled. So far, the NGOs have felt intimidated but continue to operate freely under current legislation.

Since the 1990s, the independent Center for Policy Alternatives has published reports on policy issues facing the government. Although interest groups have the ability to present reports to parliamentary committees, very few do, and there are doubts that legislators would take such reports into consideration.

In an ominous sign of the times, attacks against the media have increased since the election of the UPFA government in April 2004. Although legal and constitutional protection of the media and creative arts is strong, intimidation and attacks against the media have grown common. Beatings, arrests, police and army searches, and assassinations have become a typical feature of the post-April 2004 period. Some of the attacks have been part of the conflict between the LTTE and their opponents in the north and east, but many others have been aimed at the Sinhalese media or against Tamil media operating in the government areas. The 2005 attacks included the April 28, 2005, murder of English-language *Daily Mirror* journalist Dharmaretnam Sivaram "Taraki," the bombing of the Tamil-language *Suderoli* newspaper office in Colombo, the arrest of a *Suderoli* reporter gathering news, and an attack on the English-language *Sunday Leader* newspaper office in October.[6] These attacks, as well as the beatings of other reporters, mostly believed to have been carried out by supporters of the government coalition, have intimidated many journalists.

Sri Lanka continues to have some of the strongest anti-slander and libel laws in the world. Any journalist or public figure must be very careful to avoid language that could result in prosecution and a large fine. In addition, the violence against journalists who do not agree with the government has led to an environment in which the government can dissuade them from writing critical reports. In 2005, the Sri Lankan military pressured filmmakers to cease production of antiwar or antimilitary films.[7]

In the 1970s, the Sri Lankan government took over the Lakehouse group of newspapers. Since that time, the Lakehouse group has presented the government line in its English, Tamil, and Sinhala publications. The impact of government control on the newspaper chain shows up in the ample placement of government and other advertising in the Lakehouse papers while private newspapers have very few advertisements to run.

Recommendations

- The government must require that voters present identification to vote in national elections in order to prevent voter impersonation.
- Effective action, such as stronger protective legislation, must be taken to protect the media from attacks, arrests, and detention.
- The government should gradually divest itself of media ownership and control.
- A nonpartisan civil service should be created in order to prevent political interference in government hiring, firing, and promotion.

CIVIL LIBERTIES – 4.45

Although civil liberties have improved sharply since the early 1990s, Sri Lanka still has a serious problem with police beatings and torture. Human rights organizations have documented numerous cases of deaths of suspects in custody.[8] For example, a recent report by the Hong Kong–based Asian Legal Resource Center (ALRC) documents more than 100 cases of torture, denial of basic rights to defendants, and murder of defendants by police.[9] The report reinforces many others over the last two years documenting increased torture, murder, and denial of civil rights by the police and security forces. In recognition of human rights abuses by police and military personnel, the government increased training programs to teach service personnel proper interrogation techniques and how to protect the rights of detainees.

The judicial system maintains enough independence to prosecute suspects in the killings and beatings. Due to widespread intimidation of witnesses and victims, however, charges are often dismissed or dropped. There is a serious problem protecting witnesses who testify against police and security force personnel charged with human rights violations. Instances of threats and violence against them are numerous, especially in rape cases. A widely publicized case was the December 2004 murder of police torture victim Gerald Mervyn Perera, who died a few days before he was to testify in court. The court had already awarded him 1.7 million rupees (US$17,000). The police had failed to pay him the award, and he was returning to court to seek action to force the government to pay him the court-ordered settlement.

Another civil liberties concern is the series of attacks against unarmed Tamils in Batticaloa and Ampara districts in the east. Many of the attacks are carried out by the LTTE.[10] However, a faction of the LTTE led by Colonel Vinayagamurthi Muralidharan, alias Karuna Amman, which split with the LTTE in March 2004, has carried out a war against the LTTE and may be responsible for some of the attacks. It has been rumored that the faction receives logistical assistance and protection from the Sri Lankan security forces, specifically the army. While there is no specific evidence linking the military to the Karuna group in many of the killings, Karuna did receive assistance from the army after fleeing the Batticaloa district in April 2004 when the LTTE attacked his forces.[11] To date, few Karuna suspects have been arrested by the security forces in over 200 attacks against unarmed LTTE political officers, supporters, and offices in government-controlled areas. In the Sinhalese areas, numerous attacks by and against opposition supporters have taken place. Despite hundreds of incidents, few people have been arrested.

The Prevention of Terrorism Act (PTA), passed in 1979, allows suspects (in practice, mostly ethnic Tamils) to be held indefinitely without charges. Security forces are allowed to deny suspects access to attorneys or the opportunity to notify their relatives. Although the ceasefire agreement barred PTA arrests under the law, the courts have not yet cleared all of the cases of detainees. Some have been held for more than 10 years.

In 1960, Sri Lanka became the first nation in the world to elect a female prime minister. Despite this milestone, women still lack equal access to positions of power in Sri Lanka. The government has provided legal equality to women but has failed to uphold it in practice. Although the government has shown increasing awareness and sensitivity to sexual harassment in the past five years, sexual harassment laws enacted in 1995 have yet to show any impact. Despite a 2004 campaign to raise awareness of domestic violence, the nation still lacks legislation criminalizing the practice.[12]

Women from Sri Lanka have faced serious employment problems in the Middle East and some Western countries; numerous instances of abuse and forced conscription into prostitution have been reported. While the government condemns publicized cases of trafficking in women, it has done little to protect its citizens or apply pressure on the governments of the countries where its citizens have been victimized. The government fears that if the question of sexual and physical abuse of its citizens is raised, the countries will restrict employment opportunities for Sri Lankan nationals. Related to this is a growing problem with the importation of Southeast Asian and Eastern European prostitutes into Sri Lanka. In some cases, the women are held against their will. The most that the Sri Lankan government has done has been to occasionally fine and deport the women while usually ignoring the source of the problem.

Sri Lanka also has a serious problem with child sexual abuse. The country has become a major destination for Western Europeans and North Americans who openly solicit and travel with young boys. While strong laws exist to protect children from sexual exploitation, the government has done very little to enforce those laws or discourage the sex tourists.

The Sri Lankan constitution provides for equality under the law for all ethnic, religious, and other groups in the country, and Sri Lankan governments have traditionally been very concerned with the needs of the poor. However, in practice, this equality has been an ideal rather than a reality. Most government jobs and development projects have been distributed on the basis of patronage, which discriminates against

Tamils and Muslims in favor of governing-party supporters (who are almost always Sinhalese). As a result, ethnic minority groups have been denied equal representation in the civil service and in the receipt of development projects. Areas where minorities are in the majority do not receive a fair share of development projects and government jobs if they do not elect members of parliament (MPs) from the ruling party to parliament. In fact, the Sri Lankan civil war resulted primarily from Tamil complaints about discrimination in education, in government job hiring, and in development project placement. These problems continue to be points of tension between the government and the Tamils. Ethnic discrimination is barred by the constitution, but in practice, most employers do not hire members of ethnic communities other than their own. Further compounding the problem is the separation of the education system into Sinhalese and Tamil language schools, which results in unequal treatment and disproportionate Sinhalese representation in universities.

Of new concern is the emergence of a Sinhalese Buddhist nationalist movement that has been agitating for a change in the ceasefire agreement with the LTTE and for a law protecting Buddhism from Christian conversions.[13] Supporters of the movement believe that it is a popular uprising in support of Buddhist rights, while opponents view it as a parochial response to the challenges of modernization. In any case, the nationalists proposed legislation that would bar so-called unethical conversions to any religion, requiring all converts to notify the government of their conversion or face arrest. In addition, those using "unethical" means to convert new members could face up to five years in prison. The law would make any Christian who helps a Buddhist convert to Christianity risk prosecution. Comprising about 8 percent of the population, Sri Lankan Christians have felt threatened by the proposed legislation. Although the cabinet approved the bill and sent it to parliament, the parliament has yet to act on it.

Related to the fear of Christian activity has been an increase in attacks against Christians and Christian churches. These attacks reached a peak at the end of 2003, with a total of 30 attacks by the end of January 2004.[14] After this period of intensity, the attacks subsided in number but still continue. Nevertheless, the Sri Lankan government has usually avoided interfering in the affairs of the major religions of the country (Buddhism, Hinduism, Islam, and Christianity). All religions have traditionally been allowed to worship as they wish.

As far as other targeted groups are concerned, very little has been done to provide opportunities for people with disabilities. The high costs of providing disabled access to buildings, jobs, and education have so far discouraged efforts and rendered them unlikely to occur in the near future. In addition, penal code Section 365a criminalizes homosexual behavior. Although the anti-homosexual laws are not routinely enforced, they are often used as grounds to exact bribes or to threaten gays.

The rights of association and assembly traditionally have been supported in Sri Lanka. Demonstrations and trade union actions, although sometimes challenged by the police, are allowed, and processions are common. Nevertheless, police attacks against demonstrators have been numerous in the last two years. The demonstrations have reflected a wide array of political opinions ranging from leftists protesting the lack of jobs for university graduates to antiwar activists and groups demanding action against supposed forced conversions to Christianity. On numerous occasions police have claimed that the demonstrators became violent, while the demonstrators accuse the police of misbehavior.

The trade union movement has been hurt by the creation of trade unions by political parties to carry out party policy. When a party is in power, it benefits its trade unions and eliminates pressure from other unions. As a result, trade unions lose power and membership when "their" party is out of office and gain power and members when it is in office.[15] Sri Lanka has strong legislation protecting the rights of workers to form trade unions and to strike. In reality, however, enforcement of union recognition laws is weak, union organizers are victimized, and strong action to prevent unions occurs in the free trade zones.[16]

Recommendations
- Cases of those who have been arrested under the PTA and held without trial or charge should be examined expeditiously.
- The police and other security forces should continue to receive training on general human rights issues, particularly on acceptable interrogation techniques.
- A concerted effort should be made to investigate accusations of torture and of custodial rape or murder, and those responsible should be prosecuted.
- Adequate protection should be provided for witnesses in cases involving police and security force personnel.

- Current laws protecting worker rights to organize should be enforced in the general economy as well as in the free trade zones.

RULE OF LAW – 4.15

The Sri Lankan legal system is based on a combination of English common law, Roman-Dutch law, and local Sinhalese and Muslim law. It provides adequate protection to suspects who are deemed innocent until proven guilty.

Since 1970, the Sri Lankan judicial system has endured an ethnic civil war and two insurrections by Maoist guerrillas. During this time, it has struggled to remain independent of the government. Elected officials apply pressure on judges, which is mitigated by a strong tradition of an independent judiciary supported by the country's political leaders. Judges are protected from interference by a set of laws. However, there are many ways to circumvent the laws, and political interference continues to be a problem in the administration of justice.

Judges in the lower courts (primary courts, magistrate's courts, the district courts, and the high courts) are appointed by the Judicial Service Commission (JSC), which also dismisses and disciplines them. The JSC is composed of the chief justice and two associate justices of the Supreme Court. Because the Supreme Court and Court of Appeal justices are appointed by the president, they are often close to the president and respond to pressure. Thus, the president may have an undue amount of influence over the judges. Since 1985, all new judges have been trained by the Sri Lanka Judges' Institute.[17] The institute has also provided in-service training for sitting judges. Although the institute receives relatively limited funding, judges are reasonably well prepared for the bench.

The most serious problem judges face has been gaining access to law reports, especially copies of Supreme Court decisions. They often must make decisions without access to case law as determined by the Court of Appeal and the Supreme Court. Until recently, written decisions of the higher courts were not published in a law report and still are not available to all judges. An additional obstacle to judges' professionalism is the lack of a code of conduct. In October 2005, the Bar Association of Sri Lanka called for the creation of a code. Its development is now in its early stages.

The judicial system has struggled to deliver justice in a reasonable length of time. It is not unusual for cases, especially civil cases, to extend well beyond 10 years. The cost of maintaining legal counsel over the years of periodic hearings places litigation beyond the means of all but the richest of Sri Lankans. Thus, although the judicial system is open to all, the rich and the politically connected have undue influence over the process.

One factor helping counteract this imbalance in Sri Lankan society is the Legal Aid Commission. The commission is a statutory body created in 1978 that provides free legal assistance to suspects facing criminal charges. Suspects who earn less than 2,500 rupees per month (roughly US$25) are eligible. However, the commission is sorely underfunded, with a yearly budget of only 1.2 million rupees (US$12,000) to cover the approximately 25,000 cases it handles a year.

A new problem facing the courts has been the rise of the Colombo underworld, which often has close ties to politicians. The murder of high court judge Sarath Ambepitiya on November 19, 2004, by an underworld figure; several courtroom attacks including a grenade attack on a court in the southern city of Embilipitya on February 21, 2005; and the ambush of prison transport buses such as that in Gampaha on September 26, 2005, when three prison guards and a prisoner were killed, reflect the increase in power of the underworld and its effect on the judiciary.

Prosecutors, on paper, are independent of political pressure, although in reality the process is highly politicized. It is common for politicians to face criminal prosecution only when their party is out of power. This phenomenon has led to a profusion of political cases, some justified, some not, whenever there is a change of government.

The performance of the Sri Lankan court system in response to state violations of civil liberties has been positive. In the wake of the human rights violations in the early 1990s, the Supreme Court, in recognition of the slowness of the Sri Lankan judicial system, named itself the court of first instance in human rights cases. This has allowed the court to respond quickly to allegations of abuse.

The Sri Lankan military and police are largely independent of civilian control. The legislature oversees the security force budgets but not their activities. The president usually holds the Ministry of Defense portfolio but exercises control only when she or he feels compelled to do so for political reasons or because of international pressure.

Meanwhile, political interference with the police is rampant. This extends from promotion and control of police leaders to transfer of or retribution against individual officers for actions opposed by politicians. The political use of the security forces has become acceptable practice. For example, during the 2004 general elections, police special task force members led by a government minister fired weapons in the air in Sammanthurai, Ampara, while masked thugs attacked voters near a polling station.[18] Most police officers guarding polling stations during elections hesitate to take action against wrongdoers and leave the polling area when ordered by a politician. They realize that to defy the orders of a politically powerful individual may lead to transfer or disciplinary action.[19]

The Sri Lankan constitution and legal system give citizens strong property rights. However, political considerations determine challenges to the rights of political opponents of the government. There have been numerous cases of seizure of the property of political opponents. A further problem has been the seizure of private property in the north and east for "security" purposes. Even since the ceasefire agreement, much of this land is still held by the security forces. Large depopulated areas surround government military bases in the north and east. Many of the houses in these areas have been razed or are occupied by the security forces. In addition, security forces have allowed squatters to move onto the land they have seized. This has become a serious problem in Trincomalee district in the east.

Recommendations

- The quality of judges and their access to legal information should be improved to enhance the professionalism of the judiciary. This would include the publication and dissemination of all Supreme Court decisions and relevant Court of Appeal decisions.
- An independent panel should be created to appoint and oversee the conduct of judges.
- Further efforts should be made to ensure that court cases are resolved in a reasonable amount of time. This might include requiring judges to hear cases in the afternoon or reducing the grounds for procedural delays in court cases.
- An effective independent police board should be created to govern the police department, prevent political pressure on police officers, and make sure they enforce laws.

ANTICORRUPTION AND TRANSPARENCY – 3.71

Three significant types of corruption prevail in the Sri Lankan political system: efforts to circumvent bureaucratic red tape, personal bribe solicitation by government officials, and nepotism and cronyism. The Sri Lankan government has made a strong effort to remove the excessive bureaucracy and regulations that were a feature of the United Front government of the 1970s. Many of the government-run enterprises have been sold to the private sector. However, the state still controls a significant number of businesses. Although there are fewer regulations, many remain, allowing for bribery opportunities. The excessive slowness of the judicial system has also inspired numerous bribe attempts.

Sri Lanka has long had anticorruption laws in place, but enforcement of the laws has been a serious problem. Enforcement of anti-bribery laws is the responsibility of the Bribery Commission, which was established in 1994. It has been largely ineffective. The Bribery Commission's 2004 annual report noted a 26.7 percent increase in complaints, to a total of 4,626.[20] Despite the increase, only 787 were sent on for action. Of these, just one resulted in conviction, while 11 ended in acquittal. The other cases have not been acted on and may never be resolved.

Transparency International–Sri Lanka has noted the poor enforcement of anticorruption laws, a task that currently is divided among agencies including the Bribery Commission.[21] Whistle-blower protection legislation, a freedom-of-information act, and laws for public disclosure of assets by public officials are lacking.

Despite movement toward a free economy, nepotism and cronyism continue to be a problem. The government has enacted a number of laws to reduce conflicts of interest in the awarding of government contracts and other government expenditures, but these are largely circumvented by politicians and bureaucrats, who can easily award contracts to relatives or business associates.

Sri Lankans widely believe that corruption is rife in their society. Yet there are very few arrests for corruption. The lack of protection for whistle-blowers limits the public disclosure of corruption. Because of widespread political interference in police affairs, anticorruption laws are usually not enforced against members of the governing party. When charges are made against politicians, they are usually covered up by the government-controlled media, as well as the police authorities, who are under the control of politicians. However, with the frequent changes of government, the politicians and public officials who are protected by one government face prosecution by the next. The rights of the victims of corruption are largely ignored.

Sri Lanka has always been proud of its educational system, which is recognized as one of the strongest in Asia. Although higher education is largely free of bribery, competition is keen for admission to prestigious primary and secondary schools. As a result, there is a serious problem with parents' offering bribes to school officials.

Sri Lanka has one of the best government data reporting systems in the world. Countless reports and publications of government statistics and information are released each year. However, reporting of regulations and laws or court decisions is limited. It is very difficult to learn of government regulations without legal counsel. Without formal freedom of information legislation, information remains difficult to obtain for average citizens in Sri Lanka.

Budget debates are a highlight of the legislative process each year. The opposition mounts strong challenges, questioning all aspects of the budget. The budget process is open to public scrutiny; the yearly budget debates are well reported in the press, and most citizens follow them closely. Beyond this, though, oversight of legislation after it is passed is limited. The creation of the Center for Policy Alternatives continues to transform the legislative process by providing research and information on budget and other issues before the parliament.

The transparency of awarding government contracts and the implementation of government programs varies across the country. All information related to government contracts and bidding is public and is available to those who can take the time and effort to seek out the government ministry involved. However, outside Colombo, where most government activities take place, local populations often have no way to ascertain the scope or purpose of government activity in their area.

The distribution of foreign aid has been a contentious issue. Many allegations have arisen that aid is predominantly distributed to the area along the west coast, close to Colombo, and that the rest of the country is largely ignored. In addition, the Tamil and Muslim minorities have claimed limited disbursements of foreign aid in their areas. This problem was somewhat alleviated by the large influx of aid to help with the post-ceasefire rebuilding effort. Still, while Jaffna and the Vanni areas of the north received large amounts of assistance, the east coast appeared to receive much less.

The same complaint has followed the relief and rebuilding effort since the 2004 tsunami. Although the damage was greatest along the east coast, the per-family expenditure of funds for food in the harder hit Eastern Province was less than the per capita allocation of funds in the less severely hit southwestern coast of Sri Lanka.[22] Moreover, widespread allegations of corruption have been made over the allocation and spending of tsunami relief aid. In October 2005, the Sri Lankan auditor-general's office made a report to parliament documenting widespread fraud.[23]

Recommendations

- An appropriate mechanism should be created to ensure that foreign aid promised after the 2004 tsunami is distributed in a fair manner among the Sinhalese, Tamil, and Muslim victims of the tsunami, and between the north and east in the case of post-conflict aid.
- Government anticorruption agencies should be given more power to enforce the law.
- Legislation to protect whistleblowers should be enacted.
- The passing of freedom-of-information legislation should be made a priority.

NOTES

[1] All population data is from the 1981 census (*Statistical Abstract of the Democratic Republic of Sri Lanka,* Colombo: Government of Sri Lanka, Department of Census and Statistics, 1996, 40.) Because of the war, Sri Lanka has held only one partial census since 1981. A 2001 census did not gather information from the Tamil areas of the north and east. Because of this, there is a great deal of confusion about the current population of Sri Lanka. For instance, the 2005 internet edition of the CIA's *The World Fact Book* (Washington, D.C.: Central Intelligence Agency, 2005, http://www.cia.gov/cia/publications/factbook/geos/ce.html#People, accessed 20 and 25 October 2005) reports the partial 2001 census as an accurate island-wide census. Based on voter registration records in the Tamil areas and the partial census, this author has projected the current population percentages as the following: Sinhalese 73.6%, Sri Lanka Tamils 12.0%, Muslims 8.8% and Indian Tamils 4.9%.

2 *Final Report on Parliamentary General Election, 2nd April 2004* (Colombo: People's Action for Free and Fair Elections [PAFFREL], February 2005), http://www.lanka world.com/paffrel/Publications/Final%20Report%20on%20Parliamentary%20General %20Election%202004.pdf, accessed 25 October 2005; *FinalReport on Election Related Violence: General Election 2004* (Colombo: Center for Policy Alternatives [CPA], Center for Monitoring Electoral Violence [CMEV], December 2004), http://www .cpalanka.org/research_papers/CMEV_GE_2004_English.pdf, accessed 25 October 2005.

3 *Sri Lanka, Parliamentary Elections 2 April 2004, European Union Election Observation Mission, Final Report* (Brussels: European Union), http://europa.eu.int/comm/external_ relations/human_rights/eu_election_ass_observ/sri_lanka/final_%20report04.pdf.

4 *Final Report* (PAFFREL); Final Report (CEMV).

5 *Suderoli* is a pro-LTTE newspaper published in Colombo.

6 "Press Attack, Threatens[sic] to Free and Fair Election Environments" (Colombo: Free Media Movement [FMM], press release, 17 October 2005), http://www.freemedia srilanka.org/index.php?action=con_all_full&id=20&section=news_press.

7 "Film Makers Branded as New Terrorism" (FMM, press release, 22 September 2005), http://www.freemediasrilanka.org/index.php?action=con_all_full&id=19&section=news_ press.

8 "Sri Lanka" in *Report 2005* (New York: Amnesty International [AI], 2005), http://web .amnesty.org/report2005/lka-summary-eng. accessed 31 October 2005.

9 "Systematic and Widespread Torture by State Institutions in Sri Lanka and Absence of Effective Remedies for Victims and Their Family Members" (Hong Kong: Asian Legal Resource Center [ALRC], September 2005), posted 21 October 2005), http://www.alrc .net/doc/mainfile.php/unar_cat_sl_2005.

10 "Sri Lanka: End the Killings and Abductions of Tamil Civilians" (New York: Human Rights Watch, 24 May 2005), http://hrw.org/english/docs/2005/05/24/slanka10996 .htm, accessed 25 October 2005.

11 "UNP MP Brought Karuna to Colombo," *The Island,* 23 June 2004; Surinamala, "Inside Story of the Karuna Drama," *Sunday Leader,* 27 June 2004.

12 "Sri Lanka: Violence Against Women in Sri Lanka" (London: Women Living Under Muslim Law [WLUML], 15 August 2003, http://www.wluml.org/english/newsfull txt.shtml?cmd%5B157%5D=x-157-18552, accessed 31 October 2005.

13 For a description of the law and the issues surrounding it, see Timothy Samuel Shah and A.R.M. Imtiyaz, "A Brief on Sri Lanka's Proposed Anti-Conversion Legislation: Information, Observation and Analysis" (Washington, D.C.: LankaLiberty.com), http://www .lankaliberty.com/reports/index.html.

14 "Armed Guards for Sri Lankan Church," BBC News, World Edition, 27 January 2004, http://news.bbc.co.uk/2/hi/south_asia/3434145.stm, accessed 30 October 2005.

15 Craig Baxter, Charles H. Kennedy, Yogendra K. Malik, Robert C. Oberst, *Government and Politics in South Asia* (Boulder, CO: Westview Press, 1998), ch. 21.

16 "Sri Lanka: Annual Survey of Violations of Trade Union Rights (2004)" (Colombo: Friedrich Ebert Stiftung – Sri Lanka), http://www.fessrilanka.org/fes/Links/pdf/slaso.pdf, accessed 28 November 2005.

17 For a description of the institute, see the Sri Lankan Ministry of Justice and Law Reforms website: http://www.justiceministry.gov.lk/Sri%20Lanka%20Judges%20Institute.htm.

18 The author observed the event and investigated it as an International Election Monitor for PAFFREL.

19 Policemen guarding a polling station in Ampara District in the 2004 general elections claimed to this author that they had "taken a break" at the moment that a masked gang came and stole ballot papers from the station and did not know anything about the incident.

20 Associated Press, "Significant increase registered in bribery cases during 2004," Lanka Newspapers.com, 8 October 2005, http://www.lankanewspapers.com/news/2005/10/3902.html.

21 "TI Report on Sri Lanka calls for Independent AntiCorruption Authority and tighter rules for public tendering" (Berlin: Transparency International, press release, 12 August 2004), http://www.tisrilanka.org/Press/press.html, accessed 30 October 2005.

22 This is based on an analysis of statistics reported by the Sri Lankan Centre for National Operations (CNO).

23 "Sri Lanka: The Auditor General's report on tsunami mismanagement should not be ignored" (Hong Kong: Asian Human Rights Commission [AHRC], press release, 29 September 2005), http://www.ahrchk.net/statements/mainfile.php/2005statements/354/, accessed 28 October 2005.

TANZANIA

CAPITAL: Dar es Salaam
POPULATION: 36.5 million
GNI PER CAPITA: $300

SCORES	2004	2006
ACCOUNTABILITY AND PUBLIC VOICE:	N/A	3.82
CIVIL LIBERTIES:	N/A	3.82
RULE OF LAW:	N/A	3.37
ANTICORRUPTION AND TRANSPARENCY:	N/A	2.82

(scores are based on a scale of 0 to 7, with 0 representing weakest and 7 representing strongest performance)

Paul J. Kaiser

INTRODUCTION

Defined by the World Bank as "one of the politically most stable countries in Africa,"[1] the United Republic of Tanzania conducted its third round of multiparty elections during the fall of 2005. Despite political tensions, opposition accusations of electoral irregularities, and media reports of election-related violence on the country's Indian Ocean islands of Zanzibar since the advent of multipartism in 1992, the country has made some progress economically and, to a lesser extent, politically under the leadership of Union president Benjamin Mkapa, currently completing his second (and final) five-year term.[2]

Working closely with the World Bank, the International Monetary Fund (IMF), and key Western donors, the Mkapa government has moved forward with a vigorous economic reform agenda, dismantling the socialist *ujamaa* (translated as "familyhood") state created by Tanzania's founding father and first president, Julius Nyerere. In 2005, the Tanzanian government finalized its National Strategy for Growth and Reduction of Poverty (the Swahili acronym is MKUKUTA). This plan, which was developed through a participatory process initiated in 2000,

Paul J. Kaiser is Associate Director and Adjunct Associate Professor of Political Science at the University of Pennsylvania. He has conducted extensive field research and published widely on a range of issues related to the political and economic transition process currently under way in Tanzania.

highlighted three goals essential to the success and sustainability of the ongoing reform process: economic growth and income poverty reduction, improvements in quality of life and social well-being, and, more broadly, improvements in governance and accountability. At the macroeconomic level, recent World Bank data indicate that the reform process is beginning to pay dividends. In 1995 the inflation rate was 27.1 percent and the economic growth rate was 3.6 percent. By 2004, inflation was around 4 percent, and the growth rate had increased by over 3 percent to 6.7 percent.[3] Endemic corruption at all levels of government, and the limited impact of reforms in rural areas, however, undermine the positive effects of the economic reform process throughout the country.

The political situation is a bit more ambiguous. The United Republic of Tanzania is the product of a 1964 political union between two former British colonies: mainland Tanganyika and the islands of Zanzibar. While Julius Nyerere's Tanganyika African National Union (TANU) party had dominated the political landscape during the peaceful transition to independence in 1961, the same had not been true for Zanzibar, where contested elections in December 1963 were immediately followed by a January 1964 Zanzibar Revolution, which overthrew the ruling Arab aristocracy in favor of a nationalist African movement led by Abeid Karume.

Negotiations between Tanganyikan president Nyerere and his Zanzibari counterpart Karume shortly after this revolution resulted in the formation of the political union between what were in April 1964 two sovereign and independent countries. A Union government (a president and a 232-member National Assembly) was established with sovereign political jurisdiction over Tanganyika and Zanzibar. A separate Zanzibar government (a president, a house of representatives, and subsequently, local councils) was also created, with political power limited to internal, non-Union matters of governance. Currently, 22 Union matters are listed in the constitution, including foreign affairs, defense and security, police, emergency powers, citizenship, immigration, external borrowing and trade, and the "registration of political parties and other matters related to political parties."[4] This two-government structure has resulted in a twin transition process, one dominated by the mainland and the other based in Zanzibar.

TANU was renamed the Chama cha Mapinduzi (CCM) in 1977. This party has been the dominant political force on the mainland since independence. Founding father Julius Nyerere governed the country from independence to 1985. His presidency was followed by those of Ali Hassan Mwinyi (1985–1995) and Benjamin Mkapa (1995–2005). As of November 2005, support was strong for CCM presidential candidate Jakaya Kikwete in the December 14, 2005, elections. The October 30, 2005, elections in Zanzibar were contentious, with incumbent CCM presidential aspirant Amani Karume (son of Zanzibar's first president) narrowly defeating Seif Shariff Hamad from the opposition Civic United Front (CUF). Both elections were originally scheduled for October 30, but the unexpected death of an opposition vice presidential aspirant prompted Tanzania's National Election Commission to reschedule the Union elections.

ACCOUNTABILITY AND PUBLIC VOICE – 3.82

Multiparty politics in Tanzania are best understood in the context of the 1964 union between mainland Tanganyika and Zanzibar. Union elections have consistently reflected the will of the people in multiparty contests held in 1995 and 2000, despite the fact that local and international observers noted irregularities in both of these elections. Currently 18 registered political parties operate freely on the mainland, but their bases of support are limited to select regions and town/urban centers.[5] The incumbent, President Benjamin Mkapa, like his predecessor Ali Hassan Mwinyi, is expected to respect the two-term limit.

As of November 2005, according to many local and international press accounts, the current CCM candidate, Jakaya Kikwete, was expected to dominate a field of nine presidential candidates in the upcoming December elections.[6] The two other main presidential contenders were businessman Freeman Mbowe, from the Chama cha Demokrasi na Maendeleo (CHADEMA) party, and former economics professor Ibrahim Lipumba, from CUF. While it was highly unlikely that either of these candidates would be elected president, the opposition was expected to win some seats in a CCM-dominated parliament. There are differences among these political parties regarding public policy priorities and the pace and scope of political and economic reform, but there is a consensus that the reform process should be continued.

[*Editors Note:* The Decmber 14, 2005, presidential and legislative elections were dominated by CCM. Jakaya Kikwete received 80.3 percent of the valid votes cast, with Ibrahim Lipumba receiving 11.7 percent and

Freeman Mbowe obtaining 5.9 percent. For the National Assembly, CCM won 206 seats, CUF 19 seats, CHADEMA 5 seats, Tanzania Labour Party 1 seat, and the United Democratic Party 1 seat. CCM nominated additional 58 seats for women, CUF 11 seats, and CHADEMA 6 seats. Despite some irregularities, local and international observers declared these elections free and fair.]

The National Election Commission (NEC) has the legal mandate to organize and administer elections throughout the mainland, and the registrar of political parties is entrusted with the registration of all parties contesting in local and national elections. The NEC was accused by observers and opposition parties of poorly administering the 1995 and 2000 elections, often to the advantage of the ruling party, but given CCM's dominance on the mainland, the consensus is that the will of the people was respected in both of these contests.

The executive branch in Tanzania, comprising the president, vice president (directly elected by the people), cabinet ministers (chosen by the president from parliamentarians in the National Assembly), and prime minister (chosen by the president), is constitutionally one of the most powerful on the continent. The president has the authority to reverse judgments of the Court of Appeals through legislation. Further, through his constitutional power to appoint unelected members of parliament, he can bolster ruling-party dominance in the legislative body. A constitutional provision that reserves 30 percent of the seats for women, allocated proportionally to parties in the National Assembly based on electoral performance, enables the successful political parties to appoint additional members of parliament. Given CCM's dominance in National Assembly and presidential elections, this has enabled the newly elected CCM president to appoint a substantial number of female parliamentarians, along with 10 additional members, as stipulated in the constitution. In addition, "all key functions down to the District Commissioners are directly appointed by—and thus dependent upon—the Presidency."[7]

CCM continues to dominate the government at all levels despite the multiparty system in which it operates. As a remnant of the single-party era, and in recognition of continued CCM dominance, the ruling party plays an instrumental role in appointing high-ranking civil servants, but a substantial number of lower-level functionaries are selected based on competition and merit.

Negotiations between CCM and CUF following the contentious 1995 elections in Zanzibar culminated in the *Muafaka* (translated as "agreement") accords; a similar agreement called *Muafaka* II was reached between both parties after the elections in 2000. Neither agreement was fully implemented, leading CUF to contest the 2000 and 2005 elections. Muafaka II resulted in the amendment of the Election Act 1984, introducing a permanent voters register, abolishing the recording of voter registration numbers on the ballot counterfoil, giving the right to party/candidate agents to receive authenticated election results at the polling stations and collation centers, and limiting the role of *Shehas* (local village leaders directly appointed by the government) in the registration process.[8]

CCM Zanzibar presidential candidate Amani Karume narrowly defeated CUF's Hamad on October 30, 2005, amid accusations of an election marred by fraud and intimidation, unfair electoral laws, a biased electoral commission, a dishonest tabulation of the ballots, and limited implementation of the amendment to the Election Act.[9] There were a total of eight candidates for the presidency, but CUF and CCM dominated the elections on the islands. While all 16 registered political parties in Zanzibar had the de jure right to participate in the political process across the islands, the realities on the ground were quite different. Throughout the election campaigning process, CUF was repeatedly denied the right to organize campaign rallies; the large number of security personnel from the mainland intimidated opposition members on the CUF-dominated island of Pemba and on Unguja, where pockets of CUF supporters were outnumbered by their CCM counterparts.[10] Despite assurances by the government that CUF would have fair and equal access to the media during the campaign period, this was not the case. The CCM campaign dominated government radio, television, and print outlets, limiting coverage of opposition campaign events.[11]

Zanzibar's elections are administered by the Zanzibar Electoral Commission (ZEC), which has been repeatedly criticized by major donors, local and international observer groups, and the opposition for acting on behalf of the ruling CCM government and for ensuring the party's success on the islands at the expense of CUF. The ZEC has seven members, who include a chairperson, a vice chairperson, and an independent commissioner (nominated by the president), two commissioners nominated by CCM, and two commissioners nominated by CUF. Despite guarantees in the constitution that the ZEC should operate independently of the government, the inclusion of political appointees has politicized the body in favor of the ruling party.[12]

In addition to the direct election of representatives in a single-member, first-past-the-post electoral system, the attorney general and five other members elected by Zanzibar's House of Representatives also serve in the legislative body. Executive dominance also prevails in Zanzibar, where the president nominates 10 members of the House of Representatives (two in consultation with the opposition), and the constitution allows for the appointment of women based on the same formula as for the Union National Assembly.[13]

Throughout the Union, an array of civic groups, nongovernmental organizations (NGOs), and public policy institutes comment on, and attempt to influence, the legislative process and subsequent implementation of public policy. The major organizations focus on HIV/AIDS, law, gender equality, children's rights, the media, land rights, and human rights. These organizations operate in relative freedom, but the government does periodically, and unpredictably, intervene to limit their work if they criticize it on sensitive matters. It is often difficult to predict how the government will respond to criticisms raised by these groups. In September 2005, the Tanzanian government banned HakiElimu, a local NGO that published an August 2005 report criticizing government primary education reform efforts.[14] The Ministry of Education and Culture accused HakiElimu of "disparaging the image of our education system and the teaching profession of our country through [the] media." Subsequently, 95 local and international civil society organizations issued a "Statement Regarding Rights and Responsibilities of Government and Civil Society Organizations," which offered a detailed response to the Ministry of Education's accusations against HakiElimu.[15] The local Tanzania Education Network coordinated this response document. In contrast, organizations such as the University of Dar es Salaam–based Research and Education for Democracy in Tanzania (REDET) and Tanzania Election Monitoring Committee (TEMCO) have, over the years, offered very critical assessments of the conduct of elections with minimal interference by the government. The donor community, overall, can freely establish funded partnerships with development and advocacy organizations that engage in a wide array of activities across the country with minimal government interference.[16]

The official registration process for nongovernmental organizations, based on the Non Governmental Organizations Act, No. 24, 2002, requires NGOs to obtain a Certificate of Compliance from the Office of the Registrar of NGOs in the vice president's office. Failure to register with this office, or to comply with the other requirements of the act, is a criminal offense.[17] The registration and de-registration process for NGOs is often susceptible to political pressures, as the HakiElimu case demonstrates.

The mainland and Zanzibar have separate media policies. While both governments carefully monitor and periodically limit freedom of the press, the Zanzibar government has been especially aggressive in this regard as the government owns all radio and television stations, along with the only newspaper currently published on the islands, *Zanzibar Leo*. The Zanzibar Newspapers, News Agency and Books Act, 1988, gives the minister in charge of information the power to ban publications with minimal oversight.[18]

On the mainland, approximately 20 television stations and 30 radio stations are in operation, along with an array of newspapers, both public and private.[19] A number of laws impede the media's freedom to criticize the government openly, including the Newspapers Act, 1976; the National Security Act, 1970; and the Broadcasting Services Act, 1993. In April 2003, the National Assembly enacted the Tanzania Communications Regulatory Authority Act, which was followed in October by the release of a new policy regarding information and broadcasting. While these actions represent positive developments for media independence and freedom of expression, the government still maintains controls over the media through some of the legislation listed above. For example, the Swahili newspaper *Daima* was suspended for two days in December 2005 by the Ministry of Information for printing an unflattering photo of President Mkapa.[20] This was imposed under the Newspaper Act, which allows the minister for information and culture to prohibit any publication of any newspaper "in the public interest" or "in the interest of peace and good order."[21]

On the mainland and the islands, onerous libel suits against the press have caused concern among some advocacy groups. In February 2003, former Organization of African Unity secretary general, Dr. Salim Ahmed Salim, was awarded damages worth 1,000,000 shillings (approximately US$1,000) by the mainland High Court. This libel suit was filed by

Salim against the Kenya-based weekly *East African* newspaper for publishing an article critical of him in September 2002.[22] In October 2003, the Zanzibar High Court ruled that Zanzibar's popular *Dira,* the first independent, locally produced newspaper since the 1964 union, had printed two libelous articles about President Karume's daughter and son in January 2003. As a result, the newspaper was ordered to pay damages set at 660,000 shillings (approximately US$660).[23] Shortly afterward, the Zanzibar government suspended and the High Court subsequently banned the newspaper. The initial decision by the government to suspend *Dira* was based on the Zanzibar Newspapers, News Agency and Books Act, 1988, which empowers the government to close a newspaper that is determined to be a "threat to national security."[24] The newspaper reportedly addressed the sensitive issue of the 1964 union between mainland Tanganyika and Zanzibar islands, and it ran an article that accused the ruling party of preparing to rig the 2005 elections. The High Court did not address this issue of national security, instead ruling that the newspaper was not properly registered. In November 2004, the High Court ruled on this case again, refusing to reverse the 2003 ban.

From June 9–20, 2005, the Zanzibar government banned political columnist Jabir Idrissa from contributing to the Swahili newspaper *Rai* based on the claim that he did not have formal government accreditation as a journalist. The political opposition in Zanzibar, along with international organizations such as the Committee to Protect Journalists and Reporters Without Borders, assert that Idrissa was banned because his writings criticized the government.[25]

Overall, Tanzanians have freedom of cultural expression with minimal government interference. Two major pieces of legislation, the National Arts Council of Tanzania Act No. 23, 1984, and the Copyright and Neighboring Rights Act No. 7, 1999, provide the following government ministries and their agencies with the authority to monitor cultural expression: the Ministry of Industry and Trade (Copyright Society of Tanzania), the Ministry of Education and Culture (Department of Culture Development and the National Arts Council), and the Ministry of Natural Resources and Tourism (The National Museum of Tanzania).

Recommendations

- The Union government should initiate a process of political reconciliation in Zanzibar between CCM and CUF, assuring that the Zanzibar government thoroughly implements all of the requirements of the Muafaka II agreement.

- The Union and Zanzibar governments should facilitate a productive public discussion about the strengths and weaknesses of the current terms of the political union, with the goal of amending the constitution in a way that reflects the popular will of Tanzanians from both the mainland and Zanzibar.
- The Union and Zanzibar governments should refrain from interfering with press freedom, amending all laws that give both governments the legal authority to limit freedoms to criticize government policies and political leaders.

CIVIL LIBERTIES – 3.82

While there are no indications that the government engages in systematic torture of prison inmates, conditions inside the prisons are "harsh and life threatening" according to Robert Winslow, who developed a comprehensive website on "comparative criminology" across the world.[26] Approximately 15 prisoners sentenced to death in the Ukonga maximum security prison in Dar es Salaam protested prison conditions in December 2004. According to Amnesty International, the prisoners specifically cited poor food quality, overcrowded cells, and severe beatings by prison authorities as the reasons for the hunger strike. After the prisoners wrote a letter to the president, the minister of home affairs, and the Commission for Human Rights and Governance, central prison authorities agreed to form an inquiry team to investigate. The protesting prisoners ended their strike after meeting with the inquiry team. There are over 3,000 inmates at this prison, among them more than 90 sentenced to death after being found guilty of murder. According to official government statistics, as of August 2004, 387 prisoners were under the sentence of death, although the last execution was carried out in 1995. In April 2003, President Mkapa commuted 100 death sentences.[27]

There have been reports of prisoners waiting several years for trials because they refused, or were not able, to pay bribes to the police and court officials. In some cases, people convicted of crimes served their full sentences before their trials were held. In an effort to relieve chronic overcrowding of the prison system caused by this backlog and by the lack of adequate facilities, in February 2005 the government introduced a pilot program in six regions of the country that enables prisoners convicted for up to three years to have their sentences suspended by performing community services such as the maintenance of public roads, afforestation, environmental and water conservation, and the repair of public facilities (including hospitals and schools). According to the minister for home affairs, approximately 45,000 prisoners are being housed in facilities originally designed for a total population of 20,000.[28]

According to the Union's Preventive Detention Act No. 60, 1962 and the subsequent Preventive Detention Amendment Act No. 2, 1985, the president may order the arrest and indefinite detention (without bail) of any person who the government considers to be dangerous to national security or to the public order. While this section of the act is rarely used, arbitrary arrests and detentions are a problem in the country. According to the law, any person arrested for a crime, and not under the jurisdiction of the Preventive Detention Act and its amendment, must be charged before a magistrate within 24 hours. The police often fail to comply with this statutory requirement.[29]

While the Tanzanian government is required to protect the basic political and civil rights of men and women in the country in accordance with the constitution, the transition to multipartism and open markets has posed some challenges for the regime. The government does not have a history of implementing laws or establishing regulations that explicitly discriminate against persons based on their gender, ethnic, or religious affiliations and/or physical disabilities. Statutes are in place designed to protect persons against discrimination in employment and occupation. However, the recent political transition has resulted in the curtailment of political and civil rights for the political opposition, especially in Zanzibar (see "Accountability and Public Voice").

In terms of the political rights of women, the Union and Zanzibar governments have reserved seats for female representatives in the National Assembly and House of Representatives (see "Accountability and Public Voice"). One of the 10 candidates for president in the December 2005 Union elections, Anna Claudio Senkoro, was the first woman to run for this office. Senkoro's Progressive Party of Tanzania was not expected to obtain many votes, but the symbolic value of her campaign served to highlight the issue of civil and political rights for women in the country. More than 100 other women ran for the National Assembly.[30] Women constitute approximately 35 percent of the public service workforce, with substantially less representation at the higher levels of public administration.[31]

The Sexual Offenses Special Provision Act, 1998 prohibits the trafficking of persons for sexual purposes, with punishment for those found guilty ranging from 10 to 20 years of imprisonment or up to $300 in fines. It is reported that women have been trafficked to Zanzibar and Mombassa, Kenya, specifically to work as prostitutes. Many of those who are trafficked to work as domestic laborers are often subjected to commercial sexual exploitation. Children are often trafficked away from families to work in mines, in commercial agriculture, or as domestic laborers.[32] According to the Tanzanian Ministry of Labour and Youth Development, the International Labour Organization–supported Time-bound Program has enabled the government to rescue or prevent 30,530 children from being employed as miners, fishermen, commercial sex workers, plantation workers, and domestic servants over the past three years. According to a 2003 International Labour Organization report, 717,677 children between the ages of 5 and 17 were engaged in a variety of forms of labour in the country.[33]

Tanzania encompasses more than 130 ethnic groups. The largest group, the Sukuma, represents only 13 percent of the population.[34] Ethnic politics have not been a salient characteristic of the Tanzania state. The country's first three presidents have been from different regional, ethnic, and religious backgrounds.

While people with disabilities are not formally discriminated against, legal protection against discrimination is minimal. In addition, access to basic government social services and employment opportunities is limited due to the lack of disabled-accessible facilities in government offices.

The Tanzanian government does not have a history of placing restrictions on religious observance, religious ceremony, religious education, or the operation of faith-based organizations. However, tension between Muslims and Christians in the country appears to be increasing. These religious groups are equal in size, but some Muslims believe that Christians have dominated the political realm since independence, and some Christians fear the rise of Muslim fundamentalism in the country.[35] These tensions have not substantially impacted freedom of worship, but periodic violent confrontations between a small number of Muslims and Christians demonstrates the potential for this to happen in the future.

The Tanzanian constitution guarantees freedom of association, and the government respects the right to form and join trade unions. However, the Zanzibar government repeatedly denied the political opposition the right to organize rallies during the campaign for the October 2005 elections (see "Accountability and Public Voice"). The government does not have a record of systematically killing political opponents or peaceful activists, although there have been instances both on the mainland and in Zanzibar in which an undisciplined police force has come into violent contact with the political opposition, especially during the months leading up to national elections. During the postelection violence between CUF supporters and the local police in Pemba in January 2001, at least 31 political protesters were killed by the police, and more than 2,000 people fled to Mombassa for political refuge. This followed a large opposition political rally in Dar es Salaam, in which the defeated CUF Union presidential aspirant Ibrahim Lipumba was publicly beaten by security forces. During the 2005 election campaigns in Zanzibar, one youth was shot by the police, an act the opposition claimed had political motivations.

Recommendations

- The Union government should reform the prison system by providing fair and humane treatment for inmates in accordance with international standards. The state should also assure that all citizens charged with a crime have the opportunity to defend themselves in a timely fashion, in a court of law that does not engage in corruption or bribe taking.
- The Union and Zanzibar governments should guarantee citizens' freedom of association, especially during election campaigns, without regard to political affiliation.
- The Union government should widely publicize the problem of people trafficking and the importance of protecting the rights of women and children, thoroughly implementing and amending, where appropriate, all relevant child labor and trafficking laws so that the country is in accord with international standards.
- The Union government should carefully monitor Muslim/Christian relations in the country and develop conflict prevention mechanisms if tensions intensify into repeated violent confrontation.

RULE OF LAW – 3.37

The judicial branch of the Tanzanian government comprises the Court of Appeal of the United Republic of Tanzania, the High Courts for the Mainland and Zanzibar, and the Judicial Service Commission for the mainland. Zanzibar has a parallel system, with some cases eligible for appeal in the Court of Appeal based on the mainland. Given the strength of the executive branch, the judiciary has rarely restrained the government in politically important cases.[36] Even though the constitution provides for judicial independence, the World Bank reports that "constrained administrative independence of the Judiciary" has contributed to the "underlying weakness of the legal and judicial system."[37] Due to the power of the executive branch and the corrupt practices of many in the judiciary, prosecutors can be influenced by political pressures, and high-level government officials are rarely prosecuted for corrupt practices and other inappropriate and illegal activities. However, higher courts are beginning to assert their independence from the executive branch.[38]

The president of Tanzania has the constitutional prerogative to appoint judges to the Court of Appeal and the High Court. He also appoints the chief justice, who serves as the head of the Court of Appeal and the chief of the judiciary. The president's appointment of judges to the High Court occurs in consultation with the Judicial Services Commission (the chief justice as chairman, the attorney general, a judge of the Court of Appeal, the principal judge of the High Court, and two additional members appointed by the president). The five levels of courts combine tribal, Islamic, and British common law, with family and civil matters governed by customary law. In certain specific matters in Zanzibar and the mainland, Muslims are governed by Islamic law.

Overall, the quality of judicial services is of a low standard due to a poor legal system and regulatory framework, weak management and coordination of judicial institutions, ineffective human resources and administration, and an overall poor work environment. The IMF specifically identifies, among other things, "low competence, morale, and integrity of public sector legal personnel." In order to address these problems, in 2005 the government has developed a Legal Sector Reform Program.[39] It remains to be seen if this program will prove to be effective.

Everyone charged with a criminal offense is presumed innocent until proven guilty, and the government is supposed to provide citizens with fair, public, and timely hearings by competent, independent, and impartial tribunals. Nonetheless, citizens charged with a crime often have to wait months, and sometimes years, for a trial. Due to endemic corruption in the judicial system, justice is more quickly served for those willing to bribe police and court officers. According to the Prevention of Terrorism Act, 2002, only relevant parties are permitted to attend the trials of terror suspects, and information about the identity of witnesses who testify at these trials is not available to the public.[40] For citizens charged with a serious offense, such as murder, Tanzanian law provides for defense counsel.

The Union president serves as the commander in chief of the armed forces, and he effectively controls a military that does not have a history of intervening in the political affairs of the state. The police force (and the People's Militia Field Force, commonly referred to by its Swahili acronym FFU) falls under the legal jurisdiction of the Ministry of Home Affairs, which is responsible for maintaining law and order in the country.

In 1991, the president appointed a Commission on Land Matters that studied the land tenure system in Tanzania. Issa Shivji, an eminent professor of law at the University of Dar es Salaam, chaired this commission. Around the same time, the Ministry of Lands, Housing, and Urban Development assembled a committee to examine the same issue. After the results of these initiatives were published, a public debate ensued that resulted in the establishment of the National Land Policy.[41] Subsequently, the Land Act 1999 and the Village Land Act Nos. 4 and 5 of 1999 were passed by the National Assembly.[42] According to these acts, all land in Tanzania technically belongs to the state. However, this land can be effectively owned by Tanzanian citizens in three ways: (1) government-granted right of occupancy, (2) Tanzania Investment Centre (TIC) derivative rights that permit Tanzanians to sublease their land to local and foreign investors,[43] or (3) the leasing of granted-right-of-occupancy lands by the private sector. Right-of-occupancy periods range from 5 to 99 years, and derivative rights range between 5 and 98 years. Noncitizens can occupy land only for investment purposes.[44] While the expropriation of foreign-owned businesses was a common feature of former president Julius Nyerere's village socialism initiative enshrined in the 1967 Arusha Declaration, the last reported expropriation occurred in 1985. The ambiguities of land ownership in which all land "belongs" to the Tanzanian government, but can be "owned" by citizens, and can be "occupied" by foreign investors, are vestiges of the country's socialist past that are disincentives for foreign direct investment.[45]

Recommendations

- The Union government should reform the judiciary, specifically upgrading the quality of its judicial and legal services by increasing its support for legal education and strengthening the existing legal framework by making the process more efficient and effective.
- The Union government should demonstrate resolute political will and provide the resources necessary to enhance the effectiveness of existing institutions dedicated to eradicating corruption in the judicial branch. This can be done by thoroughly implementing the relevant existing laws and amending them where necessary, and enhancing the capacity and effectiveness of the Legal Sector Reform Program.
- The Union government should assure judicial independence from the executive branch by amending the constitution, amending existing laws, and enacting new legislation that assures the separation of powers between the two branches of government and that enhances the oversight capacities of the judiciary.
- The Union government should amend laws that deal with land ownership by citizens and noncitizens so that they are consistent with its current emphasis on promoting economic growth and development through local and foreign direct investment in the local economy.

ANTICORRUPTION AND TRANSPARENCY – 2.82

In 1975, the Anti-Corruption Squad was formed in accordance with an amendment to the Prevention of Corruption Act No. 16 of 1971. Before this squad was formed, combating corruption was the province of the police force, which was under the jurisdiction of the Ministry of Home Affairs. In 1991, a further amendment to the 1971 act resulted in the replacement of the Anti-Corruption Squad with the Prevention of Corruption Bureau.

In 1996, the Mkapa government established the Warioba Commission, which was given the mandate to examine corruption in the country and offer a set of recommendations. The final report has served as a blueprint for combating corruption in the country, with the subsequent adoption in 1999 of a comprehensive National Anti-Corruption Strategy and Action Plan (NACSAP), the appointment of a minister of good governance, and the establishment of a Commission for Ethics. Despite these efforts, corruption in Tanzania continues to be a major problem at all levels of government compounded by the limited protections offered by the government for whistle-blowers.[46] Corruption is a less serious problem in the higher education sector, which has a standardized assessment procedure for admitting and grading students.

According to Transparency International's Corruption Perceptions Index, Tanzania ranked 96th out of 146 countries in 2004 (scoring 2.8 out of 10) and 96th out of 159 (scoring 2.9) countries in 2005.[47] A recent UN report cited extensive corruption in the tax administration, judiciary, public procurement, privatization, local administration, and social services.[48] In an effort to address this issue, the Law Reform Commission has recently drafted amendments to a new Anti-Corruption Law designed to strengthen the prosecution mechanism and bring Tanzania into compliance with international treaties. This new law would provide the Prevention of Corruption Bureau with access to information and evidence necessary to conduct thorough investigations into alleged corruption by government officials. The legislation is expected to be reviewed by the cabinet no later than the end of April 2006.[49]

According the World Bank's assessment of doing business in Tanzania, the country ranks 140th out of a total of 155 countries. Of the 10 indicators cited by the Bank in the assessment, in "dealing with licenses" Tanzania rates as the "worst performer" in the world, with property registration and the payment of taxes ranking 143 and 144, respectively.[50] Despite the progress in macroeconomic reform, the government's intervention in the economy continues to create disincentives for entrepreneurship and local and foreign investment in the country. In an effort to address this, draft bills on Business Activities Registration and Reform and the Regulatory Licensing System are scheduled to be presented to the National Assembly by July 2006.[51]

While certain government institutions are designed to enforce the separation of public office from the personal interests of public servants and protect against conflict of interest in the private sector, they are weak and ineffectual. This has served to provide opportunities for pervasive corruption at all levels. Disclosure procedures are, however, required for public officials by the Declaration of Assets and Liabilities Act No. 5, 2001.[52] Information on elected public officials is supposed to be available to the public, but individuals must apply to the government to review the requested documents. The application process effectively limits public access to this information. The public does not have access to information on disclosures by civil servants.[53]

As a part of the economic reform process, the IMF has worked closely with the Tanzanian government to enhance its capacity to collect taxes in a fair and transparent manner. The autonomous Tanzania Revenue Authority (TRA) is entrusted with this responsibility and has made some progress in recent years. For example, the TRA introduced a code of conduct for its tax officials, and a new tax appeal mechanism began operation in 2001.[54] During the 2004–2005 fiscal year, tax revenue collection was 20 percent higher than in the previous year, exceeding the target amount agreed to by the Tanzanian government and the IMF.[55]

Despite the existence of a number of oversight and watchdog institutions, including the Prevention of Corruption Bureau, the Commission for Human Rights and Good Governance, and an Ethics Secretariat, government funds are often unlawfully and unwisely spent. Many of these and other institutions have the potential to provide adequate oversight functions, but they are underfunded, unable to retain well-trained officers, have overlapping mandates, and operate in a weak legal framework.[56] The mainland press often reports on high-profile cases of corruption, but these cases receive far less attention in the Zanzibar press, presumably because the government owns all of the newspapers and radio and television stations. Although there is a competitive system for awarding government contracts, this process is often beset with bribery and other corrupt practices by government officials at all levels of administration.[57]

According to the IMF, the budget-making process is "open and well-structured," with the Budget Committee and the Finance and Economic Affairs Committee responsible for legislative oversight.[58] Quarterly reports are published and subject to review by the public, and the budget process includes input by Public Expenditure Review (PER) Working Groups that are composed of representatives from government, the World Bank, other donors, and civil society organizations.[59] The

PER recently concluded that there was a "clear need to strengthen internal and external audit of public expenditure." The government proposed to accomplish this by strengthening the capacity of the National Audit Office.[60]

The government provides a legal environment for the administration and distribution of foreign assistance in the country, but disbursements by donors through the exchequer or by direct, in-kind grants made to projects and programs are often not accounted for due, presumably, to corrupt practices by government officials.[61] Despite this situation, the budget coverage of externally financed projects is, according to the IMF, "quite comprehensive."[62]

Recommendations

- The Union government should enhance the legitimacy, capacity, and effectiveness of existing oversight institutions, specifically focusing on the appropriate use of financial and in-kind foreign aid. This should be done by thoroughly implementing existing laws, amending them where necessary.
- The Union government should fully implement all of the provisions of the National Anti-Corruption Strategy and Action Plan (NACSAP), strengthen the portfolio and political capacity of the Ministry of Good Governance, and enhance the effectiveness of the Commission for Ethics.
- The Union government should facilitate an enabling environment for successful local entrepreneurs and foreign investors, specifically addressing the roadblocks to productive economic activities identified in the World Bank's "Doing Business" benchmarks for successful business development.
- The Union government should remove government officials who are not able to account for direct and/or in-kind grants made to specific Tanzanian government projects and programs.

NOTES

[1] "Tanzania Country Brief" (Washington, D.C.: World Bank, September 2005), http://web.worldbank.org/WBSITE/EXTERNAL/COUNTRIES/AFRICAEXT/TANZANIA EXTN/0,,menuPK:287345~pagePK:141132~piPK:141107~theSitePK:258799,00.html.

[2] For references to the 1995 elections, consult Paul J. Kaiser, "Power, Sovereignty, and International Election Observers: The Case of Zanzibar," *Africa Today* 46, No. 1 (Win-

ter 1999): 29–49. For the 2000 elections, see Paul J. Kaiser, "Zanzibar: A Multi-Level Analysis of Conflict Prevention," in Chandra Sriram and Karin Wermester, eds., *From Promise to Practice: Strengthening UN Capacities for the Prevention of Violent Conflict* (Boulder: Lynne Rienner Publishers, 2003), 101–33.

3 "Tanzania: Mkapa Leaves a Socialist State More Liberalised," *IRIN News* (New York: United Nations Office for the Coordination of Humanitarian Affairs, Integrated Regional News and Information Networks, 13 December 2005), http://www.irinnews.org/report.asp?ReportID=50643&SelectRegion=Great_Lakes&SelectCountry=TANZANIA

4 See *Constitution of the United Republic of Tanzania of 1977* (Dar es Salaam: The United Republic of Tanzania National Web site, 1998), http://www.tanzania.go.tz/constitutionf.html.

5 "Tanzania: Most Political Parties Sign on to Election Code," *IRIN News*, 11 August 2005, http://www.irinnews.org/print.asp?ReportID=48551.

6 Based on an analysis by the author of English and Swahili newspapers, along with VOA, BBC, and AllAfrica reports published in November 2005.

7 Jonas Ewald, "Election or Democracy? The Interface Between Economic Reforms and Democratisation in Tanzania" (Oslo, Norway: First Annual Network Conference on Actors and Approaches in Local Politics, paper, 17–19 October 2002); Rose Shayo, "Women Participation in Party Politics during the Multiparty Era in Africa: The Case of Tanzania" (Auckland Park, South Africa, EISA Occasional Paper, Number 34, July 2005).

8 "The Elections in Zanzibar, United Republic of Tanzania, 30 October 2005," *Report of the Commonwealth Observer Group* (London: Commonwealth Secretariat, 17 November 2005), 19–20, http://www.thecommonwealth.org/Templates/Internal.asp?NodeID=147130.

9 Ibid., 18; see also "The Report of the East Africa Law Society's Mission to Zanzibar of 16th to 20th May 2005" (Zanzibar, Tanzania: East Africa Law Society, 15 July 2005).

10 "The Elections in Zanzibar . . ." (Commonwealth Secretariat), 31.

11 Ibid., 35.

12 "The Elections in Zanzibar . . ." (Commonwealth Secretariat), 18.

13 Ibid., 25.

14 "Tanzania: Report Critical of Primary Education Angers Minister," *IRIN News*, 1 September 2005, http://www.irinnews.org/print.asp?ReportID=48863.

15 "Cases 2005: Africa" (New York: Committee to Protect Journalists [CPJ], 11 November 2005); "NGO Banned from Publishing Studies about Education System" (Toronto: International Freedom of Expression Exchange [IFEX], Alert, 11 October 2005).

16 For example, the Washington D.C.–based PACT (http://www.pactworld.org) organization opened an office in Dar es Salaam in 2002 and has engaged in a number of advocacy initiatives with local NGOs. PACT Tanzania (http://www .pacttz.org) and the Lawyers' Environmental Action Team (http://www.leat.or.tz) produced two Swahili/English guides for civil society organizations in Tanzania, one focusing on "policy, law and governance," and the second on the "law making process."

17 "Procedures for Registration of Non Governmental Organizations Under the Non Governmental Organizations Act, No. 24, 2002" (Dar es Salaam: United Republic of

Tanzania, Vice President's Office/Tanzania Education and Information Services, 2002), http: //www.tanedu.org/Procedures_NGO_registration.pdf.

18 Lawrence Kilimwiko, "Tanzania" (Windhoek, Namibia: Media Institute of Southern Africa [MISA], n.d.), www.misa.org/sothisisdemocracy/tanzania/tanzania.html).

19 "Reporters without Borders Tanzania 2004 Annual Report" (Paris: Reporters Without Borders, 3 May 2004), http://www.rsf.org/print/php3?id_article=10206.

20 Guardian Reporter, "Ban of Newspaper Riles MOAT ", *Guardian* (Dar es Salaam, Tanzania), 9 December 2005.

21 "Government Suspends Two Newspapers" (IFEX, December 6, 2005).

22 Kilimwiko, "Tanzania" (MISA).

23 "Weekly Paper May Have to Close Because of Heavy Fine" (Paris: Reporters Without Borders [RSF], 30 October 2005).

24 "Cases 2004: Africa" (CPJ, 1 December 2004); "Tanzania, Zanzibar Minister of State Salim Juma Osman" (Paris: World Association of Newspapers, 27 November 2003), www.wan-press.org/article3146.html?var_recherche=tanzania.

25 "Cases 2005: Africa" (CPJ, 24 June 2005); "Zanzibar Government Bans Leading Columnist" (RSF, 13 June 2005).

26 Robert Winslow, "Crime and Society: A Comparative Criminology Tour of the World: Tanzania" (San Diego: San Diego State University, n.d.), http://www-rohan.sdsu.edu/ faculty/rwinslow/africa/tanzania.html.

27 "Tanzania: Further Information: Harsh Prison Conditions/Torture or Ill Treatment/ Death Penalty: At Least 15 Prisoners on Death Row" (London: Amnesty International [AI], 26 January 2005); "Tanzania: Harsh Prison Conditions/Torture or Ill Treatment/ Death Penalty" (AI, 13 January 2005).

28 "Tanzania: Government Introduces Community Service to Decongest Prisons," *IRIN News,* 11 February 2005, http://www.irinnews.org/print.asp?ReportID=45506.

29 Winslow, "Crime and Society . . ."; see also Chris Maina Peter, "Incarcerating the Innocent: Preventive Detention in Tanzania," *Human Rights Quarterly* 19, No. 1, 113–35.

30 Cathy Matjenyi, "First Woman Runs for Tanzania Presidency," *Voice of America News,* 26 October 2005.

31 "United Republic of Tanzania: Public Administration Profile" (New York: United Nations [UN], Department of Economic and Social Affairs, Division for Public Administration and Development Management, January 2004).

32 Winslow, "Crime and Society . . ."; see also, "Tanzania: Focus on Child Labor," *IRIN News,* 13 August 2003, http://www.irinnews.org/report.asp?ReportID=35950&Select Region=Great_Lakes&SelectCountry=TANZANIA.

33 "Tanzania: Over 30,500 Rescued from Child Labour," *IRIN News,* 30 March 2005, http://www.irinnews.org/report.asp?ReportID=46377&SelectRegion=Great_Lakes&Select Country=TANZANIA.

34 "Tanzania," in *The World Factbook* (Washington, D.C.: U.S. Central Intelligence Agency [CIA], 2005), http://www.cia.gov/cia/publications/factbook/geos/tz.html#People; "Tanzania: Ethnic Groups," in *East Africa Living Encyclopedia* (Philadelphia: University of Pennsylvania, African Studies Center, 1992), http://www.africa.upenn.edu/NEH/ tethnic.htm.

35 For three very different perspectives on the emerging Muslim/Christian divide, see Hamza Mustafa Njozi, *Mwembechai Killings and the Political Future of Tanzania* (Ottowa: Globalink Communications, 2000); Lawrence E. Y. Mbogoni, *The Cross and the Crescent: Religion and Politics in Tanzania from the 1880s to the 1990s* (Dar es Salaam: Mkuki na Nyota Publishers, 2005); and Bruce E. Heilman and Paul J. Kaiser, "Religion and Identity in Tanzania," *Third World Quarterly* 23, No. 4 (August 2002): 691–709.

36 Siri Gloppen, "The Accountability Function of the Courts in Tanzania and Zambia," in Siri Gloppen, Roberto Gargarella, and Elin Skaar, eds., *Democratization and the Judiciary: The Accountability Function of Courts in New Democracies* (London/Portland, OR: Frank Cass Pub., 2004), 112–36.

37 "Project Information Document (PID), Appraisal Stage, Accountability, Transparency & Integrity Project: Tanzania" (Washington, D.C.: International Monetary Fund [IMF], Report No. AB2054, 15 December 2005), p. 3.; see also "Tanazania," in *2005 Index of Economic Freedom* (Washington, D.C./New York: The Heritage Foundation/The *Wall Street Journal,* 2005), http://www.heritage.org; and "United Republic of Tanzania: Public Administration Profile" (UN, January 2004), 14.

38 Winslow, "Crime and Society"; see also, "Tanzania: Corruption in Isles Judiciary Still Rampant," BBC Monitoring Service, 3 January 2006; "Tanzania, Country Brief" (World Bank, September 2005).

39 "Project Information Document (PID), Appraisal Stage, Accountability, Transparency & Integrity Project: Tanzania" (Washington, D.C.: International Monetary Fund [IMF], Report No. AB2054, 15 December 2005).

40 See "The Prevention of Terrorism Act, 2002" (Kampala, Uganda: East African Centre for Constitutional Development), http://www.kituochakatiba.co.ug/tzterroract.htm.

41 Dzodzi Tsikata, "Land Tenure and Women's Land Rights: Recent Debates in Tanzania" (Geneva: United Nations Research Institute for Social Development [UNRISD], Project on Agrarian Change, Gender and Land Rights, paper, September 2001).

42 Bahati Mlolo, "Land Policy Challenges for Policy Makers: Tanzania Experience" (Dar es Salaam: Ministry of Land and Human Settlements Development, n.d.).

43 The Tanzania Investment Centre was established as a result of the Tanzania Investment Act, 1997, for the purpose of providing comprehensive information about investing in the country.

44 "United Republic of Tanzania Business Guide" (Dar es Salaam: Tanzania Investment Centre, March 2002), 54.

45 "United Republic of Tanzania Business Guide" (Dar es Salaam: Tanzania Investment Centre, March 2002).

46 Medard Rwelamira and Heather Mupita, "Fighting Corruption in Tanzania: Challenges and Prospects for Partnership" (London: the Southern African Forum Against Corruption/Commonwealth Business Council, October 2003); S. J. Sitta, "Integrity Environment and Investment Promotion: The Case of Tanzania" (Addis Ababa, Ethiopia: OECD, NEPAD, and Transparency International conference, "Alliance for Integrity—Government and Business Roles in Enhancing African Standards of Living," paper, 7–8 March 2005; "Improving Enterprise Performance and Growth in Tanzania"

(Washington, D.C.: World Bank and International Finance Corporation [IFC], Investment Climate Assessment, November 2004).

47 "Corruption Perceptions Index 2004" (Berlin: Transparency International [TI]); "Corruption Perceptions Index 2005" (TI).

48 "United Republic of Tanzania: Public Administration Profile" (UN, January 2004), 14.

49 "Fourth Review Under the Three-year Arrangement Under the Poverty Reduction and Growth Facility and Request for Waiver Performance Criteria" (IMF, Africa Department, 18 July 2005), 13, 20.

50 "Doing Business—Benchmarking Business Regulations: Tanzania" (World Bank, 2005), http://www.doingbusiness.org/ExploreEconomies/Default.aspx?economyid=185.

51 "Fourth Review . . ." (IMF, 18 July 2005), 20.

52 "Assets Disclosure by Public Officials: Historical Information," Administrative & Civil Service Reform website, (Washington, D.C.: The World Bank Group, n.d.), http://www1.worldbank.org/publicsector/civilservice/assetsByCountryHistoricalALL.asp.

53 George Larbi, "Between Spin and Reality: Disclosure of Assets and Interests by Public Officials in Developing Countries" (Manchester, U.K: unpublished paper, 25 November 2005).

54 "Tanzania: Report on the Observance of Standards and Codes—Fiscal Transparency Module" (IMF, Staff Team, 1 February 2002), 7.

55 "Statement by Peter Ngumbullu, Executive Director for the United Republic of Tanzania and John Mafararikwa, Senior Advisor to Executive Director, International Monetary Fund, July 29, 2005" (Dar es Salaam: International Monetary Fund, 29 July 2005).

56 "PID: Tanzania" (IMF, Report No. AB2054, 15 December 2005).

57 Florida Henjewele, Geoffrey Mwambe, Erasto Ngalewa, and Knut Nygaard, "Local Government Finances and Financial Management in Tanzania" (Dar es Salaam: Research on Poverty Alleviation [Report No. 16], 2004), 18–19; see also "Combating Money Laundering in the SADC Sub-Region: The Case of Tanzania," in Prince M. Bagenda, *Profiling Money Laundering in Eastern and Southern Africa* (Pretoria: Institute for Security Studies [ISS], Monograph No. 90, December 2003), http://www.iss.co.za/pubs/Monographs/No90/Chap3.html.

58 "Tanzania: Report on the Observance . . ." (IMF, 1 February 2002), 10.

59 Ibid., 15.

60 "Memorandum of Economic and Financial Policies for 2005/06 and the Medium Term," submitted as an Attachment to a Letter by Basil P. Mramba, Minister of Finance, Government of Tanzania, to the Managing Director of the International Monetary Fund, 14 July 2005, Appendix I, "Fourth Review Under the Three-year Arrangement Under the Poverty Reduction and Growth Facility and Request for Waiver Performance Criteria" (IMF, Africa Department, 18 July 2005), 42.

61 "Tanzania: Report on the Observance . . ." (IMF, 1 February 2002), 8.

62 "Tanzania: Report on the Observance . . ." (IMF, 1 February 2002), 8.

UGANDA

CAPITAL: Kampala

POPULATION: 26.9 million

GNI PER CAPITA: $250

SCORES	2004	2006
ACCOUNTABILITY AND PUBLIC VOICE:	3.82	3.99
CIVIL LIBERTIES:	4.23	3.81
RULE OF LAW:	4.08	3.66
ANTICORRUPTION AND TRANSPARENCY:	3.77	3.74

(scores are based on a scale of 0 to 7, with 0 representing weakest and 7 representing strongest performance)

Nelson Kasfir

INTRODUCTION

The aspirations of Ugandans to enjoy freedom and democracy suffered significant setbacks between October 2003 and November 2005. The most important reasons for these reverses stem from the increasingly evident motivation of President Yoweri Museveni to extend his 20-year period in office despite constitutional limits and the opposition of his closest colleagues. His recent efforts to change the rules and silence his opponents bear unfortunate resemblance to those of his predecessors, Milton Obote and Idi Amin. They demonstrate the difficulties of maintaining progress toward democratization in Uganda. Ironically, the most serious threats to democracy over the last two years have resulted from Uganda's re-adoption of multiparty competition.

Uganda has always been a difficult country to govern democratically. It is deeply fragmented into ethnic, religious, and regional cleavages that greatly complicate the formation and maintenance of a legitimate ruling coalition. As his authority over his coalition members declined, each former ruler increasingly resorted to patronage and intimidation at the expense of support for the rule of law. By the time Museveni and the National Resistance Army (NRA) seized power by defeating the national army in 1986, Uganda had become a failed state without an effective

Nelson Kasfir writes frequently on Ugandan politics and development. He teaches government at Dartmouth College.

constitution, fair elections, protection from terror, autonomous judges, or honest officials.

Over the following 15 years, Museveni presided over a widely applauded political and economic recovery. A liberal and carefully balanced constitution emerged through a process of widespread popular participation. By and large, the government respected the exercise of free speech and a free press. The new parliament created by the constitution vigorously attempted to hold the government accountable for corruption, even forcing several ministers out of the cabinet and reversing some dubious transactions intended to privatize state banks and public corporations. The emphasis on frequent elections at every level of government from the village to the state, although organized without parties, may have strengthened the basis for a democratic culture.

At the same time, worrying signs of authoritarian behavior, reminiscent of Uganda's past, accompanied Uganda's recovery. The constitution legitimated a no-party system in which individuals rather than parties competed for office. Prohibiting participation by parties strengthened the hand of the president, who controlled the National Resistance Movement (NRM or "Movement"), and who could also use the institutions of government for political advantage over unorganized rivals. Museveni had ruled for 10 years before competing in an election. Corruption remained widespread throughout the new government. The president expanded his reliance on patronage to build support. He tended to make decisions without consulting parliament in regional wars fought in three border areas, in the Democratic Republic of the Congo, and in the Sudan. The army, which had been regarded as incorruptible and highly disciplined when it won power, gained a reputation for corruption and attacking civilians in battle areas—vices reminiscent of former Ugandan armies.

Nevertheless, Uganda exhibited many signs of an emerging democratic culture under Museveni. The judiciary decided several constitutional cases against the government. Members of parliament (MPs) changed many government legislative proposals before passing them. Press criticism of government actions was frequent and vocal. Constitutional commissions held the government accountable for human rights and financial improprieties. Civil society organizations campaigned vigorously for women, the environment, and peace. One of the most important milestones for democratization was the constitutional requirement that a president could serve only two terms. That meant President Museveni would have had to leave office in 2006. Had that happened, it would have been the first time in Uganda's postindependence history that one president had been replaced by another peacefully and democratically. It would have provided a fundamental demonstration that the Ugandan government respected the spirit of the rule of law as well as its regulations. Instead, in 2005 Museveni and his closest advisers clearly reversed direction. Considerable political liberalization had occurred, but it became increasingly uncertain how much had been accomplished to hold the government accountable to its citizens.

ACCOUNTABILITY AND PUBLIC VOICE – 3.99

Despite many disconcerting instances of intimidation and fraud, and the absence of participation by parties, the presidential and parliamentary elections held in 1996 and 2001 seemed to most observers to reflect broadly the will of the people. Recent events cast doubt over the prospects for the free and fair conduct of the next set of elections, scheduled for February 2006. The last two national elections were the only ones held at regular intervals since independence. Suffrage was equal and universal, with special-interest parliamentary constituencies for workers, youth, women, persons with disabilities, and the army (at present these account for 27.5 percent of MPs).[1] The electoral commission was regarded as relatively independent of the president and committed to an honest ballot count, but not always able to manage the complicated logistics involved in Uganda's complex electoral system.

In a referendum held on July 28, 2005, Ugandan voters adopted multiparty competition, casting aside the country's no-party system. While 92.5 percent supported legalizing party activity, only 47 percent of those registered voted, largely due to a boycott by the opposition, despite its strong prior support for party competition.[2] The refusal of the opposition to participate reflected their suspicion that Museveni did not favor genuine multiparty competition, but instead was manipulating the change in political systems to enable his continuation in office.

Before the July 2005 referendum, parties could register under the Political Parties and Other Organizations Act 2002, and many did. But the act prohibited any party from organizing activities below the national level. Unregistered political groups were not permitted to hold public meetings. Qualified political groups could hold meetings without seeking a permit, but the police had to be informed of the time and place. A police officer who determined that an ongoing meeting contravened the act could stop it. In 2004 and 2005, the police dispersed 21 peaceful demonstrations and public rallies.[3] The most prominent among these involved public meetings by opposition groups, including rallies demonstrating against a third term for the president, against the Movement, and an address by Major General Mugisha Muntu of the Forum for Democratic Change (FDC). On the other hand, public meetings of supporters of the Movement were not dispersed.

Passage of the multiparty referendum implied official recognition of every person's right to choose a party and join in its public meetings. Museveni, however, interpreted the consequences of the referendum narrowly. He explicitly insisted that its purpose was to increase the internal discipline of the Movement by removing doubters. As one reporter wondered, "the question therefore, is whether the Movement would actually allow a truly multiparty democracy."[4]

A few by-elections were held between 2003 and 2005. Even though no parties could campaign officially, the government used the Movement secretariat and other government resources, including intervention by the president, to support its preferred candidates. The National Resistance Movement-Organization (NRM-O) registered as a political party and chose its interim leaders in 2004. Despite their reservations about the constitutionality of required registration under the Political Parties and Organizations Act 2002, other parties registered in 2005. The FDC, a new party that included Kiiza Besigye, who had run second to Museveni in 2001, faced delays before successfully registering. Unlike the NRM-O, which was able to build on the Movement's organizational activities during the two decades of the no-party period, the other parties had a relatively short time (roughly August to November 2005) to organize their national conferences, discuss policies, elect fresh officials, and create or rebuild party structures in preparation for the 2006 elections. A new Political Parties and Organizations Act responsive to the transition to electoral participation by parties was enacted in November 2005.

Passage of the constitutional amendment that removed presidential term limits in August 2005 freed Museveni to run for another term. He accepted the nomination of the NRM-O in November 2005. President

Museveni's control over the government and the army greatly decreases the likelihood that another party can replace the Movement, which by 2006 will have been in power for 19 years. Four donors—Great Britain, Ireland, Netherlands, and Norway—signaled their alarm in 2005 over the government's unwillingness to provide a level playing field for elections by cutting their aid by small amounts.

The government will pay 45 million shillings (US$25,000) for campaign expenses to each presidential candidate (raised from 20 million in 2001). This sum is only a small fraction of what each party is likely to spend. Growth in the economy has made it possible for private interests to contribute significantly to each party's campaign. However, the NRM-O has benefited far more than any opposition party because they receive contributions from both public and private sources. Judging from the many instances of economic privileges given to investors, regulations controlling influence over campaigns are not enforced effectively.

The FDC nominated Kiiza Besigye as its presidential candidate at the end of October 2005. Two weeks later, on his return from a campaign trip, he was arrested in Kampala and imprisoned on remand on charges of treason, misprision of treason, and rape. Later, on the basis of the same allegations and despite his civilian status, he was court-martialed by a military tribunal on charges of terrorism and unlawful possession of weapons. After he received bail from the high court in November 2005, he was immediately rearrested and returned to prison on the court-martial charges. The opening of his military trial was set four days after the official date for presidential nominations. At the end of November 2005, no one knew whether the executive would allow him to continue his campaign for president.

The 1995 constitution increased the separation of powers by giving additional authority to parliament and the judiciary to check aggressive executive action, one of Uganda's most serious problems in the past. For several years following the adoption of the constitution, parliament played an unusually aggressive role in executive oversight. Unexpectedly, the no-party system gave MPs greater independence to stand up to the executive. As the restoration of parties grew more likely beginning in 2003, parliament's oversight activity diminished, although not entirely. In June 2004, five MPs were able to persuade the commercial court to issue an injunction that temporarily blocked the sale of the Uganda Commercial Bank. MPs forced the government to suspend an agreement to lease the Dairy Corporation, a state-owned company, in February 2005 until they could study its terms.[5] However, many MPs felt that the executive was often able to avoid oversight.

In a white paper issued in September 2004, the cabinet proposed numerous constitutional amendments, including the shift from the no-party to a multiparty system.[6] In October 2004, more than 240 MPs judged likely to support the government on the removal of presidential term limits and other constitutional amendments each received a 5-million-shilling payment (US$2800) in cash from Movement officials "for consultations on the White Paper" with their constituents.[7] The source of this money was never satisfactorily explained. MPs forced the withdrawal of a few of the cabinet's more significant recommendations, for example denying the president the power to dissolve parliament. On the other hand, the executive insisted on retaining special-interest seats for army MPs, who will be obligated to vote for the government after the return to multiparty politics.[8]

In general, people make their political choices without undue influence from powerful groups outside the government. However, it would be dangerous for ordinary citizens or political leaders to resist projects endorsed by the president, his inner circle, or the military, particularly soldiers involved in the war in the north. In November 2004, for example, soldiers in the Uganda People's Defense Forces (UPDF) physically assaulted four MPs conducting a meeting at an internally displaced persons (IDP) camp in the north.[9]

The autonomy of the public service is protected by the constitution. The public, health, and education service commissions generally make appointments on the basis of merit and open competition, despite the widespread reliance on patronage and corruption elsewhere in the government. In 2005, however, cases surfaced of interference in the appointments of Justus Akankwasa as assistant commissioner in the Ministry of Education and Sports and Dr. John Mulumba as the coordinator of the Project Management Unit for the Global Fund to Fight Aids, Tuberculosis and Malaria.[10] The district service commissions, which make appointments in local governments, confronted further allegations of discrimination.

The state recognizes the rights of civic and business organizations to advocate but enforces the same limitations on peaceful advocacy as it does for political organizations. Nongovernmental organizations

(NGOs) must register with the government but are not hobbled by legal requirements. Civil society organizations testify before parliamentary committees and comment publicly on government policy without official impediment. Some lobbyists believe they have significantly influenced bills considered during the past two years.[11] On the other hand, the government also makes efforts to influence the public positions taken by civil society organizations.

The government permits international NGOs to visit Uganda to investigate human rights and other alleged violations. In September 2005, the government expressed its strong disagreement with the findings of a Human Rights Watch report on northern Uganda in a press statement, but did not take stronger action against the NGO or its investigators.[12]

In 2005, the government seriously damaged its reputation for tolerance of the media and free expression. It had sought an injunction banning *The Monitor,* the leading opposition newspaper, in November 2003 from publishing details from a politically sensitive interim report of the Constitutional Review Commission.[13] In June 2004, six journalists became the first in Uganda's history to be convicted by a military court-martial for contempt of court.[14] No other serious clashes with the media occurred until August 2005, when the government temporarily closed a radio station and arrested a reporter for sedition.[15] In November 2005, the government threatened to close *The Monitor* over a story that President Museveni had offered his brother the top position in the military.[16]

Following Besigye's arrest the following week, the government banned all public reporting, demonstrations, or discussion of any aspect of his case. At the same time, the police raided *The Monitor* without a search warrant to remove an advertisement for a defense fund for Besigye, and searched all the newspaper's upcountry distribution vans.[17] There were no other reported cases involving extralegal intimidation or physical violence against journalists or other public indications of censorship during this two-year period.

Access to the internet is not regulated nor does the state hinder access, which is available through cybershops in towns throughout Uganda. The state continues to hold a controlling interest in *The New Vision* newspaper, and officials sometimes try to gain favorable coverage for the government, but aside from this arrangement, no reports indicate that the government funded official points of view or limited media access to its opponents. In general, the state protects the freedom of cultural expression as well. However, it did ban public performances of *The Vagina Monologues* in February 2005 for promoting "illegal, unnatural sexual acts, homosexuality and prostitution."[18]

Recommendations

- The government should protect the electoral process and the public's faith in its neutrality by not bringing criminal charges based on preexisting evidence against candidates for high office after campaigns have begun.
- Parliament should enforce its Rules of Procedure to discipline members who accept rewards in support of or opposition to any matter under consideration.
- The government should refrain from closing radio stations for statements made in programs they broadcast, and newspapers for stories they run.
- The government should leave the regulation of public discussion of issues related to court trials to the presiding judge.
- The police should be given explicit regulations prohibiting them from entering a media facility without a search warrant or other authorizing document signed by a judge.

CIVIL LIBERTIES – 3.81

While the 1995 constitution protects civil liberties, prohibits torture, and limits pretrial detention, its provisions were not applied uniformly between 2003 and 2005. The Uganda Human Rights Commission (UHRC), an independent government agency, and international human rights organizations documented many cases of torture throughout this period.[19] Of the 2,294 human rights cases reported to the UHRC in 2004, 488 involved torture.[20] The UHRC awarded compensation to several victims. However, the state paid the victims in only a fraction of these cases. The UHRC successfully opposed the government's recommendation to abolish it by transferring its functions to the Inspector General of Government (IGG). It argued that the cabinet's proposal would reduce "the importance of full coverage of human rights."[21] In its 2004 report to parliament, the UHRC noted that the state minister for security had admitted that torture had been used, while insisting that it would be eliminated.

The war against the Lord's Resistance Army (LRA) in the northern region led to the virtual suspension of civil liberties for over 90 percent of the rural population between 2003 and 2005.[22] More than 1.9 million people lived in IDP camps during this period. The government had forced them into these camps starting in 1996 as a measure to deprive the Sudan-based LRA of a source of supply. Soldiers routinely abused the inhabitants, who were usually too intimidated to report them. Those who complained were often subjected to arbitrary arrest followed by prolonged detention in army barracks. Few police posts exist in the camps. The judicial system in the area is crippled by vacancies. The state is unable or unwilling to protect inhabitants of the camps from attacks by the LRA, often posting small numbers of poorly armed and locally recruited militia rather than soldiers. The UHRC and other domestic human rights NGOs sometimes have provided IDPs with effective petition and redress.

Prisons continue to be seriously overcrowded, due in part to slow processing by prosecutors and courts. While suspects for serious offenses can be detained for up to 360 days, they are often held longer. Leaders and supporters of opposing political organizations, such as the FDC, were held without trial for more than two years on charges of treason and murder.[23] Two MPs representing constituencies in northern Uganda were arrested on murder charges in April 2005 and given bail.

During the 1990s, the government made important efforts to promote women's equality despite longstanding cultural and legal discrimination, particularly in marriage. However, violence against women continues at high levels. During the 2003 to 2005 period, parliamentary consideration of a domestic relations bill that would provide protection for married women was again postponed at the insistence of the government. An important provision in this bill would have criminalized marital rape, a significant mode of transmission of HIV infection to women. Other provisions would have given women and girls more security in marriage, divorce, and family property. No law currently proscribes female genital mutilation (FGM). Attempts have been made to persuade people whose cultural practices include FGM to change them, but the state does not play a significant role in such efforts.

The war in the north has taken a serious toll among women and children. The military has been unable to prevent the LRA from abducting thousands of girls and women to serve as concubines and soldiers.

The government is responsible for the IDP camps in the north. Of the people living in the IDP camps, 80 percent were women and children.[24] Rape of girls and women by government soldiers occurs frequently in the towns and all the camps.[25] Among the 63,000 inhabitants of Pabbo camp in Gulu District, 6 out of every 10 women had been "physically and sexually assaulted."[26] Mortality rates in the camps were above medically defined emergency levels, resulting in an average of 1,000 deaths per week. Aside from LRA abductions, trafficking of women was not a serious problem. Most women in Uganda work the land, but few of them have any ownership rights in it. However, by law 30 percent of all elected positions in local government from the village to the district level must be filled by women.

The constitution protects every individual's freedom to practice his or her religious and cultural beliefs. No laws sanction religious or cultural discrimination. Each ethnic group is constitutionally entitled to choose a traditional or cultural leader. Parliament has a Committee on Equal Opportunities to attend to the needs of members of marginalized groups. In general, the government does not interfere with religious practices, place restrictions on religious ceremonies, or interfere in internal administrative activities of organizations related to religious faiths, so long as it does not perceive a security issue. However, the government requires all religious organizations to register with the NGO board in the Ministry of Internal Affairs. Some observers have claimed that born-again Christians receive preference in some government positions.[27]

Religious issues have long been intertwined with politics in Uganda. Even though it takes a strong antisectarian stand, the Movement government has not been able to eliminate religious concerns from politics in local and national arenas. Officially, national leaders remain neutral in the appointment of religious or spiritual leaders. Behind the scenes, they attempt to promote candidates who favor the government.

Lack of government protection in the north exposes many religious institutions to attacks by the LRA on religious grounds. Members of the Acholi ethnic group practice a traditional healing ritual to reconcile with perpetrators of atrocities who were formerly members of the LRA. Muslims have protested provisions in the domestic relations bill requiring wives to consent to further marriages by their husband and requiring husbands who want to marry more than one wife to show that they have an adequate income to support them.

Persons with disabilities face considerable obstacles in Uganda, as in many poor countries; however, the government has demonstrated some desire to improve living conditions for these populations. Persons with disabilities are represented in parliament through five special-interest MPs who devote much of their assigned funds helping their constituents and ensuring that their voices are heard.[28] While only a small percentage of disadvantaged Ugandans can be assisted in this way, the symbolic value these MPs provide is impressive.

The right to form or join and participate in trade unions and civic associations is guaranteed by the constitution, although higher civil servants and members of the police or army are not permitted to organize. The government's interest in promoting investment, especially from foreign entrepreneurs, makes it reluctant to support workers' organizations or strikes. The government permits some businesses, including those newly privatized, to operate without recognizing unions among their workers. The state does not compel citizens to belong to any associations.

Continued interference with rallies and demonstrations by officials, particularly the police, indicates that the government has not accepted its obligation to protect the newly broadened exercise of freedom of association and assembly. The state sometimes uses excessive force to prevent or repress public protests, as it did in the days following the arrest of Besigye in November 2005.[29] In addition, security personnel and other government officials attempt to intimidate individuals holding opposition views by accusing them of associating with rebels.[30]

Recommendations
- The president should explicitly and publicly prohibit all government agencies, including the military and intelligence organizations, from the use of torture.
- The government should encourage parliament to pass the domestic relations bill as soon as possible.
- The government should instruct officers stationed in northern Uganda to enforce strict disciplinary measures to prevent soldiers from engaging in sexual misconduct against civilian women and to forbid any other violence against residents in IDP camps.
- The government should instruct the police to allow all peaceable political public meetings to proceed unless a disturbance of public

order occurs. The government should require a senior police officer to make the decision to disperse any public meeting.

RULE OF LAW – 3.66

In order to deepen the separation of powers, the constitution emphasized the independence of the judiciary. In three landmark decisions in recent years, the highest courts demonstrated their autonomy by striking down legislation on fundamental political issues. In January 2004, the Supreme Court nullified the Constitutional (Amendment) Act 2000 because parliament failed to follow its own rules of procedure by passing it without waiting 14 days between readings.[31] In June 2004, the constitutional court declared the second Referendum Act invalid, thus casting into question the referendum under which the no-party system had been extended in 2000. In November 2004, the constitutional court struck down sections of the Political Parties and Organizations Act 2002, which restricted parties' ability to organize below the national level, hold public rallies, or contest for power. The court upheld the act's requirement that parties must register. The executive branch, and particularly the president, had put high priority on each of these acts. Political opponents of the government had brought all three cases.

Building a culture of constitutionalism is an important foundation for the maintenance of the rule of law. It requires that changes in a constitution be made judiciously and on the basis of consultation with the public. In March 2005, the government introduced the Constitution (Amendment) Bill 2005, which proposed amending or repealing at least 112 constitutional provisions plus all six of its schedules.[32] In preparing this bill, the government responded to the report of the Constitutional Review Commission (CRC) that it had appointed in 2001. While the primary intention of the bill was preparation for the impending change to multiparty competition, the government included many unrelated provisions that substantively reversed decisions taken by the Constituent Assembly only 10 years earlier. None of the new provisions inserted by the cabinet had been formulated on the basis of either popular input or discussion in the CRC.

The judiciary has generally maintained its commitment to impartiality and nondiscrimination. However, this obligation has been achieved less effectively at lower levels of the judiciary, particularly in the district courts. Several years ago, in response to allegations that some judges were corrupt, the judiciary set up a Judicial Integrity Committee that held meetings with groups of civic leaders and judicial officers throughout the country to formulate policies to improve judges' performance.[33] The problem is related to inadequate compensation of judges. The recommendations of a forum of judicial officers in March 2004 stressed improvement in judicial terms of service, immediate investigation and resolution of accusations of corruption, and more legal and administrative measures to fight corruption.[34]

The executive and legislative branches generally do not interfere with judges and magistrates. Nevertheless, in a profoundly discouraging instance of intimidation of the judiciary in November 2005, approximately 30 heavily armed soldiers surrounded the High Court, blocked all exits, and attempted to force their way into the cells in preparation to rearrest 14 defendants, alleged associates of Besigye, in case they were granted bail. The principal judge later declared that "not since the abduction of Chief Justice Ben Kiwanuka from the premises of the Court during the diabolical days of Idi Amin had the High Court been subjected to such [a] horrendous onslaught."[35]

The case was an extreme example of a growing practice of the Ugandan government to court-martial civilians involved in allegations of treason in addition to indicting them in civilian courts. This practice of "double jeopardy," exposing individuals to two courts on the basis of the same factual situation, weakens the rule of law. Otherwise, government authorities tend generally to comply with court decisions, even though they sometimes have tried to negate their effect by introducing new legislation or constitutional amendments.

Judges for the High Court are recommended for appointment by a judicial service commission from among advocates who have practiced law for 10 or more years. They are usually appointed, promoted, and dismissed without bias. They are trained to judge cases fairly. However, the chair of the General Court-Martial is often not a trained lawyer, leading to unfair or injudicious decisions. In June 2004, six civilian journalists were summoned to a General Court-Martial to explain why they should not be charged but instead were immediately tried and convicted.[36] Besigye's lawyers were detained in his trial in November 2005 for arguing that the court-martial, held in an army barracks, had no jurisdiction over a civilian.[37]

The courts operate on the presumption of innocence and the right to a fair hearing, both constitutional guarantees. However, the judges have heavy dockets, and the prosecution is often poorly organized. As a result, criminal defendants often spend months and even years on remand before trial. While the constitution insulates the director of public prosecutions (DPP) from political pressures, the DPP's belated decision to bring criminal charges in the Besigye case appears to indicate that it was not fully independent. Citizens have the right to independent counsel but often cannot afford to pay for it. The state is constitutionally required to supply counsel for people who are indigent, but does not always do so. Public officials are rarely prosecuted for abuse of power.

All persons are constitutionally entitled to equal protection under the law. By and large, courts treat all persons who come before them equally. But there is considerable discrimination on the basis of ethnic origin, gender, and especially sexual orientation. The rights of women and children are often overlooked. In July 2005, the parliament approved a constitutional amendment criminalizing marriage between persons of the same sex. The state introduced antisectarian legislation soon after it came to power but rarely enforces it.

President Museveni, who retired from the military in April 2004, is in effective control of the military, police, and internal security forces. However, few observers would argue that members of the uniformed services observe the law when high political authorities order them to act otherwise, such as in the events surrounding the arrest of Besigye in November 2005. Cases are rarely brought to discipline members of the police, military, or security forces for taking bribes. Respect for human rights among members of the police, military, and security services is not frequently observed, particularly when they are stationed in a war zone. The military and intelligence services are generally not accountable to parliament. However, since the passage of the Public Finance and Accountability Act 2003, MPs have been able to review the auditor-general's (AG) analysis of classified expenditures, providing some accountability for one aspect of military activity.

The state enforces property rights and contracts in general. However, women do not have the right to own or inherit property in many circumstances. Wives and children have statutory protection in land transactions involving plots on which they are living. A proposed constitutional amendment to permit the state to take property for development purposes was withdrawn from parliament in 2005. Complaints of fraudulent land titles involving officials in the central and district land offices frequently appear in the press.

Recommendations
- The government should promote respect for the constitution by not amending it frequently or without prior public input.
- The government should prohibit military personnel from interference in court proceedings and court-martial any officers authorizing such operations.
- The government should end immediately its practice of bringing civilians before military courts-martial.
- The government should not charge any person, civilian or military, simultaneously in a civilian court and a military tribunal.
- The president should institutionalize civilian control over the military rather than retaining personal control.

ANTICORRUPTION AND TRANSPARENCY – 3.74

Starting in the late 1980s, the state radically reduced its involvement in the economy, thus eliminating many opportunities for government officials to take advantage of public funds. However, despite economic liberalization, the 2005 Index of Economic Freedom gives Uganda's regulation regime a poor rating, citing corruption as a reason why it is difficult to do business in Uganda.[38] In Uganda it takes 17 procedures to start a business, the second highest number of the 37 African countries according to the World Bank.[39]

The 1995 constitution authorized anticorruption measures, in particular to strengthen the independence of the inspector-general of government (IGG) and the AG. The IGG has the authority to investigate and prosecute cases of corruption. It handles 3,000 to 4,000 complaints annually and regularly secures corruption convictions for low-ranking public servants. In 2005, it opened an investigation into alleged malpractices in the examination process at Makerere University. The IGG's success in investigating cases, albeit mostly at lower levels of government, led to the government's unsuccessful efforts in 2005 to weaken it. The AG, who employs the largest number of professional accountants and auditors in Uganda's public sector, has a strong reputation for honest audits of government income and expenditure. The AG's auditors work inside each of the government's ministries. The AG gained the power to examine classified expenditures after passage of the Public Finance and Accountability Act 2003. During the period under review, the AG and selected MPs serving in the public accounts committee reviewed military and security expenditures for the first time.

The public accounts committee reviews the AG's reports and submits its recommendations to parliament frequently. It summons department heads to testify about problems of financial accountability the AG has found in their operations. In 2004, a fraud unit was created in the DPP to handle cases of fraud and corruption. In addition, the government has a Ministry of Ethics and Integrity, which established a Directorate of Ethics and Integrity (DEI) to coordinate policies of all the constitutional and administrative agencies pursuing corruption and to follow up on the implementation of commissions of inquiry concerning corruption.

A strengthened leadership code, adopted in 2002, requires political and civil officers to declare their assets and avoid conflicts of interest involving public bodies. The Leadership Code Act of 2002 made these declarations available to the public upon application to the IGG. In 2003, the IGG published the declarations of the president and cabinet in the newspapers. However, a 2004 court decision holding that the president did not have to dismiss officials who failed to declare their assets to the IGG undercuts the code's enforcement. The president's behavior in the case provided ambiguous signals about his support for the IGG. He dismissed Kakooza Mutale, the adviser who had not filed his declaration on time, but then submitted an affidavit to the court supporting him—a signal the judge may have found difficult to keep in perspective. During the 2003–2005 period, an ongoing courts-martial tried high-ranking military officers for inflating their payrolls with ghost soldiers. The Ministry of Education took disciplinary action against schools that padded their accounts with ghost teachers and pupils.

Purchase of goods in the public sector is an area rife with suspicions of fraud and corruption in both central and local governments. The new Public Procurement and Disposal of Public Assets Authority (PPDA), established by statute in 2003, governs transactions throughout the executive branch. It is charged with promoting transparency, fairness, and accountability in the procurement process and maintaining open and competitive bidding. Due to Uganda's extensive decentralization, district (local) governments have their own tender boards. In 2005, the Ministry for Local Government reviewed the Local Government Act to ensure that it conformed to the PPDA Act.[40] No evaluation of the PPDA was available as of November 2005.

Nevertheless, between 2003 and 2005, the climate for corruption remained favorable. As the International Monetary Fund (IMF) pointed out, although "reports on corruption show that Uganda has slightly improved its rating globally, it remains at the low end of the scale in country rankings."[41] Uganda's low ranking for corruption worsened slightly in 2005, according to Transparency International's Corruption Perceptions Index, to a score of 2.5 out of 10.[42] A persistent and widespread belief that corruption will generally not be punished is probably the most important factor in such perceptions. The government, and President Museveni in particular, demonstrates a marked lack of interest in reducing corruption, especially in cases involving high-ranking members of the government and members of the president's family. The government failed to prosecute any of the public officials identified in several commissions of inquiry, although a few were dismissed. The president reappointed and promoted two ministers (one a relative by marriage) who had been censured by parliament, even though neither of them had resolved the conflicts of interest that had led to their censures.

Moreover, the cabinet took several steps in an unsuccessful effort to strip the most active agency fighting corruption, the IGG, of its powers to prosecute offenders directly. Its proposal would have turned the IGG from an action agency into one limited to making investigations. As an MP and former minister of ethics and integrity put it, "the proposal is rendering the office cosmetic and powerless in as far as fighting corruption is concerned."[43] On the other hand, in the same proposals, the cabinet recommended and parliament subsequently established a new anticorruption court in 2005.[44]

The silence of donors over diversion of their aid is likely to embolden the government. Foreign assistance accounts for a significant proportion of both the government's recurrent and its development budgets—a total of approximately 50 percent in fiscal year 2004–2005 and 40 percent in 2005–2006. A confidential World Bank report leaked to the press in 2005 warned that it was "common knowledge and discourse among leading members of the diplomatic community in Kampala" that budgetary support provided by donors "can be diverted into classified budgets."[45] The report recommended aid cuts to Uganda. An analysis of the release of donor-supported funds by the Ministry of Education from 2002 to 2004 for building classrooms showed that the number the ministry reported it had built was only slightly more than half of those it said it had received the money to build.[46] Suspension of aid by the Global Fund to Fight Aids, Tuberculosis and Malaria for "serious mismanagement" of funds in August 2005 was a rare exception—and only temporary. In fact, the fund restored aid after the government established a commission of inquiry to investigate the fraud but before the commission had made its report and before its determination of whether any prosecutions were warranted.

Public discussion of specific cases of corruption is relatively open, even when they involve powerful government figures. The news media frequently investigate and report allegations of corruption. MPs and journalists receive tips from both military and civilian officials on the purchase of nonoperable equipment or looting by soldiers.[47] Individual MPs often expose cases through questions in parliament or through reports by committees. The Prevention of Corruption Act 1970 protects informers called as witnesses by removing their obligations to state their names or any matters leading to their discovery. Nevertheless, whistle-blowers frequently do not feel secure in publicly revealing their information in public. The access to information bill, under parliamentary consideration in 2005, proposes additional protections for whistleblowers. While the first parliamentary counsel had begun in 2005 to draft an anti–money laundering bill and a prevention of corruption (amendment) bill to cover gaps in existing laws, his slow pace raised concerns.[48] Despite a constitutional guarantee of citizens' right to know about the conduct of the government, officials often invoke the Official Secrets Act to block requests for relevant information about specific government operations.

The budget must be passed by parliament before the executive can spend funds. The Budget Act of 2001 introduced fundamental changes in the budget-making process by requiring the executive to submit preliminary estimates to parliament 10 weeks before the finance minister presented it formally. The executive was enjoined to respond specifically to changes proposed by parliamentary committees. The proposal greatly increased meaningful legislative review of the budget. Informants noticed that significant discussion and modification of specific government estimates had occurred as a result of the additional involvement of MPs. Accounting for expenditures is the task of the AG. By 2005, his office had removed most of its backlog, giving parliament the opportunity to investigate more recent allegations of executive improprieties. Both of parliament's public accounts committees energetically pursue discrepancies in government expenditures and tax collections revealed in the reports of the auditor general, forcing corrupt officials to face criminal proceedings.

Recommendations

- Whenever the government appoints any commission of inquiry to investigate corruption, it should make a public commitment to publish the report.
- The president should make a public commitment that he expects the DPP to investigate and prosecute all cases in which a commission of inquiry has produced prima facie evidence of corruption or other criminal violation.
- Parliament should promptly enact an access to information bill.
- The government should make an explicit commitment to each donor that it will prosecute any official who fails to account for a grant or loan provided by that donor.

NOTES

1 Figures calculated from the Directories (Kampala: Uganda's 6th and 7th Parliaments). Voting for women's seats will be conducted on the basis of universal suffrage in the 2006 elections.

2 Felix Osike and Milton Olupot, "92.5% Yes 7.5% No," *The Sunday New Vision* (Kampala), 31 July 2005.

3 *Seventh Annual Report* (Kampala: Uganda Human Rights Commission [UHRC], 2004), 170–72, http://www.uhrc.org/publications/1127821534chapter%2011.pdf.

4 John Kakande, "Are We Genuine About the Return to Multipartyism?" *New Vision*, 8 August 2005.

5 Richard Mutumba, "Government Suspends Dairy Deal," *The Monitor* (Kampala), 23 February 2005.

6 "White Paper on Constitutional Review," *Monitor*, 22 September 2004.

7 Henry Mukasa and Apollo Mubiru, "MP Cries Foul on Kisanja Cash," *New Vision*, 28 October 2004.

8 Hamis Kaheru, "Army to Remain in Politics," *New Vision*, 8 July 2004.

9 "MPs Violently Prevented from Discussing with their Constituencies," Human Rights House Network, 24 November 2004, http://www.humanrightshouse.org/dllvis5 .asp?id=2595.

10 Abu Mayanja, "State House Must Not Meddle in Public Affairs," *New Vision*, 6 September 2005; Henry Onoria, "Legislative and Policy Measures in Uganda vis-à-vis Practical Challenges of Compliance with [the] AU Anti-Corruption Convention" (Kampala: Transparency International [TI]-Uganda, 31 October 2005), 22, http://www.apnacafrica .org/docs/AntiCorruption%20Legislative%20and%20Policy%20Measures%20in%20 Compliance%20with%20the%20AU%20Convention.pdf.

11 Interviews conducted with two lobbyists by a Ugandan researcher during 2005.

12 "Human Rights Watch Reply to Ugandan Government Document of September 23, 2005 regarding Human Rights Watch's Report 'Uprooted and Forgotten: Impunity and Human Rights Abuses in Northern Uganda'" (New York: Human Rights Watch [HRW], 30 September 2005).

13 Victor Karamagi, "Plan to Change Media Law Spells Doom for Free Press," *Monitor*, 17 August 2005.

14 Steven Candia and Maurice Okore, "Summons Turn to Trial," *New Vision*, 20 June 2004.

15 Ibid.

16 Monitor Team, "Government Threatens to Close Daily Monitor," *Monitor*, 15 November 2005.

17 Angelo Izama, "Police Raid Monitor over FDC Advert," *Monitor*, 19 November 2005.

18 "Uganda Ban on Vagina Monologues," BBC News, 18 February 2005, http://news.bbc .co.uk/1/hi/world/africa/4277063.stm.

19 "Rights Watchdog Accuses Army of Abuses" (New York: United Nations, Office for the Coordination of Humanitarian Affairs Integrated Regional Information Network [IRIN], 29 September 2005); "State of Pain: Torture in Uganda" (HRW, vol. 16, no. 4 [A], March 2004).

20 *Seventh Annual Report* (UHRC), 21–22, http://www.uhrc.org/publications/112780 3857chapter%202.pdf.

21 "Comments on the Cabinet Proposals for the Abolition of Uganda Human Rights Commission," *Sixth Annual Report* (UHRC, Sec. 4.8, 2003), http://www.uhrc.org/publications.

22 "Uprooted and Forgotten: Impunity and Human Rights Abuses in Northern Uganda" (HRW, vol. 17, no. 12 [A], September 2005), 13.

23 Hussein Bogere, "66 FDC Members in Prison," *Monitor*, 10 May 2005.

24 "IDP Children's Death Rates over Emergency Levels, Report Says" (IRIN, 30 September 2005); "1,000 Displaced Die Every Week in War-torn North – report" (IRIN, 29 August 2005).

25 "Uprooted and Forgotten" (HRW), 32.

26 "Suffering in Silence: A Study of Sexual and Gender Based Violence (SGBV) in Pabbo Camp, Gulu District, Northern Uganda" (Gulu, Uganda: Gulu District Sub Working Group on SGBV, 15 June 2005), 1, 9, http://www.unicef.org/media/files/SGBV.pdf.

27 For example, a news report stated that in the quasi-military Special Revenue Protection Services "membership is confined to persons who are 'saved.'" David Kaiza and Julius

Barigamba, "Here Comes Janet Museveni, Sent by God to Save Uganda," *The East African* (Nairobi), 12–18 December 2005.

28 Author's interview with an MP representing persons with disabilities, Kampala, 4 July 2005.

29 Private communication from Kampala, 30 November 2005.

30 *Seventh Annual Report* (UHRC, 2004), 166.

31 Anne Mugisa and Alfred Wasike, "Ssemogerere Wins Constitution Act Petition," *New Vision,* 30 January 2004.

32 Oloka Onyango, "Constitution Bill Is Disaster in Substance," *New Vision,* 11 March 2005.

33 Onoria, "Legislative and Policy Measures," 19–20; "Third Meeting of the Judicial Group on Strengthening Judicial Integrity," Colombo, Sri Lanka, 10–12 January 2003, 8, http://www.unodc.org/pdf/crime/corruption/judicial_group/Third_Judicial_Group_repo rt.pdf.

34 "Towards Strengthening Judicial Integrity in Uganda: New Approaches–Recommendations," The 6th Annual Judicial Officers' Forum, Lake View Regency Hotel, Mbarara [Uganda], http://www.fhri.or.ug/recom.htm.

35 Solomon Muyita, Simon Kasyate, Hussein Bogerere, and Lydia Mukisa, "Armed Men Disrupt Besigye Court Case," *New Vision,* 17 November 2005; Victor Karamagi, "Judiciary under Attack: Where Will the People Run to?" Monitor, 23 November 2005. The defendants avoided rearrest by asking their sureties not to sign their bail bonds, forcing their return to the civilian prison, thus avoiding transfer to a military prison.

36 "Summons Turn to Trial," *New Vision,* 20 June 2004.

37 "Besigye Case Adjourned," *Monitor,* 24 November 2005.

38 "Index of Economic Freedom" (Washington, D.C./ New York: Heritage Foundation/ *Wall Street Journal,* 2005), http://www.heritage.org/research/features/index/country .cfm?id=Uganda.

39 From World Bank, "Doing Business in 2005, country tables, (Washington, D.C.: World Bank 2004) reported in "Striving for Good Governance in Africa: Synopsis of the 2005 African Governance Report" (Addis Ababa: UN Economic Commission for Africa, 2003), 20, http://www.uneca.org/agr.

40 Onoria, "Legislative and Policy Measures," 21.

41 Frank Nayakairu, "IMF Urges Uganda to Tackle Corruption," *Monitor,* 13 September 2005.

42 "Corruption Perceptions Index 2005" (London/Berlin: TI, 18 October 2005), http://www.transparency.org/cpi/2005/dnld/media_pack_en.pdf; Elias Biryabarema, "Is Uganda Fighting a Fruitless Battle Against Corruption?" *Monitor,* 25 October 2005. For the previous year, see the *Global Corruption Report 2005* (Berlin: TI), 237, http://www .globalcorruptionreport.org/gcr2005/download/english/corruption_research_%20I.pdf.

43 Miria Matembe, "Museveni Has No Political Will," *Monitor,* 16 October 2003.

44 Onoria, "Legislative and Policy Measures," 19.

45 Paul Busharizi, "World Bank May Cut Aid," *New Vision,* 17 May 2005.

46 Andrew Mwenda, "Between Donors and Government, Foreign Aid Is Lost Along the Way," *Monitor,* 19 July 2005.

47 Author's interview with an MP, Kampala, 4 July 2005.

48 Onoria, "Legislative and Policy Measures," 38.

UKRAINE

CAPITAL: Kiev

POPULATION: 47.1 million

GNI PER CAPITA: $970

SCORES	2004	2006
ACCOUNTABILITY AND PUBLIC VOICE:	3.48	4.85
CIVIL LIBERTIES:	3.91	4.34
RULE OF LAW:	3.32	3.65
ANTICORRUPTION AND TRANSPARENCY:	2.82	3.01

(scores are based on a scale of 0 to 7, with 0 representing weakest and 7 representing strongest performance)

Dominique Arel

INTRODUCTION

Two years ago, no one could have anticipated that the clear rise of post-Communist authoritarianism in Ukraine would be blocked by the largest street demonstrations in Europe since 1989. The Orange Revolution—the popular peaceful uprising to invalidate the fraudulent 2004 Ukrainian presidential election—was a seminal event in the post-Soviet region (Baltics excepted), as it sent a powerful message that the slide toward a noncompetitive and relatively closed system is not irreversible. In Orange Ukraine, the political trajectory is very much in the balance, with both promising signs pointing to a regime striving to achieve European standards and worrying trends reflecting durable old-regime traits.

Ukraine has made the most progress since 2004 in the realm of Accountability and Public Voice. The 2004 presidential election ultimately proved that the results of an election in oligarchic Ukraine could reflect the will of the electorate. Despite numerous reports that state employees were instructed to pressure voters to support the incumbent regime candidate, Viktor Yanukovych (a strategy known as "the use of administrative resources"), the race was in fact extremely competitive in favor of challenger Viktor Yushchenko. The Yanukovych camp, in collusion with the presidential administration and the Central Electoral Commission (CEC), was thus forced to clumsily fabricate nearly a million

---

Dominique Arel holds the Chair of Ukrainian Studies at the University of Ottawa.

votes in Yanukovych's fief of Donbas in the presidential runoff of November 21, 2004.[1] After two weeks of mass protests, the Supreme Court invalidated the vote and ordered a repeat ballot on December 26, which domestic and international observers deemed free and fair.[2] A year later, Ukraine was gearing up for a crucial parliamentary election in March 2006, but the Orange Revolution rendered the prospects of a fraudulent election almost unthinkable.

The media have opened up considerably. The *temnyky* (those presumably secret but regularly leaked instructions from the presidential administration to the broadcast media on how to treat the news of the day) vanished during the Orange Revolution.[3] While the broadcast and print media continue to lack the critical and investigative bent displayed by online media, particularly *Ukrainska pravda,* they have been used increasingly by politicians as arenas for attacks on their political opponents. When Prime Minister Yulia Tymoshenko and her allies were ousted from power in September 2005, the Tymoshenko and Yushchenko political blocs washed their political dirty linen in the media glare, amid severe charges of corruption and disloyalty.[4] This was a far more open process than, for instance, the backroom dealings of oligarchic factions that led to Yushchenko's dismissal as prime minister in April 2001, when the accusers refused to debate the merits of their case publicly.[5] This new openness of the political game, which, as in all open systems, is not always pretty, can be seen as the most immediate legacy of the Orange Revolution.

Ukraine, however, remains hampered by a weak adherence, on the part of politicians and public servants, to the rule of law. A common thread in the country's approach to the elements of democracy is an inability or unwillingness to devise practical mechanisms to enforce laws and rights. Rights are often declarative and lack supporting legislation, as in the realm of minority, language, and religious rights. When reasonably drafted in legislation, rights often remain unenforced for lack of funding, as in the deplorable conditions of detention. Even more fundamentally, the principle of separation of powers between the executive, legislative, and judicial branches—the stepping-stone of open and competitive systems—remains unclear in the minds of the Ukrainian political elite, even those of the Orange persuasion. This ambiguity is embodied by the persistently controversial role of a prosecutor general whom the amended constitution continues to endow with the power to interfere in court judgments. The temptation to circumvent the law, at all levels of the state, is rendered all the more insidious when the premier magistrate of the land is constitutionally mandated to do so.

ACCOUNTABILITY AND PUBLIC VOICE – 4.85

In the Kuchma era, the Ukrainian political system was aptly characterized as "competitive authoritarian."[6] The executive branch strove to make state officials, from those in power ministries down to local administrators, loyal to the presidential regime rather than to the institution of the presidency, through nontransparent policies ("administrative resources") not regulated by law. The system, nonetheless, rested on the legitimacy of electoral contests, a process that the regime could not entirely control. In 1999, President Kuchma was elected to a second five-year term in a campaign marred by irregularities, particularly the use of state TV as a propaganda tool. The lack of a credible challenger and Kuchma's decisive victory margin led monitoring bodies to recognize the outcome.[7] In 2004, however, all surveys indicated that former prime minister Viktor Yushchenko had a chance to defeat the incumbent regime's candidate, Viktor Yanukovych.

The election became a revolution. In an initial round of 27 candidates, Yushchenko obtained a plurality (40 percent), slightly ahead of Yanukovych, despite being essentially shut out of national TV coverage. In the second round, exit polls predicted a Yushchenko victory, but the CEC proclaimed Yanukovych the winner by a 3 percent margin, despite an obviously fraudulent turnout in Donbas (alone sufficient to account for the official Yanukovych lead) and evidence from leaked phone conversations that the presidential administration had been hacking into the CEC central server.[8] International monitoring organizations and Western governments refused to recognize the results, and the unprecedented mass protests on the Maidan, Kyiv's central square, prompted the court to invalidate the results. A repeat election, in the presence of the largest international delegation of electoral observers in history, produced a clean Yushchenko victory.

The 2004 Ukrainian election was a turning point in the post-Soviet region, as it went against the trend of a general decline in the belief that rulers could be defeated through competitive elections. (The 2003 Rose Revolution in Georgia set the precedent, but the fact that the eventual presidential victor, Mikhei Saakashvili, ran unopposed in the decisive round, after the street protests, shed some doubt on the democratic process). In 2005, Ukraine consolidated its democratic electoral credentials by passing an electoral law that, in the words of the Council of Europe, "significantly enhanced election procedures" by allowing domestic nongovernmental organizations (NGOs) to observe the elections and improving the process by which some voters are allowed to vote either at home or at a polling station different from the one assigned to their residence.[9] These two dispensations (home voting and absentee ballots) prompted the worst violations in the first two rounds of the 2004 election: numerous cases of multiple voting. The Council of Europe, however, voiced concern about a clause that would allow the electoral commission to temporarily shut down, without a court order, a newspaper or broadcast station for "slander" or the retransmission of "unconstitutional" material.[10]

The March 2006 parliamentary election was set to introduce two significant changes in electoral representation. The first is the nature of the electoral system. For the first time, all parliamentary deputies will be elected through proportional representation (PR), when electors vote for a party list rather than a specific deputy representing an electoral riding. In the previous system, used in the 1998 and 2002 parliamentary elections, half of the deputies were elected in individual ridings and the other half through party lists. In practice, most deputies elected in ridings ran as independents and then joined propresidential factions in parliament. In 2002, the propresidential bloc ran poorly in the PR seats, finishing far behind the right (Our Ukraine) and left (Communist) opposition, but nevertheless managed to achieve a majority in parliament. The pure PR system, a rarity in international practice, was adopted to prevent this infringement of electoral accountability. Many PR systems break up countries into several regional constituencies, with region-specific party lists. Ukraine opted for a single constituency (i.e., the entire country), which could raise a different problem of electoral accountability, as national party lists risk being dominated by deputies originating from major centers (Kyiv, Donetsk, Lviv).

The second major change in the electoral process is the introduction of the so-called imperative mandate of parliamentary deputies, as part of the constitutional amendments adopted on December 8, 2004 (see Rule of Law). In the past decade, the parliamentary floor resembled a stock exchange, with deputies constantly joining or leaving existing or new factions, often, allegedly, with a price tag. The process was detrimental to the consolidation of political parties and to the formation of a stable parliamentary majority. In order to achieve the latter, the new electoral law expressly forbids future deputies, all elected through party lists, to leave their party/parliamentary faction during the entire duration of their mandate. The European Union (EU's) Venice Commission has criticized this clause as potentially unconstitutional on the grounds that "Members of Parliament are supposed to represent the people and not their parties."[11] To be sure, party discipline—or deputies' obligation to vote according to the party line—is at the core of the British Commonwealth parliamentary tradition. Yet deputies, in this tradition, can leave or be expelled from a party and become independent or join another party. In an imperative mandate, recalcitrant deputies would in principle be expelled from parliament altogether, making them entirely accountable to their party. It remains to be seen whether Ukrainian political culture will tolerate the enforcement of such an inflexible and questionable rule of legislative conduct in a context in which the legitimacy of constitutional amendments itself remains cloudy.

The media has largely freed itself from the strain of executive control since the early days of the Orange Revolution. Reporters Without Borders noted a "spectacular" improvement in Ukraine's ranking in its annual press freedom index, which jumped from a ranking of 138 in 2004 to 112 in 2005.[12] National TV channels, owned by either the state or private entrepreneurs (the so-called oligarchs), now reflect a broad range of opinion. NGOs sounded the alarm in May 2005 when the Ministry of Transport and Telecommunications announced that websites would need to register with authorities and comply with guidelines regarding reporting that compromised the "honor," "reputation," and "dignity" of individuals. Media monitoring groups warned that such vague language could open the door to administrative censorship.[13] The ministry rescinded its decision in October 2005.[14] A few cases of repression against journalists were reported in the regions, such as an attack against TV reporter Natalya Vlasova in Dnipropetrovsk and the allegedly groundless arrest of weekly magazine journalist Volodymyr Lutiev in Sevastopol.[15] Reporters Without Borders argued that these incidents were indicative of a "deteriorating climate" in fall 2005 and called for legal action against those threatening press freedoms.[16] While these cases are disturbing, the Kyiv-based Institute of Mass Information, in its monthly *Press Freedom Barometer,* noted in October 2005 that all indicators of media persecution (imprisonments, attacks, threats, state pressure) were down, generally by at least half, as compared to October 2004.[17] No journalist has been murdered since the Orange Revolution.

The relaxation of media control, however, lacks a firm legal foundation. The National Television Company of Ukraine, the state-run television and radio broadcaster, has not yet been reformed, and NGOs complained that their recommendations on the nomination of new officials by the new government were totally disregarded and that the process lacked transparency.[18] The Council of Europe has called for years for the introduction of a public broadcasting service in Ukraine, in which the government would have general oversight but no direct control, along the lines of the BBC or PBS.[19] A draft law "On Public Television and Radio in Ukraine" was in preparation in 2005 and was favorably received by the British NGO Article 19,[20] but there were reports that the Yushchenko administration was split on the virtue of public broadcasting, with some officials supporting the maintenance of a state-controlled broadcasting structure.[21] In the whirlwind of mutual accusations of corruption during the government crisis of September 2005, claims were made that both archrivals Tymoshenko and Poroshenko had been lobbying for the sale of private TV stations to their respective allies. (The crisis originated from the permanent tension caused by the overlapping duties between Prime Minister Tymoshenko and Security Council Secretary Poroshenko). Whether true or not, these allegations at least suggested that the distance between government and the broadcast media remains uncomfortably narrow. As with all domains of political and social life, the translation of policy intentions and general principles of law into clear and enforceable legislation remains Ukraine's biggest challenge.

Recommendations

- To comply with European democratic standards, the government should initiate new constitutional amendments to replace the imperative mandate of deputies with more flexible rules favoring party discipline.

- To favor greater regional representation, the government should consider breaking the single PR national list into several regional lists in the next parliamentary election.
- To consolidate the gains of the Orange Revolution regarding the media, the government should prioritize the passing of a law on public broadcasting and protections for journalists.

CIVIL LIBERTIES – 4.34

The situation in penitentiaries is bleak. Amnesty International denounces an "apparently pervasive culture of impunity" among law enforcement officials in their treatment of detainees.[22] Even though Ukraine bans torture and has signed all the relevant international conventions, the use of violent methods, such as electric shocks, suffocation by the forcible use of gas masks, or the suspension of individuals from a metal pole, appears to be widespread. According to a 2004 study by the Kharkiv Institute for Social Research, two-thirds of people in police detention claimed to have been ill-treated, one-third to have received beatings, and 4 percent to have been tortured with special equipment.[23] Between July 2003 and July 2004, 436 cases of alleged torture were reported by NGOs.[24] Police brutality aside, the European Court on Human Rights has observed that "the lack of resources cannot justify prison conditions which are so poor as . . . to be inhuman and degrading."[25]

Further, very few violations of civil rights in prison are prosecuted in court. Human rights groups, in fact, claim that courts routinely condone torture by passing verdicts that rely on confessions obtained under torture. When convictions of civil rights violators do occur, they are often "disproportionately lenient."[26] A January 2005 law intends to address this lacuna by providing for more severe punishment of people who inflict torture.[27] Also noteworthy is an unprecedented decision by the Ministry of Interior to involve NGOs in a systematic program to inspect sites of detention, which has been praised by civic organizations. A culture of impunity becomes more vulnerable when exposed to public opinion.[28]

The protection of rights in Ukraine generally remains fairly weak. On a positive note, the space for political contestation has broadened noticeably since the Orange Revolution. Previously, opposition groups complained regularly of police harassment. For instance, the searches conducted on the premises of the youth civic group PORA in October 2004, prior to the first round of presidential balloting, were legally questionable.[29] Scholars argued that incidents like these were part of a general pattern of the selective use, by the executive branch, of law enforcement agencies (Tax Police, Interior Ministry, Office of the Prosecutor General) against political opponents.[30] These tactics of the so-called blackmail state ceased under Yushchenko, notwithstanding the fact that the losers of the presidential vote have regularly complained of harassment. On the whole, the state is now respectful of the right of individuals to organize and assemble autonomously.

The capacity of individuals to exercise rights related to the public recognition of groups, however, is far more ambiguous. Ukraine is often lauded for its tolerance toward religious, ethnic, and language groups, but few of its policies in that regard rest on a strict observance of rights. Since independence, religious life has flourished in Ukraine, with the number of Orthodox parishes and evangelical missions greater than in the entire Russian Federation.[31] The registration of religious organizations, however, is bureaucratically onerous and, in its excessive regulation of internal management, has been criticized as infringing on the right of these religious organizations to conduct their own affairs.[32]

Access to premises remains far and away the major problem hindering the practical realization of the right to worship collectively. Religious groups complain of delays and refusal on the part of local administrations in allocating lands for the construction of sites of worship.[33] For groups whose property had been expropriated by the Soviet regime—particularly, but not limited to, the Uniate Church—a fair mechanism of property restitution has yet to be implemented. The basic problem is that religious associations as such are not recognized as legal entities that can acquire property.[34] Only local communities (hromada) and monasteries possess such a right. Yet these communities are often solicited to change their church affiliation, given the intense competition between the four Christian churches—the Ukrainian Orthodox Church Moscow Patriarchate (UOC-MP), the Ukrainian Orthodox Church Kyiv Patriarchate (UOC-KP), the Autocephalous Ukrainian Orthodox Church, and the Uniate Church—for the enrollment of local communities, complicating the issue of restitution.[35] The legal uncertainty in the allocation of church property feeds the perception that local administrative bodies are biased in their policies with respect to rival churches. As in electoral politics, the alleged bias follows a regional pattern, with the UOC-MP complaining of discrimination in Western Ukraine and the UOC-KP of comparable mistreatment in Eastern Ukraine.[36]

Anti-Semitism is a cause for serious concern. The Global Forum on Anti-Semitism, founded by ex-Soviet dissident and Israeli government minister Natan Sharansky, noted a rise in anti-Semitic acts in Ukraine (and Russia) in 2005.[37] Yet, because the number of reported incidents is relatively small, one can question, as some other Jewish organizations in Ukraine do, whether the evidence points to a measurable increase in such acts. A clearer and more disturbing pattern, in any case, is the relative public indifference toward anti-Semitism. Anti-Semitic acts, when they do occur, tend to receive minimal coverage in the media.[38] Anti-Semitic speech, of the most blatant form, tends to be left unchallenged by state and civic bodies, even when it reaches wide audiences.

Moreover, the largest private university in Ukraine, the Inter-Regional Academy of Personnel Management (MAUP), recognized by the Ministry of Education as a PhD-granting institution, has for years distributed to all its students two glossy magazines, *Personal* and *Personal-Plius,* which regularly carry articles that attribute responsibility for the atrocities of the Bolshevik Revolution and the 1933 famine in Ukraine to Jews and use the kind of traditional anti-Semitic imagery common in Europe prior to World War II. Yet there was little reaction from government or civil society until MAUP director Heorhii Shchokin became an international embarrassment by publicly supporting Iran's call to eradicate Israel in November 2004.[39] This incident suggests that as long as a situation does not acquire an international dimension, there is little political liability in harboring unambiguous anti-Semitic views in Ukrainian domestic politics. The one visible case in which authorities attempted to shut down a newspaper on the grounds of anti-Semitism in January 2004 was widely perceived as an act of selective prosecution against a publication associated with an opposition party.[40]

In terms of language rights, Ukraine finally deposited the ratification instrument of the European Charter for Regional or Minority Languages at the Strasbourg headquarters of the Council of Europe in September 2005, two and a half years after the Ukrainian parliament ratified the charter and nearly six years after the parliament's first attempt at ratification (a vote that had subsequently been overturned by the

Constitutional Court on procedural grounds). The charter aims at codifying the rights of a critical mass of speakers of nonofficial languages to use their language in public domains. A number of minority languages in Ukraine have long been used by authorities in rural areas (Hungarian, Romanian/Moldovan), but the six-year delay in ratifying the charter is rooted in disagreements over the status of Russian, a language used as a matter of preference by nearly half of the population,[41] far more than the proportion of ethnic Russians (17 percent) or of Ukrainian citizens claiming Russian as their native language (30 percent).[42]

Russian was the de facto state language in the Soviet Union and continues to predominate in most urban areas. A political compromise was achieved in the 1996 constitution, making Ukrainian the sole state language, while guaranteeing "the free development, use and protection of Russian."[43] Yet no legislation specifies when and how Russian (or other nonofficial languages) can be used in public domains. In practice, the use of Russian continues to predominate in Eastern Ukraine, but in a legal limbo, at the discretion of civil servants.[44] The dominant view in government is that the charter does not apply to Russian, even if the law on ratification explicitly says so, and it appears most unlikely that the legal codification of the public use of languages in Ukraine will be on the agenda any time soon.

Legal mechanisms to protect visible minorities against discrimination remain lacking, although progress has been made in the preparation of a bill that would define a range of discriminatory offenses, shift the burden of proof to the defendant, and introduce a variety of evidentiary methods in court.[45] Meanwhile, some minorities find themselves at the margin of the law. Roma organizations in the western province of Transcarpathia periodically report instances of police brutality.[46] Chechens apprehended while attempting to enter the EU through Ukraine are systematically refused asylum and often deported back to Russia.[47] Human Rights Watch asserts that the amended Ukrainian law on refugees "infringes the right to seek asylum" as enshrined in the Universal Declaration of Human Rights and that the "routine use" of administrative detention "results in serious human rights violations."[48] In general, migration policy is pervaded by corruption and a lack of government resources.

Ukraine has been identified as a major country of origin for the trafficking of women and children, with the number of estimated victims in the hundreds of thousands.[49] Conviction rates are quite low; only 22 traffickers were sent to jail in 2005.[50] Once again, the absence of a well-defined mechanism to enforce general principles of law is a major problem. Reliance on witness testimony, a requirement that offenders must have crossed borders, and a presumption that female victims may have been a consenting party account for the paucity of successful prosecutions.[51] The creation of a separate Counter-Trafficking Department in the Ministry of Interior in 2005 may signal a heightened determination by the new government to stem the flow of trafficking.[52]

Recommendations
- To prevent simmering conflicts from worsening, the Ukrainian government should initiate the adoption of clear legal guidelines for the allocation of church property, including restitution, and the public use of languages, including Russian.
- Without infringing on academic freedom, the Ministry of Education should elaborate clear ethical guidelines for discriminatory speech and acts emanating from institutions whose curriculum and diploma are officially recognized by the state.
- The Ukrainian government must put an end to the culture of impunity and other instances of police brutality prevalent in sites of detention.

RULE OF LAW – 3.65

Ukraine has a serious flaw in its justice system: the excessive powers entrusted to the prosecutor general. In a modern democracy, the chief prosecutor represents the state in a court of law but must abide by the final judgment of the court. In the Soviet Union, however, the prosecutor was given a supervisory role over the work of courts. The 1996 Ukrainian constitution proclaimed the separation of judicial, executive, and legislative powers and the concomitant subordination of prosecutorial power to the courts. The Soviet-era oversight duties of the prosecutor were to be phased out by 2001, but they remained in place until the Orange Revolution.

Five days after the Supreme Court invalidated the results of the November 21 presidential vote and ordered a new round of elections (on December 3, 2004), a political compromise was concluded by the

Yushchenko and Yanukovych camps.[53] The compromise took the form of a quid pro quo. The Yushchenko party, Our Ukraine (over the strenuous objections of the Tymoshenko Bloc, which was supporting Yushchenko during the election), agreed to a constitutional amendment that would purportedly shift significant powers to the prime minister and parliament, transforming Ukraine into a parliamentary-presidential system, rather than the other way around. In return, the Yanukovych Party of Regions agreed to amend the election law by eliminating the loopholes (voting at home, voting in absentia) that allowed the worst fraudulent voting in the first two rounds. The constitutional amendments were to come into effect in January 2006.

The amendments, passed by a constitutional majority of the Verkhovna Rada (parliament), appear to have violated constitutional procedure. According to Article 159 of the constitution, a draft law introducing amendments must be considered by the Constitutional Court for its conformity to constitutional requirements before it is voted on. The court had examined a previous version of these constitutional amendments earlier in 2004, but a 1998 ruling by the court opined that all versions of a draft amendment must be examined anew.[54] The question is whether the draft amendment voted on December 8 was sufficiently altered from previous versions to require another opinion of the court. The Constitutional Court was not given an opportunity in 2005 to rule on the matter, partly because it began to lack a quorum in late 2005. Procedural maneuvers in parliament prevented the filling of court vacancies, allegedly to prevent a decision to overturn the December 8 constitutional amendment.[55] The result is a serious discredit to the rule of law. Politicians, no doubt, were under great pressure from the street, which had massively mobilized for nearly three weeks running, to break the political impasse in December 2004. Yet the circumvention of the court, and its eventual neutralization for partisan purposes, cannot but undermine the legitimacy of constitutional rule in Ukraine.

The constitutional amendments, surprisingly, reinstated the Soviet-era powers of the prosecutor general by including among his duties the "supervision [*nahliad*—in the sense of "control"] over the observance of the rights and freedoms of persons and citizens, [as well as] over the observance of laws regarding these issues by bodies of executive power, bodies of local self-government, and their officials and employees."[56] The Venice Commission, the legal arm of the Council of Europe, had warned in the strongest terms that these prosecutorial powers, detailed in drafts of constitutional amendments prepared by the government in 2003–2004, were incompatible with the rule of law and the fundamental democratic principle of the separation of powers.[57] The expansive investigative and detention powers of the office were also criticized as inherently placing the prosecutor in a conflict of interest. The danger, wrote the Venice Commission, was that "It was precisely in communist states that the prosecutor's office became a tool of repression as a result of . . . its broad scope of authority and its exemption from all supervision."[58]

The Council of Europe has been unflinching in its denunciation of this holdover of Communist legal practice, writing in no uncertain terms in its September 2005 report, that "the long overdue abolition of the general oversight should be accomplished as soon as possible" and that "this function should be transferred to the judiciary (administrative courts) and ombudsperson institution gradually."[59] The oversight functions undermine the core notion of a fair trial. By initiating the review of court judgments, the European Court of Human Rights deemed the practice incompatible with the principle of legal certainty embedded in the European Convention on Human Rights.[60]

With such expansive and unregulated powers, the prosecutor general has found himself under a permanent cloud of political controversy before and since the Orange Revolution. The most visible case was that of Georgii Gongadze, a muckracking journalist who was kidnapped and murdered in the fall of 2000. Conversations secretly recorded in President Kuchma's office allegedly link the kidnapping to high government officials.[61] For four years, the authorities impeded the investigation. On November 8, 2005, the European Court of Human Rights ruled that "the Ukrainian authorities . . . failed to investigate [Gongadze's] death [and] treated [his widow] in an inhuman and degrading manner."[62] Earlier in the year, Prosecutor General Svyatoslav Piskun, who had been reinstated in his position in December 2004, announced the capture of three low-level policemen, the alleged killers of Gongadze, and a trial was announced for 2006, but, repeating a pre-Orange pattern, there is no evidence that his office has been actively investigating the identity of whoever gave the orders.[63]

The prosecutor's handling of two critical suspects in the chain of command—former interior minister Kravchenko, who was called for questioning through the most irregular means of the mass media and found dead the day after, and Colonel Pukach, commander of the Interior Ministry's Criminal Investigations Directorate, who vanished following a leak of his imminent arrest—did little to dissipate doubts about continuing political interference and the possible existence of an immunity pact between the current and former presidents on the matter. A report written on behalf of the International Federation of Journalists found no direct evidence of political collusion yet concluded that "the Gongadze case has been conducted in such a way consistent with the existence of such an arrangement, however informal or general its terms."[64]

In the first half of 2005, the prosecutor general hauled in for questioning and detained dozens of public figures associated with the Yanukovych camp, on charges ranging from electoral fraud to separatism and extortion. The most significant arrest was that of Borys Kolesnykov, the head of the Donetsk regional council and a key official in Yanukovych's Party of Regions. People close to the Party of Regions claimed that these arrests were akin to political persecution of the opponents of the Orange Revolution and appealed to European bodies.[65] Ukrainian media and NGOs gave little credence to these grievances. The Council of Europe called for investigations to be carried out "in full compliance with European standards."[66] The fact that several of these investigations were conducted by an office endowed, as we saw, with excessive powers, and whose relationship to the presidential administration has traditionally lacked transparency, raised suspicions of a partisan operation.

In the end, no high-profile case was brought to court, and Yushchenko, seeking the support of his former rival, Yanukovych during the nomination process for his new prime minister in September 2005, signed an agreement promising amnesty to the perpetrators of electoral fraud.[67] In November, Yushchenko fired Prosecutor General Piskun (later reinstated by a court order), who claimed that his dismissal was related to his determination to investigate Yushchenko's wife on charges of corruption, a claim that Yushchenko denied.[68]

The upshot is that a constitutional arrangement that blurs the distinction between adjudicating and enforcing the law leaves the door wide open to the perception that politics trumps the law in Ukraine. An aggravating factor is the severe lack of funding that affects all levels of the judiciary, not only limiting judges in their ability to take up cases expeditiously but also rendering them more dependent on the executive branch.[69] A 2002 report on the European judicial systems found that Ukraine has one of the lowest rates of public spending on courts, with a per capita figure eight times less than that in Poland.[70] However, a significant step forward was taken in September 2005, when the Cabinet of Ministers voted to triple the salaries of judges, effective in January 2006. The Council of Europe saluted the initiative, while cautioning that the executive branch should not be in a position to influence the salary of court officials.[71]

The amended constitution upholds the right of the president to appoint professional judges to five-year terms, contributing to lasting corruption in the judiciary more broadly. Parliament elects all other judges (except those of the Constitutional Court) for permanent terms by a legally established procedure. The president also maintains the rights to establish or abolish courts of general jurisdiction (including the Supreme Court, specialized commercial courts, and military courts) and to appoint and remove chairs and deputy chairs of courts. A draft amendment to the Law on the Judicial System of Ukraine—intended to transfer this authority away from the president in order to prevent the possibility of indirect influence—was submitted to parliament in January 2005. The constitution provides an extensive list of conditions under which judges or chairs may be dismissed but clearly allocates this responsibility to the body that appointed them in the first place. The Constitutional Court, comprised of 18 judges and ultimately responsible for deciding the constitutionality of legislation, is appointed in equal shares by the president, parliament, and the Congress of Judges. However, the Constitutional Court has lacked a quorum since October 2005 as a result of parliament's failure to appoint its share of new judges, thus rendering the court's authority to consider cases obsolete.

While the law in Ukraine provides for each citizen's right to a timely, fair, and open trial, including the use of juries, this right was not respected in practice. Juries were not used over the course of 2005, and judges made most court decisions alone. Moreover, pretrial detention remains a serious problem, with defendants remaining in detention for months, or even years, before being brought to trial. Pretrial detainees often lack access to counsel due to vague legislation; while the law guarantees the right to legal defense, the stage at which a detainee has the right to consult a lawyer remains unclear, with discrepancies between Article 21 of the Criminal Procedure Code and the Law on the Police.[72]

The role of the police and the Security Service of Ukraine remains an area of significant concern but also one in which the government is taking clear steps toward reform. The police are accountable to the minister of internal affairs, whereas the internal security service forces report directly to the president. Specific changes to the criminal justice system, including an end of abusive practices by the police, are critical to Ukraine's meeting its goal of an association agreement with the European Union in 2007, as established in the three-year joint action plan for political and economic reform in the country signed by the government and the EU in February 2005.[73] To this end, the government has made noteworthy strides toward curbing police abuses by taking disciplinary action against abusive law enforcement authorities, which will hopefully enable some progress toward resolving the country's long-standing problem of police impunity.

Recommendations

- As demanded by the Council of Europe for several years, Ukraine must break with the Soviet practice of endowing the Office of the Prosecutor General with supervisory powers over court decisions. The relationship between the prosecutor general and the executive must be made more transparent.
- Vacancies on the Constitutional Court must be filled and the court must be given an opportunity to rule on the conformity of the amendments voted on December 8, 2004, with constitutional procedures.
- The Gongadze case is a litmus test for the new government's commitment to justice and due process. The government must ensure that the investigation into the instigators of the crime is unimpeded.

ANTICORRUPTION AND TRANSPARENCY – 3.01

In Transparency International's Corruption Perceptions Index 2005, it ranked in the bottom tier, 107th out of 159 countries, tying with Belarus and coming in slightly ahead of Russia and Georgia. This score was actually an improvement over the 2004 index, in which Ukraine finished at 122 out of 146 countries.[74] The expectation that the new

Orange government would usher in a more transparent style of governance most likely explains Ukraine's better performance, as it appears to be too early to judge whether the endemic petty corruption, such as bribe-taking, that has characterized Ukraine for so long, has markedly diminished.

Bribes are generally linked to a combination of overintrusive government regulation, low salaries for civil servants, and poor oversight. The scale of regulations does not appear to have diminished in 2005, as the *Wall Street Journal*/Heritage Foundation Index of Economic Freedom continued to rank Ukraine in the bottom fifth of the world on the indicator of "Regulation," citing "complex, unpredictable, burdensome, and duplicative" procedures for conducting business.[75] Prime Minister Tymoshenko announced her intention to scale back on the number of licenses issued by bureaucrats, a fertile ground for corruption, but the government's lack of cohesion on economic policy, which culminated with Tymoshenko's firing in September 2005, cast doubts on whether the policy bore fruit. Salaries of government employees, on the other hand, did increase in fiscal year 2005.

With the media no longer under pressure from the executive and political debates being conducted more openly, including among rivals within the Orange camp, allegations of corruption on a grand scale were regularly aired throughout 2005. This breakthrough in public exposure was not accompanied, however, by a change in the structural incentives for politicians and civil servants to blur the line between private and public interests. The most powerful incentive arises from the maintenance of subsidized prices and barter arrangements in the energy sector, the source of most of the private wealth accumulation in postindependence Ukraine. For as long as Ukraine has been paying below market prices for its energy, brokers have privately, and opaquely, benefited from the difference between world and fixed prices (explaining how at least two former prime ministers, Yulia Tymoshenko and Pavlo Lazarenko, made their fortunes in the late 1990s). A glaring current example is the company RosUkrEnergo, which controls the distribution of Turkmen gas to Ukraine and whose owners remained unknown in 2005.

Corruption is arguably the most pressing issue in the minds of the electorate. An American political scientist boldly argued that the mass mobilization during the Orange Revolution can be best explained as a unique opportunity for the population to manifest its rejection of pervasive corruption.[76] The inability of the Yushchenko administration to tackle the energy sector proved very damaging politically. In September, Yushchenko chief of staff Oleksandr Zinchenko stunned the nation by publicly accusing two other close Yushchenko aides, Petro Poroshenko and Oleksandr Tretyakov, of "corruption."[77] The implication was that the businessmen who financially supported the Orange demonstrations were now using their state offices to pursue private gains. Several allegations were linked to the gas distribution network. It was revealed that the Security Service of Ukraine (SBU), headed by Oleksandr Turchynov, a Tymoshenko ally, had begun, over the summer, to look into the middleman companies operating in the gas industry and that these investigations involved people close to Yushchenko, including Tretyakov.[78] Turchynov claims that he then received direct orders from Yushchenko to "stop persecuting my men" and that these investigations "were creating a conflict" with Russian President Vladimir Putin.[79]

The September allegations were denied by the accused and only briefly investigated. (The fact that an investigation into the allegations of corruption against Poroshenko was ended a few days after the firing of Prosecutor General Piskun in October 2005 did little to alter the public perception of the use of the office of the prosecutor general as a political instrument.)[80] However, they led to a decline in the popularity of Yushchenko and his political formation, Our Ukraine, to the advantage of the Tymoshenko Bloc, from where most corruption charges originated. While in the Kuchma era politicians appeared to be politically immune from their alleged corrupt behavior, in the Orange era there appears to be an electoral cost to engaging in what the public perceives as corruption. The problem is the scope of gray zones. Corruption is an elastic concept that extends from gross misdeeds, such as embezzlement, to the fuzzier realm of conflict of interest. Many of the corruption allegations that have been leveled in partisan discourse since September 2005 may turn out to have had more to do with conflict of interest than blatant corruption. Yet Ukraine lacks legal guidelines to regulate the private interests of state officials, and the process of public disclosure of revenues by these officials has little credibility.[81] This, and the continuously shady nature of energy transactions, feeds a public perception that corruption prevails among the higher-ups, undermining incentives for lower-level officials to mend their ways.

There were nonetheless a number of developments favoring government transparency in 2005. The Yushchenko administration was initially criticized for continuing the Kuchma practice of restricting access to normative acts according to criteria ("for official use only") not recognized by legislation.[82] In the first three months of 2005, President Yushchenko issued 42 decrees and two instructions that were not publicly accessible, and Prime Minister Tymoshenko issued an additional 15. The practice was terminated afterward, and the Ministry of Justice recognized its illegal nature. Hundreds of such restricted acts had been passed in the Kuchma era and were reportedly used to shield perks and benefits for political insiders; in other words, the kind of behind-the-scenes arrangements likely to fall under the rubric of corruption.[83] Yet legal guidelines establishing clear standards on the confidentiality of information are still lacking, and their lack, in practice, impedes the right of citizens to gain access to information on government activities. The lack of legislation to enforce the right to free access to information, inadequacies in the court system, and the absence of an effective mechanism to appeal against government decisions makes civic access to government information far more problematic than media access.[84]

Another potential breakthrough in government transparency was the conduct of the televised state auction of Kryvorizhstal, Ukraine's largest steel plant, in October 2005. Shortly before the Orange Revolution, the plant had been sold to a group of Ukrainian businessmen, who included Kuchma's son-in-law, Viktor Pinchuk, for $800 million, a price that was widely considered far below its market value. The 2005 auction was won by a Dutch consortium willing to pay six times that amount.[85] Kryvorizhstal was Exhibit No. 1 in the Orange government's oft-repeated promise to reopen bidding on illegal privatizations that took place in the Kuchma era. The intention to reprivatize assets, however, raised serious concerns among domestic and international entrepreneurs about the government's determination to respect property rights.[86] Torn between a more populist prime minister, who hinted at thousands of reprivatizations, and a more pragmatic president, who talked of dozens, the government was incapable in the first nine months of 2005, of devising a clear policy regarding the scope and process of reprivatization. While the fate of reprivatization remained uncertain by the end of the year, the sale of Kryvorizhstal set a high standard regarding open bidding for government contracts and property in the future.

Recommendations

- The government must strive to phase out barter arrangements and price differentials in the energy sector, thereby removing a powerful incentive for nontransparent and corrupt transactions.
- The government should elaborate clear guidelines regarding conflict of interest among state officials and ensure that their public declaration of revenues is credible with the public.
- Building on the Kryvorizhstal precedent, the government should institute a regular practice of open bidding for government contracts and property.

NOTES

[1] Lucan Way, "Ukraine's Orange Revolution. Kuchma's Failed Authoritarianism," *Journal of Democracy* 16, 2 (April 2005), 131–45.

[2] *Ukraine. Presidential Election. 31 October, 21 November and 26 December 2004. OSCE/ODIHR Election Observation Mission Final Report* (Warsaw, Poland: Organization for Security and Co-operation in Europe [OSCE], Office for Democratic Institutions and Human Rights [ODIHR], 2005), http://www.osce.org/documents/odihr/2005/05/14224_en.pdf.

[3] "Under Assault. Ukraine's News Media and the 2004 Presidential Elections" (New York and Washington, D.C.: Freedom House, Special Report, June 2004), http://www.freedomhouse.org/uploads/special_report/17.pdf.

[4] Roman Kupchinsky, "Corruption Allegations Abound," Radio Free Europe/Radio Liberty (RFE/RL), 8 September 2005, http://www.rferl.org/featuresarticle/2005/9/E539907C-99DC-419B-92BA-483C36A92B38.html.

[5] "It Is Tymoshenko Who Is Copying Kuchma," *Gazeta Wyborcza* (Poland), 15 September 2005, translated in *The Ukraine List* (UKL) 364, 7 October 2005, http://www.ukrainianstudies.uottawa.ca/ukraine_list/ukl364_15.html.

[6] Lucan Way, "The Sources and Dynamics of Competitive Authoritarianism in Ukraine," *The Journal of Communist Studies and Transition Politics.* 20, 1 (March 2004), 143–61.

[7] "Report on Ukraine's Presidential Elections: October and November 1999" (Washington, D.C.: Commission on Security and Cooperation in Europe, United States Helsinki Commission, 20 December 1999), http://www.csce.gov/index.cfm?Fuseaction=UserGroups.Home&ContentRecord_id=35&ContentType=R&ContentRecordType=R&UserGroup_id=117&Subaction=ByDate&CFID=18849146&CFTOKEN=53.

[8] Andrew Wilson, *Ukraine's Orange Revolution* (New Haven: Yale University Press, 2005).

[9] *Honouring of Obligations and Commitments by Ukraine* (Strasbourg: Parliamentary Assembly of the Council of Europe [COE], Report, Doc. 10676, September 2005), http://assembly.coe.int/Documents/WorkingDocs/doc05/EDOC10676.pdf.

[10] Ibid.

11 "Opinion on the Amendments to the Constitution of Ukraine Adopted on 8.12.2004" (Strasbourg: European Commission for Democracy Through Law [Venice Commission], 13 June 2005).

12 "Reporters Without Borders in Kiev: 'The Time for Promises is Over!'" (Paris: Reporters Without Borders [RSF], 14 November 2005), http://www.rsf.org/article.php3?id_article=15579.

13 "Adoption of Decree on Online Registration Worrying" (RSF, 26 May 2005), http://www.rsf.org/article.php3?id_article=13916.

14 "Government Rescinds Decree Requiring Online Publications to Register," (RSF, 11 October 2005), http://www.rsf.org/article.php3?id_article=13916.

15 "Journalist Beaten and Warned to Halt Investigation," *CPJ News Alert* (New York: Committee to Protect Journalists [CPJ], 7 October 2005), http://www.cpj.org/news/2005/Ukraine07oct05na.html; "Reporters Without Borders in Kiev" (RSF).

16 "Reporters Without Borders in Kiev" (RSF).

17 "Press Freedom for November 2005" (Kyiv: Institute of Mass Information), http://eng.imi.org.ua.

18 *100 dniv novoi vlady: pohliad neuriadovykh analitychnykh tsentriv* (Kyiv: Ukrainian Centre for Economic and Political Studies [UCEPS] et al., May 2005), http://www.uceps.org/img/st_img/table/746/concept.pdf.

19 *Honouring of Obligations* (COE).

20 "Memorandum on the Draft Public Service Broadcasting Law for Ukraine" (London: Article 19: Global Campaign for Free Expression, August 2005, http://www.article19.org/pdfs/analysis/ukraine-amendment-of-draft-law-on-broadcasting.pdf.

21 "Ukraine," in *Attacks on the Press in 2005* (CPJ), http://www.cpj.org/attacks05/europe05/ukraine_05.html.

22 "Public Appeal. Ukraine. Torture and Ill-Treatment in Police Detention" (London: Amnesty International [AI] Index: EUR 50/005/2005, 23 August 2005), http://web.amnesty.org/library/index/engeur500052005.

23 "'How Confessions Are Beaten Out' by Ukraine Authorities," *The Wire, AI's Monthly Magazine,* October 2005, http://web.amnesty.org/wire/October2005/Ukraine.

24 *Honouring of Obligations* (COE).

25 Ibid.

26 "Ukraine. Time for Action: Torture and Ill-Treatment in Police Detention" (AI, Index: EUR 50/004/2005, 27 September 2005), http://web.amnesty.org/library/Index/ENGEUR500042005.

27 *Honouring of Obligations* (COE).

28 "Human Rights in Ukraine One Year After The 'Orange Revolution'" (Vienna: International Helsinki Federation for Human Rights [IHF-HR], 19 December 2005), http://www.ihf-hr.org/documents/doc_summary.php?sec_id=3&d_id=4168.

29 "Appeal of the Ukrainian Helsinki Union of Human Rights," *Prava ludyny* 10 (2004), http://www.khpg.org/index.php?id=1102414656&r=2&s=2004&n=10.

30 Keith Darden, "Graft and Governance: Corruption as an Informal Mechanism of State Control" (unpublished conference paper, 2003), http://www8.georgetown.edu/centers/cdats/Graft%20and%20Governance.pdf.

31 Catherine Wanner, "Communities of the Converted: Explaining the Appeal of Evangelicalism in Ukraine," in Dominique Arel and Blair Ruble, eds., *Rebounding Identities: The Politics of Identity in Russia and Ukraine* (Baltimore: Johns Hopkins University Press, 2006).

32 Taras Antoshevs'kyi and Lesia Kovalenko, "Monitoring relihiinoï svobody v Ukraïny: osoblyvyi ohliad na mainovi pytannia" (Lviv: Ukrainian Catholic University, Institute of Religion and Society, Religious-Information Service of Ukraine [RISU], 2005), http://www.risu.org.ua/freedom/analytics/report/.

33 Ibid.

34 *Honouring of Obligations* (COE).

35 Antoshev'skyi and Kovalenko, "Monitoring" (RISU).

36 Ibid.

37 "Chyslo proiavlenii antisemitisma sokratilos' v Evrope, vyroslo v Rossii i Ukraine," *Jewish News,* 26 January 2006, http://www.jn.com.ua/Antisemitism/sohnut_2601.html.

38 "Chronicle of Anti-Semitism in Ukraine: 2002–2004" (Washington, D.C.: Union of Councils for Jews in the Former Soviet Union [UCSJ]), http://www.fsumonitor.com/stories/121404ChronicleinUkraine.pdf.

39 Per Anders Rudling, "Organized Anti-Semitism in Contemporary Ukraine: Structure, Influence and Ideology," *Canadian Slavonic Papers* 48, 1–2 (March–June 2006), 1–39.

40 Natalia A. Fedushchak, "Ukrainian News in Cross Fire," *Washington Times,* 15 February 2004.

41 Dominique Arel, "Interpreting 'Nationality' and 'Language' in the 2001 Ukrainian Census," *Post-Soviet Affairs* 18, 3 (July–September 2002), 238.

42 "Pro kil'kist' ta sklad naselennia Ukraïny za pidsumkamy Vseukraïns'koho perepysu naselennia 2001 roku" (Kyiv: State Statistics Committee of Ukraine, 2002).

43 "Constitution of Ukraine," Adopted at Fifth Session of the Verkhovna Rada of Ukraine on 28 June 1996, http://www.rada.gov.ua/const/conengl.htm.

44 Volodymyr Kulyk, *Revisiting A Success Story: Implementation of the Recommendations of the OSCE High Commissioner on National Minorities to Ukraine, 1994–2001* (Hamburg: Centre for OSCE Research [CORE], Working Paper 6, 2002), http://www.core-hamburg.de/documents/32_CORE_Working_Paper_6.pdf.

45 "Protection for Ethnic Minorities May Soon Be Closer to EU Standards," *ICPS Newsletter* (Kyiv: International Centre for Policy Studies [ICPS]), 24 October 2005, http://www.icps.com.ua/doc/nl_eng_20051024_0295.pdf.

46 "Ukrainian Police Fingerprint Roma," (Budapest: European Roma Rights Centre, 2005), http://www.errc.org/cikk.php?cikk=2203&archiv=1.

47 "Ukraine: On the Margins—Rights Violations against Migrants and Asylum Seekers at the New Eastern Border of the European Union" (New York: Human Rights Watch [HRW], Index No. D1708, 30 November 2005), http://hrw.org/reports/2005/ukraine1105/.

48 Ibid.

49 *Honouring of Obligations* (COE).

50 "Trafficking in Persons Report" (Washington, D.C.: U.S. Department of State, Office to Monitor and Combat Trafficking in Persons, 3 June 2005), http://www.state.gov/g/tip/rls/tiprpt/2005/46616.htm.

51 Vittoria Luda di Cortemiglia, "Trafficking in Minors for Commercial Sexual Exploitation. Ukraine" (Turin: United Nations Interregional Crime and Justice Research Institute [UNICRI], Action Program Against Trafficking in Minors for Sexual Purposes, 2005), http://www.unicri.it/wwd/trafficking/minors/docs/dr_ukraine.pdf.

52 *Honouring of Obligations* (COE).

53 Steven Lee Myers, "Ukrainian Justices, in Show of Independence, Order New Runoff," The New York Times, 3 December 2004. For a narrative of events during the Orange Revolution, see Andrew Wilson, *Ukraine's Orange Revolution* (Yale).

54 *Honouring of Obligations* (COE).

55 Bohdan Futey, "Crisis in the Constitutional Court of Ukraine: A Court Without Judges?" *UKL* 362, 15 September 2005, http://www.ukrainianstudies.uottawa.ca/ukraine_list/ukl362_6.html.

56 Daniel Bilak, "'The Deal'—Some Cautionary Thoughts," UKL 305, 8 December 2004; C. J. Chivers, "Ukraine's Sharp Turn Toward the West," *The New York Times,* 9 December 2004.

57 "Opinion on Three Draft Laws Proposing Amendments to the Constitution of Ukraine," Adopted by the Venice Commission at its 57th Plenary Session, Venice, 12–13 December 2003 (European Commission for Democracy Through Law [Venice Commission]), http://www.venice.coe.int/docs/2003/CDL-AD(2003)019-e.pdf; "Opinion on the Amendments to the Constitution of Ukraine Adopted on 8.12.2004," Adopted by the Commission at its 63rd Plenary Session, Venice, 10–11 June 2005 (Venice Commission), http://www.venice.coe.int/docs/2005/CDL-AD(2005)015-e.pdf.

58 "Opinion on the Draft Law Amending the Law of Ukraine on the Office of the Public Prosecutor," Adopted by the Commission at its 60th Plenary Session, Venice, 8–9 October 2004 (Venice Commission), http://www.venice.coe.int/docs/2004/CDL-AD(2004)038-e.pdf.

59 *Honouring of Obligations* (COE).

60 Ibid.

61 J. V. Koshiw, *Beheaded: The Killing of a Journalist* (Reading, UK: Artemia Press, 2003).

62 "World Press Freedom Review: Ukraine 2005" (Vienna: International Press Institute [IPI]), http://service.cms.apa.at/cms/ipi/freedom_detail-new.html?country=/KW0001/KW0003/KW0087/.

63 Simon Pirani, "The Gongadze Inquiry. An Investigation Into the Failure of Legal and Judicial Processes in the Case of Gyorgy Gongadze. Report No. 2: The Instigators Are Getting Away" (Brussels: International Federation of Journalists; Kyiv: Institute of Mass Information; et al., September 2005), http://www.ifj.org/pdfs/gongadze2.pdf.

64 Ibid.

65 Taras Kuzio, "Criminal Charges Reach Senior Leaders of Ukrainian Opposition," *Eurasia Daily Monitor,* 1 July 2005, http://www.jamestown.org/edm/article.php?article_id=2369966.

66 *Honouring of Obligations* (COE).

67 Mykhailo Wynnyckyj, "The Day the Music Died," *UKL* 363, 22 September 2005, http://www.ukrainianstudies.uottawa.ca/ukraine_list/ukl363_3.html.

[68] Andrew Osborn, "Prosecutor Who Investigated Yushchenko's Wife Is Sacked," *The Independent* (UK), 20 October 2005, http://news.independent.co.uk/europe/article320808 .ece.

[69] "Human Rights in Ukraine One Year After" (IHF-HR).

[70] *Honouring of Obligations* (COE).

[71] Ibid.

[72] Amnesty International, "Ukraine: Time for Action: Torture and Ill Treatment in Police Detention," http://web.amnesty.org/library/Index/ENGEUR500042005.

[73] "Ukraine: Time for Action: Torture and Ill Treatment in Police Detention."

[74] *Corruption Perceptions Index 2005* (Berlin: Transparency International), http://www .transparency.org/cpi/2005/dnld/media_pack_en.pdf.

[75] *2006 Index of Economic Freedom.*

[76] Joshua A. Tucker, "Enough! Electoral Fraud, Collective Action Problems, and the '2nd Wave' of Post-Communist Democratic Revolutions" (Ottawa: University of Ottawa, First Annual Danyliw Research Seminar in Contemporary Ukrainian Studies, Paper, October 2005), http://www.ukrainianstudies.uottawa.ca/pdf/P_Tucker_Danyliw05.pdf.

[77] "The Scandalous Press Conference with Zinchenko," *Ukrains'ka pravda,* 5 September 2005, translated in UKL 360, 13 September 2005, http://www.ukrainianstudies.uottawa .ca/ukraine_list/ukl360_11.html.

[78] Kupchinsky, "Corruption Allegations"; Kupchinsky, "A Conflict Over Gas And Power," RFE/RL, 12 September 2005, http://www.rferl.org/featuresarticle/2005/9/46189B83-B037-4966-910C-89F5D78ADC96.html.

[79] Kupchinsky, "Battle Against Corruption Grinds to a Halt," RFE/RL Organized Crime and Terrorism Watch, 3 October 2005, http://www.rferl.org/reports/corruptionwatch/ 2005/10/13-031005.asp.

[80] Steven Lee Myers, "Prosecutors Close Case Against Yushchenko Ally," *The New York Times,* 22 October 2005.

[81] Kupchinsky, "Corruption Allegations."

[82] *100 dniv novoi vlady* (UCEPS).

[83] "Secret Material Which The Regime Concealed Under Stamps 'Not To Be Printed' and 'Not To Be Published,'" (Kharkiv: Kharkiv Group for Human Rights Protection, 22 April 2006), http://khpg.org/index.php?id=1145710178.

[84] "Legislative Gaps Make Public Oversight of Government Bodies Difficult," *ICPS Newsletter* 31, 290, 19 September 2005, http://www.icps.kiev.ua/eng.

[85] "Country's Largest Steel Mill Sold At Auction," RFE/RL, 24 October 2005, http://www .rferl.org/featuresarticle/2005/10/B87465A5-EB07-48B0-BAEA-5E60F46F54A8.html.

[86] Anders Aslund, "The Economic Policy of Ukraine after the Orange Revolution," *Eurasian Geography and Economics* 46, 5 (2005), 327–53.

VENEZUELA

CAPITAL: Caracas

POPULATION: 26.7 million

GNI PER CAPITA: $3,490

SCORES	2004	2006
ACCOUNTABILITY AND PUBLIC VOICE:	3.64	3.00
CIVIL LIBERTIES:	4.17	4.07
RULE OF LAW:	3.21	2.98
ANTICORRUPTION AND TRANSPARENCY:	2.89	2.13

(scores are based on a scale of 0 to 7, with 0 representing weakest and 7 representing strongest performance)

Martin Edwin Andersen

INTRODUCTION

As the head of an oil rich country, President Hugo Chavez—whose own political ascendancy reflected popular disenchantment with Venezuela's exclusionary traditional political parties—has presided over the deterioration of the country's democratic institutions. Chavez's Bolivarian Revolution, which he now defines as "21st century socialism," has meant a new constitution, a new legislature, a new Supreme Court, new election officials, and purges of both the state-owned oil company and the Venezuelan armed forces. Chavez still cites combating corruption and social injustice as the leitmotif for his brand of authoritarian politics. Yet under his rule, corruption in Venezuela appears to be getting worse, coming in 130th out of 158 countries surveyed in Transparency International's 2005 Corruption Perceptions Index.

The government spent much of 2005 using the country's oil wealth to promote anti-North, anti-free trade, pro-Cuban politics abroad,[2] even

Martin Edwin "Mick" Andersen has served as Director of Latin American and Caribbean programs for the National Democratic Institute for International Affairs, as a member of the professional staff of the Senate Foreign Relations Committee, and as a Senior Advisor for Policy Planning at the U.S. Department of Justice. He is the author of *Dossier Secreto: Argentina's Desaparecidos and the Myth of the "Dirty War"* (Boulder, CO: Westview, 1993) and *La Policia: Pasado, Presente y Propuestas para el Futuro* (Buenos Aires: Sudamericana, 2001). In 2005, he was an expert witness in the Italian government's prosecution of former Chilean dictator, Captain General Augusto Pinochet, for human rights crimes.

591

as Venezuela's high levels of poverty remained constant. The growing militarization of the country's political sphere, as evidenced by the appointment of more than 300 serving and retired military officers in public posts outside of the defense sector, was accompanied by the inauguration of a blacklist of political opponents that denied tens of thousands access to state jobs and services, as well as by increases in political corruption.[3]

The decision by Venezuela's four major opposition parties to abstain from the December 2005 election contest, claiming that the National Electoral Council (CNE) is biased toward pro-Chavez parties and therefore the results would be rigged, meant that voters were faced with two real choices: staying at home or voting for parliamentary candidates loyal to Chavez. Analysts said this would show the real level of public support for Chavez. The vote could serve as a reality check on a Venezuelan president who has eliminated various institutional accountability mechanisms, even as he consolidates his political and economic power, particularly over the armed forces. However, the government's growing control over sectors of Venezuelan life, record-high oil prices, and his unbroken, albeit questionable, string of electoral victories, all appeared to make Chavez largely unassailable in the 2006 presidential election.

[*Editor's note:* In elections for the National Assembly held on December 4, 2005, in which all five main opposition parties boycotted the poll due to their lack of confidence in the electoral system's transparency and ability to guarantee the secrecy of the vote, only 25 percent of Venezuela's 14 million voters took part in a contest that resulted in Chavez's firm control over the legislative body. In the aftermath of the parliamentary election, the *Economist* noted, Venezuela was "edging toward a Potemkin democracy . . . the new assembly will be composed wholly of supporters of Mr Chávez, albeit split among several parties ."[4]]

ACCOUNTABILITY AND PUBLIC VOICE – 3.00

Venezuelan citizens can change their government democratically, although conditions for the anti-Chavez opposition make it increasingly hard to do so. Almost three-quarters of Venezuela's adult population has chosen not to participate in recent elections, despite the claim of Chavez and his supporters that they have brought large numbers of Venezuela's poor—some 68 percent of the population—into the democratic processes.[5] Campaign financing is largely unregulated, although the electoral law does explicitly prohibit advertising by any government agency in political campaigns or elections. In the most recent electoral contests, the Chavez government has significantly increased social spending in a bid to mobilize its political base.

After his election in 1998, Chavez won a national referendum on a new constitution that allowed a strengthened chief executive the right to dissolve the National Assembly and made it possible for Chavez to retain power until 2013. Meanwhile, Chavez's Assembly allies granted him special fast-track powers allowing him to decree a wide range of laws without parliamentary debate. Following approval of the new constitution, the Assembly and the Supreme Court were dismissed.

Chavez consolidated his hold on power following the defeat, amid charges of ballot rigging, of a first-ever presidential recall referendum. By mid-2004, more than four million people of some 14 million eligible voters had signed recall petitions. Chavez, however, won the referendum with 58 percent of the vote. Following the election, which was conducted in relative peace and characterized by a high turnout, opposition groups insisted that there was a large discrepancy between the official results and their own exit polls. Although some independent observers cited what they called credible reports of voter harassment—including physical intimidation and the reassignment of thousands of voters to far-away polling stations—and vote tampering, both the Organization of American States and the Carter Center in Atlanta, Georgia, said that they found no evidence of election fraud. In October 2004, regional and municipal elections, voters overwhelmingly backed pro-Chavez candidates.

In 2005, people who signed recall petitions complained that they could not get government jobs or contracts, qualify for public assistance programs, receive passports, or even receive services at local libraries.[6] Chavez also signaled his plans to remain in power for the foreseeable future; when swearing in his party's candidates for the December 4, 2005, National Assembly elections, he told them that if they were elected, they might be called on to participate in an effort to amend the constitution. Following the election, the Organization of American States highlighted the climate of "mutual distrust . . . polarization and political tension," as well as the fact that there was an "absence of strict control mechanisms of the use of public and private resources for political and electoral ends."[7]

At the national level, by 2005 there were no truly independent government institutions. Chavez's party, the Fifth Republic Movement, controls the National Assembly, as well as the Supreme Justice Tribunal (TSJ)—whose members are elected by the National Assembly to a single 12-year term—and the intelligence services. Chavez has relied heavily on supporters from within the armed forces, both on active duty and retired, to staff key executive branch and public enterprise posts. Chavez's party also controls the "citizen power," or ombudsman, branch of government, created in the 1999 constitution to fight corruption, and other checks and balances have been eliminated. In addition, according to an authoritative private risk analysis firm, in recent years there has been a "rapid increase in the numbers of Cuban political advisors, military officers and intelligence operatives in the country"—a disturbing presence, as the island country remains the last dictatorship in the hemisphere.[8]

Venezuela has a large government bureaucracy, but the civil service is not chosen through open competition or by merit. The 1961 constitution provided for a career civil service and established standards for performance, advancement, suspension, and retirement. These have been largely ignored by Chavez and his predecessors in favor of a patronage system in which the military actively participates.

The virulent rhetoric employed by official and quasi-official sources is also widely seen as tacitly approving violence against government opponents. Threats, intimidation, and physical harm to numerous persons, as well as accusations by the political opposition of illegal wiretapping of the telephones of private citizens who are members of anti-Chavez groups, are well documented.

Even though the country has one of Latin America's best-organized and most extensive communities of nongovernmental organizations, the government has done little to protect the rights of civil society. In 2000, the Supreme Court ruled that nongovernmental organizations (NGOs) that receive funding from foreign governments or whose leaders are not Venezuelan are not part of civil society. As a result, they may not represent citizens in court or bring their own legal actions. The Chavez government has also made an effort to undermine the legitimacy of reputable human rights and other civil society organizations by questioning their ties to international organizations. In 2005, the leaders of the U.S. National Endowment for Democracy–supported Sumate (a

Venezuelan civic association for the defense of electoral rights) were brought up on charges of conspiring against the government. Moreover, the ability of civic groups to offer meaningful contributions by testifying, commenting on, or otherwise influencing government policy or legislation has been reduced significantly, although the regime has created some so-called popular consultation mechanisms, such as the "Bolivarian Circles," that are largely in the hands of its partisans.

Although the constitution provides for freedom of the press, exercise of that right is difficult in practice, with press laws, in the words of one foreign journalist, "designed to be enforced selectively, and to intimidate."[10] Physical attacks, police and military raids on media outlets without judicial warrant, and criminal prosecutions against anticorruption journalists exist in a climate of violent anti-media rhetoric by the government and a significant anti-Chavez slant on the part of media owners. In July 2004, a new law was ratified that regulates the work of journalists, provides for compulsory registration with the national journalism association, and punishes reporters' "illegal" conduct with prison sentences of three to six months. A Supreme Court ruling upheld censorship laws that effectively declared laws protecting public authorities and institutions from insulting criticism to be constitutional. The Law on the Social Responsibility of Radio and TV, giving the government control over the content of radio and television programs, went into effect in December 2004, with Chavez claiming that the "Venezuelan people have begun to free themselves from . . . the dictatorship of the private media." [11]

According to an October 2005 report by the Inter-American Press Association (IAPA), there has been an increase in violence against journalists and media outlets that are critical of the government, "threatening them with the possibility of being taken over or disappearing." In September 2005, the National Telecommunications Committee (CONATEL) opened administrative proceedings against seven private television stations and 22 private radio stations for bureaucratic offenses. According to the IAPA report, the government "uses official advertising as an instrument of coercion and has become the country's 'main communicator.'" In addition, there are four national television stations backed by 25 "semi-official stations," while the airwaves are filled with 146 semi-official and alternative community radio stations. The IAPA added that the government has also created "a swarm of print media, with 72 semi-official community newspapers." In 2005, Chavez went forward with the creation of a regional media network, Telesur, in partnership with the governments of Argentina, Cuba, and Uruguay. In contrast, the government does not restrict internet access.

In July 2005, the attorney general's office initiated a criminal investigation of the Caracas-based daily *El Universal* following publication of a front-page editorial. In the piece, the newspaper decried the politicization of the criminal justice system, saying that it had lost its autonomy and become ineffective, causing the attorney general's office and the courts to lose legitimacy. The probe was justified under *desacato* (contempt) provisions that criminalize expressions deemed offensive to public officials and state institutions. In October, the Supreme Court found that a newspaper editorial did not constitute an "institutional insult" prohibited by law. It noted, however, that the constitution proscribes "the use of freedom of information and opinion to destabilize democratic institutions."[12]

Freedom of cultural expression in Venezuela has also been subjected to Chavez's views on the need for a cultural revolution, which critical intellectuals and artists say is an attempt to use cultural institutions for political profit. The president has frequently called on Latin America to establish a cultural identity outside of what he calls American cultural imperialism.[13] In 2001, Chavez fired the heads of 16 major museums and other cultural institutions, with critics charging that experienced museum curators had been replaced by the president's political cronies. The government has also censored works of art critical of the regime and of Chavez personally.

Recommendations
- The blacklisting of people for their participation in legal political movements should be outlawed, and penalties enforced against those who create such lists or use them to deny jobs or services in the public sector.
- The president and other senior government officials should refrain from highly charged, intimidating rhetoric against opponents.
- Rules and regulations governing civil society organizations should be rewritten to reflect those of a modern, democratic polity, protecting the rights of those that receive funding from foreign governments or whose leaders are not Venezuelan.

- The civil service should be reestablished according to modern international standards, with specific provisions regarding performance, advancement, suspension, and retirement.
- Restrictive and undemocratic press laws, such as the Law of Social Responsibility in Radio and Television, should be abolished.

CIVIL LIBERTIES – 4.07

The constitution and the 1999 Organic Criminal Procedures Code (COPP) provide for freedom from arbitrary arrest and detention and prohibit torture and the holding of detainees incommunicado. Officials who instigate or tolerate torture are legally liable for prosecution and the law grants victims the right to medical rehabilitation. It further prohibits so-called forced disappearances (secret abductions), stating that an individual must refuse to obey an order to commit such a crime, and provides for the prosecution of the intellectual author of the crime.

In practice, widespread arbitrary detention and torture of suspects do take place in Venezuela—although most of these cases involve criminal suspects—as well as dozens of extrajudicial killings by military security forces and the police. Such extralegal acts are often characterized officially, despite eyewitness testimony, as the result of confrontations. The independent group Venezuelan Program of Education and Action on Human Rights (PROVEA) charged that the number of those reported to have been killed by the security forces while resisting arrest increased by 300 percent in the past decade. It also said that in the past five years, the number of cases of torture has risen by 90 percent. Chavez government action against police and security officers guilty of abusing both political opponents and suspects of common crimes is virtually nonexistent. In addition, 90 percent of all investigations into human rights violations do not make it past the preliminary stages of the process.[14]

According to a 2005 report by Human Rights Watch, prison conditions in Venezuela are "cruel, inhuman, and degrading," with overcrowding a chronic problem. The penal institutions are "virtually controlled by armed gangs." Hundreds of people die each year in prison riots and inmate violence; the human rights group PROVEA has estimated that, in 2003, the murder rate in prison was 40 times the national average. In October 2005, a Caracas-based group, Observatorio Venezolano de Prisiones (Venezuelan Prison Watch), claimed that 314 prisoners were killed and 517 were wounded in violent incidents over the course of the year.[15]

State protection of Venezuelan citizens from nonstate actors has been unsuccessful for two major reasons—police ties to vigilante death squads and official connivance with leftist guerrillas from neighboring Colombia operating on Venezuelan territory. Venezuela has increasingly become a safe haven for Colombia's leftist guerrillas, and scores of Venezuelans living and working near the countries' shared borders have been the victims of armed assaults, kidnappings, and murders by the Colombian rebels. Since 2001, some 140 peasants have been killed by paramilitaries or police believed to be linked to landowners who oppose the Chavez-inspired land takeover movement (see "Rule of Law"). Few of the perpetrators have been caught or tried.[16]

The Venezuelan constitution prohibits discrimination on the basis of politics, age, race, sex, creed, or any other condition. Men and women are legally equal in marriage. A 1990 labor code stipulates that employers must not discriminate against women with regards to salaries or working conditions and offers a series of guarantees for pregnant women and new mothers. These regulations, generally enforced in the country's formal economy, are not a factor in the informal economy, which accounts for roughly half of the active labor force.

Venezuelan women increasingly participate in the country's political and economic life, making important gains in the medical and legal professions, for example. Women are more active in government and politics than in many other Latin American countries and comprise the backbone of Venezuela's sophisticated grassroots network of nongovernmental organizations. They won 20 seats in the 165-member National Assembly in the July 2000 elections, and, in 2002, four women served in the 18-member cabinet. However, they are still underrepresented in leadership positions. There is substantial institutional and societal prejudice on issues of domestic violence and rape, and work-related sexual harassment is common. The 2005 UNDP *Human Development Report* says that women make up 61 percent of professional and technical workers and 27 percent of administrators and managers. The report put the ratio of female-earned income to male-earned income at 0.42. It ranks Venezuela 58th out of 140 countries surveyed on its gender-related development index and 64th on its gender empowerment measure. Women make up about half the student body at most universities.[17]

Although the constitution prohibits trafficking in persons, victims' rights groups report that Venezuela is a source, destination, and transit country for trafficked men, women, and children. According to Survivors' Rights International, Venezuela is a country of destination for women for commercial sexual exploitation, recruited through job advertisements in major newspapers. The victims are also trafficked abroad, where their passports are taken away and they are prostituted in massage parlors and brothels. Colombian women are trafficked into Venezuela through prostitution trade networks originating in their home country.[18]

There are no laws specifically designed to prosecute all forms of trafficking in persons, and legal action is limited to the use of existing laws against forced disappearance and kidnapping. The country's underdeveloped legal framework, the rampant corruption among immigration officials—which the Chavez government has in some ways sought to reduce—and the ready availability of fraudulent official identity documents help create ideal conditions for trafficking. In recognition of the problem, in January 2005, a seminar on trafficking in persons was held in Caracas and attended by officials from the Ministries of the Interior, Justice, and Foreign Affairs, as well as by a government prosecutor and members of the coordinator unit on trafficking in persons of the Organization of American States.

Approximately 316,000 indigenous people live in Venezuela, belonging to 27 ethnic groups. The formal rights of Venezuela's indigenous peoples have improved under Chavez. The constitution created three seats in the National Assembly for indigenous people and also provides for "the protection of indigenous communities and their progressive incorporation into the life of the nation." Those rights, specifically the groups' ability to make decisions affecting their lands, cultures, and traditions and the allocation of natural resources, are seldom enforced, as local political authorities infrequently take their interests into account. The lack of effective legal rights has created an unprecedented migration of Indians to poverty-stricken urban areas.

A recent report by the International Disability Rights Monitor credits Venezuela's legal framework with protecting disability rights and says that the government appeared willing to commit itself to meeting the needs of some 927,392 Venezuelans, or 4.4 percent of the total population, who were listed as disabled in the 2001 census. Although

Venezuelan law requires newly constructed or renovated buildings to provide access and prohibits discrimination in employment and public services, by the end of 2005 there had not been a sustained effort to implement the law, or to raise public awareness on disability issues. Architectural and communications inaccessibility are among those entrenched bars that make the elimination of inequality in daily life more difficult, said the report.[19]

Freedom of religion is guaranteed by the Venezuelan constitution on the condition that its practice does not violate public morality, decency, or the public order. In general, the state protects the rights of nonbelievers and adherents of minority religious faiths and movements and refrains from restricting religious observance, ceremony, and education. Throughout 2005, however, Chavez and the leaders of the local Roman Catholic Church, who generally side with his political opposition, engaged in an escalating war of words. In August, Cardinal Rosalio Castillo Lara called the government a dictatorship; Chavez responded that the prelate was an "outlaw, bandit, immoral." In October, the Florida-based evangelical New Tribes Mission was expelled from the country, with Chavez claiming that they were "agents of imperial penetration." Two weeks later, the Church of Jesus Christ of Latter-day Saints (the Mormons) announced it was withdrawing its 220 American missionaries from the country after having faced months of trouble either renewing their visas or getting new ones. In recent years, the Mormons reported being harassed by the National Guard.[20]

Freedom of peaceful assembly and association, established in the Venezuelan constitution, have been respected by the government, although much less so since Chavez took office, particularly due to the disruption of peaceful demonstrations by government supporters. According to the Venezuelan human rights group PROVEA, while at least 49 people were injured by the security forces' monitoring of peaceful demonstrations this was a significant decrease from 2004. A March penal code revision strictly penalizes some forms of peaceful demonstration, punishing road blockages with up to eight years imprisonment and outlawing the pot-clanging protests associated with opposition movements.

The president and his supporters have sought to break what they term a stranglehold of corrupt labor leaders on the job market, claiming the old labor regime amounted to little more than employer-controlled workers' organizations. Labor activists say this tramples on the rights of private organizations and masks Chavez's intent to create government-controlled unions. Security forces frequently break up strikes and arrest trade unionists, allegedly under the watchful eye of Cuban security officials.[21] In 2003, the International Labor Organization's Committee on Freedom of Association reported "the extremely serious and urgent situation in Venezuela marked by numerous complaints of repeated violations of freedom of association for both workers' and employers' organizations." It cited the authorities' intimidating statements to the Venezuelan Workers' Confederation. It also noted serious allegations of antiunion violence, which were not investigated by the government.[22]

Recommendations

- Clear public orders to Venezuelan military, security, and law enforcement agencies should be issued that they must refrain from the use of excessive force in dealing with demonstrations and public protests.
- Torture carried out by state agents should be penalized with the same severity as murder.
- Laws specifically designed to prosecute all forms of trafficking in persons should be promulgated.
- Increased resources should be directed to improving penal conditions.

RULE OF LAW – 2.98

The civilian judiciary in Venezuela is independent by statute, although it is highly inefficient and often corrupt. The constitutional reform approved in 1999 allowed Chavez partisans to be appointed to the Supreme Court, as attorney general (public prosecutor) and as comptroller general, without following constitutionally mandated procedures. In October 2005, Venezuelan human rights groups told the Inter-American Commission on Human Rights (IACHR) that they had identified the deteriorating justice system as the reason for the growing impunity, criminality, and violence in the country.[23]

Chavez supporters in the Venezuelan legislature severely weakened judicial independence by enlarging the Supreme Court from 20 to 32 members, giving the government the opportunity to pack it in December

2004 with pro-Chavez magistrates. The Chavez partisans justified the move as a response to pro-opposition rulings, which included a decision to absolve four military officers charged with taking part in a 2002 coup attempt against Chavez. Following the new appointments to the bench, in March 2005 the court's constitutional chamber overturned the acquittals. Independent observers have characterized the reversal as "apparently without precedent in recent Venezuelan legal history."[24]

Critics contend that the autonomy and independence of the judiciary is compromised by the fact that deputy judges and prosecutors lack job security and have inadequate legal training. While 60 percent of the judges held their positions provisionally when Chavez took office, that number reached between 75 and 80 percent in 2005. On March 11, 2005, the IACHR issued a statement expressing its concern that since 2004, 436 provisional public prosecutors have been appointed. Even the new president of the Supreme Court, although minimizing the issue of job stability, admitted, "judges in the labor-law field are part of those who might be under outside pressure." Between April and June 2005, courts of law had been placed in receivership and judges and prosecutors removed in several states, a situation that led the National Assembly to ask the president of the judicial chamber of the Supreme Court for an explanation.[25]

The lower courts have also been packed with Chavez supporters.[26] The Venezuelan judicial watchdog group Foro Penal notes that more than 200 judges have been removed from their posts or retired for political reasons.[27] A number of judges were subsequently appointed who lacked legally mandated professional qualifications and whose only claims to office were their ties to members of the ruling party.

The COPP provides for the right to a fair trial, conducted publicly, and considers the accused innocent until proven guilty in a court. This is a marked change from the old inquisitorial system, based on the Napoleonic code, in which the presumption of innocence generally was not respected or accepted. However, the country's public defender program is seriously understaffed, and the ability of the accused to attend their own judicial proceedings often depends on whether they can pay prison officials to guarantee their own appearance in court.

Public and ruling party officials are rarely prosecuted for abuse of power or other wrongdoing. Chavez himself refused to comply with a 2003 Supreme Court ruling that ordered the return of control of the

Caracas police force by the federal government to the city's mayor, who belonged to the political opposition. Although the government alleges that the police force was repressing progovernment demonstrations, regime opponents say that the decision to take over the metropolitan police is in keeping with other policies pursued by Chavez that undermine the autonomy of the civilian police. In March 2005, the government amended Venezuela's criminal code by broadening laws that punish "disrespect for government authorities," a move human rights groups say could inhibit public criticism and third-party oversight.

The constitution requires equal treatment of citizens under the law. However, in practice these protections vary widely. Political opinion, social origin, and property can and do make a difference, as do the politicization of law enforcement and the administration of justice and the special status enjoyed by Chavez's supporters in the armed forces.

In July 2005, the government announced that it was broadly restructuring Venezuela's law enforcement agencies following a number of scandals, including the murder the previous month of three University of Santa Maria students. The students were shot in apparent retaliation for the death of a Military Intelligence Directorate (DIM) officer a week before, although they were not connected to the military man's death. After they were gunned down for allegedly failing to stop their cars, guns were planted on them to give the impression of an armed confrontation. An autopsy showed that two had been shot multiple times in the head. In response, Chavez ordered the abolition of the DIM and its replacement with a new agency directly under his command. The seven superiors of those who carried out the attempted cover-up of the massacre were fired. The case was still under investigation at the end of 2005.[28] Reorganization plans were also announced for the corrupt Directorate of Intelligence and Prevention Services (DISIP) and the police forces, which have ties to organized crime.

The military high command is loyal to the president rather than to the constitution and the law. Chavez uses Venezuela's armed forces as his own special instrument, positioning numerous active duty and retired military officers at all levels of the country's public administration and involving them in both domestic and international politics.[29] The 1999 constitution assigns the armed forces a significant role in the state, bypassing legislative approval of military promotions and leaving that task solely and directly with the president, thereby placing the armed forces at the service of Chavez and his political program. However, it does not provide for civilian control over the military's budget or procurement practices or for related institutional checks. A coup attempt in 2002—in which Chavez was briefly overthrown and arrested and president of the Venezuelan Federation of Chambers of Commerce installed as interim president for 47 hours before troops loyal to the deposed president rallied—prompted Chavez to sack 60 generals and replace them with unconditional supporters. During the 2004 regional elections, active duty officers openly campaigned in support of Chavez and were appointed on retirement to state and municipal posts. By 2005, nine of the country's state governors were former military men. In addition, the military's role in nontraditional missions, such as social services and public works projects, was linked to their involvement in corruption scandals that remain uninvestigated.[30] A separate system of armed forces courts retains jurisdiction over members of the military accused of rights violations and common crimes, and decisions cannot be appealed in civilian court. The Supreme Court selects candidates for military judgeships from a list provided by the minister of defense. Critics claim this process links them to the views and interests of the military high command and contributes to the impunity of the armed forces, even though the list is published. In August 2005, the National Assembly voted to create a new military reserve force whose command structure is independent of the current armed forces and which will be used to maintain internal order. Critics say they fear even further militarization of Venezuelan politics and the creation of one more instrument of political control by Chavez.[31]

Property rights are increasingly at peril in Venezuela. In 2005, the government imposed tougher terms and tighter restrictions on foreign mining and oil interests and even expropriated business interests and landholdings.[32] Chavez said that eliminating large landholdings—in a country where 60 percent of arable land belongs to 2 percent of its landowners—was part of "21st century socialism." In September, he declared: "Those who don't cooperate with us, we will apply the law and take everything. To those we expropriate land from, maybe I will give them a piece of paper that says, 'in 2030, collect from Chavez.'"[33]

Indigenous communities typically face deforestation and water pollution of their traditional lands. Few of Venezuela's approximately 316,000 indigenous people from 27 ethnic groups hold title to their land; many say that they do not want to, as they reject market concepts of individual property, preferring instead that the government recognize those lands traditionally held by them as native territories. Indigenous communities trying to defend their legal land rights are subject to abuses, including murder, by gold miners and corrupt rural police.

Recommendations

- A legal and administrative framework should be created so that judges and prosecutors have job stability and receive adequate legal training before assuming their posts.
- The amended criminal code that broadens laws that punish "disrespect for government authorities" should be struck down.
- Confiscatory laws concerning property rights should be abolished; existing disputes should be open to independent arbitration by recognized international authorities, if necessary. In addition, the government should recognize lands traditionally inhabited by native peoples as territories belonging to each respective indigenous group.
- The use of active duty and retired military officers in public administration should be significantly curbed.
- The role of the National Assembly in the oversight of the armed forces should be restored and strengthened, and the military should be subject to the scrutiny of an independent inspector general.

ANTICORRUPTION AND TRANSPARENCY – 2.13

The Chavez government came to power after indicting the former governing establishment as corrupt and elitist. Campaigning for the presidency for the first time, Chavez vowed: "I shall fry the heads of corrupt politicians once I get to power."[34] However, Venezuela remains among the most corrupt countries in the world.[35]

The Chavez government has done little to free the state from excessive bureaucratic regulations, registration requirements, and other controls that increase opportunities for corruption. Instead, it has significantly expanded the state's role in the economy in one of the most regulated economies in the world and relies on attacking persons and social sectors it considers corrupt. Good-government laws and regulations are selectively enforced against the opposition. New regulations and controls over the economy have ensured that public officials have retained the ample opportunities for personal enrichment enjoyed under the former regime. For example, Articles 12, 300, and 301 of the 1999 constitution enshrine the concept of public ownership and management of oil and other strategic industries. Following a high-profile confrontation with PDVSA, the state oil company, Chavez replaced its leadership, based on meritocracy, with his own directorate. For these and other reasons, Venezuela was categorized as a "repressed" country in the Heritage Foundation/ *Wall Street Journal* 2005 Index of Economic Freedom, ranking 146th of 155 countries surveyed.[36]

The government's role in the economy has been expanded by the Chavez government's insistence on placing real power in loyal hands— often those of military cronies. State conflict-of-interest regulations have rarely been enforced. Compliance with the April 2003 Law Against Corruption that set out in detail such conflicts and their sanction is conditioned by Chavez's party's control of all national anticorruption offices.

The 2003 anticorruption law established a citizen's right to know and set down the state's obligations to give Venezuelans a rendering of public goods and expenses three times annually, "except for that having to do with security or national defense expressly established by law." The law also requires most public employees to present a sworn declaration of personal assets within 30 days of assuming a post as well as 30 days after leaving it, allows for the extradition of corrupt officials and their prohibition from holding office in the future, and includes a prohibition on officials having secret foreign bank accounts. It is, however, observed largely in the breach.[37]

The Chavez government has taken steps to remove key economic decisions, such as the sale of national debt bonds, from meaningful legislative oversight. Rather than implementing laws and regulations ensuring open bidding, transparency, and effective competition in the award of public contracts, the regime appears to have replaced the old system, in which personal loyalties and opportunities for mutual enrichment took precedence over public interest concerns, with one that is merely a new buddy system—comprising those loyal to the president. Despite the promise contained in the new Law Against Corruption, the government does not publish expenditures in a detailed and timely fashion; in fact, such information is hard to come by.

Chavez's party controls the "citizen power"—or ombudsman—branch of government created by the 1999 constitution to fight corruption, thus making it nearly impossible to challenge the regime's autocratic use of public funds. This branch comprises the offices of the ombudsman (responsible for compelling the government to adhere to the constitution and laws), the comptroller general (who controls the revenues and expenses incurred by the government and serves as the watchdog for the national patrimony), and the public prosecutor (who provides opinions to the courts on the prosecution of criminal cases and brings to the attention of the proper authorities cases of public employee misconduct and violations of the constitutional rights of prisoners or accused persons). Although some independent institutions remain at the state and local levels to carry out investigations and prosecutions of government corruption, they are easily circumscribed by geography and resources. In addition, Venezuela has yet to enact a law protecting government whistleblowers along the lines set down in the Organization of American States' model anticorruption statutes. Venezuela's privately held media do air allegations of official corruption extensively; however, the lack of fair and balanced reporting and the country's pronounced class divisions mean that reporting about corruption is often politics by other means—discrediting one's opponents without having to debate other public policy issues or offering new solutions to vexing problems.

One Canadian writer noted that primaries in 2005 by Chavez's Fifth Republic Movement (MVR) "did more to reveal the manipulative and undemocratic workings of the MVR than to encourage any democratic opening . . . The problem stems from a simple fact . . . the old power structures, culture of clientelism and patronage systems remain."[38]

Recommendations

- The government should take specific steps to free the state from excessive bureaucratic regulations, registration requirements, and other controls that increase opportunities for corruption, which would help ensure respect for private property, reduce the role of the state in profit-making enterprises, and eliminate unnecessary procedures that hinder economic growth.
- The government should take all necessary measures to ensure that conflict-of-interest regulations are fully and fairly enforced,

strengthening the rules governing disclosure of actual, potential, or apparent conflicts and promoting public awareness of conflict-of-interest policy.

- The government should restore meaningful legislative oversight to the process of making key economic decisions.
- To restore credibility to the "citizen power" branch of government created to fight corruption, the heads of the offices of the ombudsman, comptroller general, and the public prosecutor should either be appointed by bipartisan consensus within the National Assembly or, at least in the first two instances, chosen through national elections.
- A law protecting government whistle-blowers should be enacted along the lines set down in the Organization of American States' model anticorruption statutes, in consultation with international whistle-blower protection organizations.

NOTES

1 "Corruption Perceptions Index" (Berlin: Transparency International, 2005). Venezuela was ranked 100 out of 133 countries in 2003.

2 Danna Harman, "Chávez seeks influence with oil diplomacy," *Christian Science Monitor,* 25 August 2005. According to Carlos Granier, an economist at Cedice, a Caracas think tank, cited in the *CSM* article, a Cuban-Venezuelan oil "deal" alone costs Venezuelans an estimated US$ 1.7 billion in opportunity costs in 2005—in dollar terms, the equivalent to all US official aid, including military and non-military, to Latin America.

3 Julian Brookes, "Hugo Chavez and His Bolivarian Revolution," *Mother Jones,* 4 October 2005.

4 "All power to chavismo," *Economist,* 8 December, 2005.

5 Alma Guillermoprieto, "Don't Cry for Me, Venezuela," NYRB 52, No. 15, 6 October 2005; see also, Venezuelan Gen. (ret.) Boris Saavedra, "Civil-Military Relations in Venezuela: Changing Patterns Since 1999" (St. Louis: Midwest Association of Latin American Studies [MALAS], conference paper, November 2005. "When the pro-Chavez vote is presented as a percentage of the whole electorate," Saavedra wrote, "it is reduced to a quite stable but far lower 30.3–33.4 percent . . . in the midst of extremely high abstentionism."

6 Guillermoprieto, "Don't Cry," *NYRB;* A story in the 18 April 2005 edition of VenezuelaAnalysis.com, "Venezuela's Chavez says Blacklist must be 'buried,'" reported that after "the national media had increasingly reported about individuals who were either denied government jobs or fired from their job because their name was on the list of signers in support of the recall referendum," Chavez himself said that the list, compiled by a parliamentary deputy supporter, who admitted that the list had been used to persecute supporters of the opposition, should not be used.

7 Guillermoprieto, "Gambler," *NYRB;* Organización de los Estados Americanos, "Observaciones Preliminares de la OEA sobre las Elecciones Parlamentarias en Venezuela" (press release), 6 December 2005.

8 "Venezuela: Public Opinion and the Future of the Bolivarian Revolution," *StratforWorld Terrorism Report* (Austin, TX), 12 October, 2005.

8 "Venezuela: Court Orders Trial of Civil Society Leaders" (New York: Human Rights Watch [HRW], 8 July 2005); Guillermoprieto, "Gambler," *NYRB;* "A Young Defender of Democracy Faces Chavez's Wrath," *Wall Street Journal (WSJ)*, 10 June 2005.

10 Guillermoprieto, "Don't Cry," *NYRB.*

11 "Controversy in Venezuela over new media law," *Pravda,* 9 December, 2004.

12 "Cases 2005: The Americas – Venezuela" (New York: Committee to Protect Journalists [CPJ], 2005).

13 Richard Gott, in "Hugo Chavez and His Bolivarian Revolution," *Mother Jones,* 8 October 2005.

14 "Report 2005 – Venezuela" (London: Amnesty International [AI], 2005); "Venezuela – Resumen del Pais" (HRW, January 2005); Joseph McSpedon, senior program manager, Freedom House (Washington, D.C.: U.S. Senate, Subcommittee on the Western Hemisphere, testimony, 17 November 2005).

15 "Venezuela – Resumen," (HRW); *Informe OVP, 4to trimestre 2005* (http://www.ovprisiones.org/informe3tr2005/2005-4to.html).

16 "Venezuela: Chavez targets police corruption," *Green Left Weekly* (GLW), 12 July 2005; According to an article, "Venezuelan Government Says 96 Campesinos Were Assassinated 1999 to 2004," in the 11 November, 2005 edition of *Venezuelanalysis.com:* "Venezuela's Attorney General commissioned an investigation into the murders of 138 peasant leaders, following a protest from one of Venezuela's main peasant organizations, the National Agrarian Coordinator Ezequiel Zamora (CANEZ), that the Attorney General has not done enough to prosecute those responsible."

17 "Venezuela" in "Country Fact Sheets," *Human Development Report 2005* (New York: United Nations Development Program [UNDP], 2005).

18 "Trafficking and Sexual Exploitation Between Venezuela and Ecuador," Alexandria, VA: Survivors' Rights International (SRI), 17 July 2003.

19 "Venezuela" in *International Disability Rights Monitor [IDRM] Americas 2004* (Washington, D.C. and Chicago: Center for International Rehabilitation [CIR], August 2004).

20 Juan Forero, "Mormon Church Withdraws Its Missionaries in Venezuela," *New York Times,* 26 October 2005.

21 Meghan Clyne, "Venezuela Outsources Intelligence Activities to Cuba – Caracas Provides Cheap Oil in Exchange for Surveillance of Citizens," *New York Sun,* 26 January, 2005; on Cuban security presence in Venezuela, see also Javier Corrales, "The Logic of Extremism: How Chavez Gains by Giving Cuba So Much," in *Cuba, Venezuela and the Americas: A Changing Landscape, Inter-American Dialogue,* December 2005.

22 "Latest report of ILO Committee on Freedom of Association cites Belarus, China, Colombia, Venezuela, others," International Labour Organization press release (www.ilo.org/public/english/bureau/inf/pr/2003/15.htm), 28 March 2003.

23 "Venezuela's Conscience," *The Washington Post,* 30 October 2005.

[24] "Venezuela: Rights Lawyer Faces Judicial Persecution" (HRW, 5 April 2005).

[25] "The rule of law: Is the independence of the judicial career respected?" (Caracas: Asociacion Civil Sumate, undated), http://infovenezuela.org/cap2_en_2.htm#; *El Nacional*, 3 February 2005, A-5.

[26] Guillermoprieto, "Don't Cry," *NYRB*.

[27] Edgar Lopez, "9 jueces y 10 fiscales concentran los expedients de 400 imputados politicos," *El Nacional*, 7 June 2005.

[28] "Venezuela "Chavez targets police corruption," *GLW*, Intervienen la DIMy el Cicpc por caso de estudiantes, *Radio Nacional de Venezuela*, 1 July 2005. (http://www.rnv.gov.ve/noticias/index.php?act=ST&f=2&t=19521).

[29] As leftwing Chavez biographer Richard Gott stated (*Mother Jones*, 8 October 2005): "The bureaucracy is in the hands of the middle-class opposition, and it's very difficult to get any sort of reform through the existing government machine, so Chavez does rely on the military to get things done, as his own political party"; "Paymaster General; Venezuela's armed forces," *The Economist*, 9 July 2005.

[30] Saavedra, "Civil-Military Relations in Venezuela" (Midwest Association of Latin American Studies/MALAS) op. cit.; *El Nacional*, 9 January 2005.

[31] "Venezuela, politica y diplomacia," *Informe Latinoamericano*, 31 August 2005.

[32] Jose De Cordoba, "Chavez charts a land route," *WSJ*, 18 January 2005; "Venezuela Announces Plan to Seize More Lands," *WSJ/Dow Jones Newswires*, 15 March 2005; "Venezuela Uses Seized Assets as Bargaining Chip," *WSJ*, 16 September 2005; "Apropriacion de haciendas y plantas industrials," *Informe Latinoamericano*, 14 September 2005; "Chavez ofrece compartir tierra ociosa," *Informe Latinoamericano*, 29 September 2005; "Cowing the private sector; Venezuela," *The Economist*, 3 September 2005.

[33] "Venezuela," *Hemisphere Highlights* IV, 10 (Center for Strategic and International Studies); see also, "Chavez has succeeded in redefining the debate in Latin America," *Newsweek International*, 31 October 2005.

[34] David Paulin, "Venezuelan Populist Worries Oil Industry," *International Herald Tribune*, 17 November 1998.

[35] Guillermoprieto, "Don't Cry," *NYRB*; Saavedra, "Civil-Military Relations in Venezuela" (MALAS); "Venezuela: Public Opinion," *Stratfor Daily Briefs*.

[36] According to Luis E. Lander and Margarita López Maya, in "Oil and Venezuela's Failed Coup," *Foreign Policy in Focus*, 26 April, 2002: "The naming of [leftist economist] Gastón Parra as president in February 2002 led to an open confrontation between the government and PDVSA's top management, who alleged that by sidestepping the meritocracy, Chávez was violating the traditional criteria for naming the members of the company's board of directors. This led the PDVSA leadership to call a strike that was backed by the country's key workers' and business federations, and that served as the platform for the attempted coup of April 11"; Guillermoprieto, "Don't Cry," *NYRB*.

[37] Ley Contra la Corrupcion, *Gaceta Oficial* N° 5.637 *Extraordinario*, 7 April 2003.

[38] Jonah Gindin, "Hugo Chavez and the 'New Democracy,'" *Canadian Dimension*, July/August 2005.

VIETNAM

CAPITAL: Hanoi

POPULATION: 83.3 million

GNI PER CAPITA: $480

SCORES	2004	2006
ACCOUNTABILITY AND PUBLIC VOICE:	1.30	1.63
CIVIL LIBERTIES:	2.77	3.00
RULE OF LAW:	2.36	2.75
ANTICORRUPTION AND TRANSPARENCY:	2.45	2.61

(scores are based on a scale of 0 to 7, with 0 representing weakest and 7 representing strongest performance)

Zachary Abuza

INTRODUCTION

Vietnam is a contradictory state. It is a one-party Communist state, an authoritarian regime that uses coercion and threats of violence to maintain its monopoly on power. There are no independent media, and many of the constitutionally enshrined rights, such as assembly and freedom of speech, are superceded by Article 2, which places the Vietnam Communist Party above the law. At the same time, the regime enjoys popular legitimacy as the organization that won Vietnamese independence and allows surprisingly high levels of civil society and religious freedom. Economic reforms have moved Vietnam from a centrally planned economy to one predominantly guided by the market, which has created more political space for entrepreneurs, lawyers, and others involved in the commercial sector. While there have been broad political, economic, and legal reforms, the Vietnam Communist Party remains firmly in power and countenances no opposition. Yet, individuals, especially in commercial life, have considerable freedom.

Vietnam was divided in 1954 following the Geneva Accords that saw the end of the French colonial era. After more than two decades of struggle and fighting against the U.S.-backed Republic of Vietnam regime,

Zachary Abuza is Associate Professor of Political Science and International Relations at Simmons College in Boston. He has written extensively on Vietnamese politics, human rights, and foreign policy, as well as transnational security issues in Southeast Asia.

Vietnam was formally reunified by the Communist-dominated Democratic Republic of Vietnam. The country was renamed the Socialist Republic of Vietnam and immediately began to nationalize the southern economy. Tens of thousands of officers and officials of the RVN regime were sent to reeducation camps, some for up to a decade. The forced collectivization of agriculture in the south, elimination of the south's currency, and inefficiencies of the centrally planned system led to severe economic strains. Shortages and economic dislocations were compounded by Vietnam's occupation of Cambodia from 1979 to 1989.

In 1986, the death of the last of the first generation of leaders allowed for a second generation to assume power. Vietnam embarked on a course of economic reforms known as Doi Moi, or Renovation. While Doi Moi led to macroeconomic stability, more extensive political reforms were halted because of the fall of Communism in Eastern Europe. Vietnamese economic and political reforms stalled in the mid-1990s due to political infighting and ideological debates within the Communist Party but have since regained momentum following the party's ninth congress in 2000 and the election of a new generation of leaders.

ACCOUNTABILITY AND PUBLIC VOICE – 1.63

The Socialist Republic of Vietnam (SRV) is a one-party state in which the Vietnam Communist Party (VCP) maintains a monopoly on power. The VCP does enjoy considerable popular support owing to its role in liberating the country from colonial rule, defeating the United States, and reunifying the country in 1976. While the VCP suffered a severe loss of popular legitimacy in the late 1970s–1980s due to economic mismanagement and political repression, economic reforms begun in 1986 have relegitimized the regime to a considerable degree. The VCP claims to represent the interests of all sectors of Vietnamese society. Its Central Committee—a 150-person body that is the VCP's top decision-making organ—has good provincial representation (over half of its membership) and comprises representatives from other key sectors (central government apparatus, the military, and VCP committees). Yet this is hardly full representation, and the VCP countenances no dissent or opposition to its rule.

The National Assembly (NA) has been transformed from a rubberstamp parliament into a fairly autonomous legislative body. This was due to the paucity of legal codes in the early 1990s. The transition to a more market-oriented economy necessitated the rapid codification of civil and business laws as well as the rewriting of the penal codes. The United States–Vietnam Bilateral trade agreement of 2000 and Hanoi's subsequent steps to meet the requirements for entry into the World Trade Organization have led to even greater codification and legal transparency. To meet this demand, the NA went from meeting for one brief session a year to rubber-stamping party decisions to acting as a more professional lawmaking body. It now meets biannually and maintains a larger permanent staff. The NA is slowly being transformed into a full-time legislature: currently 25 percent of the members of parliament (MPs) work full time. It is unclear whether the NA will accelerate this process in the near future. Beginning in 2005, it gained the right to draft legislation rather than simply amend or tweak laws drafted by the executive branch; before 2005, the executive drafted 97 percent of all legislation while other Communist Party organs drafted the remainder. Increases in the NA's lawmaking capacity are in line with the VCP general secretary's stated goal in 2000 to transform Vietnam into a "law-governed" society.

On the 2005 docket of the NA was a revision of the Law on Lawmaking. The key change to this law is a provision that will allow increased inputs from the citizenry during the lawmaking process. This is expected to come into force in 2006.

Despite these reforms, the NA is not independent from VCP interference. First, no political parties other than the VCP are allowed to run for office. Although independent candidates are allowed, they cannot organize into coherent opposition parties. Moreover, an arm of the Vietnam Fatherland Front is responsible for vetting all candidates. Candidates must pass a political litmus test and can be disqualified for minor reasons. Currently, only 10 percent of the 498 members are independents; the remainder are Communist Party members. Candidates are not allowed to campaign but instead are given a few public but highly regulated forums in which they can propose their platforms. In the last election, in 2002, an average of 2.3 candidates ran per seat. The Vietnam Fatherland Front is in charge of every stage of the NA electoral process.

Authorities have given increased attention to village/commune-level and provincial-level democratization. In November 1993, the NA passed revisions to the Law on Election of Deputies to People's Councils, which called for greater gender and minority representation in addition to increased numbers of candidates per seat and independent candidates. Nonetheless, the Vietnam Fatherland Front, which oversees subnational elections as well, continues to ensure control over the legislatures. In the April 2004 people's council elections, there were irregularities, including early closure of polls.

While considerable improvements have taken place at all levels of legislative capacity in Vietnam, the NA still acts in the interest of the VCP. While it has increased its oversight of personnel and budgets, as well as of certain large scandal-plagued construction/infrastructure projects (see "Anticorruption and Transparency"), it has not passed any legislation that compromises the ruling party's interests. Likewise, the Vietnam People's Army is a key political institution whose interests are never challenged. In sum, there is no viable political opposition.

Constitutionally a system of checks and balances exists, but in reality, the VCP's monopoly on power usually does not allow the system to function. For example, while on a number of occasions government or politburo-selected candidates have not been elected to the NA, and the NA has sacked a handful of cabinet-level officials, such actions are still infrequent. The judges in the Supreme People's Court must be confirmed by the NA, and available evidence suggests that all have been. While party membership is not a prerequisite for entrance into the civil service, it is essential for advancement beyond the middle ranks.

Civil society has gained more space in 2003–2005, and in the urban areas of Ho Chi Minh City and Hanoi, civil society organizations have proliferated. This is particularly true in the commercial sector, where chambers of commerce and other business associations have sprung up. These organizations have the most independence, but legal, health, and environmental organizations have more space and freedom to operate as well. Women's organizations have become involved in anti-trafficking efforts and pushing the government to take a more aggressive stance. Foreign nongovernmental organizations (NGOs) operating in Vietnam suggest that they have more space to operate and implement programs that would have been too politically sensitive a few years ago.[1] The Vietnam Bar Association is often called on to review draft legislation. The U.S. government's Star Project, which was originally established to help educate Vietnamese officials on how to implement the Bilateral Trade Agreement signed in 2000, has now become an organization to help with Vietnam's accession into the World Trade Organization (WTO).

This program has developed such a cadre of expertise that, according to some U.S. government officials, the VCP now comes to it for help in drafting laws in the economic field. The environment is more receptive for these organizations to raise issues and concerns with the NA and the government. Yet, the playing field is still not level, and the government continues to regulate the growth of civil society through a registration process for all organizations and other legal requirements. Donors are not free of state pressure and are circumscribed in their choice of counterparts and fund recipients.

Perhaps the biggest beneficiaries of more relaxed policies are public health NGOs, which have found much greater political space in the wake of the SARS crisis and the outbreaks of avian flu since 2002. The government quickly organized 1,700 health inspectors and has called on local monitoring teams to report on the spread of infections.[2] Nonetheless, foreign scientists and the World Health Organization (WHO) have all expressed concern that Vietnam is still not giving them full access to both the country and samples.[3] The threat of avian flu and the central role that Vietnam is playing as the virus mutates cannot be underestimated. The lack of openness and transparency in Vietnam regarding this issue has global implications.

The media have suffered a number of setbacks since October 2003. This is primarily for two reasons. First, the Tenth Party Congress is expected to be held in the second quarter of 2006. Party congresses are seminal events that happen roughly every five years. Historically, the year preceding a congress is marked by concerted state efforts to clamp down on the media and prevent debate over policies from becoming public. A second and related factor is that the VCP is losing its monopoly over the flow of information as internet access and usage proliferates. Current estimates put the number of internet users at roughly six to seven million out of a total population of 87 million (7 to 8 percent of the population).[4]

While freedom of expression is constitutionally enshrined (Article 69), all media remain owned or controlled by the VCP and the government. No independent media organs have been allowed. The few attempts by dissidents to publish independent journals or newspapers have met with harsh and immediate crackdowns by the state. The government uses nebulous and vague security and espionage laws in most prosecutions against journalists; "dissemination of state secrets" is the most common charge. For example, Nguyen Dan Que, who was arrested in March 2003 for publishing *Tuong Lai (The Future),* was sentenced in March 2004 to 20 years' imprisonment for "abusing democratic rights to jeopardize the interests of the state" and for violating Article 80 of the penal code for "spying."[5]

In December 2003, a former reporter for the communist party's own journal, *Tap Chi Cong San,* was tried on espionage charges for two incidents: first for submitting written testimony on the human rights situation in Vietnam to the U.S. Congress in July 2002, and second for posting an article on the internet in which he criticized the yet unratified border treaty with China.[6] In May 2004, an intermediate court upheld his seven-year sentence.[7] Other current cyber dissidents under detention are private citizens Nguyen Khac Toan and Dr. Pham Hong Son.[8]

The VCP is very concerned about the power of the internet and the ability of dissidents both to post their views and to form relationships with people overseas, especially ethnic Vietnamese. While few have access at home in Vietnam, the country has an estimated 4,000 to 5,000 internet cafés. The ministry of public security employs a large cyberforce to monitor internet traffic and block certain sites.[9] There are only a few internet service providers (ISPs). In July 2004, the ministry of public security issued Directive 71 to combat "bad and poisonous information" that was being circulated online. Under this directive, the onus for monitoring content was shifted to the owners of internet cafes. Both the failure to monitor and control access to websites deemed offensive to the state and the uploading or downloading of materials that threaten the state will result in the forced closure of the internet café. The directive prohibits any use of the internet that would either "infringe on national security" or disseminate undefined "state secrets."[10] According to Amnesty International, "ISPs and individual Internet users are obliged by law to facilitate easy access for security agencies to networks and computers. The Ministry of Culture and Information explicitly encourages individuals and Internet providers to inform on those 'violating rules' on the provision of information."[11] In April 2004, the Ministry of Public Security shut down an unlicensed news website for reprinting a BBC article on ethnic unrest in the Central Highlands. On the other hand, the government also looks to the internet as an instrument of national integration and even reform, with many ministries operating online. The government is making efforts to increase Internet access in rural areas. Thus, control over subversive aspects of the internet is a key concern for the government.

While the government has allowed the press more leeway with regard to reporting on corruption, it still sets limits, especially when the reporting goes against the party's interests. No direct criticism of the VCP or its policies is tolerated. For example, in November 2004, the editor of the online magazine *VnExpress,* Truong Dinh Anh, was fired by the Ministry of Culture and Information not because of any specific articles that he wrote on official corruption, but because he allowed readers to post their comments on a story that the website had posted about the government's purchase of 76 new Mercedeses for the biennial Asia-Europe meeting in Hanoi. More troubling was the case of Nguyen Thi Lan Anh, a reporter for the country's most progressive, and hence highest circulated, newspaper *Tuoi Tre.* Ms. Anh ran a series of stories about the monopolization of a segment of the pharmaceutical industry by a foreign investor that led to the rapid rise of drug prices.[12] She was indicted on January 5, 2005, and remains under house arrest.

The most important setback in media freedom is the new use of libel laws. In 2004, the government issued a new press law that requires journalists to pay monetary damages to individuals or organizations who have been harmed in some way as a result of their reporting, regardless of whether the reporting was accurate or not. It is unclear whether this new libel provision has been used.

In sum, there is no independent media. Although the government does not exercise direct censorship, as all media is government or party owned and all of the editorial boards must report to the party and state, there is tremendous self-censorship. Perhaps the only bright spot is the artistic freedom of painters, musicians, and other artists (less true with novelists and poets). Visual artists have considerable latitude and as a result have reached international renown.

Recommendations
- Article 2 of the constitution must be abolished, thereby ending the VCP's role as a "leading force in society."
- Media liberalization and press and internet freedoms must become a priority for the regime. The first steps would be to end internet censorship, abolish the politically motivated use of libel laws, and stop interfering in the editorial rooms of the media organs. The

government should stop using nebulous espionage and state secrets laws to prosecute political dissidents.

- The government should implement recent legal provisions that allow the citizenry to comment on draft legislation.
- The Vietnam Fatherland Front must stop interfering in national and local elections and disqualifying independent candidates deemed politically suspect by the regime. More independent candidates at the local and national level should be allowed. The NA must continue to professionalize itself and become a full-time legislature. Moreover, the NA should take advantage of new legal provisions that allow it to draft its own legislation.
- The government must allow for the development of autonomous civil society, including permitting civil society to forge partnerships with foreign counterparts.

CIVIL LIBERTIES – 3.00

Beatings, both to coerce statements and as punishments within the penal system, are routine in Vietnam. There are frequent reports that these beatings also include attacks with electric cattle prods. Evidence, however, suggests that torture is much less widespread than in the past. Prison conditions are harsh and remain well below minimum international standards, lacking proper healthcare, caloric/dietary needs, and sanitation. Convicts are forced to perform labor. On the other hand, attacks on critics of the regime are conducted by the state itself, not independent groups or organizations.

The Vietnamese government often employs detention without trial—usually house arrest—under Decree 31/CP of the Communist Party's central committee, as it has found that it attracts less international criticism than a trial. Under 31/CP, individuals can be held up to two years. Decree 89/CP allows the military to detain people without charge in certain situations. This has been used regularly in response to peasant or ethnic minority protests.

Legally speaking, the constitution enshrines full gender equality. The paternalistic nature of Vietnamese culture, however, means that women have considerably less political power and representation than men. While the representation of women in the NA is considerably better than in any other political institution, it is still quite low: 139 of 498, or 28 percent. Three cabinet members are women, but no representatives on the politburo are female. Representation at the provincial level is low. One of the hallmarks of the VCP was to eliminate feudal gender provisions in the law in the 1950s. While sex discrimination is illegal, there has never been a successful legal case to create a precedent or force a change in culture.

Trafficking is a serious problem, in particular the trafficking of "wives" to China, but the trafficking of children and contract laborers is also growing. The penal code explicitly prohibits trafficking in women and children, but the situation has become more critical in recent years. The government appears to be taking this issue more seriously. The U.S. government has sanctioned Vietnam (ranking it in Tier 2) for human trafficking but acknowledged steps it has taken to remedy the situation.[13] In late 2003, the ministry of public safety established an anti-trafficking force, and in July 2004, the government announced a national action plan to combat trafficking for commercial sexual exploitation.[14] At the same time, the Vietnamese government announced a five-year national plan that addressed all aspects of anti-trafficking efforts, including prevention, prosecution, and protection. Since 2003, there have been "142 prosecutions and 110 convictions specifically related to trafficking in women and children."[15] The International Organization for Migration has programs in northern Vietnam, and women's organizations have pushed this agenda.

Vietnam has a considerable degree of freedom of worship for individuals as long as they attend officially recognized churches. There is not, however, freedom of religion. In November 2003, the NA passed an ordinance "Regarding Religious Belief and Religious Organizations" that declares, "The State guarantees freedom of religious belief and of religion for its citizens. Nobody is permitted to violate these freedoms" (Article 1). But the ordinance outlines all the procedures for registration and the legal loopholes that the state has to curtail independent actions by the churches.[16] Six religions are recognized officially; their leadership is appointed by and accountable to the Vietnam Fatherland Front. The government curtails religious freedom at multiple levels, for example by limiting the number of students in seminaries, approving their appointments, vetting them for their political views, and funding the churches. The government is at odds with the Vatican regarding the appointment of bishops, which the VFF considers a sovereign right, although in practice Hanoi has often confirmed the Vatican's choice. There are underground churches—Cao Dai, Catholic, evangelical Christian, and Buddhist—that do not recognize the authority of the VFF. However, the Vietnamese government vigorously persecutes heads of these churches, and several leaders, such as Fr. Thadeus Van Nguyen Ly, Thich Huyen Quang, and Thich Quang Do, remain incarcerated or under house arrest.

Vietnamese leaders have historically perceived clerics (both Buddhist and Catholic) to be antiregime, and the country's history also contains some odd episodes of religion and militancy—especially among the Hoa Hao and Cao Dai sects that raised their own armies. Persecuted religious figures are often very political in their dissent.

Treatment of minorities has improved, as the VCP general secretary, Nong Duc Manh, is not Vietnamese, but ethnic Tay. The greatest civil conflicts continue to be with ethnic (concurrently religious) minorities in the Central Highlands region. Although the mass crackdowns and news blackouts that occurred in 2001–2002 have subsided, the government reacts quickly to public assembly. Summary detention is routine in the Highlands. The government has been most repressive toward ethnic minority Christians in the Central Highlands, where the government has launched an official campaign to eradicate "Dega Protestantism," which it considers to be an unofficial religion. Since 2001, the Central Highlands has seen violent crackdowns on secessionist demonstrations. Though the conflict is not religiously based, the government asserts that separatists often use their religion to "sow divisions among the people" and "undermine state and party unity." In June 2005, police tried to force residents in Gia Lai province to join the official Evangelical Church of Vietnam.[17] In addition, members of the Mennonite community have come under legal attack by security forces since March 2004.[18] At the international level, Hanoi has put intense pressure on the Cambodian regime to return ethnic Montagnards—one of the key ethnic minority groups—who fled Vietnam. The Montagnards have a palpable and not unfounded fear of persecution if they return, and Hanoi has offered them no assurances otherwise.

Vietnam received poor marks from the U.S. Commission on International Religious Freedom, which in their 2004 report designated Vietnam a "Country of Particular Concern."[19] While Vietnam chafed at the report's findings, U.S. diplomats have reported improvements in the religious climate in Vietnam as the government attempts to remove itself from the designation. In 2004–2005 the number of religious figures arrested and/or detained noticeably decreased and the Vietnamese government has also engaged in religious diplomacy, allowing the U.S.-based monk and peace activist Thich Nhat Hahn to visit Vietnam.[20] During the historic 2005 visit to Washington, D.C., by Vietnamese premier Pham Van Khai, the two sides signed the U.S.-Vietnam Agreement on Religious Freedom. The agreement was in response to the Commission on International Religious Freedom's policy recommendation that a monitoring mechanism be established.[21]

Freedom of assembly is enshrined in the constitution, but it is not protected. Although numerous unions (women's, peasants', trade, and so on) exist, they are not independent but are arms of the VFF. Individuals are not compelled to join organizations or parties. This includes the Vietnam Communist Party, which in fact is a very elite organization that comprises less than 2 percent of the overall population. The state does not permit demonstrations and public protests; were demonstrations to break out, the government would use force to disperse the protestors.

Recommendations
- The government must abolish 31/CP, which allows for administrative detention without charges, and 89/CP, which allows the military to detain people without trial.
- The government must do more to combat human trafficking. In particular, it must address the trafficking of women and children into China.
- The government must address root causes of the unrest in the Central Highlands and increase government and legal transparency. Security forces must operate with less impunity.
- The Vietnam Fatherland Front should stop interfering in the day-to-day operations of the various churches.
- The government should allow international monitors to oversee the repatriation of Montagnards from Cambodia.

RULE OF LAW – 2.75

The avowed goal of the country's paramount leader is to transform Vietnam in to a "law-governed society." To that end, legal codification has increased dramatically in recent years, has the technical proficiency of the drafters.

While there have been improvements, the judiciary is still not independent. Judges are appointed by the ministry of justice, in large part for their political loyalty and Communist Party membership. Although the legal training of judges has improved, it is still weak and not a requisite in judicial appointment. There is a serious shortfall in the number of trained legal officials—lawyers, judges, prosecutors, and court officials—and educational standards are inadequate. While judges of the Supreme Judicial Court must be approved by the NA, this has been a pro forma process.

Police often make arrests without court-issued warrants. Once indicted, individuals are presumed guilty under the constitution. The prosecutors are not independent from political interference. Legal proceedings are held swiftly—often trials last little more than a few hours. Most trials are open to the public, with the exception of politically sensitive trials of dissidents or of other national security cases. While defendants are provided legal counsel, the role of the defense lawyer is more or less to plead for a lighter sentence. The 2002 mass trial of Nam Cam, an underworld figure implicated in all sorts of criminal behavior, including drug distribution, prostitution, loan sharking, human trafficking, murder, and corruption of government officials—in which 163 defendants were tried in conjunction with Nam Cam's operations, including many government officials and two VCP Central Committee members—was thought to be a watershed in that the defense lawyers were allowed to call and cross-examine witnesses. Yet, those innovations have not been institutionalized. For example, in early July 2004, Vietnam brought two dissidents—Tran Khue, a retired academic, and Pham Que Duong, a 73-year-old military historian—to trial. The trials were swift, and the defendants had no ability to challenge the prosecution or call witnesses. According to July 2003 amendments to the legal code, defendants are entitled access to their lawyers from the time of their arrest, but this right is often ignored. The 2003 amendments also outline the investigative period that prosecutors have: three months for less serious offenses—usually for crimes with sentences under three years—up to 16 months for exceptionally serious offenses (including those that would result in sentences from 15 years to life as well as the death penalty). During the investigative period, defendants are almost always incarcerated, though this is credited to their sentence as time served.

There is a growing awareness and more frequent reporting in the state-controlled media that many court rulings were wrong and that innocent people have been incarcerated. Nonetheless, no formal process exists for those wronged to seek redress and compensation; ad hoc processes prevail. In a few instances, higher courts have questioned the rulings of the lower courts. In a recent case, the Supreme People's Court unexpectedly reduced the original 13-year sentence given to political dissident Pham Hong Son, who was convicted on espionage charges, to five years.[22] The court found that Pham's crime "was not as serious as found by the intermediate court."[23] This was the first time the Supreme People's Court made such a ruling. In general, as Vietnam is a one-party state, the courts do not rule against the VCP's interests, which sometimes—though not consistently—include anticorruption trials of party members.

Article 2 of the constitution places the VCP—and hence many of its members—above the law. However, this preferred status is slowly being eroded as more and more VCP members, including senior officers, are being prosecuted for corruption. Party position is no longer a protection, thus indicating a growing, though incomplete, acceptance of equality under the law. More important was a linguistic change in the constitution that identified the VCP as the *leading* political authority rather than the sole authority. While this does not portend a multiparty system, it does recognize the growing role of political independents and nonparty members in policy making.

In 2005, the NA debated the highly contentious issue of compensation for victims who are unjustly accused by state authorities. While citizens have the right to petition the government regarding socioeconomic issues, abuses of power, and the ill effects of laws and decrees, whistle-blowers have no protection. To that end, in 2005 the NA also debated a provision that would codify procedures, rights, and protections regarding the settlement of citizens' complaints and petitions; although it has not become law, support for this bill is gaining in the NA.

Corruption within the judiciary is a growing concern. During the course of investigations in the Nam Cam case, the former vice director of the People's Supreme Procuracy, Pham Si Chien, was arrested.[24] Chien, who had received bribes from Nam Cam, influenced investigations and trials into the underworld leader's empire.

According to the constitution, the Vietnam People's Army (VPA) is bound not just to defend the Vietnamese nation but to protect the Vietnamese Communist Party. Thus, regime survival is equated with national security. The VPA is used to put down peasant and ethnic unrest in the Central Highlands. The police are within the ministry of public security and are routinely used to crush dissent and maintain the regime's monopoly on power. The security forces show little to no respect for human rights. While there is no evidence of police or security force personnel being disciplined or held accountable for abuses of power, many have been dismissed, punished, and tried for corruption.

The issue of private property is complicated. Technically, the state owns all property. In reality, peasants hold long-term titles to their land; what were originally 15-year contracts have been extended to 30 years. This land can be passed between generations. In urban areas, individuals can hold long-term titles to their land, shops, or apartments. The state (at the central and provincial level) does appropriate land, for the most part for national development projects, but some compensation is usually paid.

Very contentious issues persist regarding property rights. First, while the media often depict the unrest in the Central Highlands as a purely ethnic or religious rights issue, it began over land disputes. Beginning in the late 1990s, the Vietnamese government offered titles to land in the minority-dominated regions to ethnic Kinh Vietnamese from the overpopulated delta regions. The provision of titled land and the establishment of coffee plantations precluded the Montagnards from engaging in their traditional *swidden* (slash and burn) agriculture. When they began to protest the titling of land, the demonstrations quickly grew to include ethnic grievances, tinged with charges of religious persecution. When Vietnamese security forces cracked down in early 2000, several hundred Montagnards fled into Cambodia, where they sought sanctuary. Second, at the village level, collective land is often appropriated by corrupt party officials or "auctioned" off to family or friends in return for kickbacks. As a result, peasants lose their social safety net, while funds that should be put in the village coffers are embezzled or misdirected. This is the single greatest cause of rural unrest.

Recommendations

- The government should maintain its commitment to transforming Vietnam into a "law-governed society" in which all citizens, regardless of race, gender, or political affiliation, are treated equally under the law. To that end, the government must make meaningful investments in human resource development in its judicial system, including the training of prosecutors, law clerks, and judges, and apply a legal qualifications litmus test to judges rather than a political litmus test.
- The NA should increase its oversight of the judicial sector, especially with regard to judicial corruption, through hearings, investigations, and prosecutions.
- The government must address political elites' abuse of power at the local level, in particular land grabs and appropriation of collective goods.
- The government should establish procedures for people unfairly or wrongly charged in legal proceedings to seek redress and compensation.

ANTICORRUPTION AND TRANSPARENCY – 2.61

The independent watchdog Transparency International (TI) consistently rates Vietnam as very corrupt by both global and regional standards.[25] In 2005, TI ranked Vietnam as the 16th most corrupt country in the Asia Pacific (out of 24) and as the 107th out of 159 worldwide. Since the late 1990s, the Vietnamese leadership has identified corruption as the single most important challenge to its legitimacy and continued rule. Anticorruption campaigns have been continual within the party's ranks, but they have been fairly ineffective and led to few prosecutions. Simply put, the VCP is unable to police itself, and without an independent media corruption will continue to dog the regime.

Nevertheless, following the trial of Nam Cam in 2002, the leadership has been able to gain traction in its anticorruption efforts. According to one press account, in October 2005, "One minister, five deputy ministers, 14 provincial chairpersons and deputy chairpersons and hundreds of ministerial department heads and company directors face[d] criminal proceedings."[26]

Beginning in 2004, Vietnam uncovered major corruption cases in four critical sectors of the economy: oil and gas, fisheries, aviation, and trade and industry. In early 2005, La Thi Kim Oanh, the former director of a state company under the ministry of agriculture and rural development, was convicted of embezzling $4.6 million and causing losses of $2.2 million.[27] She received the death penalty for her crime.[28] As a result of the scandal, Le Huy Ngoc, minister of agriculture and rural development, was forced to resign after being reprimanded by the prime minister; two of his deputies, Nguyen Thien Luan and Le Quang Ha, were arrested and sentenced to three years in prison for their involvement in the scandal. Two senior officials from the ministry of trade, Mai Van Dau (the deputy minister) and Le Van Thang, were arrested for participation in an export quota allocation scandal in the textile industry. At least two senior members of the state-owned oil firm, PetroVietnam, were arrested in 2005 on charges of corruption that cost the state millions of dollars.[29]

Vietnamese officials have used a number of tools in their counter-corruption efforts. Vietnamese law provides for two main measures for dealing with corruption: criminal punishments, including life imprisonment and the death penalty, and administrative sanctions. The government has given the media more freedom in covering corruption cases as well. In two major trials, Nam Cam (2002–2003) and La Thi Kim Oanh (2003–2004), portions of the trial were broadcast live on national television.[30]

In charge of government corruption cases is the state inspectorate agency (SIA). While the SIA has had some successes, it is under pressure to improve its operations and performance. It is currently reviewing a number of new policies, most important among them a civilian whistle-blower statute that would provide legal protections.[31] The SIA is also considering financial rewards for whistle-blowers.

Other proposals include increasing the responsibilities of state managers, especially at key state enterprises; clearly defining prohibited activities for public employees; requiring full economic disclosure for public officials; raising the transparency and democracy of state agencies; and improving coordination among state agencies responsible for anti-corruption investigations and prosecutions. None of these proposals has been enacted into anticorruption legislation.

The NA has taken a much more proactive role in anticorruption measures. During the sixth session of the eleventh NA, October to December 2004, deputies passed the Inspection Law to give investigators additional tools. During that same session, the deputies proposed establishing an independent anticorruption committee.[32] The former prime minister, Vo Van Kiet, has publicly endorsed this commission and called for full independence from party and state interference. The NA gave priority to the issue of corruption in 2005. In particular it investigated allegations of mismanagement and embezzlement in the construction of the controversial Dung Quat oil refinery in central Vietnam as well as a highly controversial and much maligned development project for the mountainous hinterland, Program 135.

The NA has gained greater oversight of the national budget; in mid-2005 discussions took place both within the assembly itself as well as in the VCP about investing it with a limited line-item veto power. The NA continues to be the most transparent political institution in the country and allows the television to air its sessions. The Office of the NA has posted several of its draft bills on the internet for public comment. The assembly has enhanced its oversight capability, investigated government officials for corruption, and sacked cabinet members for corruption and poor performance. Significantly, the government relocated the General Auditor's Office out of the executive branch and placed it in the NA.

Nevertheless, the Vietnamese political and economic system encourages corruption. First, the media are by no means independent and play no watchdog role. Second, although economic reforms have been considerable, the economy is still not governed by the market, and key sectors are highly regulated by the state and/or controlled by state-owned enterprises. While the private sector is now constitutionally recognized and entrepreneurs have legal protections, private businesses still do not compete on a level playing field and have less access than state-owned enterprises to capital, inputs, licenses, and foreign direct investment. Moreover they face limits on the hiring and firing of employees. State-owned enterprises are given almost all government contracts. Third, while the government briefly tried to impose financial disclosure procedures on its public officials starting in 1999, these quickly fell by the wayside. It was only in 2005 that discussions about reinstating these procedures were again raised. Conflicts of interest are not challenged openly. Fourth, whistle-blowers still do not have adequate incentives and protections. Fifth, corruption is highly embedded in all sectors of society. At this point gift-giving has become culturally pervasive. Sixth, there is little governmental transparency. Although budgets and other decisions are becoming more transparent as the NA gains additional oversight powers, there is a long way to go. Many budgets, policies, and issues are still categorized as "state secrets," and hence any investigation into them is a punishable offense.

There has been far less transparency in the economic sector, especially regarding open bidding and effective competition in the awarding of government contracts. Vietnam is consistently ranked by businessmen as one of the most corrupt places to do business in Southeast Asia, and kickbacks and closed tenders are commonplace. Anecdotal evidence suggests that the distribution of foreign development assistance has become more fair, transparent, and accountable. Foreign donors have greater ability to conduct audits and ensure proper end-use. However, corruption in education, in particular entry into tertiary level schools—available to less than 3 percent of the population—remains a systemic problem.

Recommendations
- The government must support the establishment of independent forces to monitor official corruption, including an independent anticorruption commission, a free press, and a stronger state inspectorate agency.
- The government must pass legislation to protect and reward whistle-blowers.
- The government must continue its efforts to privatize the state-owned sector and dismantle the overly regulated sectors of the economy that give rise to rent-seeking and corruption.
- The NA must have greater oversight over state budgets and have investigative powers into alleged misuse of public funds.

NOTES

1 Personal communications, 17 November 2005.

2 "Flu on the Wing," *The Guardian,* 15 October 2005, http://www.guardian.co.uk/bird flu/story/0,14207,1591358,00.html; Nguyen Nhat Lam, "Vietnam Suspects Two New Bird Flu Deaths," Reuters, 29 October 2005, http://www.alertnet.org/thenews/newsdesk/HAN134248.htm; "Bird Flu in Vietnam Resisting Tamiflu," Canadian Broadcasting Corporation, 30 September 2005, http://www.cbc.ca/story/science/national/2005/09/30/tamiflu20050930.html.

3 "Flu on the Wing," *The Guardian,* 15 October 2005.

4 "Socialist Republic of Viet Nam, Appeal for Cyber dissident - Nguyen Khac Toan" (London: Amnesty International [AI], 1 June 2005), http://web.amnesty.org/library/Index/ENGASA410202005?open&of=ENG-VNM.

5 "Vietnam - 2004 Annual Report" (Paris: Reporters Without Borders [RSF], 3 May 2004), http://www.rsf.org/print.php3?id_article=10227.

6 "Vietnam: Protest Trial of Dissident Charges Include Testimony to U.S. Congress" (AI, Press release No. 293, 2 January 2004), http://web.amnesty.org/library/index/ENGASA410012004; "Socialist Republic of Viet Nam, Appeal for Cyber dissident - Nguyen Vu Binh," AI, 6 January 2005), http://web.amnesty.org/library/Index/ENGASA410192005?open&of=ENG-VNM.

7 "Attacks on the Press 2004: Documented Cases from Asia for 2004" (New York: Committee to Protect Journalists [CPJ, 2005, http://www.cpj.org/attacks04/asia04/viet.html.

8 "...Cyber dissident - Nguyen Khac Toan" (AI, 1 June 2005); "Socialist Republic of Viet Nam, Appeal for Cyber dissident – Dr. Pham Hong Son" (AI, 1 June 2005), http://web.amnesty.org/library/Index/ENGASA410182005?open&of=ENG-VNM.

9 Minky Worden, "Testimony on the Human Rights Situation in Vietnam before the House Committee on International Relations" (New York: Human Rights Watch [HRW], 20 June 2005), http://hrw.org/english/docs/2005/06/21/vietna11177.htm.

10 "Attacks on the Press 2004" (CPJ).

11 ". . . Cyber dissident - Nguyen Vu Binh" (AI, 1 June 2005).

12 "Vietnam: Reporter Who Investigated Drug Company Is Indicted" (CPJ, 18 January 2005), http://www.cpj.org/news/2005/Vietnam18jan05na.html.

13 "Vietnam (Tier 2)," in *Trafficking in Persons Report* (Washington, D.C.: U.S. Department of State, June 2005) http://gvnet.com/humantrafficking/Vietnam-2.htm.

14 Previous to this National Action Plan, the issue of trafficking in women and children was a component of the 2004–2010 National Plan of Action on Protection for Children in Special Circumstances and also part of the 2000–2005 National Anti-Criminal Plan of Action.

15 "Vietnam (Tier 2)" (U.S. Department of State, June 2005).

16 "Ordinance of the Standing Committee of the National Assembly . . . Regarding Religious Belief and Religious Organizations" (HRW, unofficial translation, 2004), http://hrw.org/english/docs/2004/10/21/vietna9551.htm.

17 Minky Worden, "Testimony . . . " (HRW, 20 June 2005).

18 "Vietnam: Attack on Mennonites Highlights Religious Persecution" (HRW, 22 October 2004), http://hrw.org/english/docs/2004/10/22/vietna9552.htm.

19 "Annual Report" (Washington, D.C.: U.S. Commission on International Religious Freedom [USCIRF], May 2004), http://www.uscirf.org/countries/publications/current report/2004annualRpt.pdf.

20 Personal conversation with a congressional staffer, 21 October 2005.

21 AFP, "US-Vietnam Pact on Religious Freedom Questioned," 6 May 2005.

22 "Indictment" [unofficial translation] (Hanoi: Supreme People's Procuracy, No: 06/KSTD-AN, 10 April 2003), http://hrw.org/advocacy/internet/dissidents/phs-english.pdf.

23 "Internet Dissidents, Vietnam. Pham Hong Son" (HRW), http://hrw.org/advocacy/internet/dissidents/6.htm.

24 "Corruption in High Positions," Vietnamnet Bridge, 6 October 2005, http://english.vietnamnet.vn/spf/2005/06/449993/.

25 "Asia and the Pacific Regional Highlights Corruption Perceptions Index (CPI) 2005" (Berlin: Transparency International, 26 October 2005), http://www.transparency.org/cpi/2005/dnld/cpi2005.highlights_asia_pacific.pdf.

26 "Corruption in High Positions," Vietnamnet Bridge, 6 October 2005.

27 "Corruption trial involving two former deputy ministers opens in Vietnam," Agence France-Presse, 17 November 2003.

28 "Accustom to Corruption," *Vietnam Investment Review* (VIR), 31 October 2005, http://www.vir.com.vn/Client/VIR/index.asp?url=search.asp&key=corruption.

29 Ibid.

30 "Former Vietnam Ministers on Trial," BBC World Service, 17 November 2003, http://news.bbc.co.uk/1/hi/world/asia-pacific/3276697.stm.

31 "Accustom to Corruption," VIR, 31 October 2005.

32 Vu Long, "NA Turns Attention to Anti-Corruption," VIR, 31 October 2005, http://www.vir.com.vn/Client/VIR/index.asp?url=content.asp&doc=8607.

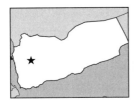

YEMEN

CAPITAL: Sanaa

POPULATION: 20.7 million

GNI PER CAPITA: $520

SCORES	2004	2006
ACCOUNTABILITY AND PUBLIC VOICE:	3.23	2.64
CIVIL LIBERTIES:	3.61	3.35
RULE OF LAW:	3.45	2.88
ANTICORRUPTION AND TRANSPARENCY:	1.85	1.93

(scores are based on a scale of 0 to 7, with 0 representing weakest and 7 representing strongest performance)

Brian Katulis with David Emery

INTRODUCTION

In the two years from the end of 2003 until the end of 2005, Yemen's overall performance on democratic governance weakened, with little progress to report on strengthening the rule of law, fighting corruption, and increasing transparency. Yemen's government severely restricted press freedom; security forces intimidated, beat, and arrested dozens of journalists who had expressed criticism of the government. The government also used a restrictive press law to jail journalists and close newspapers that had criticized the government. The government crackdown on press freedom during this two-year period represented one of the most tangible signs of a lack of progress toward democratic governance in Yemen.

Some of the government actions to limit press freedom were related to crackdowns following unrest in the country and a rebellion led by a cleric and former member of parliament. In June 2004, clashes broke out between government forces and supporters of Hussein Badreddin al-Hawthi, a prominent cleric in Yemen's Zaidi community in the northern region of Saada. Al-Hawthi, who formed an opposition group called Believing Youth, had become strongly critical of the Yemeni government's relationship with the United States, accusing the government of taking actions to please the United States at the expense of the Yemeni people.

Brian Katulis is Director of Democracy and Public Diplomacy on the National Security Team at the Center for American Progress. **David Emery** is an analyst at Freedom House.

Hundreds of people were reportedly killed in the clashes in Saada, prompting several human rights organizations to call for inquiries into reports of extrajudicial killings, mass arrests, and incommunicado detentions by government forces. Al-Hawthi was killed in September 2004, but the clashes between his supporters and government forces continued through 2005. President Ali Abdullah Saleh accused several opposition political parties of supporting al-Hawthi's insurgency. In addition to clashes in Saada, Yemen continued to face challenges in maintaining law and order from groups with links to international terrorist organizations.

Serious economic problems, including widespread poverty, continue to plague Yemen. More than 40 percent of Yemenis live below the poverty line, and economic growth has been weak. In March 2005, Yemen experienced two days of demonstrations over the introduction of a sales tax. In July, dozens of Yemenis were killed in riots when the price of fuel increased by nearly 150 percent after fuel subsidies were lifted as part of an International Monetary Fund reform program.

Despite the economic stagnation and worrying signs of backsliding on political reform, the Yemeni government continued to take steps to present the image of moving forward on democratic reform, participating in numerous international conferences on democratic development and hosting an intergovernmental regional conference on democracy, human rights, and the role of the International Criminal Court in January 2004.

ACCOUNTABILITY AND PUBLIC VOICE – 2.64

Yemen is a republic headed by a popularly elected president, with a bicameral parliament composed of a 301-seat popularly elected house of representatives and a 111-member Shura council. The house of representatives has legislative authority, and the Shura council serves in an advisory capacity. Members of the consultative Shura council are currently appointed by the president, but in September 2005, the government proposed that half of its members, along with governors and district directors, be democratically elected in the future.[1] Thus far, the legislative framework has not been amended to reflect this proposal.

On the surface, Yemen appears to have a relatively open democratic system. Regular elections have been a key feature of Yemen's political landscape since 1990. With 22 political parties, Yemenis seemingly are free to support a range of political positions. Yet in reality, Yemen's politics are monopolized by the ruling party, the General People's Congress (GPC). In 2003, the GPC increased the number of parliament seats it holds from 145 to 238.[2] In 1999, President Saleh was elected to a five-year term in the country's first nationwide direct presidential election, winning 96.3 percent of the vote. Saleh's only opponent came from within his ruling GPC party, and his term in office was extended from five to seven years in a 2001 referendum.[3]

Yemen's April 2003 parliamentary election, its third in the last decade, took place despite concerns that popular unrest resulting from the war in Iraq might lead to a postponement. International election observers noted that Yemen had made substantial improvements in electoral management and administration. On the surface, the elections were competitive, with the opposition Islah party taking seats in constituencies that were former strongholds of the ruling party. However, there were numerous problems with the election. Voter registration involved widespread fraud, and underage voting posed a ubiquitous problem.[4]

During the campaign, the election administration placed limits on the issues candidates could raise and the presentations they could make in televised campaign statements. A single member of the Supreme Commission for Elections and Referendum (SCER) was the final decision maker on what candidates could and could not say during televised appearances, with no opportunity for appeal.[5]

International and domestic election monitors and Yemeni unions noted that the ruling GPC party used state resources to influence the outcome of the vote. For example, the Ministry of Education allowed the use of schools for campaign activities.[6] In certain parts of the country, government officials threatened teachers with transfer or the loss of their jobs if they did not help the GPC in its campaign.[7] In addition, international election monitors noted that elements of the ruling GPC employed "heavy-handed and coercive measures" on Election Day.[8] Although provision exists in the law for public financing for campaigns, parties are also permitted to raise unregulated funds from private donors, a system that numerous analysts believe favors the ruling party. In addition, the GPC reportedly manipulates votes by arranging for military troops to vote in particular constituencies, even if they are not residents there.

Article 62 of the constitution and Sections 24 and 53 of the Election Law require that the populations of all constituencies be equal in size, with a variation of not more than plus or minus 5 percent.[9] Nevertheless, as drawn, the boundaries of electoral constituencies do define populations of unequal size. In addition, according to independent domestic election monitors, the judiciary did not thoroughly and carefully review election disputes; it responded to 56 separate complaints in the postelection period, taking only three days to issue its ruling, which prompted complaints that the merits of different election disputes were not carefully considered.[10] Yemen held local government elections in 2001. Although local council members are popularly elected, the 2000 Law on Local Authority allows for the appointment of the chairpersons of local councils by the president. In practice, the chairpersons hold the preponderance of power in the local councils, and the Local Authority Law does not grant substantial decision-making authority to the council members.[11]

In the 1990s, Yemen embarked on a comprehensive campaign to enhance women's political participation by placing a strong emphasis on registering women to vote. The number of women registered increased nearly seven-fold, from half a million in the 1993 parliamentary elections to over three million in the 2003 parliamentary elections.[12] However, women are vastly underrepresented in most senior leadership positions in government offices. Yemen's government has attempted to increase women's participation in government by instituting a quota system in government ministries, but women's rights activists in Yemen note that these officials are often marginalized because of societal biases against women in the workplace.

The underrepresentation of women is starkest in Yemen's elected offices. Despite the best efforts of women's rights groups to increase the number of women in parliament, only one woman won a seat in the 2003 parliamentary elections, out of a total of 301 seats.[13] The opposition Islah party did not run a single female candidate in the last parliamentary elections, and the ruling GPC party had only 10 female candidates. Out of a total of 1,400 candidates in the election, only 11 were female.[14] At the local government level, women won only 35 seats out of 6,676 in the 2001 elections.[15] There are no female judges serving in the northern part of the country.[16]

Except for certain positions in Yemen's Foreign Ministry, no merit-based competitive selection process exists for civil service positions. Minister of Civil Service and Procurement Khalid Al-Sufi decided in September 2003 to suspend all employment procedures because of corruption and bribes taken by people in charge of the hiring process. In September 2005, with financial backing from the World Bank, the government launched a new identification system in civil service that would eliminate approximately 60,000 ghost employees [people on payroll who do not perform any job] and help in the anticorruption efforts.[17]

The constitution provides guarantees to protect the rights of an independent civic sector, and for the most part the government allows civic organizations to conduct their work freely. Overall, donors to civic organizations and public policy institutes are free of pressures from the state. However, the government and parliament do not have well-developed procedures for the regular, organized, and meaningful involvement of outside groups in the formulation of laws and policy.

Security forces and other government bodies reportedly continue to threaten and harass journalists. In addition, because of the relative weakness of the state in certain regions of the country, Yemen's government offers journalists few protections from powerful tribal forces.

Article 103 of the Press and Publications Law outlaws "direct personal criticism of the head of state" and publication of material that "might spread a spirit of dissent and division among the people" or "leads to the spread of ideas contrary to the principles of the Yemeni Revolution, prejudicial to national unity or distorting the image of the Yemeni, Arab, or Islamic heritage." Critics maintain that these vague provisions, combined with the lack of a strong judiciary, create an environment in which the government can use the threat of legal sanction against journalists who are critical of government policies. A new draft media law that would abolish jail terms for journalists who criticize the president is currently under parliamentary debate; however, critics point out that separate provisions in the law could severely restrict journalists in other ways and could be used to silence opposition to the ruling party prior to the upcoming presidential election.[18]

The print media do not seem to have a strong impact across much of Yemeni society, which has an illiteracy rate estimated at 51 percent of the adult population.[19] The state maintains a monopoly over the media that matter most—television and radio.

In the two years from 2003 to 2005, Yemeni journalists faced numerous incidents involving violence, death threats, arbitrary arrest, and convictions under weak laws governing the freedom of the press. Despite a call by President Saleh in June 2004 to put an end to imprisonment penalties for press offenses, government authorities used the Press and Publications Law numerous times. These incidents point to a widespread government crackdown on criticism and dissent in this two-year period, in which prominent editors and journalists of opposition and independent newspapers have been threatened, attacked, and jailed. Yemen saw a new incident reflecting a deteriorating press freedom environment nearly every month during the period.

In February 2004, unknown gunmen entered the house of Sadeq Nasher, editor of the *Al-Khaleej* newspaper, and issued a death threat prompted by Nasher's investigations into the December 2002 assassination of political opposition leader Jarallah Omar. In February, Saleh ordered the release of Najeeb Yabli, who had been detained for writing an article in the *Al-Ayyam* daily newspaper critical of Saleh's policies. In March 2004, a Yemeni court ordered the release of journalist Saeed Thabet, who had been detained for publishing "false information" on an assassination attempt against the president's son, Colonel Ahmad Ali Abdullah Saleh. Thabet was later fined and banned from working as a journalist for six months by the western court of Sana'a. In April 2004, Ahmed Al-Hubaishy, editor of the newspaper *May 22,* a weekly that has been critical of Islamic militants, was beaten by unknown assailants.

In September 2004, Abdel Karim al-Khaiwani, editor of the prominent opposition weekly *Al-Shoura,* was convicted of incitement, insulting the president, publishing false news, and encouraging divisions within society because of a series of opinion pieces criticizing the government's actions in Saada during the clashes with Al-Hawthi's followers.[20] Hundreds were killed in the three-month uprising, which was centered in the northern mountains along Yemen's border with Saudi Arabia. Al-Khaiwani was sentenced to one year in prison, and the government suspended *Al-Shoura*'s publication for six months. The government also took steps to withdraw the license of the *Al-Hurriya* newspaper. The information ministry closed a new weekly, *Al-Neda,* for violating Article 37 of the Press and Publications Law, which requires a new newspaper or magazine to publish within six months of registration; *Al-Neda* had missed this deadline by two days.

In December 2004, five journalists received suspended prison sentences for various offenses, including publishing articles that criticized the Saudi royal family and articles that detailed corruption among Yemeni political leaders.

In the spring of 2005, several journalists in Taiz and Al-Dal'e governorates were beaten while working. The Yemeni Journalists Syndicate (YJS) denounced alleged police attacks against Mohammad Abdu Sufian, editor of the *Taiz* newspaper, Mohammad Mohsen al-Hadad, general manager of Taiz Radio and Television Bureau, and Abu Bakr Al-Arabi, general manager of Taiz Media Center.[21] In addition, YJS claimed that Mohammed Saif al-Qarari of *al-Thawrah Daily* and Abdulqader Abdullah Sa'ad of *al-Wahdah Weekly* newspapers were beaten and their cameras broken by the governor's bodyguards

In August, Jamal Amer, editor of *Al-Wasat* newspaper, was abducted and beaten by armed men who said they were acting on behalf of military officers. Government security forces ransacked the office of Associated Press journalist Ahmed Alhaj, taking files and a computer. In October, Yemeni police beat a television crew from the Arab satellite channel Al-Arabiya who were covering a strike by textile workers in Sanaa. *Al-Thawra,* the government-run daily newspaper, ran several editorials in 2005 accusing reporters critical of the government of being foreign intelligence agents.

When considered collectively, these incidents demonstrate a serious lack of commitment on the part of Yemen's government to respecting the freedom of the press, at times in failing to act to protect journalists and other times in actively harassing press activities and agents. In addition, they also point to serious structural weaknesses in Yemen's legal and governance system—the checks and balances that would offset the executive branch's lack of commitment to press freedom are not in place, leading to the jailing, beating, and threatening of dozens of journalists for expressing criticisms and dissenting views.

Recommendations

- The government should follow through on its proposal to make half of the Shura seats, as well as governor and district director posts, elected rather than appointed positions.
- The Yemeni government should amend the Law for Press and Publications to clarify or delete the numerous vaguely worded provisions on outlawed publications in Articles 137 to 153. The current draft law being debated by parliament should be amended

and clarified to ensure the press freedom and greater public debate so essential in a democratic system.

- The government should abolish the Ministry of Information and set about developing procedures and regulations to enable the establishment of private and independent broadcast media outlets in order to reduce the state's monopoly on radio and television.
- The government should redraw the electoral constituencies in accordance with the principles set by the Constitution and Election Law, providing for equal and balanced representation.
- The government should establish special mechanisms to expedite the dispute resolution and appeals process at all stages of the election cycle, either by further developing the capacity of the SCER to rule or by setting up special and independent electoral courts to arbitrate disputes in a timely, thorough, and cost-effective manner.

CIVIL LIBERTIES – 3.35

Yemen's constitution offers protections against arbitrary arrest and detention without trial, but it is ambiguous regarding the prohibition of cruel and unusual punishment. Yemen's government has stepped up efforts to reduce the incidence of torture, but violations continue, in part due to a lack of adequate training and awareness among law enforcement officials. At the same time, the government has at times seen fit to look the other way or even perpetrate such violations, all the more so during recent crackdowns related to the al-Hawthi rebellion and the antiterrorist campaign.

In March 2004, journalist Muhammed Al-Qiri was beaten after being taken into the custody of security forces for photographing arrests made by members of Political Security Unit. During his later interrogation his head was reportedly slammed into a metal bar. There has been no report of an investigation into the incident. In June 2004, certain individuals reported being tortured in pretrial detention, one of them alleging the administration of electric shocks during the interrogation.[22]

Prosecution of state officers accused of torturing and abusing prisoners is uneven. All public employees are immune from prosecution for crimes allegedly committed while on duty. The attorney general must provide special permission to prosecutors to investigate allegations against members of the security forces, and the head of the appeals court must lift the immunity before the accused is tried.

By law, detainees must be arraigned within 24 hours of arrest or be released. However, arbitrary detention does occur, sometimes because law enforcement officials lack proper training and at other times because political will is absent at the most senior levels of government.

The global war on terrorism has created pressures on Yemen to exploit all means available to counteract the threat posed by suspected terrorists. After the attacks on the United States on September 11, 2001, and amid evidence of significant al-Qaeda links in the country, Yemen's internal security forces conducted a series of mass arrests, incommunicado detentions, and deportations of foreigners, using methods that sometimes violated international human rights conventions and basic rule-of-law standards.

The constitution provides for freedom of assembly, but the government has taken steps to limit this freedom in practice. The 2003 Law of Demonstrations and Strikes limits peaceful demonstrations by requiring groups to obtain advance permission from the Ministry of Interior. In March 2004, thousands demonstrated in major cities across Yemen to protest Israel's extrajudicial killing of Hamas leader Sheikh Ahmad Yassin. However, in September 2004, the government prevented a demonstration planned by opposition parties in Sana'a against government actions in quelling the Saada rebellion. In October 2004, government security forces arrested members of the opposition Liberation Party for conducting a public demonstration.

By law, women are afforded protections against discrimination and provided with guarantees of equality under the Sharia (Islamic law). In practice, however, women continue to face pervasive discrimination in several aspects of life. For example, the Labor Law of 1995 provides safeguards against discrimination against women in the workplace, but in practice discrimination is common and women remain vastly underrepresented in the workforce. Women constitute only 22 percent of the workforce, and their participation in government jobs is much lower. Yemen's Education Act ensures equality of access to education, but Yemen has one of the largest gaps in the world between boys' and girls' primary school net attendance rates, at 67.8 percent for boys and 40.7 percent for girls.[23] The law provides for protection of women against violence, but in practice such provisions are rarely enforced. The penal code allows for leniency for persons guilty of violent assault or killing of women for alleged immodest behavior or "crimes of honor."[24]

Women who seek to go abroad must obtain permission from their husbands or fathers to receive a passport and travel. Women—unlike men—do not have the right to confer citizenship on their foreign-born spouses, and the process for conferring citizenship on children born in the country of foreign-born fathers is in practice more difficult than for children born of Yemeni fathers and foreign-born mothers. Civil society organizations and human rights monitors report that female prisoners are not released at the end of their sentences unless a male relative is present.[25]

Yemen is relatively homogeneous ethnically and racially. The Akhdam (Arabic for servants), a small group that claims to be descended from ancient Ethiopian occupiers, live in poverty and face social discrimination. The government, however, does not discriminate against this group and in fact has social and economic development programs to support its members.

Likewise, while government disability laws mandate the rights of disabled persons in the workplace, school, and elsewhere, widespread discrimination among the Yemeni public persists. In spite of government programs including the Social Welfare Fund, the Social Fund for Development, and the Fund for the Welfare of the Disabled, access for people with disabilities to services and provisions remains restricted.[26]

Article 2 of the constitution states that Islam is the religion of the state, and Article 3 declares that Islamic Sharia is the source of all legislation. Although the constitution guarantees the freedom of religion, based on Islamic Sharia, a Muslim converting to another religion is guilty of the crime of apostasy, which is de jure punishable by death. Nevertheless, no instances of government prosecution of citizens for this crime have been reported.

Overall, the state refrains from excessive interference in the appointment of religious and spiritual leaders, but it has taken some steps to prevent politicization of mosques and Islamic religious schools for extremist purposes.[27] While it offers no special protections to nonbelievers, it also does not institute policies to discriminate against them and generally respects their rights.

Yemenis have the right to form associations in "scientific, cultural, social, and national unions in a way that serves the goals of the Constitution," according to Article 58 of that document.[28] Despite its small size, Yemen has several thousand nongovernmental organizations, according to estimates from the government.

The government respects the right to form and join trade unions, and the General Federation of Trade Unions of Yemen—the main union organization, with an estimated 350,000 members in 14 unions—dominates the landscape. Critics claim that several syndicates are ineffective in protecting the interests of their members and that the government and ruling party elements have recently stepped up efforts to control the affairs of these organizations.[29]

Recommendations
- The Yemeni government should implement a comprehensive program to train law enforcement, security, and prison officials in the proper procedures for arresting, detaining, and interrogating accused individuals.
- Public officials should not have immunity for crimes committed while on duty.
- The government should amend national laws to ensure that women enjoy full equality in the law, particularly personal status laws on obtaining citizenship.
- The government should introduce laws to criminalize domestic violence against women in Yemen and work with civil society organizations to develop support structures such as shelters and counseling services to assist women who are victims of violence.

RULE OF LAW – 2.88

Despite efforts in recent years by the Yemeni government to reform the judiciary and enhance its capacity, the court system remains the weakest link of the three branches of government, susceptible to interference from the executive branch and unable to implement its rulings in many parts of the country.

In theory, Yemen's judiciary is independent. Article 149 of Yemen's constitution states that "the judicial authority is an autonomous authority in its judicial, financial, and administrative aspects, and the General Prosecution is one of its sub-bodies. The courts shall judge all disputes and crimes. Judges are independent and not subject to any authority, except the law." In practice, however, Yemen's Judicial Authority Law, which provides further definition of how the judiciary is managed, includes provisions that some legal analysts and civil society leaders argue contradict the constitutional safeguards of the judiciary's independence. Article 104 of this law assigns the president of the republic to the supreme judicial council (SJC), which manages the affairs of the judiciary. In addition to the president, the minister of justice, the deputy minister of justice, and the head of the judicial inspection board, who reports to the minister of justice, all serve on the SJC. These provisions legally enable the executive to maintain a strong degree of control over the judicial branch. More specifically, under the judicial authority law, the Ministry of Justice has a number of powers that constrain the judiciary's independence—supervising the finances, administration, and organization of the courts; reassigning judges and authorizing them to take nonjudicial jobs; selecting the number of members in the Supreme Court and courts of appeal; and defining the location and selecting the jurisdiction limits of primary courts.[30]

In addition to this most basic issue of limits on judicial independence, the judiciary suffers from a lack of adequate resources, which hinders its ability to hire and train qualified judges and implement its rulings. In rural areas, Yemenis frequently rely on traditional tribal forms of justice. A judicial reform move increased the salaries of judges as a measure to eliminate corruption, but this has not proven to be a panacea for the problem of judges taking bribes.

In January 2005, the SJC appointed 25 new judges, dismissed 22 judges without compensation and benefits, ordered more than 100 judges into early retirement, and moved several judges to different positions in an attempt to advance judicial reforms further. In addition, the Higher Judicial Council appointed 24 people to the Judicial Inspection Commission, a body that monitors the performance of judges. The new appointees included Abdullah Farwan, former chairman of the Central Organization for Control and Audit. These changes represented one of the largest shifts under a judicial reform program begun with support from the World Bank in 1997.

Yemen's law provides citizens with the opportunity for a fair and public trial and guarantees access to independent counsel. There were, however, reports of two trials that did not meet international standards of fairness in 2004.[31] Three men were sentenced to death in these trials, in which some lawyers withdrew from the defense team in protest at unfair trial conditions. Article 47 of the constitution states that the accused is innocent until proven guilty by final judicial ruling, and no law may be enacted to put a person on trial retroactively for acts committed. In practice, however, this principle is often undermined by the detention of suspects for long periods of time without trial. Article 48 of the constitution prohibits arrests made without warrant issued by a judge or prosecutor. On the other hand, government crackdowns since 2003 have often seemingly ignored the law in practice, with claims of national security overriding personal rights.

The Ministry of the Interior oversees the criminal investigative department of the police, which conducts most criminal investigations and arrests. The Ministry of Interior also maintains oversight of prison conditions for the 10,348 inmates detained in Yemen as of September 2003.[32] Prison conditions remained poor, with reports of unsanitary conditions, overcrowding, and a lack of access to medical care.[33] Unlike many other countries in the Arab world, Yemen does not have state security courts. However, the political security office (PSO), Yemen's primary internal security force, operates under the control of the president, with little or no oversight from other parts of the executive branch, the parliament, or judicial authorities.

The 2004 trials of suspects involved in terrorist attacks in Yemen were held in secret, and several human rights groups questioned the fairness of these proceedings, pointing out that defense attorneys were not permitted to meet with their clients in private and were not provided with full access to all of the evidence.

Yemen's constitution and legal framework afford all citizens equal treatment under the law. In practice, the legal system remains highly informal, with personal connections and networks frequently trumping the dictates of the law. The government's record on respecting and enforcing property rights is weak, however, particularly in parts of the country where tribal forces are stronger and government authority is limited.

The military is under the control of the executive branch. Nonetheless, tribal disputes and the prevalence of guns in society present a constant threat to the rule of law. In the 2003 parliamentary elections, police, military, and internal security services mostly refrained from interference in the political process, although opposition sources accused military or security agents of instigating disturbances in areas where opposition candidates were poised to win seats.[34] Even more worrying is the increasing frequency of reports of intimidation by military and security agents involving independent and opposition journalists. If true, this demonstrates government willingness to subvert the democratic process in order to maintain power. The upcoming presidential election will serve as an important test of the GPC's oft-voiced commitment to democracy.

Formal procedures as defined by Yemen law govern the rights and acquisition of property, though the reality, as is so often the case in Yemen, may differ markedly. Claims, particularly in southern Yemen, have arisen concerning government seizure of property and violations of property rights, with charges of unequal application of laws being levied.[35] These claims are denied by the government.[36] Yet questions over property rights extend beyond Yemenis. Skepticism among foreign businesses may discourage much-needed foreign investment.[37] In addition, while Yemen law grants its citizens inheritance and property rights, in practice women are routinely deprived of them due to tribal laws and custom.[38] A high female illiteracy rate, along with a lengthy judicial process, compounds the problems of legal redress.

Recommendations
- The Yemeni government should take further steps to decrease the potential for the executive branch's interference in the judiciary, such as transforming the SJC into a body appointed by the Shura council rather than by the president.
- Judicial authorities and the police should be more tightly linked and better coordinated to ensure that judicial rulings are fully implemented and respected.
- The government should ensure that all police and security authorities are subject to oversight and investigation from the legislative branch of government and the judiciary, as well as the executive branch.

ANTICORRUPTION AND TRANSPARENCY – 1.93

Corruption remains rife in Yemen, a fact recognized both inside and outside the country. Yemen earned a lowly 2.7 rating on Transparency

International's 2005 Corruption Perceptions Index, placing it 103 out of 159 countries surveyed—the scale ranges from a most corrupt score of 1.0 to a least corrupt score of 10.0.[39] Critics of corruption within the country are not limited to the political opposition but are also senior members of the current government, including the head of Yemen's primary audit agency, the Central Organization for Control and Auditing (COCA), and numerous ministers. Yet despite Yemen's declaring it as a top priority for the past several years, the fight against corruption has seemed to lack the political will necessary to achieve much success. The discrepancy between Yemen's established legal framework and its practical application has meant little tangible progress in this area. When a coalition of opposition parties launched an initiative in the fall of 2005 to encourage political reform in order to fight corruption, the government rejected the plan and accused those who initiated it of trying to overthrow the current regime.[40] President Saleh himself has downplayed corruption within his government, saying, "Those who raise anti-corruption slogans are themselves corrupt."[41]

Yemen's civil service and public administration suffer from overall underdeveloped institutional capacity, inefficient management systems, burdensome procedures, low salaries that tempt civil servants to resort to corruption to supplement their incomes, and an unnecessarily large number of personnel. Yemen has embarked on a reform process to eradicate bureaucratic inefficiencies and corruption in the civil service, but the efforts have been impeded in part by widespread poverty throughout the country. In July 2005, the government began a four-stage National Wage Strategy that will reward civil servants based on specific job criteria and will, in stages, increase minimum monthly salaries from 8,000 Yemeni riyals (US$41) to 20,000 Yemeni riyals (US$102).[42] As yet, it is too early to tell what effect this move will have on reducing government corruption. The government's patronage system involves "employing" thousands of Yemenis in government positions who draw double salaries, thus ensuring their loyalty to the ruling party. Many of these are tribal sheiks and military personnel.[43] Privatization has been one of the slowest components of the economic reform program, in part because of lack of proper laws and rules governing the privatization process.

Articles 118 and 136 of the constitution prohibit the president and ministers from engaging in private business of any kind. However, because Yemen currently does not require income or financial assets disclosure by government officials, enforcement relies on an honor system dependent on truthful self-reporting and self-monitoring.

COCA serves as the supreme audit institution in the country and conducts a series of regular audits of government ministries and organizations. Even though COCA officials claim that it is fully independent from the executive branch of government, the organization has failed to examine numerous allegations of high-level corruption. When sufficient evidence is gathered pointing to prosecutable cases of corruption, COCA refers them to the public funds prosecution office, as well as President Saleh's office.[44] Requests for investigations into corrupt government practices often go unanswered for long periods. Moreover, judges presiding over such cases allegedly have been complicit in corrupt practices themselves.[45]

A culture of bribery allegedly permeates the state apparatus including hospitals, schools, and universities, with little legal redress available to victims.[46] Bribes are often necessary for such basic activities as obtaining hospital treatment.[47] In fact, those who raise objections publicly often face criticism or even worse. On April 23, 2005, Jamal Amer, the editor in chief of the independent *Al-Wassat* newspaper, was abducted, interrogated, beaten, and threatened by armed men who claimed to be acting on behalf of military officers; this occurred after Amer's newspaper published an article accusing the Ministry of Education of nepotism in granting government scholarships to study abroad to the children of prominent Yemeni officials.[48] The Ministry of Interior denied involvement in the six-hour kidnapping and promised to investigate the incident, but to date no charges have been filed.[49]

Corruption costs Yemen substantial amounts of funding both internally and externally. Weak governance results in daily costs and lost revenues—COCA reported that in the first half of 2005, 55 cases of corruption resulted in financial losses exceeding 3 billion Yemeni riyals (US$15 million).[50] For example, by undervaluing imported goods and taking illegal surcharges on the undeclared amount, officials cost the government significant tax revenues. The World Bank estimates that such informal payments and other gifts necessary to do business in Yemen average nearly 9 percent of sales.[51] Yet such practices go largely unchecked by the auditing and investigative bodies charged by law with fighting corruption. In fact, opposition politicians claim that, as of the beginning of 2006, "not a single official has been punished for financial corruption so far, despite reports by COCA revealing serious financial corruption in state-run organs."[52]

However, international pressure has been mounting on Yemen to redress corrupt practices and improve governance. With the suspension of large amounts of external aid pending marked improvements in these areas—the World Bank reduced its loans from $420 million to $280 million while the U. S. government suspended Yemen from the Millenium Challenge Account Program for 2006—positive movement within the Yemen government may be starting to occur.[53] At the end of 2005, President Saleh referred two draft anticorruption laws to the government for debate calling for the establishment of an independent national inspection and monitoring commission that would follow up on corruption charges and work closely with local and foreign transparency watchdog groups. However, this anticorruption body, if created, would be supervised directly by the president, bringing into question its independence and effectiveness.

While the budget is formally introduced by the executive branch and debated by the legislative branch, President Saleh and the GPC dominate the budget-making process. Critics argue that Yemen, as one of the world's least-developed countries, spends a disproportionate amount of money on security and military issues and not enough on social issues and fighting corruption.[54] In addition, the failure to curtail the rampant corruption largely negates any legislative review and scrutiny of the budget.

On the other hand, parliament showed signs of a more active involvement in the political process in December 2004, when it delayed passage of the budget for the first time due to concerns over what opposition members saw as a lack of will within the GPC and the executive branch to institute reform and fight corruption.[55]

Although Yemen's laws require a degree of transparency and public access to information, in practice detailed accounting of expenditures rarely occurs in a timely fashion. The state offers few procedures to ensure transparency, open bidding, and effective competition in awarding government contracts. The government does provide limited information concerning its expenditures on its website; however, as the majority of Yemeni citizens do not have internet access their recourse to the information is limited.

Recommendations

- Yemen's government should introduce requirements of public disclosure of personal finances, including income, assets, and all business interests for all senior public officials such as the president, senior staff to the president, government ministers, top ministry officials, judges and other senior judicial authorities, and members of parliament.
- The government should establish formal mechanisms, such as an anonymous telephone tip line, by which government employees and individuals can report instances of alleged corruption and misuse of public resources.
- The new national higher authority to fight corruption should be fully independent of the president and the executive branch; it should be able to investigate and prosecute alleged instances of corruption and make reports thereof publicly available without fear of government interference.
- The Yemen government should actively enforce its transparency and public access to information law.

NOTES

[1] "Yemen: Year in Brief 2005 – A Chronology of Democratic Developments," IRIN-news.org, 10 January 2006, http://www.irinnews.org/print.asp?ReportID=51014, accessed 27 June 2006.

[2] "Election Guide" (Washington, D.C: Electionworld.org and International Foundation for Election Systems [IFES]), http://www.ifes.org and http://electionguide.org.

[3] "Yemen at a Glance," *Arab Political Systems: Baseline Information and Reform – Yemen* (Washington, D.C.: Carnegie Endowment for Peace, 2005), 19, 21, http://www.carnegie endowment.org/files/Yemen_APS.doc, accessed 28 June 2006.

[4] "Preliminary Statement of the NDI International Election Observer Delegation to Yemen's April 27 Legislative Elections" (Washington, D.C.: National Democratic Institute for International Affairs [NDI], 29 April 2003), 4, http://www.accessdemocracy.org/library/1584_ye_election03.pdf, accessed 3 July 2006.

[5] Interview with representatives from NDI and the IFES, Sanaa, 27 September 2003.

[6] Ibid.

[7] Interview with Ahmed Al-Sufi and Abdullah Sallam Al-Hakimi of the Yemen Institute for Development of Democracy (YIDD), Sanaa, 25 September 2003.

[8] "Preliminary Statement of the NDI," 1.

[9] Ibid., 5.

[10] Interview with Abdul Majed Al-Fahed, Executive Director of the Civic Democratic Initiative Support Foundation (CDF), Sanaa, 26 September 2003.

11 "Yemen's Constitutional Referendum and Local Elections" (New York: Human Rights Watch [HRW], February 2001).

12 Interview with Amat Al-Aleem Al-Soswa, Yemen's Minister of Human Rights, Washington, D.C., 10 September 2003.

13 Ziad Majed, et al., *Building Democracy in Yemen: Women's Political Participation, Political Party Life, and Democratic Elections* (Stockholm: International Institute for Democracy and Electoral Assistance [IDEA], 2005), 13.

14 "Review of the Annual Strategic Report: Yemen 2002–2003" (Sanaa: General Center for Studies, Research, and Publishing, 2003).

15 Mujahed Al-Mussa'abi, "National Committee for Women: Challenges & Future," *Yemen Times*, 18–24 November 2002.

16 Interview with Rashida Al-Hamdani, Chairperson of the Women's National Committee, Sanaa, 28 September 2003.

17 "YEMEN: New System to Eliminate Thousands of "Ghost" Civil Servants," IRINnews.com (New York: UN Office for Coordination of Humanitarian Affairs, 12 September 2005).

18 Joel Campagna, "Attacks, Censorship, and Dirty Tricks: In Yemen, the Press Climate is Deteriorating" (New York: Committee to Protect Journalists [CPJ], 9 March 2006), 1, http://www.cpj.org/Briefings/2006/yemen_3-06/yemen_3-06_printer.html, accessed 26 June 2006.

19 Kevin Watkins, *Human Development Report [HDR] 2005* (New York: United Nations Development Programme [UNDP], 2005), 250.

20 Campagna, "Attacks," 3.

21 Yasser Mohammed Al-Mayyasi, "Protests Against Attacks on Journalists Mount," *Yemen Times*, 12–15 May 2005, http://www.yementimes.com/article.shtml?i=841&p=front&a=1, accessed 3 July 2006.

22 Amnesty International Yemen Report, 2004, http://web.amnesty.org/web/web.nsf/print/F5AAEDDCA09FE51280256FF100588B2D.

23 "25 by 2005 Country Data: Yemen," *Gender Achievements and Prospects in Education, GAP Report: Part One* (New York: UNICEF, UN Girls' Education Initiative [UNGEI], 2005), http://www.ungei.org/gap/country.php, accessed 29 June 2006.

24 Interview with Rashida Al-Hamdani, Chairperson of the Women's National Committee, and Ramzia Al-Eryani, Yemeni Women's Union, Sanaa, 28 September 2003; "Yemen Country Profile" (UNDP, 2003).

25 Jamal Al-Admimi, *Human Rights* (Sanaa: Forum for Civil Society [FCS], December 2002), 48.

26 Samar Mujalli, "Disabled: 'We Refuse to be Like This'," *Yemen Times*, 8–11 June 2006, http://www.yementimes.com/article.shtml?i=953&p=report&a=1.

27 Ibid.

28 "The Constitution of the Republic of Yemen," *Athawabit Journal, A Quarterly Journal of Culture, Development, and Politics* (April 2002).

29 Interviews with members of the journalists' and teachers' syndicates, 25 and 29 September 2003.

[30] Jamal Al-Adimi and Faisal Asswfi, "Justice Report: Yemen 2000," *Al-Qistas* (FCS, 2000), 7.

[31] Amnesty International Yemen Report, 2004, http://web.amnesty.org/web/web.nsf/print/ F5AAEDDCA09FE51280256FF100588B2D, accessed 10 July, 2006.

[32] Interview with Rashid Jarhoom, Yemen's Deputy Minister of Interior, Sanaa, 29 September 2003.

[33] "Kenya; Ordeal in Yemen," *Africa News,* 20 September 2004, Accessed through Lexis-Nexis, 10 July, 2006.

[34] Sheila Carapico, "How Yemen's Ruling Party Secured an Electoral Landslide," *Middle East Report Online,* 16 May 2003, http://www.merip.org/mero/mero051603.html, accessed 28 June 2006.

[35] Jane Novak, "Yemen: Failure or Democracy," *Yemen Times,* 22–25 December 2005, http://www.yementimes.com/article.shtml?i=905&p=report&a=1, accessed 28 June 2006.

[36] "Yemen Envoy Seeks British Asylum," BBC News, 29 April 2005, http://news.bbc .co.uk/2/hi/uk_news/4499833.stm, accessed 23 June 2006.

[37] "Bertelsmann Transformation Index 2006 – Yemen" (Gutersloh: Bertelsmann Stiftung, 2006), 9, http://www.bertelsmann-transformation-index.de/fileadmin/pdf/en/2006/ MiddleEastAndNorthernAfrica/Yemen.pdf, accessed 28 June 2006.

[38] Arwa Al-Anesi, "Yemeni Women Deprived of Family Inheritance," *Yemen Times,* 1–4 June 2006, http://www.yementimes.com/article.shtml?i=951&p=report&a=4, accessed 28 June 2006.

[39] Corruption Perceptions Index (Transparency International, 2005).

[40] "Yemen: Year in Brief 2005 – A Chronology of Democratic Developments," IRIN-news.org, 10 January 2006, http://www.irinnews.org/print.asp?ReportID=51014, accessed 27 June 2006.

[41] Nabil Sultan, "Yemen: MPs Target Corrupt 'Government of Mass Destruction'," Internet Press Service/Global Information Network, 5 January 2006, accessed through Lexis-Nexis, 23 June 2006.

[42] Paul Garwood, "Yemen Under New Pressure to End Corruption as World Bank Cuts Support," Associated Press, 27 October 2005, 2, accessed through Lexis-Nexis, 23 June 2006; *Yemen Economic Update* (Sana'a: World Bank Group, spring 2006), 3.

[43] Kevin Whitelaw, "On a Dagger's Edge," *U.S. News & World Report* 140, 9 (13 March 2006): 38–45.

[44] Interview with Rashid Jarhoom.

[45] Christian Chaise, "Corruption Runs Parallel Economy in Impoverished Yemen," Agence France Presse, 7 May 2006, accessed through Lexis-Nexis 26 June 2006.

[46] Mohammed Hatem al-Qadhi, "Crackdown on Corruption Needs Commitment," *Yemen Times,* 28–30 November 2005, http://www.yementimes.com/article.shtml?i=898&p= opinion&a=3, accessed 28 June 2006.

[47] Mohammed Al-Asaadi and Abdul-Aziz Oudah, "Collective Efforts to Fight Corruption," *Yemen Observer,* 9 December 2005, 1.

[48] Yasser Mohammed Al-Mayyasi, "Al-Wasat Editor Abducted, and Brutally Beaten," *Yemen Times,* 25–29 August 2005, http://www.yementimes.com/article.shtml?i=871&p= front&a=1, accessed 28 June 2006.

49 "Military Source Denies Journalist Amer's Accusations," Yemen News Agency, 25 August 2005, accessed through Lexis-Nexis 28 June 2006.

50 Mohammed Al-Asaadi and Abdul-Aziz Oudah, "Collective Efforts," 1.

51 Yemen Economic Update (World Bank), 8.

52 Sultan, "MPs Target."

53 David Finkel, "In the End, a Painful Choice," Washington Post, 20 December 2005, A01.

54 Novak, "Yemen: Failure or."

55 "Yemen: Strengthening Parliamentary Institutions and Increasing Inclusive National Dialogue (04929)," CEPPS/NDI Quarterly Report: April 1 to June 30, 2005 (NDI, 2005), 3, http://pdf.usaid.gov/pdf_docs/PDACF483.pdf. accessed 28 June 2006.

ZIMBABWE

CAPITAL: Harare
POPULATION: 13 million
GNI PER CAPITA: $2,120

SCORES	2004	2006
ACCOUNTABILITY AND PUBLIC VOICE:	2.19	1.07
CIVIL LIBERTIES:	3.04	2.45
RULE OF LAW:	2.48	1.26
ANTICORRUPTION AND TRANSPARENCY:	1.86	0.88

(scores are based on a scale of 0 to 7, with 0 representing weakest and 7 representing strongest performance)

Robert B. Lloyd

INTRODUCTION

President Robert Mugabe presides over a country torn by deep political fissures, a freefalling economy, and international condemnation for human rights abuses. Despite these challenges, Mugabe's power has become more entrenched. His political resiliency has been surprising given the growing chorus of international and domestic opposition to his rule. In the past five years, the Commonwealth, the European Union, and the United States have all imposed limited sanctions against Zimbabwe. These actions were taken due to Mugabe's controversial policies of seizing commercial farmland; government-sponsored intimidation, beatings, detention, and torture of opposition supporters; and manipulation of elections. As Zimbabwe's economic crisis has deepened, the government has found it difficult to clear its debt arrears with the International Monetary Fund (IMF). The IMF, frustrated at continued nonpayment of loans, has threatened to expel Zimbabwe.

Domestic opposition, which since 2000 had posed a serious challenge to Mugabe, has experienced severe setbacks. The March 2005 legislative elections increased the control of Mugabe's ruling Zimbabwe

Robert B. Lloyd is a Professor of International Relations at Pepperdine University in Malibu, California. His primary research interests are international conflict management, international negotiation, and Africa.

African National Union–Patriotic Front (ZANU–PF) political party over the legislature. The opposition Movement for Democratic Change (MDC), led by trade unionist Morgan Tsvangirai, began to split over how best to challenge the president. Other avenues to contest the government have been closed. The government uses restrictive legislation to clamp down on prominent critics. State-owned radio, television, and newspapers dominate the country. The erosion of the independence of the judiciary continues through judicial resignations, politically compliant appointments, and paychecks battered by spiraling inflation.

Condemnation of Mugabe has not, however, been universal. South Africa, the state with the most leverage against Zimbabwe, is generally pro-Mugabe. South Africa's positive attitude is shared by many African states and organizations, which see Mugabe as a hero of Zimbabwe's war for independence, achieved in 1980. Furthermore, his land seizure policies targeting white-owned farms are viewed sympathetically by a number of other southern African states. This reservoir of goodwill has helped Mugabe weather domestic and international criticism. Within Zimbabwe, the president derives support from a tightly woven web of party elites, government positions, and private enterprises held together by a system of patronage with Mugabe at its apex.

These sources of domestic and international support have enabled Mugabe to use state power to impose his will over Zimbabweans, further strengthening his grip on the country. Force used against citizens intensified in the government acquisition of private property. Over several months in mid-2005, for example, police and security forces implemented Operation Clear the Filth, using violence to demolish a number of urban townships. It is estimated that more than 700,000 individuals lost their homes. The government also demolished thousands of informal businesses through Operation No Going Back. A new citizenship law meant many of those displaced who were of mixed national heritage found that they were no longer citizens.

Zimbabwe's political isolation and economic decline will remain for the foreseeable future. Given Mugabe's advanced age (approximately 80 years), the task of addressing the country's structural problems should come fairly soon. A post-Mugabe Zimbabwe will be a failed state marked by economic collapse, a population ravaged by HIV/AIDS, turmoil over political succession, and continued disputes over property rights.

ACCOUNTABILITY AND PUBLIC VOICE – 1.07

Zimbabwe is essentially a single-party state with a strong executive president. Party and presidential loyalties undermine effective checks and balances. While the legislature is legally autonomous from the executive, it is highly unlikely that the executive will be held accountable for any excessive exercise of power. The executive does indict party leaders on corruption charges, but these are related primarily to feuds within the ZANU–PF.

Zimbabwe has a unicameral legislature with regularly scheduled elections. ZANU–PF has held power since independence in 1980. In the March 2005 parliamentary elections, five parties fielded candidates for the 120 elected seats. The elections were generally peaceful. All registered voters were able to vote irrespective of race, color, political affiliation, or sex. In the two weeks prior to the elections the government allowed opposition parties to campaign and permitted limited—but biased—media coverage.

Compared to the 2003 vote, political violence and intimidation decreased markedly prior to the March 2005 elections. Nevertheless, there were still reports of violence against opposition party members and their supporters. One survey of opposition MDC members of parliament (MPs) and candidates found that most claimed to have personally experienced intimidation and violence from security services and ZANU–PF partisans.[1]

ZANU–PF decisively won the elections, gaining the two-thirds majority needed to amend the constitution. The MDC, its main rival, charged electoral fraud but attended the swearing-in ceremony. The British government stated that the elections were seriously flawed and thus did not represent the democratic will of the Zimbabwean voters. Independent electoral observers monitored the elections, but the government allowed into the country only groups from Africa that it believed were pro-ZANU–PF. These observers stated the vote reflected the will of the Zimbabwean people.

Of special concern were unexplained discrepancies between announced voting totals and subsequent official results, which may have affected election outcomes in 31 constituencies. The Zimbabwe Electoral Commission (ZEC), whose members were appointed by the government, could not provide a ready explanation for the discrepancies.

The impression of ZEC partiality toward the government was reinforced after it filed a court application in support of Mugabe following the president's disagreement with a court decision to let an imprisoned opposition MP run for his own seat.

The government purports to abide by democratic guidelines established by the Southern African Development Community (SADC), a regional grouping of states. Opposition political parties receive public funding. It is legal for all candidates other than the president to be criticized. The Public Order and Security Act (POSA) criminalizes false reporting and statements that "incite or promote public disorder or public violence." In addition, it also requires that police be notified in advance of any public gathering of more than two people and prohibits those that police believe could cause public disorder. An individual convicted of this crime is liable for a one-year imprisonment or a fine. The ambiguity of the language means the law essentially criminalizes political speech by the opposition. State ownership of the media makes it more difficult for opposition parties to receive any coverage and in particular favorable coverage during the campaign period.

The rise of the MDC had until recently offered increasing opportunities for rotation of power among different parties. The party's major electoral defeat in the March 2005 elections decreases the likelihood of a successful challenge to ZANU–PF dominance. Deep divisions within the MDC over strategy, tactics, and leadership now threaten its continued existence as a viable political party. The coming period will be critical in assessing whether the MDC is able to recover its strength and unity at all.

Regulations to prevent the undue influence of economically privileged interests are inadequate in the face of government efforts to retain power. Political choices through multiple parties, regularly scheduled elections, and opportunities to campaign are reduced by restrictive laws that entrench the power of ZANU–PF elites. ZANU–PF officials have been given land and businesses seized from opposition supporters, the government has faced allegations of using food to buy votes, and government-trained and -supported youth militias intimidate opposition supporters and leaders. Groups opposed to the government, such as religious organizations, white farmers, and trade unions, are actively discriminated against. Individuals who support ZANU–PF are less likely to be subject to political and legal intimidation than those who support the MDC.

Supporters of the ZANU-PF are given preference in employment opportunities and are frequently rewarded with civil service jobs. One ZANU–PF government official reportedly told the heads of government-owned companies, "Make sure you implement party directives. . . . For as long as ZANU–PF is in power, make sure you serve it."[3]

Parliament does debate legislation, allowing citizens the opportunity to become aware of impending changes. Individuals may walk into parliament to hear the debates, and the parliament's sessions are broadcast. Civic groups are allowed to comment on pending legislation, although the government does not act on views contrary to its policies.

The government has placed increasing legal restrictions on nongovernmental organizations (NGOs). Both POSA and the Access to Information and Protection of Privacy Act (AIPPA) place limits on the abilities of individuals and NGOs to speak, associate, and assemble. In December 2004, the parliament approved the Non-Governmental Organizations (NGO) Bill, which would ban foreign funding of Zimbabwean civic associations that deal with governance issues, require annual registration and the payment of fees, and prohibit foreign NGOs from engaging in the "promotion and protection of human rights and political governance issues." The act immediately drew the attention of domestic and international human rights groups. Individuals who publicly protested this law when it was under consideration were arrested.[4] However, international outcry has apparently delayed President Mugabe's signing it into law.[5]

The government exercises direct control on print and broadcast media. The state-owned Zimbabwe Broadcasting Corporation (ZBC) operates domestic radio and television stations. The government daily, *The Herald,* is widely seen as a mouthpiece of the Mugabe government. The AIPPA criminalizes the publication of false information. A government-controlled Media and Information Commission (MIC) regulates independent media by requiring the accreditation of journalists and media organizations.

In 2003, the government closed *The Daily News,* Zimbabwe's only independent daily newspaper, for failing to register with the MIC. Although the closure was overruled by the courts, *The Daily News* remains closed. Since 2003 the government has also closed *The Daily News on Sunday, The Tribune,* and *The Weekly Times.* The country now lacks an independent daily press.

The government uses security forces to enforce restrictive legislation against journalists.[6] Journalists have been beaten, detained, deported, and threatened.[7] In 2004, the Committee to Protect Journalists listed Zimbabwe as third on the list of the worst places in the world to be a journalist, just behind Cuba and Iraq.[8]

Only state-controlled media are allowed to broadcast in Zimbabwe. An independent radio station was immediately shut down by police after it opened in 2000. The station then relocated to Britain and began beaming to Zimbabwe as SW Radio Africa in 2002. Shortly before the March 2005 parliamentary elections, the Zimbabwean government allegedly began jamming the broadcast frequencies.[9]

Zimbabweans use the internet to circumvent restrictions, but the government has attempted to hinder access. In November 2003, 14 people were arrested for circulating an e-mail message criticizing President Mugabe's economic policies and urging violent demonstrations and strikes to force him from power. The e-mail had not been intercepted electronically, but a paper copy had reportedly been given to police.[10] In March 2004, the Supreme Court struck down as unconstitutional an intercept provision of a law that allowed government monitoring of telephone and internet communications. The state-owned telecommunications company subsequently began requiring internet service providers to monitor the content of customers' e-mails.[11]

Cultural expression is protected provided it is not seen as antigovernment. A prominent musician known for his outspokenness against President Mugabe, Thomas Mapfumo, is banned from state-controlled media. He distributes his music by cassette. Artists also self-censor so as to avoid antagonizing the government, and many have left the country.[12] The government verbally attacked an American film, *The Interpreter,* that many saw as anti-Mugabe. Nevertheless, the Zimbabwe Board of Censors approved the film, and it ran for two weeks in early July at Harare cinemas and is available on video.[13]

Recommendations

- The Public Order and Security Act and the Access to Information and Protection of Privacy Act provisions must be amended to allow freedom of speech and association.
- Mugabe should refuse to sign into law the restrictive Non-Governmental Organizations (NGO) Bill, approved in December 2004 by the parliament.

- The government must take steps to ensure that the Zimbabwe Electoral Commission is completely politically independent by requiring that representation reflect a range of political parties, civic groups, and business leaders.
- Voting procedures must be reformed to allow independent and unhampered verification of polling stations.
- The government should allow private ownership of print and broadcast media and repeal all restrictive legislation against the media.

CIVIL LIBERTIES – 2.45

Zimbabwe's constitution states that everyone in the country is entitled to the fundamental rights and freedoms of the individual, "whatever his race, tribe, place of origin, colour, creed, or sex." Zimbabwe has also ratified the International Convention on the Elimination of All Forms of Discrimination Against Women.[14] Constitutional provisions include sections that prohibit torture and inhuman or degrading punishment and guarantee protection from arbitrary search or entry. Later amendments, however, qualify these rights subject to "the interests of defense, public safety, public order, and public morality." In addition, "state of emergency" laws dating from the struggle for independence have been retained and employed to limit civil rights and liberties.

Zimbabwe has signed the International Covenant on Civil and Political Rights. This imposes a responsibility on Zimbabwe to enforce constitutional provisions that prohibit arbitrary arrest or detention even during times of domestic strife.[15] Nevertheless, Amnesty International reports that members of the Central Intelligence Organization and the Zimbabwe Republic Police have tortured individuals seen as opposed to the government. On October 14, 2004, Philani Zamchiya, president of the Zimbabwe National Students Union (ZINASU), stated that he had been kidnapped and assaulted by police. He escaped from a moving car. In February 2004, Lovemore Madhuku, chairman of the National Constitutional Assembly (NCA), was beaten by police with batons and dumped on the outskirts of Harare during a peaceful demonstration near the parliament. Both individuals required hospitalization, but no arrests for assault or kidnapping were made.[16]

Government security forces and politically supported youth wings are responsible for most of these attacks.[17] Training centers for ZANU–PF militia youth have been expanded. After graduation, they are deployed to various parts of the country where they set up roadblocks, harass suspected MDC supporters (at times violently), and enforce government price controls.[18] The police have not intervened in cases where they have observed attacks by the youth militia against civilians.

There are no protections against arbitrary arrest. High-profile individuals such as Morgan Tsvangirai have some due process, but less well-known political opponents are simply arrested and detained. Once arrested, they have no effective protection against long-term detention. In 2004, the government approved the Criminal Procedure and Evidence Bill, extending detention of those arrested for corruption or violating security laws from 48 hours to 21 days.[19]

For those who are incarcerated, the conditions are poor. Former MDC MP Roy Bennett, who was convicted by the parliament and jailed for eight months for pushing Justice Minister Patrick Chimasa, described jail conditions as "hellish." He claims inmates were beaten on a daily basis and were not properly clothed. Bennett himself reported that he had to stand naked in front of prison guards, was given a prison uniform covered in human excrement, and lost over 60 pounds while in jail.[20] He was never given the right to appeal the sentence.

Citizens lack effective means of petition and redress when their rights are violated. For example, a recent change in the Zimbabwe Citizenship Act requires dual citizens to renounce their foreign citizenship or lose their Zimbabwean citizenship. Zimbabweans who are not resident in the country for five years also lose their citizenship. This act clearly targets white Zimbabweans who hold British citizenship or South African residency status. The act has also stripped the citizenship of black Zimbabweans who have historical roots in neighboring African countries. Black Africans now face deportation. Importantly, there are no legal means to appeal the changes in citizenship.[21]

No widespread trafficking of women and children has been reported, although women may be transported to South Africa to work as prostitutes. In rural areas there are reports of girls being offered in compensation for interfamily disputes in accordance with traditional customs. Traditional practices such as polygamy and *lobola,* which is a mutual agreement of the price that the groom has to pay in order to marry the bride, remain legal.

Women hold seats in parliament, as government ministers, and at the local level. The ZANU–PF congress allots 30 percent of party positions and a fixed quota of the party's powerful Central Committee to women. In December 2004, President Mugabe appointed a woman, Joice Mujuru, as second vice president. There is some speculation that she may succeed Mugabe when he eventually passes from the political scene.

Zimbabwe's official language is English, but the inhabitants speak approximately 20 languages. The majority speaks Shona, and the largest minority speaks Ndebele. Multilingualism is common. Although President Mugabe is a Shona speaker, legal discrimination against minority languages does not appear to occur.[22] All major ethnic groups are represented in the government, although most belong to the Shona group. Mugabe's inner circle is increasingly drawn from the Zezeru subgroup of the Shonas.[23]

Shortly after independence in 1980, tensions flared between the Shona and Ndebele speakers, leading to a low-level civil war in which thousands of Ndebeles were killed by government forces. Mugabe cited this conflict as a reason to keep in place a state of emergency, which allowed his government to detain people (in practice mostly Ndebele) without charge. Many Ndebeles in Matabeleland, which is an area of strong MDC support, argue that the government also discriminates against them in law and employment.

The issue of who is a Zimbabwean is contentious due to the country's colonial history. The constitution devotes an entire chapter to the topic. In the early years of independence, Mugabe was careful to promote reconciliation among black and white Zimbabweans, but the government now discriminates against white Zimbabweans. Justifications for land seizures are made on explicitly racist grounds. White Zimbabweans have no right to their farms because they are white, the government argues, and therefore gained the land illegally. Black Zimbabweans whose origins were in neighboring African countries have likewise been politically disenfranchised without due process.

The constitution provides for freedom of religion, and the government generally protects this right. The majority of the Zimbabwean population is Christian, primarily Protestant. Many Christians also practice traditional African religious rites. Muslims make up less than 2 percent of the population. The Witchcraft Suppression Act provides criminal penalties for those who practice witchcraft. This law has been supported by human rights groups because it protects women accused of employing sorcery to cause harm, a serious charge in Africa. Relations have become increasingly strained between the government and churches, which the government believes are supporting the opposition MDC. Roman Catholic Archbishop of Bulawayo Pius Ncube, a prominent critic of the government, denies that he supports the opposition.[24] Ncube has received death threats but has not been arrested. There is little evidence of systematic and severe government interference in the appointment of religious leaders or the internal organization of churches, but religious leaders who do not hold Zimbabwean citizenship and are deemed opponents of the Mugabe government have been expelled.

The government allows religious instruction. One-third of the schools in the country are Christian. In addition, Christian hospitals are a major source of affordable medical care for many Zimbabweans. The government permits limited religious broadcasting over state-owned television and advertising in the government-controlled press. Public religious gatherings, however, may be restricted under POSA. For example, on September 29, 2004, nine members of a women's organization, Women of Zimbabwe Arise, were arrested and detained for two days for praying in public at Harare's Africa Unity Square. Three of the women claim that they were assaulted at the Harare Central Police Station by plainclothes officers. When the women later appeared in court, no charges were presented by the government, and they were released.[25]

There is strong social and religious disapproval of homosexuality in Zimbabwe. In the past, President Mugabe has publicly called homosexuality "un-African" and essentially a European import. Thus, practicing homosexual relations is illegal and a punishable offense.

The Disabled Persons Act was passed in 1994 for the purpose of "enhancing the educational, social and occupational interests of Zimbabweans with disabilities." In 2004, the government allocated a supplemental US$1.1 million to the National Disability Board (NDB), an advisory government policy body, to better meet the needs of the disabled. Problems have been reported concerning delivery of funds and services to the intended beneficiaries.[26] In September 2005, the parliament approved an amendment to the Zimbabwean constitution that makes discrimination based on physical disability impermissible.[27]

The constitution guarantees freedom of assembly and association, but specific clauses abrogate these rights in the interest of safety, order, and morality. Rights are further limited by legislation such as POSA. The MDC claims that police may refuse to allow a meeting on the basis that they do not have sufficient manpower to provide security.[28] The government selectively applies this restriction to the MDC, not to ZANU–PF.[29]

The Labor Relations Act allows private sector workers to form and operate unions. Unions register with the ministry of public services, labor, and social welfare. An umbrella organization, the Zimbabwe Congress of Trade Unions (ZCTU), comprises approximately 30 individual unions. Morgan Tsvangirai began his political activism as secretary-general of the ZCTU, and the government views that organization as being aligned with the MDC. The government has attempted to suppress the ZCTU through harassment, intimidation, and violence.[30] In November 2005, the entire ZCTU leadership was arrested ahead of a planned march and protest in favor of better working conditions and on behalf of people living with HIV/AIDs.[31] The government started a rival and progovernment union, the Zimbabwe Federation of Trade Unions (ZFTU), to undermine the ZCTU.

Zimbabweans are not directly compelled by the state to belong to any association. There are, however, widespread reports that a member of the ZANU–PF will get food while opposition supporters will not. Zimbabwe is currently facing food shortages due to drought and the seizure of farms. Emergency food aid is controlled by the government.

Since 2002, the government has not used excessive force against meetings provided they meet POSA regulations. The government often uses a catch-and-release policy for public protests that do not comply with POSA regulations. In October 2005, for example, opposition MDC MP Gilbert Shoko and 16 of his supporters protested Zimbabwe's fuel shortage by walking to work. The police arrested them under POSA, but all were later released.[32]

Recommendations

- The government must repeal the Criminal Procedure and Evidence Bill, which extends detention of those arrested for corruption or violating security laws from 48 hours to 21 days.

- The citizenship law should be amended to reinstate citizenship for Zimbabweans who have lived in the country for a relatively long period of time and to allow citizens to keep dual nationality.
- The government must cease using war veterans, youth militia, police, and security services to intimidate, beat, and detain civilians.
- Independent groups must have unfettered access to jails and prisoners to verify that conditions are consistent with constitutional provisions against torture and inhuman or degrading punishment.

RULE OF LAW – 1.26

The constitution provides for an independent judiciary and authorizes the president to appoint judges to the courts. Senior judges must have legal training, be experienced with Roman-Dutch law, and be fluent in English.

President Mugabe has increased executive control over the judiciary, which has nevertheless retained some independence. In 2004, for example, Zimbabwean judge Sandra Mungwira acquitted six MDC activists accused of murdering Cain Nkala, a ZANU–PF party official. After a nine-month trial, the judge called police evidence unreliable. Furthermore, the judge stated that police had assaulted the accused, denied them medical treatment for the resultant injuries, deprived them of food, and refused them proper legal assistance.[33]

Judges have resigned after the government stated it could not guarantee their security. An accused citizen may receive a fair trial, but judicial vacancies mean that trials lack timeliness.[34] Of the nearly 40 cases filed by the Movement for Democratic Change after the 2002 elections, none have been heard. Enias Magate, the head of the Magistrates Association of Zimbabwe, stated in October 2005 that many judges were experiencing financial distress due to relatively low pay. A number of judges have been charged with corruption.[35]

Under the constitution every person charged with a criminal offense is presumed to be innocent until proven guilty. Citizens have a right to independent counsel. In practice, however, the government has not allowed access to counsel for some individuals detained.[36] In high-profile cases, like the two treason trials of Morgan Tsvangirai from February 2003 through August 2005, the accused did have access to counsel. He was defended by George Bizos, who defended Nelson Mandela in his treason trial in the 1960s. In criminal cases, an indigent defendant may request legal assistance, but this is rarely granted. Zimbabweans are, however, provided an interpreter at state expense.

The erosion of the independence of the judiciary also has the effect of strengthening the political control of prosecutors. Welshman Ncube, a former University of Zimbabwe law school professor and MDC leader, argues that prosecutors are intimidated by the government and fear losing their jobs.[37]

From Mugabe on down, the political culture fosters lack of accountability to the electorate. This is reflected in periodic amnesties for government members accused of wrongdoing. The illegal seizure of land has been a ripe opportunity for political leaders to abuse their power in obtaining property. While Mugabe has periodically reiterated his support of the "one man one farm policy," no senior official has returned any land—and many own more than one farm. Public officials and ruling party leaders are not prosecuted for wrongdoing unless they run afoul of Mugabe. In February 2004, for example, James Makamba, a wealthy businessman and senior ZANU–PF member, was accused of contravening foreign exchange laws and charged with corruption under the Criminal Procedure and Evidence Bill.[38] A court dismissed all charges, but the Supreme Court reversed the decision on appeal. The Zimbabwean press speculated that Makamba's close personal relationship with Mugabe's wife had become a cause of concern for the president and was the reason for the charges. Makamba reportedly fled the country in 2005.[39]

Overall, security and military forces are accountable to the government but not to civilians. The police and security forces act on the orders of the president. Furthermore, the government has not condemned the harassment, torture, detention, and killing of Zimbabweans by these forces. The government has been careful to provide for the needs of the senior members of the military, as in large measure Mugabe's continued rule depends on their support. Top officials owe their positions to Mugabe and have received land and other benefits for their loyalty. The result of this codependence is an increasingly militaristic regime. Within the military, senior officers support the ruling ZANU–PF.

Zimbabwe allows for the private ownership of property through individual or corporate ownership but does not respect and enforce property rights. Any remaining avenues for seeking legal redress for the seizure of white-owned farms were ended with government approval of a constitutional amendment in 2005 that disallowed all appeals for the return of seized land. In the past two years, government officials have sent mixed signals on whether land may actually be owned or perhaps leased from the government.[40] Government land minister John Nkomo, in a discussion on land seizures in June 2004, stated that eventually there would be no private land in Zimbabwe. The government soon retreated, stating that no change had taken place in land policies regarding private property.[41] Nevertheless, the government seems to be indicating that mineral resources should be state owned. In 2004, President Mugabe stated, "we cannot recognize absolute ownership of our resources."[42]

Since 2004, the government has continued seizures of land, particularly commercial farms owned by white Zimbabweans. In December 2003, the government amended the Land Acquisitions Act, permitting it to acquire large agribusinesses. Four months later, the large Kondozi farm in eastern Zimbabwe was seized by the government, which evicted more than 1,500 farmworkers and their families. In December 2004, the government passed a law prohibiting farmers whose land had been seized from claiming their equipment. This law was aimed at seizing tractors needed for commercial farming. Five individuals were subsequently charged with smuggling farm equipment into neighboring Zambia. A number of white farmers have relocated to that country.[43]

In 2005, land seizures occurred for the first time in urban areas. Between May and July 2005, the government destroyed tens of thousands of shanty dwellings and street stalls in a Harare suburb. The informal settlements had been built on land previously seized from white farmers. The government stated that the purpose of the land clearance was to clean Harare of its slums and reduce crime.[44] The area was not generally considered an opposition stronghold as many ZANU–PF supporters had settled there, so independent observers differ on whether the government actions also had underlying political and economic motivations. Demolitions of township settlements were not limited to Harare but also occurred in Bulawayo, the second-largest city, and throughout the country.

A report compiled by the UN Secretary-General's special envoy Anna Tibaijuka, who conducted a fact-finding mission to Zimbabwe, estimates that the government's Operation Murambatsvina (variously translated

Operation Restore Hope or Operation Clear the Filth) left approximately 700,000 people homeless. Around 2.4 million people—some 18 percent of the population—have been affected directly or indirectly by the land clearance.[45] Human rights organizations report that evicted residents were frequently beaten by police and moved to rural areas;[46] some residents were also arbitrarily arrested, detained, and fined during the forced evictions.[47] Human Rights Watch reports that Operation Murambatsvina has disproportionately affected women, children, foreign-born persons, and people with HIV/AIDS, who are the more vulnerable groups in society. The government refused subsequent UN offers to erect temporary tents or more permanent homes, claiming they were un-African.

Recommendations
- The government must strengthen the independence of the judiciary through guarantees of security, increased pay, and appointment of qualified judges who are not politically biased in favor of ZANU–PF.
- All forced evictions and destruction of lawful enterprises must end.
- Just and timely legal procedures must be provided for those displaced to seek legal redress for loss of property. This includes the repeal of the 2005 constitutional amendment that permits the confiscation of land without legal recourse.
- Domestic and international organizations must be allowed access to populations under duress for food assessment, emergency relief, and long-term development.

ANTICORRUPTION AND TRANSPARENCY – 0.88

Since independence, the government has pursued import-substitution policies, shielding the country from imports through price controls, tariffs, and licensing. These licenses allowed profitable rent-seeking opportunities for ruling-party supporters. The government also purchased private companies as a way to boost black employment prospects. The government borrowed money to finance ailing state-owned corporations, fund social programs, and increase the size of the military. Unable to repay, Zimbabwe was cut off from private capital and sought funding from the IMF, which attached conditions to its loans.

For the past two years the IMF has warned Zimbabwe that its failure to pay past arrears on previous loans would lead to its expulsion from the organization. A last-minute payment in September 2005 averted expulsion, but there was uncertainty over the source of foreign exchange used to make this payment. The IMF subsequently announced it would visit Zimbabwe to investigate the source of the funds.[49]

The IMF reports some recent progress in government reduction of price controls but notes that the Grain Marketing Board has not been dismantled.[50] The Zimbabwean government has been addressing the differences between the official and black-market exchange rates in two ways: police crackdown and deregulation. In 2005, Operation No Going Back enforced a ban on street vendors and black marketers in the cities. In Harare, for example, police announced the arrest of 134 people for allegedly dealing in foreign currency.[51] The Reserve Bank of Zimbabwe in October 2005 deregulated the foreign exchange market, which led to rapid depreciation in the value of the Zimbabwean dollar. Official rates were approximately 56,000 to the dollar, as compared to about 5,000 to the dollar in the prior year.[52] Black-market rates for the Zimbabwean dollar as of late 2005 were approximately 90,000 to 100,000 to the U.S. dollar.[53] Inflation is increasing rapidly. In September, the inflation rate had jumped to 360 percent from an annual rate of 265 percent the previous month.[54]

The seizure of commercial farms has caused farm employment to tumble, throwing hundreds of thousands out of work and leading to food shortages. International donors estimate that up to half the population needs food aid, a figure the government disputes.[55] Foreign exchange earnings, heavily dependent on agricultural exports, have collapsed, leading to shortages of hard currency. In the past year, the government also has demolished thousands of informal businesses as part of both Operation No Going Back and Operation Clear the Filth. According to the IMF, these informal businesses arose as a result of excessive state regulation.[56] The government is now considering taking control of the mining industry. As a result of political turmoil and poor economic policies, Zimbabwe's economy has contracted in each of the past eight years. Not coincidentally, Zimbabwe has experienced emigration to neighboring states and Britain. Population figures from the 2002 census show an unexplained shortfall of about 2.5 million people out of a population of 11.6 million. While some of the population loss may be attributed to the negative impact of the AIDS pandemic on life expectancies, other countries have confirmed large influxes of Zimbabweans.[57]

The primary interest of the Mugabe government is to retain power through a system of patronage that includes access to both state and private assets. The ruling ZANU–PF party owns a wide range of businesses, allowing party elites to profit personally. ZANU–PF refuses to open the books on these companies. Private farmland confiscated from former owners has been redistributed to party leaders. The government discloses few financial details that would make its operations more transparent and help avoid any possible conflict of interest on the part of public officials. The assets of some public officials—large houses and properties—would suggest income beyond a government salary, but no financial disclosures are available to assess whether the assets were obtained in a lawful or unlawful manner.

The Zimbabwean government does not currently have an effective legislative or administrative process that promotes integrity and punishes corruption. The result is relatively high levels of corruption. Political leaders are occasionally prosecuted for corruption, but this seems related to political intrigues within the ruling circles.[58] In mid-2004, for example, the government began a corruption probe into the commercial operations of ZANU–PF. Former army officer General Solomon Mujuru focused his attention on parliamentary Speaker Emmerson Mnangagwa, who as secretary for administration was seen as responsible for ZANU–PF finances. Many political observers, however, speculated that the real reason for the investigation was to sideline Mnangagwa from possible presidential ambitions as a successor to Mugabe.[59] In Transparency International's 2005 Corruption Perceptions Index (CPI), Zimbabwe scored 2.6 out of a possible top score of 10.[60]

The deteriorating economy has negatively affected education in Zimbabwe. Pay for lecturers has lagged, increasing the opportunities for corruption and graft through the taking of bribes for admission and grades. School enrollment has fallen to less than 60 percent as Zimbabweans are increasingly unable to afford school fees. Private schools that attempted to increase their fees in response to the spiraling inflation rate were branded racist by Mugabe. Many were closed. State schools, however, were allowed to raise their rates between 200 and 2,000 percent.[61]

It is not clear whether the government and the tax administrator operate effective internal audit systems to ensure accountability of expenditure and tax collection. Given the relatively high levels of corruption in the government, lower level officials have ample incentives for both graft and its concealment. Investigative and auditing bodies do exist, but they are hampered by political pressure. Furthermore, the details of the investigative process are not always transparent.

Allegations of corruption are given wide but biased attention in the state-owned news media if it serves government interests. The lack of government transparency and an independent media make it difficult to detect cases of procurement corruption, bribes, and kickbacks. Mugabe's nephew, for example, was accused in October 2005 of illegally smuggling 30 tons of flour to neighboring Mozambique in 2003. Leo Mugabe, a ZANU–PF MP, and his wife were charged with contravening the Grain Marketing Board Act and the Customs and Excise Duty Act. His case, which received prominent coverage in the media, was eventually dropped for lack of evidence.[62]

Although anticorruption legislation and mechanisms exist through the Prevention of Corruption Act, the legal environment is generally not supportive of investigators seeking to report cases of bribery and corruption. Cases of alleged corruption have often not been pursued by the police. A 10 percent reward for whistle-blowers for recovery of funds has been stymied in bureaucracy and has merely made detection of corrupt officials more difficult.

There is a degree of legal, regulatory, and judicial transparency. The budget and other kinds of information are published. The budget is presented to parliament for questioning and approval. However, the executive has, in the past, provided figures on expected revenues and expenses that were inaccurate. No independent parliamentary audit body exists to analyze the executive's budget figures and assumptions. As Mugabe's ZANU–PF party holds a majority in the parliament, approval is normal. AIPPA allows the government to restrict access to information held by public bodies. The Defense Procurement Act allows the government to withhold important financial records from the public. The cost of the purchase of military and related equipment from China in 2004, for example, was not disclosed.

The Procurement Act makes collusion among government contractors and providers of goods or services illegal. The president can, however, limit the act at his discretion. The government's State Procurement

Board is required to invite bids from both local and international entities, but foreign firms and governments have complained of an alleged lack of transparency and fairness in the process. In some cases, contracts have been awarded to local suppliers with higher bids than foreign firms.[63]

The European Union, the United States, and Great Britain have imposed sanctions on Zimbabwe due to a number of Mugabe's policies, including his controversial land seizures, economic policies, flawed elections, and prior military intervention in Congo-Kinshasa. At this time Zimbabwe receives no foreign assistance from these states and organizations except for emergency food aid. Allegations of bias in the government's distribution of international food aid are widespread; the state denies that it politicizes the aid by giving preference to political supporters. Zimbabwe is facing severe famine due to the collapse of the farming sector through commercial farm land seizures and a drought.

Recommendations

- The government should disband the Grain Marketing Board so as to allow market forces to boost production without opportunities for rent-seeking behavior by politically well-connected individuals.
- ZANU–PF must be divested of its corporations, and the government should privatize state-owned companies.
- Anticorruption protocols of the Southern African Development Community (SADC) must be implemented.
- All budget items—including defense-related expenditures—must be published and verified by an outside auditor who is free from political influence.
- Official statements of public income and net worth should be published for all elected and high-level appointed officials. Submitting deliberately inaccurate statements should be a criminal offense.

NOTES

[1] *Playing with Fire: Personal accounts of human rights abuses experienced by 50 opposition Members of Parliament in Zimbabwe, and 28 opposition election candidates* (Johannesburg: The Zimbabwe Institute, March 2004), http://www.mdczimbabwe.org/Violence/violence.htm.

2 *Election Update 2005: Zimbabwe,* No 3, EISA (Johannesburg, South Africa, 25 April 2005), http://www.eisa.org.za/PDF/eu200503zim.pdf.

3 Itai Mushekwe, "Implement ZANU-PF directives, Manyika tells parastatal heads," *Zimbabwe Independent,* 23 September 2005, http://www.theindependent.co.zw/news/2005/September/Friday23/3244.html.

4 "Statement on the Occasion of Human Rights Day by Participants in the African Civil Society Consultation on Zimbabwe" (New York: Human Rights First [formerly The Lawyers Committee for Human Rights], 8 December 2004), http://www.humanrights first.org/defenders/hrd_zimbabwe/hrd_zim_18.htm.

5 Caiphas Chimhete, "Mugabe refuses to sign NGOs Bill" (Washington, D.C.: International Center for Not-For-Profit Law, news release, 15 April 2005), http://www.icnl.org/PRESS/Articles/2005/20050415a.htm.

6 *Cases 2005: Africa: Zimbabwe* (New York: Committee to Protect Journalists [CPJ], 14 February 2005), http://www.cpj.org/cases05/africa_cases05/zim.html.

7 *Zimbabwe - Annual Report 2005* (Paris: Reporters Without Borders [RSF], 3 May 2005), http://www.rsf.org/print.php3?id_article=13575.

8 Robyn Curnow, "'Long arm' of the government threatens media in Zimbabwe," *The International Herald Tribune,* 2 May 2005, http://www.iht.com/articles/2005/05/01/business/zim02.php.

9 "Zimbabwe private radio 'jammed,'" BBC News, 14 March 2005, http://news.bbc.co.uk/2/hi/africa/4346971.stm.

10 "Fourteen arrested for circulating e-mail message criticizing Mugabe" (RSF, 22 June 2004), http://www.rsf.org/print.php3?id_article=10710.

11 "Internet firms asked to spy on customers" (RSF, 4 June 2004), http://www.rsf.org/article.php3?id_article=10551.

12 "When laughter gets you locked up: Protest art in Zimbabwe," *The Economist,* 8 November 2003, 105.

13 "US film 'attacks' Zimbabwe," News24.com, 3 September 2005, http://www.news24.com/News24/Entertainment/Abroad/0,,2-1225-1243_1764593,00.html.

14 "Zimbabwe: Constitutional reform—an opportunity to strengthen human rights protection" (London: Amnesty International [AI], 2 February 2000), http://web.amnesty.org/library/index/ENGAFR460012000.

15 "Under a Shadow: Civil and Political Rights in Zimbabwe, A Human Rights Watch Briefing Paper" (New York: Human Rights Watch [HRW], 6 June 2003), http://www.hrw.org/backgrounder/africa/zimbabwe060603.htm#4.

16 *2005 Report on Zimbabwe, Covering Events from January to December 2004* (AI, 2005), http://web.amnesty.org/report2005/zwe-summary-eng.

17 *Zimbabwe: Covering Events from January to December 2004* (AI, 2005), Ibid.

18 Hilary Andersson, "Zimbabwe's torture training camps," BBC News, 27 February 2004, http://news.bbc.co.uk/2/hi/africa/3493958.stm.

19 "'No bail' bill passed in Zimbabwe," BBC News, 16 February 2004, http://news.bbc.co.uk/go/pr/fr/-/2/hi/world/africa/3493013.stm.

20 "'Jail Hell' over for Zimbabwe MP," BBC News, 28 June 2005, http://news.bbc.co.uk/go/pr/fr/-/2/hi/africa/4630683.stm.

21 Justin Pearce, "Zimbabwe's unwanted 'foreigners,'" BBC News, 25 August 2005, http://news.bbc.co.uk/go/pr/fr/-/2/hi/africa/4177222.stm.

22 Ethnologue 2003 (Dallas, Texas: SIL International), http://www.sil.org/; "Harare Declaration" (Harare, Zimbabwe: Intergovernmental Conference of Ministers on Language Policy, March 1997, http://www.bisharat.net/Documents/Harare97Declaration.htm.

23 "Divided we rule; Zimbabwe," *The Economist,* 15 January 2005, 52.

24 "Bishop slams Zimbabwe food claims," BBC News, 13 May 2004, http://news.bbc.co.uk/go/pr/fr/-/2/hi/africa/3711153.stm.

25 *Zimbabwe: Covering Events from January to December 2004* (AI, 2005), http://web.amnesty.org/web/web.nsf/print/B2454CF9631E895A80256FE4005EB10B.

26 "Zimbabwe: Gov't boosts spending on disabled," IRINNews.org, 2 March 2004, http://www.irinnews.org/report.asp?ReportID=39789&SelectRegion=Southern_Africa&SelectCountry=ZIMBABWE&ARG2=57658.

27 Constitution of Zimbabwe, Amendment (No. 17) Act, 2005, http://www.kubatana.net/docs/legisl/constitution_zim_amd17_050916_act.pdf.

28 "Zimbabwe Judge Slams Police," BBC News, 6 August 2004, http://news.bbc.co.uk/go/pr/fr/-/2/hi/world/africa/3541008.stm.

29 Personal interview with NGO country director who works with political opposition parties in Zimbabwe, 12 November 2005.

30 "Zimbabwe Activists Win Reprieve," BBC News, 21 November 2003, http://news.bbc.co.uk/go/pr/fr/-/2/hi/world/africa/3225682.stm.

31 "Zimbabwe Police Detain Union Leaders," CBS News, 9 November 2005, http://www.cbsnews.com/stories/2005/11/09/ap/world/mainD8DOKR583.shtml.

32 "Zimbabwe MP Held for Fuel Protest," BBC News, 6 October 2005, http://news.bbc.co.uk/go/pr/fr/-/2/hi/world/africa/4315180.stm.

33 "Zimbabwe Judge Slams Police," BBC News.

34 Joseph Winter, "Zimbabwe Judges Under Pressure," BBC News, 15 October 2004, http://news.bbc.co.uk/go/pr/fr/-/2/hi/world/africa/3743990.stm.

35 "Zimbabwe's Judges 'Going Hungry,'" BBC News, 31 October 2005, http://news.bbc.co.uk/go/pr/fr/-/2/hi/world/africa/4394102.stm.

36 "Zimbabwe Judge Slams Police," BBC News.

37 Personal interview with NGO country director who works with political opposition parties in Zimbabwe, 12 November 2005.

38 "'No Bail' Bill Passed in Zimbabwe," BBC News.

39 Violet Gonda, "Allegations that James Makamba seeks asylum in the UK," SW Radio Africa Zimbabwe, news, 15 September 2005, http://www.swradioafrica.com/news150905/makamba150905.htm.

40 "Zimbabwe Set to Nationalise Land," BBC News, 30 May 2005, http://news.bbc.co.uk/go/pr/fr/-/2/hi/world/africa/4593543.stm.

41 *Blood and Soil: Land, Politics and Conflict Prevention in Zimbabwe and South Africa* (Brussels: International Crisis Group, Africa Report No. 85, 17 September 2004), 12–13, http://www.crisisgroup.org/library/documents/africa/southern_africa/land_reform/contents_foreword_and_executive_summary.pdf.

[42] "Mugabe to Seek Mining Shares," BBC News, 14 September 2004, http://news.bbc.co.uk/go/pr/fr/-/2/hi/world/africa/3657116.stm.

[43] "Zimbabwe Judge Slams Police," BBC News.

[44] Joseph Winter, "What Lies Behind the Zimbabwe Demolitions?" BBC News, 26 July 2005, http://news.bbc.co.uk/1/hi/world/africa/4101228.stm.

[45] Anna Kajumulo Tibaijuka, *Report of the Fact-Finding Mission to Zimbabwe to Assess the Scope and Impact of Operation Murambatsvina by the UN Special Envoy on Human Settlements Issues in Zimbabwe* (New York: United Nations, 18 July 2005), http://www.unhabitat.org/documents/ZimbabweReport.pdf.

[46] "Joint Statement" (AI, the Centre on Housing Rights and Evictions [COHRE], and Zimbabwe Lawyers for Human Rights, 23 June 2005), http://www.humanrightsfirst.org/defenders/hrd_zimbabwe/forced-evict-062205.pdf.

[47] "Joint Statement" (AI, the Centre on Housing Rights and Evictions [COHRE], and Zimbabwe Lawyers for Human Rights, 23 June 2005), http://www.humanrightsfirst.org/defenders/hrd_zimbabwe/forced-evict-062205.pdf.

[48] "Zimbabwe: Mass Evictions Lead to Massive Abuses" (HRW).

[49] Shakeman Mugari, "IMF to probe Zim's source of debt funds," *Zimbabwe Independent,* 21 October 2005, http://www.theindependent.co.zw/news/2005/October/Friday21/3424.html.

[50] *Zimbabwe: Staff Report for the 2004 Article IV Consultation* (International Monetary Fund [IMF], 10 June 2004), http://66.102.7.104/search?q=cache:zix2nGf3FUMJ:www.sarpn.org.za/documents/d0001643/P1991-IMF_Zim-report_Oct2005.pdf+International+Monetary+Fund,+Zimbabwe:+Staff+Report+for+the+2004+Article+IV+Consultation&hl=en.

[51] "Illegal forex dealers nabbed," *South African Press Association,* 9 October 2005, http://www.fin24.co.za/articles/economy/display_article.asp?ArticleID=1518-25_1813813.

[52] "Africa – Currency Exchange Rates," *Mbendi,* http://www.mbendi.co.za/cyexch.htm.

[53] "Forex Barons Wrecking Economy," *Herald* (Harare), 13 November 2005, http://allafrica.com/stories/printable/200511140811.html.

[54] "Zim inflation jumps to 359.8%," *South African Press Association,* 10 October 2005, http://www.fin24.co.za/articles/economy/display_article.asp?ArticleID=1518-25_1814403.

[55] *The Politics of Food Assistance in Zimbabwe: A Human Rights Briefing Paper* (HRW, 12 August 2004), http://www.hrw.org/backgrounder/africa/zimbabwe/2004/.

[56] "Public Information Notice" (IMF, PIN 04/104, 17 September 2004), http://www.imf.org/external/np/sec/pn/2004/pn04104.htm.

[57] "Where have all the people gone? Zimbabwe," *The Economist,* 27 November 2004, 70.

[58] "Banking breakdowns," *Africa Confidential* 45, 2 (23 January 2004).

[59] "Gunning for Mnangagwa," *Africa Confidential* 45, 8 (16 April 2004)..

[60] *"Corruption Perceptions Index 2005"* (Berlin: Transparency International [TI], 18 October 2005), http://www.transparency.org/surveys/index.html#cpi.

[61] Joseph Winter, "The Rise and Fall of Zimbabwe's Schools," BBC News, 7 May 2004, http://news.bbc.co.uk/go/pr/fr/-/2/hi/world/africa/3693857.stm.

62 Lebo Nkatazo, "Mugabe's nephew cleared of corruption," *newzimbabwe.com*, 16 November 2005, http://www.newzimbabwe.com/pages/leo4.13469.html.

63 *Zimbabwe Report 2003* (Executive Office of the President of the USA, Office of the U.S. Trade Representative, 31 March 2003), http://www.ustr.gov/assets/Document_Library/Reports_Publications/2003/2003_NTE_Report/asset_upload_file492_6234.pdf.

APPENDIX 1
RECOMMENDATIONS PROGRESS REPORT

This appendix is intended to serve as a progress report on all recommendations issued in the 2004 edition of *Countries at the Crossroads.* We have asked the analysts for the countries featured in both the 2004 and 2006 editions to provide an update on each 2004 recommendation, briefly conveying whether any progress was achieved in the two-year period as well as the extent to which the governments have made an effort to reach these goals.

While the countries' records are mixed, the appendix illustrates that, in many areas in which the need for reform is most urgent, the government has taken no action at all. In other cases, it is evident that needed draft laws have been proposed but not ratified, implemented, or enforced, thus rendering such efforts largely ineffective.

We hope that this progress report will provide policy makers, government officials, and members of the media with a useful tool for identifying those issues of lasting concern in the surveyed countries as well as recognizing where progress has, in fact, been made.

ARMENIA

Accountability and Public Voice

2004: The government should implement electoral laws already on paper; measures against electoral fraud need to be strictly enforced.
2006: The November 2005 constitutional referendum suggests that Armenia's ruling elite remains unwilling to commit to these goals.

2004: The ruling elites should stop using government resources for their election campaigns.
2006: The regime again resorted to this practice in the run-up to the referendum.

2004: The authorities must give up their de facto control over electronic media by amending the broadcasting legislation and lifting the ban on A1+.

2006: The ban on A1+ has not been lifted. The amended constitution contains provisions that could make a state body granting and revoking broadcasting licenses more independent, but it will be several years before these provisions take effect.

2004: Libel should be regulated by civil, not criminal law.
2006: Libel is still regulated by criminal law.

Civil Liberties

2004: Armenia's political leadership must take real steps to eliminate the widespread ill-treatment of criminal suspects in custody.
2006: The government has taken no action in this area.

2004: Security officials guilty of human rights abuses must face punishment. Jail terms for such crimes must be lengthier. Armenian courts must stop ignoring defendants' claims of physical abuse.
2006: The government has taken no action in this area.

2004: Reform of Armenia's code of administrative offenses, which has proved to be a powerful tool for political repression, is urgently needed. The authorities should draw up a new code from scratch and avoid enforcing controversial provisions of the existing one in the interim.
2006: The Soviet-era code remains in force, and the authorities continue to apply it arbitrarily.

Rule of Law

2004: Armenia's parliament should be given the authority to confirm or block judicial appointments made by the president. This will require corresponding changes to the constitution.
2006: No such changes have been made in the constitution.

2004: The president should be stripped of his constitutional right to sack virtually all judges.
2006: The constitution has been amended to restrict this authority.

2004: Armenia should enhance judicial oversight of criminal investigations conducted by police and prosecutors. The courts must stop rubber-stamping practically all pretrial detentions requested by the prosecutors.
2006: The government does not seem to have done anything to make the courts less subservient to the prosecutors.

2004: Legal amendments are needed to bring the system of criminal justice, still based on Soviet-era practices, closer to Western standards.
2006: The corresponding constitutional amendments are a step in the right direction but unlikely to be sufficient.

2004: The government must work harder to combat the rampant corruption in the judiciary and law enforcement agencies.
2006: The government has taken no action in this area.

Anticorruption and Transparency

2004: The authorities must fight corruption in earnest. That means investigating and punishing corrupt government officials regardless of their position and political connections. All necessary laws are in place, but they need to be enforced. Any anticorruption drive must encompass the law enforcement agencies, where graft is rampant and particularly damaging to public confidence.
2006: The government has taken no action in this area.

2004: Parliament should pass stronger legislation to combat illegal practices, including a law on conflict of interest. Also, the existing law on financial disclosure must be amended to allow for the verification of officials' financial statements.
2006: No such legislation has been passed by parliament.

2004: The Audit Chamber should be given more powers to inspect any government agency. Its critical findings should automatically entail parliamentary and/or criminal inquiries.
2006: The chamber remains hamstrung by a lack of authority and remains susceptible to political pressure from parliament leadership.

2004: Government bodies should become more open to the media. A freedom of information law would be very useful.
2006: Such a law has been enacted, but its positive impact on government transparency has not become visible yet.

AZERBAIJAN

Accountability and Public Voice

2004: The government must engage in meaningful consultation with the civic sector in a more open political space.

2006: No action has been taken.

2004: Election observers' monitoring practices should be brought into line with Council of Europe standards. Toward this end, the government should remove the ban on election monitoring for local NGOs that receive financial support from international sources.
2006: The government removed the ban shortly in advance of the 2005 parliamentary elections, which was a positive step. In the future, the authorities must ensure that independent NGOs can monitor the election process without interference.

2004: The government should take steps to bring fairness to the composition of the Central Election Commission, which now disproportionately weights its membership toward the ruling YAP party.
2006: No action has been taken.

2004: Measures should be taken to reform and render television and radio licensing procedures more transparent, including the formation of a board not appointed or otherwise controlled by the president to oversee such licensing.
2006: No action has been taken.

2004: The state should ensure that public television and radio meet appropriate standards of programming independence under the direction of a politically diverse board of eminent persons from the broad political spectrum, including opposition figures.
2006: Azerbaijan's first public-service broadcasting channel (ITV) came into being in August 2005, three months before the 2005 parliamentary elections. Candidates did have more free airtime than in past election cycles, a welcome step that should be institutionalized going forward. However, the imbalance in the composition of the nine-member public broadcasting steering committee that oversees programming content and strategy raises serious questions as to whether ITV can fulfill its promise as a truly independent voice in Azerbaijan's media.

Civil Liberties

2004: The authorities must ease the profound institutional control that cuts across all sectors of Azerbaijani society. A major step in this regard would be support for a more resilient civil society, from both the Azer-

baijani authorities and the international donor community, with a goal of broader and more meaningful political participation.
2006: No action has been taken.

2004: The government should facilitate and encourage smoother registration and compliance procedures for NGOs.
2006: While the Ministry of Justice's response time to NGO applications has improved since the law on the registration of legal entities was passed in 2003, questions remain about the fairness with which NGO applications are evaluated and the basis on which registration is denied.

2004: The authorities should make needed amendments to national legislation with respect to countertrafficking measures, particularly in devising aggressive state policies against trafficking and eliminating contradictions between the constitution and the criminal code, which impede implementation of international treaties at the national level.
2006: In June 2005, Azerbaijan's parliament adopted a law on fighting human trafficking, which included provisions for appointment of a new national coordinator empowered to oversee the establishment of several special rehabilitation centers designed to aid victims of human trafficking. These and other provisions of the law need to be fully implemented.

Rule of Law

2004: The judicial selection process should be reformed in accordance with the requirements of Azerbaijan's membership in the Council of Europe.
2006: In 2005, the authorities established a new system for testing and approving judges and approved the first class of judges under this new system, which contains a range of safeguards.

2004: An independent, self-governing bar association, as envisioned in legislation passed in 1999, should be created.
2006: No action has been taken.

2004: Steps to enhance judicial independence and transparency are crucial. Toward this end, resources should be devoted to increased staffing and to case-tracking systems that would make information available for public records.
2006: No action has been taken.

Anticorruption and Transparency

2004: To combat the pervasiveness of official corruption, the government should make a priority of passing the Draft Law on Corruption and ensure that its provisions are implemented once in force.
2006: A law on combating corruption was adopted in January 2004. However, the authorities have yet to implement the range of provisions contained in this law.

2004: To bring greater integrity to the election process, candidates for public office should comply with the letter and the spirit of the election code's provisions requiring financial declarations, and noncompliance should bring swift and certain consequences.
2006: No action has been taken.

BAHRAIN

Accountability and Public Voice

2004: The government needs to end all policies that dilute or skew the electoral process. In particular, the ongoing practice of granting voting rights to a select group of non-Bahrainis with close ties to the regime should be replaced with a nondiscriminatory and transparent process of conferring naturalization and full citizenship rights on a broad spectrum of long-term residents in the country.
2006: The government has taken no steps to address this issue, although the National Assembly has begun to discuss the problem of political naturalization in a serious fashion.

2004: The government of Bahrain should continue to make high-ranking officials available to the local press.
2006: Official press briefings and question-and-answer sessions continue to take place on a regular basis.

2004: The international community should actively intervene on behalf of reporters and editors who face civil or criminal charges for writing or publishing reports that are factually true yet politically sensitive or otherwise unflattering to the regime.
2006: Various civic groups have written letters to the Bahraini government regarding specific cases but no such active intervention by the international community has occurred.

2004: The Kingdom of Bahrain should rescind the restrictive Press and Publications Law of 2002 and replace it with regulatory legislation drafted by the national assembly, in consultation with professional journalists, human rights organizations, and press freedom groups.
2006: The 2002 Press and Publications Law remains in force.

Civil Liberties

2004: The regime must uphold its commitment to liberal principles and follow through with political and legal reforms.
2006: Progress toward political liberalization has slowed markedly, although municipal and parliamentary elections are scheduled to take place in May and October 2006.

2004: Police and intelligence service personnel should be trained to recognize and accept civil liberties as a matter of general principle. Officers who develop and implement ways to respond to nonviolent public demonstrations without the use of excessive force should be rewarded.
2006: Police response to popular demonstrations has become less brutal, although this trend does not appear to have been codified.

2004: Ambiguity concerning the legality of exiling political dissidents needs to be clarified.
2006: While exile is not currently being used to punish political dissidents, the issue remains legally ambiguous. The amended constitution of 2002 protects citizens from any imposed limitations on their freedom of movement but does not explicitly guarantee that Bahraini citizens will not be forced into exile.

2004: Contradictions regarding family and personal status law between state and religious courts, particularly with respect to women, must be resolved.
2006: Such contradictions persist, and women are routinely treated differently from men in both civil and religious court proceedings.

2004: The government should expand both educational and employment opportunities and social services for the most disadvantaged groups in Bahraini society and recognize the dangers inherent in situations in which opulent wealth and conspicuous consumption exist alongside widespread poverty and despair.

2006: High levels of unemployment and restricted educational opportunities continue to plague the local Shiite community.

2004: The government must rescind Decree Number 56 (granting blanket immunity from criminal and civil prosecution to any official suspected of inflicting torture or otherwise violating human rights in the past) and thoroughly investigate and punish perpetrators of torture.
2006: Decree Number 56 remains in force.

Rule of Law

2004: The government of Bahrain must create a coherent network of judicial institutions that replaces arbitrary procedures, deliberations, and rulings with predictable, transparent, and routine proceedings.
2006: Uncertainty continues to pervade the operations and deliberations of the judicial system, which remains divided into two separate branches (the civil law courts and the Sharia courts).

2004: Judges and public prosecutors who hold their positions due to personal ties to the ruling family should be replaced with professional jurists who have completed formal education in the law.
2006: The legal system remains firmly in the hands of senior members of the ruling family, and the king maintains the right to appoint all judges by royal decree.

2004: Private property rights must be codified and respected, and long-standing forms of community property should be legally defined and registered in ways that protect them from abrupt confiscation.
2006: The government has taken no steps in this direction.

Anticorruption and Transparency

2004: The government of Bahrain should act in accordance with the terms of the National Action Charter and take concrete steps to heighten the transparency of all contracts and agreements drawn up by state agencies.
2006: State officials have done little to heighten the transparency of contracts and agreements, although the National Assembly has begun to discuss such measures.

2004: Financial and administrative auditing and monitoring structures that are envisaged in law should be rapidly created, operate transparently, and be allocated sufficient resources to conduct thorough investigations.
2006: Auditing of government operations remains rudimentary.

CAMBODIA

Accountability and Public Voice

2004: The government should end election violence and intimidation, guarantee candidates equal and fair news coverage, and ensure the unbiased dissemination of information by village chiefs.
2006: The government has taken no action in this area; however, no elections were held in the surveyed period.

2004: Electoral reform needs to continue, particularly improvement of registration and complaints processes, as well as reform of the NEC and its provincial counterparts.
2006: The government has taken no action in this area.

2004: Voter education should be strengthened emphasizing the role of elections and the legislature, appropriate official complaints channels, and the rights and responsibilities of voters.
2006: The government has facilitated international assistance in this area, including voter education and the strengthening of domestic election monitoring capacity.

2004: The government should take measures to improve government accountability and transparency, including establishing regular channels for government dialogue with civil society on policy making, merit-based civil service appointments, and assistance to strengthen the monitoring role of the National Assembly.
2006: The government has facilitated internationally funded programs to strengthen the technical capacity of the National Assembly and reform the civil service but has not established regular dialogue with civil society organizations.

2004: The government must desist from interfering with and intimidating the media and ensure that media licensing procedures are not subject to bias.

2006: The government has taken no action in this area.

Civil Liberties

2004: State leaders must make a genuine commitment to end impunity and to invest resources sufficient to promote change in state and social practices.
2006: The government has reiterated its commitment to ending impunity but has not matched such statements with substantive action.

2004: The government should fully and promptly investigate allegations of state torture and ensure appropriate prosecution and punishment, including through an effective Khmer Rouge Tribunal. Practical measures aimed at preventing torture are necessary, such as regular and independent prison inspections, guaranteed access to prisoners, and procedures to make evidence obtained through torture inadmissible in court.
2006: The government has made progress toward establishing the Khmer Rouge Tribunal but has not implemented effective systems to prevent or investigate torture.

2004: Police and prison detention conditions must be improved, including food, clothing, and health care.
2006: The government has facilitated some international assistance to improve prison conditions and engaged in dialogue with international partners on prison reform but has not significantly improved conditions in detention.

2004: Greater efforts should be made to reduce discrimination against women and ethnic minorities, particularly Vietnamese.
2006: The government has continued efforts to better integrate gender issues into government policy formulation and has enacted a Law on Domestic Violence but has not taken steps to ameliorate discrimination against ethnic Vietnamese.

2004: Efforts to combat human trafficking and the sexual and commercial exploitation of women and children need to be increased.
2006: Despite continued statements of commitment, the government has not stepped up efforts in this area.

Rule of Law

2004: State leaders must commit themselves to ending executive interference in the judiciary.
2006: The government has taken no action in this area.

2004: The government should upgrade the legal framework by enacting the draft penal code, code on criminal procedure, civil code and code on civil procedure, and subsidiary regulations.
2006: The government committed itself at the December 2004 Consultative Group meeting to enacting these laws but has made little progress toward this end.

2004: The government should expedite the structural reform of judicial institutions, including amending laws to clarify the organization and functioning of courts.
2006: The government has committed itself to amending the Organic Law on the Organization and Functioning of the Courts, which is still under revision by the Ministry of Justice.

2004: Judicial professionalism should be improved, including through training to improve trial procedures.
2006: The government has taken steps to improve training for judicial officials, including the establishment of a Royal School of Judges and Prosecutors in November 2003.

2004: Judicial corruption must be addressed, including through the establishment of an independent anticorruption commission; support for independent monitoring of the judiciary; improved transparency of criminal processes, including mandated presence of lawyers for the accused and prohibition of trial judges' reviewing evidence prior to trials; and strengthening the ability of the judiciary to resist corruption through improved personal security and adequate remuneration.
2006: The government has taken no action in this area.

2004: Access to justice should be improved through the establishment of a state-funded legal aid program.
2006: The government has taken no action in this area.

Anticorruption and Transparency

2004: The government should seek to end the culture of impunity by imposing stiff anticorruption measures, such as enacting laws on anticorruption, assets declaration, and conflict of interest; establishing an independent anticorruption commission; ensuring the independence of the National Audit Authority (NAA) and strengthening its technical capacity; and prioritizing the establishment of an independent ombudsman's office.

2006: The government has made further, slow progress on the draft anticorruption law, which would establish an anticorruption commission, and the technical capacity of the NAA has been improved through international assistance.

2004: The civil service needs reform, including increased salaries and extensive education to change entrenched behavior. This can be funded by a streamlining of the civil service and by foreign aid.

2006: The government has continued to make incremental progress toward civil service reform, with international assistance.

2004: The parliamentary processes should be improved, especially with respect to the capacity of the legislature to monitor government performance and conduct meaningful dialogue with constituents.

2006: Efforts to strengthen the capacity of the National Assembly to monitor government performance have continued with international assistance. Capacity remains weak, however, and processes to ensure meaningful interaction with constituents have not been implemented.

2004: Public finance reform should continue, particularly of public procurement and budget reconciliation procedures.

2006: The government has continued to make incremental progress in this area, with international assistance.

2004: Access to information needs improvement, including through enacting freedom of information legislation and strengthening the information infrastructure.

2006: At the 2004 Consultative Group meeting, the government committed itself to preparing a legislative framework to facilitate access to state information and to improve access to information but has not yet demonstrated progress in either area.

EAST TIMOR

Accountability and Public Voice

2004: Top priority must be given to setting a date, or date range, for the first parliamentary election and to passing laws to govern the electoral process.
2006: Elections have been set for 2007, but no such laws have been developed.

2004: The government should set up a professional independent body accountable to parliament to administer the election. The new election body should evaluate the previous election to highlight specific problems that need to be addressed.
2006: Electoral authority has been established under the State Administration Ministry, answerable to the minister.

2004: East Timor's leaders must be extremely vigilant about their conduct and their respect for separation of powers, the independence of the judiciary, and freedoms of speech and the media.
2006: The need for vigilance is ongoing.

2004: A journalists' media commission should be encouraged in order to provide a voice for the media, and laws to project journalists should be introduced.
2006: The government has proposed an amendment to the Penal Code that would criminalize defamation; the president can still veto the decree. The establishment of a media council is under active discussion.

Civil Liberties

2004: More steps are needed to reduce detentions, including a systematic review of existing prisoners and expedited hearings for cases that have extended beyond a reasonable standard of detention.
2006: Improvements have been made, especially with 72-hour hearings. Yet further reforms are needed.

2004: In cooperation with civil society, the East Timor government should invest in workshops to promote mutual understanding among ethnic groups to reduce future conflict and address existing prejudices.
2006: No government workshops have been held on ethnic conflict, and the issue is not seen as an immediate priority.

2004: Police officers and military forces should have human rights training and greater exposure to professional security forces.
2006: The police and military have received human rights training, and exposure to international security forces is ongoing. Further methods of entrenching a human rights approach to policing must still be considered.

2004: More effort needs to be directed to educating the population on new laws, and incidents of bias need to be strongly condemned.
2006: The government has made no progress in this area.

Rule of Law

2004: Efforts should be made to address deficiencies in the legal sector, including inadequate language skills and professional training. Such efforts should include recruitment of additional prosecutors, training in administrative skills and records management, and increased funding for the Office of Public Defenders.
2006: Many measures are being implemented in the legal sector, and its deficiencies are recognized and being addressed gradually in partnership with donors.

2004: The East Timor government must improve legal representation for suspects through the expansion of legal aid programs.
2006: Public defenders are undergoing training.

2004: The use of Portuguese as the official language of the legal system— at least in the short term—should be reconsidered.
2006: This issue has not been reconsidered.

2004: International personnel should have a greater role in the judicial system on a temporary basis, and care should be taken to promote the transfer of skills to East Timorese.
2006: International judges, prosecutors, and legal advisers are assisting the legal system.

Anticorruption and Transparency

2004: The establishment of the constitutionally mandated ombudsman, or Provedor de Justiçia, and the resources necessary to support the office are urgently needed. If, as is the case in the judicial system, personnel are insufficiently trained, the government of East Timor should request

international assistance to help run the office of the ombudsman, with a special emphasis on training East Timorese as soon as possible.
2006: An ombudsman has been appointed, an office established, and staff training undertaken. International assistance is being provided to the office.

2004: The government should introduce tougher measures to address corruption and introduce protection for whistle-blowers.
2006: Anticorruption measures are being addressed but are not yet in place. No whistle-blower protection has been achieved.

2004: Open bidding should be used in all government contracts, and the terms of public contracts should be made available to the public.
2006: This goal has not yet been achieved.

2004: Strict measures should be introduced into the bureaucracy involving conflicts of interest and nepotism.
2006: This goal has not yet been achieved.

2004: The government should set up an anticorruption agency.
2006: Corruption is handled by the Office of the Inspector General and/or by the ombudsman.

GEORGIA

Accountability and Public Voice

2004: The government must ensure that serious past irregularities, including ballot-box stuffing and biased media coverage, are not repeated in future elections and that the results reflect the true will of the people.
2006: The January 2004 presidential and March 2004 parliamentary elections marked an improvement over the November 2003 elections in several respects, including progress in the administration of the election process, greater secrecy of the ballot, and efforts to increase the participation of national minorities.

2004: Greater participation of ethnic minorities and women in the political process should be encouraged through steps including improved availability and access to Georgian language courses for minorities and public education efforts for both groups.
2006: There has been some progress in this area. In addition to efforts to encourage national minorities to participate in the political process,

the government has created several initiatives including free language classes and the rebroadcasts of Georgian television news programs in translation.

2004: The government should take more active steps to ensure the independence of the country's media by, among other things, repealing libel and slander legislation used to intimidate journalists into not publishing reports critical of the government. In addition, the authorities must thoroughly investigate and pursue violence against journalists perpetrated by police and nonstate actors.

2006: Progress in this area has been limited. In June 2004, libel was decriminalized and the parliament passed the Law on Freedom of Speech and Expression, which shifted the burden of proof in defamation cases to the plaintiff. However, the government continues to exercise indirect control over the media, and journalists are still subjected to extralegal intimidation and violence.

Civil Liberties

2004: To help address the prevalence of ill-treatment of detainees and suspects by law-enforcement officials, victims should be given the opportunity to make complaints before a judge regarding torture during investigations.

2006: The government has taken several important steps to address torture and ill-treatment of detainees. For example, a measure was passed stipulating that testimonies obtained in pretrial detention could be used as evidence only if the defendant confirms their truthfulness in court.

2004: A law on religion should be adopted that would provide legal protections for all religious groups, and prompt legal action should be taken against those who attack members of minority faiths.

2006: No formal law has been adopted; however, the government has successfully prosecuted and convicted several individuals guilty of crimes against religious minority groups.

2004: Women who are victims of sexual assault or trafficking should have access to basic assistance services.

2006: No significant progress has been made in this area.

2004: The government should, when financially possible, provide members of minority ethnic groups with greater opportunities to learn Georgian and integrate more fully into Georgian society.

2006: The government has created several initiatives to this end, including rebroadcasts of Georgian television news programs in translation and free legal consultations for ethnic Armenian populations in certain regions.

Rule of Law

2004: The rule of law in Georgia must be strengthened by increasing the number of qualified judges and providing them with adequate and timely financial compensation to reduce instances of bribery.

2006: Some progress has been reported. Most notably, judges' salaries have been raised.

2004: Documented complaints of judicial corruption should be investigated by an independent body, and appropriate disciplinary measures should be taken.

2006: No significant improvement has been recorded.

2004: The rights of detainees should be enforced, including informing them promptly of the charges against them and providing them access to attorneys of their own choosing as required by law.

2006: Despite several legal provisions, the rights of detainees are still frequently abused.

2004: Courts should not be permitted to make convictions based on confessions that have been extracted under torture.

2006: New measures have been passed to tackle this issue. For example, testimonies obtained in pretrial detention can now be used as evidence only if the defendant confirms their truthfulness in the court. In addition, witness testimonies obtained outside the courtroom can now be read during a trial only if the witness agrees to it while in the court.

Anticorruption and Transparency

2004: Having recently established high-profile mechanisms to address the country's endemic corruption, the government must take further steps to produce concrete results, including implementing key recommendations of the anticorruption council. As part of this process, the internal auditing mechanisms of government agencies should be strengthened, and the tax code should be simplified to prevent confusion and opportunities for the exercise of undue discretion by tax and customs officials.

2006: The government has made notable progress in its attempts to combat corruption. For a more detailed description see the "Anticorruption and Transparency" section of the 2006 Georgia report.

2004: Adequate safeguards should be provided for whistle-blowers exposing corrupt activities, including witness-protection programs.

2006: The government has instituted certain protections for whistle-blowers through the Law on Freedom of Speech and Expression

2004: Widespread corruption in the educational system must be tackled through such measures as the adoption of standardized entrance examinations and increased government financing for state schools.

2006: The government recently introduced standardized university entrance exams, which are evaluated by independent agencies instead of universities, as was previously the case.

2004: Government accountability and transparency can be enhanced by providing the public with more comprehensive and timely information on draft legislation and policies.

2006: The government has taken limited steps in this direction, although some NGOs complain that the government still does not provide enough time for public discussion when important decisions are made.

GUATEMALA

Accountability and Public Voice

2004: The government needs to institute adequate campaign finance laws.

2006: Although the government has begun to tackle electoral reform, campaign finance laws have been set aside awaiting second-generation reforms expected in 2006.

2004: The government should do more to protect the freedom of speech. This requires a crackdown on clandestine groups that have targeted those committed to exposing abuses and pursuing justice.

2006: Harsh libel laws have been successfully challenged in the courts, contributing to the establishment of a climate more conducive to freedom of speech. Yet the government has done little to crack down on clandestine groups.

2004: Indigenous and women's groups are formulating concrete proposals designed to foster greater political participation. Enhanced government collaboration with these groups would help contribute to the expanded political participation of women and the Mayan population. **2006:** The government has displayed a willingness to collaborate with women and indigenous sectors and to table legislation designed to remedy their marginalization. Yet legislation has not resulted in the concrete policy initiatives still much needed to address continued socioeconomic, political, and cultural discrimination.

Civil Liberties

2004: A willingness to identify, confront, and root out the clandestine groups responsible for much of the country's violence would represent a positive first step.
2006: The government has taken no action in this area.

2004: The newly elected administration should endeavor to collaborate directly with civil society to alleviate residual forms of discrimination. Many of the reforms required are outlined in the indigenous and socioeconomic accords but await action; in other cases, legislation introduced, such as the language law, must translate into genuine reform.
2006: Some progress has been achieved, although the scale of the problem requires more concerted attention and action.

2004: Attention should be paid to enacting comprehensive education reforms that both improve access for disadvantaged groups and permit the revision of curriculums in ways that tackle persistent prejudice.
2006: Education legislation designed to address prejudice and discrimination has been introduced; efforts still need to be made to support the development of curriculums and to improve access.

Rule of Law

2004: The 2004 budget must be revised to permit the strengthening of key judicial institutions, including the civilian police and the court system.

2006: The government has taken no action in this area.

2004: The further expansion of rural tribunals, incorporation of customary law, and provision of services in indigenous languages, along with the revival of the public defender's office, could persuade Mayan communities that the legal process serves their needs, thereby diminishing rural violence.
2006: The government has taken no action in this area.

2004: The judicial system requires further modernization to speed up and streamline the trial process.
2006: The government has taken no action in this area.

2004: Judicial autonomy must be enhanced. This could be achieved by the introduction of legislation designed to depoliticize judicial appointments and by a commitment to enabling judicial officials to perform their tasks—tackling impunity and working to guarantee that justice is served—without threat to their lives and livelihood.
2006: The government has taken no action in this area.

Anticorruption and Transparency

2004: The government must observe the significant fiscal reforms recently introduced and pass tightened and further laws that guard against conflict of interest and enhance governmental transparency.
2006: The government has failed to make any progress in this area.

2004: The government must provide an environment in which judicial investigations into graft can proceed unimpeded.
2006: Judicial investigations into graft have begun, but they have often been stymied by the politicization of the judiciary as well as bribes and intimidation of prosecutors and presiding magistrates.

2004: The UN Commission to Investigate Illegal Armed Groups and Clandestine Security Apparatus should be established promptly, and its findings and recommendations translated into swift actions that not only target previous administrations but safeguard against future acts of corruption.
2006: This measure has not yet been introduced.

INDONESIA

Accountability and Public Voice

2004: The parties have agreed to modify the system of closed-list proportional representation. However, the parties maintain control over the ranking of candidates on the lists. Further movement toward an open list is necessary.

2006: In the 2004 elections, an "open-list proportional representation" system was used in which voters could vote for a single individual as well as for a party. The system was complex, however, and had little impact on the outcome, with the result that party rankings of candidates tended to prevail.

2004: Making more information available about political party financing and government operations would enable civic groups to mobilize public pressure more effectively in order to enhance accountability between elections.

2006: Little progress has been made in this area; civil society groups and monitoring bodies complain that party finances are still not transparent.

2004: Continuing efforts are needed to protect journalists and their right to report freely on critical issues, including internal conflicts such as that in Aceh.

2006: Little progress has been made in this area.

Civil Liberties

2004: The government must provide training for current police and new recruits in areas ranging from basic policing skills and tactics to the handling of complex investigations into transnational threats, such as terrorism and human trafficking, as well as political and financial corruption.

2006: Police training is improving, in part with the assistance of donor countries, but the challenges remain enormous.

Rule of Law

2004: The most pressing need is to disable the court mafia that involves judges, prosecutors, and defense attorneys in the regular fixing of cases.

2006: Some steps have been taken to improve probity in the judicial system, but the court mafia remains entrenched.

2004: Enhanced training for judges and prosecutors in applying and interpreting the law is necessary, particularly in areas such as corruption and human rights. However, court officials also need a more supportive political environment in order to work effectively.
2006: Training of judges and prosecutors is improving slowly. The political environment has not changed markedly.

2004: Civil society must be strengthened to help reduce the rewards for fixing cases. This means not just enhancing the capacity of government watchdog groups but raising awareness among the general public about the rights to which they are entitled and the opportunities available to them to pursue justice.
2006: Civil society monitoring requires further strengthening. Awareness of legal remedies among the general public remains low, while alienation from the legal system is common.

Anticorruption and Transparency

2004: The government should make use of information such as asset declarations to hold officials legally and politically accountable.
2006: While there has been a slight overall improvement in government efforts to eradicate corruption, assets declarations are still not used as the basis of investigations and prosecutions.

JORDAN

Accountability and Public Voice

2004: Both the executive and legislative branches of government should be popularly elected, and citizens should have guaranteed access to pending legislation and regulations.
2006: Little action has been taken in this area. An unrepresentative parliament was elected in 2003 under rules similar to those that have existed since 1993.

2004: In the next several years, Jordan should initiate a broad public dialogue on the legislative election law and consider whether to abolish the one-person, one-vote electoral system in favor of a system that would strengthen political parties.

2006: The king formed the National Agenda Committee to discuss such reforms, but its dialogue is not public, and its proposals are not yet fully known.

2004: Jordan should consider redrawing its electoral districts so that the number of legislators per district is based on population.
2006: No action has been taken.

2004: Jordan should reduce restrictions on the press, including repealing legislation that criminalizes defamation or insult of the royal family and public officials; eliminating capital requirements for newspapers; abolishing mandatory membership for journalists in the Jordan Press Association; liberalizing the broadcast media; and refraining from direct and indirect censorship, including any review and prior censorship of books and periodicals.
2006: No action has been taken, although the National Agenda may address some of these issues.

Civil Liberties

2004: The government should publicly acknowledge complaints of torture and police misconduct, perform thorough and impartial investigations of complaints, establish civilian review boards, and prosecute alleged perpetrators where the evidence merits.
2006: No action has been taken, and complaints have mounted.

2004: To increase further the accountability of state officials for human rights violations, the National Human Rights Centre should be granted the authority to conduct investigations and file lawsuits on behalf of private citizens.
2006: No action has been taken.

2004: The Jordanian government should continue its commendable efforts to promote women's equality by pressing for additional legal reform and working to eliminate such barriers to women's advancement as domestic violence.
2006: Parliament has rejected reforms, and legislation awaits upper and lower house compromise.

2004: Jordan should repeal the August 2001 temporary law on public gatherings in favor of more reasonable and less restrictive regulations.

2006: No action has been taken.

2004: The state should streamline and reduce the reporting and disclosure requirements for civil society organizations and permit them to take stances on policy matters and advocate for reform.
2006: Government campaigns against freedom of association and expression have increased.

Rule of Law

2004: High-level Jordanian officials, including King Abdullah, should make clear to judges and other officials, including members of the security forces, that interference in the judiciary will not be tolerated.
2006: No action has been taken.

2004: The government should consider granting the Higher Judicial Council full authority to appoint judges. To increase transparency in the judicial appointment process, the government should publicize widely lists of judicial candidates and eventual appointees.
2006: No action has been taken.

2004: The government should improve the quality of training for judges and continue its efforts to increase the efficiency of the judicial system, both by computerizing court activities and implementing alternative forms of dispute resolution.
2006: A judicial ethics code has been created, but no implementation or supervision is apparent.

2004: The government should repeal the temporary legislation that grants overly broad authority to the prime minister to refer cases to the state security court and implement measures to ensure that all defendants receive timely access to counsel.
2006: No action has been taken.

2004: The military and the Government Intelligence Directorate should be subject to greater civilian oversight. Ministers supervising these ministries should be civilians or surrender their commissions.
2006: No action has been taken.

Anticorruption and Transparency

2004: The government should continue to investigate and prosecute officials who have engaged in corruption, but it should do so in civil courts and in a transparent manner.
2006: No action has been taken.

2004: The state should take additional steps to reduce corruption, such as enacting mandatory financial disclosure laws for public officials and reforming the civil service, including enacting a civil servants' ethics code.
2006: No action has been taken.

2004: Jordan should increase the transparency of state institutions and actions. Positive measures would include opening the budgets of the royal court and armed forces to legislative scrutiny and enacting freedom of information legislation.
2006: No action has been taken.

2004: Jordan should continue to implement the e-government project and take steps to ensure that most citizens have access to electronic government services.
2006: No action has been taken.

2004: The Jordanian government should permit greater civil society involvement in efforts to eradicate corruption and to encourage uninhibited media reporting on corruption stories.
2006: No action has been taken.

KAZAKHSTAN

Accountability and Public Voice

2004: In order for free and fair elections and free media to flourish, the government must cease using both legal and extralegal means to control and suffocate scrutiny and dissent.
2006: The opposition had more opportunities to participate in the 2005 election than in the 2004 legislative elections, but the government continues to use legal and extralegal means to stifle opposition.

2004: The government must end its crackdown on political opposition groups and discard the proposed law on elections.
2006: Some modifications have been introduced.

2004: It is vital that the new law on media and elections not reverse the direction of media and electoral reform in Kazakhstan.
2006: The president vetoed a new antidemocratic media law.

2004: The government needs to address criticisms by opponents about changes to proposed laws and allow for a more open and democratic debate.
2006: There appears to be some increase in public debate, but it does not meet the standards of a democratic society.

2004: The government must cease instigating lawsuits and using threats and coercion in its efforts to stifle the media and opposition.
2006: The government has taken no action in this area.

2004: Registration thresholds for political parties should be lowered, and banned parties should be allowed to resume their activity.
2006: Thresholds remain, but some previously unregistered groups have been registered or have found other means of participation.

2004: Lawyers, judges, and journalists must be better trained to understand press freedoms and the enforcement of constitutional protections with respect to elections and the media.
2006: Education of the public and media by election commissions was better in 2005 than in 2004, but still insufficient.

Civil Liberties

2004: The government needs to continue its progress in improving gender equality within the republic.
2006: The government has focused on education to achieve gradual shifts in women's public roles.

2004: A more progressive law on NGOs than the one proposed is necessary; the restrictive language in the present version must be altered to demonstrate Kazakhstan's willingness to sustain and support civil society.
2006: No such law has been passed. As a result of international pressure, however, the Constitutional Council vetoed two laws on NGOs in August 2005 that would have gone even further to limit the rights of independent nongovernmental groups.

2004: Torture in any form must be criminalized, and laws pertaining to torture must be upheld by authorities. Officials who engage in torture must be prosecuted criminally.
2006: There is little evidence that Kazakhstan is giving priority to this issue.

2004: Kazakhstan's application to be chair of the OSCE should be used by the international community as leverage to encourage reform and to force the government to address civil liberties infringements.
2006: Kazakhstan has demonstrated the limited applicability of this strategy, reminding the international community of the relative paucity of levers available for use in rich states that are slow reformers but not active abusers.

Rule of Law

2004: Constitutional amendments are necessary to make the judiciary free from undue influence by the executive branch and not subject to pressures from the justice ministry.
2006: The government has taken no action in this area.

2004: An intense review of the judicial system as it functions today is imperative in order to address the many areas in which it is ineffective and is operating unlawfully by not upholding the laws as they are designed to be implemented and practiced.
2006: The government has taken no action in this area.

Anticorruption and Transparency

2004: A viable legal framework that enforces anticorruption laws without political favoritism or arbitrariness is a required first step for Kazakhstan to take toward controlling corruption.
2006: There has been some small progress in this area. While the necessary anticorruption laws are in place, enforcement remains uneven. Most high-profile corruption prosecutions are politically motivated, though the defendants may truly be guilty. Anecdotal evidence suggests the courts are becoming more effective at prosecuting corrupt low-level officials.

2004: All sectors of the government must be held accountable for corruption, including the executive branch; if Nazarbayev is not held

accountable for enforcing policies he himself claims to support, it is highly unlikely the rest of society will take them seriously.
2006: There has been no progress in this area.

2004: The government also needs to direct more attention to education funding and support for transparent practices within education in order to prevent young people from growing up using bribery and other forms of corruption to get through school.
2006: Some progress has been made in this area, and the government's promise to provide 3,000 scholarships per year for foreign training of Kazakh students and postgraduates should lead to substantial progress in the future.

2004: Kazakhstan's desire to join the WTO may offer a way for the international community to establish incentives for the government to enforce and uphold anticorruption measures and increase government transparency.
2006: Kazakhstan has made significant progress in its WTO accession bid, and this could lead to future anticorruption measures and increased transparency.

KENYA

Accountability and Public Voice

2004: The government should ensure that the constitutional review process move forward quickly and refrain from interfering.
2006: The review process did move ahead, but parliament and the government significantly altered the final version, which was defeated in the November 2005 referendum.

2004: The proposed constitution should include provisions reducing executive power.
2006: The final, government-influenced draft significantly reduced the powers of the prime minister, a position that was included in the previous draft precisely to limit executive power.

2004: The media council should have a status similar to that of the Law Society of Kenya, which was established by an act of parliament but which exercises its functions independently and is part of civil society.
2006: Legislation to this effect is being considered.

2004: Electoral reform should include addressing the wide disparities in constituency size.
2006: The Electoral Commission is to undertake a review of constituency boundaries in 2006.

2004: The Electoral Commission's independence and funding should be increased.
2006: The commission has continued to consolidate its independence.

2004: The government should close the vast urban-rural gap in access to information that limits the ability of millions of people to receive adequate information.
2006: A number of initiatives are underway, but their impact remains unclear.

2004: Campaign finance reforms must be passed.
2006: Relevant legislation is being considered but has not yet been introduced into Parliament.

Civil Liberties

2004: Human rights training should be integrated into all levels of law enforcement.
2006: Human rights training occurs only on a sporadic, ad hoc basis.

2004: The government should ensure that any legislation designed to combat terror not circumscribe civil liberties.
2006: The government continues to give official support to draft legislation that could circumscribe civil liberties.

2004: The public policy process in general, and specifically the constitutional reform initiative, should place particular emphasis on promoting women's and disadvantaged minorities' rights.
2006: These issues remain on the public policy agenda, although not with sufficient priority. The defeated draft constitution included provisions in this regard.

2004: The constitution should provide that international human rights conventions be automatically incorporated into domestic law on ratification by the state.
2006: There is no such constitutional provision.

2004: Adequate resources should be provided to the judicial system to ensure that international norms regarding length of detention without trial and prison population size be respected.
2006: Insufficient resources continued to be devoted to eliminating human rights deficiencies in the judicial system.

2004: Justice must be shown to the victims of politically motivated ethnic clashes.
2006: Although there has been some criticism of a relative lack of government attention to this, it has not recently been a high-profile issue.

Rule of Law

2004: Constitutional reform must include the creation of an independent judiciary.
2006: The draft constitution, which did not go far enough in this direction, was defeated; no other progress has been made.

2004: The government should either create an independent commission or strengthen the Judicial Service Commission to monitor judicial performance and appointments.
2006: No such action has been taken.

2004: The judicial system must receive increased resources, as it is the cornerstone of good governance.
2006: The judicial system continues to be significantly underfunded.

2004: The government should take enforcement measures to address corruption and inefficiency in the justice system, including access to legal services by all citizens, especially disadvantaged minorities.
2006: Little progress has been made.

Anticorruption and Transparency

2004: The government should promote legislation that allows Kenyans broader access to information, protects those who would report corruption, and allows for judicial review.
2006: Such legislation is under consideration.

2004: The culture of impunity needs to end, and major cases of corruption need to be prosecuted.

2006: A number of major corruption cases have come to light. Some are being prosecuted, yet these prosecutions have yielded no significant results.

KYRGYZSTAN

Accountability and Public Voice

2004: The Central and Territorial Election Commissions must be freed from executive control.
2006: The government is considering proposals to this end but no action has been taken.

2004: The government must demonstrate rather than merely promise political reform, ending the autocracy.
2006: The postrevolutionary government has ended autocracy.

2004: The use of show trials against members of the opposition must end.
2006: There were no show trials in 2005.

Civil Liberties

2004: The government must ensure that reforms to Kyrgyz institutions and laws yield improved state-society relations.
2006: The government has launched a process to amend and improve the constitution as well as initiated positive new media legislation, but it has taken only tentative steps toward reforming corrupt law enforcement bodies.

Rule of Law

2004: Freeing the judiciary's budget from executive control, increasing the salaries of Kyrgyz judges, and liberating magistrates from executive influence—in both their appointments and their tenure—is essential.
2006: No formal legislation along these lines has been enacted yet, but the government has recognized the problems and promised laws to strengthen the courts and weaken the power of state prosecutors.

2004: The government must free the Kyrgyz courts from executive intervention and manipulation.

2006: The executive has ended the practice of blatantly pressuring judges for particular verdicts.

Anticorruption and Transparency

2004: New initiatives to allow a real measure of local budgeting for the regions must be carried out in practice.
2006: A real measure of local budgeting has not been implemented, but the new government has not yet had the opportunity to present its first post-revolution budget.

2004: Economic decisions should be shifted from migratory state appointees, who are rotated from region to region and thus rarely have vested interests in the oblasts where they are temporarily posted, to local governments, which currently have few real powers.
2006: Steps toward this goal have been taken with promises of an administrative reform in 2007 that would abolish the provincial level of government and leave a three-tier system of central, district, and village authorities.

MALAYSIA

Accountability and Public Voice

2004: Malaysia's Election Commission should be made independent, a first step toward which might involve removing it from the prime minister's department.
2006: The Election Commission has not been subjected to any reforms and was widely criticized for mismanagement during the 2004 general election.

2004: Campaign financing and expenditures should be subjected to clearer regulation.
2006: No such regulations have been adopted.

2004: Civil service recruitment should gradually be widened, providing a larger pool of candidates by which to restore bureaucratic quality.
2006: Prime Minister Abdullah Badawi appears to attach greater importance to the standing and integrity of the civil service, but few meaningful reforms have yet been undertaken.

2004: The Printing Presses and Publication Act should be abolished in order to encourage greater media freedom.
2006: Controls over the print and electronic media during the period under review have not been significantly loosened.

Civil Liberties

2004: The Internal Security Act and the Emergency Ordinance should be repealed and replaced by better police work and open trial proceedings.
2006: Prime Minister Abdullah has continued strongly to defend the principle of preventive detention.

2004: The University and University Colleges Act should be repealed and the Police Act loosened. In this way, various elements of civil society could keep the government more closely accountable.
2006: Restrictions on student participation in political life remain tightly enforced.

2004: In view of the gains made by the Malay community over the past several decades, the New Economic Policy (NEP) should be further scaled back in order to alleviate minority grievances.
2006: The tone of the NEP has been softened under its various successor programs, though most of the quotas benefiting the Malay community remain in place. In fact, United Malays National Organization Youth in 2005 demanded that these quotas be more rigorously enforced.

Rule of Law

2004: The independence of Malaysia's judiciary should be restored through impartial recruitment and promotion of judges. To this end, the government should consult more closely with the Malaysian Bar Council.
2006: The judiciary has displayed greater independence in its decisions in political cases, more often ruling in ways that have benefited opposition leaders. Recruitment and promotion still appears, however, to be deeply politicized.

2004: Judges require more training in order to rule effectively in complex commercial cases.

2006: With the passing of the Asian currency crisis and subsequent attempts to deal with nonperforming loans, issues over training in commercial cases appear less pressing. It is doubtful, however, that training has been significantly improved.

2004: The Attorney-General's Chambers should display more accountability to the public by disclosing its criteria for initiating and dropping proceedings.
2006: The operating style of the Attorney-General's Chambers appears to have changed little.

2004: The partisanship of the police force should be reduced by making the home ministry more accountable to parliament.
2006: The police have not been made any more accountable to parliament.

2004: The ineffectiveness with which the police confront street crime might be stemmed by recruiting more officers, hiring across ethnic lines, and increasing pay scales.
2006: Little improvement in police effectiveness in crime fighting or reduction in corruption can be expected before the recommendations of the Police Commission are fully adopted.

Anticorruption and Transparency

2004: Malaysia's Anti-Corruption Agency should be free to investigate cases of corruption in nonpartisan ways, and the Integrity Management Committee should be given enforcement powers.
2006: During the period under review, the ACA has carried out a few unprecedented and high-profile corruption investigations, but executive dominance still appears to seriously hinder its activities. The Integrity Management Committee has made few gains.

2004: Whistle-blowers should not be threatened with prosecution under the Official Secrets Act (OSA).
2006: The OSA remains in force, although a prominent opposition figure was acquitted on OSA charges during the period under review.

2004: Officials and politicians should be required to declare their assets publicly.

2006: New regulations over disclosure of assets by MPs have been put in place, but they remain laxly enforced.

2004: Government contracts should be awarded through open bidding.
2006: Prime Minister Abdullah has given greater attention to the need for open bidding involving GLCs, but greater transparency remains sporadic.

2004: The expenditures of Petronas should be specified in the federal budget.
2006: Petronas's internal dealings remain only partly disclosed through annual reports.

2004: The government should introduce pending legislation in a timelier fashion, allowing more consistent public scrutiny.
2006: The government's methods of introducing legislation and seeking feedback from the public have changed little.

MOROCCO

Accountability and Public Voice

2004: Senior officials appointed by the king to key public positions must be accountable to the government.
2006: No progress has been made.

2004: Institutional reforms are necessary to improve the legislative, regulatory, and inquiry ability of the parliament.
2006: There is no indication of recent institutional reforms to improve the workings of the parliament, although a program to strengthen parliamentary committees is under way.

2004: The tasks, internal regulations, and division of labor between the parliament's two chambers must be clarified and institutionalized.
2006: The official website of the parliament's two chambers makes no note of new regulations, and no other indication of new regulations could be found.

2004: Legal reforms should include progressive civil liberties and press codes, a coherent law on political parties, and a simple and fair electoral code.

2006: The media continue to work within the framework of Dahir No. 1-02-207 of October 3, 2002; new legislation on political parties was passed in October 2005 to simplify the process of party creation; the trend of reversing civil liberties in the name of counterterrorism continues; and the electoral code has not changed since 2003.

2004: The party system must be completely reorganized to enhance the independence of the parties from the central administration, democratize their internal structure, and improve their representation capacity.
2006: The party system was not reorganized, although the new law on political parties, 36-04, passed by parliament in October 2005, provides for restructuring the political field.

Civil Liberties

2004: Gender equity, freedom of conscience and belief, and protection of Berber culture and language must be clear and explicit in the constitution.
2006: Gender equity and freedom of worship are stated in the constitution and have been strongly supplemented by the passage of the new Family Law in January 2004. More can be done to ensure the protection of Berber language and culture.

2004: Legal reforms must clearly define and proscribe torture and cruel treatment in all situations. The use of statements extracted under torture must be prohibited in clear and specific terms.
2006: Torture is forbidden under Moroccan law; parliament passed two laws in October 2005 that criminalize torture.

2004: An independent and transparent truth and reconciliation commission should be established to fully compensate and rehabilitate victims of human rights abuses, investigate unsolved cases, address clearly the state's responsibility, and put an end to continued impunity, especially in cases of current violations.
2006: The government established an Equity and Reconciliation Commission in 2004 to address its past, with rehabilitation and compensation available for victims who request it; however, no investigation into the crimes is available, as perpetrators continue to enjoy immunity, and cases of post-1999 victims of torture fall outside the commission's mandate.

Rule of Law

2004: The role, powers, and composition of internal supervisory and disciplinary bodies such as the Inspection Générale and the Conseil Supérieur de la Magistrature must be expanded and improved.
2006: There have been no reforms of the role, powers, and composition of such internal supervisory and disciplinary bodies as the Conseil Supérieur de la Magistrature, and no clear indication can be found of recent reforms of the Inspection Générale.

2004: To improve judicial performance and bring the problem of petty corruption in the judicial process under control, procedures should be simplified and decision making and execution accelerated through consolidation of various courts and jurisdictions into single court systems.
2006: Morocco continues to have different courts and jurisdictions and has not consolidated them into single court systems.

2004: The training of the justice corps should be increased and its performance improved by offering incentives to qualified students, revising teaching standards, and requiring professional training as part of the curriculum.
2006: Professional training has been made available to certain magistrates, legal experts, and civil servants of the Ministry of Justice. There is no indication of incentives to qualified students, revised teaching standards, or required professional training as part of the curriculum.

Anticorruption and Transparency

2004: The government must allow public access to official information.
2006: Public access to information continues to be limited.

2004: The administrative functioning of the regime must be more transparent.
2006: Administrative reform is still needed to increase transparency.

NEPAL

Accountability and Public Voice

2004: Once democracy is restored, state radio and television should be placed under the control of an independent broadcasting board.

2006: The government has taken no action in this area; instead, the situation has grown worse; democracy has not been restored and the clampdown on the independent media has become more severe.

2004: Full merit-based hiring and promotion in the civil service should be introduced.
2006: The situation has worsened: Maoists are targeting and assassinating civil servants, and the government is failing to protect civil servants in the provinces.

2004: There should be an end to the licensing of journalists.
2006: The licensing of journalists continues.

2004: The king's role in politics should be curbed.
2006: The king's role in politics has increased.

Civil Liberties

2004: The government should institute human rights training for the army and police.
2006: Effective training has not been implemented, the human rights situation has worsened, and the army and police's human rights violations have become more severe.

2004: To prevent the indefinite detention of suspected Maoists, apparent loopholes in the Terrorism and Disruptive Activities Ordinance (TADO) need to be closed.
2006: The government has taken no action in this area; the detention situation has worsened.

2004: The special committees set up under TADO to coordinate local counterinsurgency efforts should be disbanded.
2006: The government has taken no action in this area.

2004: Reform is needed for laws on property and in other areas that discriminate against women.
2006: Nepalese law generally recognizes citizens' rights to private property, but the government has not yet addressed the right to citizenship by descent through the mother or the existence of discriminatory inheritance and property laws.

2004: To the extent resources permit, the government should hire more labor inspectors—and pay them adequately—to enforce labor laws better.
2006: The government has taken no action in this area.

Rule of Law

2004: The king's role as army commander and in appointing judges needs to end.
2006: The king's role has increased.

2004: Increased funding for judicial salaries and legal texts is needed to improve court administration.
2006: The government has taken no action in this area.

Anticorruption and Transparency

2004: Foreign auditors should be hired to monitor customs and other key revenue sources—an admittedly drastic solution to a seemingly intractable corruption problem.
2006: The government has taken no action in this area.

2004: The government budget and other key financial statements should be more broadly published and distributed.
2006: The government has taken no action in this area.

2004: The size of the civil service should be reduced, perhaps through attrition, creating a leaner but better-paid bureaucracy.
2006: The government has taken no action in this area; however, civil service numbers are falling as civil servants in the rural areas are being deliberately harassed and killed by Maoists, resulting in a significant number of deaths and voluntary resignations.

2004: Procedures for public access to routine documents need to be streamlined.
2006: The government has taken no action in this area.

NICARAGUA

Accountability and Public Voice

2004: Investigative journalism should be encouraged, for example through training for journalists.
2006: No action has been taken.

Civil Liberties

2004: The state must fully implement legal changes passed over the past few years.
2006: The executive and judicial branches have made significant progress in implementing the principal change, which is the new penal procedure code. But the government has only spottily shouldered its responsibilities regarding new legislation on the rights of citizens on the Atlantic Coast (regulations to the Autonomy Statute and the Land Demarcation Law) and done very little to help people with disabilities.

2004: Laws protecting women and children must be passed and enforced.
2006: Such laws do not exist; the Nicaraguan legislature has avoided passage of the equal opportunities law for women and the criminalization of child prostitution.

Rule of Law

2004: Greater investment of resources in judicial training and infrastructure is needed.
2006: Given that many foreign donors have withdrawn financial assistance from the judicial system in recent years (after engagement in the 1990s), overall judicial training and infrastructure have not advanced much. However, specific training continues in the new procedure code and for public prosecutors and defenders.

2004: The new Judicial Organic Law, the criminal procedures code, and a new penal code should be enforced in order to increase judicial independence and legitimacy.
2006: Passage of a reformed penal code is still pending in the Assembly. The Law of the Judicial Career, passed in late 2004, which bears most

directly on the issue of judicial independence, also has not been implemented. The criminal procedures code, extended to all cases at the end of 2004, has helped reduce arbitrary detentions and established an oral accusatory system for criminal proceedings.

Anticorruption and Transparency

2004: To open up the functioning of the government to public scrutiny, the state must engage in ongoing campaigns that bring government-related news to the media. The state must play a proactive role in sharing information with the people, perhaps through regular news releases as well as town-hall–style meetings revealing the accomplishments of and challenges faced by the government.
2006: The Bolaños government has modestly reinforced its efforts to bring its achievements to public attention and has held local-level meetings with citizens, mainly outside the capital, both to inform them of policy and to solicit inputs into the National Development Plan.

2004: Greater transparency in government is necessary through public scrutiny of officials' records followed by dismissal or prosecution and conviction, when merited. Those government officials found guilty of malfeasance must be subject to the same penalties as the average citizen.
2006: The weaknesses in the probity law for public servants and the lack of legislative action on the draft access to information law have resulted in little growth in the public scrutiny of officials' actions. The extreme politicization of the judicial system has significantly hindered its action in processing corruption cases, allowing almost complete impunity and proving galling to the citizenry.

NIGERIA

Accountability and Public Voice

2004: The Independent National Electoral Commission (INEC) should enjoy genuine autonomy and be funded adequately through an autonomous budget to administer elections properly.
2006: INEC remains deeply vulnerable to executive influence, including executive control of its budget, which is chronically underfunded.

2004: State-controlled media must be accessible to all electoral candidates on an equitable basis and should be permanently controlled by an autonomous broadcast authority to guard against partisan bias.
2006: State-controlled media remains dominated by the party in power, but some coverage of the opposition appears on national networks; local televised media is largely beholden to the state governors. Private print media are more independent but subject to selective financial and political influence, while private television and radio stations have also seen increased government interference of late.

2004: Licenses for private broadcasting should be made more easily available and provision for community radio stations established.
2006: No government action has been taken in this area.

Civil Liberties

2004: Implementation of constitutional and legal provisions must be improved, especially in the handling of protests, strikes, and related forms of group political expression, in treatment of detainees and prisoners, and regarding women's rights.
2006: The government announced that it would release half of all the nation's prisoners, and human rights groups won a number of precedent-setting cases to improve the protection of women's rights under the Nigerian Sharia code, but associational rights have deteriorated markedly.

2004: The government must act forcefully at all levels to curb political militias and related political vigilantism and end official impunity for acts of violence by security forces.
2006: Militia activity has grown bolder and better armed, and security force impunity has only been curbed at the margins.

2004: Official and NGO efforts to educate citizens regarding their rights and remedies if those rights are not respected should be increased.
2006: Government information campaigns have been limited, while targeted NGO efforts have made progress in some communities.

Rule of Law

2004: The judicial branch should be financially independent of the executive, receiving funds directly from the federal budget, and be adequately funded to allow the proper administration of justice.

2006: The National Judicial Council receives funds directly from the federal budget, but the executive continues to release such appropriations as it sees fit, and state and federal executives control significant ancillary funding needs, such as transportation, courtroom necessities, and so on.

2004: Members of the government cannot be allowed impunity for legal transgressions and must abide by court decisions. Workshops and seminars to instill these values should include high government officials.

2006: Several governors, the inspector-general of police, a minister, and other high-level politicians have been arrested or dismissed for corruption, although worrisome political motives have been tied to a number of these cases, and government officials have shown an occasional unwillingness to abide by unfavorable court decisions. Donor-sponsored ethics workshops have been well attended and soon forgotten.

2004: Independent civilian oversight of police must be strengthened to discourage abuses and political manipulation of police.

2006: Human rights NGOs are working with the police to improve community policing practices, and the police have instituted a number of community dialogue channels in some areas, but their seriousness or effectiveness to date appears anecdotal.

Anticorruption and Transparency

2004: The Independent Corrupt Practices Commission (ICPC) must be made truly independent and take up its prescribed role as watchdog over malpractice from any sector.

2006: The ICPC undertook few prosecutions in 2004–2005 and was largely eclipsed by the highly effective Economic and Financial Crimes Commission, which showed increasing willingness to hound high-level corruption but also some danger of politicization by late 2005.

2004: The capacity of the executive's budgetary process needs to be strengthened, including the capacity of the Auditor-General's Office, to help increase accountability and public knowledge and voice.

2006: The President's Due Process Unit improved the procurement process for the 15 percent of the budget over which it had authority, but the larger budgetary process remains obscure.

2004: Legislative staff training should be increased, and offices should be modernized (including computerizing the offices of the budget, appropriations, and related committees with oversight responsibilities) to help keep the executive branch honest and accountable.

2006: National legislative staffs have generally improved in skills and performance, and the National Assembly has improved its technological resources, but its ability to challenge the presidency remains limited, and state assemblies have been largely controlled by the governors.

2004: The Office of the Auditor-General should be independent of the presidency and the legislature, in terms of both appointment and funding. Its budget should derive directly from the federal accounts.

2006: The auditor-general's office has been firmly under presidential control since 2003.

2004: Robust freedom of information laws easily enforceable in the courts should be adopted to ensure the public's access to government information.

2006: The House of Representatives passed the Freedom of Information Act in 2004, and the Senate appears close to passing it as well.

2004: Any sale of state assets should be closely monitored to ensure that benefits accrue to the Nigerian people and not unduly to well-connected private individuals.

2006: Powerful politicians traded accusations that they had benefited from government privatization efforts, particularly in the telecommunications and steel industries.

PAKISTAN

Accountability and Public Voice

2004: The government should resist the military's intervention in constitutional governance, which undermines popular political participation.

2006: The government has taken no action in this area.

2004: The Legal Framework Order should be rescinded in order to pave the way for restoration of civilian rule.

2006: The government has taken no action in this area.

2004: General Musharraf should adhere to his roadmap for democracy and genuinely transfer power to the elected parliament and government.

2006: The government has taken no action in this area.

2004: The legal and practical restrictions on major political parties should be withdrawn.
2006: The government has taken no action in this area.

2004: For their part, the political parties should reach agreement on a political code of conduct that prevents the winner-take-all politics of the past that has facilitated military intervention.
2006: No action has been taken in this area.

2004: The internal wing of Inter-Services Intelligence (ISI) should not be allowed to interfere in the affairs of political parties or civil society organizations.
2006: The government has taken no action in this area.

2004: The government should withdraw the new press laws, and legal measures should, instead, be introduced to protect journalists and punish officials intimidating them or otherwise interfering with the constitutional guarantees of freedom of the press.
2006: The government has taken no action in this area.

2004: The Council of Pakistan Newspaper Editors and the All Pakistan Newspapers Society should be involved in any new legislation relating to the media.
2006: The government has taken no action in this area.

Civil Liberties

2004: The ISI's role in supporting Islamic militant groups should be brought to an end, making it possible progressively to eliminate sectarian and religious militancy.
2006: The government has taken no action in this area.

2004: The government should seek the cooperation of major political parties to repeal the hudood ordinance and amend the blasphemy laws.
2006: The government has taken no action in this area.

2004: The broad powers of the National Accountability Bureau (NAB) should be restricted in accordance with the normal penal and criminal procedure codes.
2006: The government has taken no action in this area.

2004: The ban on student unions and the limitations on political parties and trade unions should be removed.
2006: The government has taken no action in this area.

Rule of Law

2004: The independence of Pakistan's judiciary should be restored through appointment of judges of good repute.
2006: The government has taken no action in this area.

2004: The process of appointments to the superior judiciary should be made more transparent, possibly involving the Pakistan Bar Council and open hearings before a parliamentary committee.
2006: The government has taken no action in this area.

2004: The present confrontation between the bar and the judiciary must be brought to an end.
2006: The government has taken no action in this area.

2004: The military's interference with law enforcement and judicial proceedings should be rolled back, along with the abolition of parallel courts and prosecution bodies.
2006: The government has taken no action in this area.

2004: The duplication in the jurisdictions of the Federal Investigation Agency (FIA) and NAB should be eliminated.
2006: The government has taken no action in this area.

2004: Funding and training for law enforcement and the judiciary should be increased.
2006: The government has taken no action in this area.

2004: Security and Intelligence services should not be allowed to remain above the law.
2006: The government has taken no action in this area.

2004: More judges should be appointed to clear the extensive backlog in lower courts.
2006: The government has taken no action in this area.

Anticorruption and Transparency

2004: The government must hold both the military and the judiciary accountable if efforts against corruption are to bear fruit.
2006: The government has taken no action in this area.

2004: NAB should not be used for the political purpose of discrediting politicians and civilian administrators. Appointment of its personnel should be subjected to checks and balances and its jurisdiction should be extended to the military and the judiciary.
2006: The government has taken no action in this area.

2004: Improvements in pay scales for civil servants and judges are necessary to curtail the environment for corruption.
2006: The government has taken no action in this area.

2004: Secrecy in government should be minimized.
2006: The government has taken no action in this area.

2004: The scope of the Freedom of Information Ordinance must be expanded and an enforcement mechanism should be provided.
2006: The government has taken no action in this area.

SIERRA LEONE

Accountability and Public Voice

2004: The government must undertake difficult political negotiations with paramount chiefs, the existing (and not popularly elected) basis for local governance.
2006: The government introduced elected local governments, though the duties and political relations of this new layer of administration remain confused vis-à-vis paramount chiefs.

2004: The government should take a minimalist approach to monitoring professional standards of journalists, leaving this task as much as possible to the Sierra Leone Association of Journalists (SLAJ).
2006: The government continues to monitor professional standards of journalists, although the introduction of a degree program in journalism at the University of Sierra Leone represents an advance. Recent politically motivated prosecutions indicate a need to repeal the seditious libel law.

2004: Measures should be taken to encourage broader diffusion of newspapers, which still do not circulate widely outside the capital, to promote political debate.
2006: The government has taken no action in this area. Private merchants provide limited distribution of newspapers in the three provincial capitals.

Civil Liberties

2004: Police training and more vigorous prosecution of police abuse of citizens are basic measures necessary to improve the government's record for protecting existing rights.
2006: Government action in this area has been limited.

2004: Rehabilitation of the country's court system will be necessary to provide citizens with means to redress inconsistent enforcement of rights.
2006: Aside from extending limited court services to areas previously in rebel hands, the government has taken little action in this area.

2004: A mechanism must be put in place to ensure the country's impoverished majority of access to government institutions.
2006: The government has taken no action in this area.

Rule of Law

2004: The movement of fighters across international borders in the region must end, as it threatens renewed violence for Sierra Leone.
2006: Concrete positive steps have been taken to monitor regional security threats.

2004: Departure of UN peacekeepers should be delayed if security situation in Guinea deteriorates.
2006: Given the departure of peacekeepers at the end of 2005, careful attention needs to be paid to ensure coordination of security forces and the UN peacekeeping mission in Liberia. Political developments in Guinea bear close monitoring in the event of a political transition there.

2004: The government needs to secure protection for members of the Special Court, given the court's intent to prosecute individuals who still enjoy high standing among non-state armed groups.

2006: The government protects the Special Court against potential threats by supporters of defendants. International agencies and the Nigerian Government brought Charles Taylor to the court to answer charges, increasing the court's legitimacy of in the eyes of many Sierra Leone citizens.

Anticorruption and Transparency

2004: The prosecutorial weakness of the Attorney General's Office, as well as the weak mechanisms permitting those who are charged to pursue their legal rights, must be addressed as part of a broader reform of the judiciary.
2006: Very limited government action has been taken in this area.

2004: The government must provide greater political support for oversight and investigative agencies.
2006: Limited gains have been made in promoting investigations of the Anti-Corruption Commission. This agency needs to be encouraged to pursue cases more vigorously.

2004: The state needs to provide better public access to information about government-funded programs.
2006: The government has not taken practical action in this area.

SRI LANKA

Accountability and Public Voice

2004: The establishment of a viable, effective, and independent electoral commission is needed to ensure that future elections are not marred by political violence and allegations of corruption.
2006: No action has been taken.

2004: Media independence could be strengthened by a gradual divestiture of state ownership of media outlets.
2006: No divestiture has been made.

2004: The formation of an independent media council that could serve as a mechanism for the self-regulation of the media sector should be expedited.

2006: No action has been taken.

Civil Liberties

2004: Cases of those who have been arrested under the Prevention of Terrorism Act (PTA) and held without trial or charge should be examined expeditiously.
2006: There has been progress in resolving these cases, but many still remain to be heard.

2004: The police and other security forces should receive training on general human rights issues, particularly on acceptable interrogation techniques.
2006: The police and security forces have received some training, but additional assistance is needed.

2004: A concerted effort should be made to investigate accusations of torture and custodial rape or murder, and those responsible should be prosecuted.
2006: No action has been taken.

2004: The government should take steps to enhance prosecution of trafficking in women and children by more aggressively investigating and prosecuting cases under already existing legislation.
2006: No action has been taken.

Rule of Law

2004: Planned improvements to address the quality of judicial staff and their access to legal information to enhance the professionalism of the judiciary must be followed through.
2006: The quality of judges and their access to legal information remains an area of much-needed improvement.

2004: The political impasse over the question of the dismissal of present chief justices should be resolved as expeditiously as possible.
2006: This issue has not been resolved but has disappeared with the change in government in 2004.

2004: Larger structural changes to the judiciary should be considered, such as giving an independent panel the power of appointing judges or

changing the criteria for membership in the Judicial Service Commission (JSC).
2006: No action has been taken.

Anticorruption and Transparency

2004: Most important, priority should be given to establishing a mechanism to ensure that the potential influx of foreign aid that was promised at the June 2003 Tokyo donors' conference be disbursed in a fair and transparent manner.
2006: No action has been taken, although the issue has been delayed by political problems and elections.

2004: Existing anticorruption laws, such as the DALL, need to be strictly enforced, and existing institutions, such as the Bribery Commission, need to be allowed to function fully and effectively—if necessary by giving them additional powers and resources, such as their own investigative staff.
2006: There has been no apparent improvement in this area.

2004: Legislation offering protection for whistle-blowers is needed.
2006: No action has been taken.

2004: The passing of freedom-of-information legislation should be made a priority.
2006: No action has been taken.

2004: Accountability would be improved if mechanisms were put in place to require that all proposed legislation be made available to the public for their scrutiny and comment.
2006: No mechanisms have been created.

UGANDA

Accountability and Public Voice

2004: The most important reform to increase political accountability in Uganda would be the retirement of President Museveni at the end of his current term, the last one he is permitted under the constitution.
2006: President Museveni orchestrated the removal of term limits, the formation of a new political party, and his nomination as its presidential candidate.

2004: The reappointment of the original chair of the electoral commission, Stephen Akabway, would help restore the independence and authority of that commission.

2006: The regime retained the current chair, Dr. Badru Kiggundu. At this point, changing the chair would reduce, not increase, independence. Kiggundu has shown some independence.

2004: A hands-off government policy toward criticism by journalists would strengthen both the norms of government accountability and support for the government.

2006: The government has moved in the opposite direction by interfering with the media.

Civil Liberties

2004: The government should introduce a policy of effective and prompt punishment for all human rights violations caused by members of all security services.

2006: The government has taken no action in this area.

2004: A human rights component should be inserted into the security forces' training programs, with required refresher courses offered biannually. Soldiers in the original National Resistance Army (NRA) were effectively trained to respect the rights of all civilians, and this memory and the pride of officers from that time could be drawn upon.

2006: The government has taken no action in this area.

2004: All paramilitary security forces should be disbanded.

2006: The government has taken no action in this area.

2004: Laws meeting the constitutional standards of equality of women with men should be passed and actively implemented, particularly those giving women the right to land ownership, the right to a share of marital property upon divorce, and the right to inherit property from their husbands.

2006: The government has taken no action in this area.

2004: Ending the war with the Lord's Resistance Army (LRA) is essential for ending the human rights abuses caused by both armed forces. The best chance for a peaceful settlement would be the adoption of a

consistent government policy to support independent negotiations by Acholi church officials and respected elders with the leaders of the LRA.
2006: The government appeared to be on the verge of successful negotiations at the end of 2004; however, the negotiations collapsed.

2004: The cabinet should withdraw its September 2003 proposal on cost-savings grounds to merge the Uganda Human Rights Commission (UHRC) with the inspector general of government because a merger is likely to reduce vigorous protection of constitutional rights.
2006: Outcries from Parliament and civil society caused the cabinet to withdraw these proposals.

Rule of Law

2004: The government should strengthen the rule of law through the president's commitment that all criminal cases not involving the military during active combat will be tried before the judiciary.
2006: The government has taken no action in this area.

2004: The government should expand its staffing in the police and the office of Director of Public Prosecutions (DPP) to reduce the number of prisoners on remand and thus accelerate trials.
2006: The government has taken no action in this area.

2004: The executive should instruct the police and intelligence agencies not to re-arrest acquitted defendants without evidence of a completely different charge.
2006: The government has taken no action in this area.

2004: Increasing the budget and staff of the UHRC would improve the willingness of government departments to comply with legal norms.
2006: The government has taken no action in this area.

2004: The government should commit its departments to applying the Anti-Terrorism Act only after thorough investigation.
2006: The government has taken no action in this area.

Anticorruption and Transparency

2004: The Inspector General of Government (IGG) and the auditor-general have built effective and trusted governmental accountability

structures for transparency and against corruption since 1995; doubling the budgets of both would probably save the government money over-all and would strengthen the culture of accountability.
2006: The government has taken no action in this area.

2004: The government must prevent the corrupt diversion of foreign aid.
2006: The government has taken no action in this area.

2004: Public officials and their relatives should be prohibited from acquiring properties through privatization.
2006: The government has taken no action in this area.

UKRAINE

Accountability and Public Voice

2004: Proposals for constitutional amendments, specifically those creat-ing a parliamentary system, should undergo a thorough and indepen-dent examination and be subjected to an authentic, public, and nationwide consultation process. These amendments should not be allowed to take effect in a way that circumvents the electoral rights of citizens or benefits incumbents.
2006: Constitutional amendments were passed in December 2004 fol-lowing a political agreement between the Yushchenko and Yanukovych camps enabling a repeat vote of the presidential election. Several aspects of the constitutional reform have been criticized by the Council of Europe, and the legitimacy and efficacy of the amendments remain unclear.

2004: Salaries of civil servants should be increased.
2006: There is evidence that the new government has already, or is in the process of, implementing this recommendation.

2004: Government policy on consultation with civic groups should be refashioned to strengthen links and afford civic groups access to officials and the rights to comment on policy and legislation.
2006: Civic groups still complain of not being listened to, but signifi-cant progress has been noted regarding the openness of the Ministry of Internal Affairs toward NGOs.

2004: Legislation to keep the government at arm's length from the media should be linked to any government funding of media, which should be supported on a nonpartisan and broad basis. An ombudsperson for freedom of the media should be introduced to guarantee and protect the rights of journalists against government interference. The issuing of temnyky (theme directives to the media) must cease.

2006: Direct interference of the executive in media reporting, including the issuing of temnyky, has ceased. However, the government's determination to create a public broadcasting service in line with European standards remains unclear.

Civil Liberties

2004: Government officials and law-enforcement personnel require more effective and higher-quality training and education in civil liberties.

2006: International NGOs continue to deplore the pervasive mistreatment, including torture, of detainees and prisoners in the law enforcement system.

2004: Laws must be enforced consistently (not selectively), and those responsible for violating the rights must be prosecuted and punished.

2006: While the rule of law remains, on the whole, weakly enforced, the blunt use of law enforcement organs, such as the tax police and Ministry of Interior troops, against political opponents, has considerably diminished.

2004: The parliament and its investigative/monitoring functions must be expanded; resources should be given to parliamentary committees to investigate and monitor wrongdoing, corruption, and violations of the law in both the government and the police/militia structures.

2006: Little progress has been recorded. The parliamentary investigative commission on Gongadze was prevented from delivering its report.

2004: A witness-protection program must be implemented, and funding and support to the ombudsperson's office increased.

2006: This recommendation does not appear to have been heeded.

2004: The registration process for civic groups must be simplified and clarified.

2006: This recommendation does not appear to have been heeded.

2004: The government should issue an annual report—through its ombudsperson's office—on hate crimes and hate speech with a section addressing responses by authorities to these rights violations.
2006: This recommendation does not appear to have been heeded.

Rule of Law

2004: Legislation and ethics governing the separation of the executive and parliament from the judiciary must be strengthened and enforced; those who violate these regulations must be investigated and held accountable.
2006: The Office of the Prosecutor General continues to blur the separation between the executive and the judiciary. To the dismay of the Council of Europe, the amended constitution continues to endow the prosecutor general with the powers to supervise court rulings and enforce laws.

2004: The quality of judges' training needs improvement.
2006: There was evidence during the Orange Revolution that several judges had benefited from Western-funded NGO training.

2004: The redress mechanism by which judges are held accountable when they violate rights of defendants must be strengthened.
2006: There does not appear to be noticeable progress on this process yet.

2004: Compliance with court decisions must be enforced, and those who are in contempt must be punished.
2006: International NGOs have continued to underline the persistent problem of unenforced court rulings.

2004: The Security Service of Ukraine (SBU) should be subject to scrutiny by a parliamentary oversight commission to ensure that the agency is not politicized and its functions are not abused by the president's office.
2006: Parliamentary oversight powers remain weak.

Anticorruption and Transparency

2004: Law enforcement officials should receive improved training and education concerning their responsibilities and clearer instruction about what activities should be considered illicit and corrupt.

2006: There does not seem to be evidence of greater clarity on this issue among law-enforcement officials.

2004: An independent extragovernmental agency that includes representatives of major political parties, including the opposition, should be set up for tackling intra-systemic corruption and organized crime.
2006: This recommendation was not heeded.

2004: Detailed conflict-of-interest guidelines need to be established and enforced in the executive, judicial, and legislative branches, and violators should be prosecuted.
2006: The accusations surrounding the sudden firing of Tymoshenko and of several top aides, with Orange politicians accusing each other of corruption, have starkly exposed the absence of conflict-of-interest guidelines in government.

2004: Independent ethics commissions governing members of the executive, judiciary, and parliament should be reinforced.
2006: This recommendation was not heeded.

2004: Naftohaz, the gas monopoly, should be subject to an independent auditing system and parliamentary scrutiny.
2006: The relationship between the highly lucrative oil and gas import business and the private interests of government officials remains murky. Parliamentary scrutiny remains weak, and no independent auditing system has been established.

VENEZUELA

Accountability and Public Voice

2004: The government should immediately embark upon a series of good-faith gestures to defuse Venezuela's highly polarized political atmosphere. In particular, both the president and other senior government officials should refrain from highly charged, intimidating rhetoric against opponents.
2006: The government has taken no action in this area.

2004: The government should work with the international community to ensure that the recall petition process is both transparent and overseen by neutral third parties.

2006: The government allowed access to international observers.

2004: The president's practice of bypassing the National Assembly should come to an end, and that body should be held accountable to modern parliamentary standards regarding transparency, openness, and accessibility.
2006: The National Assembly continues to work under the president's direction and without modern standards.

2004: Venezuela should live up to its international obligations regarding press freedom; in this regard, it might be useful for both private and publicly owned media to open themselves up to opposing points of view in a time frame or manner accessible to the greatest number of viewers/ listeners/readers.
2006: The government has taken no action in this area.

2004: The use of agents from nondemocratic countries within Venezuela's intelligence, security, and police apparatuses is unacceptable in a true democracy and should stop.
2006: The government has taken no action in this area.

Civil Liberties

2004: Police and security officers guilty of abuses against suspects of common crimes must be punished.
2006: The government has taken no action in this area.

2004: Clear public orders to Venezuelan military, security, and law enforcement agencies should be issued that they must refrain from the use of excessive force in dealing with demonstrations and public protests.
2006: The government has taken no effective action in this area.

2004: In communities or regions where Native Americans represent a significant percentage of the population, the government should allow greater use of traditional law.
2006: The government has taken no action in this area.

2004: A specific law enabling prosecution for the trafficking of persons should be passed, and increased efforts should be made to enforce relevant existing statutes.
2006: The government has recognized the importance of trafficking in persons as a policy issue.

Rule of Law

2004: Stronger steps are necessary to ensure that newly appointed judges are consensus candidates enjoying community-wide approval and not the representatives of a particular political party or interest.
2006: The government has taken no action in this area.

2004: Increased efforts are needed to ensure that improvements continue in the justice system, including concrete steps to guarantee that the police and security forces are not used for partisan political purposes.
2006: The government has taken no action in this area.

2004: The military's role in internal security must be limited to extraordinary circumstances in which civilian law enforcement proves unable to meet the challenge faced. The president's use of military cronies to staff non-military government agencies should come to an end.
2006: The government has taken no action in this area.

2004: Members of the armed forces should be subject to civilian courts in all cases except those concerning the lawful fulfillment of their duties as part of the military.
2006: The government has taken no action in this area.

2004: Laws governing private property rights need to be strengthened and enforced.
2006: The government has taken no action in this area.

Anticorruption and Transparency

2004: To restore credibility to the citizen-power branch of government created to fight corruption, the heads of the offices of the ombudsman, comptroller general, and the public prosecutor should be either appointed by bipartisan consensus within the national assembly or, at least in the first two instances, chosen through national elections.
2006: The government has taken no action in this area.

2004: The Chávez government should make a concerted effort to free the state from excessive bureaucratic regulations, registration requirements, and other controls that provide continued opportunities for corruption.
2006: The government has taken no action in this area.

2004: A law protecting government whistle-blowers should be enacted along the lines set down in the Organization of American States' model anticorruption statutes.
2006: The government has taken no action in this area.

VIETNAM

Accountability and Public Voice

2004: The Communist Party must end its position as the leading force in society.
2006: The government has taken no action in this area.

2004: Ensuring press freedoms, including unrestricted internet, must be a high priority.
2006: The government has taken no action in this area.

2004: The national assembly needs strengthening through professionalization, in particular to bring in more full-time parliamentarians and to educate its members and staff.
2006: The government has taken steps to improve the professionalization of its legislators and their permanent staff and has increased the number of full-time parliamentarians.

Civil Liberties

2004: The government must allow for the development of autonomous civil society.
2006: The government has allowed some modest developments in civil society, especially in the commercial and legal sectors, although they remain politically constrained.

2004: The government must allow for the functioning of independent churches, permitting monks and other religious leaders to independently distribute aid.
2006: The government has taken no action in this area.

2004: The policy of administrative detention under CP/31 is a real danger to the development of human rights.
2006: The government has taken no action in this area.

Rule of Law

2004: Vietnam requires legal reform and legal training, as further reform is constrained by the lack of qualified personnel.
2006: The government has invested in limited human resource development in the legal sector and has been more willing to accept international assistance in this area.

Anticorruption and Transparency

2004: Only a free press can force the leadership to police itself. The regime must therefore encourage press freedom.
2006: The government has taken no action in this area.

2004: Vietnam needs further economic reforms, such as the complete marketization of the economy, privatization of state-owned enterprises, and the further development of the private sector.
2006: The government has increased the scope of its economic reform program, allowed for more privatization of state-owned assets, and given more leeway to the private sector, though key economic sectors remain dominated by state-owned enterprises and overly regulated by the state.

2004: Government needs to ensure greater transparency, which would allow for increased monitoring of governmental activities.
2006: The government has taken no action in this area.

YEMEN

Accountability and Public Voice

2004: The Yemeni government should enhance the training, direction, and oversight of local election officials to ensure that they can fulfill their responsibilities. For the long term, the Yemeni government should invest in measures to depoliticize the electoral administration, such as creating an election administration staffed with properly trained civil servants.
2006: The Supreme Commission for Elections and Referendum (SCER), with the support of the International Foundation for Elections (IFES) and the United Nations Development Program (UNDP), has held two training courses for administrative personnel for the purpose of carrying out free, neutral, and transparent elections. However, more should

be done to de-politicize the electoral administration in the long term – SCER continues to be dominated by the ruling GPC party.

2004: The electoral constituencies should be redrawn in accordance with the principles set by the Constitution and Election Law.
2006: SCER has discussed but not yet acted upon redistricting.

2004: Special mechanisms should be established to expedite the dispute resolution and appeals process at all stages of the election cycle, either by further developing the capacity of the SCER to rule or by setting up special and independent Electoral Courts to arbitrate disputes in a timely, thorough, and cost-effective manner.
2006: While SCER has worked to improve the impartiality and transparency of future elections in Yemen, independent Electoral Courts have yet to be set up. With the help of international organizations, SCER has cleansed the voter registry of numerous double entries and underage names, but no amendments to electoral law in order to establish special mechanisms have been made.

2004: The Law for Press and Publications needs to be amended to either clarify or delete the numerous vaguely worded provisions on outlawed publications in Articles 137 to 153.
2006: The Law for Press and Publications has not been amended and continues to be used to restrict press freedom. The government abandoned a 2003 draft media law due to strong criticism from international press-freedom watchdog groups. A new draft law under debate in parliament would amend the original law but has been criticized as vague and potentially restrictive.

2004: The government should develop procedures and regulations to enable the establishment of private and independent broadcast media outlets in order to reduce the state's monopoly over radio and television.
2006: The state continues to maintain a monopoly over radio and television and has rebuffed attempts to establish private television channels.

Civil Liberties

2004: The Yemeni government should implement a comprehensive program to train law enforcement, security and prison officials on the proper procedures for arresting, detaining, and interrogating accused individuals.

2006: Minor steps have been taken in this area, such as a rehabilitation training course for policemen administered by the European Union in December 2005, which included lectures about human rights and respect. However, continued reports of harassment and poor treatment of prisoners suggest that a strong need for a national comprehensive training program in this area still exists.

2004: Public officials should not have immunity for crimes committed while on duty.
2006: There has been no legal change in this area.

2004: The government should amend national laws to ensure that women enjoy full equality in the law, particularly personal status laws on obtaining citizenship.
2006: No such changes in national laws have been made.

2004: The clause in the Penal Code that allows for leniency for persons guilty of so-called "crimes of honor" should be eliminated.
2006: The government has taken no legal action to change this clause.

2004: School attendance should be mandatory for all students, both male and female, until the age of 15.
2006: The law provides for universal, compulsory, and free education for children ages 6 to 15, but it is still not uniformly enforced, and school attendance remains low.

Rule of Law

2004: The Yemeni government should take steps to decrease the potential for the executive branch's interference in the judiciary, such as removing the President from the Supreme Judicial Council (SJC).
2006: In June 2006, President Saleh issued a decree removing himself as head of the SJC and appointing Supreme Court Chief Justice Essam al-Samawi in his stead. Yet, the executive branch retains the power to appoint or remove SJC members. No legislative action has been taken to reduce executive power in this area.

2004: Judicial authorities and the police should be more tightly linked and better coordinated to ensure that judicial rulings are fully implemented and respected.
2006: No significant improvements have been made in this area.

2004: The government should ensure that all police and security authorities are subject to oversight and investigation from the legislative branch of government and the judiciary, as well as the executive branch.
2006: The police and security authorities ultimately remain subject to executive oversight, which has been uneven at best. No substantial changes in the law have been made to strengthen legislative and/or judiciary responsibility and power in this area.

2004: Suspects allegedly involved with terrorist organizations should be either charged with a crime or released if insufficient evidence exists.
2006: While some suspects in the war on terror have been released after renouncing extremist views and engaging in religious dialogue with Islamic figures, others continue to be held without charge or trial.

Anticorruption and Transparency

2004: Yemen's government should introduce requirements of public disclosure of personal finances, including income, assets, and all business interests for all senior public officials such as the president, senior staff to the president, government ministers, top ministry officials, judges and other senior judicial authorities, and members of parliament.
2006: No government action has been taken in this area.

2004: Formal mechanisms should be established, such as an anonymous telephone tip line, by which government employees and individuals can report instances of alleged corruption and misuse of public resources.
2006: No government action has been taken in this area.

2004: The government should create a body that is fully independent of the president and the executive branch to investigate and prosecute alleged instances of corruption, and make the reports of investigations publicly available.
2006: New draft laws establishing a national higher authority to monitor and fight corruption are under debate by parliament. However, in their current form these laws would give the president direct authority over the new commission.

ZIMBABWE

Accountability and Public Voice

2004: A new constitutional commission needs to work closely with all sectors of society, including the National Constitutional Assembly (NCA). The new constitution needs to separate clearly the judicial, legislative, and executive branches of government; clear limits on the powers of the executive merit special attention. A strong bill of rights is necessary to secure the liberty of citizens.

2006: Recent amendments to the constitution did not address these concerns. The creation of a new senate actually allowed for greater executive influence in the legislative branch.

2004: The rights of all political parties to engage in the political process must be supported and the winner-takes-all culture that has marked Zimbabwe must end. The ruling party must negotiate with, rather than jail, the political opposition.

2006: The ruling party significantly reduced physical harassment of opposition political parties in 2005 elections; the government withdrew treason charges against opposition leader Morgan Tsvangirai but took steps to strengthen its grip on power.

2004: The government needs to repeal the Public Order and Security Act (POSA) and the Protection of Privacy Act (AIPPA).

2006: The government did not repeal the POSA or the AIPPA.

2004: The government must allow foreign correspondents back into the country and permit international and domestic election observers free access during elections.

2006: The government continues to place severe restrictions on foreign correspondents and now determines which international election observers are allowed into the country.

Civil Liberties

2004: Policy proposals to foster respect for civil liberties must be aimed directly at government failure to uphold constitutional rights and liberties. Therefore, short-term policies should focus simply on protection of human life, including through the disbandment of youth militias.

2006: Training centers for youth militias have been expanded, and police have not intervened in cases in which they have been reported as observing attacks against citizens.

2004: Government leaders must be prosecuted for using war veterans, youth militia, police, and security services to intimidate, beat, and detain civilians.
2006: Government leaders have not been prosecuted for the use of security forces to intimidate, beat, or detain civilians.

2004: NGOs must be permitted to function freely.
2006: The parliament approved a new NGO bill that further restricts NGOs. Although this bill has not been signed by President Robert Mugabe, it nevertheless indicates government attitudes toward NGOs.

2004: Constitutional freedoms of association, assembly, and speech must be upheld.
2006: The government continues to use restrictive legislation to curtail freedoms of association, assembly, and speech.

Rule of Law

2004: Policies that respect the rule of law must focus on the protection of property and the courts. The government needs to return all land taken from Zimbabweans and develop an independent commission to deal with issues of land reform in a transparent and constitutional manner.
2006: The government approved a constitutional amendment ending legal challenges to land seizures and broadened its attack on property rights through its demolition of urban townships.

2004: The government needs to stop politicizing the courts by placing close political supporters in judgeships.
2006: The government has continued politicizing the courts through the appointment of political supporters.

2004: Judges must apply the constitution justly, resisting government interference.
2006: Judges are still under pressure from the executive but have nevertheless shown some continued independence.

Anticorruption and Transparency

2004: The government needs an outside audit of its finances, the creation or reinvigoration of government oversight agencies in both the executive and legislative branches, and open financial disclosure of the ZANU-PF family of companies.

2006: The government has not reformed its auditing procedures to ensure effective and transparent oversight of government agencies and ZANU-PF-related businesses.

2004: The government must implement the anticorruption protocols of the Southern African Development Community (SADC) and of its 2001 Malawi Summit. These must be accompanied by stronger compliance mechanisms.

2006: The government has not implemented any of the anticorruption protocols of the SADC and of its 2001 Malawi Summit.

2004: It is necessary to divest the government of its state-owned enterprises and system of state licensing to end economic incentives for political corruption.

2006: The government has neither divested itself of state-owned companies nor ended licensing and other regulatory incentives for political corruption.

2004: Legislation that examines instituting methods of accountability in procurement is necessary to end the incentives for fraud.

2006: There has been no reform of government procurement processes to reduce incentives for fraud.

2004: The government must ensure international accountability in the distribution of food aid by allowing the United Nations and other international and domestic organizations the ability to monitor the food's distribution.

2006: The government has refused to allow the United Nations or other independent organizations to monitor food distribution freely.

APPENDIX 2
SURVEY METHODOLOGY

The Freedom House *Countries at the Crossroads* survey provides a comparative evaluation of government performance in four touchstone areas of democratic governance: Accountability and Public Voice, Civil Liberties, Rule of Law, and Anticorruption and Transparency. This survey examines these areas of performance in a set of 30 countries that are at a critical crossroads in determining their political future.

Crossroads evaluates two different sets of 30 countries bi-annually, with the 2004 countries covered in each even-numbered year and the 2005 countries covered in odd-numbered years. The 2006 edition is the third in the *Countries at the Crossroads* series; it evaluates the same 30 countries initially examined in the 2004 edition, providing an opportunity for a year-on-year analysis and assessing the extent to which this group of countries is backsliding, stalling, or improving in terms of democratic governance. The timeframe for events covered is October 1, 2003, through November 30, 2005.

In cooperation with a team of methodology experts, Freedom House designed a methodology that includes a questionnaire used both to prepare analytical narratives and for numerical ratings for each government. The survey methodology provides authors with a transparent and consistent guide to scoring and analyzing the countries under review and uses identical benchmarks for both narratives and ratings, rendering the two indicators mutually reinforcing. The final result is a system of comparative ratings accompanied by narratives that reflect both governments' commitment to passing good laws and also their records on upholding them.

The survey's methodology was created for the 2004 edition by a committee of senior advisers from the academic and scholarly communities. Its members were Larry Diamond, Hoover Institution; Adrian Karatnycky, Freedom House; Paul Martin, Columbia University; Rick Messick, the World Bank; Ted Piccone, Open Society Institute; Louise Shelley, American University; Jay Verkuilen, University of Illinois, Urbana-Champaign; Ruth Wedgwood, Johns Hopkins University; and Jennifer Windsor, Freedom House. In consultation with the committee, the Freedom House staff revised and updated the methodology for 2005 and 2006. Most notably, a new subsection on property rights has been included under the Rule of Law section and the subsection on the rights of women, ethnic, and religious minorities has been separated into two distinct subsections under Civil Liberties.

Freedom House enlisted the participation of prominent scholars and analysts to author the survey's country reports. In preparing the survey's written analyses with accompanying comparative ratings, Freedom House undertook a systematic gathering of data. Each country narrative report is approximately 6,500 words. Expert regional advisers reviewed the draft narrative reports, providing written comments and requests for revisions, additions, or clarifications. Authors were asked to respond as fully as possible to all of the questions posed when composing the analytical narratives; thus, the country narrative reports help inform the numerical scores.

For all 30 countries in the survey, Freedom House, in consultation with the report authors and academic advisers, has provided numerical ratings for the four thematic categories listed above. Authors produced a first round of ratings for each subcategory by evaluating each of the questions and assigning scores on a scale of 0–7. The regional advisers and Freedom House staff systematically reviewed all country ratings on a comparative basis to ensure accuracy and fairness. All final ratings decisions rest with Freedom House.

Scores are assigned on a scale of 0–7, where 0 represents weakest performance and 7 represents strongest performance. These ratings allow for comparative analysis of reform among the countries surveyed and are valuable for making general assessments of the level of democratic governance in a given country; they should not be taken as absolute indicators of the situation in a given country.

In devising a framework for evaluating government performance, Freedom House sought to develop a scale broad enough to capture degrees of variation so that comparisons could be made between countries in the current year, and also so that future time series comparisons might be made to assess a country's progress in these areas relative to past performance. These scales achieve an effective balance between a scoring system that is too broad—which may make it difficult for analysts to make fine distinctions between different scores—and one that is too narrow—which may make it difficult to capture degrees of variation between countries and therefore more difficult to recognize how much a given government's performance has improved or eroded over time.

Narrative essays and scoring were applied to the following main areas of performance, which Freedom House considers to be key to evaluating the state of democratic governance within a country:

ACCOUNTABILITY AND PUBLIC VOICE

- Free and fair electoral laws and elections
- Effective and accountable government
- Civic engagement and civic monitoring
- Media independence and freedom of expression

CIVIL LIBERTIES

- Protection from state terror, unjustified imprisonment, and torture
- Gender equity
- Rights of ethnic, religious, and other distinct groups
- Freedom of conscience and belief
- Freedom of association and assembly

RULE OF LAW

- Independent judiciary
- Primacy of rule of law in civil and criminal matters
- Accountability of security forces and military to civilian authorities
- Protection of property rights
- Equal treatment under the law

ANTICORRUPTION AND TRANSPARENCY

- Environment to protect against corruption
- Existence of laws, ethical standards, and boundaries between private and public sectors
- Enforcement of anticorruption laws
- Governmental transparency

In addition to the main subject matter areas, authors were asked to prepare an Introduction, giving a brief history of the country and outlining key issues in its development. At the end of each of the four major category sections, the authors provide succinct recommendations for the regime to take with respect to areas of most immediate and pressing concern. Moreover, for the first time, in 2006, the authors were required to follow up on the recommendations made in the previous edition and evaluate whether any progress had been made.

SCORING RANGE

The *Countries at the Crossroads* survey rates countries' performance in each of the four major subject areas on a scale of 0 to 7, with 0 representing the weakest performance and 7 the strongest. The scoring scale is as follows:

Score of 0–2 Countries that receive a score of 0, 1, or 2 ensure no or very few adequate protections, legal standards, or rights in the rated category. Laws protecting the rights of citizens or the justice of the political process are nonexistent, rarely enforced, or routinely abused by the authorities.

Score of 3–4 Countries that receive a score of 3 or 4 provide few or very few adequate protections, legal standards, or rights in the rated category. Legal protections are weak and enforcement of the law is inconsistent or corrupt.

Score of 5 Countries that receive a score of 5 provide some adequate protections, legal standards or rights in the rated category. Rights and political standards are protected, but enforcement may be unreliable and some abuses may occur. A score of 5 is considered to be the minimally adequate performance in the rated category.

Score of 6–7 Countries that receive a score of 6–7 ensure nearly all adequate protections, legal standards, or rights in the rated category. Legal protections are strong and are usually enforced fairly. Citizens have access to legal redress when their rights are violated, and the political system functions smoothly.

APPENDIX 3
2006 METHODOLOGY QUESTIONS

1. Accountability and Public Voice

a. Free and fair electoral laws and elections

    i. Is the authority of government based upon the will of the people as expressed by regular, free, and fair elections under fair electoral laws, with universal and equal suffrage, open to multiple parties, conducted by secret ballot, monitored by independent electoral authorities, with honest tabulation of ballots, and free of fraud and intimidation?

    ii. Are there equal campaigning opportunities for all parties?

    iii. Is there the opportunity for the effective rotation of power among a range of different political parties representing competing interests and policy options?

    iv. Are there adequate regulations to prevent undue influence of economically privileged interests (e.g., effective campaign finance laws), and are they enforced?

b. Effective and accountable government

    i. Are the executive, legislative, and judicial branches of government able to oversee the actions of one another and hold each other accountable for any excessive exercise of power?

    ii. Does the state system ensure that people's political choices are free from domination by the specific interests of power groups (e.g., the military, foreign powers, totalitarian parties, regional hierarchies, and/or economic oligarchies)?

    iii. Is the civil service selected, promoted, and dismissed on the basis of open competition and by merit?

    iv. Is the state engaged in issues reflecting the interests of women; ethnic, religious, and other distinct groups; and disabled people?

c. Civic engagement and civic monitoring

    i. Are civic groups able to testify, comment on, and influence pending government policy or legislation?

    ii. Are nongovernmental organizations free from legal impediments from the state and from onerous requirements for registration?

    iii. Are donors and funders of civic organizations and public policy institutes free of state pressures?

  d. Media independence and freedom of expression

    i. Does the state support constitutional or other legal protections for freedom of expression and an environment conducive to media freedom?

    ii. Does the state oppose the use of onerous libel, security, or other laws to punish through either excessive fines or imprisonment those who scrutinize government officials and policies?

    iii. Does the government protect journalists from extra-legal intimidation, arbitrary arrest and detention, or physical violence at the hands of state authorities or any other actor, including through fair and expeditious investigation and prosecution when cases do occur?

    iv. Does the state refrain from direct and indirect censorship of print or broadcast media?

    v. Does the state hinder access to the internet as an information source?

    vi. Does the state refrain from funding the media in order to propagandize, primarily provide official points of view, and/or limit access by opposition parties and civic critics?

    vii. Does the government otherwise refrain from attempting to influence media content (e.g., through direct ownership of distribution networks or printing facilities; prohibitive tariffs; onerous registration requirements; selective distribution of advertising; or bribery)?

    viii. Does the state protect the freedom of cultural expression (e.g., in fictional works, art, music, theater, etc.)?

2. Civil Liberties

  a. Protection from state terror, unjustified imprisonment, and torture

    i. Is there protection against torture by officers of the state, including through effective punishment in cases where torture is found to have occurred?

    ii. Are prison conditions respectful of the human dignity of inmates?

   iii. Does the state effectively protect against or respond to attacks on political opponents or other peaceful activists?

   iv. Are there effective protections against arbitrary arrest, including of political opponents or other peaceful activists?

    v. Is there effective protection against long-term detention without trial?

   vi. Does the state protect citizens from abuse by private/non-state actors?

  vii. Do citizens have means of effective petition and redress when their rights are violated by state authorities?

b. *Gender equity*

    i. Does the state ensure that both men and women are entitled to the full enjoyment of all civil and political rights?

   ii. Does the state take measures, including legislation, to modify or abolish existing laws, regulations, customs, and practices that constitute discrimination against women?

  iii. Does the state take measures to prevent trafficking in women?

  iv. Does the state make reasonable efforts to protect against gender discrimination in employment and occupation?

c. *Rights of ethnic, religious, and other distinct groups*

    i. Does the state ensure that persons belonging to ethnic, religous, and other distinct groups exercise fully and effectively all their human rights and fundamental freedoms (including ethnic, cultural, and linguistic rights) without discrimination and with full equality before the law?

   ii. Does the state take measures, including legislation, to modify or abolish existing laws, regulations, customs, and practices that constitute discrimination against ethnic, religious, and other distinct groups?

  iii. Does the state make a progressive effort to modify or abolish existing laws, regulations, customs, and practices that constitute discrimination against disabled people?

  iv. Does the state make reasonable efforts to protect against discrimination against ethnic, religious, and other distinct groups in employment and occupation?

  d. *Freedom of conscience and belief*
   i. Does the state accept the right of its citizens to hold religious beliefs of their choice and practice their religion as they deem appropriate, within reasonable constraints?
   ii. Does the state refrain from involvement in the appointment of religious or spiritual leaders and in the internal organizational activities of faith-related organizations?
   iii. Does the state refrain from placing restrictions on religious observance, religious ceremony, and religious education?
  e. *Freedom of association and assembly*
   i. Does the state recognize every person's right to freedom of association and assembly?
   ii. Does the state respect the right to form, join, and participate in free and independent trade unions?
   iii. Are citizens protected from being compelled by the state to belong to an association, either directly or indirectly (e.g., because certain indispensable benefits are conferred on members)?
   iv. Does the state effectively protect and recognize the rights of civic associations, business organizations, and political organizations to organize, mobilize, and advocate for peaceful purposes?
   v. Does the state permit demonstrations and public protests and refrain from using excessive force against them?

3. **Rule of Law**
  a. *Independent judiciary*
   i. Is there independence, impartiality, and nondiscrimination in the administration of justice, including from economic, political or religious influences?
   ii. Are judges and magistrates protected from interference by the executive and/or legislative branches?
   iii. Do legislative, executive, and other governmental authorities comply with judicial decisions, which are not subject to change except through established procedures for judicial review?
   iv. Are judges appointed, promoted, and dismissed in a fair and unbiased manner?

     v. Are judges appropriately trained in order to carry out justice in a fair and unbiased manner?

b. *Primacy of rule of law in civil and criminal matters*

     i. According to the legal system, is everyone charged with a criminal offence presumed innocent until proven guilty?

     ii. Are citizens given a fair, public, and timely hearing by a competent, independent, and impartial tribunal?

     iii. Do citizens have the right and access to independent counsel?

     iv. Does the state provide citizens charged with serious felonies with access to independent counsel when it is beyond their means?

     v. Are prosecutors independent of political direction and control?

     vi. Are public officials and ruling party actors prosecuted for the abuse of power and other wrongdoing?

c. *Accountability of security forces and military to civilian authorities*

     i. Is there effective and democratic civilian state control of the police, military, and internal security forces through the judicial, legislative, and executive branches?

     ii. Do police, military, and internal security services refrain from interference and/or involvement in the political process?

     iii. Are the police, military, and internal security services held accountable for any abuses of power for personal gain?

     iv. Do members of the police, military and internal security services respect human rights?

d. *Protection of property rights*

     i. Does the state give everyone the right to own property alone as well as in association with others?

     ii. Does the state adequately enforce property rights and contracts, including through adequate provisions for indigenous populations?

     iii. Does the state protect citizens from the arbitrary and/or unjust deprivation of their property (e.g., Does the state unjustly revoke property titles for governmental use or to pursue a political agenda?)?

e. *Equal treatment under the law*

     i. Are all persons entitled to equal protection under the law?

    ii. Are all persons equal before the courts and tribunals?

   iii. Is discrimination on grounds of gender, ethnic origin, nationality, and sexual orientation prohibited and prosecuted by the state?

4. Anticorruption and Transparency

  a. Environment to protect against corruption

     i. Is the government free from excessive bureaucratic regulations, registration requirements, and/or other controls that increase opportunities for corruption?

    ii. Does the state refrain from excessive involvement in the economy?

   iii. Does the state enforce the separation of public office from the personal interests of public officeholders?

   iv. Are there adequate financial disclosure procedures that prevent conflicts of interest among public officials (e.g., Are the assets declarations of public officials open to public and media scrutiny and verification?)?

    v. Does the state adequately protect against conflicts of interest in the private sector?

  b. *Existence of laws, ethical standards, and boundaries between private and public sectors*

     i. Does the state enforce an effective legislative or administrative process designed to promote integrity and to prevent, detect, and punish the corruption of public officials?

    ii. Does the state provide victims of corruption with adequate mechanisms to pursue their rights?

   iii. Does the state protect higher education from pervasive corruption and graft (e.g., Are bribes necessary to gain admission or good grades?)?

   iv. Does the tax administrator implement effective internal audit systems to ensure the accountability of tax collection?

  c. *Enforcement of anticorruption laws*

     i. Are there effective and independent investigative and auditing bodies created by the government (e.g., an auditor general or ombudsman) and do they function without impediment or political pressure?

    ii. Are allegations of corruption by government officials at the national and local levels thoroughly investigated and prosecuted without prejudice?

    iii. Are allegations of corruption given wide and unbiased airing in the news media?

    iv. Do whistleblowers, anticorruption activists, investigators have a legal environment that protects them, so they feel secure about reporting cases of bribery and corruption?

d. *Governmental transparency*

    i. Is there significant legal, regulatory, and judicial transparency as manifested through public access to government information?

    ii. Do citizens have a legal right to obtain information about government operations, and means to petition government agencies for it?

    iii. Does the state make a progressive effort to provide information about government services and decisions in formats and settings that are accessible to disabled people?

    iv. Is the executive budget-making process comprehensive and transparent and subject to meaningful legislative review and scrutiny?

    v. Does the government publish detailed and accurate accounting of expenditures in a timely fashion?

    vi. Does the state ensure transparency, open-bidding, and effective competition in the awarding of government contracts?

    vii. Does the government enable the fair and legal administration and distribution of foreign assistance?

ABOUT FREEDOM HOUSE

**Freedom House is an independent private organization
supporting the expansion of freedom throughout the world.**

Freedom is possible only in democratic political systems in which governments are accountable to their own people, the rule of law prevails, and freedoms of expression, association and belief are guaranteed. Working directly with courageous men and women around the world to support nonviolent civic initiatives in societies where freedom is threatened, Freedom House functions as a catalyst for change through its unique mix of analysis, advocacy and action.

- **Analysis.** Freedom House's rigorous research methodology has earned the organization a reputation as the leading source of information on the state of freedom around the globe. Since 1972, Freedom House has published *Freedom in the World,* an annual survey of political rights and civil liberties experienced in every country of the world. The survey is complemented by an annual review of press freedom, an analysis of transitions in the post-Communist world, and other publications.

- **Advocacy.** Freedom House seeks to encourage American policy makers, as well as other governments and international institutions, to adopt policies that advance human rights and democracy around the world. Freedom House has been instrumental in the founding of the worldwide Community of Democracies, has actively campaigned for a reformed Human Rights Council at the United Nations, and presses the Millennium Challenge Corporation to adhere to high standards of eligibility for recipient countries.

- **Action.** Through exchanges, grants, and technical assistance, Freedom House provides training and support to human rights defenders, civil society organizations, and members of the media in order to strengthen indigenous reform efforts in countries around the globe.

Founded in 1941 by Eleanor Roosevelt, Wendell Willkie, and other Americans concerned with mounting threats to peace and democracy, Freedom House has long been a vigorous proponent of democratic values and a steadfast opponent of dictatorships of the far left and the far right. The organization's diverse Board of Trustees is composed of a bipartisan mix of business and labor leaders, former senior government officials, scholars, and journalists who agree that the promotion of democracy and human rights abroad is vital to America's interests abroad.